Innovative Economic, Social, and Environmental Practices for Progressing Future Sustainability

Chai Lee Goi
Curtin University, Malaysia

IGI Global
PUBLISHER of TIMELY KNOWLEDGE

A volume in the Practice, Progress, and
Proficiency in Sustainability (PPPS) Book Series

Published in the United States of America by
IGI Global
Engineering Science Reference (an imprint of IGI Global)
701 E. Chocolate Avenue
Hershey PA, USA 17033
Tel: 717-533-8845
Fax: 717-533-8661
E-mail: cust@igi-global.com
Web site: http://www.igi-global.com

Library of Congress Cataloging-in-Publication Data

Names: Goi, Chai Lee, 1976- editor.
Title: Innovative economic, social, and environmental practices for progressing future sustainability / Chai Lee Goi, editor.
Description: Hershey, PA : Engineering Science Reference, [2022] | Summary: "This book explores the current practice in economic, social, and environmental sustainable development, which continues to prove its importance in our lives as it affects all aspects of them"-- Provided by publisher.
Identifiers: LCCN 2021037633 (print) | LCCN 2021037634 (ebook) | ISBN 9781799895909 (hardcover) | ISBN 9781799895916 (paperback) | ISBN 9781799895923 (ebook)
Subjects: LCSH: Sustainable development. | Economic development--Environmental aspects.
Classification: LCC HC79.E5 I51495 2021 (print) | LCC HC79.E5 (ebook) | DDC 338.9/27--dc23
LC record available at https://lccn.loc.gov/2021037633
LC ebook record available at https://lccn.loc.gov/2021037634

This book is published in the IGI Global book series Practice, Progress, and Proficiency in Sustainability (PPPS) (ISSN: 2330-3271; eISSN: 2330-328X)

British Cataloguing in Publication Data
A Cataloguing in Publication record for this book is available from the British Library.

For electronic access to this publication, please contact: eresources@igi-global.com.

Practice, Progress, and Proficiency in Sustainability (PPPS) Book Series

Ayman Batisha
International Sustainability Institute, Egypt

ISSN:2330-3271
EISSN:2330-328X

Mission

In a world where traditional business practices are reconsidered and economic activity is performed in a global context, new areas of economic developments are recognized as the key enablers of wealth and income production. This knowledge of information technologies provides infrastructures, systems, and services towards sustainable development.

The **Practices, Progress, and Proficiency in Sustainability (PPPS) Book Series** focuses on the local and global challenges, business opportunities, and societal needs surrounding international collaboration and sustainable development of technology. This series brings together academics, researchers, entrepreneurs, policy makers and government officers aiming to contribute to the progress and proficiency in sustainability.

Coverage

- Environmental informatics
- Green Technology
- Global Business
- Technological learning
- Intellectual Capital
- Global Content and Knowledge Repositories
- Innovation Networks
- ICT and knowledge for development
- Knowledge clusters
- E-Development

IGI Global is currently accepting manuscripts for publication within this series. To submit a proposal for a volume in this series, please contact our Acquisition Editors at Acquisitions@igi-global.com or visit: http://www.igi-global.com/publish/.

The Practice, Progress, and Proficiency in Sustainability (PPPS) Book Series (ISSN 2330-3271) is published by IGI Global, 701 E. Chocolate Avenue, Hershey, PA 17033-1240, USA, www.igi-global.com. This series is composed of titles available for purchase individually; each title is edited to be contextually exclusive from any other title within the series. For pricing and ordering information please visit http://www.igi-global.com/book-series/practice-progress-proficiency-sustainability/73810. Postmaster: Send all address changes to above address.

Titles in this Series

For a list of additional titles in this series, please visit: http://www.igi-global.com/book-series/practice-progress-proficiency-sustainability/73810

Technological Development and Impact on Economic and Environmental Sustinability
Yilmaz Bayar (Bandirma Onyedi Eylul University, Turkey) Mahmut Unsal Sasmaz (Usak University, Turkey) and Omer Faruk Ozturk (Usak University, Turkey)
Engineering Science Reference • © 2022 • 300pp • H/C (ISBN: 9781799896487) • US $215.00

Handbook of Research on Monitoring and Evaluating the Ecological Health of Wetlands
Ashok K. Rathoure (Akone Services, India)
Engineering Science Reference • © 2022 • 370pp • H/C (ISBN: 9781799894988) • US $295.00

Blockchain Technologies for Sustainable Development in Smart Cities
P. Swarnalatha (Vellore Institute of Technology, India) and S. Prabu (Pondicherry University, India)
Engineering Science Reference • © 2022 • 285pp • H/C (ISBN: 9781799892748) • US $215.00

Impacts of Climate Change and Economic and Health Crises on the Agriculture and Food Sectors
Vítor João Pereira Domingues Martinho (Polytechnic Institute of Viseu, Portugal)
Engineering Science Reference • © 2022 • 420pp • H/C (ISBN: 9781799895572) • US $195.00

Handbook of Research on Resource Management and the Struggle for Water Sustainability in Africa
Innocent Simphiwe Nojiyeza (University of Zululand, South Africa) Oliver Mtapuri (University of KwaZulu-Natal, South Africa) Prosper Bazaanah (University of Johannesburg, South Africa) and Edzisani Ellen Netshitozwi (Office of the Chief Justice, South Africa)
Engineering Science Reference • © 2022 • 437pp • H/C (ISBN: 9781799888093) • US $295.00

Innovative Strategic Planning and International Collaboration for the Mitigation of Global Crises
Gabriela Antošová (University College of Business in Prague, Czech Republic)
Information Science Reference • © 2022 • 327pp • H/C (ISBN: 9781799883395) • US $195.00

Handbook of Research on Changing Dynamics in Responsible and Sustainable Business in the Post-COVID-19 Era
Cristina Raluca Gh. Popescu (University of Bucharest, Romania & The Bucharest University of Economic Studies, Romania & The National Institute for Research and Development in Environmental Protection (INCDPM), Romania & National Research and Development Institute for Gas Turbines (COMOTI), Romania)
Business Science Reference • © 2022 • 512pp • H/C (ISBN: 9781668425237) • US $315.00

IGI Global
PUBLISHER of TIMELY KNOWLEDGE

701 East Chocolate Avenue, Hershey, PA 17033, USA
Tel: 717-533-8845 x100 • Fax: 717-533-8661
E-Mail: cust@igi-global.com • www.igi-global.com

EDITORIAL ADVISORY BOARD

Table of Contents

Detailed Table of Contents

Communication in the commercial banking sector in Nepal is carried out very poorly in correspondence. Practicing effective banking communication makes work easier, faster, comfortable, and accurate as a mediator between bank, customer, government, shareholder, suppliers, client, board of directors, and employees. The purpose of this chapter is to provide insight on how the banking communication system operates in Nepal, how effective those techniques and tools are, and thereby proposes policy recommendations for improvising banking communication. The chapter uses extensive desk reviews followed by related literature to understand the field of study. In the demand side, providing time to address customer problems, adopting effective communication measures, and increasing banking facilities increase awareness in banking communication, while, on the supply side, in order to improve the banking system, the banks should focus on financial service management, adopting e-banking and organizational regulation policies for customer satisfaction.

Existing economic systems have encouraged overconsumption by constantly inspiring consumers to have more. With these consumption habits, it has been understood that it is not possible to maintain present living standards for many years, and as a result, sustainability discussions have emerged. One of the most fundamental components of these sustainability discussions is the "sustainable consumption" approach. Sustainable consumption proposes to meet the needs of today's humanity without compromising the ability of future generations to meet their needs in order to leave a livable world for them. At this point, the aim of this study is to discuss sustainable consumption from the perspective of economic theory and to examine it within the framework of consumer behavior. For this purpose, the titles of consumption, consumer behavior, consumption society, sustainability, sustainable consumption, consumer behaviors in sustainable consumption and reasons for sustainable consumption failure, and suggestions for solutions are discussed in detail in the study.

This chapter empirically examines the (asymmetric) impacts of economic complexity on Turkey's Ecological and Carbon Footprints by employing the augmented nonlinear autoregressive distributed lag (augmented NADL) method for the 1981-2017 period. This chapter's findings are as follows. First, nonlinear cointegration exists between economic complexity and environmental damage. Second, economic complexity has a significant long run asymmetric impact on Turkey's Ecological and Carbon Footprints. Third, in the long run, positive developments in economic complexity increase environmental damage in Turkey, whereas the impact of negative developments is insignificant on Turkey's environmental deterioration. Fourth, significant short run asymmetries regarding economic complexity's effect exist only in the Ecological Footprint model. Lastly, in the short run, positive developments in economic complexity decrease environmental damage, while negative developments intensify it. In line with the empirical findings, some policy recommendations are made.

Although energy concepts and climate change are highly present on everyone's life, educational systems are in cases still lacking on their curricula the teaching of what energy is, how it is produced, and what is the relationship between energy use and climate change. It is suggested by the many that a society which is not literate about energy will never be capable of using it more effectively. This chapter presents a research performed with more than 100 participants from different backgrounds and age ranges with three different learning activities to educate on energy with different rationales including digital technologies. The authors measured the beliefs and intentions before and after the activity. They found that overall the values were high and there was no significant gain after the activity. Also, they found that learners experienced similar learning with all activities, but that engagement was significantly higher with the embodied activity.

In the quest of fostering green consumer behavior, companies are developing green marketing communications. However, do green consumer behaviors gets influenced by such marketing practices or it is result of green consumption values? The research-based chapter answers this question by developing a conceptual model against the background of green consumer behavior theories. The explanatory

Preface

INTRODUCTION

This book, *Innovative Economic, Social, and Environmental Practices for Progressing Future Sustainability*, offers conceptual frameworks, empirical studies and case studies focusing on sustainable development that meets the needs of the present without compromising the ability of future generations to meet their own needs. Sustainable development is a long-term solution to how we plan our indefinite progress in the future, and the concept covers a broad scope of environmental, social, and economic developments. Sustainable development is the ideal vision of the future and requires further study and consideration.

This book is ideal for academicians, researchers, practitioners, policymakers, government officials, decision-makers, instructors, and students.

CONTENTS OF THE BOOK

The handbook presents a collection of 17 chapters that explore strategic issues in environmental, social, and economic developments.

Chapter 1, titled "Assimilation of Communication Deviance in Customers and Bankers Appraisal of Commercial Banks in Kathmandu, Nepal" (authors: Udaya Paudel and Niranjan Devkota), focuses on the important issue on the effective communication practice in the commercial banking sector in Nepal. Their findings show that the cooperative level of the bank, language used and various services are the major factors affecting customers' perception of banking communication. Fourteen recommendations are put forward for improving communication management for the banking sector.

Chapter 2, titled "Consumer Behavior and Sustainable Consumption in Economic Theory" (author: Mikail Kar), discusses consumer behavior is of vital importance for sustainability. Consumer behavior is discussed within the framework of a five-stage process logic: identification of needs, identification of alternatives, evaluation of alternatives, purchase decision and post-purchase evaluation. At each stage, sustainable consumption should be taken into consideration. Sustainable consumption behaviors in consumer behavior are examined by dividing them into direct consumption of natural resources and indirect consumption of natural resources.

Chapter 3, titled "Does Achieving Economic Complexity Impede Turkey's Environmental Sustainability? Asymmetric Evidence From the Augmented NADL Approach" (author: Alper Karasoy), examines the (asymmetric) impacts of economic complexity on Turkey's Ecological and Carbon Footprints by employing the augmented nonlinear autoregressive distributed lag (augmented NADL) method for the

1981-2017 period. The findings show that although achieving economic complexity seems to benefit Turkey's environmental performance in the short run, it worsens Turkey's environmental quality in the long run. Also, the findings reveal that development and sustainability policies in Turkey are shortsighted and tend to sacrifice Turkey's long-run environmental sustainability at the expense of short-term gains. Finally, even though Turkey's economic complexity index values have stayed above zero during the 1981-2017 period, the level of economic complexity remained considerably low compared to developed countries.

Chapter 4, titled "Evaluation of Engagement and Desirability of Different Teaching Techniques of Energy Concepts: How to Rise Energy Literacy of the General Public in Educational Institutions" (authors: Alfonso Ramallo and José A. Ruiperez-Valiente), presents research performed with more than 100 participants from different backgrounds and age ranges with three different learning activities to educate on energy with different rationales, including digital technologies. The researchers found that citizens' activities embodying and visualizing the energy they generate can be a great way to engage them more meaningfully with an issue than passive or interactive content like books or games.

Chapter 5, titled "Green Consumption Values and Consumer Behavior: Evidence From Singapore" (authors: Stella Tan Char Ern, Omkar Dastane, and Herman Fassou Haba), discusses and comprehends green consumption value and consumer behavior from the perspective of green marketing communication in Singapore. The findings imply that managers should enhance green consumption values, which can foster consumer behavior. Therefore, offering and highlighting consumption values is more relevant rather than focusing much on marketing communication aspects. Furthermore, the findings have indicated that customers are more focused on buying green products and are highly concerned about environmental safety. Therefore, it is recommended that products must be co-branded by the companies in a new direction concerning green friendliness. Another recommendation is to adopt the development strategy, which is used for sustainable growth of the economy and sustainable consumption is known as sustainable development and the environment is protected by it.

Chapter 6, titled "Green Intellectual Capital in the Spanish Wine Industry" (authors: Bartolomé Marco-Lajara, Patrocinio Zaragoza-Sáez, Javier Martínez-Falcó, and Eduardo Sánchez-García), analyzes the different factors influencing the formation of GIC in wine companies and addresses the three dimensions of GIC in the wine industry. Based on the findings, the researchers proposed the wine industry choose the most suitable intangible resources for the environmental management of wineries. One of the main challenges for managers in understanding the role of intangible resources - and not only tangible ones - in the environmental management of wineries. Once they recognize the value of GIC, they must take the lead in promoting environmental initiatives and empowering employees to participate in the winery's environmental management proactively. In addition, the establishment of incentives that reward best environmental practices can improve the environmental performance of wineries.

Chapter 7, titled "Improving Society as a Business Strategy: A Review From a Strategic Management Perspective" (author: Yeşim Kurt), analyzes highlights some business strategy issues - what strategic corporate social responsibilities are and how the relationship with the business strategy can be integrated into the business? Strategic CSR is associated with carrying out activities to improve society, not only to improve society but also to consider the interests of the business. The author also highlights the future research directions of the topic. This includes the extent to which companies are aware of this concept, how they react to these activities, whether CSR can be applied strategically, and how it is integrated into the business are among the topics worth investigating. Another potential issue to consider is developing performance measurement indicators that reveal the effects and results of Strategic CSR.

Chapter 8, titled "Innovation as a Management Question: Can Innovation be Managed?" (authors: Haneen Allataifeh and Sedigheh Moghavvemi), highlights the importance of innovation management, which has been progressively covered in the management literature in the last thirty years. The authors highlight rationales and processes to manage innovation and contribute to broadening the themes and focus of future research.

Chapter 9, titled "Local Perspectives of Sustainable Urbanism: Solutions Based on Spanish Legislative Model" (author: Maria Jesus Garcia), discusses that planning can establish a subjective use different from materialized use. It should be noted that for a plan to have content adjusted to the restoration parameters in the sense that it promotes the maintenance of constructions and buildings, its determinations must maintain the balance between the use already materialized and the use susceptible of appropriation that results from the planning.

Chapter 10, titled "Low Carbon Cities: Sustainable Urban Development in Malaysia" (author: Chai Lee Goi), reviews the current sustainable urban development and the implementation and planning of low carbon cities in Malaysia. The author recommends that a holistic approach should encompass not only energy policy but also social, economic, and ecological aspects of sustainable development. To realise the country's vision, the experts, the government, and political leadership all need to come together.

Chapter 11, titled "Organizational Structural Construct Based on a Framework for Reliability, Safety, and Deployment of Organizational Resources" (author: José Vargas-Hernández), analyzes an organizational resilience framework leading to the development of a structural construct of organizational resilience for the evaluation of organizational resilience performance. The concept of organizational resilience emerging from cognitive, ecology and engineering sciences, among others, confirms that the creation and development of an organizational resilience framework for structural construct can be supported by elements based on the flexibility of organizational culture, organizational safety and reliability, the promotion elements, and the deployment of organizational resources.

Chapter 12, titled "Sustainable Luxury Fashion: From Owning to Sharing" (author: Fayrene Chieng), discusses that luxury brands with a history of high quality, heritage, artisanship, and durability are more likely to uphold social and environmental values. Luxury fashion brands must credibly promote the true values to consumers so that they can understand how those values align with principles of sustainable development.

In order to determine the current land use characteristics, Chapter 13, titled "The Future of Capability Building in Sustainable Development" (authors: José Vargas-Hernández and Elsa Patricia Orozco-Quijano), recommends the important to conduct some database analysis from primary and secondary sources. This approach allows cities to broaden their vision by considering the multiple functions of a specific site and defining its various components by comparing data with other cities.

Chapter 14, titled "Sustainable Resilience in Urban Land Use" (author: Chabi Gupta), discusses that for the future of capability building in sustainable development, leaders should promote their employees' digital, cognitive, social, emotional capabilities and adaptability and resilience. Due to Covid19, the working environment is expected to change dramatically over the next ten years, and people in practically every function and industry will need to learn new skills.

Chapter 15, titled "Towards a Sustainable Future of Marketing Management Praxis in Rural Destination Space" (author: Samuel Adeyinka-Ojo), discusses that sustainable destination branding and relationship-based building approach are crucial in understanding future marketing management and efforts, especially in rural tourism destinations.

Chapter 16, titled "Understanding How Entrepreneurship Innovation Solve Women's Challenges in the Arab Region: Omani Women Entrepreneurs Model" (authors: Fadi Abdel Muniem Ahmad Fattah and Hussam Al Halbusi), outlines the Omani government's long-term plan, Visions 2020-2040, for enhancing and encouraging women's involvement in SMEs to maximize returns, create employment opportunities, and reduce market and institutional failures. Overall, this chapter provides a road map for policymakers to embark on appropriate administrative regulations and laws to facilitate Omani women's involvement in entrepreneurship.

Last but not least, Chapter 17, titled "Unlock the Next Level of Green: GREEFE for Organizational Sustainable Innovation" (author: Ying Ying Tiong), proposes a GREEFE framework to connect the fundamental elements of hotel marketing (green marketing mix: green products, green price, green promotion and green place) with safety measures. Green brands are perceived by travellers as more trustworthy and high-quality, with safety measures being a must-have criterion for hotels.

Happy reading!

Chai Lee Goi
Curtin University, Malaysia

Acknowledgment

I would like to express my sincere gratitude to the chapter contributors for their hard work. I also would like to thank members of the Editorial Advisory Board for their support and their advice and guidance during the process of preparing this book.

Finally, thanks to IGI Global editorial/production team for the assistance.

Chai Lee Goi
Curtin University, Malaysia

Chapter 1
Assimilation of Communication Deviance in Customer and Banker Appraisals of Commercial Banks in Kathmandu, Nepal

Udaya Raj Paudel
Quest International College, Pokhara University, Nepal

Niranjan Devkota
https://orcid.org/0000-0001-9989-0397
Quest Research Management Cell, Quest International College, Pokhara University, Nepal

ABSTRACT

Communication in the commercial banking sector in Nepal is carried out very poorly in correspondence. Practicing effective banking communication makes work easier, faster, comfortable, and accurate as a mediator between bank, customer, government, shareholder, suppliers, client, board of directors, and employees. The purpose of this chapter is to provide insight on how the banking communication system operates in Nepal, how effective those techniques and tools are, and thereby proposes policy recommendations for improvising banking communication. The chapter uses extensive desk reviews followed by related literature to understand the field of study. In the demand side, providing time to address customer problems, adopting effective communication measures, and increasing banking facilities increase awareness in banking communication, while, on the supply side, in order to improve the banking system, the banks should focus on financial service management, adopting e-banking and organizational regulation policies for customer satisfaction.

DOI: 10.4018/978-1-7998-9590-9.ch001

INTRODUCTION

Effective banking communication can strengthen the connection between customer, suppliers, stakeholders, managers, client, employees, board of directors, neighbor, community and nation (Thussu, 2018; Parajuli et al., 2020). In communication, numerous of barriers are formulated such as perceptual barriers, language barriers, emotional barriers, physical barriers and cultural barriers (Van Eemeren & Grootendorst, 2016). Effective communication fosters ideas and builds common ground to develop complex interpersonal relationships. The communication pattern has changes telephone, email and fax into instant messaging/ chat, virtual words, social networking sites, wikis, twitter, blogs in the workplace which become very beneficial to transfer information from one place to another place and save data and information. (B.K. et al., 2019, Austin & Pinkleton, 2015) argued that human capital are strong foundation for any organization with verbal and non-verbal communication and for banks as well. Communication media are important in attracting attention, holding attention, and increasing the information's accessibility and its impact on consumer perception (Herr et al., 1991; Bucăţa & Rizecu, 2017). Communication between senders and receivers of the information is considered to be an important process (Mohr & Nevin, 1990; Haroon & Mallik, 2018; Paudel et al., 2021). Banks communicate distinctly among the customers that will help in improving satisfaction among customers and each customer will have distinct effects of the same information communicated (Schlich, 2012; Şeitan, 2017). Thus, banking communication considers the emotional impact of the message along with the actual information and factual content in good banking operation (Van Staden et al., 2007).

Although banks and their services have been advancing in Nepalese commercial banks customer satisfaction in terms of communication is still a far cry (Gautam & Dhital, 2004; Shrestha et al., 2018). Shrestha (2018) stated that updating and listening to customers in an effective way leads to customer satisfaction and loyalty among customer towards the bank and customer still feels employees of bank require training on communication. Similarly, Sapkota et al. (2018) analyzed role of information communication technology in Nepalese banking industry show pros and cons of using information and communication technology in Nepalese banks. (Gaire, 2018; Parajuli et al., 2019) concluded that communication has significant role in the satisfaction of customers and banks should continuously keep reviewing and monitoring the communication strategies and practices in his study; effectiveness of internet banking system and clients satisfaction. Till date various discussions and research are made on customers' perception on banking communication in Nepal. Gautam & Dhital (2004) covered customer satisfaction in Nepalese commercial banks; prospects and challenges of e-banking in Nepal (Banstola, 2007); Application of management control system in Nepalese commercial banks (Rijal, 2006); Role of information communication technology (ICT) in Nepalese banking sector (Sapkota et al., 2018).

In their study (Moore et al., 2018; Ishaq Bhatti et al., 2011) revealed that communication strategies could be improved when the bank merged the communication department and marketing department and work together for the common vision. These process scales up the internal and external communication in the banking sector. Moreover, Aral et al. (2013) today, advance information technology has tremendously progressed and changed the banking industry. The automation and revolutionary changes changed financial and banking scenario globally. The availability of ATM, smart chips embedded with microprocessor chip, Electronic Data interchange (EDI) bring revolutionary changes in banking sector (Berger, 2018). Thus, understanding-banking communication becomes crucial part in banking sector.

In the context of Nepal the study on how consumer perceives banking communication is still noble and effective area for the study. Kharel et al. (2019) mentioned that every stakeholder have right to get relevant information, interact and communicate. However, it is also seen that banks responsiveness to convey information regarding various banking products, services, updates will help in increasing customer satisfaction among the communication services provided by the bank. Hence, the present study aims to fulfill this gap. Still several questions are unanswered in context of banking communication in Nepalese commercial banks with respect to customers and their satisfaction like: How have been banks communicating with customers? How aware are customers on banking communication? What can be the factors affecting customers understanding on banking communication? What are the barriers for effective communication? What management strategy can be adopted for effective banking communication? What factors are taken into consideration while making strategies for effective banking communication? Therefore, the aim of this paper is to extrapolate the gap in banking communication among "A" grade banks of Nepal.

Historically, Nepal Bank Limited was established in 1937. After 53 years Nabil Bank Ltd has introduced the service of credit card in 1990s. After that Himalyan Bank introduced Automated Teller Machine and Telephone in (1995). Mostly, the banking sector have to wait for nearly 65 years for internet banking where Kumari Bank launched internet banking for the first time in Nepal in 2002 (Mishra, 2008). In the context of Nepal, the customers are adopting traditional method of banking still they are not shifted entirely into new approach. Lack of knowledge, awareness and familiarity about online banking technology become primary reason for the customers' reluctance to use the e- banking services (Pikkarainen et al., 2004). Moreover, customer are also getting problems from banking communication regarding internet security, theft or loss of password, concerned about the private information, online infrastructure, training about internet banking, trust issues, electricity problems and adoption of internet banking in the country (Khatri & Dhungel, 2013). Banking communication builds employees 'culture and increase effectiveness and productivity of employees, which assists to create brand name, honesty and reliability (Akmajian, et al., 2017). Thus, the paper aims to explore the communication gap revealed through bankers' and customers' experience on banking communication in commercial banks, and thereby recommends the effective communication measures to avoid the barriers.

The remaining body of the paper is organized in four parts. In the next section, literature review is discussed which is followed by methodology used, then the results and discussions of the study are presented before conclusion and recommendations.

LITERATURE REVIEW

Banking Communication: Customer Perception

Banking communication can be urged as the way bank listen, serves, convey and understand information and issue of customers through proper means and techniques Hoque et al. (2018). Modern banking practice started in Nepal since 1937 AD as mentioned by Pant (2016) and it was after the establishment of Nepal Bank Limited as per Gajurel & Pradhan (2012). According to report of NRB (2018) there are 28 commercial banks, 33 development banks, 65 finance companies and 14 saving and credit cooperatives existing in Nepal. As per the source of NRB (2016) there are total 229 financial institutions including 187 BFIs of "A" "B" "C" and "D" categories. For better communication practices, bank should have free flow of information among all the stakeholders (Walther, 1988). Amiri (2015) observed that communication in banks helps its employees and customers in having knowledge about various strategic decisions that are implemented or going to be implemented by bank, banking policies and procedures, various issues related with bank and the way to get out of those issues. It further helps in achieving solidarity among bank and customers and is able to achieve necessary information. B.K. et al. (2019) stated that customer privacy, customer welfare, data security, community relation are strong foundation for sustainable development and this can be related to the banking business in relation to customers as well.

Banking communication provides a medium for customers to express their needs, perspectives and judgments on the services being provided by banks (Blythe, 2008; Shrestha et al., 2018; Parajuli et al., 2020). Banstola (2007) found that level of education seems affecting the adoption and use of e-banking. Similarly, Customer feel satisfied if they can enjoy proper facility of ATM, credit cards, if they don't have to wait for longer time (Gautam & Dhital, 2004). Agarwal & Garg (2012) depicted that face to face communication is most trusted form of communication as perceived by customers whereas, Dharmavaram & Nittala (2018) concluded banks should give proper training to customer service employees who interacts with customers and responds to their problem. Banking communication literatures are available which shows banking relation with their customers. In 1990s banking sector generates word of mouth communication in service market place (Glynn Mangold et al., 1999) which demands professionalism in service sector. Now, communication has advanced level and in Nepal all banks are providing ICT service (Sapkota et al., 2018). Tan & Teo (2000) argues that attitudinal and perceived behavioral control factor drives intention to adopt internet.

The literature shows that banking communication has been crucial matter for banks these days and similar efforts are being shown by banks around the globe to improve their communication practices. However, in Nepalese context banks seems to be improving in the part of communication hence, a sincere study on banking communication helps to reveal out the perception of customer. It further helps policy makers and banking organizations to handle with the ongoing situation.

Banking Communication and Employee Relation

The globalization has changed on the development of organizational management and increase intense competition. The modern technology has raise employees performance by using advance communications technology. Both organization and human are social being which are interlinked with each other (Austin &Pinkleton, 2015). Effective communication improves job satisfaction, which directly improves in productivity. Thus, organizational communication and worker performance integrate different units and functions of an organization Communicating performance standard and expectation regularly observe activities of employees and provide them feedback (Aral et al., 2013). Moreover, effective internal communication successfully manages the strategic management of organization in order to engage employees and achieve objectives. Communication identifies corporate strategy, which drives organization towards their goal and objective. The means of communication set common goal in the organization, which focuses on achieving desired objectives in organization (Ahmad, 2006; Alleyne et al., 2007).

Effective communication between employees increase trust in organizations, which leads to the success on business organization. The relationships with supervisors and coworkers exchange all the information, which is best practice of communication. Generally, communication management maintains the connection between employees to employees and employees to organization. Thus, it increases performance of organization effectively and efficiently (Hargie et al., 2002; Kurland & Bailey, 2000). Furthermore, management hesitates to practice effective communication, which becomes problematic for the organization as it develops lack of data and weak action plans. Most of the managers are poor at communication is one of the defect of organization. Their improper communication leads to the organizational losses (Power &Rienstra, 1990). Their unfriendly behavior might create problem of motivation. As a result their working efficiency will be decrease. Thus, banking communication plays vital role to help managers to investigate real issues and problem in organization. With the passage of time, communication becomes tools to coordinate internal control system and drive organization into successful path (Thomson &Hecker, 2001; Sadia et al, 2016).

The flow of communication create organizational goal, values, objective which helps to prepare strategies in organization. There is positive relationship between communication and employees (Smythe, 1996; Thomas et al., 2009). Moreover, effective communication increase overall organizational functioning, foundation of sound management, greater coordination and effective interaction among workers. Now, the placement of e-banking communication in bank improves performance of workers and increase efficiency in work (Svensson, 2004). Shrestha et al. (2019) stated that quality work life also impacted on how worker communicates in their organization. So, banks should focus in effective communication.

METHODOLOGY

This research has been conducted by using a mixed method of analysis, considering the communication status in commercial banks of Nepal. Content analysis was done by reviewing studies and grey literature as available from a thorough internet surfing. For the larger picture of the study, the researchers have drawn secondary information from past to the recent communication related publications. The primary data based findings were drawn from the previous cross-sectional researches on the banking customer side with 403 respondents (Parajuli, 2019) and 326 bankers (Shrestha, 2019). Hence, the research mainly focuses on descriptive methodology and desk review.

Theoretical Debate on Banking Communication

Communication determines the success of banking sector (Hill & Alexander, 2001) so that there are numerous literatures, communication models and theories discussing it as integral part of banking sector and customer satisfaction (Ammari et al., 2017; Rijal, 2005; Banstola, 2007; Sapkota et al., 2018; Khatri & Dhungel, 2013; Alawni et al., 2015) with especial emphasis on customer retention, loyality and information flow (Lassar et al., 2000; Goode & Moutinho, 1996; Gautam & Dhital, 2004; Laukken et al., 2009; Alawni et al., 2015).

Theorists and communication experts have invented and experimented many models. Al-Fedagahi (2012) states Shannon and Weaver model of communication related to transmission of information from sender to receiver with the help of medium. These days major way to create strong customer base and relation with customers is good communication tactics used by banks. Flensburg (2009) developed a model: Structure plus data equals to information. When certain information is flowed by bank to customers they visualize the information and create certain perception on the matter communicated. Lenski model (2010) helps to understand relationship between information and knowledge. How bank disseminate the information and how customers perceive the information generated by banks and are acknowledged by customers can be accessed in the study. Saussure's speed circuit model (2003) gives priority to natural language stating there is no place for message as it connects only receivers and senders but focus on language systems stored in brains of individual language users' (Daylight, 2017). The study depicts how natural languages in the brains of employees or customers are conveyed to each other.

Further, the language stored in general model of communication formulated by Gerbner (1956) deals with two dimensions of communication: perceptual and means and control and is processed through operation of coding and decoding. In this study the perception of employees, communication correspondence and customers are taken into consideration. The mentioned theories deal how effective communication can lead banks to attract and retain customers. The communication practiced by banks helps to create image, reputation and trust among the customers (Narteh & Odoom, 2015; Guo, 2018). The advancement of information and communication technology is improving in working styles of banking sector. The banks and financial institutions are improving technological sector to sustain in competitive banking sector. The latest technology adopted by bank and financial institutions are electronic banking where activities have been performed on the basis of electronic channels through mobile phone, internet, telephone etc (Sharma, 2011). Sikdar et al. 2015 revealed that e-banking service is the combination of conventional banking, social computing and internet banking. Moreover, e- banking focuses on profitability and performance of employees. It is clear that banks are shifted to electronic banking to cut costs maintaining reliable customer services. Now days, banking industry being the spirit of financial sector banking system has been used by most of the bank in overall the world (Mansour et al. 2016). Banking system works for achieving goals and shape the strategy for competitive advantage through financial service management, digitalization, networking, responsiveness, human resource management, corporate culture and organizational regulation (Rus et al., 2016; Yaseen & Qirem, 2017; Ishaq Bhatti et al., 2011).

RESULTS AND DISCUSSION

In the study of Italinan banks, Cavallone and Modina (2013) assert that in this competitive banking age communication has been crucial factor in order to attract and retain customers helping to create long term value focusing on transparency, response speed and advisory-based sales. Kirakosyan and Dănăiaţă (2014) further state better communication is important for better relationship with customers in the study conducted in Romania. Likewise, communication in banks of Nepal has also been increasing and strengthening as it is found to build good customer base in today's competitive market age. As similar to our study, Sapkota et al. (2018) state that latest services used by customers in Nepalese commercial banks are SMS banking, m-banking, E-banking and utility bills payment. Information and telecommunications have advanced in Nepalese commercial banks and major advancement are in the field of ATM, Mobile banking, internet banking. These have been possible because of banks' consistent efforts of making customers aware on various banking facilities (Banstola, 2007). The study by Lenka et al. (2009) shows that Customer satisfaction has enhanced and encouraged in banks of India through improvement in various aspects of communication. It is also revealed that maximum customer satisfaction is generated from quick service, easy transaction environment in bank, reasonable service charges, well-maintained ATM, timely and helpful SMS/e-mails by banks, safety, convenience, adequate branch networks, modern equipment used by bank (Nupur, 2010; Muyeed, 2012). However, Vyas & Raitani (2014) mention that critical areas because of which customers switch the banks are improper communication about facilities provided by banks, service quality, effective advertisements competition, response to customers and price rates.

Piric et al. (2017) state that customers' perception strongly influences customer loyalty, communication, market share and profitability of the banking business. In the study conducted by Gautam & Dhital (2004), they find that respondents perceive that their banks are neither neglecting them nor providing wonderful facilities and services but in contrast this study shows that the scenario has improved to certain extent and banks have started giving attention and preference to consumers knowing that consumers are building blocks for the flourishment and enhancement of profitability and services of banks. Major determinants that customer look forward while their banks communicate with them are how the employees of the bank interact, behave with them, problem faced while transacting in bank, the way banks disseminate the information and the ways they handle various issues and grievances of customers, hassle in updating their account and consistency of communication by banks.

Additionally, major expectation of customers from bank is to get information on time accurately. 31.03% customers expects bank to provide information timely. 25.78% customers have faced hassle in account update, therefore, to minimize the hassle quick service, digital service, automatic update; prior information can be adopted by banks where 26.98% customers responded that providing prior information regarding updates and amendments would be effective in order to minimize hassle in account update. Likewise, while asking about suggestion for improvement in banking services majority of customers (22.17%) suggest banks to disperse proper and timely information for improving their services.

This study covers banking communication from customers and bankers' perceptions on recommending effective communication measures by identifying the communication gap as the first study of this details in Nepalese banking communication context. In the earlier studies, conceptual frameworks were developed to identify dependent and independent variables necessary for moving the study forward.

Banking services are expanding due to globalization, economic instability and technological process. With the globalization, technological change and economic crisis maintaining banking system become challenging jobs (Rus et al. 2016). Banks are equally promoting to develop competitive advantages through smooth running of banking system that mainly include administrative, technical, regulatory system and human resources. The advancement of information and communication technology is improving in working styles of banking sector. The banks and financial institutions are improving technological sector to sustain in competitive world. The latest technology adopted by bank and financial institutions are electronic banking where activities have been performed on the basis of electronic channels through mobile phone, internet and telephone (Sharma, 2011). Likewise, the advancement of technology has direct impact in changing the styles of banking styles. The banking industry has been changed into the digitalization and networking technologies to deliver quality service at lower cost with high quality, satisfying customer and stakeholder. Sikdar et al. (2015) revealed that e-banking service is the combination of conventional banking, social computing and internet banking. Moreover, e-banking focuses on profitability and performance of employees.

Moreover, banks are shifted to electronic banking to cut costs maintaining reliable customer services. Now days, banking industry being the spirit of financial sector banking system has been used by most of the bank in overall the world (Mansour et al. 2016). Moreover, financial industry shows direct connection with the economic revolution. Financial industries are promoting technological innovation for the economic development of Nation. Economic evolution is based on monitoring managers, mobilizing savings, managing risks, evaluating projects, and facilitating transactions. Banking management system maintains good relation with employees to understand employee characteristics.

Banking communication is becoming important measure how bank performs in relation to set of customer requirement and how customers are being more concerned about information and service provided by banks (Hill & Alexander, 2001; Paudel et al., 2020). As stated in earlier studies by Lassar et al. (2000), Goode & Moutinho (1996), Gautam & Dhital (2004), Laukken et al. (2009) with increasing competition among banks, they have started increasing focus on customer satisfaction and customer retention by improving information flow, service quality and communication patterns. The impact of bank communication depends upon customer satisfaction, customer loyalty driven from the communication information offered by banks (Alawni et al., 2015). The impact on bank communication can be negative if employees of the organization are not committed to their work and they do not communicate well with the customers as well which will result in customers switching the bank and minimizing customers (Ammari et al., 2017). Rijal (2006), Banstola (2007), Sapkota et al. (2018), Khatri & Dhungel (2013) argue that communication practices, methods used by banks are likely to determine either customers will have positive or negative influence towards bank.

Similarly, significant improvements on communication models can be observed in various studies. Employees' behavior is the crucial part of bank, which derives the attitude of employees toward organization. The behavior of employees is generally determined by performance, effort, social influence, perceived e-banking service quality and motivation (Yaseen & Qirem, 2018). The behavior of employees, attitude, performance and efforts are the factors which create positive and negative thoughts of employees. These factors should monitor time and again to refresh and run the organization smoothly. This paper also mentions issues related to employee's behavior discussing about communication culture, responsiveness and organizational culture in detail. Similarly, responsiveness is major factor which advocate cleanliness, reduce resource wastage and protect environment. Whereas, organizational culture can be promoted through gender equality, equal distribution of power, stereotyping, class, manner, racism, customs, language and anxiety.

The majority of accounts holder's use internet services for the daily use. The globalization has transformed clerical work into electronic process. Over viewing the current scenario, core banking service facilities management becomes major issues of discussion. The awareness about internet banking, its benefit and security become prominent factor where employees need to understand clear in order to make customers clear about the banking service. The electronic banking can perform various banking activities through electronic channels like internet, mobile and telephone. Thus, banks are launching different technologies such as Automated Teller Machine (ATM), Internet banking, Mobile Banking, Telephone Banking and point of sales which save time and increase effectiveness in organization (Khatri and Dhungel, 2013). Banking communication shows relationship between communication management and overall banking communication. The proper banking management communication emphasizes to create customer satisfaction and bank loyalty. Financial institution like banks encourage to promote banking communication management because it fosters economic development as it manages risks, monitor managers, evaluate project, mobilize saving and facilitating transaction. Moreover, effective communication successfully collaborates the interpersonal relationship with employees and increase working efficiency. They focus on both commercial and individual customer through qualitative service. Thus, the importance of banking communication is increasing day by day in banking system in Nepal.

CONCLUSION AND RECOMMENDATIONS

This research study concludes that cooperative level of bank, language used and various services offered by banks were found to be factors affecting customers and bankers' perception in banking communication. 61.62% respondents are yet unaware about communication system being used by banks so that banks should provide timely and proper information for improvement in banking services. Banking communication mirrors the true pictures of organizations; hence, communicative skills of banking officials should be effective. It seems that male employees are higher than female employees and majority are highly educated and yet they are poor in managerial communication process. Also, female managers should not be discriminated and nullified for higher-level positions. Thus, banks should learn to attract customers, use updated technology, follow effective communication rules and increase awareness level of both employees and customers. Therefore, banking communication management depends on banking system, employees' behavior and core-banking service facilities. Communicating schemes, addressing problems, listening ATM problems are positively correlated so that proper attention in informing and updating customers about changes regarding banking activities are required.

The following recommendations are put forward for improving communication management for banking sector policy makers, people as prospective employees, related monetary organizations, industries and government at large:

1. **Using bias-free language:** Language reflects the way we think, believe and make perspective. To establish good relation with customers, bankers must also appear fair by avoiding gender bias, racial and ethnic bias, age bias and disability factors.
2. **Customers' awareness program:** As 61.62% banking customers are unaware about advanced communication system adopted by banks, promotional campaigns should be initiated to aware customers about various tools, strategies, system used by banks to communicate with customers. In order to run these kinds of programs bankers association Nepal, NRB and banks can join hands together. 31.03% customers expects to get proper information in time about various updates made by banks, therefore, timely information to customers regarding changes, update and problems seen in their account should be conveyed by banks which would help them in earning trust of customers increasing their loyalty towards bank and minimizing hassle in account updates.
3. **Building strong relationship between banks and customers**: In order to evoke trust with banking customers, bankers should demonstrate honesty, objectivity, sincerity; awareness of audience needs and demonstrate impressive performance through effective communication style. Allocating sufficient time to the customers for addressing their genuine problems can build strong relationship with them.
4. **Improving in customer service:** As per the findings of the study 22.17% respondents state that banks need to improve their services and communication. Initiations can be taken by analyzing expectations and needs of customers, addressing their queries properly and providing them secured, friendly environment and better facilities. For the purpose NRB can build specific guidelines for banks particularly helping to ease customers in their communication.
5. **Composing appropriate message correspondence:** The quality of message determines the successful execution. Bankers should control style and tone by using conversational tone, avoiding obsolete and pompous language, avoiding preaching and bragging, and using plain English in place of incomprehensible language. In composing message it is quite important to nitpicking, using functional and content words, concreteness denotative and connotative focus communicate well. In written messages, bankers should use simple sentence, craft unified and coherent paragraphs, and add transitional elements.

6. **Regulating bodies should administer banking communication policies:** While reviewing various literatures in order to ease the study, various policies, reviews of Government of Nepal like SDGs policies, Information Act, Government of Nepal communication policies, National information and communication technology policies are made. These policies cover certain aspects of communication and can be linked with communication being practiced in banks. However, if NRB would initiate and formulate communication policies specifically for banking and financial institutions then that would ease banks to follow the policy and implement effective communication which can be proved to be fruitful for customers, NRB, banking and financial institutions.
7. **Organizing staff development programs on banking communication:** The overall awareness level on banking communication displayed 46% employees are moderately aware about banking communication, 37% employees are highly aware and 12% are low aware about banking communication. Thus, the bankers are moderately aware about banking communication because they are busy in office hour but they are required to improve communication. Moreover, the pressure also adds mental stress on their mind. They concentrate more on fulfilling targets rather than understanding issues related to communication.
8. **Avoiding gender biasness in the growth of the employees:** The awareness level on banking communication based on sex illustrates 45% of female employees and 55% male employees are aware about banking communication. In an organization both the gender are prominent factors for smooth running of business. Top-level managers take most of the decisions and male employees mostly occupy those positions where female employees are slightly backward in taking decisions and policies making activities due to male chauvinistic culture. The organizations should provide opportunities to female employees to utilize the creative skills and talents of the women.
9. **Bridging the communication barriers for conflict resolution:** The frequency level indicates that 76% of employees are facing conflict with customers and employees frequently. Moreover, 52% of employees face multi-cultural difficulties in the organization. The main reason behind conflict is poor communication, competition, difference in work environment, individual differences, more power, difference in objectives, lack of well defined responsibility, language problem, incompatible goals, structure of organization, disruptive mentality and so on. Therefore, in order to manage conflict and multicultural difficulties employees should practice for negotiation and fairness, non-threatening behavior, respect, trust and support, honesty and accountability, responsible parenting, shared responsibility, economic partnership, harmonization, teamwork, collaboration, effective communication and co-ordination in their work.
10. **Promoting e-banking communication and use of ICTs:** The human behaviors resist changing their work patterns. Digitalization has shifted traditional method of banking communication. Banks are using papers excessively in daily basis that can be controlled through promotion of e-banking communication. Only 40% of employees are adequately known about the update version of e-banking system. They are still having inadequate information about new electronic facilities provided by e-Sewa like viber banking, bank smart, fone banking and vendor machine. They are unaware about update version of banking system as they think the existing technology has sufficient to promote e-banking communication.
11. **Considering the customer centered communication:** Improvement of customer and employee satisfaction is the major tool, which creates goodwill of the organization. The satisfied customers and employees spread positive word of mouth. The e-banking practice has accelerated service delivery in bank, which satisfies both customers and employees. The study also reveals that 80%

of the employees are satisfied with the modern technologies as it decreases their handwork. The age group between 20-40 are satisfied with modern technology and above 40 years age group of employees are still not satisfied with modern technology as they feel hesitation to practice e-banking. On the other hand, only 60% of employees are satisfied with e-banking practice. Thus, for the greater acceptance, communication should be audience centred.

12. **Prioritizing in digitalization, data security and documentation:** Banks have major issues on data security and privacy maintenance. A per findings, banks has to face 23% of data security and privacy issues. Bank and financial institutions are highly regulated industries operating numerous transactions daily. Banks are trusted as data security and privacy management. In spite of these e-banking services, facilities increase the problem of security and privacy management issues. Hackers are getting more active and committed cyber crime. These kinds of challenges might lose the trust of client. Therefore, to make customer aware about daily transaction their data are maintained time and again.
13. **Following green banking policy:** Environment conservation is corporate social responsibilities of banks. The banks need to focus on promotion of green banking policy. The result shows that banks promote green banking practice through reducing paper consumption by 54%, recycle waste by 31%, sponsor tree plantation by 29%, protect environment by 46%, reduce stationary cost by 58%. Thus, still bank use excessive amount of papers daily, only less percentage of waste are used for recycle and sponsor tree plantation. Thus, bank should focus on practice of green banking policy, which helps to promote social responsibility, advocate cleanliness, reduces resource wastage, support government law and upholds ethics in business.
14. **Ethno relativism:** Cross-cultural trainings should be provided to the employees so that they respect others' cultures as well. They become neutral and understand that all the cultures have their good aspects and their negative aspects as well. It will help them to avoid ethnocentrism and xenophobia, and they can coordinate and communicate well in teams. While working in banks, if they have this view then this can help to establish better relation among employees for desired output.

Thus, if we can assimilate the communication gap in customers and bankers, the nexus can bring career success, growth of business, strong decision making, faster problem solving, precaution of potential problems, steadier workflow, increased productivity, strong business relationships, persuasive marketing messages, enhances professional images, lower employee turnover, better financial results and strengthens organizational relations.

Limitation of the Study and Future Research

The limitation of this study is the use of purposive sampling technique; other sampling techniques could help in better sample selection. The study only insights the communication pattern, practice and perception on commercial banks and their customers so, this study cannot be used to generalize overall banking and financial market of Nepal. And, both traditional and modern means of communications are being practiced by present commercial banks in Nepal. The issue requires further investigation as to find out best way of communication that banks can practice in order to satisfy and aware their customers about communication techniques being practised by banks to facilitate them. Also, the study does not look how customers of ''B", "C", "D" grade financial institutions perceive communication being flowed by their respective organizations and what strategies those organizations are following to ease communication procedure for their customers. Hence, further research can be conducted including all licensed financial institutions by NRB for attainment of better output and the role those financial institutions are playing in order to ease communication with their customers. This study was conducted in Kathmandu valley only, so further research might be conducted in other areas as well so that bigger picture on how customers across Nepal perceive banking communication can be analyzed. Likewise, monetary loss occurred due to fault in bank's technology were only included in present study but loss can occur in other forms rather than monetary as well so, loss of time, value that might have occurred due to banks fault can also in included in further studies.

REFERENCES

Agarwal, S., & Garg, A. (2012). The importance of communication within organizations: A research on two hotels in Uttarakhand. *Journal of Business and Management*, *12*, 30–49.

Ahmad, A. H. (2006). Auditing communication satisfaction among academic staff: An approach to managing academic excellence. *Business Review (Federal Reserve Bank of Philadelphia)*, *5*(1), 330–333.

Akmajian, A., Farmer, A. K., Bickmore, L., Demers, R. A., & Harnish, R. M. (2017). *Linguistics: An introduction to language and communication*. MIT press.

Al-Fedaghi, S. (2012). A conceptual foundation for the Shannon-Weaver model of communication. *International Journal of Soft Computing*, *7*(1), 12–19. doi:10.3923/ijscomp.2012.12.19

Alawni, M. S., Yusoff, R. Z., Al-Swidi, A. K., & Al-Matari, E. M. (2015). The relationship between communication, customer knowledge and customer loyalty in Saudi Arabia insurance industry companies. *Mediterranean Journal of Social Sciences*, *6*(1), 315–318. doi:10.5901/mjss.2015.v6n1p318

Alleyne, C., Kakabadse, A., & Kakabadse, N. (2007). Using the HR intranet: An exploratory analysis of its impact on managerial satisfaction with the HR function. *Personnel Review*, *36*(2), 295–310. doi:10.1108/00483480710726154

Amiri, M. (2015). Internal communication: Perception and opinions of bank employees. *Academie Royale Des Sciences D Outre-mer Bulletin Des Seances, 4*(5), 17-22.

Ammari, G., Alkurdi, B., Alshurideh, A., & Alrowwad, A. (2017). Investigating the impact of communication satisfaction on organizational commitment: A practical approach to increase employees' loyalty. *International Journal of Marketing Studies*, *9*(2), 113–133. doi:10.5539/ijms.v9n2p113

Aral, S., Dellarocas, C., & Godes, D. (2013). Introduction to the special issue—social media and business transformation: A framework for research. *Information Systems Research*, *24*(1), 3–13. doi:10.1287/isre.1120.0470

Austin, E. W., & Pinkleton, B. E. (2015). *Strategic public relations management: Planning and managing effective communication campaigns*. Routledge. doi:10.4324/9781315754833

B. K., A., Mahato, A., Thapa, S., Rai, A., & Devkota, N. (2019). Achieving Nepal's sustainable development goals (SDGs) by effective compliance of corporate governance. *Quest Journal of Management and Social Sciences*, *1*(1), 50–72. doi:10.3126/qjmss.v1i1.25974

Banstola, A. (2007). Prospects and challenges of e-banking in Nepal. *Journal of Nepalese Business Studies*, *4*(1), 96–104. doi:10.3126/jnbs.v4i1.1034

Berger, A. A. (2018). *Media and communication research methods: An introduction to qualitative and quantitative approaches*. Sage Publications.

Blythe, J. (2008). *Essentials of marketing*. Pearson Education.

Bucăţa, G., & Rizescu, A. M. (2017). The role of communication in enhancing work effectiveness of an organization. *Land Forces Academy Review*, *22*(1), 49–57. doi:10.1515/raft-2017-0008

Cavallone, M., & Modina, M. (2013). Customer perception of bank communication: Evidence and implications. *Corporate Ownership and Control*, *10*(4), 299–307. doi:10.22495/cocv10i4c3art1

Daylight, R. (2017). Saussure and the model of communication. *Semiotica*, *2017*(217), 173–194. doi:10.1515em-2016-0038

Dharmavaram, V., & Nittala, R. (2018). Service quality and customer satisfaction in online banking. *International Journal of Online Marketing*, *8*(2), 45–56. doi:10 4018/IJOM.2018040103

Flensburg, P. (2009). An enhanced communication model. *The International Journal of Digital Accounting Research*, *9*(15), 31–43.

Gaire, A. K. S. (2018). Effectiveness of internet banking system and clients satisfaction: evidence from Surkhet, Nepal. *Technology, 1*(1), 10-21.

Gajurel, D. P., & Pradhan, R. S. (2012). Concentration and competition in Nepalese banking. *Journal of Business. Economics*, *1*(1), 5–16.

Gautam, T., & Dhital, M. S. (2004). Customer satisfaction in Nepalese commercial banks. *Journal of Management and Development Review*, *1*(2), 1–18.

Gerbner, G. (1956). Toward a general model of communication. *Audio Visual Communication Review*, 171-199.

Glynn Mangold, W., Miller, F., & Brockway, G. R. (1999). Word-of-mouth communication in the service marketplace. *Journal of Services Marketing*, *13*(1), 73–89. doi:10.1108/08876049910256186

Goode, M., & Moutinho, L. (1996). The effects of consumers age on overall satisfaction: An application to financial services. *Journal of Professional Services Marketing*, *13*(2), 93–112. doi:10.1300/J090v13n02_07

Guo, Y. (2018). Implementing relationship banking strategies and techniques and improving customer value. *Finance and Market, 2*(2).

Hargie, O., Tourish, D., & Wilson, N. (2002). Communication audits and the effects of increased information: A follow-up study. *The Journal of Business Communication, 39*(4), 414-436.

Haroon, H., & Malik, H. D. (2018). The Impact of organizational communication on organizational performance. *Journal of Research in Social Sciences*, *2*(1), 140–156.

Herr, P. M., Kardes, F. R., & Kim, J. (1991). Effects of word-of-mouth and product-attribute information on persuasion: An accessibility-diagnosticity perspective. *The Journal of Consumer Research*, *17*(4), 454–462. doi:10.1086/208570

Hill, N., & Alexander, J. (2001). Handbook of customer satisfaction and loyalty measurement. *International Journal of Retail & Distribution Management*, *29*(7), 347–347. doi:10.1108/ijrdm.2001.29.7.347.1

Hoque, M. E., Nik Hashim, N. M. H., & Razzaque, M. A. (2018). Effects of communication and financial concerns on banking attitude-behaviour relations. *Service Industries Journal*, *38*(13-14), 1017–1042. doi:10.1080/02642069.2018.1428954

Ishaq Bhatti, M., Zafarullah, M., Awan, H. M., & Bukhari, K. S. (2011). Employees' perspective of organizational service quality orientation: Evidence from Islamic banking industry. *International Journal of Islamic and Middle Eastern Finance and Management*, *4*(4), 280–294. doi:10.1108/17538391111186537

Kharel, S., Magar, S., Chaurasiya, N., Maharjan, S., & Rijal, C. P. (2019). Transparency and accountability in the Nepalese corporate sector: A critical assessment. *Quest Journal of Management and Social Sciences*, *1*(1), 1–25. doi:10.3126/qjmss.v1i1.25972

Khatri, J. R., & Upadhyaya-Dhungel, K. (2013). Internet banking in Nepal: Use and challenges. *Banking Journal*, *3*(2), 57–77. doi:10.3126/bj.v3i2.8544

Kirakosyan, K., & Dănăiaţă, D. (2014). Communication management in electronic banking. Better communication for better relationship. *Procedia: Social and Behavioral Sciences*, *124*, 361–370. doi:10.1016/j.sbspro.2014.02.497

Kurland, N. B., & Bailey, D. E. (2000). Telework: The advantages and challenges of working here, there, anywhere, and anytime. *IEEE Engineering Management Review*, *28*(2), 49–60.

Lassar, W. M., Manolis, C., & Winsor, R. D. (2000). Service quality perspectives and satisfaction in private banking. *Journal of Services Marketing*, *14*(3), 244–271. doi:10.1108/08876040010327248

Laukkanen, T., Sinkkonen, S., & Laukkanen, P. (2009). Communication strategies to overcome functional and psychological resistance to Internet banking. *International Journal of Information Management*, *29*(2), 111–118. doi:10.1016/j.ijinfomgt.2008.05.008

Lenka, U., Suar, D., & Mohapatra, P. K. (2009). Service quality, customer satisfaction, and customer loyalty in Indian commercial banks. *The Journal of Entrepreneurship*, *18*(1), 47–64. doi:10.1177/097135570801800103

Lenski, W. (2010). Information: A conceptual investigation. *Information (Basel)*, *1*(2), 74–118. doi:10.3390/info1020074

Mansour, I. H. F., Eljelly, A. M., & Abdullah, A. M. (2016). Consumers' attitude towards e-banking services in Islamic banks: The case of Sudan. *Review of International Business and Strategy*, *26*(2), 244–260. doi:10.1108/RIBS-02-2014-0024

Mishra, B. B. (2008). *The development of e-payment and challenges in Nepal*. Academic Press.

Mohr, J., & Nevin, J. R. (1990). Communication strategies in marketing channels: A theoretical perspective. *Journal of Marketing*, *54*(4), 36–51. doi:10.1177/002224299005400404

Moore, P. M., Rivera, S., Bravo-Soto, G. A., Olivares, C., & Lawrie, T. A. (2018). Communication skills training for healthcare professionals working with people who have cancer. *Cochrane Database of Systematic Reviews*, *2018*(7), 1–120. doi:10.1002/14651858.CD003751.pub4 PMID:30039853

Muyeed, M. A. (2012). Customer perception on service quality in retail banking in developing countries-a case study. *International Journal of Marketing Studies*, *4*(1), 116–122. doi:10.5539/ijms.v4n1p116

Narteh, B., & Odoom, R. (2015). Does internal marketing influence employee loyalty? Evidence from the Ghanaian banking industry. *Services Marketing Quarterly*, *36*(2), 112–135. doi:10.1080/15332969.2015.1014237

Nepal Rastra Bank. (2016). *Directives, Notification: Banks & FIs Regulation, Categorization of Banks.* Retrieved from https://www.nrb.org.np/bfr/bfrdirectives.php?vw=15

Nepal Rastra Bank. (2018). *Directives, Notification: Banks & FIs Regulation.* Retrieved from https://www.nrb.org.np/bfr/bfrdirectives.php?vw=15

Nupur, J. M. (2010). E-banking and customers' satisfaction in Bangladesh: An analysis. *International Review of Business Research Papers, 6*(4), 145-156.

Pant, B. (2016). *Financial Inclusion in Nepal: Policy Review and Prescriptions* (No. 34). NRB Working Paper.

Parajuli, S., Paudel, U. R., & Devkota, N. (2020). Banking Communications: A Perceptual Study of Customer Relations. *South Asian Journal of Social Studies and Economics*, *8*(3), 23–34. doi:10.9734ajsse/2020/v8i330212

Parajuli, S., Rajbhandari, S., Joshi, A., Sujan, K. C., & Bhandari, U. (2019). Transforming corporate governance through effective corporate social responsibility (CSR) and social entrepreneurship orientation in Nepal. *Quest Journal of Management and Social Sciences*, *1*(1), 26–49. doi:10.3126/qjmss.v1i1.25973

Paudel, U. R., Parajuli, S., Devkota, N., & Mahapatra, S. K. (2020). What determines customers' perception of banking communication? An empirical evidence from commercial banks of Nepal. *Global Economy Journal*, *20*(4), 1–21. doi:10.1142/S2194565920500190

Paudel, U. R., Puri, S., Parajuli, S., Devkota, N., & Bhandari, U. (2021). Measuring Cultural Diversity Impact in Hospitality Industry Leadership: Managerial Communication Perspective from Five Star Hotels in Kathmandu Valley, Nepal. *Journal of Tourism & Adventure*, *4*(1), 75–88. doi:10.3126/jota.v4i1.40680

Pikkarainen, T., Pikkarainen, K., Karjaluoto, H., & Pahnila, S. (2004). Consumer acceptance of online banking: An extension of the technology acceptance model. *Internet Research*, *14*(3), 224–235. doi:10.1108/10662240410542652

Pirić, V., Martinović, M., & Barac, Z. (2018). A study on customer's perception of Croatia's banking industry. *UTMS Journal of Economics (Skopje)*, *9*(2), 169–180.

Power, M., & Rienstra, B. (1999). Internal communication in new corporate conglomerates: Developing a corporate communication model for loosely coupled businesses in local government. *International Journal of Public Sector Management*, *12*(6), 501–515. doi:10.1108/09513559910301757

Rijal, S. (2006). Application of management control system in Nepalese commercial banks. *Journal of Nepalese Business Studies*, *3*(1), 92–99. doi:10.3126/jnbs.v3i1.486

Rus, S., Mocan, M., Ardelean, B. O., Ivascu, L., & Cioca, L. I. (2016). Conceptualization and examination of success factors in the banking system. *Procedia Economics and Finance*, *39*, 679–684. doi:10.1016/S2212-5671(16)30289-1

Sadia, A., Salleh, B. M., Kadir, Z. A., & Sanif, S. (2016). The relationship between organizational communication and employees productivity with new dimensions of effective communication flow. *Journal of Business and Social Review in Emerging Economies*, *2*(2), 93–100. doi:10.26710/jbsee.v2i2.35

Sapkota, N., Paudel, N., Subedi, D. K., Bhattarai, R., & Shrestha, R. (2018). Role of information communication technology (ICT) in Nepalese banking industry. *American Scientific Research Journal for Engineering, Technology, and Sciences*, *42*(1), 75–88.

Schlich, B. (2012). *The customer takes control: global consumer banking survey 2012*. Ernst & Young.

Şeitan, R. (2017). Organizational discourses-A literature review. *Acta Universitatis Danubius Communication, 11*(2).

Sharma, H. (2011). Bankers' perspectives on e-banking. *Global Journal of Research in Management*, *1*(1), 71-85.

Shrestha, P. (2018). Service quality and customer satisfaction: Evidence of Nepalese banks. *NCC Journal*, *3*(1), 121–133. doi:10.3126/nccj.v3i1.20254

Shrestha, S., Devkota, N., Paudel, U., Bhandari, U., & Parajuli, S. (2020). Bankers' Communication Know-how: An Analysis from Commercial Banks of Kathmandu valley. *Quest Journal of Management and Social Sciences*, *2*(1), 80–99. doi:10.3126/qjmss.v2i1.29023

Shrestha, S., Thapa, S., Mangrati, L., Devkota, P., Rai, R., & Adhikari, K. (2019). Quality of work life (QWL) situation in the Nepalese corporate sector. *Quest Journal of Management and Social Sciences*, *1*(1), 119–145. doi:10.3126/qjmss.v1i1.25977

Sikdar, P., Kumar, A., & Makkad, M. (2015). Online banking adoption: A factor validation and satisfaction causation study in the context of Indian banking customers. *International Journal of Bank Marketing*, *33*(6), 760–785. doi:10.1108/IJBM-11-2014-0161

Smythe, J. (1996). The changing role of internal communication in tomorrow's company. *Managing Service Quality*, *6*(2), 41–44. doi:10.1108/09604529610109756

Svensson, G. (2004). Interactive service quality in service encounters: Empirical illustration and models. *Managing Service Quality*, *14*(4), 278–287. doi:10.1108/09604520410546815

Tan, M., & Teo, T. S. (2000). Factors influencing the adoption of Internet banking. *Journal of the Association for Information Systems*, *1*(1), 5–14. doi:10.17705/1jais.00005

Thomas, G. F., Zolin, R., & Hartman, J. L. (2009). The central role of communication in developing trust and its effect on employee involvement. *The Journal of Business Communication, 46*(3), 287-310.

Thomson, K., & Hecker, L. (2001). Value-adding communication: Innovation in employee communication and internal marketing. *Journal of Communication Management (London), 5*(1), 48–58. doi:10.1108/13632540110806668

Thussu, D. K. (2018). *International communication: Continuity and change*. Bloomsbury Publishing.

Van Eemeren, F. H., & Grootendorst, R. (2016). *Argumentation, communication, and fallacies: A pragma-dialectical perspective*. Routledge. doi:10.4324/9781315538662

Van Staden, E., Marx, S., & Erasmus-Kritzinger, L. (2007). *Corporate communication: getting the message across in business*. VanSchaik.

Vyas, V., & Raitani, S. (2014). Drivers of customers' switching behaviour in Indian banking industry. *International Journal of Bank Marketing, 32*(4), 321–342. doi:10.1108/IJBM-04-2013-0033

Walther, J. B. (1988). Communication satisfaction in the bank: An audit evaluation. *The Journal of Business Communication, 25*(3), 79-86.

Yaseen, S. G., & El Qirem, I. A. (2018). Intention to use e-banking services in the Jordanian commercial banks. *International Journal of Bank Marketing, 36*(3), 557–571. doi:10.1108/IJBM-05-2017-0082

Chapter 2
Consumer Behavior and Sustainable Consumption in Economic Theory

Mikail Kar
Bursa Uludag University, Turkey

ABSTRACT

Existing economic systems have encouraged overconsumption by constantly inspiring consumers to have more. With these consumption habits, it has been understood that it is not possible to maintain present living standards for many years, and as a result, sustainability discussions have emerged. One of the most fundamental components of these sustainability discussions is the "sustainable consumption" approach. Sustainable consumption proposes to meet the needs of today's humanity without compromising the ability of future generations to meet their needs in order to leave a livable world for them. At this point, the aim of this study is to discuss sustainable consumption from the perspective of economic theory and to examine it within the framework of consumer behavior. For this purpose, the titles of consumption, consumer behavior, consumption society, sustainability, sustainable consumption, consumer behaviors in sustainable consumption and reasons for sustainable consumption failure, and suggestions for solutions are discussed in detail in the study.

INTRODUCTION

Economic theory is built on the assumption that human needs are unlimited and resources are scarce. In order to meet these unlimited needs for many years, production and consumption have been made by ignoring the scarcity of natural resources. Today's economic systems, which started to be shaped by the industrialization process, encouraged consumers to consume irresponsibly and unconsciously, by suggesting that they should not settle for less and have more. The production and consumption structure envisaged by these systems has increased its influence especially in the second half of the 20th century, causing many ecological problems to emerge. In other words, humanity has used resources as much as possible in order to produce more, consume more and earn more, and it has caused the pollution and

DOI: 10.4018/978-1-7998-9590-9.ch002

destruction of nature. It has been realized that it will not be possible to sustain the increase in growth and development with these consumption habits for many years, and it has been evaluated that the change has become a necessity. In other words, the limited natural resources used to meet the unlimited needs of people at this point made it necessary to harmonize the environment and the economy.

Humanity, which did not attach sufficient importance to the environmental issue for many years, started to notice and take into account ecological problems from the beginning of the 1970s, with the increasing environmental problems. In the literature that started to emerge in this period, the existing economic approach was questioned and it was stated that a new economic understanding should be developed that did not disturb the functioning of the ecological system. At this point, there has been a transition from the economic understanding focused on maximum growth to the idea of sustainable development. As one of the most fundamental components of these sustainability discussions, the "sustainable consumption" approach comes to the fore. Sustainable consumption is a form of consumption that is based on the use of the world's resources within the limits of sustainability and seeks ways to minimize the damage to natural life. In other words, it is the consideration of environmental concerns in consumption. The way to leave a livable world to future generations will be possible by focusing on how economic activities such as the selection, use and disposal of products and services can be carried out in a way to gain social and environmental gain.

The aim of this study is to discuss sustainable consumption from the perspective of economic theory and to examine it within the framework of consumer behavior. Although sustainability is a concept that economics has brought to the interdisciplinary literature, the sustainable consumption approach has been discussed more intensively in other disciplines and has not been adequately addressed in the context of economic theory. In this respect, this study makes an important contribution to the literature by processing sustainable consumption from the perspective of economic theory. This study is structured in seven sections in line with the stated purpose. After this general introduction, which is the first section, consumption, consumer and consumer behavior are examined in the second section. In the third section, the consumer society and sustainability approach are discussed. In the fourth section, the sustainable consumption approach is shared. In this section, sustainable consumption is examined with its definition, scope, process and actors. In the fifth section, consumer behaviors in sustainable consumption are discussed. In the sixth section, the causes of failure in sustainable consumption and solution suggestions are examined. In the conclusion part, which is the seventh section, a general evaluation is made by making a summary.

CONSUMPTION AND CONSUMER BEHAVIORS

Consumption and Consumer

Consumption, with the most general approach, is the activity of meeting the needs of living things in order to survive. Humans, as a species of these creatures, consume throughout their lives. When it comes to consumption in economics, people's consumption is meant. Consumption is one of the main focuses of economic theory. There are different definitions of consumption in the literature. Consumption, which can be expressed as simply using and destroying something, is broadly defined as all the material and moral values spent for the fulfillment of many legitimate and illegitimate needs of human beings in terms of physiological, biological, social and cultural aspects. In fact, to understand simply with the economic theory approach, consumption is the use of produced goods and services by people in line with their needs and wants. The perpetrator (person) who performs the expressed economic consumption activity is called the consumer. The consumer, in its most general terms, means the person who buys or uses the products and services for the end-use purpose. With a clear expression from the perspective of economic theory, the consumer is the person who has the need to be satisfied and the spending power (Bocock, 1993; Griskevicius & Kenrick, 2013).

The history of the concepts of consumption and consumer dates back to as old as the history of humanity. A person becomes a "consumer" by starting to consume from his birth, and this situation ends with the death of the individual. Since the conditions of each period are different, this situation is also reflected in people's understanding of consumption. In the early periods of history, that is, in the pre-agricultural revolution period, hunter-gatherer people who lived as nomadic people only consumed without producing. The consumption concept of these people consists of meeting the most basic necessities such as eating, drinking, heating and sheltering. However, over time, with the effect of settled life, industrialization and technological developments with the agricultural revolution, people started to consume in order to meet their socio-cultural and psychological needs as well as meeting their compulsory needs. As a result, in the literature, consumption and consumers are historically divided into two periods, the period when people are only consumers and the period when people are both producers and consumers. The second period is divided into three periods: the agricultural post-revolutionary period, in which consumption is at the forefront, the post-industrial revolution period, in which production is at the forefront, and today's global information technology period, in which consumption is the focus (Solomon, 1995; Bocock, 1993).

Consumer Behaviors

Behavioral science is an approach that systematically examines human behavior with scientific methods by making use of the analysis methods of different disciplines. At this point, consumer behavior investigates the purchasing behaviors of consumers related to economic decisions and the economic and psychological factors that are effective in these behaviors, and tries to explain the cause and effect relationships. With its widely accepted definition, consumer behavior is defined as the field of study that examines the processes related to the selection, purchase, use or disposal of goods and services and the factors affecting these processes in order to satisfy the wants and needs of individuals or groups. Consumer behavior, on the one hand, is influenced by the consumer's individual needs, motives, learning process, personality, perceptions, attitudes and beliefs; On the other hand, it emerges with the influence of sociocultural factors such as culture, social class, reference group and family in the society of which the consumer is a member (Wilkie, 1994; Bocock, 1993; Griskevicius, 2013; Solomon, 1995).

It is possible to evaluate the characteristics of consumer behavior under six main headings. Consumer behavior,

- -is the behavior that is motivated to achieve a goal such as the satisfaction of certain needs and wants.
- -is a dynamic process consisting of pre-purchase activities, purchasing activities and post-purchase activities.
- -is complex and varies in timing.
- -deals with different roles such as initiator, influencer, decision maker, buyer and user.

- -is affected by internal and external factors.
- -may differ for different people as a natural result of personal differences.

The consumer's decision-making mechanism is quite complex and how it works is not fully known. Because each person exhibits a unique behavior structure. Many variables come into play during decision making, and the number and impact of these variables may differ from person to person. With a general approach, the factors that affect consumer behavior are examined in three classes as personal factors, socio-cultural factors and psychological factors (Wood & Hayes, 2012; Solomon, 1995).

- *-Personal factors (demographic factors):* Age, gender, occupation, education level, marital status, income level, etc.
- *-Socio-cultural factors:* Family, social class, cultures, social subcultures etc.
- *-Psychological factors:* Personality, learning, motivation, perception, belief, attitudes, etc.

In the beginning, consumer behavior studies focused only on purchasing, today this concept is handled more within the framework of process logic. The consumer behavior process can be examined in five stages with a general approach (Munthiu, 2009; Solomon, 1995).

- *-Identifying the need:* The purchasing decision process starts with the identification (recognition) of the need. The consumer realizes his need when he feels a difference between his current situation and the situation he wants to be. If the consumer feels a significant difference between his current state and his desired state, he moves on to the second stage of the consumption process.
- *-Identifying alternatives:* At this stage, which is the second stage, the consumer begins to learn about various goods and services that can meet his needs. In the light of the information obtained, consumption alternatives are determined.
- *-Evaluation of alternatives:* At this stage, the consumer may be faced with many different alternatives depending on the type of product. At this stage, the consumer tries to determine the most suitable one by comparing these alternatives in terms of price, quality and other features.
- *-Purchasing decision:* At this stage, the consumer decides to buy or not buy the product or service they need. Every consumer is expected to make a decision to purchase the product or service that will satisfy their needs at the highest level.
- *-Post-Purchasing Evaluation:* At this stage, the consumer evaluates the satisfaction level depending on the relationship between the expected performance of the good or service and the performance obtained after consumption. This evaluation enters the consumer's decision function as a separate determining factor in subsequent decision stages.

CONSUMER SOCIETY AND SUSTAINABILITY

Consumer Society

The change in information and technology has brought a new economic order based on consumption instead of the economic understanding based on production. The goal is no longer to maximize production, but to maximize consumption. In the past, approaches that were against excessive and unnecessary consumption; has begun to attribute meanings such as success, pleasure, fun and freedom. Consumption has become the criterion of a good life. In the new culture, the modern consumer has come to harbor negative prejudices against those who do not consume enough. Increasing living standards and excessive consumption have become the main indicators of power and happiness. The society shaped by this new understanding is called the consumer society (Slater, 1997; Featherstone, 1991; Droge, 1993).

The consumer society is a concept that started to be used in the 1950s and 60s to express the developed western societies that identified the basis of existence with ownership. With this concept, it is expressed how these societies consume more and more and how they form their social identities with the objects they own and consume. In consumer societies, consumers who make consumption a lifestyle are encouraged to consume continuously in all areas of life (Slater, 1997; Featherstone, 1991; Droge, 1993).

At this point, the basic features of the consumer society can be expressed under eight main headings; In consumer societies,

- -consumers consume more in their spare time due to the rising level of welfare.
- -working hours are gradually decreasing, so consumers can find more leisure time to consume.
- -individuals form their social affiliation through consumption.
- -aesthetic elements come to the forefront in the daily lives of individuals.
- -consumption is seen as a lifestyle.
- -consumption models are based on social classes.
- -consumer rights rise to a more important position than citizenship rights.
- -everyday life becomes commercialized.

Sustainability

Realizing, albeit late, that they have disrupted the ecological balance because of their actions, humanity began to feel the necessity of changing something after the second half of the 20th century. Expressing that environmental capacity was exceeded for the first time in the post-World War II period by the scientific community led to debates on whether the population and consumption should be limited or not. At this point, the necessity of starting a new era in which environmental pressures will be reduced has begun to be voiced and the concept of sustainability has entered the literature (Schaefer & Crane, 2005; Chappells & Trentmann, 2015).

Sustainability is generally not completely exhausting a resource or using the resource in a way that does not cause harm (Schaefer and Crane, 2005). The World Commission on Environment and Development defines the concept of sustainability as the ability of people to meet their current needs without affecting the amount and form of resources that will meet the needs of future generations (WCED, 1991). In the Maastricht agreement, sustainability is defined as follows; to protect and improve environmental quality, to protect human health, to ensure the rational use of natural resources, and to address and evaluate all environmental problems at an international level. According to the International Union for Conservation of Nature (IUCN), the UN Environment Program (UNEP) and the World Wide Fund for Nature (WWF), sustainability is improving the quality of life so that it remains within the carrying capacity of the life-supporting natural systems in the environment. The Sustainable Enterprise Center (2010) defines sustainability as a way of doing business that generates profits without harming people and the planet. The term sustainability; emerged from the urgent need to use the earth's resources in such a way that humans and other species can acceptably exist on earth in the future (Haron et al., 2005; Schaefer & Crane, 2005).

Even though sustainability efforts are a little different from today's meaning when we look at them historically, human beings first showed the first examples of sustainability efforts by protecting the areas they consider sacred, some animals and forests. For example, in the 15th century, Venice implemented forest protection laws to prevent deforestation and prevent future timber shortages. In the 1700s, the use of timber, especially by poor people, was prohibited due to the fear of timber shortages in Europe. In the 1790s, England stopped its exports to Canada with the fear of a shortage of coal, which was the most important mine of the period. In the 18th and 19th centuries, various conservation laws were enacted in Germany to prevent the destruction of forests and at the same time to ensure the continuity of the society's needs such as wood and water. Sustainability in its current sense has been brought to the agenda with many reports, papers, commissions and conferences held at the international level after the second half of the 20th century and has been transformed into a global concept (Chappells & Trentmann, 2015; Haron et al., 2005). The key milestones of this process are summarized below.

- -In 1968, the Club of Rome was established with the mission of "World Problematic". Under the title of "Limits to Growth", the Club of Rome prepared future scenarios and prepared a report on rapid industrialization, population growth, malnutrition and poverty, non-renewable resources, scarcity and finally environmental degradation.
- -In 1972, the Stockholm Environment Conference (1972), the first environmental conference organized by the United Nations, was held.
- -In 1983, the report named "Our Common Future" was prepared by the World Commission on Environment and Development (WCED) consisting of participants from 20 different countries and presented to the United Nations General Assembly in 1987. The Brundtland Report went down in history as the first study in which the amounts of natural resources were calculated at the national, regional and global level.
- -In 1992, Agenda 21 The United Nations Conference on Environment and Development was held in Rio de Janeiro. With this conference, it is aimed to implement the Brundtland report and to draw attention to the environmental damage caused by consumption.
- -In 1997, the Kyoto Protocol established the targets and mechanisms necessary for the implementation of the "United Nations Framework Convention on Climate Change". Accordingly, as an emission target, the emissions of the 40 most industrialized countries should be reduced by at least 5% between 2008 and 2012 compared to 1990 levels.
- -In 2000, the "Millennium Summit" was held by the United Nations in New York with the participation of 149 heads of state and senior officials from more than 40 countries. At the end of the summit, the "United Nations Millennium Declaration" was announced.
- -In 2002, the World Sustainable Development Summit was held in South Africa. Important decisions were taken at the summit in five areas such as water projects, energy, health, agriculture, protection of biodiversity and ecosystem management. At the summit, also known as Rio+10, what has been done since the "Rio Earth Summit" was discussed.
- -In 2012, world leaders came together at the "Rio+20" meeting to advance sustainable development 20 years after the "World Sustainable Development Summit" and agreed on important principles.

- -In 2015, the United Nations Sustainable Development Summit (2015) was held in New York. The aim of this summit is to build on the Millennium Development goals taken at the previous Millennium Summit and to realize the unachievable goals.

SUSTAINABLE CONSUMPTION

Definition and Scope

According to the United Nations Environment Program (1995), sustainable consumption is not to endanger the needs of future generations by minimizing the use of natural resources and substances that pollute the environment, while using products that meet basic needs and improve the quality of life. There are many different definitions in the literature that lead to similar results. According to the definition made by DEFRA (2003), sustainable consumption is the economic and social developments that meet the demands and needs of current and future generations, while ensuring that they reach a better quality of life and without exceeding the limits of the world ecosystem (DEFRA, 2003). Paavola (2001) also defined sustainable consumption as consumption behaviors that have very few harmful environmental effects compared to other consumption behaviors. According to Hertwich (2002), sustainable consumption is the consumption of products that are produced in a durable and repairable way that will create less waste by using less natural resources and energy, and that can be recycled to a large extent or whose waste will not be harmful to the environment. Sustainable consumption is not only to consume less, but also to consume differently, more efficiently and to have a better quality of life. Sustainable consumption is an umbrella term that gathers many key issues such as meeting needs, improving quality of life, increasing productivity, minimizing waste (Vermeir & Verbeke 2006; Mont & Plepys, 2008; Zhao & Scroeder, 2010; DEFRA, 2003; Abdulrazak & Quoquab, 2018; Marzouk & Mahrous, 2020; Rezvani et al., 2018; Prendergast & Tsang, 2019; Piligrimiene et al., 2020).

In the studies carried out to reveal the scope of sustainable consumption, there are two main ways: reducing the consumption level and changing consumption behaviors (towards sustainable consumption) (Fuchs & Lorek, 2005; Schaefer & Crane, 2005; Mont & Plepys, 2008). The first solution is to reduce the overall consumption level. Avoidance of consumption is the most sensitive behavior in terms of sustainability. Studies show that satisfying needs without purchasing or using any product is the most effective action in the environmental context. The second solution states that more environmentally sensitive consumption behaviors should be exhibited, in other words, existing consumption behaviors should be made more sustainable. For example, the consumption of products that are produced using fewer resources, require less energy, and are almost entirely made of recyclable materials, explains the actions towards this solution. If it is not appropriate to avoid or reduce consumption to meet a person's need, then he must fulfill this need by consuming products that have less ecological effects than others. This behavior means that there is a need to move towards sustainable products (Han & Hansen, 2012; Vermeir & Verbeke 2006; OECD, 2002; Abdulrazak & Quoquab, 2018; Rezvani et al., 2018; Prendergast & Tsang, 2019; Piligrimiene et al., 2020).

Emerging Factors

Sustainable consumption approach came to the fore in the second half of the 20th century, especially towards the end, and it increased its place in discussions day by day. Sustainable consumption started to take place in the literature with the 1960s, but in general terms, it came to the agenda for the first time in the Agenda 21-Rio Earth Summit organized in 1992, and the content and details of the concept were reported. In the 4th Chapter of Agenda 21, titled "Changing Consumption Patterns", it is emphasized that people can lead their lives at high standards only by using less natural resources in the world. "Transforming Our World: 2030 Agenda for Sustainable Development", which was adopted at the United Nations Development Summit held in 2015, has been one of the goals it has set to be achieved by 2030, the issue of securing sustainable consumption patterns. In addition to the historical emergence of sustainable consumption, there are factors that have revealed the sustainable consumption approach, brought it to the agenda and turned it into a hot topic of goals and objectives, which have been pointed out before. These factors can be expressed under two main headings as environmental factors and social factors (Zhao & Scroeder, 2010; Lee, 2014; Abdulrazak & Quoquab, 2018; Kapoor & Dwivedi, 2020; Park & Lin 2020; Rezvani et al., 2018; Prendergast & Tsang, 2019)

- *-Environmental factors:* The leading environmental factors that are effective in drawing attention to sustainable consumption; greenhouse gas effect, global warming, ozone layer depletion, usage intensity of water resources, production of solid waste, intensity of use of forest resources, organic agriculture.
- *-Social factors:* Industrialization, consumer awareness, welfare levels of countries and insufficient education are the leading social factors that bring sustainable consumption to the agenda.

Major Actors

In order for the sustainable consumption policy to achieve the desired success or at least move forward in line with the target, the actors who are party to the policy should act together in parallel with the integrated policies. For sustainable consumption, the actors have duties that are complementary to each other. There are many actors of sustainable consumption, but in general, four main actors can be mentioned: international organizations, states, companies and consumers (Mont & Plepys, 2008; OECD, 2002; Han & Hansen, 2012; Geiger et al., 2018; Kapoor & Dwivedi, 2020; Marzouk & Mahrous, 2020; Prendergast & Tsang, 2019; Piligrimiene et al., 2020).

- *-International organizations:* Sustainable consumption has been brought to the agenda with the initiatives of international organizations and they will be one of the most important actors in its success. This problem, which has emerged as a global problem, should be tackled with a global approach. At this point, international organizations play a key role in addressing the problem and solution with a global approach. Many organizations established since the emergence of the sustainability paradigm have enabled studies on sustainable consumption. UN Environment Programme (UNEP), The United Nations Commission on Sustainable Development (UNCSD), Sustainable Consumption Research Exchange (SCORE), The Collaborating Centre on Sustainable Consumption and Production(CSCP), European Environment Agency (EEA), Sustainable Production and Consumption Movement (SPAC), North American Sustainable Consumption

Alliance (NASCA), World Wide Fund for Nature (WWF), The Yale Center for Environmental Law and Policy (YCELP), The Center for International Earth Science Information Network (CIESIN), and Lifestyles of Health and Sustainability (LOHAS) are some of them. The United Nations (UN), European Union (EU) and OECD are three very important actors that should be especially mentioned in terms of the work of international organizations.

- *-States:* States with regulatory and sanction power are among the most important actors in the realization of the desired change towards the goal of sustainable consumption. The state contributes greatly to the sustainable consumption process through ways and methods such as legal regulations, inspections, incentive policies and education campaigns. At the point of state intervention, the first issue that should be noted is taxes. The state can reduce the consumption of certain products by imposing high taxes on certain products or increase the consumption of those products by lowering the tax rates of environmentally friendly products. The second important topic that should be mentioned within the scope of the state role is incentive policies. At this point, various incentives can be given to companies, other public institutions and consumers, so that they act in accordance with the concept of sustainable consumption. In this context, it is possible to increase the level of knowledge and awareness of decision makers about the environmental and economic potential of sustainable consumption through education.
- *-Firms:* Firms that carry out the design, production and supply processes of the goods and services that are the subject of consumption are another important actor of sustainable consumption. It is very difficult to shape the approaches of companies whose main purpose is profit maximization and therefore trying to minimize their costs, with a sustainable consumption approach. In the literature, it is stated that there are various changes that companies will make in order to contribute to the sustainable consumption process. The first of these is vision and mission changes. They can provide support and direction to all other actors with social responsibility projects that companies will carry out with a focus on environmental issues. It is necessary to establish a corporate reputation that serves sustainability. For this, it is necessary to reshape the views underlying the company's values, principles and reasons for existence with an understanding of sustainability. Secondly, new technology and application development, which is called eco-innovation in the literature, can be counted. Under eco-innovation, important topics such as environmental management systems, pollution prevention, cleaner production, and life cycle management are discussed. Eco-innovation basically refers to the transition from the traditional firm model to the firm model that takes environmental concerns into the decision function.
- *-Consumers:* Consumers form the heart of sustainable consumption. There are many tasks that international organizations, states and companies have to do for the success of the sustainable consumption strategy, but in the end, all of them aim to direct consumer behavior at the point of sustainability. Considering that demand is the main driving force of the system, the situation can be better understood. If the consumer accepts sustainable consumption and shapes the decision function for the success of this strategy, other actors will take steps to make the process successful. It is not easy to initiate sustainable behaviors and to ensure the sustainability of these behaviors. The difference between consumers' claimed desire to change and their actual behavior must be eliminated. For this, consumers need to understand the connections between production, consumption and destruction systems, and the environmental effects caused by these structures and be sensitive to these issues. Society's attention should be drawn to the fact that the world has limited resources, despite the ever-increasing population and lifestyle based on high consumption.

The necessity of using these resources as effectively as possible and recovering them as much as possible after use should be made accepted by the members of the society. Individuals' awareness of the environmental and social impacts of their own consumption will prompt many to reevaluate their consumption preferences.

Sustainable Consumption Process

The consumption process is discussed in the second part of the study with five different stages. These stages should be reviewed within the scope of sustainable consumption strategy and what changes can be made should be evaluated (Haron et al., 2005; Reisch et al., 2013; Hale, 2018; Mont & Plepys, 2008; Abdulrazak & Quoquab, 2018; Kapoor & Dwivedi, 2020; Marzouk & Mahrous, 2020; Piligrimiene et al., 2020).

The first step is to identify the need. An important step of the sustainable consumption approach is the quantitative reduction of consumption. At this point, the first thing the consumer should do is clarify whether the situation in question is a need or a desire. A significant contribution will be made to the process by avoiding non-essential consumption. In other words, the first step in the sustainable consumption process is to give up that consumption process if possible.

The second step is to identify alternatives. If the consumer has decided to move forward in the consumption process, what he has to do is to keep this consumption process in a sustainable consumption behavior as much as possible. At this point, sustainable consumption criteria should be an indispensable prerequisite while determining alternatives. This will ensure that the possibilities that will harm the process are eliminated at the very beginning of the process.

The third step is the evaluation of alternatives. Sustainable consumption is a policy that should always be carried forward as an active process. Among the identified alternatives, an evaluation should be made at the point of determining the one that satisfies the needs of the consumer and is most suitable for sustainable consumption at the same time.

The fourth step is to make the purchasing decision. At this point, the consumer can still give up on buying or go back to the previous steps and start the process again in a more suitable way for sustainable consumption. Therefore, before making a purchase decision, he should review the evaluations of the product in question and make sure that the purchase he will make does not limit the alternatives of future generations while meeting his own needs. Instead of buying and consuming, it should also look at the alternatives of renting or second-hand use, if possible.

The fifth step is the post-purchase evaluation process. In this process, it should be acted in a way that minimizes the waste load of the related consumption on the nature. Information about recycling processes should be obtained. If the post-consumption waste is not to be recycled, it should be disposed of or stored properly. It should be ensured that the lessons learned from this consumption in terms of sustainability are used in subsequent purchases.

CONSUMER BEHAVIORS IN SUSTAINABLE CONSUMPTION

At the center of the understanding of sustainable consumption is consumer behavior, which this study also focuses on. Considering the fact that more than half of the environmental problems in developed countries are caused by individual consumption behaviors, it becomes clear how effective individual consumption behaviors are on environmental problems. Therefore, individual consumption behaviors should be considered as the main determining factor in explaining sustainable consumption. While analyzing consumer behavior in sustainable consumption policy in the literature, consumption of natural resources of consumers is handled with two different classifications. These are direct consumption of natural resources and indirect consumption of natural resources (Wolff & Schönherr, 2011; Zhao & Scroeder, 2010; Quoquab & Mohammad, 2017; Haron et al., 2005; Siegrist et al., 2015; Vringer et al., 2017; Abdulrazak & Quoquab, 2018; Geiger et al., 2018; Kapoor & Dwivedi, 2020; Marzouk & Mahrous, 2020; Rezvani et al., 2018; Prendergast & Tsang, 2019; Piligrimiene et al., 2020).

- *-Sustainable consumption behavior in direct consumption of natural resources:* Some of the natural resources are used directly by final consumers, not as intermediate goods in production. Water, oil, natural gas are the best-known examples of these natural resources (Trudel, 2019; Hale, 2018; Wolff & Schönherr, 2011; Zhao & Scroeder, 2010; Vringer et al., 2017).

The first thing to consider in direct consumption of natural resources is water, which is an indispensable source of life. For a sustainable world, water has a much more important place than all other resources. Water is indispensable for life to continue. The wasteful use of water by consumers who have easy and cheap access to water causes the world's water resources to be consumed rapidly. A consumer can provide significant support to a sustainable consumption policy by taking simple measures in his daily water consumption. Examples of these are taking a short shower instead of taking a long bath, not leaving the tap open while shaving or brushing teeth, washing the dishes in the dishwasher, turning off the water while soaping hands, choosing water efficient fixtures, shower heads, taps and reservoirs.

Oil can be considered as a second direct natural resource consumption. Uncontrolled use of oil causes both rapid consumption of oil resources and pollution of the air. In order for consumers to act in accordance with the sustainable consumption policy, they need to pay attention to their oil consumption. Examples of effective measures for the consumption of oil resources within the limits of sustainability; using less cars, preferring bicycles, walking or public transportation, taking advantage of the opportunities of technology to do some work online or by phone instead of traveling for every job.

The third natural resource that should be mentioned is natural gas. Some of the measures that can be taken to consume the natural gas resource at a sustainable level are as follows: Reducing the heat setting of the heater when leaving the house for a long time, lowering the heater setting at night, lowering the temperature setting of unused rooms, trying to dress tight before raising the heat setting of the heater, not keeping windows open for long periods of time, to insulate the doors, walls, roofs and windows of the house, prefer an energy efficient heating system.

- *-Sustainable consumption behavior in indirect natural resource consumption:* In addition to consuming natural resources directly, consumers also indirectly consume natural resources by consuming industrial goods and services. At this point, the goods and services they will choose are an important component of the success of the sustainable consumption policy. In the literature, this subject is examined under five headings: behaviors related to sustainable product preferences, behaviors related to recycling, behaviors related to product sharing, behaviors related to product rental and behaviors related to voluntary simplicity (Macdiarmid et al., 2016; Quoquab & Mohammad, 2017; Haron et al., 2005; Siegrist et al., 2015).

Behaviors related to sustainable goods and service preferences is a subject that includes many subtitles such as organic, long-lasting, ecologically labeled and local goods preferences. Organic products are products in which genetic engineering, artificial fertilizers, preservatives, colorants, additives, chemical coating and brightening agents and chemical packaging materials are not used in their cultivation or processing. The use of these organic products allows both to save many natural resources and to make wastes much less and harmless. Preferring long-lasting products is another type of sustainable choice of goods and services. Increased product lifespan means slower consumption of natural resources. The fact that consumers pay attention to the ecological label of the goods they buy is another situation that reveals sustainable consumption behavior. Preferring local goods is also important for sustainable consumption. Each good is loaded with energy, and moving the good over long distances increases the energy of that product. Therefore, the sustainability vision requires choosing local alternatives of a commodity whenever possible.

Behaviors related to recycling are another very important part of sustainable consumption policy. It is possible to divide the consumption behaviors of consumers, which are subject to recycling, into three: Preferring products made from recycled materials, preferring products whose wastes are almost entirely recyclable, and sending the wastes generated as a result of use to recycling. Applying these three ways will both reduce the use of natural resources, provide longer-term use of resources for different purposes, and enable the reduction and preservation of wastes in nature.

Another sustainable consumption behavior is product sharing. These behaviors can be expressed as the sharing of a single product by a group of two or more individuals instead of each individual purchasing a separate product for their own use. Just as books in libraries can be used jointly by a large number of individuals, it is also possible for certain products to be shared. Shared use of cars, lawn mowers, electrical appliances can be given as examples of product sharing. However, here is a sharing made with ecological concerns, not for obligatory and economic reasons.

Behaviors related to renting products include the behaviors of individuals to tend to service consumption by renting them, instead of purchasing certain products and owning them, with the motive of sustainable consumption. Using the service provided by the car rental company instead of buying a car can be given as an example of this type of behavior. If renting is preferred instead of purchasing, the maintenance and repair expenses of the relevant product will also belong to the manufacturer. This will allow products to be produced in a way that is longer lasting, more durable, requires less maintenance and repairs, can be easily repaired and recycled. Thus, the indirect effects of the efforts of individuals who lead to a sustainable consumption behavior on the sustainable production process of the companies may also occur.

Behaviors related to voluntary simplicity is one of the important actions to change the existing consumption behaviors towards sustainability. The concept of voluntary simplicity has emerged not only as a consumption-oriented approach, but as a philosophical movement and lifestyle to discover the real meaning of life. This emerging voluntary simplicity movement should not be confused with poverty, which is considered as compulsory simplicity. Voluntary simplicity is to remove some consumptions from your life as a lifestyle while there is the opportunity to consume completely. In other words, it is basically changing the definition of need. Material simplicity, self-determination, ecological sensitivity, humane scale, and individual development are included in the literature as the five main values that form the basis of the voluntary simplicity lifestyle.

REASONS FOR SUSTAINABLE CONSUMPTION FAILURE AND SUGGESTIONS FOR SOLUTIONS

At this point, it is clear that the 2030 sustainable consumption targets are far away and cannot be achieved at this rate. Discussing the slow process of the process and the root causes of the failures is very necessary in order to evaluate what can be done to adopt the sustainable consumption approach. At this point, the main causes of these problems are discussed below, and then solutions are offered (Dietz & Neumayer, 2007; Princen, 2003; Wolff & Schönherr, 2011; Quoquab & Mohammad, 2017; Macdiarmid et al., 2016; Siegrist et al., 2015; Trudel, 2019; Hale, 2018; Vringer et al., 2017).
The main causes of the problems can be counted as follows.

- *-Lack of will:* Some behaviors of sustainable consumption actors are only verbal. In particular, states say that they will support these policies and pass laws, but they do not give up on the maximum economic growth target and continue their administration in line with short-term goals with the old understanding. Firms also do not give up their profit maximization and cost minimization targets. The majority of consumers do not abandon their excessive consumption habits as long as they have financial means. These factors are among the most important reasons for the failure of the process.
- *-Insufficient risk analysis:* Adequate risk analyzes are not carried out, experts who can work on this subject are not adequately trained and employed. It cannot be demonstrated by scientific analyzes that not changing the behaviors will cause significant problems and that even small changes will create significant differences. Actors focus on the current situation and the short-term future, and the bad scenarios mentioned are considered to be rather long-term predictions and are ignored.
- *-Insufficient financial resources:* It is one of the basic behaviors of the elected authorities to transfer resources to policies that provide short-term and voting potential instead of long-term policies. At this point, sufficient financial resources cannot be provided for the sustainable consumption policy, which is a long-term process, and some necessary investments cannot be made for the success of the process.
- *-Inadequacy of environmental laws:* States are the actors responsible for enacting laws related to the process, supervising practices and penalizing when necessary. However, the prolongation of the enactment of the laws, the unclear and comprehensible laws, or the very light penalties hinder the process. In addition, the fact that the process is mostly not delegated to independent authorities causes the process to be abused and unsuccessful.

The mentioned failure should not be seen as an absolute failure and it should be considered that the process is in progress, albeit slowly. At this point, it is clear that the above-mentioned reasons must be reversed in order to continue the process more quickly and effectively. In addition, taking the following steps will be effective in increasing the success of the process (Joshi & Rahman, 2015; Wolff & Schönherr, 2011; Dietz & Neumayer, 2007; Macdiarmid et al., 2016; Trudel, 2019; Hale, 2018; OECD, 2002).

- *-Using the market mechanism:* In order for a sustainable consumption policy to be successful, the process must somehow find a response within the market mechanism. Each actor of the process makes a cost-benefit evaluation. In addition to the long-term return, if the short-term return of this policy is high and the cost is low, the policy will find a response. Social costs and social benefits must be calculated and included in the price mechanism. These can be done through incentive policies, polluting permits, and taxes. Using existing markets, creating non-existent markets and developing inadequate markets will make significant contributions to the process.

- *-Independent regulatory agencies:* Independent regulatory agencies were established to make regulations, implement regulations and supervise regulations as a solution to many problems after the second world war. Since sustainable consumption policy is a long-term process, it should be freed from the influence of the political approach that pursues short-term policies and the interest groups that are easy to put pressure on the political approach. Independent institutions are the most basic and effective solution to this problem.
- *-Creating public opinion:* The success of this process can be achieved not through top-down policies, but through innovations demanded from the base. As mentioned before, the economy is now demand-based. In other words, the power is in the hands of the consumer and their demands will be met. If consumers can be put at the center of sustainable consumption and persuaded, both companies and the state will have to take a step at this point. However, if the process is left to the product differentiation strategies of the companies and the vote expectations of the politicians, it is very difficult to get results.
- *-Determining compliance indicators:* In order to monitor how sustainable policies work and what the results are, some indicators should be selected. For success, these indicators must be measurable, understandable and easily observable. In this respect, it is necessary to determine and share indicators that can observe the process both in countries and regions and globally.

The solution proposals mentioned above directly or indirectly concern all actors of the process. Considering the importance of consumers in sustainable consumption, particular attention should be paid to consumers. In order for sustainable consumption to be more successful, there are a number of steps that consumers must take (OECD, 2002; Joshi & Rahman, 2015; Dietz & Neumayer, 2007). The important ones are as follows;

- -Consumers should be organized in order to reach an effective result on the protection of nature.
- -Families should raise awareness of their children on sustainable consumption from the very first years.
- -Household waste should be reduced and classified for recycling.
- -The distinction between need and desire should be clarified.
- -Care should be taken when purchasing and using cleaning materials.
- -Reducing the use of cars, public transport should be preferred.
- -Environmental impacts should be included in the decision function when adopting new technologies.
- -Care should be taken when using water.
- -Solar energy should be used.

FUTURE RESEARCH DIRECTIONS

The field of study on sustainable consumption is quite broad and weak. Much work can be done in this area. Academic studies to be carried out can both contribute to the academic literature and support sustainable consumption. First of all, studies based on extensive empirical analysis can be done with comprehensive data. Results from these studies should be reported and communicated to all actors in simple language. The results obtained should be compared at certain scales between regions and countries, differences should be revealed and how successful examples can be followed should be evaluated. Empirical studies can be performed on different socio-economic groups and participation can be reported according to socio-economic status. Based on this information, specific strategies can be developed for different groups. Studies to determine the factors and effect levels that affect sustainable consumption behavior will also make important contributions to the literature and the process.

CONCLUSION

With the struggle of human beings to increase the quality of life and make their life easier, technology has developed and industrialization has grown rapidly thanks to the new and fast production methods introduced. This change and transformation has brought a new economic understanding based on consumption instead of the economic order based on production. This new economic approach has revealed consumer societies that identify the basis of existence with possession, make consumption a lifestyle and seek constant satisfaction through consumption. However, these high consumption activities have reached dimensions that disrupt the balance of the world. The race of humanity to consume more creates pressure on natural resources, causing them to be polluted and destroyed. These developments necessitated the revision of the approach of maximum satisfaction of consumer needs, which is the main focus of economics. As a result, the limited natural resources used to meet the unlimited needs of people necessitated the harmonization of the environment and the economy.

At the beginning of the 1970s, with the effect of increasing ecological problems, natural resource problems began to be noticed. The existing situation was questioned and it was discussed that a new economic approach should be developed that does not disturb the functioning of the ecological system. These discussions were developed under the sustainability approach as a framework concept. An important component of sustainability is sustainable consumption. Sustainable consumption is not to endanger the needs of future generations by minimizing the use of natural resources and substances that pollute the environment, while using goods that meet basic needs and increase the quality of life. This is a form of consumption that is based on the limited use of the world's existing resources and tries to find solutions that will reduce any negative impact on the environment. The main purpose is to maintain and, if possible, increase the living standards of the present without spending the living standards of future generations. Sustainable consumption is a process that can be achieved with the active participation of many actors, including international organizations, states, firms and consumers. These actors have tasks that have a complementary relationship between each other in the process.

This study discussed sustainable consumption from the perspective of economic theory and examined it within the framework of consumer behavior. Consumer behavior is of vital importance for sustainability. Because in the end, one of the main causes of the problem is consumer behavior, and these behaviors will form an important part of the solution. Consumer behavior investigates the purchasing behavior of consumers related to economic decisions and the factors that affect these behaviors, and tries to explain the cause and effect relationships. In the literature, consumer behavior is discussed within the framework of a five-stage process logic: identification of needs, identification of alternatives, evaluation of alternatives, purchase decision and post-purchase evaluation. At each of these stages, a sustainable consumption approach should be taken into account. Sustainable consumption behaviors in consumer behavior are examined by dividing them into two as direct consumption of natural resources and indirect consumption of natural resources. There are three basic behaviors that consumers should do in a sustainable consumption approach. These are reducing, reusing and recycling. Reducing means reducing the amount of consumption by separating needs from wants. Reusing includes the activities of using a product using it as long as possible, using it by renting, using it jointly, using it with a different product, or using it by having it repaired, instead of using it once and throwing it away. Recycling refers to the use of renewable products by making them useful again with the recycling method.

It is very valuable for human beings to understand their mistakes and take steps to compensate them as much as possible, even if it is late. When sustainable consumption policies started to be discussed, it was known that this would be a long-term process and it would be very difficult to convince, persuade and comply with states, societies and markets. For now, the distance covered should not be underestimated, despite being quite far from the targets set. At this point, among the main reasons for the failure of the process, the inadequacies of willpower, risk analysis, financial resources and environmental laws come to the fore. In order to carry out the process more quickly and effectively, steps should be taken such as eliminating these inadequacies and using the market mechanism, establishing independent regulatory institutions, forming public opinion and determining compliance indicators.

REFERENCES

Abdulrazak, S., & Quoquab, F. (2018). Exploring consumers' motivations for sustainable consumption: A self-deterministic approach. *Journal of International Consumer Marketing*, *30*(1), 14–28. doi:10.1080/08961530.2017.1354350

Bocock, R. (1993). *Consumption* (1st ed.). Routledge. doi:10.4324/9780203313114

Chappells, H., & Trentmann, F. (2015). Sustainable consumption in history: Ideas, resources and practices. In L. A. Reisch & J. Thøgersen (Eds.), *Handbook of research on sustainable consumption* (pp. 51–70). Edward Elgar. doi:10.4337/9781783471270.00011

DEFRA. (2003). *Changing patterns: UK government framework for sustainable consumption and production*. DEFRA.

Dietz, S., & Neumayer, E. (2007). Weak and strong sustainability in the SEEA: Concepts and measurement. *Ecological Economics*, *61*(4), 617–626. doi:10.1016/j.ecolecon.2006.09.007

Droge, C., Calantone, R., Agrawal, M., & MacKoy, R. (1993). The consumption culture and its critiques: A framework for analysis. *Journal of Macromarketing*, *13*(Fall), 32–45. doi:10.1177/027614679301300205

Featherstone, M. (1991). *Consumer culture and postmodernism*. Sage.

Fuchs, D. A., & Lorek, S. (2005). Sustainable consumption governance: A history of promises and failures. *Journal of Consumer Policy*, *28*(3), 261–288. doi:10.100710603-005-8490-z

Geiger, S. M., Fischer, D., & Schrader, U. (2018). Measuring what matters in sustainable consumption: An integrative framework for the selection of relevant behaviors. *Sustainable Development*, *26*(1), 18–33. doi:10.1002d.1688

Griskevicius, V., & Douglas, T. K. (2013). Fundamental motives: How evolutionary needs influence consumer behavior. *Journal of Consumer Psychology*, *23*(3), 372–386. doi:10.1016/j.jcps.2013.03.003

Hale, L. A. (2018). At home with sustainability: From green default rules to sustainable consumption. *Sustainability*, *10*(1), 249. doi:10.3390u10010249

Han, Y., & Hansen, H. (2012). Determinants of sustainable food consumption: A meta-analysis using a traditional and a structural equation modeling approach. *International Journal of Psychological Studies*, *4*(1), 22–45. doi:10.5539/ijps.v4n1p22

Haron, S. A., Paim, L., & Yahya, N. (2005). Towards sustainable consumption: An examination of environmental knowledge among Malaysians. *International Journal of Consumer Studies*, *29*(5), 426–436. doi:10.1111/j.1470-6431.2005.00460.x

Hertwich, E. (2002). Life-cycle approaches to sustainable consumption. *Workshop Proceedings Interim Report, International Institute for Applied Systems Analysis*.

Joshi, R., & Rahman, Z. (2015). Factors affecting green purchase behaviour and future research directions. *International Strategic Management Review*, *3*(1-2), 128–143. doi:10.1016/j.ism.2015.04.001

Kapoor, K. K., & Dwivedi, Y. D. (2020). Sustainable consumption from the consumer's perspective: Antecedents of solar innovation adoption. *Resources, Conservation and Recycling*, *152*(1), 1–12. doi:10.1016/j.resconrec.2019.104501

Lee, K. M. (2014). Predictors of sustainable consumption among young educated consumers in Hong Kong. *Journal of International Consumer Marketing*, *26*(3), 217–238. doi:10.1080/08961530.2014.900249

Macdiarmid, J. I., Douglas, F., & Campbell, J. (2016). Eating like there's no tomorrow: Public awareness of the environmental impact of food and reluctance to eat less meat as part of a sustainable diet. *Appetite*, *96*, 487–493. doi:10.1016/j.appet.2015.10.011 PMID:26476397

Marzouk, O. A., & Mahrous, A. A. (2020). Sustainable consumption behavior of energy and water-efficient products in a resource-constrained environment. *Journal of Global Marketing*, *33*(5), 1–19 do i:10.1080/08911762.2019.1709005

Mont, O., & Plepys, A. (2008). Sustainable consumption progress: Should we be proud or alarmed? *Journal of Cleaner Production*, *16*(4), 531–537. doi:10.1016/j.jclepro.2007.01.009

Munthiu, C. M. (2009). The buying decision process and types of buying decision behaviour. *Sibiu Alma Mater University Journals*, *2*(4), 27–33.

OECD. (2002a). *Policies to promote sustainable consumption: An overview. Policy Case Studies Series*. OECD.

OECD. (2002b). *Towards sustainable household consumption: Trends and policies in OECD countries. Policy Case Studies Series*. OECD.

Paavola, J. (2001). Towards sustainable consumption: Economics and ethical concerns for the environment in consumer choices. *Review of Social Economy*, *59*(2), 227–248. doi:10.1080/00346760110036175

Park, H. J., & Lin, L. M. (2020). Exploring attitude–behavior gap in sustainable consumption: Comparison of recycled and upcycled fashion products. *Journal of Business Research*, *117*, 623–628. doi:10.1016/j.jbusres.2018.08.025

Piligrimiene, Z., Zukauskaite, A., Korzilius, H., Banter, J., & Dovalien, A. (2020). Internal and external determinants of consumer engagement in sustainable consumption. *Sustainability*, *12*(4), 1–20. doi:10.3390u12041349

Prendergast, G. P., & Tsang, A. S. L. (2019). Explaining socially responsible consumption. *Journal of Consumer Marketing*, *36*(1), 146–154. doi:10.1108/JCM-02-2018-2568

Princen, T. (2003). Principles for sustainability: From cooperation and efficiency to sufficiency. *Global Environmental Politics*, *3*(1), 33–50. doi:10.1162/152638003763336374

Quoquab, F., & Mohammad, J. (2017). Managing sustainable consumption: Is it a problem or panacea? In W. L. Filho, D. M. Pociovalisteanu, & A. Q. Al-Amin (Eds.), *Sustainable Economic Development: Green Economy and Green Growth*. Springer. doi:10.1007/978-3-319-45081-0_7

Reisch, L., Eberle, U., & Lorek, S. (2013). Sustainable food consumption: an overview of contemporary issues and policies. *Sustainability: Science, Practice and Policy*, *9*(2), 7–25.

Rezvani, Z., Jansson, J., & Bengtsson, M. (2018). Consumer motivations for sustainable consumption: The interaction of gain, normative and hedonic motivations on electric vehicle adoption. *Business Strategy and the Environment*, *27*(8), 1272–1283. doi:10.1002/bse.2074

Schaefer, A., & Crane, A. (2005). Addressing sustainability and consumption. *Journal of Macromarketing*, *25*(1), 76–92. doi:10.1177/0276146705274987

Siegrist, M., Visschers, V. H., & Hartmann, C. (2015). Factors influencing changes in sustainability perception of various food behaviors: Results of a longitudinal study. *Food Quality and Preference*, *46*, 33–39. doi:10.1016/j.foodqual.2015.07.006

Slater, D. (1997). *Consumer culture and modernity*. Polity Press.

Solomon, M. R. (1995). *Consumer behaviour: Buying, having and being*. Allyn & Bacon.

Trudel, R. (2019). Sustainable consumer behavior. *Counselling Psychology Review*, *2*(1), 85–96.

Vermeir, I., & Verbeke, W. (2006). Sustainable food consumption: Exploring the consumer "attitude-behavioral intention" gap. *Journal of Agricultural & Environmental Ethics*, *19*(2), 169–194. doi:10.100710806-005-5485-3

Vringer, K., Heijden, E. V. D., Soest, D. V., Vollebergh, H., & Dietz, F. (2017). Sustainable consumption dilemmas. *Sustainability*, *9*(6), 942. doi:10.3390u9060942

Wilkie, W. (1994). *Consumer behavior*. John Wiley & Sons,Inc.

Wolff, F., & Schönherr, N. (2011). The impact evaluation of sustainable consumption policy instruments. *Journal of Consumer Policy*, *34*(1), 43–66. doi:10.100710603-010-9152-3

Wood, W., & Hayes, T. (2012). Social influence on consumer decisions: Motives, modes, and consequences. *Journal of Consumer Psychology*, *22*(3), 324–328. doi:10.1016/j.jcps.2012.05.003

Zhao, W., & Scroeder, P. (2010). Sustainable consumption and production: trends, challenges and options for the Asia-Pacific region. *National Resources Forum*, *34*, 4-15.

ADDITIONAL READING

Caeiro, S., Ramos, T. B., & Huisingh, D. (2012). Procedures and criteria to develop and evaluate household sustainable consumption indicators. *Journal of Cleaner Production*, *27*, 72–91. doi:10.1016/j.jclepro.2011.12.026

Corrigan, P. (1997). *The sociology of consumption*. Sage.

Featherstone, M. (1991). *Consumer culture and postmodernism*. Sage.

Heiskanen, E., & Pantzar, M. (1997). Toward sustainable consumption: Two new perspectives. *Journal of Consumer Policy*, *20*(4), 409–442. doi:10.1023/A:1006862631698

Kalmykova, Y., Rosado, L., & Patrício, J. (2016). Resource consumption drivers and pathways to reduction: Economy, policy and lifestyle impact on material flows at the national and urban scale. *Journal of Cleaner Production*, *132*, 70–80. doi:10.1016/j.jclepro.2015.02.027

McCracken, G. (1988). *Culture and consumption*. Indiana University Press.

Nash, H. A. (2009). The European Commission's sustainable consumption and production and sustainable industrial policy action plan. *Journal of Cleaner Production*, *17*(4), 496–498. doi:10.1016/j.jclepro.2008.08.020

Nava, M. (1991). Consumerism reconsidered: Buying and power. *Cultural Studies*, *5*(2), 157–173. doi:10.1080/09502389100490141

Prothero, A., & Fitchett, J. A. (2000). Greening capitalism: Opportunities for a green commodity. *Journal of Macromarketing*, *20*(1), 46–55. doi:10.1177/0276146700201005

Salzman, J. (1997). Sustainable consumption and the law. *Environmental Law (Northwestern School of Law)*, *27*, 1243–1293.

Scholl, G., Rubik, F., Kalimo, H., Biedenkopf, K., & Söebech, O. (2010). Policies to promote sustainable consumption: Innovative approaches in Europe. *Natural Resources Forum*, *34*(1), 39–50. doi:10.1111/j.1477-8947.2010.01294.x

Stevens, C. (2010). Linking sustainable consumption and production: The government role. *Natural Resources Forum*, *34*(1), 16–23. doi:10.1111/j.1477-8947.2010.01273.x

Tanner, C., & Kast, S. W. (2003). Promoting sustainable consumption: Determinants of green purchases by Swiss consumers. *Psychology and Marketing*, *20*(10), 883–902. doi:10.1002/mar.10101

United Nations. (2012). Rio+20. In proceedings of the united nations conference on sustainable development. Rio de Janeiro, Brazil: United Nations.

United Nations. (2015). Transforming our world: The 2030 agenda for sustainable development. Paris, France: United Nations.

KEY TERMS AND DEFINITIONS

Consumer: The consumer is the agent (person) who has the need to be satisfied and the power to spend and who performs the economic consumption activity.

Consumer Behavior: Consumer behavior refers to the purchasing behavior of consumers and the factors that affect these behaviors and the cause-and-effect relationships between them.

Consumer Society: Consumer society is a concept that has been used to express developed western societies that identify the basis of existence with possession.

Consumption: Consumption is the use of goods and services produced to meet needs.

Recycling: Recycling is the use of renewable products by making them useful again with the recycling method.

Reducing: Reducing means to see the needs before the wants and to reduce the amount of consumption quantitatively.

Reusing: Reusing is using a product as long as possible, rather than using it once and throwing it away.

Sustainability: Sustainability is the ability of people to meet their current needs without affecting the amount and form of resources that will meet the needs of future generations.

Sustainable Consumption: Sustainable consumption is a form of consumption that is based on the use of the world's resources within the limits of sustainability and seeks ways to minimize the damage to natural life.

Chapter 3
Does Achieving Economic Complexity Impede Turkey's Environmental Sustainability?
Asymmetric Evidence From the Augmented NADL Approach

Alper Karasoy
https://orcid.org/0000-0001-9447-3375
Afyon Kocatepe University, Turkey

ABSTRACT

This chapter empirically examines the (asymmetric) impacts of economic complexity on Turkey's Ecological and Carbon Footprints by employing the augmented nonlinear autoregressive distributed lag (augmented NADL) method for the 1981-2017 period. This chapter's findings are as follows. First, nonlinear cointegration exists between economic complexity and environmental damage. Second, economic complexity has a significant long run asymmetric impact on Turkey's Ecological and Carbon Footprints. Third, in the long run, positive developments in economic complexity increase environmental damage in Turkey, whereas the impact of negative developments is insignificant on Turkey's environmental deterioration. Fourth, significant short run asymmetries regarding economic complexity's effect exist only in the Ecological Footprint model. Lastly, in the short run, positive developments in economic complexity decrease environmental damage, while negative developments intensify it. In line with the empirical findings, some policy recommendations are made.

INTRODUCTION

Continuous economic growth cannot be explained merely by accumulated physical and/or human capital but by an economy's innovative and productive capacity (Hausmann & Hidalgo, 2011: 309). In today's world, development and growth are defined by shifting an economy's capabilities towards producing

DOI: 10.4018/978-1-7998-9590-9.ch003

and exporting more complex products (Felipe et al., 2012). As a result, economic complexity (diversification), which shows the productive knowledge an economy contains by examining the diversity and the ubiquity of its exported products (Hausmann et al., 2014: 18), has gained momentum in the recent empirical literature.

Besides being a robust predictor of growth and development, economic complexity is also claimed to be a limiting factor for income inequality and beneficial for stability (Hartman, 2013; Hartmann et al., 2017). Given these benefits, one of the main goals for developing countries should be to achieve economic complexity. However, the impact of achieving economic complexity and development can be detrimental to environmental sustainability in developing nations, and this seems to be the case for Turkey.

Since the beginning of the 1980s, partly due to the globalization process it experienced, Turkey's economic complexity index (*ECI*) increased. Turkey's ECI values turned from negative (-0.088 in 1980) to positive (0.065 in 1981) and increased almost by three folds from 1981 (0.065) to 2017 (0.176) (OEC, 2021b). Nevertheless, for the same period, Turkey's environmental problems also worsened. For instance, Turkey's per capita Ecological Footprint that shows the demand on nature intensified by more than 1.7 times from 1981 (2.023 global hectares [gha]) to 2017 (3.509 gha). Additionally, Turkey's Carbon Footprint showed a similar pattern, and it also increased more than three times from 1981 (0.725 *gha* per capita) to 2017 (2.233 *gha* per capita) (*Global Footprint Network National Footprint Accounts*, 2020).

Given the abovementioned facts, the main objective of this research will be to estimate the effect of economic complexity on Turkey's Ecological and Carbon Footprints. The empirical literature on this subject is relatively novel and limited, as discussed in the subsequent sections. This research will attempt to fill this gap for the Turkish case considering the period 1981-2017. Because economic complexity is received as a new instrument for achieving economic development for both developed and developing countries, examining this phenomenon can provide fresh evidence and insights to policymakers and researchers. Additionally, this research will employ a novel method called the augmented nonlinear autoregressive distributed lag (augmented NADL) approach. The main advantage of this approach is that it allows both dependent and independent variables to be integrated at the level. Further, given that asymmetric impacts exist, this method differentiates between the effects of positive and negative shocks in the ECI on Turkey's environmental performance. In other words, this chapter aims to empirically assess whether positive and negative developments in Turkey's ECI had different or similar impacts on its Carbon and Ecological Footprints by comparing the signs and magnitudes of these developments.

This chapter is designed as follows. The next section shortly reviews trends in Turkey's Ecological and Carbon Footprints and ECI. Section 2 summarizes the conceptual framework and relevant literature. Section 3 introduces selected data, the augmented NADL method, and models. Section 4 takes up empirical findings, and the last section is dedicated to the conclusion.

TRENDS IN TURKEY'S ECOLOGICAL FOOTPRINT, CARBON FOOTPRINT, AND ECONOMIC COMPLEXITY INDEX

In this section's first subsection, Turkey's Carbon and Ecological Footprints of consumption are graphically shown in comparison to the Carbon and Ecological Footprints of Asia. In the following sub-section, Turkey's ECI scores are graphed to compare them to the ECI scores of Japan and Germany.

The Trends in Turkey's Ecological and Carbon Footprints

The Ecological Footprint is defined as "*the amount of biologically productive area directly and indirectly demanded on a continuous basis by humanity to provide the energy and material resource flows used and to assimilate the wastes generated (i.e., CO_2 emissions), given prevailing technologies and resource management practices*" (Fath et al., 2020: 302). The Ecological Footprint is calculated in *gha.* According to Moran et al. (2008: 472), "*a global hectare represents a hectare of land with world average bioproductivity*". Expressing the Ecological and Carbon Footprints in gha makes direct comparisons possible between different countries or regions (Lin et al., 2018: 3).

In this chapter, similar to the majority of other empirical studies, the Ecological Footprint of consumption is employed. The Ecological Footprint of consumption is measured by subtracting the Ecological Footprint of export from the Ecological Footprint of production and adding the Ecological Footprint of import to the Ecological Footprint of production (Borucke et al., 2013: 523). The Ecological Footprint can be classified into six categories: fishing grounds, cropland, grazing land, forest, built-up land and carbon uptake. The first four categories represent the lands required to produce animal, plant, fiber and wood-based products for consumption. Further, built-up land is the area required for infrastructure-related needs such as cities, roads, and shelter. The last category, carbon uptake, is the biologically fertile space required to sequester carbon emissions emitted as a result of human activities (Fath et al., 2020: 302). By using carbon uptake, the Carbon Footprint is calculated (see Galli et al., 2014).

In this chapter, besides the Ecological Footprint of consumption, Carbon Footprint is employed as another environmental degradation proxy. The main reason for this is that among the Ecological Footprint categories, Carbon Footprint is the most dominant in Turkey. For instance, in 2016 and 2017, Carbon Footprint made up roughly 61% and 64% of the total Ecological Footprint, respectively [according to Global Footprint Network (2021) data]. In **Figure 1,** Asia's and Turkey's Ecological and Carbon Footprints are shown.

Figure 1. Asia's and Turkey's Ecological and Carbon Footprints for the 1981-2017 period
Source: Global Footprint Network (2021)

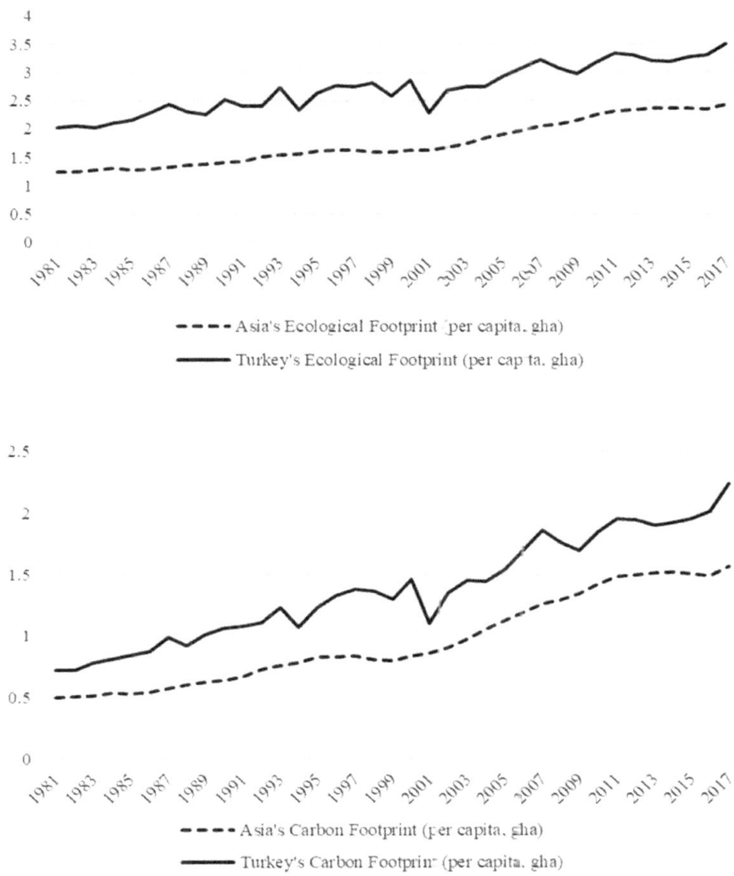

In the first graph of Figure 1, the Ecological Footprints of Asia and Turkey are shown for the 1981-2017 period. Throughout the period, Turkey's per person Ecological Footprint was above Asia's per person Ecological Footprint. This indicates that an average Turkish resident left more Ecological Footprint than an average Asian person. Also, on average, a Turkish citizen left 1.07 (gha per capita) more Ecological Footprint than an Asian person. The first graph in Figure 1 also shows the increasing trend in the Ecological Footprints of both Turkey and Asia. Nevertheless, the rate of environmental deterioration seems to be higher for Turkey than for Asia. The second graph in Figure 1 presents the Carbon Footprints. Similar to the first graph, throughout the sample period, Turkey's per capita Carbon Footprint stayed higher than Asia's. However, the increasing trend in Carbon Footprints seems steeper than Ecological Footprint for both Turkey and Asia. Further, on average, a Turkish person left more Carbon Footprint than an Asian person. In summary, both graphs indicate that Turkey's environmental performance shows a decreasing trend and Turkey's environmental decline is higher than the average environmental decline in Asia.

The Trend in Turkey's Economic Complexity Index

Economic complexity shows a society's productive knowledge that it can mobilize. Further, economic complexity indicates an economy's ability to possess and incorporate knowledge by examining its productive output (Hausmann et al., 2014: 18). Moreover, the economic complexity index utilized in this chapter is calculated by considering Turkey's export products. The calculation method is proposed and executed by Hausmann et al. (2014) and Hidalgo & Hausmann (2009), and the data is published by OEC (2021). The index is calculated by considering two parameters with respect to a country's export products: (i) their ubiquity and (ii) their diversity (Hausmann et al., 2014: 20). Typically, if a country's economic complexity is high (i.e., the economic complexity index value is high), this country's products have relatively high diversity and low ubiquity. By the same token, if a country's economic complexity is low, then its outputs possibly have low diversity and high ubiquity (Hartmann et al., 2017: 77).

Figure 2. Economic complexity indices of Turkey, Japan, and Germany for the 1981-2017 period
Source: The Observatory of Economic Complexity (OEC, 2021)

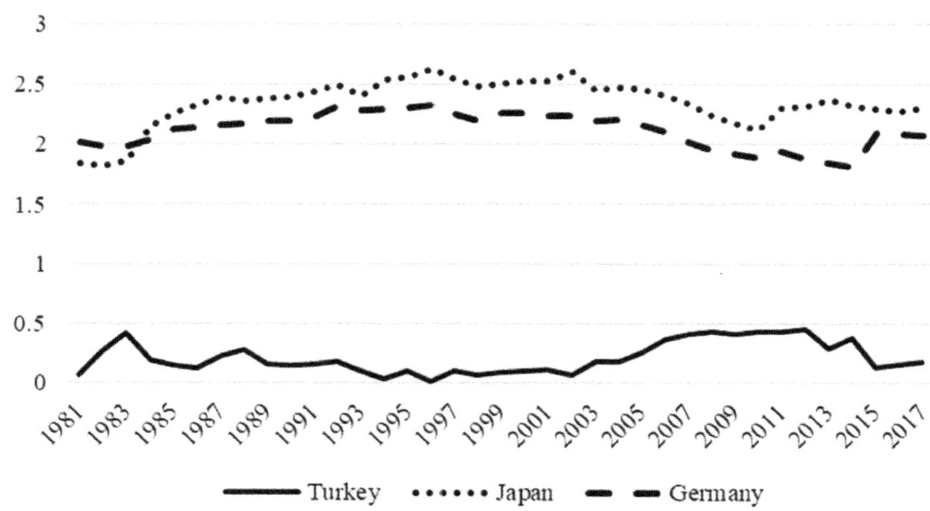

Turkey's economic complexity index is shown in Figure 2 with the indices of Germany and Japan for the 1981-2017 sample period. The reason for selecting Japan and Germany besides Turkey is that these two countries had the highest index values (i.e., the most complex economies) in 2017 [according to the OEC (2021) database].

Figure 2 shows that Turkey's economic complexity is considerably lower than Japan's and Germany's. Nonetheless, Turkey's economic complexity had never been below zero during the 1981-2017 period. Furthermore, even though Turkey's economic complexity increased at the beginning of the 1980s, it decreased in the later periods and stayed more or less stable through the mid-1990s and in the beginning of the 2000s. However, in the 2003-2008 period, Turkey's economic complexity had constantly increased. Finally, Figure 2 also shows that compared to the 2014 value, Turkey's economic complexity index stayed relatively low in the 2015-2017 period. In short, Figure 2 indicates that Turkey's economic complexity is significantly lower than its developed counterparts. Also, Turkey's economic complexity experienced some ups and downs through the sample period, yet it was always positive.

THEORETICAL FRAMEWORK AND LITERATURE SURVEY

The previous empirical literature on environmental economics heavily focuses on the impact that income imposes on environmental deterioration. Further, this impact is frequently estimated by testing the validity of the environmental Kuznets curve hypothesis (EKCH), which proposes that income may have an inverted-U impact on environmental pollution (Grossman & Krueger, 1991; Panayotou, 1993). According to the EKCH, unless a threshold level of income is reached, increases in economic growth would lead to environmental degradation. However, after a threshold level of income, higher income levels would result in minor environmental damage, as a possible result of increases in technological development, demand for a better environment, environmental expenditures, and these expenditures' effectiveness (Panayotou, 1993).

The empirical literature on testing the validity of the EKCH is colossal (see Shahbaz & Sinha, 2019 for a detailed survey), but only recently, economic complexity, which is considered to be a robust predictor of income, has been employed as an explanatory factor of environmental sustainability or energy demand. Depending on the existing level of economic development, achieving economic complexity can either benefit or worsen environmental performance. Romero & Gramkow (2021: 4) claim that a fully developed productive system and higher productive capabilities can lead to better green innovations; in other words, more economically complex countries tend to develop technological solutions to their environmental issues more easily. Additionally, economic complexity is positively associated with technological absorption; therefore, for developed economies with higher economic complexities, it is possible to expand their green technology absorption capacities (Romero & Gramkow, 2021: 4).

However, according to Gozgor & Can (2016), if a developing country is attempting to achieve continuous economic growth by increasing its export products' diversity (i.e., its economic complexity), this process would boost the volume of economic activities. Subsequently, increases in the scale of economic activities would result in higher energy demand and environmental damage (Gozgor & Can, 2016: 21595). Further, because limited economic complexity corresponds to limited export product diversity and technical productivity, intersectoral technology spillovers in developing countries with limited economic complexities might also be rather low (Fang et al., 2019: 12182). In other terms, limiting the environmental damage while achieving economic complexity might be difficult in developing nations, as technological spillovers to cleaner technologies and energy-efficient production systems may not occur.

In line with these propositions, empirical studies that investigated the effect of economic complexity on environmental performance produced mixed results. Gozgor & Can (2016) investigated how export product diversification impacts Turkey's carbon emissions by employing the dynamic ordinary least squares (DOLS) estimator. Their findings showed that higher product diversification leads to higher emission levels in Turkey. Further, Gozgor & Can (2017) conducted another study on China by employing the linear autoregressive distributed lag (linear ARDL) approach and found that higher export quality leads to lower emission levels. This study's result is supported by Can & Gozgor's (2017) study on France. In that study, the authors again employed the DOLS estimator to examine the economic complexity's impact on carbon emissions.

Shahbaz et al. (2019) investigated the roles of education and the diversity of exports on the United States of America's (USA) energy use for the 1975-2016 period. They applied the bootstrap ARDL test and the vector error correction method (VECM) and found that both education and export diversification decrease energy use in the long run. Additionally, their findings also indicated that there is a bi-directional causality between energy demand and export diversification. Moreover, Neagu & Teodoru (2019) examined the economic complexity-energy consumption-greenhouse gas emissions link for a panel of the European Union (EU) countries. They employed the fully modified ordinary least squares (FMOLS) and DOLS estimators and discovered that in the long run, economic complexity is positively associated with greenhouse gas emissions. Further, for the 25 selected EU countries, Neagu (2019) studied if the EKCH is valid regarding the economic complexity's impact on carbon emissions by employing the FMOLS and the DOLS methods. Their results showed that economic complexity has an inverted-U shape effect on emissions validating the EKCH. Fang et al. (2019) analyzed the impact of export products' quality on carbon dioxide emissions for a panel of 82 developing countries for the 1970-2014 period. Their panel fixed effects estimation findings showed that export products' quality increases carbon emissions in developing economies. Doğan et al. (2019) revealed the impact of exporting sophisticated products on carbon emissions in 55 lower-middle-, higher-middle-, and high-income economies for the 1971-2014 period using panel quantile estimation methods. Their findings showed that economic complexity positively contributes to pollution in lower-middle-income and higher-middle-income economies, whereas it decreases pollution in high-income economies.

Can et al. (2020) studied how the diversity of export products influenced the environmental quality of 84 developing economies during the 1971-2014 period. Their long run analyses are based on the panel ARDL, DOLS, and FMOLS approaches. Their findings indicated that higher diversity of export products in developing countries lead to more carbon emissions in the long run. Furthermore, Neagu (2020) investigated the economic complexity's influence on the Ecological Footprint for the selected 48 complex economies via the FMOLS and the DOLS approaches. Their findings showed that economic complexity's impact on Ecological Footprint is positive.

For a sample of 63 developing and developed economies, Shahzad et al. (2020) empirically researched the influence of export diversification on CO_2 emissions for the 1971-2014 period. The findings of their analyses produced mixed results. Their (unrestricted) fixed effects estimates showed that product diversification decreases emissions in all three panels [namely, the world (whole sample of selected countries), developing, and developed panels]. At the same time, their system-generalized method of moments (*system-GMM*) estimation findings revealed that product diversification reduces emissions in the panel of all countries yet increases emissions in the sub-panels of developed and developing economies. By using the panel quantile methods and annual data spanning the 1971-2014 period, Dogan et al. (2020) estimated the influence of economic sophistication on carbon emissions for 63 developed and developing countries. Their estimation results showed that economic complexity has heterogeneous effects on environmental degradation.

In a more recent study, Wang et al. (2021) empirically studied how renewable energy use and export quality impact carbon emissions in two panels: (*i*) top ten renewable energy producers and (*ii*) top ten economies that have the highest ECI scores. Methodologically, they used panel cointegration tests, the DOLS and the FMOLS estimators, and panel Granger causality test. Their estimation results showed that, in both panels, export quality induces carbon dioxide emissions in the long run. Boleti et al. (2021) analyzed economic complexity's effect on various environmental performance indicators in 88 developed and developing countries using a fixed-effects two-stage least squares/instrumental variables (FE 2SLS/

IV) approach. Their results indicated that improving economic complexity leads to better overall environmental performance. Nevertheless, economic complexity worsens air quality. In another study, Iqbal et al. (2021) researched the effects of export diversification, fiscal decentralization, and environmental technology-related innovations on carbon dioxide emissions in 37 Organization for Economic Co-operation and Development (OECD) economies for the 1970-2019 period. Their augmented mean group (AMG) analysis showed that export diversification has a long run positive impact on emissions, indicating that the diversity of the export products worsens environmental quality in these OECD economies.

In another recent study, Shahzad, Fareed, et al. (2021) examined energy consumption, economic complexity, and the Ecological Footprint nexus for the USA by employing the quantile ARDL (QARDL) approach and quantile causality analysis. They examined the 1965-2017 period by using quarterly data. Their findings from the quantile analyses revealed that both economic complexity and energy use increase the USA's Ecological Footprint and bi-directional causalities exist between the variables of interest. Romero & Gramkow (2021) showed that economic complexity decreases greenhouse gas (GHG) emissions in 67 economies via the fixed effects and system-GMM estimators.

Regarding the energy demand-economic complexity link, Bashir et al. (2020) examined the impact of export product diversification on energy and carbon intensities of 19 OECD countries. In their examination, they considered the 1990-2015 period and used various panel data estimation methods such as sequential estimation, quantile regression, difference GMM, and system GMM approaches. Their main findings revealed that (export) product diversification decreases both carbon and energy intensities in the long run. Sharma et al. (2021) studied the impacts of technological innovation and export diversification on renewable energy deployment for the BRICS nations. Their analysis used panel data methods, including the cross-sectionally augmented ARDL method (CS-ARDL), and considered the 1990-2018 period. Their long run findings revealed that export diversification positively contributes to the deployment of renewable energy. Shahzad et al. (2021) empirically investigated the impact of export product diversification on energy demand for 10 newly industrialized countries (NICs) for the 1971-2014 period. Their GMM, FMOLS, DOLS, and feasible generalized least squares (FGLS) estimation results showed that diversifying export products limits overall energy consumption. Shahzad, Lv, et al. (2021) empirically researched how export diversification impacts renewable energy use for the emerging seven (E-7) and the group of seven (G-7) countries by employing the FGLS and the FMOLS methods. Their findings were mixed and showed that export diversification imposes nonlinear influences on renewable energy demand.

This literature review points out several results and gaps. First, economic complexity's influence on environmental deterioration is mixed. Based on this chapter's literature survey, it is possible to postulate that achieving economic complexity in developed countries is generally beneficial to their environmental performance, while the same process is generally harmful to the environment in developing countries. Second, empirical studies on Turkey are rather limited. Conducting more empirical studies on the Turkish case would provide fresh insights to policymakers in Turkey and other developing nations to decide what should be done to achieve economic complexity and preserve or improve environmental quality at the same time. Lastly, nonlinearities and asymmetries are mostly ignored in previous research. Distinguishing the impacts of positive and negative developments in economic complexity allows observing if both types of developments have similar or different impacts on Turkey's long run environmental performance because depending on these impacts, policy propositions can significantly differ. This chapter's main aim is to fill these gaps.

DATA, MODEL, AND EMPIRICAL APPROACH

Data and Model

This chapter utilizes annual data covering the period 1981-2017. As a result of the limited sample size, two bivariate models are employed in this study—namely, the Ecological Footprint and the Carbon Footprint models. As the names suggest, the former uses Turkey's Ecological Footprint as the dependent variable, whereas the latter employs Turkey's Carbon Footprint. These (nonlinear) models are mathematically shown in equations (1) and (2):

$$LEFPC_t = \lambda_1 + \lambda_2 LECI_t^{Positive} + \lambda_3 LECI_t^{Negative} + u_t \# \tag{1}$$

$$LCFPC_t = \delta_1 + \delta_2 LECI_t^{Positive} + \delta_3 LECI_t^{Negative} + u_t \# \tag{2}$$

In equations (1) and (2), EFPC shows the per-person Ecological Footprint of consumption (in *gha*), and CFPC shows the per-person Carbon Footprint (in *gha*) in Turkey. The *ECI* is Turkey's economic complexity index. The letter *L* shows that logarithms of the time series are utilized. Terms λ_1 and δ_1 are the constants. Also, λ_i and δ_i for $i=2,3$ show the coefficients to be estimated. Time series for EFPC and CFPC are obtained from Global Footprint Network (2021), and ECI is retrieved from OEC (2021). Also, summary statistics and graphs of the employed variables are reported in the appendix section. Lastly, $LECI_t^{Positive}$ and $LECI_t^{Negative}$ are the cumulative sums of positive and negative changes in *LECI*, respectively. They are calculated as follows:

$$\begin{aligned} LECI_t^{Positive} &= \sum_{k=1}^{t} \Delta LECI_k^{Positive} = \sum_{k=1}^{t} \max\left(\Delta LECI_k, 0\right); \\ LECI_t^{Negative} &= \sum_{k=1}^{t} \Delta LECI_k^{Negative} = \sum_{k=1}^{t} \min\left(\Delta LECI_k, 0\right) \# \end{aligned} \tag{3}$$

Empirical Method: The Augmented Nonlinear Autoregressive Distributed Lag (Augmented NADL) Bounds Testing Approach to Cointegration and Estimation

This chapter employs the nonlinear autoregressive distributed lag (NADL) approach of Shin et al. (2014) and extends it by utilizing the $F^{Regressors}$*-test* on the lagged regressor(s) that is proposed by McNown et al. (2018) and Sam et al. (2019). The NADL approach is an improved version of the (linear) ADL approach developed by Pesaran et al. (PSS) (2001). The reasons for selecting this method can be stated as follows: (i) it is a suitable method for limited sample sizes, (ii) it is applicable if both regressor(s) and regressand are either *I(1)* or *I(0)* processes, but not an *I(2)* process. In other words, it can be applied if the time series is level stationary or first difference stationary. Lastly, (iii) the endogeneity issue has limited effects on the testing procedure (McNown et al., 2018: 1510).

The NADL's central premise consists of using the cumulative sums of the time series, and this approach is based on the suggestion by Granger & Yoon (2002: 5), which assert that the components (i.e., sums of the positive and negative changes) of the variables can have a long run association. Therefore, they state that hidden cointegration is a simple case of nonlinear long run association (Granger & Yoon, 2002: 2). Based on this, Shin et al. (2014) use the components that are shown in equation (3) to modify the (linear) ADL method of PSS (2001). The NADL version of the model in equation (1)[1] to be tested for cointegration can be shown as follows:

$$\Delta LEFPC_t = \lambda_0 + \lambda_1 LEFPC_{t-1} + \lambda_2^{Positive} LECI_{t-1}^{Positive} + \lambda_3^{Negative} LECI_{t-1}^{Negative} + \sum_{j=1}^{m-1} \lambda_{4,j} \Delta LEFPC_{t-j} + \sum_{k=0}^{n-1} \left(\lambda_{5,k}^{Positive} \Delta LECI_{t-k}^{Positive} + \lambda_{6,k}^{Negative} \Delta LECI_{t-k}^{Negative} \right) + u_t \quad (4)$$

Similar to the PSS (2001) study, Shin et al. (2014) approach to cointegration relies on two tests. The first one is an F-test on the coefficients of lagged regressors and regressand. Namely, $H_0: \lambda_1 = \lambda_2^{Positive} = \lambda_3^{Negative} = 0$ against $H_a: \lambda_1 \neq \lambda_2^{Positive} / \lambda_3^{Negative} \neq 0$ should be tested. The second one is a t-test on the coefficient of the lagged regressand. In this approach, $H_0: \lambda_1 = 0$ *against* $H_a: \lambda_1 \neq 0$ is tested. In the next stage, both test statistics are compared to their respective upper-bound critical values that are put forward by PSS (2001). Typically, if the test statistics are significant, then the cointegration is confirmed.

However, PSS (2001) claims that there can emerge two degenerate cases from this approach. Firstly, the F-test result can be significant, yet the coefficient of lagged regressand variable might be insignificant (i.e , $\lambda_1 = 0$) while the coefficients of lagged regressors might be significant (i.e., $\lambda_2^{Positive} \neq \lambda_3^{Negative} \neq 0$). This is called the degenerate lagged regressand variable case. Secondly, the reverse case might be valid. In other words, the coefficient of lagged regressand variable might be statistically significant (i.e., $\lambda_1 \neq 0$), whereas the lagged regressors' coefficients can be insignificant (i.e., $\lambda_2^{Positive} = \lambda_3^{Negative} = 0$). This case is named the degenerate lagged regressors case (Sam et al., 2019: 138). To prevent the first issue, the abovementioned *t-test* on the lagged regressand variable is offered by the PSS (2001) study. To solve the second case, PSS (2001) offers the assumption that the regressand should be an *I(1)* process (i.e., stationary in its first difference) (McNown et al., 2018: 1512). Nonetheless, unit root tests can provide disputing results making the assumption that regressand should be *I(1)* ambiguous.

To bypass this assumption and related issues, McNown et al. (2018) and Sam et al. (2019) provide a third test on the lagged regressors, which is called in this chapter as the $F^{Regressors}$*-test*. In this additional test, $H_0: \lambda_2^{Positive} = \lambda_3^{Negative} = 0$ against $H_a: \lambda_2^{Positive} \neq \lambda_3^{Negative} \neq 0$ is tested. In the following phase, the obtained $F^{Regressors}$*-statistic* is compared to the finite sample critical values in Sam et al. (2019). If this test statistic is significant, the significance of the coefficients of the lagged regressors would be confirmed.

To summarize, three bounds tests that are explained above should be applied to determine cointegration. In order to confirm cointegration, all three tests' results should be significant. Otherwise, the long run association cannot be validated [see Sam et al. (2019) for further details].

If cointegration is validated, the long run coefficient for the positive developments and its significance are calculated by the $-\lambda_2^{Positive} / \lambda_1 = 0$ restriction. The coefficient for negative developments and its significance are calculated by $-\lambda_3^{Negative} / \lambda_1 = 0$. Furthermore, the long run (a)symmetry is decided by a Wald test which assesses whether the equation $\lambda_2^{Positive} = \lambda_3^{Negative}$ holds. In the same vein, the existence of a short run symmetry is tested via $\sum_{k=0}^{n-1} \lambda_{5,k}^{Positive} = \sum_{k=0}^{n-1} \lambda_{6,k}^{Negative}$ [for further details, see Shin et al. (2014)].

EMPIRICAL RESULTS

Before testing for long run association, stationarity properties of the selected time series should be determined. In this respect, this empirical chapter utilizes three stationarity tests, namely, the augmented Dickey-Fuller (ADF), the Kwiatkowski-Phillips-Schmidt-Shin (KPSS), and the Phillips-Perron (PP) unit root tests proposed by Dickey & Fuller (1979), Kwiatkowski et al. (1992), and Phillips & Perron (1988), respectively. The findings of these tests are reported in Table 1.

Table 1. Results of the unit-root tests

Tests→	ADF		PP		KPSS	
Variables ↓	Level	1st difference	Level	1st difference	Level	1st difference
LEFPC	-5.5735***	-	-5.5955***	-	0.0686	-
LCFPC	-4.5333***	-	-4.5581***	-	0.1052	-
$LECI^{Positive}$	-1.5092	-6.5972***	-1.6075	-6.5832***	0.1229*	0.1238
$LECI^{Negative}$	-1.5437	-6.4455***	-1.5438	-6.4120***	0.1561**	0.1566

*Notes: Test equations include constant and trend in levels, and constant in first differences. *, **, and *** indicate significance at 10%, 5%, and 1% levels, respectively.*

According to findings in Table 1, dependent variables (i.e., LEFPC and LCFPC) do not contain unit roots. In other words, all three stationarity tests indicate that the dependent variables of both models are stationary in levels. In contrast, the independent variables ($LECI^{Positive}$ and $LECI^{Negative}$) are stationary in their first differences [i.e., they are I(1)]. These results are consistent across all the unit root tests. As the dependent variables are I(0), and the explanatory variables are I(1), the augmented NADL method should be employed. The augmented NADL method allows the dependent variable to be stationary by utilizing an additional F-test (i.e., the $F^{Regressors}$-*test*) on the coefficients of the lagged explanatory variables.

In the following stage, the existence of (nonlinear) cointegration for the proposed models can be established via the three bounds tests that are explained in the previous section. The results of the three bounds tests with their respective upper bound critical values for the Ecological Footprint model are reported in Panel A of Table 2, and the results for the Carbon Footprint model are reported in Panel A of Table 3. For both models, both F-tests' statistics are higher than their respective 1% upper bound critical values, and t-tests' statistics are lower than the 1% upper bound critical value (i.e., -5.016 & $-4.849 < -4.1$). These results indicate that a nonlinear long run association exists between environmental degradation and economic complexity in both models. In short, the test results show that nonlinear cointegration exists in both models.

Given that nonlinear long run association exists, whether economic complexity has asymmetric impacts on the Ecological and Carbon Footprints in the short and long runs should be tested. This is done by testing if the coefficients of positive and negative developments in the economic complexity index (ECI) are significantly different. The results of these tests are reported in Panels B and C of Tables 2 and 3 for each model. For the Ecological Footprint model, in both long and short runs, asymmetries exist for the ECI. In other words, positive and negative developments in the ECI have significantly varying impacts on Turkey's Ecological Footprint in the long run and the short run. For the Carbon Footprint model, asymmetries for the ECI exist only in the long run, as the Wald test for short run (a)symmetry is not significant. In short, the ECI asymmetrically impacts Turkey's Carbon Footprint only in the long run.

Table 2. The NADL results for the Ecological Footprint model

A) Cointegration Tests	**Test statistics**	**Upper Bound Critical Values (10%, 5%, 1%)**	
F-test	8.395***	4.14, 4.85, 6.36	
t-test	-5.016***	-3.21, -3.53, -4.10	
$F^{Regressors}$-test	9.291***	4.54, 5.90, 9.16	
B) Long-run Asymmetry	**Test statistic**	**p-value**	
$LECI_{LR}^{Wald\ test}$	58.5578***	0.0000	
C) Short-run Asymmetry	**Test statistic**	**p-value**	
$LECI_{SR}^{Wald\ test}$	9.5615***	0.0048	
D) Long-run Results	**Coefficients**	**Test statistics**	**p-values**
$LECI^{Positive}$	0.0389**	2.6311	0.0144
$LECI^{Negative}$	0.0024	0.1475	0.8839
E) Short-run Results	**Coefficients**	**Test statistics**	**p-values**
Constant	0.5624***	5.189429	0.0000
$\Delta LECI_{t-1}^{Positive}$	-0.0733**	-2.2996	0.0301
$\Delta LECI_{t-4}^{Positive}$	-0.0667***	-4.5994	0.0001
$\Delta LECI_{t-2}^{Negative}$	-0.0704**	-2.2595	0.0328
ECT_{t-1}	-0.6897***	-5.0162	0.0000
F) Diagnostic Tests		**Test statistics**	**p-values**
Serial Corr.		5.9726	0.2012
Ramsey RESET		0.7143	0.4063
J-B Normality		2.2962	0.3172
B-P-G Heterosked.		8.6123	0.1966
ARCH Heterosked.		0.8169	0.9362
Adjusted R^2		0.5734	
CUSUM & CUSUMSQ		Stable & Stable	

*Notes: *** and ** show 1% and 5% significance levels, respectively. Maximum lag length is 4. J-B: Jarque–Bera, B-P-G: Breusch-Pagan-Godfrey, B-G: Breusch-Godfrey. Critical values for F-test and t-test are retrieved from Pesaran et al. (2001). Critical values for F*-test are retrieved from Sam et al. (2019).*

Table 3. The NADL results for the Carbon Footprint model

A) Cointegration Tests	Test statistics	Upper Bound Critical Values (10%, 5%, 1%)	
F-test	7.844***	4.14, 4.85, 6.36	
t-test	-4.849***	-3.21, -3.53, -4.10	
$F^{Regressors}$-*test*	10.04***	4.54, 5.90, 9.16	
B) Long-run Asymmetry	**Test statistic**	**p-value**	
$LECI_{LR}^{Wald\ test}$	117.5899***	0.0000	
C) Short-run Asymmetry	**Test statistic**	**p-value**	
$LECI_{SR}^{Wald\ test}$	0.0099	0.9214	
D) Long-run Results	**Coefficients**	**Test statistics**	**p-values**
$LECI^{Positive}$	0.1334***	3.2061	0.0039
$LECI^{Negative}$	0.0564	1.2798	0.2134
E) Short-run Results	**Coefficients**	**Test statistics**	**p-values**
Constant	-0.1063**	-2.0701	0.0499
$\Delta LECI_{t}^{Positive}$	0.0701*	1.8408	0.0786
$\Delta LECI_{t-1}^{Positive}$	-0.1225***	-3.2488	0.0035
$\Delta LECI_{t-4}^{Positive}$	-0.0813***	-4.6128	0.0001
$\Delta LECI_{t}^{Negative}$	-0.0365*	-1.8199	0.0818
$\Delta LECI_{t-2}^{Negative}$	-0.1037**	-2.7804	0.0106
ECT_{t-1}	-0.5597***	-4.8486	0.0001
F) Diagnostic Tests		**Test statistics**	**p-values**
Serial Corr.		6.583086	0.1596
Ramsey RESET		0.439857	0.5141
J-B Normality		4.6841*	0.0961
B-P-G Heterosked.		6.4352	0.5986
ARCH Heterosked.		1.8496	0.7634
Adjusted R^2		0.5834	
CUSUM & CUSUMSQ		Stable & Stable	

*Notes: ***, **, and * show 1%, 5%, and 10% significance levels, respectively. Maximum lag length is 4. J-B: Jarque–Bera, B-P-G: Breusch-Pagan-Godfrey, B-G: Breusch-Godfrey. Critical values for F-test and t-test are retrieved from Pesaran et al. (2001). Critical values for F*-test are retrieved from Sam et al. (2019).*

The magnitudes of the impacts of positive and negative developments in the ECI for the long run are respectively reported in Panel D of Tables 2 and 3 for each model. For both models, in the long run, only positive shocks in the ECI have significant impacts on the Ecological and Carbon Footprints of Turkey. For the Ecological Footprint model, a 1% positive shock in the ECI corresponds to an almost 0.04% increase in Turkey's Ecological Footprint in the long run. While the ECI has the same impact on Carbon Footprint, the magnitude is much higher. For instance, a 1% positive development in the ECI results in an 0.133% increase in Turkey's Carbon Footprint in the long run. To summarize, the long run (asymmetric) findings in this chapter show that only positive developments in the ECI significantly intensify Turkey's environmental deterioration, and this intensifying impact is much higher in the Carbon Footprint model.

The short run coefficients for negative and positive developments in the ECI are shown in Panel E of Tables 2 and 3. While the short run asymmetry exists only in the Ecological Footprint model, the short run coefficients of positive and negative developments in the ECI have different signs. More specifically, in both models, while the positive shocks to the ECI in the short run decrease environmental pollution (i.e., Ecological and Carbon Footprints), negative shocks in the ECI decrease it. For instance, in the Ecological Footprint model, a 1% positive shock in Turkey's ECI corresponds to a cumulative decrease in Turkey's Ecological Footprint by 0.14% [This is calculated by adding the short run coefficients of $LECI^{Positive}$: *(-0.0733) + (-0.0667)*]. Further, a 1% percent negative shock in the ECI corresponds to a 0.07% increase in Turkey's Ecological Footprint in the short term.

This chapter's empirical findings can be outlined as follows. First, in both proposed models, nonlinear cointegration exists between economic complexity and environmental damage indicators. Second, Turkey's economic complexity has significant asymmetric impacts on its Ecological Footprint in both the short run and the long run. Third, economic complexity exerts significant asymmetric impacts on Turkey's Carbon Footprint only in the long run. Fourth, in the long run, only positive developments in Turkey's ECI intensify Carbon and Ecological Footprints, while negative shocks do not exert any significant impacts on Turkey's environmental degradation indicators. Finally, in the short run, positive developments in Turkey's ECI decrease its environmental degradation, whereas negative developments in the ECI worsen its environmental degradation.

This chapter's results show that while achieving economic complexity benefited Turkey's environmental quality to some degree in the short run; the same process hurt Turkey's environmental quality in the long run through the sample period. The long run empirical findings of this chapter which show that economic complexity harms environmental performance is approximately in line with the findings of Can et al. (2020), Doğan et al. (2019), Fang et al. (2019), Gezgor & Can (2016), Iqbal et al. (2021), Neagu (2020), Neagu & Teodoru (2019), Shahzad, Fareed, et al. (2021), and Wang et al. (2021).

Moreover, in Panels E and F of Tables 2 and 3, error correction terms' (ECTs') coefficients and the results of the diagnostic tests are respectively presented for each model. In accordance with the expectations, the ECTs' coefficients are significant and negative in both models. Also, diagnostic tests for both estimated models generally indicate that serial correlation, heteroskedasticity, functional form, and non-normal distribution problems are absent. Lastly, to confirm parameters' stability, the CUSUM (cumulative sum of recursive residuals) and the CUSUMSQ (cumulative sum of squares of recursive residuals) tests of Brown et al. (1975) are used. The graphical results of these tests are reported in the appendix sections of this chapter. Both test results reveal that parameters are stable in both the Ecological Footprint and the Carbon Footprint models. This result indicates that the estimation results can be utilized for policy analysis and recommendations.

CONCLUSION

Achieving persistent and sustainable economic development requires improving the diversity of export products (i.e., economic complexity) of a country. However, the effect of achieving economic complexity on environmental sustainability is empirically under-searched. Given that improving economic complexity can be a key instrument for developing economies to catch up with the developed ones, examining economic complexity's environmental ramifications can provide new insights to policymakers. In this regard, Turkey is a solid and limitedly examined case. Turkey experienced a globalization process since the beginning of the 1980s, which somewhat improved Turkey's economic complexity while worsening its environmental performance. As visual analysis presented in this chapter shows, Turkey's economic complexity index had never been below zero during the 1981-2017 period. However, its level of economic complexity had remained significantly lower compared to Germany's and Japan's economic complexities. Also, during the same period, Turkey's Ecological Footprint and Carbon Footprint had noticeably increased.

This chapter aimed to empirically analyze how Turkey's economic complexity affected its environmental performance during the 1981-2017 period. To fulfill this aim, two bivariate models are formed, and the augmented NADL method is utilized to econometrically estimate these models. The reason for selecting the augmented NADL is four-folds. First, this method allows both independent and dependent variables to be I(0) and/or I(1) processes. Second, this method allows testing nonlinear long run association among the variables. Third, this method is suitable for testing the asymmetric impacts of positive and negative shocks in economic complexity on the selected environmental damage proxies (i.e., Ecological and Carbon Footprints) in both the short run and the long run. Last but not least, in the empirical literature, nonlinearities and asymmetries have been rarely considered when examining the effects of economic complexity on environmental damage. It is crucial to observe nonlinear cointegration and asymmetric impacts of economic complexity because depending on the magnitude and the significance of the asymmetric effects, sustainable policy suggestions and analyses can considerably vary.

This empirical chapter's main findings are as follows. First, nonlinear cointegrations exist between Turkey's economic complexity and its Ecological Footprint, and between Turkey's economic complexity and its Carbon Footprint. Second, long run asymmetries exist with regard to economic complexity's impacts on Ecological and Carbon Footprints. However, only positive shocks in economic complexity significantly increase both footprint indicators in the long run, negative shocks in economic complexity do not impose any significant influence on environmental deterioration. Third, in the short run, significant asymmetries exist only in the Ecological Footprint Model. Further, according to short run findings, while positive developments in economic complexity benefit the environmental performance, negative developments worsen it in both models.

This chapter's empirical findings show that although achieving economic complexity seems to benefit Turkey's environmental performance in the short run; it worsens Turkey's environmental quality in the long run. The empirical findings in this chapter also reveal that development and sustainability policies in Turkey are shortsighted and tend to sacrifice Turkey's long run environmental sustainability at the expense of short-term gains. Additionally, even though Turkey's economic complexity index values have stayed above zero during the 1981-2017 period, the level of economic complexity remained considerably low compared to developed countries.

Policymakers in Turkey should consider long run consequences when planning and executing sustainability and environmental policies. In addition, Turkey's economic complexity level should be further increased, yet this should not be done to protect only the short-term (environmental) interests. Encouraging product diversification by incentivizing green sectors or the sectors that adopt environmentally friendly production practices may partly limit the negative long run ramifications of economic complexity on the environment. Given that there is currently an upsurge in global demand for sustainable goods (ClimateAction, 2021), diversifying Turkey's export products towards green goods can ensure long run sustainability while increasing the level of economic complexity. Moreover, innovations and investments towards sustainable products and production technologies should be encouraged through financial incentives and subsidies to increase Turkey's economic capabilities and ensure long run environmental sustainability. Furthermore, innovations in renewable energy production and deployment should be incentivized. Karasoy (2019) empirically revealed that alternative energy's effect on Turkey's carbon emission levels is relatively limited. Therefore, it is feasible to claim that incentivizing the deployment of renewable (or alternative) energy through innovations would improve Turkey's long run environmental performance.

Future research should focus on other developing countries to examine whether economic complexity has similar or different (asymmetric) impacts on these countries' long term environmental sustainability. Additionally, multivariate models can also be employed to investigate the direct and/or intermediating roles of possible additional variables on the environment.

REFERENCES

Bashir, M. A., Sheng, B., Doğan, B., Sarwar, S., & Shahzad, U. (2020). Export product diversification and energy efficiency: Empirical evidence from OECD countries. *Structural Change and Economic Dynamics*, *55*, 232–243. doi:10.1016/j.strueco.2020.09.002

Boleti, E., Garas, A., Kyriakou, A., & Lapatinas, A. (2021). Economic Complexity and Environmental Performance: Evidence from a World Sample. *Environmental Modeling and Assessment*, *26*(3), 251–270. doi:10.100710666-021-09750-0

Borucke, M., Moore, D., Cranston, G., Gracey, K., Iha, K., Larson, J., Lazarus, E., Morales, J. C., Wackernagel, M., & Galli, A. (2013). Accounting for demand and supply of the biosphere's regenerative capacity: The National Footprint Accounts' underlying methodology and framework. *Ecological Indicators*, *24*, 518–533. doi:10.1016/j.ecolind.2012.08.005

Brown, R. L., Durbin, J., & Evans, J. M. (1975). Techniques for Testing the Constancy of Regression Relationships over Time Source. *Journal of the Royal Statistical Society. Series B. Methodological*, *37*(2), 149–192. doi:10.1111/j.2517-6161.1975.tb01532.x

Can, M., Dogan, B., & Saboori, B. (2020). Does trade matter for environmental degradation in developing countries? New evidence in the context of export product diversification. *Environmental Science and Pollution Research International*, *27*(13), 14702–14710. doi:10.100711356-020-08000-2 PMID:32052330

Can, M., & Gozgor, G. (2017). The impact of economic complexity on carbon emissions: Evidence from France. *Environmental Science and Pollution Research International*, *24*(19), 16364–16370. doi:10.100711356-017-9219-7 PMID:28547378

ClimateAction. (2021). *WWF: Huge rise in demand for sustainable goods during Pandemic - Climate Action*. https://www.climateaction.org/news/wwf-huge-rise-in-demand-for-sustainable-goods-during-pandemic

Dickey, D. A., & Fuller, W. A. (1979). Distribution of the Estimators for Autoregressive Time Series With a Unit Root. *Journal of the American Statistical Association*, *74*(366), 427. doi:10.2307/2286348

Dogan, B., Madaleno, M., Tiwari, A. K., & Hammoudeh, S. (2020). Impacts of export quality on environmental degradation: Does income matter? *Environmental Science and Pollution Research International*, *27*(12), 13735–13772. doi:10.100711356-019-07371-5 PMID:32030594

Doğan, B., Saboori, B., & Can, M. (2019). Does economic complexity matter for environmental degradation? An empirical analysis for different stages of development. *Environmental Science and Pollution Research International*, *26*(31), 31900–31912. doi:10.100711356-019-06333-1 PMID:31489548

Fang, J., Gozgor, G., Lu, Z., & Wu, W. (2019). Effects of the export product quality on carbon dioxide emissions: Evidence from developing economies. *Environmental Science and Pollution Research International*, *26*(12), 12181–12193. doi:10.100711356-019-04513-7 PMID:30835064

Fath, B. D., Jørgensen, S. E., & Cole, M. (Eds.). (2020). *Managing Human and Social Systems*. CRC Press. doi:10.1201/9781003053514

Felipe, J., Kumar, U., Abdon, A., & Bacate, M. (2012). Product complexity and economic development. *Structural Change and Economic Dynamics*, *23*(1), 36–68. doi:10.1016/j.strueco.2011.08.003

Galli, A., Wackernagel, M., Iha, K., & Lazarus, E. (2014). Ecological Footprint: Implications for biodiversity. *Biological Conservation*, *173*, 121–132. doi:10.1016/j.biocon.2013.10.019

Global Footprint Network. (2021). *Open Data Platform*. https://data.footprintnetwork.org/#/countryTrends?type=BCpc,EFCpc&cn=223

Global Footprint Network National Footprint Accounts. (2020). http://data.footprintnetwork.org

Gozgor, G., & Can, M. (2016). Export product diversification and the environmental Kuznets curve: Evidence from Turkey. *Environmental Science and Pollution Research International*, *23*(21), 21594–21603. doi:10.100711356-016-7403-9 PMID:27519900

Gozgor, G., & Can, M. (2017). Does export product quality matter for CO2 emissions? Evidence from China. *Environmental Science and Pollution Research International*, *24*(3), 2866–2875. doi:10.100711356-016-8070-6 PMID:27838907

Granger, C. W. J., & Yoon, G. (2002). *Hidden Cointegration*. SSRN Electronic Journal. doi:10.2139srn.313831

Grossman, G. M., & Krueger, A. B. (1991). *Environmental Impacts of a North American Free Trade Agreement*. National Bureau of Economic Research Working Paper Series. No. 3914. doi:10.3386/w3914

Hartman, D. (2013). A global comparative perspective on innovation and economic diversification in Turkey. In İstanbul Policy Center (pp. 1–28). Istanbul Policy Center (IPC).

Hartmann, D., Guevara, M. R., Jara-Figueroa, C., Aristarán, M., & Hidalgo, C. A. (2017). Linking Economic Complexity, Institutions, and Income Inequality. *World Development*, *93*, 75–93. doi:10.1016/j.worlddev.2016.12.020

Hausmann, R., & Hidalgo, C. A. (2011). The network structure of economic output. *Journal of Economic Growth*, *16*(4), 309–342. doi:10.100710887-011-9071-4

Hausmann, R., Hidalgo, C. A., Bustos, S., Coscia, M., Simoes, A., & Yildirim, M. A. (2014). *The Atlas of Economic Complexity: Mapping Paths to Prosperity*. The MIT Press. doi:10.7551/mitpress/9647.001.0001

Hidalgo, C. A., & Hausmann, R. (2009). The building blocks of economic complexity. In *Proceedings of the National Academy of Sciences of the United States of America* (Vol. 106, Issue 26). 10.1073/pnas.0900943106

Iqbal, N., Abbasi, R., Shinwari, R., Guangcai, W., Ahmad, M., & Tang, K. (2021). Does exports diversification and environmental innovation achieve carbon neutrality target of OECD economies? *Journal of Environmental Management*, *291*, 112648. doi:10.1016/j.jenvman.2021.112648 PMID:33940360

Karasoy, A. (2019). Drivers of carbon emissions in Turkey: Considering asymmetric impacts. *Environmental Science and Pollution Research International*, *26*(9), 9219–9231. doi:10.100711356-019-04354-4 PMID:30721434

Kwiatkowski, D., Phillips, P. C. B., Schmidt, P., & Shin, Y. (1992). Testing the null hypothesis of stationarity against the alternative of a unit root. How sure are we that economic time series have a unit root? *Journal of Econometrics*, *54*(1–3), 159–178. doi:10.1016/0304-4076(92)90104-Y

Lin, D., Hanscom, L., Murthy, A., Galli, A., Evans, M., Neill, E., Mancini, M., Martindill, J., Medouar, F.-Z., Huang, S., & Wackernagel, M. (2018). Ecological Footprint Accounting for Countries: Updates and Results of the National Footprint Accounts, 2012–2018. *Resources*, *7*(3), 1–22. doi:10.3390/resources7030058

McNown, R., Sam, C. Y., & Goh, S. K. (2018). Bootstrapping the autoregressive distributed lag test for cointegration. *Applied Economics*, *50*(13), 1509–1521. doi:10.1080/00036846.2017.1366643

Moran, D. D., Wackernagel, M., Kitzes, J. A., Goldfinger, S. H., & Boutaud, A. (2008). Measuring sustainable development— Nation by nation. *Ecological Economics*, *64*(3), 470–474. doi:10.1016/j.ecolecon.2007.08.017

Neagu, O. (2019). The Link between Economic Complexity and Carbon Emissions in the European Union Countries: A Model Based on the Environmental Kuznets Curve (EKC) Approach. *Sustainability*, *11*(17), 1–27. doi:10.3390u11174753

Neagu, O. (2020). Economic Complexity and Ecological Footprint: Evidence from the Most Complex Economies in the World. *Sustainability*, *12*(21), 1–18. doi:10.3390u12219031

Neagu, O., & Teodoru, M. (2019). The Relationship between Economic Complexity, Energy Consumption Structure and Greenhouse Gas Emission: Heterogeneous Panel Evidence from the EU Countries. *Sustainability*, *11*(2), 1–29. doi:10.3390u11020497

OEC. (2021a). *Economic Complexity Legacy Rankings (ECI) Legacy Rankings | OEC - The Observatory of Economic Complexity*. https://oec.world/en/rankings/legacy/eci

OEC. (2021b). *OEC - The Observatory of Economic Complexity*. https://oec.world/en/resources/methods#eci

Panayotou, T. (1993). *Empirical tests and policy analysis of environmental degradation at different stages of economic development* (Wep 2-22, WP:238; ILO Working Papers). International Labour Organization. https://econpapers.repec.org/RePEc:ilo:ilowps:992927783402676

Pesaran, M. H., Shin, Y., & Smith, R. J. (2001). Bounds testing approaches to the analysis of level relationships. *Journal of Applied Econometrics*, *16*(3), 289–326. doi:10.1002/jae.616

Phillips, P. C. B., & Perron, P. (1988). Testing for a Unit Root in Time Series Regression. *Biometrika*, *75*(2), 335–346. doi:10.1093/biomet/75.2.335

Romero, J. P., & Gramkow, C. (2021). Economic complexity and greenhouse gas emissions. *World Development*, *139*, 105317. doi:10.1016/j.worlddev.2020.105317

Sam, C. Y., McNown, R., & Goh, S. K. (2019). An augmented autoregressive distributed lag bounds test for cointegration. *Economic Modelling*, *80*, 130–141. doi:10.1016/j.econmod.2018.11.001

Shahbaz, M., Gozgor, G., & Hammoudeh, S. (2019). Human capital and export diversification as new determinants of energy demand in the United States. *Energy Economics*, *78*, 335–349. doi:10.1016/j.eneco.2018.11.016

Shahbaz, M., & Sinha, A. (2019). Environmental Kuznets curve for CO2 emissions: A literature survey. *Journal of Economic Studies (Glasgow, Scotland)*, *46*(1), 106–168. doi:10.1108/JES-09-2017-0249

Shahzad, U., Doğan, B., Sinha, A., & Fareed, Z. (2021). Does Export product diversification help to reduce energy demand: Exploring the contextual evidences from the newly industrialized countries. *Energy*, *214*, 118881. doi:10.1016/j.energy.2020.118881

Shahzad, U., Fareed, Z., Shahzad, F., & Shahzad, K. (2021). Investigating the nexus between economic complexity, energy consumption and ecological footprint for the United States: New insights from quantile methods. *Journal of Cleaner Production*, *279*, 123806. doi:10.1016/j.jclepro.2020.123806

Shahzad, U., Ferraz, D., Doğan, B., & Aparecida do Nascimento Rebelatto, D. (2020). Export product diversification and CO2 emissions: Contextual evidences from developing and developed economies. *Journal of Cleaner Production*, *276*, 124146. doi:10.1016/j.jclepro.2020.124146

Shahzad, U., Lv, Y., Doğan, B., & Xia, W. (2021). Unveiling the heterogeneous impacts of export product diversification on renewable energy consumption: New evidence from G-7 and E-7 countries. *Renewable Energy*, *164*, 1457–1470. doi:10.1016/j.renene.2020.10.143

Sharma, R., Shahbaz, M., Kautish, P., & Vo, X. V. (2021). Analyzing the impact of export diversification and technological innovation on renewable energy consumption: Evidences from BRICS nations. *Renewable Energy*, *178*, 1034–1045. doi:10.1016/j.renene.2021.06.125

Shin, Y., Yu, B., & Greenwood-Nimmo, M. (2014). Modelling Asymmetric Cointegration and Dynamic Multipliers in a Nonlinear ARDL Framework. In R. C. Sickles & W. C. Horrace (Eds.), Festschrift in Honor of Peter Schmidt (Vol. 44, Issue 0, pp. 281–314). Springer New York. doi:10.1007/978-1-4899-8008-3_9

Wang, Z., Ben Jebli, M., Madaleno, M., Doğan, B., & Shahzad, U. (2021). Does export product quality and renewable energy induce carbon dioxide emissions: Evidence from leading complex and renewable energy economies. *Renewable Energy*, *171*, 360–370. doi:10.1016/j.renene.2021.02.066

ENDNOTE

1 The augmented NADL procedure in this chapter is explained for the Ecological Footprint model. The procedure is the same for the Carbon Footprint model.

APPENDIX 1

Table 4. Summary statistics

	LEFPC	LCFPC	LECI_POSITIVE	LECI_NEGATIVE
Mean	0.9944	0.2869	6.3724	-5.4522
Median	1.0091	0.3048	7.588960	-7.2512
Maximum	1.2554	0.8035	10.3615	0.0000
Minimum	0.7055	-0.3231	1.4186	-9.3616
Std. Dev.	0.1573	0.3121	3.3708	3.2118
Skewness	-0.1784	-0.2079	-0.2323	0.4784
Kurtosis	1.8956	1.9451	1.2949	1.5214
J-B Norm.	2.0205	1.9290	4.6845*	4.6524*
Probability	0.3641	0.3812	0.0961	0.0977

*Notes: * shows significance at 10% level.*

Figure 3. Graphs of the employed time series

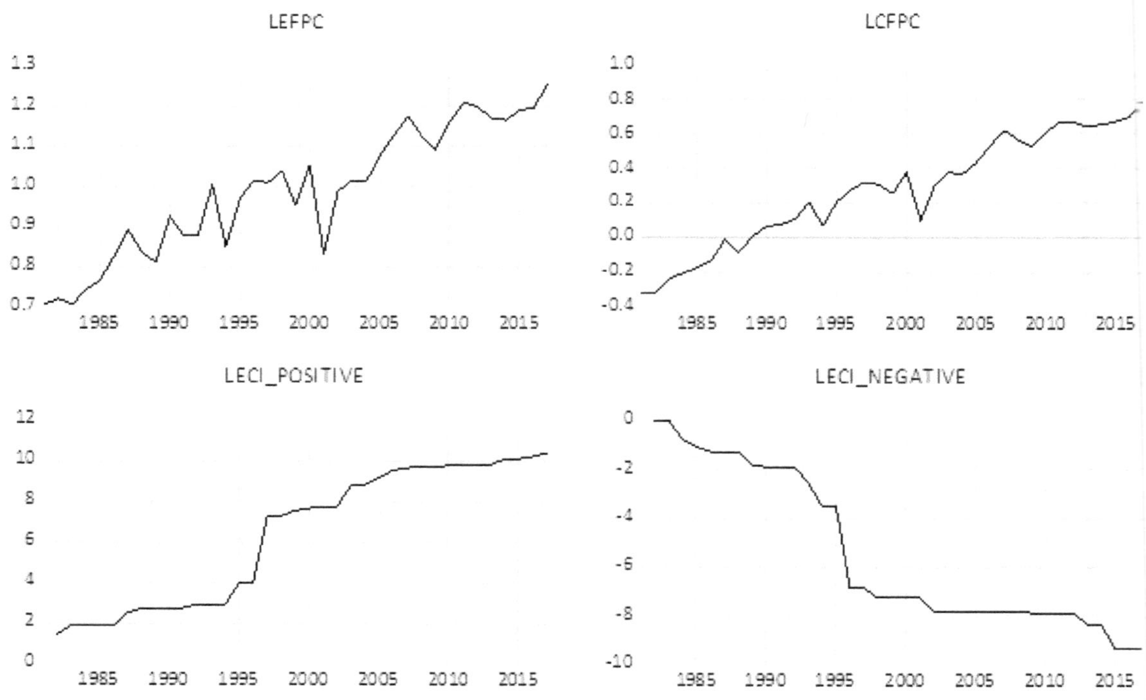

APPENDIX 2

Figure 4. Graphs of The CUSUM and CUSUMSQ tests for the Ecological Footprint model

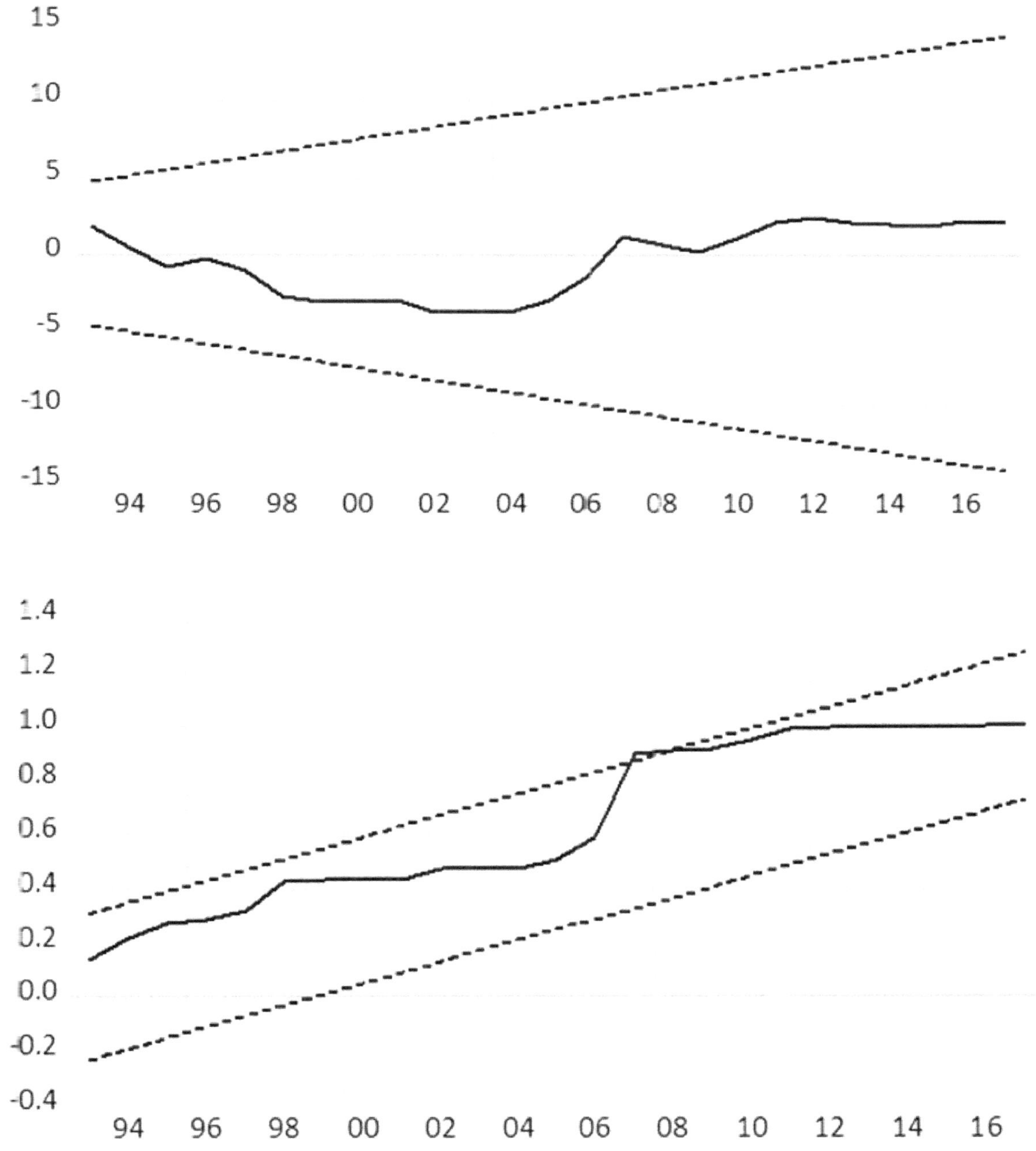

Figure 5. Graphs of The CUSUM and CUSUMSQ tests for the Carbon Footprint model

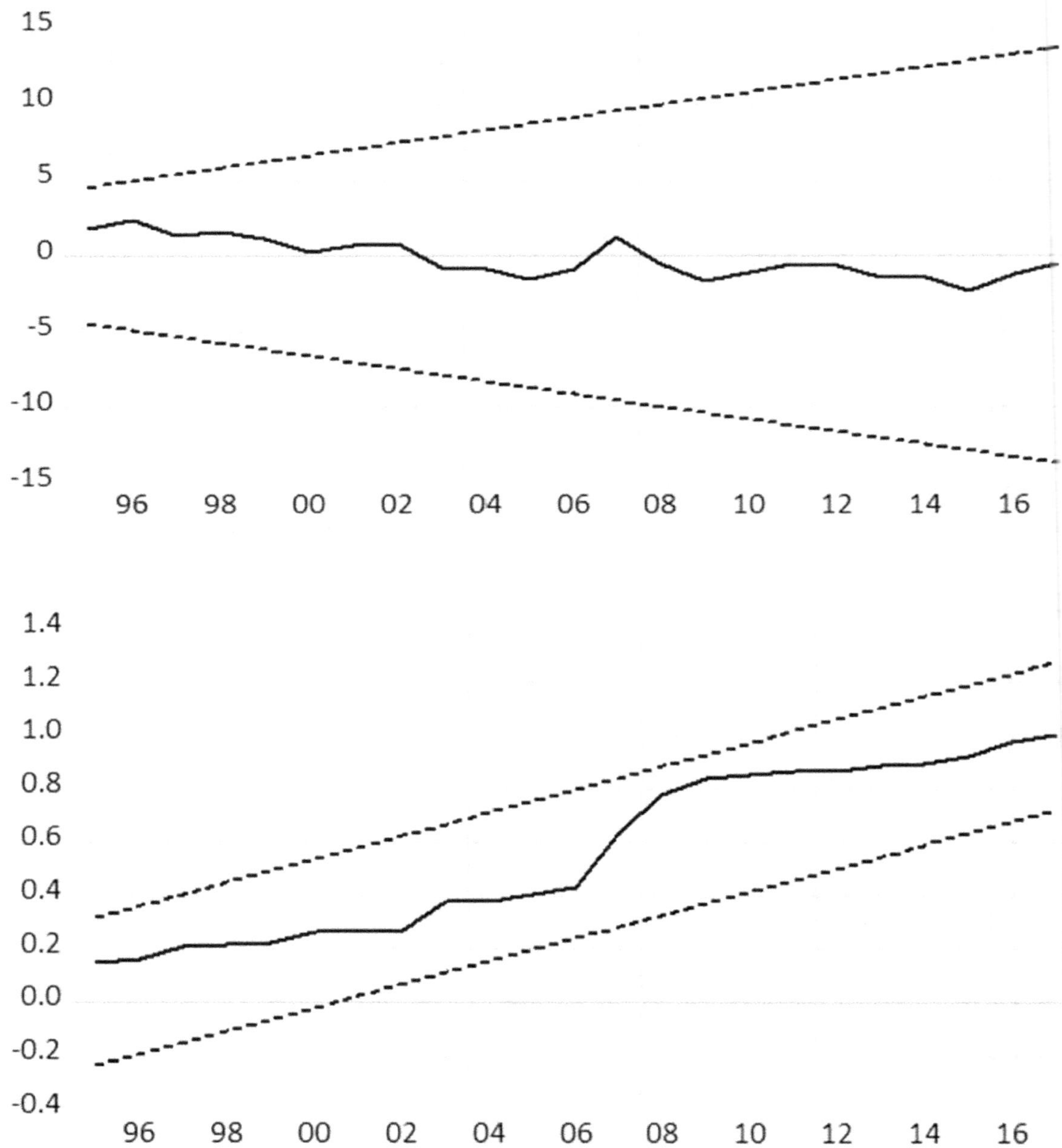

Chapter 4
Evaluation of Engagement and Desirability of Different Teaching Techniques of Energy Concepts:
How to Raise the Energy Literacy of the General Public in Educational Institutions

Alfonso P. Ramallo-González
Universidad de Murcia, Spain

José A. Ruiperez-Valiente
https://orcid.org/0000-0002-2304-6365
Universidad de Murcia, Spain

ABSTRACT

Although energy concepts and climate change are highly present on everyone's life, educational systems are in cases still lacking on their curricula the teaching of what energy is, how it is produced, and what is the relationship between energy use and climate change. It is suggested by the many that a society which is not literate about energy will never be capable of using it more effectively. This chapter presents a research performed with more than 100 participants from different backgrounds and age ranges with three different learning activities to educate on energy with different rationales including digital technologies. The authors measured the beliefs and intentions before and after the activity. They found that overall the values were high and there was no significant gain after the activity. Also, they found that learners experienced similar learning with all activities, but that engagement was significantly higher with the embodied activity.

DOI: 10.4018/978-1-7998-9590-9.ch004

INTRODUCTION

It is a usual perception that energy use related concerns such as carbon emissions or energy efficiency are gaining popularity over the last decades. This has been mainly driven by a rather generalized view of the need to reduce energy generation from fossil fuels. Scientific evidence has been pointing to the fact that energy savings come only if the population targeted have a working knowledge about how energy is used and why it has to be used efficiently. Therefore, it is vital to the sustainable future of the planet to raise awareness on this issue and explore the potential of different methodologies to accomplish this objective.

This book chapter aims at describing a real-world experience that will be of great use on the evaluation of different educational activities on the field of energy literacy, environmental education and climate change. The evaluation has been done with structured questionnaires and state of the art statistical analysis of the results.

BACKGROUND

Energy Savings and Citizen Awareness

According to the latest report of the International Panel of Climate Change (IPCC), the world is undertaking a series of changes in its climate which are resulting in serious concerns for the future of society (IPCC, 2016). This fact that now counts with a majoritarian consensus across the scientific community, is permeating into the political agendas, and the goals of policy makers and institutions in most countries around the globe.

There are several initiatives that aim at reducing the energy use to lower down the carbon emissions, and that promote the use of renewable energy to make the emissions carbon neutral, or non-existent. At a global scale, the International Energy Agency is joining efforts agglutinating highly recognized academics and other influential agents into its annexes. These are world-wide projects looking into specific facets of the issue that may help in the fight against emissions. At a European scale, the Horizon 2020 stream of funding and the LIFE program have had a substantial weight on promoting initiatives that will help with the objectives or reducing carbon emissions.

Although these projects are having a substantial effect, a great deal of the scientific literature is pointing towards the fact that energy use reduction will have to be human-centric, and that only if we promote that citizens have low-energy habits, the objectives will be fulfilled (Mogles et al, 2018). This comes in contrast with the generally low citizens' awareness of the concept of climate change, and more particularly their role to stop this challenge that society is confronting today. Several studies are starting to appear to bridge the gap of knowledge in energy and climate change. Some of these studies aim at developing the science that will allow to create educational frameworks that will ensure more educated citizens in energy matters.

Dewaters and Powers have been highly influential on the field of energy education (Dewaters & Powers, 2013). In their work, they stablish measuring criteria for the cognitive, affective and behavioral dimensions of literacy. They focus on secondary students, what has been for many authors considered the level at which a course on energy could be placed. Dewaters and Powers consolidate in their work the concept of Energy Literacy that has been used ever since often, and that defines well the concept that this paper is built around.

The idea of teaching energy to the general public goes beyond the works of Dewaters and Powers. Lawrenz et al., proposed in 1988 an education of energy that would include affective and cognitive dimensions. In this way it would be possible to form a society willing to save energy. With this work, Lawrenz was stablishing that energy literacy had to be induced considering more than the cognitive aspect.

Although the relationship between what students learn in the classroom and what they do in their daily life is complex, we firmly believe that learning energy matters thanks to a good motivation and engagement is sin-equa-non condition to change behaviors towards a greener society. More can be seen in this relationship on Jensen (2002). However, the cognitive aspects that make people have an environmental behavior are still to be understood (Culen & Volk 2000).

Energy Literacy

When looking at the concept of literacy, Hirsch (1988) considers literacy as a share wealth of knowledge that allows to communicate with each other and understand the world around us. We can consider therefore energy literacy as the cognitive features that will allow us to make more effective the communications about energy matters such as energy efficiency or climate change.

We currently live in a highly technological society, but it was not that long ago, that even knowledge about science was not that popular. Science and technology have had a great spread during the last decades, and although that spread has been led by researchers and technologists, the general population is now familiarized with basic knowledge of science such as the concept of DNA, gravity, or electricity. Concepts related to climate and energy, however have proven to be more difficult to naturally spread across the general public.

Energy has always been a concept which is difficult to define. Energy can have many different representations, and it can be considered in the form of chemical energy, potential energy, kinetic energy, and so forth. This together with the fact that it is immaterial, could make more difficult to conceptualize energy. Depending on the country, the sources of primary energy have been very different, but after the industrial revolution, fossil fuels have been the main source of primary energy that has been transformed in heating, electricity, or other forms of energy. The oil crisis of the 70's placed oil as a critical source of energy in the minds of all citizens, and this had a twofold effect: (1) society understood that oil was at the center of modern society, and (2) the dependency on oil started rising environmental concerns.

These beliefs have been evolving, and researchers have found that the awareness of energy and environmental concerns have grown differently in different regions. The report of the European Commission (European Commission, 2009) has shown that from 32% to 82% of European citizens, consider climate change a serious issue, as pointed out by (Christensen and Knezek, 2015). One of the reasons for the disparity of these results could be the existence (or absence) of environment contents in the curricula of students (Choi et al., 2010). Considering that currently a great deal of information in social media is fake or inaccurate. One could think that it is more necessary than ever to find for a trusted conduit to educate students on environmental issues.

Enacting Change (Better Intentions or Desire to Self-Learn More about the Topic)

The fact that beliefs have a great impact on behavior can be perceived directly by many, but there also exist the theoretical framework that proves it. Azjen's theory of planned behavior (Azjen 1991) explains that the behavior id built over intention, control and beliefs. The theory of Azjen can be seen as a cascade of attributes. People that have a positive intention, beliefs, and perceive the possibility of carrying out that behavior, are likely to do it, if any of the steps fail, then the behavior will not occur.

The guidelines of the Government Social Research of the UK, has stablished a series of guidelines that show effective strategies to trigger a change in behavior thanks to interventions. This work agglutinates the learnings that have been acquired in a variety of studies within different topics (GSR, 2008). The framework proposed as more successful is based on nine principles. As the framework is for any kind of intervention that aims to change behavior.

When making an intervention, the behavior to be changed is identified, and the actors and actions relative to that are identified in order to direct the intervention. In our case, the identification of audience led to students in the latest years of High School and students in the early years of university. This social group will build the society of the near future, and changing their intention towards environmental issues will have a large effect in the next decades. In this regard, the work of (Darnton et al., 2007) shows that, when tackling energy efficiency concerns, the effects seem to vary according the specific measure being chosen.

Another pillar of changing behavior is the creation of models. Models are mental artefacts that allow us to understand a phenomenon. As human behavior is rather complex, models tend to isolate a given operation of behavior in a specific aspect. This principle selects a model that will be the basis used to build the intervention. In our case and due to previous successful experiences, we have chosen the theory of planned behavior by Azjen. This model has been used in the past by the authors in Mogles et al. (2015) with good results. The models represent the factors that will have to be taken into consideration for the definition of the intervention. In that respect, Shove (2003) has shown that the factors chosen for the behavior of energy consumption could be socio-technical regimes, in terms of energy efficiency behaviors Wilson and Dowlatabadi et al. (2007) have considered the factors to be information, cost, and incentives; Thogersen (2007) however, considered personal norms to be the factor for pro-environmental behavior. These factors underpin the justification of selecting the theory of planned behavior for an intervention as the one chosen here.

Incorporating Energy in Curriculum (Mainly at Primary/Secondary School Levels)

The works of DeWaters and Powers were the stepping stone for inserting the topic of energy in the curricula of mandatory education. The questionnaires developed by them can give an idea of the necessity of educating the students in this regard. Some countries have made the teaching of energy matters a reality in recent years.

Although in the United States there have been pioneers in the education of energy, there are several countries in which the energy resources are central for the economic activity of the country. This has placed an emphasis on the inclusion in the curricula of energy matters, which is the case of the Gulf Arab States. The work of Qandile et al. (1998) included in the late 90's solar energy in the curricula of school science, when most countries where still rather behind in the literacy of energy and even more in solar energy. With this indicative, the Gulf Arab States managed to homogenize the knowledge of the current society on matters as important as the renewable energies available in their territory.

In the UK, the energy literacy of students in high schools has also been the focus of scientific studies. The work of Cotton et al. (2015) shows a large study (1136 responses) in which students' energy literacy was evaluated to define an effective intervention that could improve the knowledge on this topic of future generations. The findings of the work show that for bringing together the formal and informal curricula into effective improvement of energy literacy the 4Es model has to be adopted to enable, engage, exemplify and encourage. The results of the investigation we present here, aligns with this principle as it will be shown later in the manuscript.

The work of Maddock and Kriewaldt (2014) shows the developments in this area in the Australian territory. In this case, they used the territorial dimension of the situation of the students to help the understanding to the energy matters. They used the geographic curriculum in Australia to insert the knowledge about energy. The study showed that concepts such as energy and society, growth and sustainability and energy and environmental change, could arise within this subject. It is not unexpected that the topic of energy literacy is related to climate change and sustainability. Interestingly, the work of Maddock and Kriewaldt shows that in the case of introducing in the curricula the energy literacy, the degree at which the education in energy is enhanced is highly dependent on the knowledge and capacity of teachers.

Teaching Methodologies

Anticipating to the lack of energy professionals in the near-to-come society of the United States, Chen et al. investigated the possibility of enhancing the knowledge of people at an early stage via summer programs (Chen et al., 2014). This was oriented to middle and high school students, and included basic concepts on renewable energy. The experience was evaluated designing and carrying out these summer programs and evaluating the learning of the students via questionnaires. The results indicated that this method was an effective way of enhancing energy literacy, but also, it showed that school students had improved their image towards the degrees on engineering. Although this method is an effective way of increasing energy literacy, it does not contribute to widespread the knowledge as it would do in compulsory secondary education.

In the case of including education at high school level, Visa et al. (2008) developed an integrated approach. In this work, the authors show the results of the Comenius Socrates project that aimed at the development of a tool that would help the teaching of energy related matters at high school levels. This is one of the earlier tools with this purpose, but a substantial number of tools have been created later (as the ones used in this research).

MAIN FOCUS OF THE CHAPTER

Issues, Controversies, Problems

The exploration of the related work has raised the energy and climate challenges that we are facing, and how to educate and raise awareness across the population in order to mitigate this issue. This has led to the following research questions that were investigated in the work presented on this paper.

1. An analysis of the change in beliefs and intentions after conducting different types of learning activities related to energy concepts and climate change.
2. An evaluation of the learning and engagement experienced after performing different types of learning activities related to energy concepts and climate change.

METHODOLOGY

The methodology consisted of setting up three activities based on different learning methodologies and making them available to 103 total participants at random. The participants interacted with the activity that had been chosen randomly for them. They filled a detailed designed-for-purpose questionnaire and they were asked afterwards to fill a second version of the survey. Each aspect of the methodology is explained in detail in the following subsections.

Case Study and Context

The activity took place within the context of the project "ODSesiones" at the University of Murcia. This is a project that seeks to raise awareness and promote the objectives for sustainable development of the United Nations. The 17 Sustainable Development Goals (SDGs) represent the skeleton of the 2030 Agenda for Sustainable Development of the United Nation. These objectives were accepted by all member states on 2015 and aim at having a global view of the development of the planet that brings peace and prosperity. The 17 objectives are defined considering that the sustainability has to come as a global change in which the different aspects of the wellbeing of the global population has to be achieved (UN, 2017).

Among the university community and society within the region of Murcia, one of the activities that comes out from this project was the organization of monthly events by the different faculties. Each monthly event is devoted to a specific sustainability or social transformation aspect.

Our case study took place in one of these events, and it was organized by the Faculty of Computer Science. The topic of this event was focused on energy sustainability, more specifically, we initially had a talk on technologies to save energy, and then we organized the interactive workshop on energy consumption that we describe next as the core of this research. The interactive workshop had three stations with different activities all placed next to each other. We established the stations in the hall of the Faculty of Computer Science what is an open space close to 300 ^{m2}. The activity was previously advertised by the university through common institutional channels (newsletters, social networks, and so on), so that students and staff members would come by to participate.

Incentives

The participants of the experiments came from different faculties as prior to this session we advertise these incentives in the university newsletter. There were two incentives: one was an energy-saving LED lightbulb, and the second was the participation on a raffle. The LED light has an approximated value of 2€, and the raffle gave the possibility of winning a set of headphones of a value of around 200€.

Experimental Design

We designed a factorial experiment with the objective of analyzing the potential effects of three types of learning activities with different pedagogical bases. We designed our workshop on energy consumption so that it included as the experimental condition one of these learning activities. We randomly assigned participants to one of the three activities and encouraged participation through the incentive system. The experimental case study had the following phases:

1. **Introduction:** When a participant came to our station to do the activity, we made a brief introduction of five minutes explaining what they would need to do as part of the activity. If they decided to stay, then we would move to the next phase.
2. **Pre-test**: In the pre-test questionnaire the participants responded a series of questions regarding demographics and background, as well as the beliefs and intentions constructs. As part of the pre-test they also fulfilled a consent form to participate in the study so that their data could be used for research purposes.
3. **Activity (experimental condition):** Participants were randomly assigned to one of the three activities, so they completed either the booklet, the bicycles or the interactive game activity, and only one of those.
4. **Post-test:** After participants completed the activity, they responded to a post-test. In this post-test, they again responded to the questions related to beliefs and intentions constructs, in order to analyses the variation after conducting the activity. Additionally, they also responded to questions related to the learning and engagement experienced with the activity.
5. **Incentive:** All the participants that completed the aforementioned phases received as a reward a LED lightbulb, and they entered the raffle where one of them could receive a set of headphones as a prize.

We selected three learning activities with different pedagogical bases to analyses differences in the variation of the beliefs and intentions constructs, as well to analyses the perceptions of students in terms of learning and engagement experienced. The three activities were the following ones:

- **Passive content:** This activity involved a passive consumption of contents by reading a booklet on energy consumption (see Figure 1a). The booklet is one of the outcomes of Project FIESTA[1], an Intelligent Energy Europe Program project with 19 partner institutions from five European countries that has the aim at cutting the energy consumption of families with children. Because of this, the booklet is designed to be understandable for all audiences, and it is created with plenty of infographics and mnemonic rules to facilitate the understanding of the energy concepts and to make it more appealing. The document used was the "FIESTA Energy Efficiency Guide for Families", that was reduced to create a shorter document. Pages 1 (front page), 8 (Energy consumption depending on use), 9 (Energy consumption of appliances), 16 (energy saving advice), 17-18 (reduce heating), 19-20 (reduce cooling), 28-29 (lighting), 36-37 (how to help the environment), 44-46 (summary).

Figure 1. Example of infographic from the booklet

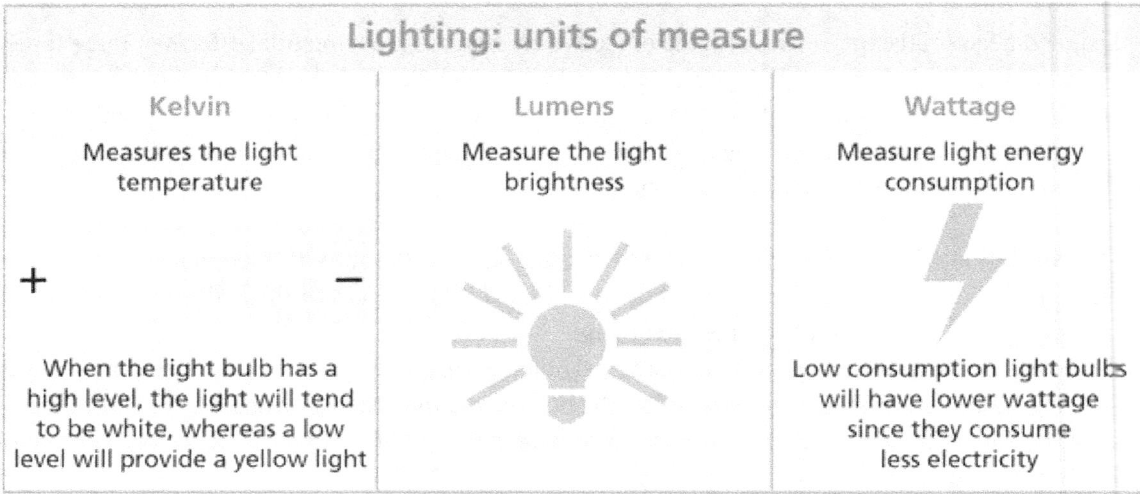

- **Embodied activity:** This activity involved students experiencing the effort required to generate energy in an embodied way (see Figure 1b). They had to cycle on a bike that had three different bulbs connected to a dynamo. One was a normal incandescent bulb, another one was a LED domestic light-bulb, and the last one was a set of electronic LEDs. Therefore, it was trivial to light the electronic LEDs (around 30mW) easy to cycle enough to light the LED domestic light-bulb (6W), and it was truly difficult for the incandescent light to light up (60W, only two participants managed to turn it orange). They had a switch to commute between the three different bulbs. This embodied activity can help students to transfer energy from a physical activity effort to an electricity context, hence encouraging them to do a mindful use of electricity.
- **Interactive digital activity**: This activity involved an interactive game that helped make the learning process more playful (see Figure 1c). The game used was one of the series called "The My Sust House Games" within the project sust. of Architecture and Design Scotland (A+DS). More specifically, it was the one called Environment and Building game[2]. The game has been designed to be used on a learning session of about 30 minutes. The game challenges the participants to plan the design of a building having to select building materials, insulation, power and heating. The game has been designed to be "usable" for people above the age of 12. During the design of the building, the player can see the impact on the energy consumption of the house depending on their decisions. Also the cost and the balance.

Finally, image in Figure 2d shows the overall scenario where the case study took place with active participants in each one of the activity stations.

Figure 2. Overview of the different activities

Instrument Design

This research required of an instrument that allowed us to measure the response to a series of constructs which are indicatives of the energy literacy, the attitudes toward energy use and environmentalism and other related concepts. In our case this took the form of a questionnaire. We have created our own instrument to ensure that the evaluation was accurate, and no extra length was given to the questionnaire. In this regard, we have prioritized using items that have been previously used and validated in past research. When necessary, we have adapted the item text to our context. We have the following constructs:

- **Demographics:** We have five items about the demographics of participants regarding gender, age, level of education, area of knowledge and current work status. These items were retrieved from previous questionnaires from MITx and HarvardX systematically used for their massive open online courses (Chuang & Ho, 2016).
- **Background:** We have three items regarding the background of participants in terms of energy consumption. These items have been retrieved from a previously validated questionnaire on energy literacy (DeWaters, 2013).
- **Beliefs:** We have six items regarding their beliefs about climate change and the potential impact we can have on it. We selected six items from the previous validated questionnaire from Christensen & Knezek (2015). There is one reversed item.

- **Intentions:** We selected four items regarding their intentions for climate. Since previous research has theorized the relationship between intentions and behavior (Montaño & Kasprzyk, 2015), we can use these questions to envision future potential actions of the participants regarding energy consumption. We took the four items from Christensen & Knezek (2015) as well. There are three reversed items.
- **Learning:** We selected four items to evaluate the three activities in regards to learning. We took these items from the WBLT Evaluation Scale, which has been already validated (Kay, 2011).
- **Engagement:** We also selected four items to evaluate the three activities in regards to the engagement that learners experienced. We also took these items from the WBLT Evaluation Scale (Kay, 2011).

The specific items for each one of these constructs can be reviewed in Appendix A. Finally, we randomized the survey question order of background, belief, intentions, learning and engagement constructs, instead of grouping the questions by construct, since based on previous research (Goodhue & Loiacono, 2002), this seems to provide better results in terms of Cronbach's alpha reliabilities. Since all of these items have been already validated by the previous studies, we have not conducted an additional validation within this study.

Data Collection and Validation of Participants per Experimental Condition

As part of this case study, we collected data from 103 participants. The main demographic highlights are: We have 74% male and 24% female. In terms of age, 76% of the participants have from 18 to 24 years, 10% have 25-34 years and 11% 35-54 years. In terms of occupation 71% are full time students, and 29% are either full-time workers or they both work and study. In terms of level of education 22% already have a master or doctorate and 76% have either a bachelor degree or are completing one. Finally, 90% of the students belong to engineering or technology knowledge area. Therefore, the majority of participants are young and are studying an engineering degree (or already have it), three out of four participants will be male, which is a demographic distribution that makes sense considering the current ratio of the Faculty of Computer Science at UMU.

The participants were distributed almost equally per condition with 34 participants for the booklets, 36 for the bicycles and 36 for the interactive computer game. To confirm that the demographics were equitably distributed across the three conditions, we conducted Chi-Squared tests for the distribution of gender, age, work status, level of education and knowledge area, and all of the tests were non-significant, indicating that there was no difference between the demographic distributions across the experimental conditions.

In terms of the background of the participants, we have an average value of 3 (SD 1.2) for "*With frequency I talk with family...*", an average value of 2.3 (SD 0.9) for "*I consider myself an expert...*", and an average value of 3.6 (SD 0.9) for "*... I always try to save energy*". We analyzed the differences in these distributions across experimental groups applying a MANOVA test, and the non-significant results ($F = 0.5$, $p = 0.75$) indicate that there are no differences in the background responses of the participants per condition.

Therefore, we can conclude that the participants of each one of the experimental conditions have similar demographics and background, and that the methodology was executed correctly to ensure the validity of the results.

RESULTS

The experiment performed on this investigation produced valuable results which gave light to the research questions. In this section, the results from the detailed analysis are explained.

Analysis of Beliefs and Intentions

This first section of the results aims to answer the research question regarding the potential change in the beliefs and intentions after conducting the different learning activities. Figure 3 shows the results for the pre- and post-test for both beliefs and intentions for each experimental condition.

First, in terms of the beliefs on the left of Figure 3, there is a clear agreement with average values of around 4.75 regarding the existing evidence of climate change, however, it does go below to around 4 for the belief in the impact that individual actions can have. The overall change of the beliefs taking all activities together was not large, with only two of the items, "Impact in 10 years" ($t = 2.7$, $p < 0.01$) and "Actions of individuals" ($t = 2.1$, $p = 0.01$) being significant based on a t-test, but with small size effects. We analyses if there are significant differences in the change of beliefs for the different learning activities, and we find that there are no significant differences based on a MANOVA test ($F = 1.2$, $p = 0.29$). Therefore, we conclude that in general there were no significant differences in the change of beliefs based on the different learning activities, and that the overall change in the beliefs was low.

Second, in terms of the intentions (on the right of Figure 3), the participants raised "Efforts on problems" as the most important one. The overall change of the beliefs is significant for only two items, "Effect quality environment" ($t = 2.66$, $p < 0.01$) and "Work to solve problems" ($t = 4.9$, $p < 0.1$) based on t-tests. On this, we found again, that there are no significant differences between this change of the intentions based on the different learning activities based on a MANOVA test ($F = 0.16$, $p = 0.99$). Therefore, we conclude that the change in the intentions was significant for only two items which were "Effect quality environment" and "work to solve problems" and that there were no differences between the learning activities.

Figure 3. Bar plot with the average value of the responses for each item, with the beliefs on the left and the intentions on the right. The rows are split based on the experimental learning activity. The green column shows the average value in the pre-test and the red column the average value in the post-test. The error bars are based on the +/- SD

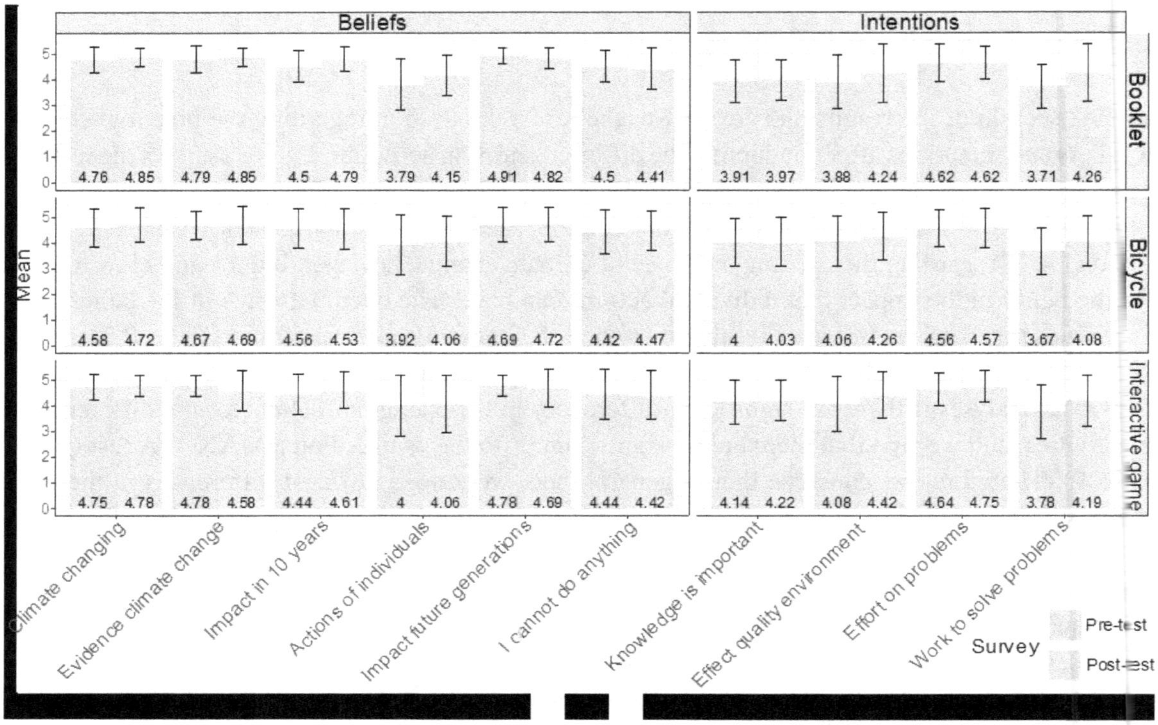

Evaluation of Learning Activities

This second section of the results is focused on the research question regarding the differences in learning and engagement between the three experimental learning activities. Figure 4 shows the results of evaluating the learning items on the left and engagement items on the right, for each learning activity.

First, in terms of the evaluation of the learning, we see that in general participants thought that the activities were useful for learning purposes with an average value for all items around four. We do not observe statistically significant differences between these responses for each separate learning activity based on a MANOVA test ($F = 0.96$, $p = 0.46$). Second, regarding the engagement with the activities, we do see significant differences between the results of the three learning activities based on a MANOVA test ($F = 3.8$, $p \ll 0.01$). In terms of engagement, the bicycle activity was regarded clearly as the most engaging of the three.

Therefore, we can conclude that there were no significant differences in terms of the learning experienced by the participants on the three activities, but they felt that the bicycle was the most engaging activity.

Figure 4. Bar plot with the evaluation in terms of learning on the left, and engagement on the right, of each one of the learning activities

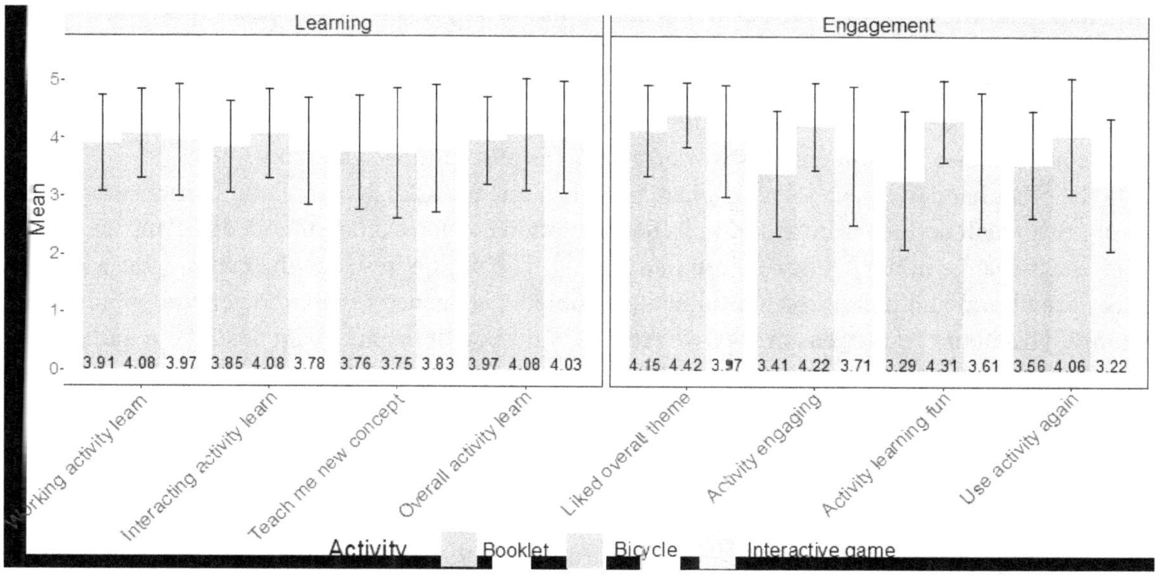

FUTURE RESEARCH DIRECTIONS

The results of this research have shown that the embedded activity provide advanced performance on a variety of aspects of the educational experience. This is interesting because it is a natural trend on this digital era to use software and other digital technologies to teach complex concepts. Considering the good results, we consider a promising new line of research the comparison of different embedded activities to teach concepts related not only to energy, but also to the environment and climate change. Energy has a clear implication, as the exercise performed by the participants is directly the matter of the test, but with climate change concepts, it is more likely that the subject will be separated to the phenomenon to a larger extent.

CONCLUSION

We can see from the results that the population examined has a very strong baseline belief of the existence of climate change. It might be for this reason that the activity has not being seen to produce a significant increase on this specific belief. On the other hand, it is easy to believe that someone that does not support this environmental event, will not change opinion after a short intervention like this one.

As a general impression, the cohort used on this experiment shows a rather high initial awareness on topics like energy and climate change. This comes with no surprise as the engineering students tend to have more self-motivation to learn about these topics. On this regard, it should be considered that when applying these findings to the general public, one should expect lower average scores on the general facets of energy awareness and literacy.

With respect to the belief about how important are individual actions, and how much effect they may have over climate change, this indicator is also rather high, and as in the previous case the value does not increase significantly after the activity. This is more worrying as the resources used were designed specifically to show people how to save energy, and to directly remark the consequences of their actions. Nevertheless, it should be taken into consideration, that the value of this believe was already pretty high. This is indicative perhaps, that to gain support on this objective once it is that high, stronger interventions are needed. We recommend this work direction as part of the future work.

On the other hand, we have seen a higher change on intentions than on beliefs. Participants might be noticing that small actions from individuals of population can have a larger collective impact. This can in turn enact change in the habits of these individuals. The region in which the experiment was done is highly agricultural and therefore environmental problems influence highly the general population and economy. This could be the reason why we have seen that, with the adequate push the population may change their intention to make an impact on the environment as a whole (as what they see surrounding them an agricultural environment], is more visible than the global climate change which is to this extent invisible). This is an interesting finding considering that specific contextual environmental problems can be drivers for a more general conduct of the individuals according to the results we found on this respect.

With respect to the evaluation of the activities in terms of learning and engagement. This was a core research question of our study. As seen on the introduction, energy concerns are about to be included on the curricula world-wide, and thus we need to further explore different teaching methodologies and types of activities to transfer the knowledge of such concepts in depth. We did not observe significant differences in learning, but it was statistically significant than the most engaging activity was the bicycles. This is an important insight as it reinforces the philosophy of "learning by doing." Even though the reported learning was equivalent, a crucial aspect that educational centers need to pursue is generating engagement, as this will imply self-motivation of students to stay up to date and therefore the creation of environmentally friendly citizens. This is important because some research suggests that when students engage more deeply on an activity, they can learn more (such as Bryson and Hand (2007) or Dunleavy and Milton (2018)). Future work can aim to combine activities of different nature during educational events, to alternate between more engaging activities and those that can provide more structured contents. We would also like to raise some limitations of our work. The main one is due to our biased population sample, most of the attendants where university students or staff, and therefore, most of them are highly educated individuals. Additionally, since it took place in a computer science faculty, the majority of them also had an engineering mindset. Therefore, our sample is not representative of the whole population.

The results of this work provide a better understanding about the beliefs of the cohort under study. Although the results should be extrapolated carefully to the general public due to possible bias of the sample, it is important to take into account those beliefs as they will be the origin of the day-to-day habits of the citizens. Being able to design educational systems that ensure a certain level of beliefs on the people will lead to a society that is more concerned with current environmental and energy issues. This more educated society can adapt their habits, leading to a noticeable reduced energy use, and ultimately a mitigation of climate change.

Our findings suggest that the profiles with a rather technical flavor tend to have already quite a good level on energy literacy, positive intentions and beliefs to improve climate change, even if they do not have dedicated courses on high schools (as it is the case in Spain). Still, it will be necessary to create citizens that are aware and literate about energy concepts, and we have seen that embodied activities can be a great tool for engagement. The results showed that the activities on which the citizens have a way of "visualizing" and embodying the energy they produce can be an ideal way to engage them more meaningfully with the issue than consuming passive or interactive contents like books or games. We did not observe an important change in beliefs or intentions with any of the activities, partially due to the fact that these values were already quite high.

This idea of making citizens more aware of energy use can improve over the following years thanks to new technologies, such as IoT technologies and devices/apps that can help track the amount of energy consumed, and thanks to the raise of hybrid (man-power / electric) transportation systems such as scooters or bicycles. One can anticipate that society may learn more about energy as a by-side effect of the new paradigm. It is interesting to see that also a strong tool is the reminder to the general population that small actions can have an effect, not only on the global climate change, but also on the local environment. This has been seen to motivate the people and make them more prone to adopt environmentally friendly behaviors.

Educational institutions such as high-schools and universities should leverage some of the lessons learned. Future research should aim to keep exploring different ways to engage citizens with energy-related activities, analyzing how these can affect their beliefs and habits, so that this can eventually have a positive effect on climate. The future of the planet might depend on changing the behavior of their inhabitants.

ACKNOWLEDGMENT

ARG would like to thank the funding of the Spanish Ministry of Economy and Competitiveness through PERSEIDES (ref. TIN2017-86885-R), Horizon 2020 Project PHOENIX (grant number 893079) and project ONOFRE of the Ministry of Science and Innovation of the Government of Spain, with code: PID2020-112675RB-C44.

REFERENCES

Azjen, I. (1991). The Theory of Planned Behaviour. *Organizational Behavior and Human Decision Processes*, *50*(2), 179–211. doi:10.1016/0749-5978(91)90020-T

Brad Maddock and Dr Jeana Kriewaldt. (2014). *Post-primary education and energy literacy: an analysis of the potential for geography curricula to contribute to Australian students' energy literacy* (Vol. 27). Geographical Education.

Bryson, C., & Hand, L. (2007). The role of engagement in inspiring teaching and learning. *Innovations in Education and Teaching International*, *44*(4), 349–362. doi:10.1080/14703290701602748

Chen, C., Tomsovic, K., & Aydeniz, M. (2014, July). Filling the Pipeline: Power System and Energy Curricula for Middle and High School Students Through Summer Programs. *IEEE Transactions on Power Systems*, *29*(4), 1874–1879. doi:10.1109/TPWRS.2013 2293752

Christensen, R., & Knezek, G. (2015). The Climate Change Attitude Survey: Measuring Middle School Student Beliefs and Intentions to Enact Positive Environmental Change. *International Journal of Environmental and Science Education*, *10*(5), 773–788.

ChuangI.HoA. (2016). *HarvardX and MITx: Four years of open online courses—fall 2012-summer 2016.* Available at SSRN 2889436. doi:10.2139/ssrn.2889436

Cotton, D. R. E., Miller, W., Winter, J., Bailey, I., & Sterling, S. (2015). Developing students' energy literacy in higher education. *International Journal of Sustainability in Higher Education, 16*(4), 456–473. doi:10.1108/IJSHE-12-2013-0166

Darnton, A. (2007). *15 Principles for Practice from Behavioural Theory.* Andrew Darnton for the Energy Saving Trust.

DeWaters, J. (2009). Energy literacy survey: A broad assessment of energy-related knowledge. Attitudes and Behaviors. Clarkson University.

DeWaters, J., & Susan, E. (2011). Powers, Energy literacy of secondary students in New York State (USA): A measure of knowledge, affect, and behavior. *Energy Policy, 39*(3), 1699–1710. doi:10.1016/j.enpol.2010.12.049

Dunleavy, J., & Milton, P. (2008). Student engagement for effective teaching and deep learning. *Education Canada, 48*(5), 4–8.

Goodhue, D. L., & Loiacono, E. T. (2002, January). Randomizing survey question order vs. grouping questions by construct: An empirical test of the impact on apparent reliabilities and links to related constructs. In *Proceedings of the 35th Annual Hawaii International Conference on System Sciences* (pp. 3456-3465). IEEE. 10.1109/HICSS.2002.994385

IPCC. (2014). Climate Change 2014: Synthesis Report. Contribution of Working Groups I, II and III to the Fifth Assessment Report of the Intergovernmental Panel on Climate Change. IPCC.

Kay, R. (2011). Evaluating learning, design, and engagement in web-based learning tools (WBLTs): The WBLT Evaluation Scale. *Computers in Human Behavior, 27*(5), 1849–1856. doi:10.1016/j.chb.2011.04.007

Mogles, N., Walker, I., Ramallo-González, A. P., Lee, J., Natarajan, S., Padget, J., Gabe-Thomas E., Lovett, T., Ren, G., Hynieswska, S., & Coley, D. (2017). How smart do smart meters need to be? *Building and Environment, 125*, 439–450. doi:10.1016/j.buildenv.2017.09.008

Montaño, D. E., & Kasprzyk, D. (2015). Theory of reasoned action, theory of planned behavior, and the integrated behavioral model. *Health behavior: Theory, research and practice, 70*(4), 231.

Qandile, Y. A., & Sabry, M. A. (1998). Guidelines for the treatment of solar energy topics in the unified science curricula of the Gulf Arab States. *Renewable Energy, 14*(1–4), 401–414. doi:10.1016/S0960-1481(98)00096-2

Shove, E. (2003). *Comfort, Cleanliness and Convenience.* Routledge.

Thøgersen, J. (2007). The motivational roots of norms for environmentally responsible behaviour. *Proceedings of the Nordic Consumer Policy Research Conference*, 1-16.

UN. (2017). *SDG Index and Dashboards report 2017 – Global Responsibilities, International spill-overs in achieving the goals.* BertelsmannStiftung. Available at: https://sdgs.un.org/sites/default/files/publications/24862017SDGIndexandDashboardsReportfull.pdf

Visa, I., Perniu, D., Alimisis, D., Visa, M., Cardon, L., & Bakay, E. (2008). Integrated Approach of Sustainable Energy Education and Research for Pre-University Curricula. *Bulletin of the Transilvania University of Brasov, Series I. Engineering and Science*, *1*(50), 287–292.

Wilson, C., & Dowlatabadi, H. (2007). Models of Decision Making and Residential Energy Use. *Annual Review of Environment and Resources*, *32*(1), 169–203. doi:10.1146/annurev.energy.32.053006.141137

APPENDIX 1: QUESTIONNAIRE

This appendix provides the text of different items grouped by construct. First, in terms of the demographic construct, we included the following items:

- What is your gender?
    - Female
    - Male
    - Other
- What is your year of birth? (e.g. 1985)
    - Numeric input field
- What is your current employment status?
    - Employed
    - Unemployed
    - Student full time
    - Retired
    - Other
- What is the highest level of education you have completed?
    - Doctorate
    - Masters
    - Bachelors
    - Secondary/High school
    - Elementary/Middle school/Jr. High or lower
- If you have studied or are studying higher education studies, which knowledge area includes those studies?
    - Engineering or technology
    - Basic sciences
    - Health or social sciences
    - Humanities, history, religion or education

Find next the items regarding the background, beliefs, intentions, learning and engagement. Note that the order of the items here does not represent the one presented to the participants, as explained in the Instrument Design section.

Evaluation of Engagement and Desirability

Table 1.

Indicate your level of agreement with the following questions	Level of agreement				
Background					
With frequency I talk with my family and friends about saving energy to mitigate climate change.	1	2	2	4	5
I consider myself an expert with respect to knowledge about energy and climate change	1	2	3	4	5
With respect to mitigating climate change, I consider that I always try to save energy.	1	2	3	4	5
Beliefs					
I believe our climate is changing.	1	2	3	4	5
I believe there is evidence of global climate change.	1	2	3	4	5
Global climate change will impact our environment in the next 10 years.	1	2	3	4	5
The actions of individuals can make a positive difference in global climate change.	1	2	3	4	5
Global climate change will impact future generations.	1	2	3	4	5
We cannot do anything to stop global climate change.	1	2	3	4	5
Intentions					
Knowing about environmental problems and issues is important to me.	1	2	3	4	5
I do have no effect on the quality of the environment.	1	2	3	4	5
It is a waste of time to work to solve environmental problems.	1	2	3	4	5
There is not much I can do that will help solve environmental problems.	1	2	3	4	5
Learning					
Working with the activity helped me learn.	1	2	3	4	5
The interaction with the activity helped me learn.	1	2	3	4	5
The activity helped teach me a new concept.	1	2	3	4	5
Overall, the activity helped me learn.	1	2	3	4	5
Engagement					
I liked the overall theme of the activity.	1	2	3	4	5
I found the activity engaging.	1	2	3	4	5
The activity made learning fun.	1	2	3	4	5
I would like to use the activity again.	1	2	3	4	5

ENDNOTES

1 http://www.fiesta-audit.eu/en/the-project/

2 http://www.mysusthouse.org/game.html

Chapter 5
Green Consumption Values and Consumer Behavior:
Evidence From Singapore

Stella Tan Char Ern
Anglia Ruskin University, UK

Omkar Dastane
https://orcid.org/0000-0002-9921-859X
FTMS Global, Malaysia

Herman Fassou Haba
Université du Québec à Trois-Rivières, Canada

ABSTRACT

In the quest of fostering green consumer behavior, companies are developing green marketing communications. However, do green consumer behaviors gets influenced by such marketing practices or it is result of green consumption values? The research-based chapter answers this question by developing a conceptual model against the background of green consumer behavior theories. The explanatory research design with quantitative research method was employed. Empirical data was collected using self-administered online questionnaire from 234 Singaporean consumers of green products. Collected data was then subjected to a range of analysis techniques using IBM SPSS AMOS 24. The findings suggest that green consumption values have stronger impact on consumer behavior as compared to that of marketing communication. However, impact of both independent variables was found to be positive and significant. In addition, it was identified that no mediating effect of marketing communication exists in relationship between green consumption values and consumer behavior.

DOI: 10.4018/978-1-7998-9590-9.ch005

INTRODUCTION

Over the last few decades sustainable development has become important topic. In layman's term sustainable development means that to meet the requirement of people without harming the environment or atmosphere. In other words, sustainability can be reflected as concept of using the resources and completing the requirement of human not only in present but also in the indefinite future which reflect that to meet human needs without depleting the resources. There are three mains constitute of this sustainability development (Yue, Sheng, She, & Xu, 2020). First one is environmental sustainability, second one is sociopolitical sustainability and third one is economic sustainability. The development of human life from all aspects affecting sustenance is called sustainability. It involves social equity, environmental quality, economic prosperity and these three are well-known dimensions of sustainability which means that between various competing goals resolving the conflicts.

Nowadays the concept of sustainability has been evolved as the field to protect the resources of world and at the same time by this agenda the depletion of resources at worldwide can be controlled in a better way. As to protect the depletion of resources at global level is very important and these days to ensure the sustainable development one of the key business strategies has taken the shape of green marketing (White & Simpson, 2013). From social marketing the concept of green marketing has been evolved. To make a product or resource environmentally friendly the concept of green marketing is being used. This is a part of marketing business in which the general interest of whole society is considered rather than focusing on the individual interest to satisfy the particular customers. This is very significant point which should be kept in mind while making the policies of an organization and setting the goals because these kinds of activities affect the business. The trend of greening the companies has been gained famed in business world (Haws, Naylor, Coulter, & Bearden, 2012).

The process of promoting the services or products by keeping their environmental benefits in view is called 'Green marketing'. These kinds of services or products can be environmentally friendly in itself or these are produced in that way which is itself environmentally friendly these products could be manufactured in a sustainable fashion. Distribution, pricing, and product development are included in the strategies of these kind of products or services (Victor, Thoppan, Nathan, & Maria, 2018). By green marketing the sales of a company can be enhanced and this also very helpful in reducing the production and operating costs of a company because by adopting this concept the usage of energy can be reduced. Green consumer behavior is very important in the field of green marketing, as the communication of green marketing had been found to impact consumer behavior and increase the awareness of green consumptions, this study will try to find out the real impact of green consumption values in Singapore and knowing whether it is stronger than that of marketing communication as it shall be recommended to scholars, academicians and managers.

It is insightful to discuss about the research context of green marketing consumption around the world. Comprehensively, there are several studies pointing out the explanation of green consumers' value and behavior in general (Shukla, 2015; Zhao et al, 2020; Tezer & Bodur, 2021). As the study of Zhao et al, (2020) tries to understand the mapping of green consumption knowledge via meta-analysis followed and supported by the study of Tezer and Bodur, (2021), which is an important one to comprehend the green consumption effect based on the method of green products utilization in order to improve the consumption experience of consumers. Nevertheless, there are several other studies which are specific to rich countries or developed countries as the demand of green consumptions in those countries are high.

The study of Shabbir et al (2020), tries to understand green marketing approaches and its impact on the behavior of consumers towards the environment based on a case study of United Arab Emirates, Tan et al, (2016) also tries to understand the barriers of green consumptions behaviors in Australia and New Zeeland leading at knowing the role of consumers' green perceptions. The study of Banyte et al (2020), elaborated deeply the understanding of sustainable consumption behavior in the United Kingdom, the avenues for innovative solutions from the perspective of home and the workplace. There are also few studies done in Singapore such as the study of Pittayachawan et al. (2014) on the prospect of consumers participation in corporate environmental management programs in Singapore and Australia. Furthermore, on the context of the research it is important to know that few studies had been done in developing countries due to not having high demand of green products' consumptions in those countries, which is a research gap that shall be considered. However, this study is going to be taking into consideration the exploration of consumers' values and behaviors of green products in Singapore focusing on these key areas of consumptions which are Green Consumption, Green Communication and Consumer Behavior.

Nowadays there is a time when awareness about the environmental concern, there is a green war cry which developed due to sustainability, people are more aware about the pros and cons of the products and services which are not environmentally friendly and now youth as a green consumers prefer those products and services which are good quality, affordable and green. The current research will gather more prominent options about sustainability in products. No one can doubt the significant impact and benefit of green products and consumptions to our current world and environment, nevertheless there are some problematic factors negatively impacting the rise of green consumptions in the world (Jesuthasan, 2020). As the climate skeptics in the world is one of the most problematic factors stopping the rise of green consumptions specially in Singapore, some consumers do not believe about the devasting consequences of the environment due to their behavior in terms of consumptions (Liam et al, 2021).

This problematic factor led to climate change skepticism as a family of arguments rejecting, disputing and questioning the orthodox view of climate issue and change their behavior for green consumption. So long as the mind of the consumers in this category of group in Singapore does not change, it is important to know that it can lead to the non-adaptation of green products and services in Singapore. It is known that even though Singapore has demonstrated some important regulation to fight the impact of climate change, they need to do much better to change the mind of the people for green consumption (Akter, Krupnik, & Khanam, 2017).

Secondly, price has been an important issue nowadays for green product consumptions in the world and even in Singapore, because the price of buying green product by consumers is four times or even five times higher than the price of other consumers' products. This problematic factor is making green product not accessible to the low-income families in Singapore and even some middle-income family in the country (Nekmahmud & Fekete-Farkas, 2020). As the problem shall be addressed for the purpose of tackling it, right now it impacts dramatically consumers consumptions of green products in Singapore and in some other parts of the world. In brief, the main two problematic factors for green consumptions' values and consumers behaviors are climate change skepticism and the expensiveness of green products.

Therefore, on one hand, companies are trying to boost green consumer behavior through green marketing communications. On the other hand, consumers with strong green consumption values appreciate purchase of green products. It is imperative to understand what among these two matters most to enhance green consumer behavior so that managers can focus on developing appropriate value proposition and communicate the same effectively. Yet the relationship of green marketing with the green consumption value and consumer behavior requires insightful investigation – therefore this research investigates these variables for predicting the concerns of sustainability based on green marketing, consumer behavior and green consumption value.

Singapore, a densely populated Southeast Asian country, is one of the top ten most globalized cities in the world. Singapore is a free-market economy with GDP of USD 340 billion as of 2020. Although, Singapore has western orientation, it firmly remains in its Asian roots. It provides unique context regarding natural resource management as an urbanized, low-lying tropical island. Singapore is susceptible to the problem of rising sea levels and other effects of climate change (IPCC, 2012; NCCS, 2012). Therefore, to combat the threats of climate change, the environmental authorities in Singapore have leveraged on state-owned mass media to initiate several communication campaigns aimed at raising awareness and motivating environmentally responsible behavior among the public. In addition, Singapore is one of the most wired countries in the world with minimum government regulation towards internet. This gives opportunities to citizens, corporations, and free media to express concerns over environmental issues to enhance pro-environmental behavior of consumers.

On the flip side, Singapore has recorded the highest carbon footprint per capita among the Asia-Pacific countries. As all the community started to concern about environmental issues, Singapore also has adopted many green campaigns to induce the citizen to sustain the environment. For instance, '3Rs' campaign, 'bring your own bag campaign' etc. demonstrating green communication by government as well as corporations. Our study examines pro-environmental behavior in Singapore. Singapore's mix of East and West offers a unique context to study effects of the media system and societal norms on individuals' pro-environmental behaviors.

The objectives of the research study are as follows: to investigate the impact of green marketing communication among Singaporean consumers' behavior, to investigate the impact of green consumptions on Singaporean consumers' behavior, to investigate the impact of green consumptions on Singaporean consumers' behavior mediated by green marketing communication. The research questions of the study are as followed: what is the impact of green consumptions to green marketing communication among Singaporean consumers? What is the impact of green consumptions on Singaporean consumers' behavior? What is the impact of green consumptions on Singaporean consumers' behavior mediated by green marketing communication?

LITERATURE REVIEW

Theoretical Background

In the field of marketing and consumer behaviors, several scholars have tried to define terms such as green marketing, consumer behavior and green consumption value. This academic literature is going to lay out the definitions of related key terms. Green marketing, it is the sustainability concept of marketing trying to promote products or services which can be environmentally safe and fight climate change, this type of marketing includes a broad range of product or service operations including modification of the product or service, sustainable packaging, changes of production process and the modification of advertisement to demonstrate sustainability (Horne, 2009). In brief, scholars concluded that green marketing is the practice of developing and advertising a product or a service based on their perceived environmental sustainability (Adawiyah, 2017; Yang & Zhao, 2019). There are some relations between green marketing and the term green marketing communication, the study, Ganganaboina and Riaz (2017) referred green marketing as green marketing communication, therefore the term green marketing communication is investigated as green marketing and both terms are used interchangeably reflecting the same concept.

Consumer behavior, it is a very important term in the field of behavioral marketing, studying and understanding buyers before, and several scholars have defined consumer behavior in their manner, but they all came to a conclusion that it is the study of individuals, or organizations or groups and the whole activities associated with their purchase intention in terms of utilizing and disposing the services and goods drive by their preferences, attitudes and emotions (Hubert & Kenning, 2008). Knowing that this research study is focused on the consumer behavior of green consumption purchase intention. Green consumption value, being a new concept of perceived value of green products or services, it has recently raised in popularity because it tries to determine how favorably consumers can assess environmentally friendly products on non-environmental factors assessment for predicting their preference of product, that is why it is defined as the tendency to express the value of environmental protection through consumer's buying behavior and consumption behavior (Haws, Winterich, & Naylor, 2014).

Review of Key Theories

One of the foundations of studies in the context of consumer behavior was Consumer Choice theory which shows influence of economic aspects on consumer behavior. The theory suggests that consumers' choice depends on the budget they must make purchases from available alternatives. This theory has underlying principle that consumers are completely rational. On the other hand, theory of consumption values by Sheth et al. (1991) suggests that behavior of consumers is a function of various consumption values such as functional, social, conditional, epistemic, and emotional. Fishbein and Ajzen (1975) developed the Theory of reasoned Action (TRA) to explain behavioral intentions. The theory effectively explains and develops understanding of the psychological and cognitive processes involved in consumers' contextual decision-making. In turn, Theory of Planned Behavior (TPB) links an individual's beliefs and behaviours, adding to TRA by incorporating the concept of perceived behavior control (Ajzen, 1991), leading to a better result in the purchase intention model's predictability.

In short, the theories used to explain green behavior have largely focused on economic influences (for example, Consumer Choice Theory), on consumption values influences, such as quality, appeal, emotions, among other factors (for example, Theory of Consumption Values), on psychological and cognitive influences (TRA), or on beliefs influences (TPB). In the specific context of pro-environmental free behavior, following key aspect and theories need to be reviewed to incorporate those in predicting green consumer behavior.

Pro-social Behavior

Prosocial behavior is a cooperative act that describes actions which will protect or enhance the well-being of others (Weinstein & Ryan, 2010), and includes interventions of great utility, such as in the case of activities aiming for environmental preservation. Welte and Anastasio (2010) add that the social context in which an individual finds him or herself can limit, support, or even disrupt individual goal seeking behavior, by imposing certain rules and values, which then become attached to certain decisions.

Green Consumption Values

Haws et al. (2014, p. 337) introduced the concept of green consumption values defining it as "the tendency to explore the value of environmental protection through one's purchases and consumption behaviors". They explored and developed a method to understand differences across consumers who do and who do not value preserving and conserving the environment, as part of their consumption behavior. The construct of green consumption values can be understood as the tendency to express the value of environmental protection through one's purchases and consumption behaviors.

Green Communication

Traditionally manufacturers have communicated the environmentally friendly characteristics of their products to consumers through advertising. This has led to the growth of a significant segment of well-informed green consumers who exert pressure on producers with criticism about the type of communication delivered (Maniatis, 2016). However, this group is small in relation to the number of consumers who need to be influenced to adopt greener consumption and who represent a potential market. When consumers have a low interest in certain kinds of goods or are reluctant to adopt a certain behavior recommended, from a marketing point of view, adopting specific and appropriate communication strategies when targeting these groups of individuals is vital.

Empirical Evidence

Yue et al (2020), trying to study consumer environmental responsibility on green consumption behavior in China, mediated by environmental concern and price sensitivity, primary data was collected for the study with a sample of 680 respondents. The findings of the study demonstrated that environmental responsibility has a positive impact on environmental concern and has different positive effects on green consumption intention, environmental concern has a positive impact on green consumption intention and also play a partial mediation role in the relationship between environmental responsibility and green consumptions intention. However, price sensitivity in their research study had played a negative moderator role in the relationship among environmental responsibility, environmental concern and green consumption intention.

Shabbir et al (2020), study on green consumption approach and their impact on consumer behavior towards the environment based on a case study of the United Arab Emirates (UAE), with 359 samples of consumers using self-administered and structured questionnaire. The data analysis method used by the researcher was confirmatory factor analysis (CFA) and structural equation modelling (SEM) in order to analyze the data, it was found that green marketing has a significant impact on consumers belief. Paco et. al (2019) studied several models of green consumer marketing and found out an optimum model to predict the consumer behavior which is usually difficult to achieve. By conducting and testing several constructs, it was found out that general prosocial attitudes have a direct and greatest impact over composition values of green products. Paco et. al (2019) also discovered that green marketing seems to have a positive impact on the buying behavior of consumers.

Singh (2015) carried out a survey on the term 'green business': A pattern modification in the world of standard business with a vision of grasping bionomical process, situational workable and green marketing as a green business strategy procedure. The investigator has done intellectual research and reached the fact that huge number of brands is using green marketing as a green business strategy. One major setback is that brands which are using green marketing as a green business strategy must make sure that their actions are not harming the customers. It was also discovered that; brands are supposed to describe the ecological advantages clearly and completely. Hasan and Ali (2015) carried out a study on the topic 'The effect of green businesses with a vision of representing the viewpoint of several writings and surveys of two aspects (green creativity and green advertisement) which will have effect on the corporation's execution. The investigators discovered that green advertisement and green creativity have an optimistic effect on the organization's execution.

Literature Gap and Research Framework

In the field of green marketing, there had been a lot of studies done by scholars and researchers in terms of understanding green consumption values and consumer behaviors. Nevertheless, there are few studies which had been done in Singapore, this research study is going to investigate the consumer behavior and green consumption values associated with green marketing communication leading to fill the literature gap that exist in the field of green marketing. However, this study is going to be taking into consideration the investigation of consumers' values and behaviors of green products in Singapore focusing on these key areas of consumptions which are Green Consumption, Green Communication and Consumer Behavior. As this research study is going to be an enormous contribution in the field of green consumption values and green marketing communication.

The research framework presents a visual description of the theoretical ground of this research. Such as the literature review investigated, green communication, green consumption value, and consumer behavior as the three main variables, predicting the sustainability of a business based on green marketing opportunities. Research framework is developed based on theoretical investigations carried out in the above section. The same is displayed in Figure 1.

Figure 1. Conceptual framework

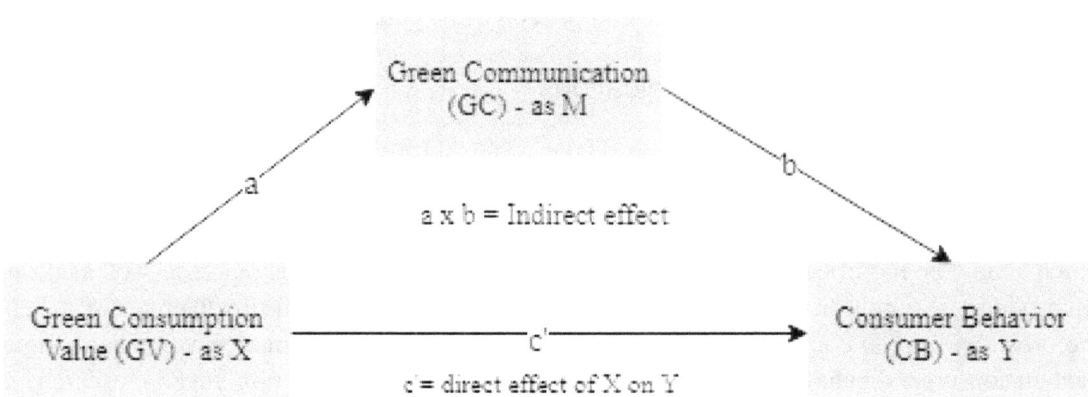

Hypotheses Development

Green Marketing Communication and Consumer Behavior

Green marketing communication is associated with the communication of green products by appropriate advertisement techniques that aim to increase the awareness about eco-friendly products to its targeted market (Ganganaboina & Riaz, 2017). Since the term green marketing is also termed as green marketing communication, therefore this term is interchangeably used in this research (Ganganaboina & Riaz, 2017). Paco et al (2019) studied several models of green consumer marketing and found out an optimum model to predict the consumer behavior which is usually difficult to achieve. By conducting and testing several constructs, it was found out that general prosocial attitudes have a direct and greatest impact over composition values of green products. Paco et. al (2019) also discovered that green marketing seems to have a positive impact on the buying behavior of consumers. From this perspective, the first hypothesis of the research study is going to be as follow:

H_1: Green marketing communication has a positive impact on Singaporean's consumer behavior

Green Consumption Value and Consumer Behavior

Consumption values and perceived value influences consumer behavior to great extend according to several studies (Animashaun, Tunkarimu, & Dastane, 2016; Hoe, Dastane & Selvaraj, 2018). Green consumption value is concerned with the preference of people towards green products, related to their purchasing inclination for green products (Choshaly, 2019). Michaud and Llerena (2010) stated that customers give more value to the original products rather than the re-made ones until they become aware of its effect on environment. There is no proof present that customers will pay a grand for the green or environmentally friendly products. Moreover, presenting the environmental data to customers has an impact on their willingness to pay for the original product; there is a drastic decrease in their WTP for the original or harmful product. These research show that businesses must trigger the environmental sense of their consumers for them to attain relevant marketing procedures for their green products. From this perspective, the first hypothesis of the research study is going to be as follow:

$H_{2:}$ Green consumption value has a positive impact on Singaporean's consumer behavior

Mediating Role of Green Communications

Narula (2016) researched the impact of contemporary literary statistics upon the behavior of green consumer and its green marketing. According to Narula and Desore (2016), the behavior of green consumer is a thoroughly researched topic however the research is generic by nature. According to the author, the research should be modified to fill the gap between the perceptions of customers as well as developing green products, recognition of green sectors, managing green goods and the involvement of stakeholders in the process of green communication. to understand that green consumption value has a significant impact on consumers' behavior mediated by green marketing communication, several research had supported the hypothesis (Peattie & Crane, 2005). From this perspective, the first hypothesis of the research study is going to be as follow:

H_3: Green marketing communication mediates relationship between green consumption value and consumer behavior

RESEARCH METHODOLOGY

The purpose of the research methodology is to lay down the structure to follow in order to analyze the data aiming at answering the research questions. The design of research is based on positivism research philosophy reflecting the testing of real world experiences on the basis of people's preferences – moreover the theoretical approach of this research is deductive that reflects the application of theory for presenting the research outcomes – also, the data analysis is preferred with quantitative approach – therefore based on deductive logic and quantitative research positivism research philosophy is the accordant implementation for this research (Saunders et al., 2016). From that perspective, the data collection method in this study is primary data collection which is done with a self-administered survey questionnaire.

A questionnaire was designed as the research instrument for collecting data. The design of research instrument was based on 5 parts, such as the first part based on analyzing the consumer preference for purchasing products. The second part was based on demographics. And the last three parts were based on the investigation of research variables. For the investigation of research variables 7-point likert scale was used. Table 1 represents the depiction of research variables according to the number of items and the adopted reference for preparing the items:

Table 1. Research instrument

Research Construct	Reference	Number of Items
Green Marketing Communication	(Paço et al., 2019)	6
Green Consumption Value	(Emekci, 2019)	6
Consumer Behavior	(Tan et al., 2016)	5

The main target of the questionnaire was given out to potential consumers of green products aged under 18 to 55+ with no exception to race or ethnicity. This age range is selected as consumers more than 18 years old are generally self-dependent in decision making as well as willingness to purchase. Current study is about adult consumers which makes this age range appropriate for this study. The responses of the questionnaire were collected through convenience sampling as this sampling technique offers several benefits such as low-cost, time saving and less efforts. The sampling technique was adopted based on the ease of researcher, and also the restriction of COVID-19 isolation – therefore with convenience sampling the data was distributed to the population that was conveniently targeted by researcher.

For this, the survey was distributed to the people involved in the social circle of the researcher, spread over entire Singapore. The self-administered online questionnaire was prepared using Google Form and circulated through online medium. The targeted population of estimated with 250 responses, yet 237 responses were obtained. Collecting the data of the research study, ethical issues were considered during the process, as no data was manipulated for the purpose of achieving the desire result of the study, and there has never been an action taken in terms of data cooking and the privacy of the participants of the questionnaire were protected in accordance with the privacy laws of data collection.

Statistical analysis was carried out when the data was collected through a questionnaire, there had been the use of demographic classification, descriptive statistics, confirmatory factor analysis (CFA) and structural equation modelling (SEM). Confirmatory factor analysis helped to comprehend and explain the model fitness which is being used in this study. The outcomes of the research were concerned with the determination of the general scope of green products among consumers. For this structural equation modelling predicting the significance and insignificance of the relationship between endogenous and exogenous construct was carried out. Structural equation also helped to understand and explain the mediating role of green marketing communication (Hair et al, 2014).

ANALYSIS, RESULT AND DISCUSSION

Demographic Analysis

The overall sample of 237 respondents is assessed for their respective demographic characteristics. Following discussion presents a descriptive analysis for this information. For gender, the results showed that 56.5% of the respondents were female, where 42.6% of respondents were male persons, and 0.8% of the respondents didn't find suitable to share their gender. Yet, from the distribution of gender it can be observed that the results included a valid distribution of gender approximately accordant division for male and female participants. Age distribution was assessed with six groups of age, such as respondents under 18 years, 18-24 years, 25-34 years, 35-44 years, 45-54 years, and 55+ years. The results obtained showed that 6.3% of respondents were under 18 years, where 28.3% of respondents were from the age group 18-24, 51.5% of the respondents were from the age group 25-34, 9.3% were between 35-44 years, and 2.1% and 2.5% were from 45-54 and 55+ age groups. It showed that mostly respondents were from the age group 25-34.

The demographics for race/ethnicity showed that 85% of respondents were Chinese, 5.1% were Malays, and 1.3% was Indian and White or Caucasian, whereas 7.2% of respondents were from another race. This showed that major part of our target population was Chinese. For describing the income of the respondents, it was observed that 30-35% of respondents were having annual income within the range of under SGD 15,000, between SGD 15,000 and SGD 29,999, and between SGD 30,000 and SGD 49,999, whereas only 3.8% of respondents were having income about SGD 50,000 and SGD 74,999. The demographic distribution for education of respondents showed that about 48.5% of the respondents were holding bachelor's degree, whereas 20.7% of the respondents were holding Polytechnical Diploma or other diploma, and 12.7% of the respondents were holding post-secondary education and 8.9% of the respondents were holding lower secondary and upper secondary education. Along with this, the least of the respondents, i.e., 1.7% and 0.8% were holding master's and PhD degree respectively. The obtained data for employment history of respondents showed that 74.7% were full-time employed, 19.8% were students in search of opportunities, and 2.5% and 3% were retired and part-time employed respectively

Normality Test

To determine the sample data showing normal distribution the process of normality analysis is performed. According to the size of sample that is greater than 50, the D'Agostino's K2 test was performed for the collected sample size of 237 respondents. The results are displayed in table 2. For this the values of kurtosis and skewness were analyzed. Also, according to the rule of thumb by Hair et al. (2006), the acceptance criterion was set for the range -1 to +1 for skewness and kurtosis values. Along with this, the range if -2 to +2 is also considered acceptable for normal univariate distribution (George & Mallery,

2010), for this, the following results were generated. As observed from the results, the value lies within the range of -1 to +1, and hence considered as acceptable. Therefore, the sample data for this research is validated as normal distribution.

Table 2. Normality test

	N	Min	Max	Mean	Std. Deviation	Skewness		Kurtosis	
						Statistic	Std. Error	Statistic	Std. Error
GV1	237	1	7	4.38	1.331	-.112	.158	-.389	.315
GV2	237	1	7	4.26	1.377	-.040	.158	-.457	.315
GV3	237	1	7	5.13	1.254	-.458	.158	.240	.315
GV4	237	1	7	5.16	1.373	-.498	.158	-.068	.315
GV5	237	1	7	4.43	1.221	.152	.158	-.058	.315
GC1	237	1	7	3.88	1.418	.049	.158	-.385	.315
GC2	237	1	7	3.61	1.388	.164	.158	-.284	.315
GC3	237	1	7	4.05	1.488	.108	.158	-.384	.315
GC4	237	1	7	4.03	1.504	.131	.158	-.489	.315
GC5	237	1	7	3.65	1.488	.111	.158	-.535	.315
CB3	237	1	7	4.57	1.378	-.230	.158	-.367	.315
CB4	237	1	7	3.81	1.679	.115	.158	-.715	.315
CB5	237	1	7	5.81	1.392	-.913	.158	-.092	.315
Valid N	237								

Reliability Test and Analysis

Reliability analysis carries significant importance for predicting the validation of internal consistency of the data set. For this, Cronbach's Alpha, Average Value Extraction, and Composite reliability test, are considered accordant and performed in this study. For this, the level of acceptability is applied, that is presented in the table below: Table 3 presents the results obtained by performing Cronbach's Alpha reliability analysis:

Table 3. Cronbach alpha reliability values

Construct	Number of items	Cronbach's Alpha
Green Consumption Value	5	0.906
Green Communication	5	0.934
Consumer Behavior	3	0.729
Total	13	0.928

As observed, the Cronbach's Alpha value is considered as excellent for 0.9 and above, whereas 0.7 and above is considered as acceptable. Based on this scale, the values for Cronbach's Alpha are accordant and meet the criteria of acceptability. Therefore, the research instrument is considered as viable and reliable for this purpose.

Confirmatory Factor Analysis

The assessment for the accuracy and reliability of data was also confirmed by performing CFA analysis. For this, the deployment of CFA analysis is considered a viable approach while performing validity test for multiple-items' construct. AMOS 24 virtual framework provides a resourceful infrastructure for carrying out this analysis. Also, the provision of inter-correlation freedom for constructs makes AMOS a suitable platform for performing this analysis. Figure 2 displays measurement model generated by performing CFA analysis with AMOS version 24 software:

Figure 2. Measurement model

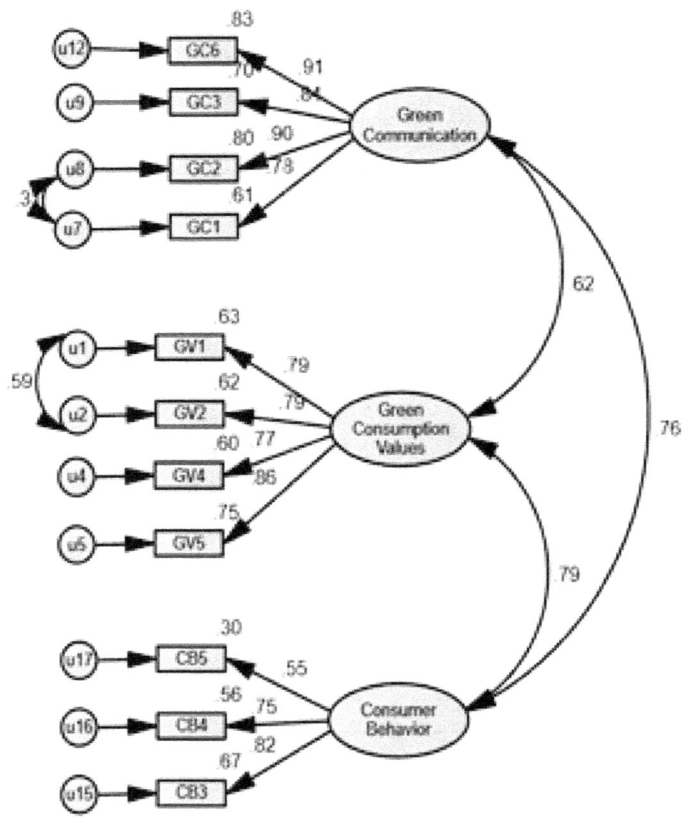

Also, for estimating the acceptability of the CFA analysis, the particular indices were selected considering providing valid approach for confirming viability of the constructed model. For this, the selected indices included CMIN/Df (chi-square over degree of freedom), CFI (comparative fit index),

GFI (Goodness-of-fit index), IFI (incremental fit index), TLI (Tucker-Lewis's index) and RMSEA (root mean square error approximation). For all the selected indices, the acceptability scale by Hair et al. (2010) was deployed. The similar procedure was followed by several authors in the past (Dastane, 2020; Donni et al., 2018; Pei & Dastane, 2020). Table 4 shows the obtained values from the default model created by AMOS and the acceptability scale for the selected indices values:

Table 4. Model fit indices of measurement model

Model Fit Factors	CMIN/DF	RMSEA	IFI	TLI	GFI	CFI
Acceptability Criteria	< 3.00	< 0.08	< 9.00	< 9.00	< 9.00	< 9.00
Default Model Value	2.800	0.087	0.960	0.942	0.911	0.959
Decision	Acceptable	Acceptable	Acceptable	Acceptable	Acceptable	Acceptable

The results showed that model is fit, as the default model values are fit within the acceptability scale of Hair et al. (2010).

Validity Assessment

Divergent validity of the measurement model is assessed by factor loadings of the factors the constructs. Table 5 displays factor loadings of all items. As the factor loadings are more than 0.5 for all items, divergent validity is said to be achieved (Awang, 2012)

Table 5. Validity assessment

Items	Consumer Behavior	Green Consumption Values	Green Communications
CB3	.818		
CB4	.748		
CB5	.552		
GV5		.864	
GV4		.775	
GV2		.787	
GV1		.795	
GC1			.782
GC2			.897
GC3			.840
GC6			.912

Next, assessment of discriminant validity is conducted. Discriminant validity is the extent to which a construct is truly distinct from other constructs, thus high discriminant validity provides evidence that a construct is unique and captures some phenomenon other measures do not (Hair et al., 2010). CFA provides two common ways of assessing discriminant validity first correlation between any two construct and second by the comparison of AVE. However, the most popular test is the correlation between two constructs therefore this research did make use of it. It was then identified based on such parameter that the measurement model achieves discriminant validity.

Structural Equation Modeling (SEM)

Direct Impact

As, validating of data was obtained by the reliability, discriminant validity and convergent tests. Therefore, the study determines the implementation of measurement model is appropriate for testing the path of coefficients describing the relationship of the developed model (Dandagi et al, 2016). For this, the structural model testing was carried out, and AMOS version 23 was used for creating the model. Figure 3 displays model generated for SEM:

Figure 3. Structural model – Direct impact>

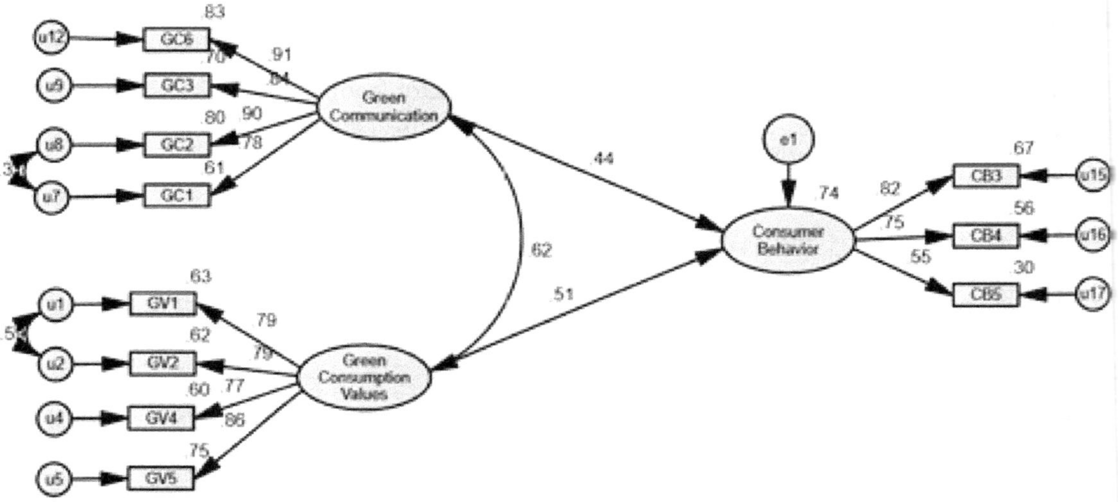

The confirmation for the accuracy of the model was based on the selection of acceptability scale for accordant indices. Based on this, the indices such as CFI, TLI, GFI, CMIN/DF, and RMSEA were selected. Also, the scale of acceptability was deployed according to the description by Hair et al. (2010). The following table presents the results for the selected indices values, within acceptability range, and the default model values as obtained after generating the model. The above presented results for the selected indices value show that it lies within the acceptability scale. Therefore, the SEM is considered as well converged, and defines apt fitness validating the accuracy of the research parameters. Results are displayed in table 6.

Table 6. Model fit indices of structural model

Model Fit Factors	CMIN/DF	RMSEA	IFI	TLI	GFI	CFI
Acceptability Criteria	< 3.00	< 0.08	< 9.00	< 9.00	< 9.00	< 9.00
Default Model Value	2.800	0.087	0.960	0.942	0.911	0.959
Decision	Acceptable	Acceptable	Acceptable	Acceptable	Acceptable	Acceptable

Results of hypotheses testing for direct impact are presented in following table 7:

Table 7. Hypotheses testing – direct impact

No.	Dependent		Independent	Beta Value	P Value	Remarks
H1	Consumer Behavior	←	Green Communications	.442	0.000	Significant
H2	Consumer Behavior	←	Green Consumption Values	.511	0.000	Significant

Mediation Analysis

Mediating variable of green marketing communication was then inserted and structural model was developed as displayed in figure 4. The procedure for mediation analysis was followed as recommended by Awang (2012) and as demonstrated by several authors in the past (Fook & Dastane, 2021; Hui et al., 2020).

Figure 4. Structural model – mediating impact

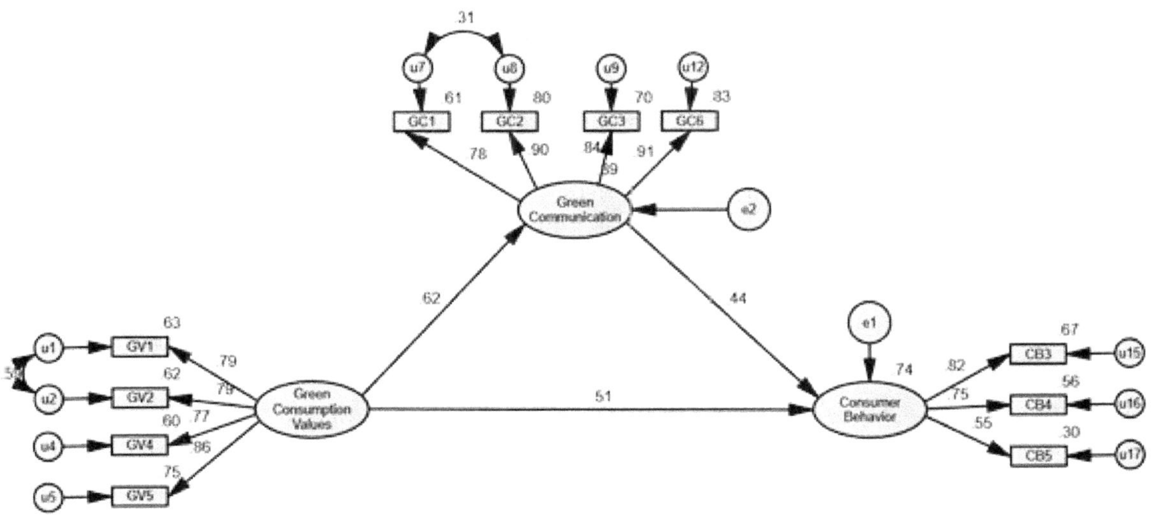

Result of hypotheses testing for mediating effect is presented in following table 8:

Table 8. Hypotheses testing – mediating impact

Dependent		Independent	Beta Value	P Value
Green Communications	←	Green Consumption Values	0.624	0.000
Consumer Behavior	←	Green Communications	0.442	0.000
Consumer Behavior	←	Green Consumption Values	0.511	0.000

Discussion

From the perspective of the findings based on the statistical analysis of the structural equation modelling (SEM), to find out the impact of green marketing communication on consumer behavior. First of all, it demonstrates that there is positive impact of 0.442 which means with 1% change in independent variable, 42.2% change is expected in dependent variable. Furthermore, there is a statistical significance with a P-value which is lower than 0.001 $p < 0.001$ 001 predicting a significant relationship and accepting the hypothesis H_1. Therefore, aligning the findings with theoretical research, we can therefore claim that the concepts of becoming more responsible and environmentally sustainable, green revolutions and protection of environment to have a sustainable lifestyle have been considered as the natural response of the World to meet the objectives of business. Moreover, the findings can be supported by empirical evidence based on the study of Paco et al (2019) studied several models of green consumer marketing and found out an optimum model to predict the consumer behavior which is usually difficult to achieve. By conducting and testing several constructs, it was found out that general prosocial attitudes have a direct and greatest impact over composition values of green products. Paco et. al (2019) also discovered that green marketing seems to have a positive impact on the buying behavior of consumers.

Green consumption value has been an important exogenous construct of this research study, in order to find its impact on consumer's behavior, there has been a demonstration of the relationship based on linear correlation between green consumption value and consumer's behavior. The equation of regression model indicates the beta value as 0.511, predicting a positive impact of consumer behavior on green marketing communication – whereas the value of $p < 0.001$ indicates a significant relationship, resulting with the acceptance of hypothesis 2. Comprehensively, the acceptance of the second hypothesis can be supported by the study of Michaud and Llerena (2010) stated that customers give more value to the original products rather than the re-made ones until they become aware of its effect on environment. There is no proof present that customers will pay a grand for the green or environmentally friendly products. Moreover, presenting the environmental data to customers has an impact on their willingness to pay for the original product; there is a drastic decrease in their WTP for the original or harmful product.

Green marketing communication does not mediate the relationship between green consumption value and consumer behavior, has been statistical proven so that the third hypothesis of this research study shall be rejected. The paths (effect, i.e., *a*), from green value consumption to green marketing communication was obtained with statistically significant and positive ($b = 0.6441$, $se = 0.624$, $p < 0.001$). Also, the (direct effect, i.e., *c'*), from green value consumption to consumer behavior was obtained with statistically significant and positive ($b = 0.4129$, $se = 0.511$, $p < 0.001$). On the other hand, the effect *(b)* of green marketing communication on consumer behavior is statistically significant and positive (b = 0.3921, se = 0.442, $p < 0.001$). Also, the value of indirect effect (IE) was found as '0.275', (where, IE = a x b) that is statistically significant for both paths. Therefore, it is observed that green marketing communication does not mediate the relationship between consumer behavior and green consumption value – hence the hypothesis H_3 is rejected.

Overall, it can be seen that the impact of green marketing communications on green consumer behavior is relatively less than that of green consumption values. In addition, green marketing communication does not mediate the relationship between green consumption values and green consumer behavior.

CONCLUSION

Conclusively, this research study has explained and comprehended green consumption value and consumer behavior from the perspective of green marketing communication in Singapore. The research questions of the study had been answered with the findings of the study had demonstrated that the research objectives of the study had been attainted, supported with statistical analysis in terms of hypotheses testing and support of empirical evidence.

First, understanding the impact and the relationship between green consumption value and consumer behavior, it is important to know that the findings of the study had answered to the question of the study with a significant p-value and strong empirical evidence. It is preceptor by many industries that customers show willingness to buy goods at competitive prices and no value is associated for those products which are environmentally friendly. It is felt by them that there is a vital role of government in making the environment of business green and show responsibility, there is no role of customers and legislations (Charter & Polonsky, 2017).

Secondly, comprehending the impact and the relationship between green marketing communication and consumer behavior, it is important to mention that the findings of the study had answered to the question of the study with a significant p-value and strong empirical evidence. Effect of environment on packaging and manufacturing, resources availability and consumption's value are taken into consideration in green marketing. Purchases of raw material and selection of vendor is also involved in green marketing. Attitudes and visions of customers are also observed in green marketing to be better brand so that they can demand customers which are conscious regarding environment (Dangelico et al, 2017).

Thirdly, investigating the role of green marketing communication as a mediator between green consumption value and consumer behavior, the findings of this study found out the insignificant role of green marketing communications as a mediator. Overall, green consumption values dominate green consumer behavior irrespective of green marketing communications. Although, there is positive significant impact of marketing communication on consumer behavior, it does not mediate relationship between green consumption values and consumer behavior.

The findings imply that managers should work towards enhancing green consumption values which in turn can foster consumer behavior. It is more relevant to offer and highlight consumption values rather than focusing much on marketing communication aspects. The results have indicated that customers are more focused on buying the green products and have a high concern about the environment safety. Therefore, it is recommended that products must be co-branded by the companies in a new direction concerning with green friendliness. Another recommendation is to adopt the development strategy which is used for sustainable growth of economy and sustainable consumption is known as sustainable development and environment is protected by it.

The study is limited with its scope for determining consumer perception preferring green products. The research provided resourceful outcomes realizing the high inclination of consumer preference for environmentally friendly products – yet the scope of research can be further expanded by analyzing the approach of companies for preferring the development of green products and the accordant strategies adopted by companies for green communication. Therefore, this provides the future direction for this research for observing the case according to company's preferences and analyzing its impact on consumer behavior. Furthermore, there can be more studies done in other countries for the purpose of comparing the results of those studies with this current study. Future studies can also uncover various dimensions of green consumption values to develop a scale to measure the same.

REFERENCES

Adawiyah, W. R. (2017). Determinants Of green Marketing quality practices among Small Medium Enterprises (SMEs). *Jurnal Ekonomi Dan Keuangan Ekuitas*, *1*(2), 240–258.

Akter, S., Krupnik, T., & Khanam, F. (2017). Climate change skepticism and index versus standard crop insurance demand in coastal Bangladesh. *National Center for Biotechnology Information, 17*, 2456-2466.: doi:10.1007/s10113-017-1174-9

Animashaun, A., Tunkarimu, T., & Dastane, O. (2016). Customer perceived value towards convenience stores in malaysia: The influence on customer satisfaction, loyalty and retention. *Journal of Marketing and Consumer Behaviour in Emerging Markets*, *2*(4), 4–27.

Awang, Z. (2012). Research methodology and data analysis (2nd ed.). UiTM Press.

Banyte, J., Salciuviene, L., Dovaliene, A., Piligrimiene, Z., & Sroka, W. (2020). Sustainable Consumption Behavior at Home and in the Workplace: Avenues for Innovative Solutions. *Sustainability Mdpi Journal*, *12*, 6564.

Beiser-McGrath, L., & Bernauer, T. (2021). *Current surveys may underestimate climate change skepticism evidence from list experiments in Germany and the USA*. Academic Press.

Charter, M., & Polonsky, M. (2017). *A Global Perspective on Greening Marketing Practice* (1st ed.). Routledge.

Choshaly, S. H. (2019). Applying innovation attributes to predict purchase intention for the eco-labeled products. *International Journal of Innovation Science*, *11*(4), 583–599.

Dandagi, S., Bhushi, U., Bagodi, V., & Sinha, D. (2016). Strategic management of technical university: Structural equation modelling approach. *Journal of Modelling in Management*, *11*(1), 75–90.

Dangelico, R., Pujari, D., & Pontrandolfo, P. (2017). Green Product Innovation in Manufacturing Firms: A Sustainability-Oriented Dynamic Capability Perspective. *Business Strategy And The Environment, Wiley Blackwell*, *26*(4), 490–506.

Dastane, O. (2020). Impact of Digital Marketing on Online Purchase Intention: Mediation Effect of Customer Relationship Management. *Journal of Asian Business Strategy,* 142-158.

Donni, R., Dastane, O., Haba, H. F., & Selvaraj, K. (2018). Consumer perception factors for fashion M-commerce and its impact on loyalty among working adults. *Business and Economic Review*, *8*(2), 168–192.

Emekci, S. (2019). Green consumption behaviours of consumers within the scope of TPB. *Journal of Consumer Marketing*, *36*(3), 410–417.

Fook, A. C. W., & Dastane, O. (2021). Effectiveness of Loyalty Programs in Customer Retention: A Multiple Mediation Analysis. *Jindal Journal of Business Research*, *10*(1), 7–32.

Ganganaboina, A., & Riaz, S. (2017). *Communication of Green Marketing Strategies for Creating Consumer Awareness: A study of grocery retail sector in Sweden*. University of Gavle.

George, D., & Mallery, M. (2010). *SPSS for Windows Step by Step: A Simple Guide and Reference* (10th ed.). Pearson.

Hair, J. F. (2010). *Multivariate data analysis: a global perspective*. Person Prentice Hall.

Hair, J. F., Black, W. C., Babin, B. J., Anderson, R. E., & Tatham, R. L. (2006). *Multivariate data analysis* (Vol. 6). Pearson Prentice Hall.

Hair, J., Hult, T., Ringle, C., & Sarstedt, M. (2014). *A Primer on Partial Least Squares Structural Equation Modeling (PLS-SEM)*. Sage Publications, Inc. (Thousand Oaks).

Haws, K. L., Naylor, R. W., Coulter, R., & Bearden, W. O. (2012). Keeping it all without being buried alive: Understanding product retention tendency. *Journal of Consumer Psychology*, *22*(2), 224–236.

Haws, K., Winterich, K., & Naylor, R. (2014). Seeing the world through GREEN-tinted glasses: Green consumption values and responses to environmentally friendly products. *Journal of Consumer Psychology*, *24*(3).

Hoe, J., Dastane, O., & Selvaraj, K. (2018). Predicting consumer perception and its impact on purchase intention for residential property market. *Journal of Technology Management and Business*, *5*(2).

Horne, R. E. (2009). Limits to labels: The role of eco-labels in the assessment of product sustainability and routes to sustainable consumption. *International Journal of Consumer Studies*, *33*, 175–182.

Hubert, M., & Kenning, P. (2008). A Current overview of Consumer Neuroscience. Journal of Consumer Behavior, 7(4-5), 272-292.

Hui, S. C. S., Dastane, O., Johari, Z., & Roslee, M. (2021). Enhancing Online Repurchase Intention via Application of Big Data Analytics in E-Commerce. In *Handbook of Research on Innovation and Development of E-Commerce and E-Business in ASEAN* (pp. 395–434). IGI Global.

Jesuthasan, M. (2021). *Explainer: The Climate Crisis and Singapore*. New Naratif.

Michaud, C., & Llerena, D. (2010). Green Consumer Behaviour: An Experimental Analysis of Willingness to Pay for Remanufactured Products. *Business Strategy and the Environment.*

Narula, S. A., & Desore, A. (2016). Framing green consumer behavior research: Opportunities and challenges. *Social Responsibility Journal, 12*(1), 1–22.

Nekmahmud, M., & Fekete-Farkas, M. (2020). Why Not Green Marketing? Determinates of Consumers' Intention to Green Purchase Decision in a New Developing Nation. *Sustainability Mdpi Journal, 12*, 7880.

Paço, D., Shiel, A., & Alves, C. (2019). H. A new model for testing green consumer behaviour. *Journal of Cleaner Production, 207*, 998–1006.

Peattie, K., & Crane, A. (2005). Green marketing: Legend, myth, farce or prophesy? *Qualitative Market Research, 8*(4), 357–370.

Pei, T. J., & Dastane, O. (2021). Digital Technology in Retail: Impact on Shopper Satisfaction. In Handbook of Research on Disruptive Innovation and Digital Transformation in Asia (pp. 187-213). IGI Global.

Pittayachawan, S., Abareshi, A., Hon Kam, B., & Teo, L. (2014). Green consumerism: a study on the prospect of consumers participation in corporate environmental management programs. *Conference Paper.*

Saunders, M., Lewis, P., & Thornhill, A. (2016). *Research Methods for Business Students* (7th ed.). Pearson.

Shabbir, M., Sulaiman, M., Al-Kumaim, N., Mahmood, A., & Abbas, M. (2020). *Green Marketing Approaches and Their Impact on Consumer Behavior towards the Environment—A Study from the UAE.* Sustainability Mdpi Journal.

Shukla, S. (2021). Green Marketing: Promoting Green Consumerism for Sustainable Development. *Prestige E-Journalof Management And Research, 2*(1), 2350–1316.

Tan, L., Johnstone, M., & Yang, L. (2016). Barriers to green consumption behaviours: The roles of consumers' green perceptions. Australian And New Zealand Marketing Academy, 1441-3582.

Tezer, A., & Bodur, H. (2020). The Green consumption Effect: How Using Green Products Improves Consumption Experience. *The Journal of Consumer Research, 47.* Advance online publication. . doi:10.1093/jcr/ucz045

Victor, V., Thoppan, J., Nathan, R., & Maria, F. (2018). Factors Influencing Consumer Behavior and Prospective Purchase Decisions in a Dynamic Pricing Environment—An Exploratory Factor Analysis Approach. *Social Sciences Mdpi Journal, 7*(153).

White, K., & Simpson, B. (2013). When do (and don't) normative appeals influence sustainable consumer behaviors? *Journal of Marketing, 77*(2), 78–95.

Yang, Y.-C., & Zhao, X. (2019). Exploring the relationship of green packaging design with consumers' green trust, and green brand attachment. *Social Behavior and Personality, 47*(8), e8181.

Yue, B., Sheng, G., She, S., & Xu, J. (2020). Impact of Consumer Environmental Responsibility on Green Consumption Behavior in China: The Role of Environmental Concern and Price Sensitivity. *Sustainability Mdpi Journal, 12*(2074).

Zhao, G., Geng, Y., Sun, H., Tian, X., Chen, W., & Wu, D. (2020). Mapping the knowledge of green consumption: A meta-analysis. *Environmental Science and Pollution Research International*, *27*, 44937–44950. PMID:33001398

ADDITIONAL READING

Halder, P., Hansen, E. N., Kangas, J., & Laukkanen, T. (2020). How national culture and ethics matter in consumers' green consumption values. *Journal of Cleaner Production*, *265*, 121754.

Yan, L., Keh, H. T., & Wang, X. (2021). Powering sustainable consumption: The roles of green consumption values and power distance belief. *Journal of Business Ethics*, *169*(3), 499–516.

Mutum, D. S., Ghazali, E. M., & Wei-Pin, W. (2021). Parallel mediation effect of consumption values and the moderation effect of innovativeness, in predicting the influence of identity on green purchasing behavior. *Journal of Consumer Behaviour*, *20*(3), 827–844.

KEY TERMS AND DEFINITIONS

Green Consumers: Consumers who are aware of their obligations towards planet and society and therefore follow principles of responsible purchasing of products and services which can minimize negative impact on the environment and people are termed as green consumers.

Green Marketing: Green marketing refers to marketing of green products to encourage green consumer behavior.

Green Products: The products which are presumed to be safe for planet and people. Such products have minimum negative impact on the environment.

Green Services: The services that benefit the sustainability of the planet and conserve natural resources can be termed as green services.

Chapter 6
Green Intellectual Capital in the Spanish Wine Industry

Bartolomé Marco-Lajara
https://orcid.org/0000-0001-8811-9118
University of Alicante, Spain

Patrocinio Zaragoza-Sáez
University of Alicante, Spain

Javier Martínez-Falcó
https://orcid.org/0000-0001-9004-5816
University of Alicante, Spain

Eduardo Sánchez-García
University of Alicante, Spain

ABSTRACT

The present research analyzes the different factors that influence the formation of green intellectual capital (GIC) in wine companies, contributing to the academic literature in a remarkable way, since to the authors' knowledge, no research has been identified that addresses such typology of organizational intangibles in the wine industry. Through a case study, the research indicates that, from a green human capital (GHC) point of view, workers' knowledge derived from environmental awareness sessions or seminar attendance are key to enhance this set of intangibles. As for green structural capital (GSC), circular economy programs, carbon and water footprint measurement computer systems, and eco-efficient facilities are clear examples that enable the formation of this dimension of the GIC. Finally, the analysis of green relational capital (GRC) highlights the importance of the company-stakeholder link for the proper environmental management of the winery.

DOI: 10.4018/978-1-7998-9590-9.ch006

INTRODUCTION

Wineries are facing increasing pressures to improve their environmental sustainability (Santini et al., 2013; Gilinsky et al., 2016), as the environment, the community and the local economy can be negatively affected by their activity. The wine industry faces several exogenous factors that threaten its survival, such as: rising energy prices, water scarcity, increasing environmental awareness of stakeholders or climate change (Guthey & Whiteman, 2009; Hertsgaard, 2010). These factors, together with the proactive attitude of winemakers, can drive the adoption of sustainable practices that subsequently culminate in product innovation, pollution prevention and the efficient management of natural resources (Carrillo-Hermosilla et al., 2010), in order to obtain a sustainable competitive advantage over time (Porter & Van Der Linde, 1995).

In this context, sustainability in the wine industry goes from being an option to a necessity. The concept of sustainability was first made known worldwide through the report *Our Common Future* by the World Commission on Environment and Development (WCED, 1987), an entity belonging to the United Nations commonly known as the Brundtland Commission. This commission related sustainability to environmental integrity and social equity, coining the term sustainable development as "development that meets the needs of the present without compromising the ability of future generations to meet their own needs" (WCED, 1987, p. 43). Subsequently, the 1992 Earth Summit in Rio de Janeiro would lead to a broad acceptance of this definition by business leaders, politicians, and NGOs (Dyllick & Hockerts, 2002). For organizations, this new approach implied the challenge of simultaneously improving social and human well-being while reducing their environmental impact (Sharma & Ruud, 2003).

Sustainable organizations try to find a sweet spot between their harmful environmental and social impacts and the economic profitability generated by their activity (Nguyen & Slater, 2010). They are aware of the social and environmental impacts of their activity, acting responsibly to minimize any negative impacts and stay in business (Phyper & MacLean, 2009). This may involve several strategies, such as reducing pollutants and waste, making processes and products more efficient, or even working to ensure that the company does not deplete its own supply chain. In the wine industry, the notion of sustainability is cemented in various official documents from the International Organization of Vine and Wine (OIV), outlining its definition (OIV, 2004), guidelines (OIV, 2008) and basic principles (OIV, 2016). In addition, wine regions have created their own frameworks to adapt sustainability in their territories. In this sense, sustainable viticulture frameworks are seen as a green response towards customer and market demands, as well as a strategic way to position the territory.

These new frameworks are characterized by requiring companies to make their productive activity compatible with the protection of the environment and the proper management of natural resources (Buysse & Verbeke, 2003), allowing companies to realize that they must address the environmental challenge through the generation of new knowledge that will enable them to follow a sustainable development approach and, as a consequence, improve their competitiveness in the business environment of which they are part (Boons et al., 2013). Thus, in order to accumulate and use their knowledge, companies adopt different approaches that are manifested through the different dimensions of Intellectual Capital (IC), these are: human capital, structural capital and relational capital (Davenport & Prusak, 1998). In this sense, the IC that incorporates environmental aspects, Green Intellectual Capital (GIC), was introduced by Chen (2008), becoming an incipient field of study at present (Yong et al., 2019).

The motivation for this research is based on two basic premises. First, the correct management of GIC allows companies to identify their level of environmental responsibility. Secondly, GIC facilitates environmental action through the knowledge achieved, for example, through cooperation and the creation of green alliances with various environmental groups or the generation of a corporate culture based on green values. Based on these ideas, and using the case study applied to a winery, this paper aims to answer the following research question: What factors influence the formation of GIC capital in wine companies?

The paper contributes to the literature in several ways. First, GIC represents a new starting point for incorporating environmental practices in organizations, as GIC overcomes the shortcomings of conventional approaches to environmental management systems by considering the intangible assets of organizations. Second, we conducted an in-depth case study to identify a sequence of steps that managers can follow to develop effective environmental management. Third, no previous research addressing GIC in the wine industry has been identified.

The present research is structured as follows. First, after this brief introduction, Section 2 presents the theoretical framework, providing a theoretical review on sustainability in the wine industry and the GIC construct since its birth. Section 3 explains the methodology followed in the empirical part to address the research question. Section 4 presents the main results obtained in the research. Section 5 presents the conclusions drawn from the study, highlighting the most relevant contributions. Finally, Section 6 discusses the limitations of the research and future lines of research.

BACKGROUND

Sustainability in the wine industry has been of great interest to the OIV, which has laid its foundations in official reports. Sustainable viticulture was first defined by Resolution CST 1/2004 as a "global strategy on the scale of grape production and processing systems, incorporating at the same time the economic sustainability of structures and territories, producing quality products, taking into account the requirements of precision in sustainable viticulture, the risks to the environment, the safety of products and the health of consumers and the valuation of heritage, historical, cultural, ecological and aesthetic aspects" (OIV, 2004). Subsequently, this definition was improved by Resolution CST 1/2008, which sets out a series of steps for environmental assessment in terms of production, processing and packaging: (1) location; (2) biodiversity; (3) varietal selection; (4) solid waste; (5) soil management; (6) energy use; (7) water management; (8) air quality; (9) wastewater; (10) neighboring land use; (11) human resources management; (12) use of agrochemicals (OIV, 2008). Recently, Resolution 1/2016 established the General Principles of Sustainable Viticulture, including the three dimensions of the Triple Bottom Line (OIV, 2016).

These new regulatory frameworks have increased the environmental awareness of wineries, driving the development of new knowledge that allows them to follow a sustainable approach and, consequently, improve their competitiveness (Boons et al., 2013). To accumulate and use their knowledge, wineries can adopt different approaches under the three dimensions of intellectual capital (IC): human, structural, and relational capital (Davenport & Prusak, 1998). However, IC that incorporates sustainable concepts, such as GIC, has only recently been introduced in the literature and needs further theoretical and empirical development. GIC enables organizations to implement stringent international regulations, meet the growing environmental awareness of consumers and create value for the organization (Huang & Kung, 2011). For this reason, its role is critical to ensure the success of the Sustainable Development Goals (SDGs) promoted by the United Nations (Yadiati, 2019).

Definitions of GIC are scarce in the management literature. On the one hand, Chen (2008), who is the creator of the construct, defined it as the total set of intangible assets, knowledge and capabilities related to environmental protection or green innovation at the individual and organizational level within an organization. Liu (2010), on the other hand, defined it as the integration of green and environmental knowledge sources into the organization to enhance its competitive advantage. Similarly, López-Gamero et al. (2011) conceived it as the sum of all the knowledge that an organization can leverage in the environmental management process to gain a competitive advantage. The following is a detailed analysis of each of the dimensions that make up the GIC: Green Human Capital (GHC), Green Structural Capital (GSC) and Green Relational Capital (GRC).

First, Chen (2008) points out the distinctive value of GHC by defining it as the body of knowledge, skills, abilities, experiences, and commitments of employees about environmental protection and/or green innovation that is embedded in employees rather than organizations. GHC enables an organization to recognize its intangible assets related to the environment, helping to implement green strategies in each competitive environment. Therefore, GHC has been considered as one of the main strategic resources to gain sustainable competitive advantages in today's dynamic organizational environment (Yusoff et al., 2019). Furthermore, higher GHC contributes to a greater extent to the development of a green organization, as environmental knowledge and skills are embedded in it (Yong et al., 2019).

Secondly, structural capital is conceived as the set of knowledge held by the non-human assets of an organization, among which we can highlight organizational charts, databases, technology, and process instructions (Jardon & Martos, 2012). Chen (2008), for his part, defined GSC as organizational assets that show concern for environmental protection or green innovation within the company. Jardon & Dasilva (2017) suggest that organizational concern for environmental aspects is not modified by human capital alone, as it requires the support of organizational culture and systems to increase the level of environmental awareness in the organization. Widener (2005) states that an organization with poor systems and procedures cannot achieve its full performance. In contrast, an organization with strong structural capital has a strong supportive environment that motivates its employees to generate new knowledge (Florin et al., 2003).

Thirdly, Chen (2008) defined GRC as the set of intangible assets based on the existing relationships between the organization and suppliers, customers, network members and partners to improve the company's environmental management and thus gain a competitive advantage. Relational capital refers to an intangible asset focused on nurturing and preserving relationships with any organization, individual or group that can influence a company's position in the market. Therefore, it is paramount for organizations to align their interests with those of their stakeholders to survive and remain competitive. Longoni & Cagliano (2018) assert that the needs of different stakeholders can be addressed through the management of green supply chains. Furthermore, other research also highlights green supply chains and the environmental perspective as powerful tools to meet stakeholders' needs (Zhu et al., 2013; Luthra et al., 2016; Jabbour et al., 2019). Therefore, GRC plays an important role in building strong and lasting relationships between suppliers and organizations. Table 1 shows all empirical research indexed in the Web of Science database addressing GIC from the founding of the construct to the present day.

Table 1. Empirical literature on GIC

Authors	Journal	Industry	Country
Chen (2008)	Journal of Business Ethics	Electronics Industry	Taiwan
López-Gamero et al. (2011)	Business Strategy and the Environment	Various Industries	Spain
Huang & Kung (2011)	Management Decision.	Manufacturing industry	Taiwan
Baresel-Bofinger et al. (2011)	International Journal of Knowledge-Based Development	Various Industries	Greece
Chang & Chen (2012)	Management Decision.	Manufacturing industry	Taiwan
Chen & Chang (2013)	Quality & Quantity	Manufacturing industry	Taiwan
Delgado-Verde et al. (2014)	Knowledge Management Research & Practice	Manufacturing industry	Spain
Chang (2016)	Corporate Social Responsibility and Environmental Management	Manufacturing industry	Taiwan
Jirawuttinunt (2018)	St. Theresa Journal of Humanities and Social Sciences	Various Industries	Thailand
Xu (2019)	Fresenius Environmental Bulletin	Manufacturing industry	China
Yong et al. (2019)	Journal of Cleaner Production	Manufacturing industry	Malaysia
Yusoff et al. (2019)	Journal of Cleaner Production	Manufacturing industry	Malaysia
Bag & Gupta (2019)	International Journal of Manpower	Automotive industry	South Africa
Yong et al. (2019a)	Journal of Management Development.	Manufacturing industry	Malaysia
Yusliza et al. (2020)	Journal of Cleaner Production	Manufacturing industry	Malaysia
Malik et al. (2020)	Sustainability	Manufacturing industry	Pakistan
Song et al. (2020)	European Journal of Innovation Management	Various Industries	China
Zaragoza-Sáez et al. (2020)	Journal of Sustainable Tourism	Hospitality Industry	Spain
Shoaib et al. (2021)	Cogent Business & Management	Food industry	Pakistan
Ma et al. (2021)	SAGE Open	Various Industries	China
Mansoor et al. (2021)	Journal of Intellectual Capital.	Manufacturing industry	Pakistan
Amores-Salvad6 et al. (2021)	Journal of Intellectual Capital.	Manufacturing industry	Spain
Ullah et al. (2021)	Environmental Science and Pollution Research	Manufacturing industry	China
Rehman et al. (2021)	Technological Forecasting and Social Change	Manufacturing industry	Malaysia
Trevlopoulos et al. (2021)	Environment Systems and Decisions	Metal Industry	Various countries
Ali et al. (2021)	Journal of Intellectual Capital	Manufacturing Industry	Pakistan
Albertini (2021)	Journal of Intellectual Capital	Various Industries	Various countries
Wang & Juo (2021)	Business Strategy and the Environment	Electronics Industry	Taiwan

Source: own elaboration

As can be seen, more than half of the research analyzed (57.14%) is contextualized in the manufacturing industry, even though this is not the most knowledge-intensive industry. This can be explained by the interest aroused by this industry, given its capacity to generate employment and wealth in the economy. Furthermore, the link between the industry and the country under analysis deserves special attention, as the research data come from the idiosyncratic industries of each country. Proof of this is the case of the electronics industry in Taiwan (Chen, 2008; Wang & Juo, 2021), the manufacturing industry in China (Ullah et al., 2021), or the hospitality industry in Spain (Zaragoza-Sáez et al., 2020). It is also important to note that there is only one research focused on the food industry, that of Shoaib et al. (2021). However, these authors use a sample of 287 dairy companies, which shows the need to analyze GIC in other sub-industries of the food industry such as the wine industry, as there are no previous studies that have carried out this task.

METHODOLOGY

Sample

Sampling is crucial for the case study, as the choice of the sample undoubtedly influences the results to be drawn from the research (Miles & Huberman, 1994). A single case has been selected to gain a deeper and broader understanding of the phenomenon under study (Chetty, 1996). For the selection of the case, environmental leaders within the wine industry were identified. According to academic literature, environmental leaders are organizations that take the lead in reducing the environmental impact of their activities and have achieved recognition of being green compared to their competitors (Runhaar et al., 2008). For the selection of the winery, we adopted the following criteria. Firstly, it had to be an ISO 14001 and Wineries for Climate Protection (WfCP) certified winery as a reflection of its environmental proactivity. Secondly, they had to have integrated environmental issues earlier than other companies in the wine sector. Thirdly, they had to be a winery with wide national and international recognition in the environmental field. After a first screening, it was decided to select Bodegas Luzón for meeting the three criteria previously adopted.

Data Collection and Analysis

The case method has been widely used in the social sciences (Burewoy, 1991), as empirical data collected through this method allows for reconceptualization and extension of theory. The case study carried out consists of three phases: (1) literature review, (2) case study analysis and (3) data collection. First, the first phase consisted of exploring the academic literature related to GIC. Secondly, a thorough description of the Bodegas Luzón case was carried out to identify its suitability for the present research. Thirdly, given the qualitative nature of the research, triangulation was used for data collection in order to increase the validity of the study and corroborate the conclusions drawn from it (Denzin, 1978). To carry out the triangulation, three sources of data were used: (1) in-depth interview with the environmental manager, Maria Dolores Garcia Martinez, and the winemaker, Vicente Micó Galbis (joint interview); (2) direct observation (visit to the winery and contact with employees); (3) access to both internal winery documentation (environmental statements, newsletters, website, etc.) and external documentation (press, corporate videos, etc.). The interview began by asking general questions to delve deeper into the history of the winery and its environmental commitment at a general level. As the interview progressed, the degree of specificity of the questions increased, asking, for example, about each of the dimensions of the GIC and their relationship with the winery's environmental management (see Appendix 1). The interview lasted 1 hour and was recorded in its entirety for subsequent transcription. During the visit to the facilities, it was possible to talk to other members of the company's staff, who also highlighted some of the environmental tasks they carried out. Data collection was stopped when the additional data resulted in a minimal understanding of the phenomenon under study (Lee, 1999). Once the transcription was completed, the interviewees' opinions on the first draft were analyzed to check its validity. The interviewees checked and accepted the transcripts of their interviews. Finally, a table summarizing the results of the study was produced.

RESULTS

The origins of Bodegas Luzón date back to 1841, the year in which Don José de Molina, commander of the Royal Army in the Spanish colony of Manila (Philippines), decided to return to his homeland: Jumilla. It was then that he took over the responsibility for the lands inherited from his father, providing them with the necessary infrastructure for wine production. The land was christened by Don José de Molina as Finca Luzón, in memory of the island where he was stationed for so long. This estate would later be inherited by his daughter Doña Ana Josefa Molina Gil, who did the same with her first-born daughter, Doña Carmen Guillén, leaving the winery linked to the female branch of the family from then onwards. In 2005, the Fuertes family took over the winery's historical legacy by acquiring it, one of the major milestones since its foundation. As the winemaker of Bodegas Luzón points out, "the acquisition of the winery by the Fuertes family was a great step forward in the development of both the winery and the Jumilla Denomination of Origin".

The winery currently has around 450 hectares of its own vineyards and another 1,000 hectares of vineyards managed by farmers, 80% of which are organically grown. The main grape variety they work with is Monastrell, a characteristic grape mainly in the Denominations of Origin (DOs) of the Region of Murcia (DO Jumilla, DO Yecla, DO Bullas) and in the DOs of Alicante and Almansa, as this type of grape needs a warm climate and good sunlight to ripen. Among the wines produced by Bodegas Luzón, the following stand out: Altos de Luzón, Alma de Luzón, Por Ti, Luzón Colección Blanco, Luzón Colección Rosado, Luzón Colección Monastrell, Luzón Colección Garnacha Tintorera, Luzón Colección Roble and Luzón Colección Crianza. They have also recently committed to the production of organic wines such as Verdecillo, Verdecillo Blanco, Luzón Ecológico Blanco and Luzón Organic, making them a benchmark winery in terms of sustainability. Thus, in 2009 they obtained the ISO 14000 certificate, becoming one of the first Spanish wineries to hold this environmental quality label and a national benchmark in sustainability due to their proactive attitude to initiate such sustainable practices. In the words of the winemaker:

"All the sustainable practices we have done in the winery are proactive, it is a long-term investment, because if you do it well and you execute it properly, the money comes back. Everything is returnable, whether in sales or image, but it is not short term, it is very long term. Therefore, if you don't develop sustainable actions with the long term in mind, they won't work. You need a very strong initial investment without knowing when it will be returnable. In fact, neither at the beginning nor now do we know with certainty the exact return. But we do know that it gives us an added quality in terms of image, organization, work, cleanliness, hygiene, improvement, and costs. But we have internalized all these actions after ten years of work. You can't do this to get money back the next day, because you don't even know when it's going to come back, and you might lose it."

As explained above, the blocks that make up the GIC are: the GHC, the GSC and the GRC. The factors that influence the formation of the three blocks of environmental intangibles for the case studied are set out below (see Table 2). On the one hand, as far as the GHC is concerned, it is worth highlighting the efforts made by the winery to integrate environmental values among its workers. Bodegas Luzón invests in training courses to provide its workers with green knowledge that allows the organization to reduce costs (through the efficient use of resources) and differentiate itself (through its high specialization in sustainable practices), attends trade fairs in the sector to detect new trends in the wine industry, makes the codified knowledge of the organization available to its workers through the code of conduct and good practices, and fosters motivation, job satisfaction and a sense of belonging to the group among its workers through managerial integrity, as its good environmental practices enable it to activate a transformative mechanism among workers: learning by imitation.

As far as the GSC is concerned, there are different factors that influence its construction. The winery has annual circular economy programmes to achieve the Triple R premises: reduce, reuse and recycle, it has its own computer systems to measure its water footprint and carbon footprint, it has eco-efficient facilities, it has prestigious certifications that endorse its commitment to the environment, such as the ISO 14000 and the Wineries for Climate Protection certificates, it has a brand with wide international recognition for its environmental work and its organic wines, has a flat organizational structure that facilitates the transmission of green knowledge, the values of its organizational culture are framed within the pillars of sustainability and it carries out annual R&D&I projects to improve the sustainability of the winery, which are subsequently translated into tangible results for the organization, such as the launch of wine without added sulphites and wine with low levels of sulphur.

As far as the GRC is concerned, Bodegas Luzón is part of a large number of associations and agreements that enable the organisation's environmental knowledge to be obtained and updated, such as: its membership of the Jumilla DO, the Jumilla Wine Business Association (ASEVIN, for its acronym in Spanish), the Jumilla Wine Route, the Murcia Institute for Agricultural and Food Research and Development (IMIDA, for its acronym in Spanish), the Integrated Centre for Agricultural Training and Experiences (CIFEA, for its acronym in Spanish) in Jumilla or the research and training agreements with Spanish universities such as the University of Cartagena, the University of Murcia and the University of Valencia. The winery also requires green certificates from its suppliers to be able to work with it, with the aim of establishing a green supply chain.

Table 2. Dimensions of GIC in Bodegas Luzón

GREEN INTELLECTUAL CAPITAL		
GREEN HUMAN CAPITALGREEN STRUCTURAL CAPITAL	Training courses	Environmental Manager: "The winery offers annual training to all its employees. On an environmental level, they are trained in good environmental practices in order to save resources." Winemaker- "At the company level it is very important to have these environmental awareness programmes because imagine the waste of resources if, for example, a worker were to leave the lights on in the winery. All the awareness-raising work that the organization does adds up to achieve our annual targets."
	Trade fairs	Environmental Manager: "We have a national and international sales team that is in charge of trade fairs and other commercial actions." Winemaker: "We participate in what we see as most interesting for our business in order to progress."
	Good practice manuals	Environmental Manager: "When a worker is hired, he/she is given initial training and, subsequently, the code of conduct and the code of good environmental practices are handed over to him/her."
	Motivation, job satisfaction and sense of belongingCircular Economy Programme	Winemaker: "The workers are motivated and satisfied in the winery because we care about the things that are happening, in water consumption, in electricity consumption... Things as simple as throwing a piece of paper on the floor and picking it up make us all feel that sustainability is ours. If the workers see that I arrive and throw a piece of paper on the floor, that I leave the light on or that I have the tap running, they will do the same."Winemaker: "We have a circular economy programme through which we develop different practices. For example, the stalks are reused for bedding, cattle feed and even as fertiliser for the vineyards. The wastewater that comes out goes to irrigate the vineyard, to the entrance garden, etc." Environmental Manager: "The last circular economy project we have carried out relates to the wastewater that is generated when the tanks are cleaned with soda. Previously, this water with soda was stored and taken away, and now we have a tank where this water is introduced, and this water then goes to the winery's treatment plant."
	IT systems to measure carbon and water footprints	Winemaker: "We have our own programmes created by the winery's IT team. There are people dedicated every day to measuring and counting the waste that is generated."
	Eco-efficient facilities	Winemaker: "We currently have solar panels, and we are going to install more. We are going to be self-sufficient in solar energy when we do the installation in September." Environmental Manager: "Our energy right now comes from wind power; we have the guarantee from our distributor that it is renewable. However, a study has been carried out and the process of installing the solar panels is underway."
	Brand	Winemaker: "At the user level I think that people, especially in Spain, still don't link the Bodegas Luzón brand with sustainable wine. On the other hand, in the European and American markets they do value it. In Spain, the value is being given by the distributor, but I think that the end consumer still does not associate Bodegas Luzón with sustainability. This is a task that we still have to develop."
	Certifications	Environmental Manager: "We are ISO 14000 and WineriesforClimateProtection (WfCP) certified, plus certified organic wine and vegan."
	Organisational structure	Winemaker: "The structure is quite flat, the management encourages us to develop new ideas on all environmental issues. Also, when we knock on their door it is always open."
	Proposal box	Winemaker: "We have a formal and informal suggestion box, because we have an APP where we have a suggestion box and a message button. But, in the end, everything formal is difficult to use, or at least people don't use it. In the warehouse we listen to everyone, because in the end we are a small company where the manager has coffee with us and is just one of us."
	Organisational culture	Winemaker: "The values at the winery have been clear from the beginning: improvement, innovation and excellence. We are a food company whose forte is constant improvement through the pillars of sustainability."

Continued on following page

Table 2. Continued

GREEN INTELLECTUAL CAPITAL		
	Investments in R&D&I	Winemaker: "We take part in all the R&D&I projects that add value to us. Many of these projects have helped us to launch new products on the market, which today are an important pillar to sustain the structure of the winery."
	Innovation performance	Environmental Manager: "The latest innovation has been the wine without added sulphites. An ecological wine, totally natural. We have been developing the necessary technology to be able to market sulphite-free wine for some time and it is now a reality. In addition, at the beginning of the year we did a study of the purification plant which has allowed us to consume less energy." Winemaker: "For example, we did a study for organic wines with low levels of sulphites and we are currently making our 12-month organic crianza wine. This study, in particular, has helped us to know why we were combining so much sulphur, why we were oxidizing the wine so much, and so on. We are now selling wine with twelve months of ageing with sulphur dioxide of 70 million matches when before it was 130."
GREEN RELATIONAL CAPITAL	Relations with institutions	Environmental Manager: "We are in ASEVIN, the Jumilla Wine Route, the DO JUMILLA, the IMIDA and the CEBAS. We also receive students from the University of Valencia, from Murcia, and we are currently developing a research project with the University of Cartagena."
	Relations with customers and suppliers	Environmental Manager: "In the winery we have suppliers who have ecological certificates and we have much more peace of mind and security. Also, as we calculate our carbon footprint, we try to buy from the closest suppliers, because of the transport issue. For cardboard we ask that they have their forest sustainability certificates, for paper and ink we ask that the suppliers certify that the inks are non-toxic, we use the lightest bottles possible, etc. We ask for a series of requirements that are related to the triple dimension of sustainability." Winemaker: "To engage with our customers we use all kinds of media, from trade fairs, LinkedIn, Instagram, to face-to-face meetings. Everything is valid if the customer is serious."

Source: own elaboration

CONCLUSION

This research aims to analyze the different factors influencing the formation of GIC in wine companies, contributing to the academic literature in a remarkable way, since, to the best of our knowledge, no research has been identified that addresses the three dimensions of GIC in the wine industry.

The results indicate that, from the GHC point of view, the winery analyzed has codes of good environmental practices, organizes training and environmental awareness sessions, attends seminars and workshops to improve its green knowledge and fosters motivation and a sense of belonging to the group through the integrity of its managers' environmental practices. As for the GSC, the company has a circular economy program, IT systems to measure its carbon and water footprint, eco-efficient facilities, a brand linked to sustainability in foreign markets, certifications that endorse its environmental commitment, a flat organizational structure through which green knowledge flows, a proposal box to pass on suggestions to management, an organizational culture built on the pillars of sustainability, constant innovations in R&D&I and, as a result, the implementation of green innovations. Finally, the GRC analysis reveals that the company-stakeholders link is very important, as the winery develops various alliances to improve its green knowledge and, consequently, its environmental management.

The approach proposed in this research can help to choose the most suitable intangible resources for the environmental management of wineries. Moreover, several practical implications for the management of wine companies emerge from the work. One of the main challenges for managers is to understand the role of intangible resources - and not only tangible ones - in the environmental management of wineries. Once they recognize the value of GIC, they must take the lead in promoting environmental initiatives, empowering employees to proactively participate in the winery's environmental management through environmental awareness sessions, attendance at seminars and workshops, etc. In this sense, the establishment of incentives that reward best environmental practices can improve the environmental performance of wineries.

Based on the research results, we encourage managers to foster cooperation between their different stakeholders, as cooperation agreements allow companies to exchange information on environmental issues, helping to improve the company's ability to engage in proactive environmental practices. Furthermore, green certifications will improve the company's image and may increase the demand for wines, as this type of certification positively affects consumers' memory and perception of the products' characteristics. Therefore, one of the most relevant practical implications of the study is that winery managers should promote the achievement of the Wineries for Climate Protection and Organic Wine certificates, in order to improve their GIC.

FUTURE RESEARCH DIRECTIONS

Despite the important contributions made in the paper, it is important to highlight the existence of some limitations. The main limitation is related to the impossibility of establishing comparisons in the single case study and the fact that the winery analyzed stands out as an environmental benchmark within the wine industry. To overcome this limitation, as a future line of research we intend to carry out a multiple case study to analyze both wineries that act as environmental leaders and those that do not take on this role, and thus be able to establish the similarities and differences in GIC between the two groups of companies.

ACKNOWLEDGMENT

This research has not received any specific grant from any public, commercial, or non-profit sector funding body. However, we would like to sincerely thank Bodegas Luzón for allowing us to enter their facilities, allowing us to conduct an in-depth interview with two of its members and providing us with all the documentation necessary to carry out the research.

REFERENCES

Albertini, E. (2021). What are the environmental capabilities, as components of the sustainable intellectual capital, that matter to the CEOs of European companies? *Journal of Intellectual Capital.*

Ali, W., Jun, W., Hussain, H., Khan, N., Younas, M., & Jamil, I. (2021). Does green intellectual capital matter for green innovation adoption? Evidence from the manufacturing SMEs of Pakistan. *Journal of Intellectual Capital.*

Amores-Salvadó, J., Cruz-González, J., Delgado-Verde, M., & González-Masip, J. (2021). Green technological distance and environmental strategies: the moderating role of green structural capital. *Journal of Intellectual Capital*.

Bag, S., & Gupta, S. (2019). Examining the effect of green human capital availability in adoption of reverse logistics and remanufacturing operations performance. *International Journal of Manpower, 41*(7), 1097–1117. doi:10.1108/IJM-07-2019-0349

Baresel-Bofinger, A., Ketikidis, P., Koh, S., & Cullen, J. (2011). Role of 'green knowledge' in the environmental transformation of the supply chain: The case of Greek manufacturing. *International Journal of Knowledge-Based Development, 2*(1), 107–128. doi:10.1504/IJKBD.2011.040628

Boons, F., Montalvo, C., Quist, J., & Wagner, M. (2013). Sustainable innovation, business models and economic performance: An overview. *Journal of Cleaner Production, 45*, 1–8. doi:10.1016/j.jclepro.2012.08.013

Burawoy, M. (1991). Reconstructing social theories. In *Ethnography Unbound*. University of California Press.

Buysse, K., & Verbeke, A. (2003). Proactive environmental strategies: A stakeholder management perspective. *Strategic Management Journal, 24*(5), 453–470. doi:10.1002mj.299

Carrillo-Hermosilla, J., Del Río, P., & Könnölä, T. (2010). Diversity of eco-innovations: Reflections from selected case studies. *Journal of Cleaner Production, 18*(10-11), 1073–1083. doi:10.1016/j.jclepro.2010.02.014

Chang, C. (2016). The determinants of green product innovation performance. *Corporate Social Responsibility and Environmental Management, 23*(2), 65–76. doi:10.1002/csr.1361

Chang, C., & Chen, Y. (2012). The determinants of green intellectual capital. *Management Decision, 50*(1), 74–94. doi:10.1108/00251741211194886

Chen, Y. (2008). The positive effect of green intellectual capital on competitive advantages of firms. *Journal of Business Ethics, 77*(3), 271–286. doi:10.100710551-006-9349-1

Chen, Y., & Chang, C. (2013). Utilize structural equation modeling (SEM) to explore the influence of corporate environmental ethics: The mediation effect of green human capital. *Quality & Quantity, 47*(1), 79–95. doi:10.100711135-011-9504-3

Chetty, S. (1996). The case study method for research in small-and medium-sized firms. *International Small Business Journal, 15*(1), 73–85. doi:10.1177/0266242696151005

Davenport, T., & Prusak, L. (1998). *Working knowledge: How organizations manage what they know*. Harvard Business Press.

Delgado-Verde, M., Amores-Salvadó, J., Martín-de Castro, G., & Navas-López, J. E. (2014). Green intellectual capital and environmental product innovation: The mediating role of green social capital. *Knowledge Management Research and Practice, 12*(3), 261–275. doi:10.1057/kmrp.2014.1

Dyllick, T., & Hockerts, K. (2002). Beyond the business case for corporate sustainability. *Business Strategy and the Environment*, *11*(2), 130–141. doi:10.1002/bse.323

Florin, J., Lubatkin, M., & Schulze, W. (2003). A social capital model of high-growth ventures. *Academy of Management Journal*, *46*(3), 374–384.

Gilinsky, A. Jr, Newton, S., & Vega, R. (2016). Sustainability in the global wine industry: Concepts and cases. *Agriculture and Agricultural Science Procedia*, *8*, 37–49. doi:10.1016/j.aaspro.2016.02.006

Guthey, G., & Whiteman, G. (2009). Social and ecological transitions: Winemaking in California. *Emergence*, *11*(3), 37–48.

Hertsgaard, M. (2010). What climate change means for wine industry. *Wired Science*.

Huang, C., & Kung, F. (2011). Environmental consciousness and intellectual capital management: Evidence from Taiwan's manufacturing industry. *Management Decision*, *49*(9), 1405–1425. doi:10.1108/00251741111173916

Jabbour, C., De Sousa Jabbour, A., & Sarkis, J. (2019). Unlocking effective multi-tier supply chain management for sustainability through quantitative modeling: Lessons learned and discoveries to be made. *International Journal of Production Economics*, *217*, 11–30. doi:10.1016/j.ijpe.2018.08.029

Jardon, C., & Dasilva, A. (2017). Intellectual capital and environmental concern in subsistence small businesses. *Management of Environmental Quality*, *28*(2), 214–230. doi:10.1108/MEQ-05-2015-0085

Jardon, C., & Martos, M. (2012). Intellectual capital as competitive advantage in emerging clusters in Latin America. *Journal of Intellectual Capital*, *13*(4), 462–481. doi:10.1108/14691931211276098

Jirawuttinunt, S. (2018). The Relationship between Green Human Resource Management and Green Intellectual Capital of Certified ISO 14000 Businesses in Thailand. *St. Theresa. Journal of the Humanities and Social Sciences*, *4*(1), 20–37.

Liu, C. (2010, October). Developing green intellectual capital in companies by AHP. In *2010 8th International Conference on Supply Chain Management and Information* (pp. 1-5). IEEE.

Longoni, A., & Cagliano, R. (2018). Inclusive environmental disclosure practices and firm performance. *International Journal of Operations & Production Management*, *38*(9), 1815–1835. doi:10.1108/IJOPM-12-2016-0728

López-Gamero, M., Zaragoza-Sáez, P., Claver-Cortés, E., & Molina-Azorín, J. (2011). Sustainable development and intangibles: Building sustainable intellectual capital. *Business Strategy and the Environment*, *20*(1), 18–37. doi:10.1002/bse.666

Luthra, S., Garg, D., & Haleem, A. (2016). The impacts of critical success factors for implementing green supply chain management towards sustainability: An empirical investigation of Indian automobile industry. *Journal of Cleaner Production*, *121*, 142–158. doi:10.1016/j.jclepro.2016.01.095

Ma, Y., Chen, S., & Ruangkanjanases, A. (2021). Understanding the Antecedents and Consequences of Green Human Capital. *SAGE Open*, *11*(1), 1–11. doi:10.1177/2158244020988867

Malik, S., Cao, Y., Mughal, Y., Kundi, G., Mughal, M., & Ramayah, T. (2020). Pathways towards sustainability in organizations: Empirical evidence on the role of green human resource management practices and green intellectual capital. *Sustainability*, *12*(8), 3228. doi:10.3390u12083228

Mansoor, A., Jahan, S., y Riaz, M. (2021). Does green intellectual capital spur corporate environmental performance through green workforce? *Journal of Intellectual Capital*.

Miles, M., & Huberman, A. (1994). *Qualitative Data Analysis. An Expanded Sourcebook* (2nd ed.). Sage.

Nguyen, D., & Slater, S. (2010). Hitting the sustainability sweet spot: Having it all. *The Journal of Business Strategy*, *31*(3), 5–11. doi:10.1108/02756661011036655

OIV. (2004). *Resolution CST 1/2004-Develpment of Sustainable Vitivinivulture*. Pareis.

OIV. (2008). *Resolution CST/2008-OIV Guidelines for Sustainable Vitiviniculture: Production, Processing and Packaging of Products*. Verone/it.

OIV. (2016). *Resolution CST 518/2016-OIV General Principles of Sustainable Vitiviniculture - Environmental - Social - Economic and Cultural Aspects*. Brento Gonçalves.

Phyper, J., & MacLean, P. (2009). *Good to green: managing business risks and opportunities in the age of environmental awareness*. John Wiley & Sons.

Porter, M., & Van der Linde, C. (1995). Green and competitive: Ending the stalemate. *Harvard Business Review*, *72*(3/5), 97–118.

Rehman, S., Kraus, S., Shah, S., Khanin, D., & Mahto, R. (2021). Analyzing the relationship between green innovation and environmental performance in large manufacturing firms. *Technological Forecasting and Social Change*, *163*, 120481. doi:10.1016/j.techfore.2020.120481

Runhaar, H., Tigchelaar, C., & Vermeulen, W. J. (2008). Environmental leaders: Making a difference. A typology of environmental leaders and recommendations for a differentiated policy approach. *Business Strategy and the Environment*, *17*(3), 160–178. doi:10.1002/bse.520

Santini, C., Cavicchi, A., & Casini, L. (2013). Sustainability in the wine industry: Key questions and research trends a. *Agricultural and Food Economics*, *1*(1), 1–14. doi:10.1186/2193-7532-1-9

Sharma, S., & Ruud, A. (2003). On the path to sustainability: Integrating social dimensions into the research and practice of environmental management. *Business Strategy and the Environment*, *12*(4), 205–214. doi:10.1002/bse.366

Shoaib, M., Abbas, Z., Yousaf, M., Zámečník, R., Ahmed, J., & Saqib, S. (2021). The role of GHRM practices towards organizational commitment: A mediation analysis of green human capital. *Cogent Business & Management*, *8*(1), 1870798. doi:10.1080/23311975.2020.1870798

Song, W., Yu, H., & Xu, H. (2020). Effects of green human resource management and managerial environmental concern on green innovation. *European Journal of Innovation Management*, *24*(3), 951–967. doi:10.1108/EJIM-11-2019-0315

Trevlopoulos, N., Tsalis, T., Evangelinos, K., Tsagarakis, K., Vatalis, K., & Nikolaou, I. (2021). The influence of environmental regulations on business innovation, intellectual capital, environmental and economic performance. *Environment Systems & Decisions*, *41*(1), 163–178. doi:10.100710669-021-09802-6

Ullah, H., Wang, Z., Bashir, S., Khan, A., Riaz, M., & Syed, N. (2021). Nexus between IT capability and green intellectual capital on sustainable businesses: Evidence from emerging economies. *Environmental Science and Pollution Research International*, *28*(22), 27825–27843. doi:10.100711356-020-12245-2 PMID:33515153

Wang, C., & Juo, W. (2021). An environmental policy of green intellectual capital: Green innovation strategy for performance sustainability. *Business Strategy and the Environment*, *30*(7), 1–14. doi:10.1002/bse.2800

WCED. (1987). World commission on environment and development. *Our Common Future*, *17*(1), 1–91.

Widener, S. (2006). Associations between strategic resource importance and performance measure use: The impact on firm performance. *Management Accounting Research*, *17*(4), 433–457. doi:10.1016/j.mar.2005.10.002

Xu, A. (2019). Study on human resource management of sewage treatment enterprises. *Fresenius Environmental Bulletin*, *28*(12), 10035–10039.

Yadiati, W., Nissa, N., Paulus, S., Suharman, H., & Meiryani, M. (2019). The role of green intellectual capital and organizational reputation in influencing environmental performance. *International Journal of Energy Economics and Policy*, *9*(3), 261–268. doi:10.32479/ijeep.7752

Yong, J., Yusliza, M., Jabbour, C., & Ahmad, N. (2019a). Exploratory cases on the interplay between green human resource management and advanced green manufacturing in light of the Ability-Motivation-Opportunity theory. *Journal of Management Development*, *39*(1), 31–49. doi:10.1108/JMD-12-2018-0355

Yong, J., Yusliza, M., Ramayah, T., & Fawehinmi, O. (2019). Nexus between green intellectual capital and green human resource management. *Journal of Cleaner Production*, *215*, 364–374. doi:10.1016/j.jclepro.2018.12.306

Yusliza, M., Yong, J., Tanveer, M., Ramayah, T., Faezah, J., & Muhammad, Z. (2020). A structural model of the impact of green intellectual capital on sustainable performance. *Journal of Cleaner Production*, *249*, 119334. doi:10.1016/j.jclepro.2019.119334

Yusoff, Y., Omar, M., Zaman, M., & Samad, S. (2019). Do all elements of green intellectual capital contribute toward business sustainability? Evidence from the Malaysian context using the Partial Least Squares method. *Journal of Cleaner Production*, *234*, 626–637. doi:10.1016/j.jclepro.2019.06.153

Zaragoza-Sáez, P., Claver-Cortés, E., Marco-Lajara, B., & Úbeda-García, M. (2020). Corporate social responsibility and strategic knowledge management as mediators between sustainable intangible capital and hotel performance. *Journal of Sustainable Tourism*, 1–23. doi:10.1080/09669582.2020.1811289

Zhu, Q., Sarkis, J., & Lai, K. H. (2013). Institutional-based antecedents and performance outcomes of internal and external green supply chain management practices. *Journal of Purchasing and Supply Management*, *19*(2), 106–117. doi:10.1016/j.pursup.2012.12.001

ADDITIONAL READING

Atkin, T., Gilinsky, A. Jr, & Newton, S. K. (2012). Environmental strategy: Does it lead to competitive advantage in the US wine industry? *International Journal of Wine Business Research*, *24*(2), 115–133. doi:10.1108/17511061211238911

Atkin, T., Wilson, D., Thach, L., & Olsen, J. (2017). Analyzing the impact of conjunctive labeling as part of a regional wine branding strategy. *Wine Economics and Policy*, *6*(2), 155–164. doi:10.1016/j.wep.2017.10.003

Baiano, A. (2021). An Overview on Sustainability in the Wine Production Chain. *Beverages*, *7*(1), 15. doi 10.3390/beverages7010015

Gilinsky, A., Santini, C., Lazzeretti, L., & Eyler, R. (2008). Desperately seeking serendipity: Exploring the impact of country location on innovation in the wine industry. *International Journal of Wine Business Research*, *20*(4), 302–320. doi:10.1108/17511060810919425

Marco-Lajara, B., Seva-Larrosa, P., Martínez-Falcó, J., & Sánchez-García, E. (2021). How Has COVID-19 Affected The Spanish Wine Industry? An Exploratory Analysis. *Natural Volatiles & Essential Oils Journal*, *8*(6), 2722–2731.

Marco-Lajara, B., Seva-Larrosa, P., Ruiz-Fernández, L., & Martínez-Falcó, J. (2021). The Effect of COVID-19 on the Spanish Wine Industry. In *Impact of Global Issues on International Trade* (pp. 211–232). IGI Global. doi:10.4018/978-1-7998-8314-2.ch012

Merli, R., Preziosi, M., & Acampora, A. (2018). Sustainability experiences in the wine sector: Toward the development of an international indicators system. *Journal of Cleaner Production*, *172*, 3791–3805. doi:10.1016/j.jclepro.2017.06.129

Montella, M. M. (2017). Wine tourism and sustainability: A review. *Sustainability*, *9*(1), 113. doi:10.3390u9010113

Mozell, M. R., & Thach, L. (2014). The impact of climate change on the global wine industry: Challenges & solutions. *Wine Economics and Policy*, *3*(2), 81–89. doi:10.1016/j.wep.2014.08.001

KEY TERMS AND DEFINITIONS

Green Human Capital: A set of knowledge, skills, and abilities of employees related to environmental protection and green innovation.

Green Intellectual Capital: A set of intangible assets held by both individuals and the organization that are intended to protect the environment and foster green innovation in the organization.

Green Relational Capital: Intangible assets based on the existing relationships between the organization and its stakeholders.

Green Structural Capital: Intangible assets owned by the organization and aimed at environmental protection and eco-innovation in the company.

ISO 14000: A set of rules governing the environmental management of companies.

Protected Designation of Origin: A distinction whose purpose is to identify a product originating from a specific place, whose quality is fundamentally due to a particular geographical environment, with the natural and human factors inherent to it.

Sustainability: Development that meets the needs of the present without compromising the ability of future generations, ensuring a balance between economic growth, environmental care, and social well-being.

APPENDIX 1

This section presents the questions asked to both the winery's environmental manager and the winemaker at the winery's facilities on August 15, 2021. This section presents the questions asked to both the winery's environmental manager and the winemaker at the winery's facilities on August 15, 2021. As can be seen, the interview was structured in four blocks: (1) history and generic data, (2) GHC, (3) GSC and (4) GRC.

1. History and generic data
    a. When was the winery founded?
    b. What do you consider to be the most important milestones of the organization?
    c. How many hectares of vineyards does the winery manage?
    d. What is the area of organic vineyards?
    e. What is the current situation of the winery?
    f. How have you been able to combat the difficulties arising from COVID-19?
2. GHC
    a. Do employees attend seminars, workshops, events to improve their knowledge about sustainability in the industry?
    b. Does the organization participate in industry trade fairs?
    c. Does the organization have a manual of good practices, environmental statements, explicit commitments to improve its environmental performance?
    d. How would you assess the motivation of employees in the winery to make it a benchmark for sustainability?
    e. Do you consider that being a sustainable winery improves the employee's working situation?
    f. Since when has the organization been firmly committed to the sustainability of the winery?
3. GSC
    a. Are there recycling programs in the organization?
    b. Are there emissions control programs in the winery?
    c. What systems are used to measure the carbon and water footprint?
    d. Are there waste and energy reduction plans?
    e. How is the waste generated in the winery reused? In relation to the question, Do you have circular economy programs?
    f. How do the facilities of the winery facilitate the efficient use of energy?
    g. Do you consider that there is a link between the Bodegas Luzón brand and sustainability on the part of the consumer?
    h. Is there a department or person in charge of sustainability in the winery?
    i. Does it have certificates that endorse its commitment to sustainability?
    j. What is the organizational structure like? Is it hierarchical or flat?
    k. What values of the organization do you consider that favor the winery's sustainability?
    l. Does the winery invest in R&D?
4. GRC
    a. Does the winery participate with other associations to improve the environment?
    b. Does the winery collaborate with its suppliers to improve its environmental targets?

c. Do you take into account green certifications when collaborating with your suppliers?
d. Do you have collaboration agreements with universities?
e. How do you relate to your customers? Do you organize events to get to know their tastes and their preference for organic wine?

Chapter 7
Improving Society as a Business Strategy:
A Review From a Strategic Management Perspective

Yeşim Kurt
https://orcid.org/0000-0002-9827-2471
Kırklareli University, Turkey

ABSTRACT

The subject of this study is strategic corporate social responsibilities. The study aims to explain the meaning of this concept, its relationship with strategy, and how it can be integrated into the business. In order to achieve these goals, a strategic management approach is used. According to the results discussed in the research, social responsibilities that aim to improve society should not be chosen and implemented by chance. These activities are associated with the corporate strategy of the business, prioritizing the important stakeholder groups of the business. At the end of this process, while corporate social responsibilities gain a strategic value, they can contribute to the sustainability of both the society and the business. In other words, they give the business a competitive advantage that is difficult to imitate.

INTRODUCTION

The concept of corporate social responsibility (CSR) began to be discussed in the 1950s, continued to spread in the 1960s, and in the 1980s, with the effect of the changes in the structure of the society, it reached a stage where it dominated the business world and academic literature (Jamali, 2007, p. 3). During this process, there was a paradigm shift towards the social assistance expected from the states at the beginning. This shift has emerged with the questioning of how businesses should approach the needs of society. The questioning of the place of businesses in society over the years has led to new responsibilities in society. Because many different stakeholders of the society have come to expect businesses to produce answers to various problems of the society. This expectation has increased so much over time

DOI: 10.4018/978-1-7998-9590-9.ch007

that businesses have become obliged to perform responsible behaviors in social and environmental issues (Bhattacharyya, 2010, p. 83; Orlitzky et. al., 2011, p. 3).

Today, businesses continue to feel this intense pressure to rebuild public trust in various contexts and remain competitive in the global economy (Jamali, 2007, p. 3). Efforts by businesses to manage these pressures and improve society have been associated with the concept of corporate social responsibility. Carroll (1991) classified these responsibilities as economic, legal, ethical, and voluntary responsibilities. Social responsibility activities are carried out by businesses for various reasons, especially the benefits of voluntary corporate social responsibilities to the business are discussed in various studies (Galbreath, 2009, p. 3-4). In addition to the benefits highlighted by the research, there are also some costs that such responsibilities bring to the business. The effective management of these costs and the ability of businesses to protect the interests of their shareholders while contributing to society has given a strategic meaning to the concept of corporate social responsibility. Studies revealing this relationship have started to create literature called strategic corporate social responsibility.

According to the strategic corporate social responsibility approach, the most important thing for businesses is profit maximization. In other words, businesses should realize social responsibilities in areas where they will benefit (Siegel & Vitaliano 2007, p. 3). Accordingly, opportunity costs should be borne, which will not only benefit society but also provide a competitive advantage to businesses (Yuen & Lim, 2016, p. 50). This strategic view is related to an approach that will provide more rational returns to the business while managing the pressures on businesses. Every expenditure made for corporate social responsibility activities means a cost for the business. As a result of bearing these costs, while creating added value to the society and social environment, on the other hand, strategic results should be obtained that will bring economic gain and competitive advantages to the business. This is possible by evaluating the business strategy and social responsibility activities together and integrating these activities into the business strategy (Bhattacharyya, 2010, p. 83-84). In other words, the CSR strategy should be transformed into a structure that supports the corporate strategy of the businesses (Yu & Liang, 2020, p. 1). Corporate social responsibilities should be used as a strategic value that contributes to the sustainable competitiveness of businesses. In this way, it will also contribute to the corporate sustainability of the businesses (Kim et. al., 2018, p. 1).

At this point, managers should determine strategies for how their businesses can be more socially responsible, ecologically sustainable, and economically competitive. Today, managers should develop skills in integrating social responsibility strategies into their businesses' strategies (Orlitzky et. Al., 2011, p. 3). Therefore, when planning CSR activities, managers should focus on these activities from a strategic perspective (Bhattacharyya, 2010, p. 83-84).

The strategic paradigm transformation summarized here for the concept of CSR, the effects of this transformation on businesses, the strategies required to plan and manage this transformation, and the roles of managers in this process emerge as an important research topic. For all reasons, evaluating the concept of CSR with a strategic management perspective and explaining the concept of strategic CSR in all its aspects is considered a subject worth investigating (Yu & Liang, 2020, p. 1). With this research, it is planned to contribute to the calls for eliminating the need for theoretical, methodological, or practical studies in this field (Sousa, et. al., 2010, p. 295).

For these reasons, it is planned to explain various concepts and relations related to the subject in this book chapter. These can be summarized as follows:

- What is strategic corporate social responsibility?

- What is the relationship between strategy, strategic management, and strategic corporate social responsibility?
- How is strategic corporate social responsibility integrated into the business?

THE CONCEPT OF STRATEGIC CORPORATE SOCIAL RESPONSIBILITY

The concept of corporate social responsibility first emerged with the questioning of the social role of businesses after industrialization. The deterioration of the natural balances in the environments in which businesses are established, the emergence of problems such as environmental noise and air pollution, the discussion of the rights of workers in unhealthy conditions, led businesses and managers to take on responsibilities that will alleviate these effects and contribute to less pressure from the society (Sert, 2012, p. 35; Lantos, 2001, p. 9).

Whether the responsibility of businesses should be to their shareholders or society; The benefits or harms of such behaviors to the business have continued to be discussed by many researchers both in the business world and in the academic literature for many years. This concept, which evolved from social responsibilities to corporate social responsibility in this process, started to be handled with a new paradigm and a strategic approach in the 1980s and 1990s. With the impact of globalization and increasing competition, business managers have forced business managers to re-examine the nature, scope, and direction of CSR activities and led to the development of Strategic CSR. According to this strategic view of corporate social responsibilities, such behaviors represent a strategic choice for businesses (Balıkçıoğlu & Karacaoğlu, 2007, p. 125; Bhattacharyya et. al., 2008, p. 267). Accordingly, there may not always be a mismatch between social responsibilities and the profitability of businesses, and if such responsibilities are turned into an opportunity, results will be obtained for the interests of both the business and the society (Jamali, 2007, p. 8-10). For this reason, businesses that turn to social responsibilities with a strategic approach will also contribute to their sustainability (Yönet, 2005). So what exactly is strategic corporate social responsibility? How can it contribute to the sustainability of businesses? This chapter of the book seeks answers to these questions.

With this strategic view, corporate social responsibilities are not just a tool for businesses to manage corporate pressures or the costs incurred for social responsibilities. It is much more than that. It is now a strategic tool for businesses that can provide them with various advantages. For this reason, strategic corporate social responsibilities have become one of the fundamental parts of strategic planning. Strategic CSR is associated with strategic actions that reveal the competitiveness and shared values of businesses (Gültekin, 2015, p. 21-24).

According to the Strategic CSR approach, there is a win-win strategy for both businesses and different stakeholder groups that make up the society (Siegel & Vitaliano, 2007). Because strategic social responsibility, which benefits both the business and the society, is done to achieve strategic goals. It is believed that my actions are good for both the business and the society (Gültekin, 2015). Therefore, strategic CSR is aimed at realizing the strategic goals of the business; It is based on the view that good work and aid do benefit society as well as businesses. Thanks to strategic CSR, businesses "give back" some of their earnings back to their target audiences because they believe that this method is the most correct way for their financial interests. In other words, while helping their social stakeholders, they also help their shareholders (Yönet, 2005, p. 247-251; Gültekin, 2015).

Accordingly, in strategic CSR, unlike traditional CSR, CSR activities that are compatible with their business strategies, goals, and objectives are preferred, not random segments of the society. This situation, which manifests itself in the form of social responsibility efforts for some businesses only towards consumers or customers, is carried out only for the target market by some, the usage area and places of the product come to the fore in some, and it may turn to potential customers in some (Yönet, 2005, p. 247-251). According to the strategic CSR approach, CSR activities, which are unrelated to the business objectives and corporate strategies of the business, are related to the inability to use resources and opportunities correctly and to lose the opportunity to create value (McElhaney, 2009, p. 34). According to this approach, no business can solve all the problems of society, nor can it bear these costs. For this reason, it is meaningful for the business to address the problems that are most closely related to its business, both in terms of the effective use of its resources and the benefit it provides to society. CSR provides a competitive advantage only if it is evaluated with this Strategic approach (Belu & Manescu, 2013; Yu & Liang, 2020, p. 2-3). This strategic choice and process, which will provide tangible long-term benefits to the business, will mediate both the economic sustainability of the business and the sustainability of the society (Heslin & Ochoa, 2008, p. 126; Bhattacharyya et. al., 2008, p. 267).

There are various definitions of strategic CSR that are similar to each other. It is a business strategy embedded in the culture and operations of the business, integrated with the core business objectives and core competencies of the business, designed to create business value and positive social change from the very beginning (McElhaney, 2009, p. 35). According to one definition, strategic CSR is explained as a strategic resource that provides a competitive advantage to the business (Kim, et. al., 2018, p. 2-3). In addition to improving society, strategic CSR emphasizes the commercial or strategic value of CSR and is explained as an activity that should be implemented (Bhattacharyya et. al., 2008, p. 267). Strategic CSR refers to a strategic perspective where benefits to stakeholders are planned while considering the interests of the business, their unique needs are met or their problems are resolved, and it refers to a process in which positive reactions are aroused from these stakeholders. (Yu & Liang, 2020, p. 2-3). In summary, strategic CSR is a business strategy that is compatible with the profit-seeking of businesses, while making shareholders happy on the one hand, and making different segments of the society happy on the other. In other words, strategic CSR is the intention to expect long-term benefits by using certain talents and resources of the business in a way that will provide both organizational and social benefits.

In addition to all these explanations and definitions, to better understand strategic CSR, it is necessary to reveal the main aspects that differ from CSR. Table 1 shows this comparison:

Table 1. Comparison of traditional and strategic corporate social responsibilities

Strategic Dimensions	Traditional CSR	Strategic CSR
Visibility	Irrelevant: Doing good is its reward e and is profitable in the long run.	Building customer and stakeholder awareness of product with CSR value-added.
Appropriability	Irrelevant: Doing good is its reward e and profitable in the long run.	Manage stakeholder relations to capture value-added for the firm.
Voluntarism	Participate in social action beyond that demanded by the firm's interests and the law.	Participate in action beyond social that demanded by law.
Centrality	Irrelevant: Doing good is tied to social need and not to core business mission	Create value via product/ service innovation linked to social issues.
Proactivity	Anticipate changes in social issues.	Anticipate changes in social issues that present market opportunities.

Source: (Husted, & Allen, 2007, p. 598).

According to the table, strategic CSR differs from traditional CSR, consistent with the explanations in this section. Accordingly, strategic CSR, unlike the traditional, serves a strategic purpose that is related to the customer, the desire to create value, the interests of the business and its shareholders, and the target market. To make this relationship more understandable, it will be useful to give examples of strategic CSR. For example, California-based outdoor and sportswear manufacturer Patagonia represents a business that has created a new market for CSR products. Patagonia set out to be an eco-friendly supplier of outerwear equipment and began manufacturing its garments with recycled polyethylene terephthalate (PET). As a result of this environmentally friendly marketing, Patagonia's clothing began to sell for approximately 50% or more than its competitors (Husted & Allen, 2007). Similarly, the corporate social responsibility practices of Kraft, a food business, in preventing hunger; Nation' Bank's efforts in economic development and the revitalization of Charlotte; eye care business LensCrafter donating eyeglasses to low-income families; Assistance of ADT security systems to women survivors of violence in their safety; examples of these behaviors. Training assistance to eliminate the disadvantages of Microsoft's information technologies; The help of Barnes and Noble bookstore to increase literacy can be given as an example of corporate social responsibilities that businesses carry out concerning their strategies (McAlister and Ferrell, 2002' cited by Balıkçıoğlu & Karacaoğlu, 2007, p. 127).

To understand why CSR activities have turned into a strategic paradigm and relate to business strategy, it is necessary to discuss the relationship of this approach with strategic management. The following section covers this discussion.

THE RELATIONSHIP BETWEEN CORPORATE SOCIAL RESPONSIBILITY AND STRATEGIC MANAGEMENT

Strategic management is about decisions and practices that will provide businesses with a long-term competitive advantage and contribute to their sustainability. Strategic CSR activities also help businesses to achieve an advantageous position against their competitors in terms of competition and to secure this for a certain period (Bhattacharyya, 2010, p. 86; Kurucz, et. al., 2008). Achieving this depends on the compatibility of CSR activities with the corporate and business strategies and objectives of the business. For this reason, CSR activities should also be handled with a strategic approach and evaluated as a part of strategic management. Because CSR is a field of activity that is closely related to the basic strategies of businesses, helps the business to manage its relations with its stakeholders, and mediates to create new-product-market opportunities, and it is a critical resource that allows businesses to create strategic advantages. For this reason, strategists and managers should consider CSR values both for their businesses and for all their stakeholders in the strategy formulation process (Sousa Filho, et. al., 2010, p. 296; Galbreath, 2009, p. 4-5). CSR can also be seen as a long-term investment tool. For this reason, it is an area of activity that should be handled and managed with strategic objectives (McWilliams, et. al , 2006, p. 7). In summary, CSR should be compatible with the culture, structure, and processes of the business and should be included in the strategic management process as a value creation process. The relationship between CSR and strategic management highlighted here and the importance of this relationship are discussed below with various concepts:

Value Creation: CSR activities are claimed to be the best or easiest path to value creation and profitability. Achieving this is about going beyond the simple approach that CSR is inherently profitable. According to the strategic management approach, the key to success is the effective management of

CSR activities and the creation of a competitive advantage that results in value creation. Value is created when consumers are willing to pay a premium for the business's products and services, based on their position and involvement in certain social issues. Value creation occurs when business resources are combined in new ways to increase potential productivity. Therefore, value creation is necessarily about innovation. Strategic management researchers have argued that CSR can provide opportunities for innovation. However, not all market-based projects will create value, and not all CSR projects will create value. Understanding how CSR activities create value for business rather than costs requires considering CSR as a strategic value creator (Husted & Allen, 2007). For this reason, CSR activities should be considered as one of the fields of activity in the value chain of the business (market, logistics, production, human resources, etc.) and in this way, orientation towards competitive advantage. In other words, it is necessary to integrate CSR into all value-producing policies and practices of the business in the strategic context (Gürol, et. al., 2010). As a result, the desired economic value from strategic CSR can be created (Husted & Allen, 2007).

Competitive Strategy: There is a strong relationship between business competitive strategy and CSR practices, according to the strategic management approach (Husted, & Allen, 2007). In other words, CSR practices are strategic activities for businesses (Bhattacharyya, 2010, p. 84). Addressing CSR activities in a strategic sense, that is, taking responsibilities that will benefit the business's strategy on the agenda, provides commercial benefits for businesses. This situation is mostly associated with cost leadership and differentiation strategies from competitive strategies. According to this view, while carrying out Strategic CSR activities, the company's product-production activities, etc. There are improvements in the fields, and reductions in production and sales costs can be experienced. Thus, strategic CSR activities can lead to cost advantages and thus help a firm to follow its "Cost Leadership" strategy (Porter and Kramer, 2006). Similarly, carrying out strategic CSR activities can help project the image of a socially responsible and environmentally conscious business. This helps to differentiate the business from other businesses. At the same time, it can lead to product differentiation for businesses that turn to produce more environmentally friendly products or distribution channels and go the way of product renewal, and it will also contribute to the follow-up of differentiation strategy by separating them from other businesses (Bhattacharyya, 2010, p. 86; Pollach, 2015, p. 58).

Customer Relational Benefits: Consumers or customers believe that a reliable and honest business will produce better products, and they tend more towards the products of those businesses. In the minds of some customers, CSR is seen as a sign of honesty and reliability. For this reason, CSR practices are also considered as a form of product differentiation, an advertising form to create or maintain brand loyalty (Siegel & Vitaliano, 2007, p. 7; Balıkçıoğlu & Karacaoğlu, 2007). Moreover, strategic CSR goes beyond customer loyalty and focuses on creating relational benefits by creating social and economic values, strengthening cooperation and trust relations between the customer and the business. Strengthening relational benefits can also be an important factor in increasing the profit of the business, creating sustainable relationships, and reducing the cost in creating shared value (Kim, et. al., 2018, p. 17; Manasakis, et. al., 2014, p. 3).

At the same time, CSR applications are a tool to create new markets when done strategically. Businesses that find a way to engage with the world's poorest citizens are helping to alleviate poverty and improving their economies, while at the same time turning this into an advantage, creating new customers and markets for their products. For example, Aravind Eye Hospitals in India perform 200,000 cataract surgeries per year for approximately US$50 per patient. These hospitals have made millions of dollars profit from these transactions that they have carried out under the name of responsibility, well below the market. These hospitals, which increased their productivity and benefited from economies of scale, also contributed to the re-visit of hundreds of thousands of people. This has contributed to the Indian economy by allowing them and their caregivers to return to the workforce (Heslin & Ochoa, 2008).

Organizational Learning: Strategic CSR activities offer businesses opportunities to learn from the projects they invest in, use this knowledge to build businesses' core competencies, and improve social or environmental conditions at the same time. Therefore, strategic CSR activities can be considered as learning laboratories to examine different ideas, methods, and processes without time pressure and other typical constraints in the delivery of commercially contracted products and services (Heslin & Ochoa, 2008, p. 129). In this approach, CSR activities prioritized based on strategic intentions have often been described by researchers as "investments" comparable to those made in R&D or employee training, because such activities have the potential for significant future gains due to the instructive nature of the process. It can also provide advantages in identifying trends or changes in the market in a business and contributes to the business moving quickly to be at the forefront of change. Finally, such CSR activities can help businesses build proactive competencies by improving their skills, processes, and systems that increase organizational readiness for change, fluctuations, and crises (Michelon, et. al., 2013, p. 83).

Stakeholder Theory: CSR activities concern business management as a strategic intervention to manage reputational risks from stakeholders and thereby enrich and improve business opportunities (Bhattacharyya et. al., 2008, p. 267-268). For this reason, managers, corporate leaders, or strategists turn to CSR activities to meet stakeholder expectations or manage pressure from stakeholders, and this interest continues to increase. NGOs, suppliers, business employees, managers, customers, government, media, competitors, etc. are the parties that make up the internal and external stakeholder group and need to be managed. (McWilliams, et. al., 2006, p, 2). Because CSR activities, unlike many other business activities, affect both internal and external stakeholders. This aspect of CSR activities brings a strategic perspective to CSR. (Bhattacharyya, 2010, p. 83-84). Managing relations with stakeholders is also related to being respected and respected in their eyes. Strategic CSR practices are an effective tool in creating this perception. This image and reputation that businesses gain through CSR practices strengthen their relations with their stakeholders (Heslin & Ochoa, 2008, p. 130). Because as a result of this kind of strategic CSR activity, the commitment and motivation of the internal stakeholders of the business increase, while the external stakeholders contribute to the good management of the environmental relations of the business (Bhattacharyya, 2010, p. 83-84). A business that does not meet the expectations of its stakeholders will lose the reputation capital it has accumulated over time. Considering that strategic CSR is an important tool to meet the needs of various stakeholders, a business with a strong corporate reputation should also continue to use strategic CSR to maintain or improve its corporate reputation (Yu & Liang, 2020, p. 4). At the same time, this positive reputation created as a result of all these, because it cannot be imitated, gives businesses a competitive advantage by distinguishing them from their competitors (Michelon, et. al., 2013, p. 83). This superiority contributes to the sustainability of the business.

Resource Dependence Theory: According to this approach, the positive relationships of businesses with their internal and external environments are valuable, rare, inimitable, and non-substitutable resources that provide a sustainable competitive advantage to the business (Michelon, et. al., 2013, p. 83). For this reason, applications that develop these relationships are also extremely important for businesses. When CSR activities are considered from a strategic perspective, they are difficult to imitate strategic resources that will contribute to the sustainability of businesses (Barba-Sánchez & Atienza-Sahuquillo, 2010, p. 1157). For this reason, CSR activities, which have strategic importance, should be managed effectively and the scarce resources and capabilities of the business should be transformed into an input for strategic success. In other words, for the profit maximization of the business, the level of resources to be allocated to CSR activities should be determined, cost-benefit analyzes should be made and resources should be allocated to CSR strategies that are compatible with the business's strategy (Orlitzky, et. al., 2011). In summary, according to the resource-based view, a strategic approach should be taken when allocating business resources to CSR activities, and the result of these activities should be considered as an important and inimitable resource for the long-term sustainability of the business.

Transaction Cost Theory: There are also explanations about CSR in this theoretical approach. Transaction cost theory emphasizes stakeholder management to increase stakeholder satisfaction, rather than assuming that CSR is costless. Accordingly, managers should carry out social responsibility efforts by monitoring stakeholder groups and having their satisfaction investigated. Executing these efforts requires managers to consider transaction costs in their decision-making processes in the short term. In the long run, CSR reduces transaction costs (Orlitzky, et. al., 2011, p. 8).

INTEGRATION OF STRATEGIC CORPORATE SOCIAL RESPONSIBILITIES INTO BUSINESS

There is a strong link between strategic CSR and the long-term sustainability of the business. Therefore, integrating these activities into the business will have positive results on the long-term competitive advantage of the business. As emphasized in the previous sections, it is possible to talk about strategic CSR activities at the point where CSR activities are related to business strategy. The establishment of this relationship is possible with integration.

There are critical issues in the business integration of these activities. According to various sources, these are related to strategic CSR plans on issues such as helping the general strategy of the business, developing strategic resources and capabilities for the business, maintaining the position of the business in the market, creating new product-market opportunities, managing the stakeholder relations of the business. (Bhattacharyya, 2010, p. 86; McElhaney, 2009, p. 36-37; Sousa Filho, et. al., 2010, p. 297-298). In this section, the integration of Strategic CSR into the business is explained with the following steps:

- Linking to business strategy
- Associating with senior management
- Linking with values, mission, and vision
- Planning resources
- Associating with the market
- Prioritizing stakeholders
- Realizing collaborations
- Determining performance indicators

Linking to Business Strategy: A business can gain value and gain a competitive advantage through socially responsible activities, but achieving this depends on acting strategically and linking CSR with corporate strategies. In other words, the CSR activities of the business are directly related to the main corporate strategy and the main field of activity (Sousa Filho, et. al., 2010, p, 297-298). How to do this, how CSR can be better integrated into the strategy of the business, emerges as a suggested subject to investigate (Galbreath, 2009, p. 9). At this point, at the very core of integration, leaders, and managers should go for a planning and organization path by considering how many CSR activities they will perform are related to business strategies.

Associating with Senior Management: To ensure full integration, it is necessary to ensure the dedication and support of the senior management in this regard. CSR should be managed as a core business strategy, such as marketing, research and development, capital expenditure, and talent management strategies. Corporate social responsibility should report to a senior leader in the business rather than staying out of the corporate foundation. The board of directors of the business should be responsible for CSR strategy as they are responsible for other business strategies such as accounting, finance, and marketing. The business's senior leadership and management, including the board of directors, must make and be involved in a unique, sound, and public commitment to CSR. Innovative businesses like Timberland, for example, have board committees that oversee corporate responsibility, and Gap takes board members on factory tours in China to see the value of supplier code of conduct and audits. In general, the higher the CSR reporting to the top management of the business, the more relevant the senior management is to this issue, the closer it is to creating value as a strategy (McElhaney, 2009, p. 36).

Linking with Values, Mission, and Vision: Concepts such as mission-vision-values, which are related to why a business exists, how it sees itself, how it looks from the outside, what it wants to do, where it wants to reach in the future, with what behavioral patterns it wants to get there, are the basic tools of managing the perceptions of the business in the eyes of stakeholders. For this reason, they also play a critical role in the integration of CSR into the business.

In this case, the reflection of CSR activities on the values, mission, and vision of the business is also vital in transforming these activities into a strategy (McElhaney, 2009, p. 36). For example, The Body Shop manufactures cosmetic products that do not harm animals as part of its mission. Here, The Body Shop has addressed a social issue – cruelty to animals – by relating it to its business strategy and reflecting it on its mission (Galbreath, 2009, p. 10).

Planning Resources: Resources are an important aspect of the strategy. It is important to plan the resources of the organization in a way that will increase organizational performance. In the integration of strategic CSR activities into the business, it is necessary to plan the tangible and intangible resources, assets, talents, and skills that will be required for such activities effectively and efficiently. Therefore, in the context of the CSR strategy, resource specificity should be provided for the resources that will be needed. Here, specificity is related to the degree of accessing the desired resources and using them at the desired time (Galbreath, 2009, p. 16-17).

Associating with the Market: For a CSR activity to become strategic, it must be carried out by establishing a relationship with the business's market and target market. Thanks to this relationship, the business can catch new product-market combinations in the future (Bhattacharyya et. al., 2008, p. 274). Analyzing target markets, identifying market segments, and developing products that will appeal to them are also related to CSR. Because when evaluating market segments strategically, a new variable must be taken into account, which is social dynamics and social expectations. Social dynamics refer to the underlying expectations of a particular market segment. This requires the ability to meet the hidden needs of customers in the market and to offer products and services that will bring them superior value Strategic CSR activities should be planned and implemented to serve this purpose. Businesses should embrace unmet social needs and social issues as a real opportunity for innovation, rather than seeing them as threats to be underestimated or factors they can ignore. Here, it innovates by utilizing the knowledge gained from target markets, target customer needs, and unmet social needs and/or social problems that directly affect these markets and customers (Galbreath, 2009, p, 13-16). Seeking innovative solutions for competitive advantage will mediate innovation (Sousa, et. al., 2010, p. 297-298). In other words, social problems should be evaluated as business opportunities, and competitive advantage should be sought by associating them with market problems (Bhattacharyya et. al., 2008, p. 273).

Prioritizing Stakeholders: Managing stakeholder relations effectively leads to a competitive advantage that is difficult to imitate. Businesses that develop relationships based on honesty, mutual trust, and cooperation with stakeholders argue that they are in a better position to gain an advantage than businesses that do not. This is because it takes time to develop trust and cooperation among stakeholders, leading to mutually beneficial exchanges of value (Galbreath, 2009; Jamali, 2007).

The stakeholder relations of the business constitute the network of relations related to the field of activity. Therefore, Strategic CSR activities should also be closely related to stakeholders (Bhattacharyya et. al., 2008, p. 268). Given the wide range of stakeholders of businesses, it is important to identify the relevant and important stakeholders of a business. When determining this, critical factors such as the power, legitimacy, and urgency of the stakeholders should be considered. When a business carries out a CSR activity related to a stakeholder that it considers as a priority, this CSR activity must meet the needs and wishes of the relevant stakeholder. If this is insufficient, stakeholder dissatisfaction ensues. The more strategic CSR activities are integrated into the corporate strategies and plans of the business, the more the demands of the stakeholders can be met. For this reason, business managers or leaders should identify the most important stakeholder groups of the business before carrying out strategic CSR activities and focus on the responsibilities that stand out for them (Bhattacharyya et. al., 2008, p. 269).

Realizing Collaborations: Effective realization of CSR strategies may sometimes require the coming together of different stakeholder groups and different talents. Partnerships may be required to effectively manage these activities and to carry out large-scale responsibilities associated with the business's strategy. Because no one can be enough alone for big social issues like AIDS or global warming. Partnerships between businesses or with non-governmental organizations can also be effective in terms of sharing risks, branding, and gaining prestige in such responsibilities (McElhaney, 2009, p. 39).

Determining Performance Indicators: Strategic CSR also needs to be integrated into performance systems. Therefore, clear performance indicators should be developed to obtain CSR measures. CSR performance metrics include reputation improvement, market growth, brand perception, employee engagement, increased sales, etc. dimensions can be considered. . If there are no effective performance measures, there will be no way to prove that the strategy is effective, which will jeopardize the long-term sustainability of the strategy (McElhaney, 2009, p. 37).

The adoption of the important steps briefly highlighted in this section by managers and leaders is important for businesses to integrate strategic CSR activities into the business and manage these activities effectively. In a study investigating the obstacles to the successful implementation of Strategic Corporate Social responsibilities, remarkable results were found in parallel with the steps highlighted in this section (Yuen & Lim, 2016). According to the research, the barriers to the integration of Strategic CSR activities in the maritime sector are as follows:

- *Lack of Resources:* Lack of resources, including finance, human capital, knowledge, and expertise, are a common barrier to CSR implementation.
- *Lack of Strategic Vision:* Lack of strategic vision is often attributed to a lack of commitment from top management. CSR needs to be directed, formalized, and promoted from the top of the organizational chart. One way to express commitment to CSR is to incorporate it into a company's mission, vision, goals, and objectives. Failure to do so stands as a barrier to CSR integration.

- *Lack of Performance Indicators:* Measurement systems are required to measure the benefits of implementing CSR. However, CSR is a fuzzy terminology and different meanings are attributed by the managers. It is often used interchangeably with concepts related to sustainability, corporate governance, business ethics, and corporate citizenship. As a result, differing views on CSR may present difficulties for managers in deriving concrete management actions on the implementation of CSR. Currently, there are limited social and environmental measurement indicators. The lack of development of measurement parameters to understand the effects of CSR activities on the business is an obstacle to the understanding and application of this concept.
- *The Low Willingness of Customers Towards CSR Activities*: Accordingly, shipping companies in the maritime sector are not rewarded appropriately and adequately as a result of CSR activities. Although there is no willingness to pay extra for the result of CSR activities in the sector, it is stated that there may be penalties in case of lack of these activities. The existence of this complexity, the fact that businesses that perform Strategy CSR activities are not rewarded enough stand as a barrier to the adoption and implementation of these practices.

SOLUTIONS AND RECOMMENDATIONS

This research has been tried to explain what strategic corporate social responsibilities are and how the relationship with the business strategy can be integrated into the business. According to the results of the research, the fact that strategic corporate social responsibilities gain a truly strategic meaning and serve the interests of the business while benefiting the society, on the one hand, depends on various critical factors. The realization of these factors is closely related to business managers, leaders, and strategies. Various suggestions can be made to these critical actors for the sustainability of the business. First, strategic corporate social responsibilities are closely related to the corporate and competitive strategies of the business. Due to this relationship, corporate social responsibilities that are formed by chance should not be realized, and activities that will contribute to the basic strategies of the business should be directed. It is seen that strategic CSR activities are closely related to senior management. Therefore, the commitments adopted by them towards these activities should be made and found by the top management in the organizational chart just like other strategic activities. At the same time, these activities should be reflected in the vision-mission and values of the business. Resource planning should be done so that these activities can be effectively managed at the targeted times. For these activities to make a strategic difference, it is necessary to associate them with the market, as well as to determine the priority stakeholders of the business and to gain reputation in these areas. In addition, the realization of strategic KSS activities on a large scale may require strategic cooperation. In such cases, cooperation with reputable institutions and businesses should be supported. Effective performance indicators should be determined to understand the effects and results of all these activities. To successfully monitor this process, units for strategic corporate social responsibilities should be established in the business. In summary, these activities should be directed with a strategic approach and the competitive advantages that can be gained as a result and the value to be created should be realized. The benefits that will emerge under these conditions will provide competitive advantages for businesses that are difficult to imitate.

FUTURE RESEARCH DIRECTIONS

Strategic CSR is as important for researchers as it is for the business world, and it attracts more and more attention day by day. Although the roots of the concept of social responsibility are very old, Strategic Corporate Social responsibilities still have an area that is up-to-date and needs improvement. The extent to which businesses are aware of this concept, how they react to these activities, whether CSR can be applied strategically, and how it is integrated into the business are among the topics worth investigating. There is also a lack of effective measurement indicators for understanding and analyzing the results of these activities. For this reason, it is recommended to develop performance measurement indicators that reveal the effects and results of Strategic CSR.

CONCLUSION

As emphasized in this study, Strategic CSR is associated with carrying out activities to improve society, not only to improve society but also considering the interests of the business. The most basic point that distinguishes this behavior from traditional corporate social responsibilities is to invest in the areas that are thought to be most beneficial to the business, not in a random way, but the realization of the company's main goals and strategies. This choice points to the relationship with strategic management. According to the strategic management approach, if corporate social responsibilities can be applied in a way that provides a competitive advantage to the business, it emerges as a value that is difficult to imitate and contributes to sustainability. The emergence of this value is related to balancing stakeholder relations, associating social responsibilities with corporate and competitive strategies of the business, creating relational benefits for customers, managing stakeholder relations-resource dependencies and transaction costs, and also qualifying these activities as an organizational learning process. These relationships, on the other hand, make corporate social responsibilities a strategic tool for the business, differentiate them from their competitors, create cost leadership opportunities for them or contribute to their corporate sustainability by obtaining new product-market opportunities. Achieving this contribution is possible through the successful integration of strategic corporate social responsibilities into the business. Ensuring this integration will provide the business with gains in both financial and reputation management, thus providing competitive advantages that are difficult to imitate for the business. These advantages will create a unique value that contributes to the sustainability of both the business and the society.

REFERENCES

Balıkçıoğlu, B., & Karacaoğlu, K. (2007). Sosyal Bir Ürün Olarak Topluma Pazarlanan Hayırseverlik: Stratejik Hayırseverlik [Philanthropy that Is Marketed to Society as A Social Product: Strategic Philanthropy]. *Gazi Üniversitesi İktisadi ve İdari Bilimler Fakültesi Dergisi*, *9*(2), 121–141.

Barba-Sánchez, V., & Atienza-Sahuquillo, C. (2010). Integration of the environment in managerial strategy: Application of the resource-based theory of competitive advantage, dynamic capabilities, and corporate social responsibilities. *African Journal of Business Management*, *4*(6), 1155–1165.

Belu, C., & Manescu, C. (2013). Strategic corporate social responsibility and economic performance. *Applied Economics*, *45*(19), 2751–2764. doi:10.1080/00036846.2012.676734

Bhattacharyya, S. S. (2010). Exploring the concept of strategic corporate social responsibility for an integrated perspective. *European Business Review, 22*(1), 82–101. doi:10.1108/09555341011009025

Bhattacharyya, S. S., Sahay, A., Arora, A. P., & Chaturvedi, A. (2008). *A toolkit for designing firm-level strategic corporate social responsibility (CSR) initiatives.* Social Responsibility. doi:10.1108/17471110810892802

Carroll, A. B. (1991). The pyramid of corporate social responsibility: Toward the moral management of organizational stakeholders. *Business Horizons, 34*(4), 39–48. doi:10.1016/0007-6813(91)90005-G

Galbreath, J. (2009). Building corporate social responsibility into strategy. *European Business Review, 21*(2), 109–127. doi:10.1108/09555340910940123

Gültekin, N. (2015). Sosyal Sorumluluk: Fedakarlık Mı? Stratejik Mi? [Evaluatıon Of Socıal Responsıblıty Applıcatıons Of Private Educatıon Instıtutıons]. *Ekonomi ve Yönetim Araştırmaları Dergisi, 4*(1), 10–30.

Gürol, Y., Büyükbalcı, P., Yasemin, B. A. L., & Berkin, E. (2010). Kurumsal Sosyal Sorumluluk Kavramı Ve Gelişmekte Olan Ülkelerde Konuya Bakış [Concept of Corporate Social Responsibility and a Perspective on the Issue in Abstract Develoiing Country Context]. *İstanbul Üniversitesi Siyasal Bilgiler Fakültesi Dergisi*, (43), 135-162.

Heslin, P. A., & Ochoa, J. D. (2008). Understanding and developing strategic corporate social responsibility. *Organizational Dynamics, 37*(2), 125–144. doi:10.1016/j.orgdyn.2008.02.002

Husted, B. W., & Allen, D. B. (2007). Strategic corporate social responsibility and value creation among large firms: Lessons from the Spanish experience. *Long Range Planning, 40*(6), 594–610. doi:10.1016/j.lrp.2007.07.001

Jamali, D. (2007). The case for strategic corporate social responsibility in developing countries. *Business and Society Review, 112*(1), 1–27. doi:10.1111/j.1467-8594.2007.00284.x

Kim, M., Kim, B., & Oh, S. (2018). Relational benefit on satisfaction and durability in strategic corporate social responsibility. *Sustainability, 10*(4), 1104. doi:10.3390u10041104

Kurucz, E. C., Colbert, B. A., & Wheeler, D. (2008). The business case for corporate social responsibility. The Oxford handbook of corporate social responsibility, 83-112.

Lantos, G. P. (2001). The boundaries of strategic corporate social responsibility. *Journal of Consumer Marketing, 18*(7), 595–632. doi:10.1108/07363760110410281

Manasakis, C., Mitrokostas, E., & Petrakis, E. (2014). Strategic corporate social responsibility activities and corporate governance in imperfectly competitive markets. *Managerial and Decision Economics, 35*(7), 460–473. doi:10.1002/mde.2635

McElhaney, K. (2009). A strategic approach to corporate social responsibility. *Leader to Leader, 52*(1), 30–36. doi:10.1002/ltl.327

McWilliams, A., Siegel, D. S., & Wright, P. M. (2006). Corporate social responsibility: Strategic implications. *Journal of Management Studies, 43*(1), 1–18. doi:10.1111/j.1467-6486.2006.00580.x

Michelon, G., Boesso, G., & Kumar, K. (2013). Examining the link between strategic corporate social responsibility and company performance: An analysis of the best corporate citizens. *Corporate Social Responsibility and Environmental Management*, *20*(2), 81–94. doi:10.1002/csr.1278

Orlitzky, M., Siegel, D. S., & Waldman, D. A. (2011). Strategic corporate social responsibility and environmental sustainability. *Business & Society*, *50*(1), 6–27. doi:10.1177/0007650310394323

Pollach, I. (2015). Strategic corporate social responsibility: The struggle for legitimacy and reputation. *International Journal of Business Governance and Ethics*, *10*(1), 57–75. doi:10.1504/IJBGE.2015.068685

Porter, M. E., & Kramer, M. R. (2006). The link between competitive advantage and corporate social responsibility. *Harvard Business Review*, *84*(12), 78–92. PMID:17183795

Sert, N. Y. (2012). Benefit Perception About the Understanding of Corporate Social Responsibility in Private Sector in Turkey: Using Web Sites for Announcing of Corporate Social Responsibility Activities. AJIT-e. *Bilişim Teknolojileri Online Dergisi*, *3*(9), 31–50.

Siegel, D. S., & Vitaliano, D. F. (2007). An empirical analysis of the strategic use of corporate social responsibility. *Journal of Economics & Management Strategy*, *16*(3), 773–792. doi:10.1111/j.1530-9134.2007.00157.x

Sousa Filho, J. M. D., Wanderley, L. S. O., Gómez, C. P., & Farache, F. (2010). Strategic corporate social responsibility management for competitive advantage. *BAR - Brazilian Administration Review*, *7*(3), 294–309. doi:10.1590/S1807-76922010000300006

Yönet, E. (2005). Kurumsal Sosyal Sorumluluk Anlayışında Son Dönemeç: Stratejik Sorumluluk [The Last Turn Of Corporate Socıal Responsıbılıty: Strategıc Responsibility]. *Balıkesir Üniversitesi Sosyal Bilimler Enstitüsü Dergisi*, *8*(13), 239–264.

Yu, S. H., & Liang, W. C. (2020). Exploring the determinants of strategic Corporate social responsibility: An empirical examination. *Sustainability*, *12*(6), 2368. doi:10.3390u12062368

Yuen, K. F., & Lim, J. M. (2016). Barriers to the implementation of strategic corporate social responsibility in shipping. *The Asian Journal of Shipping and Logistics*, *32*(1), 49–57. doi:10.1016/j.ajsl.2016.03.006

ADDITIONAL READING

Afrin, S. (2013). Traditional vs. strategic corporate social responsibility: In pursuit of supporting sustainable development. *Journal of Economics and Sustainable Development*, *4*(20), 1–6.

Ansoff, H. I., Kipley, D., Lewis, A. O., Helm-Stevens, R., & Ansoff, R. (2018). *Implanting strategic management*. Springer.

Best, R., de Valence, G., & Langston, C. (2007). *Strategic management*. Routledge.

Jones, T. M. (1980). Corporate social responsibility revisited, redefined. *California Management Review*, *22*(3), 59–67. doi:10.2307/41164877

Lasserre, P. (2017). *Global strategic management*. Macmillan International Higher Education.

Matten, D., & Moon, J. (2004). Corporate social responsibility. *Journal of Business Ethics*, *54*(4), 323–337.

Rumelt, R. P., Schendel, D., & Teece, D. J. (1991). Strategic management and economics. *Strategic Management Journal*, *12*(S2), 5–29. doi:10.1002mj.4250121003

Sayekti, Y. (2015). Strategic corporate social responsibility (CSR), company financial performance, and earning response coefficient: Empirical evidence on Indonesian listed companies. *Procedia: Social and Behavioral Sciences*, *211*, 411–420. doi:10.1016/j.sbspro.2015.11.054

Werther, W. B. Jr, & Chandler, D. (2005). Strategic corporate social responsibility as global brand insurance. *Business Horizons*, *48*(4), 317–324. doi:10.1016/j.bushor.2004.11.009

Werther, W. B. Jr, & Chandler, D. (2010). Strategic corporate social responsibility: Stakeholders in a global environment. *Sage (Atlanta, Ga.)*.

KEY TERMS AND DEFINITIONS

Competitive Strategy: It is the position taken for profitability and sustainability, which contributes to the competitive advantage of the business against their competitors in the same sector.

Corporate Sustainability: It is a set of practices aimed at ensuring that social, environmental, and economic issues are carried out in a balanced manner in the management of the business's relations with its stakeholders, thus contributing to the access of the business to the resources it will need in the future.

Mission: A concept that expresses the main reason for the existence of an organization, its main purpose, and is related to today.

Reputation Management: It is the process related to how the business is perceived in the eyes of all its stakeholders, and the creation of the desired image and identity. By creating the impression of a reliable, transparent, responsible, and good organization, businesses make reputation management.

Stakeholder Theory: The theory based on the belief that there are various stakeholder groups in which businesses are in an open system, that they affect and are affected by, that these groups have various expectations and that these expectations will be managed in a balanced way to contribute to the sustainability of the business.

Strategic Corporate Social Responsibility: Social responsibility practices that are related to the business strategies of the business, aimed at the target market of the business and its primary stakeholders, creating value for both the business and the society.

Strategic Management: A collection of decisions and practices that will take the business to where it wants to be in the future, provide a competitive advantage to the business, enable the business to manage its relations with its environment as desired, and contribute to maximizing its profits.

Value Creation: What is important to the customers of the business is the outputs that differentiate the business from other businesses in the eyes of customers. Thanks to these outputs, which are the result of the routines, skills, and abilities of the organization, a value is created for the targeted group.

Vision: The position that the business wants to be in the future, imagined and expressed as more successful and attractive than today.

Chapter 8
Innovation as a Management Question:
Can Innovation Be Managed?

Haneen Abdallah Allataifeh
https://orcid.org/0000-0001-5737-9507
University of Malaya, Malaysia

Sedigheh Moghavvemi
University of Malaya, Malaysia

ABSTRACT

Whilst the need for innovation is imperative, it is not clear how to manage its process. This is due to the lack of consensus on what an innovation process should look like, variations in the contexts at which innovation is examined, as well as the variations in the means of developing those models. The challenge in managing innovation mainly revolves around the stages of search, selection, and implementation. Issues emerge when organizations develop "routines" for these activities and when these core routines become core rigidities that are embedded and built up into structures, processes, and policies. Hence, we have to deal with a dynamic context by reviewing routines and editing, adding, and adapting to them. Despite the need to formalize and routinize the innovation process, the dynamic environment surrounding innovation should not be kept out of the innovation equation. This chapter sheds light on what is called contextual innovation management and the need to adopt an agile approach in managing innovation.

INTRODUCTION

The topic of innovation management has been progressively addressed in management literature. The question that the literature debated for a long time is: Can innovation be managed? (Tidd & Bessant, 2018). Innovation is a universal activity linked to growth and survival, and is understood as a process. This understanding shapes the way by which innovation can be managed. The innovation underlying process is seen to be common to all organizations. At the process core, certain activities and stages

DOI: 10.4018/978-1-7998-9590-9.ch008

exist (Cohn, 2013). The challenge that any organization faces is finding proper ways of managing the innovation process to provide good solutions to the renewal problem. Different conditions may lead to different solutions. Despite these variations, the main pattern of innovation as stages and phases remains the same (Tidd & Bessant, 2018).

It may appear that innovation cannot be managed due to its complicated, uncertain, and apparently random process. Issues exist in developing and polishing new knowledge, adapting and integrating it to new products/processes, supporting and diffusing the innovation, and gaining market acceptance and sustainability. Thus, the innovation process represents the place where, if anything can go wrong, there's a very good chance that it will (Fagerberg et al., 2012; Rafols et al., 2012). Scholarly research in innovation over the years shows that, despite technical challenges, the majority of innovations fail because of weaknesses in the way the process is managed. Success in innovation appears to depend on two key elements: Technical resources (e.g., knowledge, human resources, and financial resources) as well as the capabilities the company possesses to manage these resources (Tidd & Bessant, 2018).

Several scholars emphasize that innovation management is a learned capability. They believe that an "underlying pattern of success" can be found for innovation. Although the failure rate of innovation is not low, some innovation succeeds. Some companies seem to have learned how to manage and respond to innovation in a successful way. This means that a successful pattern of innovation management can improve chances of success (O'Reilly et al., 2019; Oliva & Kotabe, 2019). Although innovation will remain unpredictable and complex, finding a proper management pattern for its process will create favorable conditions under which companies can successfully find solutions for multiple challenges. Therefore, innovation is a management question (Tidd & Bessant, 2018).

Creating a pattern for innovation management activities brings up the concept of routine. Organizations create a specific pattern of behavior that becomes "the way we do things around here" as an outcome of reinforcement and repetition. These patterns become part of the organizational culture. This routine depends on the learning capability of the organization and emerges due to continuous experiments and accumulated experience around what seems to work well (Tidd & Bessant, 2018). Thus, successful innovation management is fundamentally about creating, enforcing, and improving effective routines. Learning to do this comes from recognizing and understanding effective routines (whether developed in-house or observed in another enterprise) and facilitating their emergence across the organization (Tidd & Bessant, 2018).

How the innovation process should be managed depends on how an organization looks at innovation (Eveleens, 2010; Kotsemir et al., 2013). The first step in being able to manage innovation is to successfully influence the innovation process, which is extremely vital (Chenhall & Moers, 2015). This issue has been explored by empirical research at successful companies explaining how they manage innovation (Eveleens, 2010). Once an understanding on how the innovation process can be positively influenced, the next step is to make a best practice model. Then, this knowledge can be used in practice to actively manage the process (Meissner & Kotsemir, 2016). This management basically means to alter the factors to increase the quality and efficiency of the innovation process and to decrease the time it takes and the chance of failure. Good innovation research is therefore constantly moving from theory to practice and back to theory. Innovation models described in literature are based on empirical research or theory (Langendahl et al., 2016). This chapter aims at analyzing innovation management models, and investigating if an innovation management process can/should be framed in a model of defined steps and practices. It also shed lights on, what is called, contextual innovation management and the need to adopt an agile approach in managing innovation.

INNOVATION PROCESS MANAGEMENT

Innovation management is a topic that has been progressively covered in the management literature in the last thirty years. The reason for practitioner and academic interest is seemingly due to the imperative need of innovation to organizational growth and survival (Eveleens, 2010).

It is well-known that organizations with persistent success at managing innovation outpace their peers in in financial performance and growth (Tidd & Thuriaux-Alemán, 2016). Yet, innovation management is neither automatic nor easy. It demands knowledge and skills, and knowledge that goes beyond the standard management experience and toolkit. In addition, innovation management is not the simple application of management and business disciplines to innovation, rather it has advanced as a growing and distinct body of knowledge, practice, and experience (Tidd & Bessant, 2018).

Whilst the need for innovation is imperative, it is not clear how to manage its process (Seebode et al., 2012). According to Dankbaar (2003), innovation management can be defined as the process of routinizing "what can only be partially routinized" (p. XI), and providing the needed environment and structure for creativity. Innovation literature has highlighted several frameworks for what can be called "best practice" innovation–a set of routines to organize, select, and implement stages of an innovation process. Key aspects include well-defined criteria and approaches to allocate resources and make decisions and stage gate platforms to review and validate these decisions (Seebode et al., 2012). This process of innovation management has evolved over time.

After the development of innovation concepts, innovation and innovation process models have started to evolve. Innovation models are recognized as a simplified representation of how innovation happens in reality. There is a wide variation among innovation process and innovation management models. This is due to the lack of consensus on what an innovation process should look like, variations in the contexts at which innovation is examined, as well as variations in the means of developing those models. For instance, a descriptive innovation model generated for companies of information and communication technologies8 will not be the same as an innovation model describing innovation in food and beverages industry (Eveleens, 2010). Although innovation process models vary widely, all models understand that innovation activities can be visualized and described in process models (Kotsemir et al., 2013). Over the years, the understanding of innovation processes has considerably changed. Two main innovation process approaches can be distinguished in literature, namely the innovation management approach and the innovation conceptual approach. The following two subsections describe these approaches.

Innovation Management Approach

This approach does not revolve around the innovation development in term of activities. Rather, it focuses on the emergence and development of strategies for innovation management under various political and socioeconomic conditions. Rothwell's (1994) five-generations model is considered as the most famous example of innovation management models (Figure 1). Rothwell distinguished five generations of innovation models and explained their evolutionary development and the underlying policy making, management strategy, and socioeconomic framework. While other major studies related to innovation management models evolution are available (e.g., Cagnazzo et al., 2008; Jacobs & Snijders, 2008; Niosi, 1999; Verloop & Wissema, 2004), Rothwell's model is one of the most comprehensive ones.

Figure 1. Generations of innovation management models

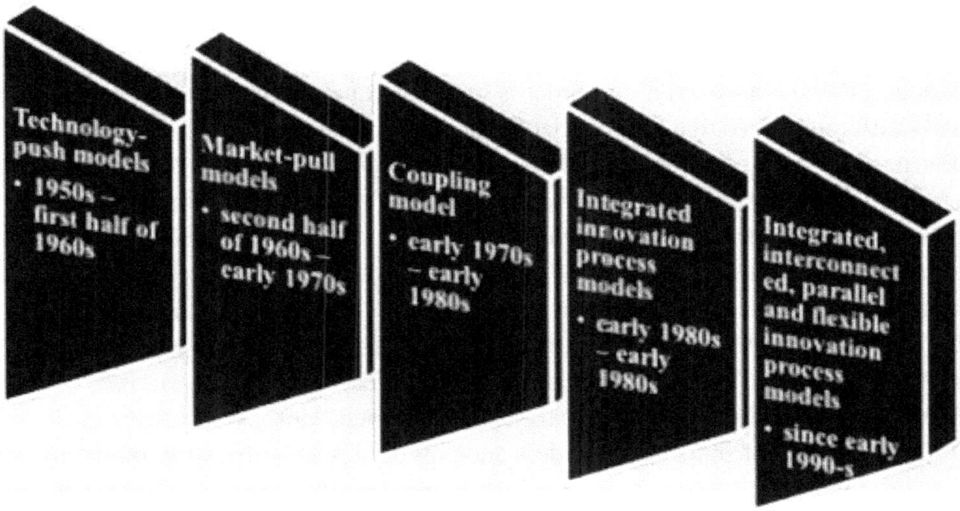

Technology push models represent the first generation of innovation management models. These models assume that the emergence of new industries stem from new technological opportunities. These technological opportunities led to the regeneration of old sectors via the implementation and diffusion of technology to improve production quality and productivity. This generation had enjoyed large employment opportunities, increased prosperity, and the booming of new electronic and automobile products. The logic behind the first-generation models was that the better the R&D as an input, the more success the products as an output (Kotsemir et al., 2013). These models assume a linear industrial innovation process, starting from scientific discovery, passing by the development of technological product, and ending with product commercialization. However, the transformation process in this generation of models became the object of study (Carter & Williams, 1958) and, later on, it formed the fundamental focus for the fifth-generation models along with the role of market in the transformation processes, based on which the innovation milieu models were built in the 2000s (Rothwell, 1994).

The second-generation models were developed in the late 1960s. They demonstrated that innovation as an outcome of R&D activities is aimed at creating value for the customers through satisfying their needs. Therefore, the "market-pull" models stressed how technologies take part in declaring growth of new markets and helped in balancing supply and demand in new product markets. This generation still assumes that existing technologies are the bases for new product development. Hence, innovation had been yet perceived as a linear process. Nevertheless, these models differ from the first-generation models in assuming that the identification of market needs comes first, before discovering technological opportunities (Kotsemir et al., 2013). The main drawbacks of this approach are the focus on the implementation of short-term R&D projects and the risk of being trapped in an exploitative type of innovation with limited capacity to develop and adapt to explorative innovation markets or technology (Hayes & Abernathy, 1980).

Third-generation models started with Mowery and Rosenberg (1979) revealing the significance of a company's functional interaction in the process of innovation. Thereafter, Rothwell et al. (1985) prolonged the linear innovation approach to link businesses with the market and research institutions in the so-called "coupling model." This model conjugated both first- and second-generation models and was grasped as an atypical and extreme innovation process model. The coupling model focused intensely on the interaction between market needs and technological capabilities within the company's framework. Rothwell et al. (1985) claimed that the process may be sequential but not continuous, as it consists of functionally different stages that are interdependent and interacting.

The fourth generation of models is the integrated process model. This generation considers innovation as a parallel chain linked process in which a company's functions are linked through feedback loops (Kline & Rosenberg, 1986). This generation witnessed enormous technology growth, new IT-based manufacturing equipment emergence, and shortening of product life cycles. During these years, companies started engaging in strategic alliances (Contractor & Lorange, 1988; Dodgson, 1993; Hagedoorn, 1990) and focusing on technological accumulation, core businesses, and key technologies (Waterman & Peters, 1982). These activities were accompanied with great networking activities of innovative small and medium enterprises (Docter & Stokman, 1987; Rothwell, 1991).

The fifth generation of innovation models adds on the fourth-generation model the strategic component, such as the integration of the cooperating companies, the growth information and communication technologies and networks utilization (Rothwell, 1992). This model possesses parallel, integrated, interconnected, and flexible characteristics of the innovation process. It was known that a company's successful innovation strategies were impelled by integrated and parallel development processes, early and strong vertical linkages, and the use of electronics-based design and information systems. Integrated innovation models are characterized by the strong existence of collaborative research, R&D joint ventures and R&D-based alliances. This led to improvements in innovation development efficiency and speed (Kotsemir et al., 2013).

The "sixth-generation" model appeared with the emergence of the open innovation paradigm (Chesbrough, 2006). This paradigm spots the light on the significance of knowledge inflows and outflows to speed up internal innovation and widen the market coverage for external innovation use, respectively. Open innovation presumes that companies should integrate external knowledge with internal knowledge, and internal paths with external paths to market (Chesbrough, 2006). Thus, innovations are no longer seen only as a process. Indeed, it can be described by the collective participation of different actors (e.g., suppliers, R&D facilities, and customers), in which different actors have different degrees of participation.

Innovation Conceptual Approach

This approach focuses on the conceptual core of models, and examines their theoretical backgrounds along with their pros and cons. The best possible example of conceptual models is Marinova and Phillimore's (2003) comprehensive analysis. The analysis of previous studies reveals that the majority of scholars focused on the historical development of one single type of innovation model, namely the national innovation system (Godin, 2009; Sharif, 2006) or the regional innovation system (Asheim et al., 2011; Iammarino, 2005). On the other hand, Marinova and Phillimore's (2003) comprehensive work involves the entire progress of innovation models since the earliest stages. Some scholars have analyzed innovation models by themselves, such as theoretical and conceptual constructs. Other scholars have analyzed the theoretical background for each generation of the models, the explanatory strength of the models, and the potential directions for future development of the models (Meissner & Kotsemir, 2016).

In the conceptual approach of innovation, Marinova and Phillimore (2003) identified six generations of innovation models (Figure 2).

Figure 2. Generations of innovation models

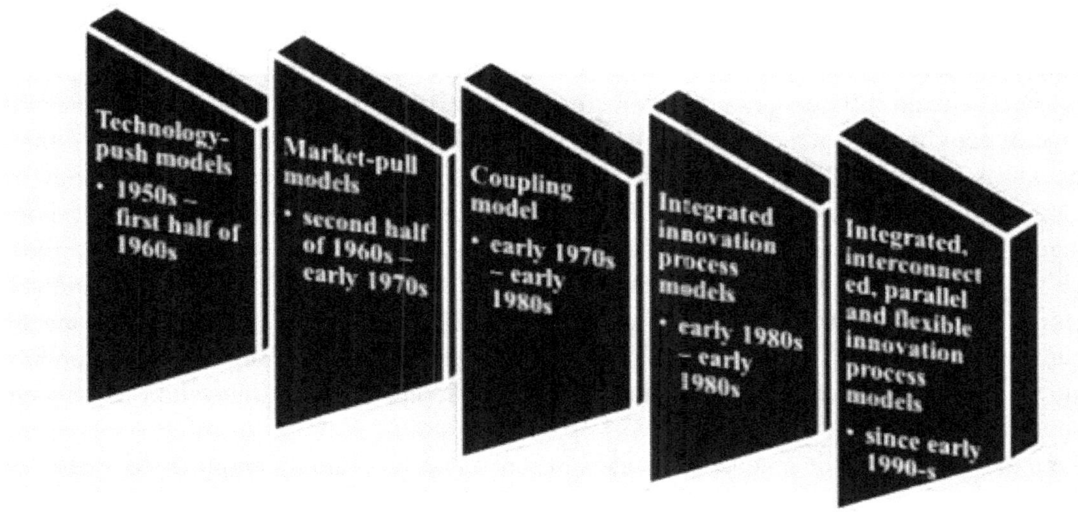

The black box innovation model stems from the Solow production function. Solow's (1957) model was the earliest attempt to incorporate technological progress within the economic equation. Innovation was presupposed to be an outcome of technological advances that drive economic growth. The black box model presumes that the process of innovation by itself is not important. Rather, it focuses on innovation inputs and outputs, such as financial investment in R&D as an input and new technological products as an output. It is debated that the utilization of timely adjusted and appropriate management activities is the only determinant for success (Mansfield, 1995). Ultimately, this understanding drove researchers to examine the relation between technology, industrial development, and science. This resulted in the reliance of policymakers on market to support technological developments. In this generation, innovation held narrower comprehension that was exclusively limited to R&D. Thus, there was a need to unlock the black box to internally investigate it (Kotsemir et al., 2013).

The linear innovation models emerged for the purpose of unlocking the innovation black box, bringing into focus certain processes that can develop new technologies and stimulate learning. It was foreseen that innovations pave the road to new policies formulation, that could encourage R&D leading to new product development via the use of sequential process, such as step-by-step activities that result in technologies adoption by markets. This was seen in three main models: The science push model, the technology push model, and the need pull model. The science push model postulates that technological advancement is an outcome of science-based discoveries (Kotsemir et al., 2013). This advancement leads to diffusion of new products/processes to the market (Rothwell et al., 1985). The technology push model assumes that the entrepreneur is the important actor who takes risk and gets over challenges to gain the monopolistic advantages of the introduction of new ideas. The need pull model is a market-driven model that emphasizes that existing demand is the only driver of innovation (Rothwell et al., 1985). The linear models are clear and simple representation of innovation that has set the direction for further innovation research advancement (Meissner & Kotsemir, 2016).

The third-generation interactive models are based on the main cons of antecedent models. Previous models excessively simplified the complex interactions between technology, science, and market. This generation models were perceived to give a profounder comprehension and a deeper description of all the actors and features of the innovation process. They also provide a new understanding of innovation; they view it as a process that is subcategorized into separate yet interacting stages (Kotsemir et al., 2013). The main differentiation of interactive models is the assumption that innovation is not the outcome of activities anymore; instead, innovation can also happen at different positions through the process (Kotsemir et al., 2013). The nature of this process is no longer linear and sequential, rather it is iterative and circular (Rothwell et al., 1985). The interactive models combined both technology push and market pull approaches in a comprehensive model. By doing so, a more nuanced and complete approach was developed, solving the issue of the actors and factors engaged in innovation. Nonetheless, the interactive models failed to identify the driving forces for innovation, the factors underlying different companies' performances, learning strategies of companies, and the role of the external environment in innovation success. Due to these weaknesses, the next generation of innovation models emerged (Kotsemir et al., 2013).

The fourth generation of innovation models explains that innovation complexity demands interactions between different agents within the company as well as cooperation amongst different companies. This generation approach is distinct in its examination of innovation from a system perspective, which emphasizes on interconnectedness, interactions, and synergies. It suggests that companies who do not hold enough resources to develop innovation can take advantage from forming a network relationship with other companies and organizations (Kotsemir et al., 2013). The main factors for this network success are the innovation systems and their interconnectedness and means of interaction. The most famous innovation system model was the innovation national system (Freeman, 1991; Nelson, 1993).

The system models explained the small company's role in innovation, the ways small companies can survive the competition and pressures from larger companies, the synergetic effects of innovation networks, variations among nations and role of governments. Further, the system models pointed out specific patterns of technological, scientific, and industrial specialization, as well as learning patterns for various countries (Kotsemir et al., 2013). These features were described in concepts of innovation chains for manufacturer-distributor relationships (Dodgson, 1993), innovation complexes for the integration of companies (Gann, 2000), strategic networks/alliances for long-term strategic contracts between companies and third parties from external environment (Sako, 1992), regional networks with a focus on geographic location of innovators (Dodgson, 1993) and regional systems of innovation on the influence of specific regional environment on the modes of innovation processes (Braczyk, Cooke, Heidenreich, & Krauss, 1998). The system models have been broadly used to describe the innovation process. However, this approach has certain drawbacks. For instance, it does not consider the lifetime of innovation networks, the potential of networks for innovation promotion in large companies, the meaning and mechanism of building trust in the innovation network, ways of achieving concurrent competition and cooperation, and the role of regulatory environments and governments in establishing convenient conditions for such interactions (Kotsemir et al., 2013).

The evolutionary models are the fifth generation of innovation conceptual approaches. This approach emerged to overcome the main drawbacks of previous approaches that were recognized as failures in neoclassical economics to deal with dynamic qualitative changes and weak explanatory power of the mechanical metaphor adopted in orthodox economic thinking for innovation dynamics. These models pay special attention to the external environment surrounding innovation and technological development (e.g., market structures, patent regimes, natural environment, and standards and regulations). Evolutionary models argue that the concept of innovation involves change (Kotsemir et al., 2013). Although innovation decisions are partially dependent on price consideration, the most essential condition for change is imperfections. Evolutionary models also assume that innovation outcomes are largely determined by the evolutionary process, and this process is just as significant as the R&D outcomes. Also, evolutionary models suggest that companies can be self-organized dynamic systems (Dosi & Orsenigo, 1994). Evolutionary models help explain the problem of "bounded rationality." It examines the processes of failure of generally fit technologies and the success of "overlooked" technologies (Tisdell, 1995), and sheds light on the value of diversity (Dowrick, 1995). Generally, these models highlight the schemes of decision-making and the modes of participants' interaction during innovation processes. Concepts such as technological imperatives (Rosenberg, 1976), innovation avenues (Sahal, 1981), technological trajectories (Biondi & Galli, 1992), technological paradigms (Dosi & Orsenigo, 1994), and technoeconomic paradigms (Freeman, 1991) are associated with the evolutionary models. These concepts mutually claim that communication between key actors and adaptive capability are key elements to gain regulating stability in the innovation process. These models trigger further advancement in research, as they accentuate the urge to explain the supporting mechanisms for the continuousness of old models and the introduction of new balance in modeled innovation processes. These models also accentuate the urge to describe the turning points in the innovation process within the framework of the evolutionary models (Meissner & Kotsemir, 2016).

The last approach is the innovation milieu models. This approach stresses on innovation regional clusters, high-tech development, and the role that geographical location plays in generating knowledge (Keeble & Wilkinson, 2017). Territorial organization plays a crucial role in the innovation process. Innovation is identified as being geographically localized, and innovation processes depend on specific resources that vary across different locations (Longhi & Keeble, 2017). Thus, the milieu model focuses on "active-territorial relationships" (e.g., the role of intercompany interactions in fostering innovation, various territorial socioeconomic factors, such as local private or public organizations, a certain culture and representation process, and a dynamic local collective learning process) (Camagni, 1991). The innovation milieu approach pays special attention to the success factors of small and medium enterprises, mechanisms through which particular regions bring on a considerable number of small innovative companies, and explains how various regions possess different paths and patterns in developing knowledge and transferring high technology. This pattern is prevailing in the innovation clusters approach that identifies groups of innovative companies located in one region, the learning regions approach, and the collective learning concept (Keeble & Wilkinson, 2017). The key argument of these models is learning. Indeed, these models stress that the core feature of any economy is learning. Accordingly, successful regions are characterized by providing certain combinations of organizations and institutions to support learning and knowledge development by local companies through conscious as well as unconscious mechanisms (Kotsemir et al., 2013).

In conclusion, all models of innovation process mutually stress on the essential role of innovation sources or triggers that have changed considerably in the theory of innovation processes. Yet, the understanding of the innovation process has deepened overtime. For instance, the understanding of innovation sources has changed, as well as the different stages/phases of the process have been redefined, ultimately. Moreover, the comprehension of the innovation process has moved from the linear sequential view into the integrated dynamic view. The individual phases have been seen to overlap and a backward feedback loop has been added to better describe the process. The literature points out that interactive models enrich research development regarding knowledge and technology transfer through the process of innovation development. All approaches of innovation models differentiate between the origins of the market phase. Based on this, the innovation process is expected to finish at the intersection between the product/process development cycle and the market cycle. The market cycle, on the other hand, is categorized into innovation diffusion and adoption. In the diffusion phase, an early communication of the innovation is understood, followed by the diffusion of innovation in the market. Diffusion includes both geographical and industrial or markets diffusion. Innovation adoption refers to the actual use of the product/process by end-users (Rogers, 1995). At this stage, innovation can be disregarded because of unfulfilled expectations, substitution technologies or other reasons linked to further use of the technology. In the early generations of innovation approaches, the source of innovation was viewed to be technological breakthroughs that will lead automatically to demand generation (technology push). The key attributes of this early generation of innovation models is the linear sequence view of innovation process that starts from research and ends in the market. Presently, the prevalent thinking of innovation is that it is the outcome of varied relationships of diversified actors, organizations, and entities in a paradigm of open innovation.

FORMAL INNOVATION PROCESS: THE DEBATE OF HINDER OR HELP

To date, all innovation management models assert the main role of innovation sources (triggers) and the meaning of these triggers, which have been considerably altered from one generation to another. Additionally, the understanding of the way the innovation process is developed has deepened over time, and the various stages of the process have been considerably redefined. Throughout the years, researchers have started to shift their understanding of innovation as a linear sequential process towards viewing it as an iterative process that consists of integrated and overlapping stages with backward loops. All innovation approaches differentiate among the origins of the market stage, whereby the innovation process is considered complete at the transition from the stage of development to the stage of marketing that is initiated with the first economic use of the developed product/service (Meissner & Kotsemir, 2016). The market stage is divided into innovation diffusion and innovation adoption. Diffusion includes distributing the innovation geographically within particular markets or industries (Organisation for Economic Cooperation and Development, 1997). Adoption includes the actual use of innovation by users (Rogers, 1995). Initially, innovation was widely viewed to be the outcome of technological breakthroughs that can automatically create demand. The essential character of these first-generation models is the presumed linear sequence of stages from research to marketing. Nowadays, innovation is predominantly viewed as the outcome of multiple interactions of various organizations and entities in an open environment (Meissner & Kotsemir, 2016).

The challenge of innovation management is mainly around the stages of search, selection, and implementation. Issues emerge when organizations develop "routines" for these activities, and when these core routines become core rigidities that are embedded and built up into structures, processes, and policies (Seebode et al., 2012). At this point, organizations tend to create selection environment and become associated with specific market and technological trajectories that effectively bound their routines. Hence, organizations start to favor established incumbents as they have already established within that environment and have created effective and well-rehearsed routines. However, this can also mean that organizations are unable of searching and exploring in new and alternative environments (i.e., lack the ability to "think outside the box"). Consequently, "core competencies" can turn to be "core rigidities" that hinder organizations from dealing with changing conditions. The issue is problematic since various degrees of novelty demand various solutions to the search, select or implement questions, and attempting to manage these simultaneously may create tensions across the corresponding organization (Seebode et al., 2012).

For instance, in the search stage, there is a long-standing debate in the innovation literature over exploration and exploitation innovation types. Both types are search behaviors; exploitation is mainly incremental, that is it relies on adaptive learning, whereas exploration is radical, and generative learning (Benner & Tushman, 2003). Similarly, the selection stage can be routinized in terms of decision criteria and rules and portfolio techniques. Under distributive conditions associated with the emergence of a new market or a radical technology, organizations with routinized selection activities face a major challenge when, for example, allocation rules for internal resource become unhelpful and can actively militate against placing bets on the new options since they are far outside the organization's "normal" framework (Seebode et al., 2012). Henderson and Clark (1990) argued that moving to new configurations with new knowledge arrangements and sets poses challenges for established incumbents. Thus, the questions is: Does having a formal innovation process hinder or help in managing innovation?

Having a formal innovation process model is under the debate of "help or hinder;" one research stream believes that formal processes increase the potential of innovation success, while the other stream suggests that it may limit innovation opportunities. The stream that opposes the effectiveness of formal innovation processes advocates that innovation approaches such as stage-gate are designed for steady and stable conditions and can be useless in innovation environment that is rapid changing and uncertain. In contrary, the stream that supports the effectiveness of formal processes contends that formal approaches tend to lower the risk of innovation and remove elements and ideas that are unlikely to possess market appeal (Peter & Colm, 2016). This argument consents with Bonner's (2005) and Cooper's (2001) propositions that formal processes are significant to coordinate and control innovation projects.

This argument is consistent with Cooper's (2001) and Bonner's (2005) contention that such processes are important for coordinating and controlling NPD innovation projects (Bonner, 2005; Cooper, 2001). Akroyd et al.'s (2009) work implied that the main imperative in managing innovation is to scale down uncertainty to a state where conventional management approaches are convenient, or to a point where it becomes obvious that the project must be abandoned. Hence, formal innovation management processes are able to help achieve this (Akroyd et al., 2009).

However, organizations that adopt a formal innovation management approach are challenged with the need to tailor innovation processes to contextual factors, such as organization size, resources, growth objectives, and competitive context. In general, while the adoption of formal innovation processes might not secure benefits in regard to revenue, a formal management approach is a significant step to develop an innovation capability. A formal innovation process can correlate with innovation best practices in larger organizations, such as having R&D budgets, innovation strategies, and cross-functional teams. For this main reason, organizations may consider it fruitful to put in place a dedicated formal process that facilitates innovation (Peter & Colm, 2016). Yet, the theory of innovation capability argues that organizations have to deal with a dynamic context by reviewing routines and editing, adding, and adapting to them. Hence, despite the need to formalize and routinize the innovation process, the dynamic environment surrounding innovation should not be kept out of the innovation equation (Seebode et al., 2012).

CONTEXTUAL INNOVATION MANAGEMENT

Different innovation process models have been developed to help organizations manage their innovation activities with suitable measurement tools and techniques. Originally, innovation process models, such as the stage gated model, can facilitate the management of innovation projects; yet, they are unable of providing a comprehensive strategic look at innovation throughout the organization and its surrounding environment (Cohn, 2013).

Many researchers have indicated their dissatisfaction with one-size-fits-all approach of innovation management (Cohn, 2013; Salerno et al., 2015). For example, Shenhar (2001) asserted the nonexistence of a single approach that fits all the cases of project management. Studies suggested that several organizations adopt different models of innovation processes (Gomes & Salerno, 2010; Vohora et al., 2004). This indicates that other arrangements than "search-select-implement" are possible and may be desirable (Salerno et al., 2015).

The theoretical foundation for "one size does not fit all" has been acknowledged as the "contingency theory" (van der Duin et al., 2014). This theory indicates that an organization is required to adapt to particular factors, in order to be successful: "The essence of te contingency theory paradigm is that organizational effectiveness results from fitting characteristics of the organizations, such as its structure, to contingencies that reflect the situation of the organization" (Donaldson, 2001, p.1). In a contextual innovation management, various contingency variables can influence the innovation process, and various types of management approaches can be identified for different contexts (van der Duin et al., 2014).

There is an intense distinction between universalistic innovation approach and contextual innovation management. The universalistic innovation approach assumes the existence of one set of success factors that explains organizational success in all similar contexts. Several scholars have attempted to distinguish the success factors that justify why some organizations are more successful than others. Based on these identified success factors, one generic model of innovation process has been proposed. In contextual innovation management, the context is interpreted in terms of several contextual factors that influence the organization and its innovation management. These contextual factors have been extensively studied, yielding various factors, such as the nature of innovation, the pattern of technological change, the nature of market, the level of complexity and uncertainty, and culture (van der Duin et al., 2014).

Innovations vary along at least five contextual factors: Type of innovation and its degree of novelty, size and type of the innovative organization, and the sector/ environment in which the innovation is pursued. The main categorization of contextual factors can be stated as follows:

- **Type of Innovation:** Research shows that different management approaches are needed for different types of innovations (van der Duin et al., 2014). Several authors differentiate between product innovation, process innovation, and service innovation. Tidd and Bessant (2018) consider four general classifications of innovation: Product innovation (changes in the products/services that a company offers); process innovation (changes in the approach in which these products/services are developed and delivered); position innovation (changes in the context in which the products/services are introduced); paradigm innovation (changes in the implicit mental models in which the company frame what it does).
- **Innovation Degree of Newness:** Innovation runs from minor improvements toward radical changes that may change the way people perceive and use innovation. Some of these changes are normal, but some of them are too radical and can change the societal basis. More often, innovation

takes place in incremental fashion (exploitative innovation). Products are seldom disruptive or "new to the world." Thus, process innovation has primarily consisted of optimization (Eveleens, 2010).

- **The Innovative Organization Size:** Organizational size was found to impact the way innovation is carried out and developed. Management of innovation in small companies was found to be different compared to large companies (Albors-Garrigos et al., 2018).
- **Type of Organization:** A difference has been found between innovation in a private company and innovation that happens in public institutes. It is proposed that innovation management in public organizations is different to that in private companies, yet the comparison between both is not often made (Hartley, 2006). In addition, organizations running in the consumer market require different innovation approaches than those operating in the business market (Ortt & Smits, 2006).
- **Type of Industry:** Studies claim that innovation processes are managed differently in different industries. The stability and dynamism of the environment were found to determine the management style and the innovation novelty (Eveleens, 2010). For example, the pharmaceutical sector is highly regulated, hence innovation processes tend to be constrained by obligatory rules and regulations. Meanwhile, in the software sector, innovation processes are much more trial-and-error-based (van der Duin et al., 2014).
- **Type of Culture/Country:** Studies emphasized that different cultures have developed different innovation practices. Some of these differences are related to different cultural orientation (e.g., a collective vs. an individual orientation). Other variations are related to institutions and regulations (e.g., variations in intellectual property protection).

The categories of contextual factors are not independent. For example, in the gaming industry, most organizations are small in size, indicating the association between industrial type, innovation, and organization (van der Duin et al., 2014). Overall, there is a huge variation among innovations, and the way it should be managed depends on how people or organizations look at it. It is imperative to consider the contextual dimensions upon deciding the innovation management models and approaches, as they can explain what management approaches should be adopted in certain situations (Eveleens, 2010).

Considering contextual variables in managing innovation does not necessarily means coming up with a unique innovation management model, different innovation process variants can be embraced in the well-known platform of a stage-gate innovation process. Such platform can be considered as a valuable tool in establishing a contextual innovation management practice, since it enables freedom to vary and allows a balance to be developed in terms of effectiveness and efficiency in innovation management (van der Duin et al., 2014).

The advantage of adopting a common innovation management platform is that deviations in the innovation process can be explicitly assessed and discussed. However, the challenge of adopting a platform approach in managing innovation is to develop a defined set of process variants that can fit the varying contexts (van der Duin et al., 2014).

In sum, the initial step in innovation management is to recognize and define the contextual dimensions that may influence the innovation process. Then, this knowledge can be employed to successfully manage the process. This management indicates the need to alter and tweak the process to improve the quality, boost the efficiency of the innovation process, and minimize the chances on failure (Eveleens, 2010). This calls for management agility, which is discussed in the following section.

INNOVATION MANAGEMENT: AGILE APPROACH

In the 2000s, the concept of agile organization emerged in harmony with the various evolutionary trends, such as collaborative vision, innovation, digital transformation, and data-based management. Agile organizations are those that are capable of continually adapt and adjust their strategic direction to create, generate, and maintain value, in a dynamic and highly uncertain environment (Oliva & Kotabe, 2019). Teece et al. (2016) defined the agile organization as an organization that is able to redirect and reimplement its resources in an effective and efficient way to capture, protect, and create value under uncertain external and internal circumstances.

Organizations that have survived over time and have stayed active are those that developed a vision, mission, and formalized values in the past, and were able to reinvent themselves to meet the business demands and generate value to their stakeholders. Therefore, organizations that develop the capability to adapt to changes in the business environment are those that beat the competition and win customers (Porter & Kramer, 2011). In a dynamic and highly uncertain environment, organizations are required to develop differentiated capabilities to properly interpret changes, instantly plan and establish suitable strategies, allocate the needed resources to meet opportunities, and constantly control the process, generally expediating the cycle of planning, organizing, executing, and controlling (Oliva & Kotabe, 2019). Generally, organizations operating in different domestic and international markets are exposed to different changes triggered by legal, economic, technological, social, and political forces. Many of these forces can have divergent or convergent direction and intensity, and agile organizations need to develop their capabilities to recognize changes and modify their processes to meet the peculiar demands of various business environments (Contractor et al., 2016; Gaur et al., 2014). Thus, the Teece et al.'s (1997) dynamic capability theory is helpful as it indicates organizational ability to build, integrate, and reconfigure external and internal expertise to rapidly address changes in the surrounding environment.

Overall, the agile organization is the one that reacts and acts rapidly by modifying its structure, strategies, products/services, processes, and controls in response of the dynamically changing business environment. Being so, the dynamic capability concept is linked to the aim of converting the organization into an agile one. Dynamic capabilities provide organizations with the ability to recognize opportunities in the business environment; the ability to adapt to meet new demands; and the ability to constantly develop tangible and intangible assets (Teece et al., 2016). In this context, startups can be considered as agile organizations with capabilities to take various risks, due to their inherently high risk-tolerance that reflects their innovation-driven objectives, structures, strategies, and design that can accomplish success or failure (Teberga et al., 2018). The knowledge management is one of the management practices that support the dynamic capabilities of agile organizations. The practice of acquiring, defining, storing, disseminating, assessing, and applying knowledge prepares organizations and triggers internal changes. Thus, organizations that have the ability to learn are the readiest ones to adapt to the requirements of business environment. Knowledge and continuous monitoring of the surrounding environment allow the organization to identify threats and opportunities. The ability to convert tacit and explicit knowledge potentializes the organization to alter its structure and processes. Similarly, managed knowledge allows the organization to boost internal innovation and to develop and transform tangible and intangible assets in response to the dynamic needs of the business environment (Natalicchio et al., 2017).

CONCLUSION

Most of the innovation challenges are not new, but the context is ever-changing. Current challenges are better met by reverting to the fundamental themes of innovation management, instead of reinventing frameworks and fads. In literature, there are different innovation management processes in regard to content and structure, and there are significant variations in scope among the studied projects. This reinforces the need for a contingent management perspective. This chapter argues that contextual management is necessary to successfully manage innovation processes. More specifically, contextual innovation management is about positioning innovation activities in a better order to meet changes in the environment. Thus, it contributes by reducing the risk of innovation and improving the efficiency of its processes. Overall, contextual innovation management leans toward contingency, rather than universalism. Hence, the concept of success factors in innovation literature tends to work in certain context and might not be applicable in others. Subsequently, the contingency perspective in innovation management contradicts the overly simplistic innovation approaches that the management literature often advocates.

In conclusion, no single innovation process can be successfully employed in all types of innovation projects. Instead, the literature offers a broad spectrum of innovation models that enable organizations to better manage various types of innovation projects. Each organization encounters different challenges upon innovating (e.g., different technologies, markets, and institutional environments). Accordingly, the innovation process tends to differ based on each organization's ecosystem. These variations impact the initiation and closure of each specific innovation process. Moreover, there are variations in the innovation processes in regard to the formality, which does not indicate that informality is related to the lack of process.

This chapter provided insights into how to correctly manage innovation processes. The authors concluded that innovation can be managed by following an innovation process model that defines and organizes the innovation activities and, at the same time, enables the organization to respond to different contextual variables that tend to influence the innovation process. The authors highlighted that there are rationales and processes to manage innovation, other than the traditional ones. This contributes to broadening the themes and focus of future research. This chapter focused on contingencies and agility; further investigations are needed in these areas to improve the systemic view of innovation processes that are connected to environments of dynamisms and uncertainties.

REFERENCES

Akroyd, C., Narayan, S., & Sridharan, V. (2009). The use of control systems in new product development innovation: advancing the 'help or hinder' debate. *ICFAI Journal of Knowledge Management, 7*(5-6), 70-90.

Albors-Garrigos, J., Igartua, J. I., & Peiro, A. (2018). Innovation management techniques and tools: Its impact on firm innovation performance. *International Journal of Innovation Management, 22*(06), 1850051. doi:10.1142/S1363919618500512

Asheim, B. T., Smith, H. L., & Oughton, C. (2011). Regional innovation systems: Theory, empirics and policy. *Regional Studies, 45*(7), 875–891. doi:10.1080/00343404.2011.596701

Benner, M. J., & Tushman, M. L. (2003). Exploitation, exploration, and process management: The productivity dilemma revisited. *Academy of Management Review*, *28*(2), 238–256. doi:10.5465/amr.2003.9416096

Biondi, L., & Galli, R. (1992). Technological trajectories. *Futures*, *24*(6), 580–592. doi:10.1016/0016-3287(92)90118-Y

Bonner, J. M. (2005). The influence of formal controls on customer interactivity in new product development. *Industrial Marketing Management*, *34*(1), 63–69. doi:10.1016/j.indmarman.2004.07.004

Braczyk, H.-J., Cooke, P. N., Heidenreich, M., & Krauss, G. (1998). *Regional innovation systems: the role of governances in a globalized world*. Psychology Press.

Cagnazzo, L., Taticchi, P., & Botarelli, M. (2008). A literature review on innovation management tools. *Revista de Administração da Universidade Federal de Santa Maria*, *1*(3), 316–330.

Camagni, R. (1991). *Innovation networks: spatial perspectives*. Belhaven-Pinter.

Carter, C. F., & Williams, B. R. (1958). *Investment in innovation*.

Chenhall, R. H., & Moers, F. (2015). The role of innovation in the evolution of management accounting and its integration into management control. *Accounting, Organizations and Society*, *47*, 1–13. doi:10.1016/j.aos.2015.10.002

Chesbrough, H. W. (2006). The era of open innovation. *Managing Innovation and Change, 127*(3), 34-41.

Cohn, S. (2013). A firm-level innovation management framework and assessment tool for increasing competitiveness. *Technology Innovation Management Review*, *3*(10), 6–15. doi:10.22215/timreview/731

Contractor, F., Yang, Y., & Gaur, A. S. (2016). Firm-specific intangible assets and subsidiary profitability: The moderating role of distance, ownership strategy and subsidiary experience. *Journal of World Business*, *51*(6), 950–964. doi:10.1016/j.jwb.2016.09.002

Contractor, F. J., & Lorange, P. (1988). Why should firms cooperate? The strategy and economics basis for cooperative ventures. *Cooperative Strategies in International Business, 1*, 3-30.

Cooper, R. (2001). *Winning at New Products; Accelerating the Process from Idea to Launch*. Perseus Books.

Dankbaar, B. (2003). *Innovation management in the knowledge economy* (Vol. 7). World Scientific. doi:10.1142/p288

Docter, J., & Stokman, C. (1987). *Innovation strategies of small industrial companies. In Innovation: Adaptation and Growth*. Elsevier.

Dodgson, M. (1993). Learning, trust, and technological collaboration. *Human Relations*, *46*(1), 77–95. doi:10.1177/001872679304600106

Donaldson, L. (2001). The contingency theory of organizations. *Sage (Atlanta, Ga.)*.

Dosi, G., & Orsenigo, L. (1994). Macrodynamics and microfoundations: an evolutionary perspective. Economics of Technology, 91-123.

Dowrick, S. (1995). *Economic approaches to innovation*. Edward Elgar Publishing.

Eveleens, C. (2010). Innovation management; a literature review of innovation process models and their implications. *Science*, *800*, 900–916.

Fagerberg, J., Fosaas, M., & Sapprasert, K. (2012). Innovation: Exploring the knowledge base. *Research Policy*, *41*(7), 1132–1153. doi:10.1016/j.respol.2012.03.008

Freeman, C. (1991). Networks of innovators: A synthesis of research issues. *Research Policy*, *20*(5), 499–514. doi:10.1016/0048-7333(91)90072-X

Gann, D. (2000). *Building innovation: complex constructs in a changing world*. Thomas Telford. doi:10.1680/bicciacw.25967

Gaur, A. S., Kumar, V., & Singh, D. (2014). Institutions, resources, and internationalization of emerging economy firms. *Journal of World Business*, *49*(1), 12–20. doi:10.1016/j.jwb.2013.04.002

Godin, B. (2009). National innovation system: The system approach in historical perspective. *Science, Technology & Human Values*, *34*(4), 476–501. doi:10.1177/0162243908329187

Gomes, L. A. V., & Salerno, M. S. (2010). Modelo que integra processo de desenvolvimento de produto e planejamento inicial de spin-offs acadêmicos. *Gestão & Produção*, *17*(2), 245–255. doi:10.1590/S0104-530X2010000200003

Hagedoorn, J. (1990). Organizational modes of inter-firm co-operation and technology transfer. *Technovation*, *10*(1), 17–30. doi:10.1016/0166-4972(90)90039-M

Hartley, D. (2006). Excellence and enjoyment: The logic of a 'contradiction'. *British Journal of Educational Studies*, *54*(1), 3–14. doi:10.1111/j.1467-8527.2005.00331.x

Hayes, R. H., & Abernathy, W. J. (1980). Managing our way to economic decline. Harvard Bus. Rev., 58(4).

Henderson, R. M., & Clark, K. B. (1990). Architectural innovation: The reconfiguration of existing product technologies and the failure of established firms. *Administrative Science Quarterly*, *35*(1), 9–30. doi:10.2307/2393549

Iammarino, S. (2005). An evolutionary integrated view of regional systems of innovation: Concepts, measures and historical perspectives. *European Planning Studies*, *13*(4), 497–519. doi:10.1080/09654310500107084

Jacobs, D., & Snijders, H. (2008). *Innovation routine: how managers can support repeated innovation*. Stichting Management Studies.

Keeble, D., & Wilkinson, F. (2017). *High-technology clusters, networking and collective learning in Europe*. Routledge. doi:10.4324/9781315188904

Kline, S. J., & Rosenberg, N. (1986). An overview of innovation. The positive sum strategy: Harnessing technology for economic growth. *The National Academy of Science, USA*, *35*, 36.

Kotsemir, M., Abroskin, A., & Meissner, D. (2013). *Innovation concepts and typology–an evolutionary discussion*. Higher School of Economics Research Paper No. WP BRP, 5.

Langendahl, P.-A., Cook, M., & Potter, S. (2016). Sustainable innovation journeys: Exploring the dynamics of firm practices as part of transitions to more sustainable food and farming. *Local Environment*, *21*(1), 105–123. doi:10.1080/13549839.2014.926869

Longhi, C., & Keeble, D. (2017). High-technology clusters and evolutionary trends in the 1990s. *High-technology clusters, networking and collective learning in Europe*, 21-56.

Mansfield, E. (1995). Innovation, technology and the economy. *Management Science*, *34*(10), 6.

Marinova, D., & Phillimore, J. (2003). Models of innovation. In S. L. Vautor (Eds.), The international handbook on innovation (pp. 44-53). Elsevier. doi:10.1016/B978-008044198-6/50005-X

Meissner, D., & Kotsemir, M. (2016). Conceptualizing the innovation process towards the 'active innovation paradigm'—Trends and outlook. *Journal of Innovation and Entrepreneurship*, *5*(1), 1–18. doi:10.118613731-016-0042-z

Mowery, D., & Rosenberg, N. (1979). The influence of market demand upon innovation: A critical review of some recent empirical studies. *Research Policy*, *8*(2), 102–153. doi:10.1016/0048-7333(79)900_9-2

Natalicchio, A., Ardito, L., Savino, T., & Albino, V. (2017). Managing knowledge assets for open innovation: A systematic literature review. *Journal of Knowledge Management*, *21*(6), 1362–1383. doi:10.1_08/JKM-11-2016-0516

Nelson, R. R. (1993). *National innovation systems: A comparative analysis*. Oxford University Press on Demand.

Niosi, J. (1999). Fourth-generation R&D: From linear models to flexible innovation. *Journal of Business Research*, *45*(2), 111–117. doi:10.1016/S0148-2963(97)00230-0

O'Reilly, N. M., Robbins, P., & Scanlan, J. (2019). Dynamic capabilities and the entrepreneurial university: A perspective on the knowledge transfer capabilities of universities. *Journal of Small Business and Entrepreneurship*, *31*(3), 243–263. doi:10.1080/08276331.2018.1490510

OECD. (1997). *Oslo manual—Guidelines for collecting and interpreting innovation data* (2nd ed.). OECD.

Oliva, F. L., & Kotabe, M. (2019). Barriers, practices, methods and knowledge management tools in startups. *Journal of Knowledge Management.*

Ortt, J. R., & Smits, R. (2006). Innovation management: Different approaches to cope with the same trends. *International Journal of Technology Management*, *34*(3-4), 296–318. doi:10.1504/IJTM.2006.009451

Peter, R., & Colm, O. G. (2016). Innovation processes: Do they help or hinder new product development outcomes in Irish SMEs? *Irish Journal of Management*, *35*(1), 104–107.

Porter, M. E., & Kramer, M. R. (2011). Creating shared value. *Harvard Business Review*.

Rafols, I., Leydesdorff, L., O'Hare, A., Nightingale, P., & Stirling, A. (2012). How journal rankings can suppress interdisciplinary research: A comparison between innovation studies and business & management. *Research Policy*, *41*(7), 1262–1282.

Rogers, E. M. (1995). Diffusion of Innovations: modifications of a model for telecommunications. In *Die diffusion von innovationen in der telekommunikation* (pp. 25–38). Springer. doi:10.1007/978-3-642-79868-9_2

Rosenberg, N. (1976). *Perspectives on technology*. CUP Archive. doi:10.1017/CBO9780511561313

Rothwell, G., Rothwell, R., & Zegveld, W. (1985). *Reindustrialization and technology*. ME Sharpe.

Rothwell, R. (1991). External networking and innovation in small and medium-sized manufacturing firms in Europe. *Technovation*, *11*(2), 93–112. doi:10.1016/0166-4972(91)90040-B

Rothwell, R. (1992). Developments towards the fifth generation model of innovation. *Technology Analysis and Strategic Management*, *4*(1), 73–75. doi:10.1080/09537329208524080

Rothwell, R. (1994). Towards the fifth-generation innovation process. *International Marketing Review*, *11*(1), 7–31. doi:10.1108/02651339410057491

Sahal, D. (1981). Alternative conceptions of technology. *Research Policy*, *10*(1), 2–24. doi:10.1016/0048-7333(81)90008-1

Sako, M. (1992). *Price, quality and trust: Inter-firm relations in Britain and Japan*. Cambridge University Press. doi:10.1017/CBO9780511520723

Salerno, M. S., de Vasconcelos Gomes, L. A., Da Silva, D. O., Bagno, R. B., & Freitas, S. L. T. U. (2015). Innovation processes: Which process for which project? *Technovation*, *35*, 59–70. doi:10.1016/j.technovation.2014.07.012

Seebode, D., Jeanrenaud, S., & Bessant, J. (2012). Managing innovation for sustainability. *R & D Management*, *42*(3), 195–206. doi:10.1111/j.1467-9310.2012.00678.x

Sharif, N. (2006). Emergence and development of the National Innovation Systems concept. *Research Policy*, *35*(5), 745–766. doi:10.1016/j.respol.2006.04.001

Shenhar, A. J. (2001). One size does not fit all projects: Exploring classical contingency domains. *Management Science*, *47*(3), 394–414. doi:10.1287/mnsc.47.3.394.9772

Solow, R. M. (1957). Technical change and the aggregate production function. *The Review of Economics and Statistics*, *39*(3), 312–320. doi:10.2307/1926047

Teberga, P. M. F., Oliva, F. L., & Kotabe, M. (2018). Risk analysis in introduction of new technologies by start-ups in the Brazilian market. *Management Decision*, *56*(1), 64–86. doi:10.1108/MD-04-2017-0337

Teece, D., Peteraf, M., & Leih, S. (2016). Dynamic capabilities and organizational agility: Risk, uncertainty, and strategy in the innovation economy. *California Management Review*, *58*(4), 13–35. doi:10.1525/cmr.2016.58.4.13

Teece, D. J., Pisano, G., & Shuen, A. (1997). Dynamic capabilities and strategic management. *Strategic Management Journal*, *18*(7), 509–533. doi:10.1002/(SICI)1097-0266(199708)18:7<509::AID-SMJ882>3.0.CO;2-Z

Tidd, J., & Bessant, J. (2018). Innovation management challenges: From fads to fundamentals. *International Journal of Innovation Management*, *22*(05), 1840007. doi:10.1142/S1363919618400078

Tidd, J., & Thuriaux-Alemán, B. (2016). Innovation management practices: Cross-sectorial adoption, variation, and effectiveness. *R & D Management*, *46*(S3), 1024–1043. doi:10.1111/radm.12199

Tisdell, E. J. (1995). *Creating inclusive adult learning environments: Insights from multicultural education and feminist pedagogy*. DIANE Publishing.

van der Duin, P. A., Ortt, J. R., & Aarts, W. T. (2014). Contextual Innovation Management Using a Stage-Gate Platform: The Case of P hilips S having and B eauty. *Journal of Product Innovation Management*, *31*(3), 489–500. doi:10.1111/jpim.12109

Verloop, J., & Wissema, J. G. (2004). *Insight in innovation: Managing innovation by understanding the laws of innovation*. Elsevier.

Vohora, A., Wright, M., & Lockett, A. (2004). Critical junctures in the development of university high-tech spinout companies. *Research Policy*, *33*(1), 147–175. doi:10.1016/S0048-7333(03)00107-0

Waterman, R. H., & Peters, T. J. (1982). *In search of excellence: Lessons from America's best run companies*. Harper & Row.

ADDITIONAL READING

Goller, I., & Bessant, J. (2017). *Creativity for innovation management*. Taylor & Francis. doi:10.4324/9781315630588

Maital, S., & Seshadri, D. V. R. (2012). *Innovation management: strategies, concepts and tools for growth and profit*. SAGE Publications India.

Shane, S. (Ed.). (2009). *The handbook of technology and innovation management*. John Wiley & Sons.

Brem, A., & Viardot, E. (2017). Revolution of innovation management: Internationalization and business models. In *Revolution of Innovation Management* (pp. 1–13). Palgrave Macmillan. doi:10.1057/978-1-349-95123-9_1

Allataifeh, H., & Moghavvemi, S. (2021). The Individual Dimension of Digital Innovation: The Altered Roles of Innovation Agents and Market Actors. *Sustainability*, *13*(16), 8971. doi:10.3390u13168971

Brem, A., & Viardot, E. (2017). Revolution of innovation management: Internationalization and business models. In *Revolution of Innovation Management* (pp. 1–13). Palgrave Macmillan. doi:10.1057/978-1-349-95123-9_1

KEY TERMS AND DEFINITIONS

Agile Innovation Management: Is the process of managing innovation by rapidly responding and adapting to the dynamic environment through modifying the organization's strategies, structure, products/services, processes, and controls.

Contextual Innovation Management: Is the practices and techniques of managing the successful implementation of the innovation process under the consideration of contextual factors that may influence the implementation process.

Innovation: Is the process of generating idea and converting it into a product/service that can add value to the relevant stakeholders.

Innovation Management: Is the practices and techniques that organizations pursue to ensure a successful implementation of the innovation process.

Innovation Process: Is the activities that an organization need to pursue to convert an innovative idea into a valuable product/service.

Chapter 9
Local Perspectives of Sustainable Urbanism:
Solutions Based on the Spanish Legislative Model

Maria Jesus Garcia Garcia
Open University, UK

ABSTRACT

The protective actions of restoration, especially when they affect urban spaces formally declared as areas of restoration, must have an urban reflection and be projected and reflected in the corresponding planning and management techniques. Planning legislation provides the instruments and the proper techniques to make urban planning adjusted to the parameters of the restoration performing actions that seek to promote the rational use of the natural and cultural resources, in particular the territory, the soil, and the urban and architectural heritage that are the support, the object, and the scene of the quality of life. Urban restoration as restoration of urban spaces requires urban treatment. Urban planning must not only deal with the growth and expansion of population centers, but also with the action on the interior of cities to adapt them to the new demands of higher quality of life in an urban context that allows the enjoyment of adequate housing with adequate spaces and equipment.

INTRODUCTION

After a few years of uncontrolled urban development, the public authorities seem once again interested in urban restoration policies. The urban planning model based on uncontrolled urban growth seems to have come to an end, more because of economic problems than because of the pernicious effects of all kinds that it has generated. In this cyclical alternation of public policies it seems that the time has come again to return to the virtues of urban restoration. However, it is not the first time that the public authorities show their interest in it. The successive housing plans that have been approved both at the regional and state levels have opted for restoration, financing and subsidizing actions in this regard, and during the nineties there were several local administrations that created restoration offices determined

DOI: 10.4018/978-1-7998-9590-9.ch009

to promote these actions. However, currently the interest in restoration is no longer limited only to the norms on development, of individual scope and little economic importance, but splashes the urban legislation, to propose a model of urban restoration with the participation of public powers, but also of the private sector to channel the activity of a sector that has been badly damaged as a result of the urban model of recent years. It is about turning urban restoration into a profitable urban activity. Restoration policies seem to be resurfacing not so much because of their virtues or because of their adaptation to constitutional objectives, as because of the exhaustion of an urban model of unsustainable development. From these premises, the following questions are analyzed.

The term restoration is synonymous with re-enabling or restoring to a property the conditions of use that it has lost. When we refer to urban restoration we are talking about a set of both public and private actions that fall on both the urbanized and built-up heritage of cities and that are aimed at restoring the conditions of use and utility to the properties or spaces (Kennedy C, Cuddihy J, Engel-Yan J, 2020). These are actions that are supported by the built heritage, mainly destined for a residential purpose, but also the urbanized heritage and the urban spaces deteriorated in their elements due to the passage of time, lacking the necessary public endowments, which have lost their original functionality and are in an advanced state of physical deterioration with the economic and social implications derived from these processes. Very fundamentally the spaces that are affected are the historic centers of the cities, although urban restoration is not sticks exclusively to this context, but manifests itself in t more general terms, such as a need to rehabilitate degraded urban spaces and to preserve the properties that should be the object of preservation. Urban restoration affects the deteriorated or degraded heritage of cities and tries to recover these elements, but it also has a broader purpose, to the extent that it is crossed by social and economic objectives. Thus, the restoration processes are intended to maintain the existing population in these areas, avoiding their eviction, and at the same time they intend to economically and functionally revitalize these spaces by implanting in them activities and services, public and commercial uses, etc. that are demanded by society and that they endow them with a new functionality. Thus, urban restoration is transcended by numerous economic, sociological, etc. factors that are articulated on the premise of the physical and material recovery of urban spaces and the elements that make them make up.

The Constitution links the right to decent housing and the right to an adequate environment with the regulation of land uses. But it also advocates the rational use of natural resources. Urban planning must be oriented towards restoration to comply with the constitutional precept, given that restoration does not consume land and allows to take advantage and use, reuse the existing heritage (Freytag T, Gössling S, Mössner S, 2019).

In short, and as established in the statement of reasons of state Law 7/2015, October 30th, which approves the revised text of the Land Law, seeks to promote the rational use of the natural and cultural resources, in particular the territory, the soil and the urban and architectural heritage that are the support, the object and the scene of the quality of life.

Likewise, the same legal text also states in its explanatory statement that "the urban land— the city already made-also has an environmental value, as a collective cultural creation that is the object of a permanent recreation, so its characteristics must be an expression of its nature and its management must favor its restoration and encourage its use".

All this shows an interest in the restoration of the consolidated urban fabric, for the city already made. Urban restoration as restoration of urban spaces requires urban treatment. Urban planning can not only deal with the growth and expansion of population centers, but also with the action on the interior of cities to adapt them to the new demands of higher quality of life in an urban context that allows the enjoyment of adequate housing with adequate spaces and equipment.

Recent legislation, both at the state and regional levels, has affected the treatment of restoration, establishing some provisions that tend to favor these actions. In addition to the techniques and instruments it makes available for restoration, it allows the resources obtained by the Administration derived from urban management to be used to finance these actions.

Thus, the Urbanism Law 7/2015, Octubre 30th, extends the purposes of the municipal land heritage (Webster C, Lai LWC, 2003), allowing the alienation of the land of the same to be used for restoration operations. This is evident in article 86 of this Law, which establishes that the income obtained by the Administration as a result of the alienation of land will be used for the conservation and extension of the municipal land heritage or by specific agreement of the competent body for the following purposes:

- Obtaining and executing local endowments on consolidated urban land.
- Actions of public initiative of urban renewal, interior reform or restoration of housing.
- Relocation and return expenses
- Purchase and, where appropriate, restoration of buildings for protected housing or public facilities.

And these same provisions are extended by the urban planning legislation to the event that there is the replacement of the use that corresponds to the Administration by its economic equivalent that can be used for the same purposes.

The restoration actions are also contemplated by the urban regulations on the occasion of the regulation of the reserve of land for the construction of protected housing (Law 8/2013, June 26th). According to this regulation, the General Urban Plans and in accordance with them the development planning instruments must establish in sectors or units of unconsolidated or developable urban land whose characteristic use is residential, land reserves for the construction of protected housing. However, according to the same article, when it is not possible to establish these reservations, they may be replaced by restoration actions outside the scope of action.

In any case, a certain scepticism about the possibility that through the generality of these precepts the expected results will be obtained cannot be overemphasized. It is not the first time that the standards take urban restoration as a reference, however the experience of recent years shows that the economic benefits of uncontrolled urban growth have won over to restoration. Restoration policies therefore seem to resurface not because of their virtues or their adaptation to constitutional precepts, but because of the exhaustion of an urban development model that no longer gives more of itself.

In any case, the current interest of the public authorities in this option is undeniable, which gives rise to their intervention from very different points of view, both regulatory and management. In this sense it can be said that the various forms of administrative activity are projected in a more complete way on the restoration activity, although it can be said that urban restoration is primarily urban restoration (Wolman A, 1965).

Thus, to the extent that the restoration consists of actions on the public spaces of urbanization or redevelopment we are talking about a public function that can be managed both directly and indirectly (Chance T, 2009)). In contrast to urban renewal or urbanisation of developable land, where the economic benefits are substantial and stimulate private investment and indirect management systems, in the case of restoration, the absence of profitability retracts private subjects from carrying out these actions, resulting in the need for greater investment by the public sector that thus supplements the inhibition of the private sector.

In other cases, the restoration actions are carried out by the administration, but the Administration, based on the interest they have, intervenes by encouraging these activities or checking their compliance with the law.

Hence the need to delimit the competences in the field of restoration to specify which public administrations are competent to act in the matter and what their level of intervention must be.

BACKGROUND

Because of the importance of the actions being carried out, two types of restoration can be distinguished: isolated restoration and integrated restoration. The first is the one that considers the object on which it falls in its own individuality, without major implications or connections with the surrounding elements. On the contrary, integrated restoration is one that considers the element on which it is projected included in a larger space in which it is integrated. Integrated restoration is the restoration of urban spaces. It does not dispense with the restoration of individual elements, but those are taken into consideration insofar as they are included in an urban context that interests to revitalize and their effects transcend the individual element on which they fall to be projected on the physical space that contains it.

The distinction mentioned is of fundamental importance because it affects the transcendence of the actions that are going to be developed, and the breadth of them, conditioning the techniques used and the legal instruments put at the service of restoration.

Restoration of Individual Elements

It is the restoration of buildings and homes intended primarily for residential use that aims to provide housing with the necessary living conditions for that residential use and is carried out by the owners or holders of some right over the property on which it acts.

In this type of restoration, the public activity usually consists of financing and promotion activities based on economic incentives, the main exponent of which is usually the provision of subsidies.

It can be distinguished between restoration actions that seek to achieve a structural and constructive adaptation of those others that are aimed at achieving a functional adaptation. By structural adaptation works are understood all those that provide the house with constructive security conditions, so that its stability, resistance, firmness and solidity is guaranteed. This is to ensure that the property meets sufficient guarantees of security and stability.

With regard to those works of restoration aimed at achieving the functional suitability, it should be noted that the criterion that guides the performance of the same is based on the achievement of habitability, integrating in this concept, according to the Law 8/2013, June 26th the improvement of the conditions of access of people with disabilities, the existence and proper functioning of health services, electrical installations, sanitation and plumbing, heating, smoke extraction and ventilation, actions related to thermal and acoustic insulation and those that promote energy saving systems. As can be seen, this is an ecological and sustainable restoration (Batty M, 2013).

The restoration is usually voluntary in these cases and is limited by the duty of conservation of the owner and the declaration of ruin that are configured as duties consubstantial with the property right.

Integrated Restoration or Restoration of Urban Spaces

In urban spaces restoration involves a set of actions that involve the protection, conservation, restoration and improvement of its urban fabric, through the enhancement and more appropriate use of the urbanized and built heritage contained in its perimeter.

In these areas, restoration actions go beyond the purely material or physical perspective, so that they also have a social or economic dimension of recovering degraded environments. Thus, for example, it is a question of maintaining the existing population, improving their living conditions and especially the quality of housing and the promotion of economic activities compatible with the aforementioned objectives. the State Housing Plan states that protected restoration actions must ensure social diversity and rehousing of the resident population. The Law of the Community of Madrid on degraded urban spaces (Allen C, Clouth, 2012) also includes restoration actions proposals to revive the activity in the degraded area, with special reference to the maintenance of existing functions and, in particular, trade and crafts and the creation of new ones, taking into account the socio-economic, cultural and technical structure of the area.

In short, the restoration of these spaces aspires to the achievement of a plurality of social and community purposes (improvement or recovery of urban complexes or rural areas, of economic and social activities and the living conditions of their residents) but always on the budget of an action on urban spaces and the elements that compose them.

Normally the restoration processes will be carried out on urban land consolidated by the building located in the historic center of the cities. However, areas or neighbourhoods that are undergoing a process of deterioration or degradation may also undergo restoration. We can talk about suburbs or slums, outskirts of cities not coinciding with the historic Center and where the limits to restoration will not be as intense as in the historic centers.

This configuration of the urban space as an object of restoration requires in any case an urban instrument (urban planning) that delimits the affected space and that foresees these actions in the framework of urban planning, which leads us to consider the restoration from an urban perspective

RESULTS AND DISCUSSION

The term restoration is primarily coined by the state and regional regulations that address the financing of public housing and urban planning policies. But to the extent that it affects urban spaces and configures urban planning, it has an urban vocation that must be contemplated by this sectoral legislation.

The protective actions of restoration, especially when they affect urban spaces formally declared as areas of restoration, must have an urban reflection and be projected and reflected in the corresponding planning and management techniques.

Planning legislation provides the instruments (plans) and the proper techniques to make a urban planning adjusted to the parameters of the restoration performing actions that tend to increase the endowments, to the estate or redevelopment of urban spaces and even the construction of houses subjected or not to a regime of protection to the public (Donatiello JE, 2015).

The restoration has a clear urban vocation, and that urban vocation is made effective through planning. The plans, transferred by the budgets of the restoration, affect the urban spaces, the city already consolidated, and order it in the indicated sense. The development of restoration actions through urban planning through planning has the following effects:

- It allows to configure urban planning in advance based on a plurality of actions that do not appear disconnected from each other, but integrated within the framework of general forecasts that is only possible to establish if there is an urban figure that anticipates these contents.
- The planning contemplates the rehabilitated element not in its own individuality but in the framework of a broader urban context that interests to rehabilitate, so that its effects go beyond the individual plane to produce broader effects.
- Determines the result of the provision and promotion activity that will tend to develop within the framework of the coordinates laid down by the plan.
- It is able to integrate the different sectoral rules that affect the same urban space and combine the different declarations and legal regimes to which they are subject with the urban planning of the same. Thus regulations on restoration, areas of integrated restoration for promotion purposes, regulations on historical heritage, declaration of cultural interest, etc.
- The plans establish the distinction between consolidated and unconsolidated urban land, which determines the form of execution of the restoration actions, the subjects involved in it and the duties of the affected owners.

Contrary to what it might seem, a planning that starts from rehabilitating premises is not characterized by the extreme maintenance of the existing patrimonial elements, but also admits alterations of the same (demolition, substitutions), as long as these actions are informed by rehabilitating purposes. Urban planning can contribute to promote the restoration and conservation of buildings basically in two ways:

- Not creating urban expectations higher than those already existing.
- Establishing a duty to rehabilitate.

It should be borne in mind that degraded urban spaces have traditionally been considered from the urban perspective, mainly through internal reform operations, although it is not until relatively recent dates when urban legislation and urban plans adopt the perspective of restoration and are transcended by their objectives.

There is no single typology of urban planning with the capacity to influence the restoration, but there can be several urban figures that adapt to these objectives (Adhya A, Plowright P, Stevens J 2011). In any case, it should be noted that urban restoration actions require detailed planning that can be provided by different plans.

For example, general plans if they contain a detailed arrangement. Law 8/2013, June 26th provides that the general plan may delimit one or several traditional historical centers where the urban planning does not allow the indiscriminate replacement of buildings and requires that their conservation, implementation, reform or renovation harmonize with the historical typology.

In the absence of such a detailed arrangement, the approval of the relevant special plan will be required (Moroni S, 2015). The special plans of interior reform have been the figure of planning that has usually affected the urban fabric already consolidated, that is, in the city already made to undertake operations of interior reform (Roggema R, 2012a). But its content has not always been transcended by the purposes of restoration. On the contrary, sometimes such planning has served to carry out renovation operations that are totally opposed to those of restoration (Alfasi N, Portugali J 2007).

In any case, and transcended by these purposes and objectives, the special interior reform plans are well adapted to the actions of urban restoration. Thus, among the objectives of the aforementioned plans are: decongestion or renewal of urban land use, creation of urban development and community equipment, sanitation of unhealthy neighborhoods, resolution of traffic or aesthetic problems and improvement of the urban environment or public services or other similar purposes (Cohen J, Stewart I, 1994)).

All these purposes coincide to a large extent with the objective scope of restoration, but at the same time the breadth of the expression other similar purposes, allow the objectives of these plans to be extended to other purposes related to it.

The approval of special plans for the protection of cultural heritage is unavoidable in those cases in which the affected urban space has been declared a site of cultural interest. Article 59 of the Law 8/2013, June 26th establishes that the declaration of set of cultural interest will determine the obligation of the city council to draft a number of special plans for the protection and, where appropriate, sanitation and renovation of the affected area (Sharifi A, 2016), in accordance with the provisions of the cultural heritage legislation.

This type of plan clearly shows its capacity to integrate the different rules and legal regimes that coexist in the same urban space (De Roo G, Hillier J, van Wezemael J, 2020). Aragonese legislation is a good example. Aragonese Cultural Heritage states that the special plan will establish for all public uses the priority order of its installation in buildings and spaces that are suitable for them. This same planning will determine the areas of restoration. Urban renovations will be possible but only if they involve an improvement with the territorial and urban environment. At the same time the planning will establish the limits to the restoration in accordance with the cultural legislation. The replacement of buildings is therefore considered exceptional and may only be carried out when it contributes to the general conservation of the complex. In any case, the urban alignments will be maintained.

On some occasions urban spaces subject to restoration are the subject of a formal declaration by the administration, giving rise to the concept of restoration area. It is in these cases when the link between restoration and urban planning is most clearly seen.

This expression refers to a space legally delimited by an administrative declaration on which the various restoration actions are planned and affected. The legal delimitation to which we refer is carried out through an administrative act that establishes the presence in the area subject to the declaration of the necessary requirements to confer such character.

The declaration of restoration area is a complement to urban planning. Through them, the aim is to complement the urban perspective from which degraded urban spaces have traditionally been contemplated, and allow the coordination of the activity of the different public administrations, especially with regard to the financing of actions carried out in these urban contexts.

Keep in mind that the statement of area of restoration involves the determination by the Administration of certain physical circumstances that are present in the urban space, but does not by itself the capacity to implement the interventions planning to need to undergo spatial domains on which it acts, interventions that have come previously determined for the plan.

The restoration areas therefore constitute the space on which the restoration actions previously defined by the planning are projected, hence the importance of having the appropriate determinations in this regard prior to the declaration. Article 55 of the State Housing Plan (RD 801/2005, of 1 July) is clear in this regard, since it states that the protected restoration actions must "conform to the regulations of the current urban planning that is applicable...».

CONCLUSION

The urban restoration presents the peculiarity that it affects spaces on which there is consolidated building where there is an urban development already materialized on which the urban planning is projected.

For its part, planning can establish a subjective use different from the materialized use. In this way, it should be noted that for a plan to have a content adjusted to the parameters of restoration in the sense that it promotes the maintenance of constructions and buildings, it is necessary that its determinations maintain the balance between the use already materialized and the use susceptible of appropriation that results from the planning. Thus two magnitudes appear on whose balance will depend the decisions of individuals when it comes to the verification or not of restoration actions. They are ultimately entrusted with the verification or not of voluntary restoration interventions

The rupture of the equation between both magnitudes can be given by two circumstances:

1. By the need to proceed with the legal duty to cede the land in which the corresponding use is located to the city council as a result of the realization of restoration actions. Situation already seen in the previous section
2. As a result of a modification of the planning that involves the alteration of the uses and intensities foreseen in the previous arrangement. Indeed, the modification of the planning can lead to an imbalance between the use susceptible of appropriation and the materialized and patrimonialized use in those cases in which the urban planning alters the uses or intensities foreseen in the previous planning. To favor the conservation of the properties, the planning must avoid creating expectations higher than those already existing (increases in use) and must tolerate certain situations previously defined based on the previous management when the materialized use exceeds the objective use foreseen by the plan. This provision is contained in Article 102.2 of Spanish urban planning legislation. Thus in the isolated operations of restoration whenever the buildings are conserved, if it gives the circumstance that the edificability materialized historically exceeds the objective use, such edificability will be taken as a reference of subjective use.

Indeed, the alteration of the use susceptible of appropriation with respect to the already patrimonialized and materialized is a factor of considerable importance for the decision to verify restoration actions.

In urban land consolidated by the urbanization, subject to isolated actions, the appropriate use refers to the plot. And if the materialized use is higher than the objective use marked by the planning, the materialized use will be taken as a reference of the subjective use, as long as the building is preserved and it is not in a situation of out of order

This provision favors the conservation and restoration of buildings, especially once the legal duty of conservation and restoration has ceased, since it allows to maintain the materialized use as long as the property in question is maintained (Shafiea FA, Dasimah O, Karuppannanb S 2013).

Also the urbanism state Law 7/2015, octuber 30th establishes special treatment to the unique properties of the cultural heritage. The general Plan may provide that the destination of the unique properties of cultural heritage and protected by the planning applications in hospitality and commercial to not consume the area corresponding to the execution unit or sector.

On the other hand, this legislation allows, within the framework of the provisions of the state legislation, that the urban development that has to be transferred to the city council can be replaced by its economic equivalent (transitional provision second b) of the Land Law).

4. Other urban duties inherent in restoration: the duty of conservation and the duty of restoration (Roggema R, 2015))

The duties of conservation and restoration oblige owners to maintain their properties in conditions of safety, health and safety, accessibility and adornment, and to keep the goods in a condition to serve for their use to the extent of the legal duty of conservation.

These duties of conservation and restoration are established in the basic legislation, specifically article 9 of the T. R. of the Land Law, establishes them within the duties and burdens that make up the essential content of the property right.

For its part, article 31 of the same Law states that failure to comply with the duties of building or restoration will entitle for expropriation for failure to fulfill the social function of the property or for the application of the regime of forced sale or replacement.

The duty of conservation reaches and is enforceable to the owner up to the limit provided for in the urban legislation. However, it must be borne in mind that the limit of the duty of conservation is not established in the basic state legislation, unlike what happened in the previous regulation, so that the autonomous regulations will establish the aforementioned limits.

Planning legislation autonomic based on these forecasts state ends up shaping the content of these duties, establishing in the majority of cases, a regime more benevolent to the conservation of the property as set forth in the regulations of state (first in the Revised Text of the Land Law of 1992 and later, after the declaration of unconstitutionality of article 247 of the mentioned legal text, for in article 183 of the Revised Text of the Land Law of 1976), where the declaration of ruin entailed as a legal consequence the demolition of the property. In this sense, the regional legislation has had an impact both in the regulation of the scenarios that may lead to the declaration of ruin (yet very linked to economic criteria), as in the legal consequences of that declaration, that allow the owner to preserve or demolish, through the intervention of the Administration to which they are recognized ability to alter the physical state of ruin.

A good example of these statements is Spanish urban planning legislation that distinguishes between the limit of the duty of conservation of the owner and the limit of the duty of conservation of the property.

The limit of the legal duty of conservation for the owner is constituted by an economic magnitude and is reached when the conservation work exceeds half the value of the buildings, excluding the soil under section 186.2 of the urban legislation. The economic limit of the duty of conservation that is demanded to the owner is constituted by the 50 percent of the value of the buildings excluding the soil. Or what is the same, the only thing that can be imposed on the owner is a conservation that does not exceed 50 percent of the value of the property.

However, the assessment of this limit does not automatically determine the declaration of ruin and subsequent demolition, but once the same has been established, the owner can choose between requesting subsidies or aid to the administration in the part that exceeds the previous limit, or requesting the declaration of ruin of the buildings. It must be borne in mind that the limit of 50% of the value of the building that marks the cessation of the duty of conservation coincides with the first assumption of ruin, physical ruin. On the other hand, the assumptions of technical ruin can also be traced back to economic criteria.

In short and always before the declaration of ruin, it allows the owners to choose either to request the formal declaration of ruin or for the conservation of the property with the limit to their charge of 50 percent of the value of the building, paying the administration the remaining part.

The declaration of ruin marks the limit of the duty of conservation of the property. The binomial ruin demolition is maintained so that declared the ruin proceeds the demolition of the property, but to declare the ruin it is necessary to take into consideration two circumstances: material, physical or factual and formal, consisting in the assessment by the Administration of such circumstances.

For this reason the declaration of ruin is subject to the will of the Administration, since concuringthe factual situation of ruin in a property, the Administration can prevent the declaration of it through the alteration of the physical state of the property by initiating the necessary conservation works to eliminate the state of ruin and all the possible effects derived from it. The owner must pay the amount of the works corresponding to half of the value of the buildings, excluding the land. Again, the owner is subject to a limit of 50 percent of the value of the building, and the Administration must pay for the works in the amount that exceeds that percentage. This demonstrates the involvement of the Administration in the duty of conservation.

REFERENCES

Adhya, A., Plowright, P., & Stevens, J. (2011). Defining sustainable urbanism: towards a responsive urban design. In *Proceedings of the conference on sustainability and the built environment*. King Saud University.

Alfasi, N., & Portugali, J. (2007). Planning rules for a self-planned city. *Planning Theory*, *6*(2), 164–182. doi:10.1177/1473095207077587

Allen, C., & Clouth, S. (2012). *A guidebook to the green economy*. UNDESA.

Batty, M. (2013). *A new science of cities*. MIT Press. doi:10.7551/mitpress/9399.001.0001

Birkmann, J., Garschagen, M., Kraas, F., & Quang, N. (2010). Adaptive urban governance: New challenges for the second generation of urban adaptation strategies to climate change. *Sustainability Science*, *5*(2), 185–206. doi:10.100711625-010-0111-3

Chance, T. (2009). Towards sustainable residential communities; the Beddington zero energy development (BedZED) and beyond. *Environment and Urbanization*, *21*(2), 527–544. doi:10.1177/0956247809339007

Cohen, J., & Stewart, I. (1994). *The collapse of chaos: discovering simplicity in a complex world*. Penguin Group Ltd.

De Roo, G., Hillier, J., & van Wezemael, J. (Eds.). (2020). *Complexity and planning: systems, assemblages and simulations*. Ashgate Publishing. doi:10.4337/9781786439185

Donatiello, J. E. (2015). The world's population: An encyclopedia of critical issues, crises, and ever-growing countries. *Reference and User Services Quarterly*, *54*(4), 85. doi:10.5860/rusq.54n4.85b

Drury, F. (2019). *Enchanting photos of the abandoned village taken over by hippies living in fairytale houses in the Spanish mountains*. MailOnline. http://www.dailymail.co.uk/news/article-3139295/Enchanting-photos-abandoned-village-taken-Spanish-hippies-living-fairytale-houses-mountains.html

Freytag, T., Gössling, S., & Mössner, S. (2019). Living the green city: Freiburg's Solarsiedlung between narratives and practices of sustainable urban development. *Local Environment, 19*(6), 644–659. doi:10.1080/13549839.2013.868872

Girardet, H. (1996). *The GAIA atlas of cities: new directions for sustainable urban living*. Gaia Books Limited.

Habitat, I. I. I. (2016). *Revised zero draft of the new urban agenda*. https://www.habitat3.org/zerodraft

Kennedy, C., Cuddihy, J., & Engel-Yan, J. (2020). The changing metabolism of cities. *Journal of Industrial Ecology, 11*(2), 43–59. doi:10.1162/jie.2007.1107

Kennedy, C., Pincetl, S., & Bunje, P. (2010). The study of urban metabolism and its applications to urban planning and design. *Environmental Pollution, 159*(8–9), 1965–1973. PMID:21084139

Kreimer, A., Arnold, M., & Carlin, A. (Eds.). (2003). *Building safer cities: the future of disaster risk*. The International Bank for Reconstruction and Development/The World Bank.

Moroni, S. (2015). Complexity and the inherent limits of explanation and prediction: Urban codes for self-organising systems. *Planning Theory, 14*(3), 248–267. doi:10.1177/1473095214521104

Roggema, R. (2012a). *Swarm planning: the development of a spatial planning methodology to deal with climate adaptation* [PhD thesis]. Delft University of Technology.

Roggema, R. (2012c). Shifting paradigms. In R. Roggema (Ed.), *The design charrette: ways to envision sustainable futures*. Springer.

Roggema, R. (2014). Towards enhanced resilience in city design: A proposition. *Land (Basel), 3*(2), 460–481. doi:10.3390/land3020460

Roggema, R. (2015). Three urbanisms in one city: Accommodating the paces of change. *Journal of Environmental Protection, 6*(09), 946–956. doi:10.4236/jep.2015.69084

Searns, R. M. (1995). The evolution of greenways as an adaptive urban landscape form. *Landscape and Urban Planning, 33*(1), 65–80. doi:10.1016/0169-2046(94)02014-7

Shafiea, F. A., Dasimah, O., & Karuppannanb, S. (2013). Urban metabolism: a research methodology in urban planning and environmental assessment. *Proceedings of the 1st international conference on research methodology for built environment and engineering*.

Sharifi, A. (2016). From garden city to eco-urbanism: The quest for sustainable neighborhood development. *Sustainable Cities and Society, 20*, 1–16. doi:10.1016/j.scs.2015.09.002

Webster, C., & Lai, L. W. C. (2003). *Property rights, planning and markets*. Edward Elgar.

Wolman, A. (1965). The metabolism of cities. *Scientific American, 213*(3), 179–190. doi:10.1038scientificamerican0965-178 PMID:14338520

World Commission on Environment and Development. (1987). *Our common future*. Oxford University Press.

Chapter 10
Low Carbon Cities: Sustainable Urban Development in Malaysia

Chai Lee Goi
https://orcid.org/0000-0003-0131-2818
Curtin University, Malaysia

ABSTRACT

The main objectives of the research are to review sustainable urban development and the implementation and planning of low carbon cities in Malaysia. Malaysia embarked on an aggressive approach to sustainable development with the introduction of the New Economic Policy (NEP) in 1970. The implementation of the New Economic Model (NEM) in 2009 further strengthened sustainable development to achieve three key goals: high income, inclusivity, and sustainability. It is aligned with the Sustainable Development Goals (SDGs) and sustainable urban development. Malaysia embarked on a goal to reduce CO2 emissions by 40% in 2005 and 45% by 2030. To achieve this goal, several policies and plans have been planned and implemented, such as the National Green Technology Policy (2010), the Renewable Energy Act (2011), the National Energy Efficiency Action Plan (NEEAP) (2015), the Low Carbon Cities Framework (LCCF) (2011), the Green Technology Application for the Development of Low Carbon Cities (GTALCC) (2016), and the National Low Carbon Cities Masterplan (NLCCM) (2021).

INTRODUCTION

In 1950, only 30% of the world's population lived in urban areas. Then, the total population increased to 55% in 2018 (United Nations Department of Economic and Social Affairs, 2018). By 2050, two-thirds of the global population will live in cities, with Asia and Africa accounting for 90% of the urban population growth. Urban populations continue to grow and have greater material prosperity, leading to an increase in consumption of resources and energy, as well as waste generation. 70% of cities are affected by climate change, while nearly all cities are at risk. The average temperature is predicted to rise between 1.2°C and 1.6°C by 2050 (Lee, 2019).

DOI: 10.4018/978-1-7998-9590-9.ch010

The total population in Malaysia is 32.7 million in 2021. Of that number, 77.3% of the population lives in urban areas (Department of Statistics Malaysia, 2021). 13 cities in Malaysia with high population densities. These include Kuala Lumpur, Seberang Perai (Penang), Kajang (Selangor), Klang (Selangor), Subang Jaya, (Selangor) Georgetown (Penang), Ipoh (Perak), Petaling Jaya (Selangor), Kuching (Sarawak), Selayang (Selangor), Shah Alam (Selangor), Iskandar Puteri (Johor), Seremban (Negeri Sembilan), Johor Bahru (Johor). Also, the majority of Malaysia's factories are located in industrial zones that are spread across the country but are particularly abundant in states such as Selangor, Penang and Johor (Crowe, n.d).

Malaysia embarked on the journey of sustainable development in the 1970s with the introduction of the New Economic Policy (NEP), which aimed to eradicate poverty and restructure societal imbalances. Malaysia formulated its New Economic Model (NEM) in 2009, which solidified its commitment to pursue sustainable development based on three principles: high income, inclusivity, and sustainability. These three elements reflect the three elements of the 2030 Agenda for Sustainable Development (the 2030 Agenda), encompassing economic, social, and environmental components. It is critical to note that the Eleventh Malaysia Plan (11MP) is aligned with most of the global Sustainable Development Goals (SDGs) (Economic Planning Unit, 2017).

According to Somasundram et al. (2018), air pollution is one of the five most worrying challenges of urban society. Air pollution has become a significant problem in Malaysia due to industrialisation. As a result of industrial growth, many harmful particles have permeated into the atmosphere. Industrial expansion has turned the quality of air from healthy to worse (Usmani et al., 2020). A review of air pollution in Malaysia conducted by Afroz et al. (2003) discussed that the air pollutants mainly involved Carbon monoxide (CO), Sulphur Dioxide (SO2), Nitrogen Dioxide (NO2), Ozone (O3), and Suspended Particulate Matter (SPM). Most of the pollution in urban and industrial areas has been caused by land transportation and industrial emissions. In addition, another reason that causes pollution in Malaysia and occurs almost every year is open burning sources. In 2019, the total amount of carbon monoxide emissions was 2.24 million metric tons (Müller, 2021)

A city is a complex system comprised of various aspects such as industry, environment, economy, infrastructure and multi-layered governance. In order for a city to move to a low carbon city, these elements must take part in low carbon transformation (Wu et al., 2021). Sustainable urban development has an important role to play to reduce carbon emissions. Cities in Malaysia are in dilemma to decouple its economic growth and carbon emissions, or risk being locked into unsustainable development pathways (Green Technology Application For The Development of Low Carbon Cities, 2019).

The main objectives of the research are to review sustainable urban development, and the implementation and planning of low carbon cities in Malaysia.

SUSTAINABLE URBAN DEVELOPMENT

In sustainable urban development, Yuan et al. (2011) summarised the idea of low carbon development into 3 phases as shown in Figure 1. The low carbon development involves low carbon economy, low carbon society, low carbon city, low carbon community and low-carbon life.

Figure 1. Three phases of low carbon development
Source: Yuan et al. (2011)

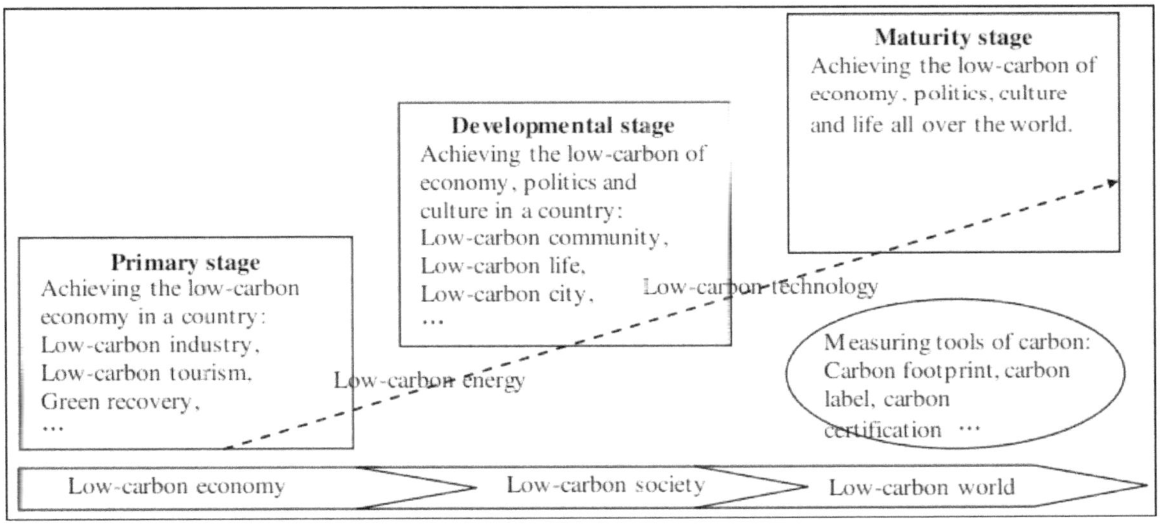

At the COP 21 in Paris in 2015, cities were acknowledged for the first time as key players in climate change. At the third summit of the United Nations on housing and sustainable urban development - Habitat III - held in Quito, Ecuador, in October 2016, the New Urban Agenda laid out global objectives and orientations for sustainable urban development. In Sustainable Development Goals (SDGs), Goal 11 – 'Sustainable Cities and Communities', the 2030 Agenda points out the significant contribution cities make to achieving the sustainable development goals (International Climate Initiative, n.d). Thus, the concept of Low Carbon City (LCC) was adopted as a means of dealing with environmental degradation caused by rapid urbanisation (Abdul Rahman, 2020).

Sustainable urban development has emerged numerous urban settlement theories such as healthy city, sustainable city, low-carbon city, transit-oriented city, compact city, smart city, green city and liveable city. Each theory has different concerns in different areas, but all share one central idea and ultimate goal: achieving maximum development with minimum resource consumption and environmental impact to ensure the well-being of both humans and the earth (Tang and Lee, 2016).

"Sustainable urban development is perceived as improving the quality of life in a city, including ecological, cultural, political, institutional, social and economic components without leaving a burden – e.g., the result of a reduced natural capital and an excessive local debt, on the future generations – and thus forming the sustainable city" (Jenks and Dempsey 2005; Yigitcanlar 2010b; While et al. 2010; Flint and Raco 2012; Yigitcanlar and Teriman, 2014).

Tang and Lee (2016) incorporated 10 major global urban sustainability rankings/ standards that corresponded to the three fundamental capacities of sustainable urban development (Refer Figure 2):

- To maintain environmental quality and carrying capacity.
- To support socio-economic development and management.

- To provide sufficient services and livelihoods to all current and future inhabitants.

Figure 2. Sustainable urban development
Source: Tang and Lee (2016)

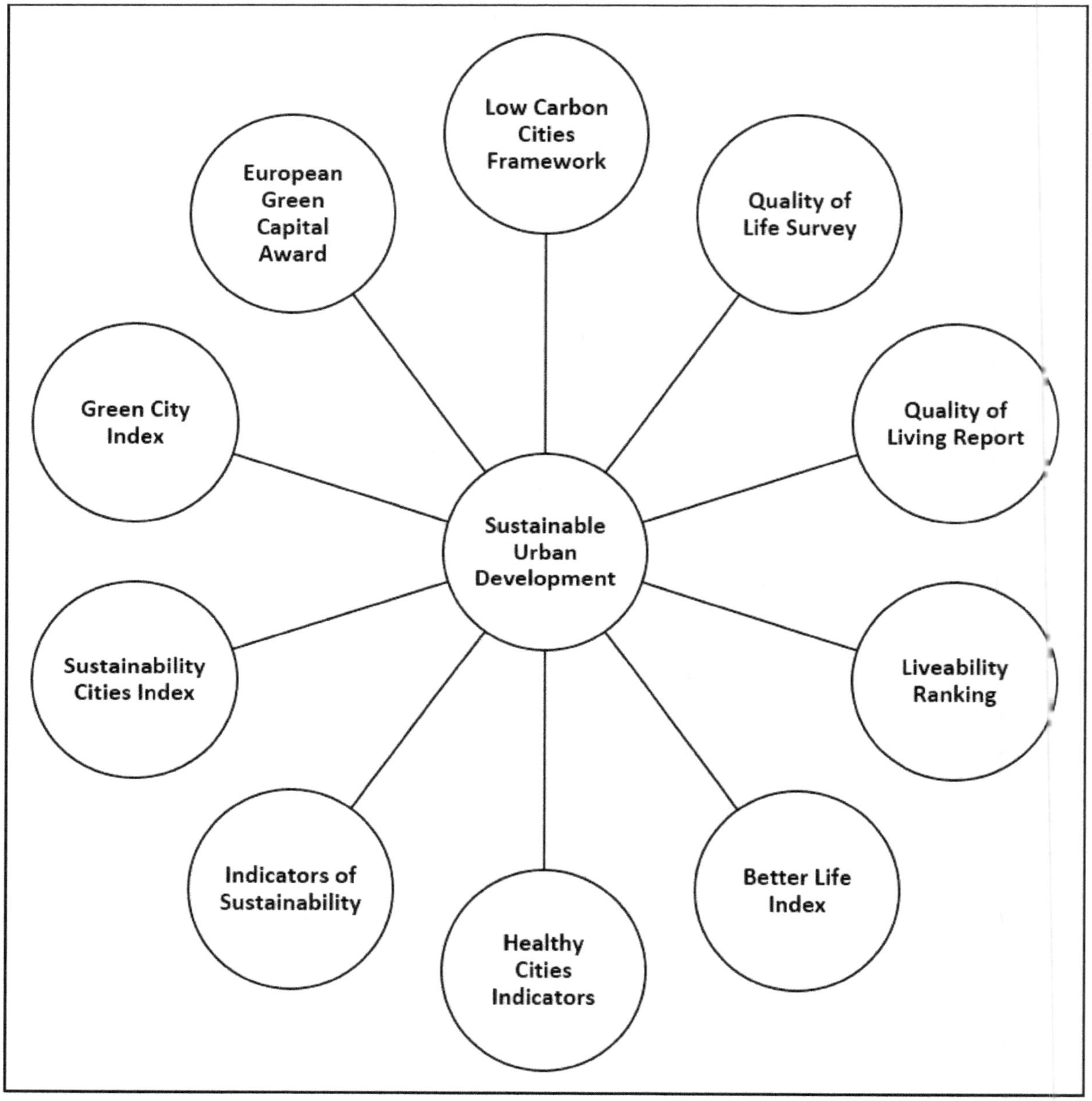

Malaysia recognises that the comprehensive implementation of Sustainable Development Goals (SDGs) will require the mobilisation of resources, including manpower, capacity building, physical spaces, and funding. Since Malaysia's national development plan has always been geared towards economic, social and environmental agenda, the implementation of Sustainable Development Goals (SDGs) in Malaysia is aligned with the five-year national development plan (Economic Planning Unit, n.d) (Refer to Figure 3).

Figure 3. The SDGs governance structure in Malaysia
Source: Economic Planning Unit (n.d)

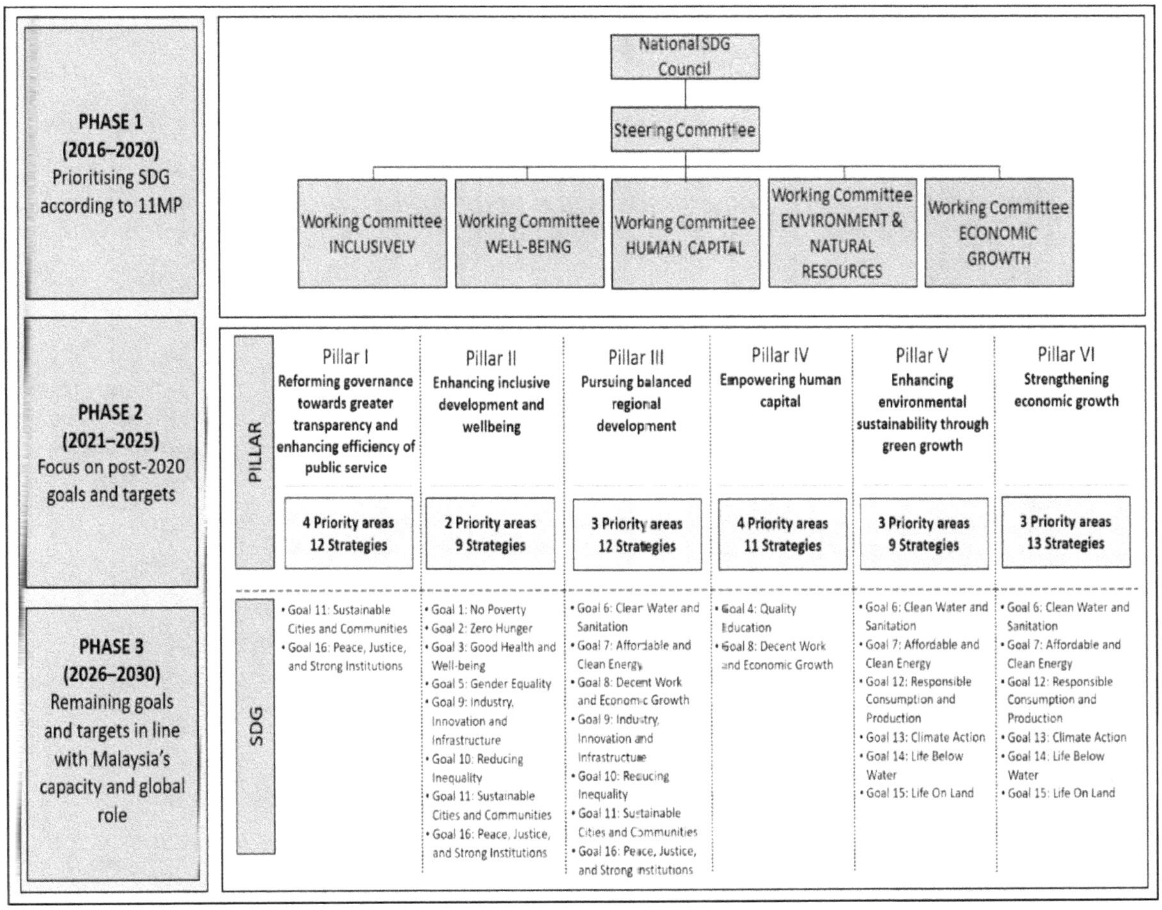

DEFINING A LOW CARBON CITY

The term low carbon city is a term used to encompass a range of approaches to sustainable urbanism including a variety of sustainable urbanism theories used at different scales and depending on the local context. A low carbon city is an urban model incorporating concepts of ecological and sustainable urbanism and resilience theory, combined with practical solutions (Refer to Figure 4) (Lehmann, 2013).

Figure 4. The aspects of sustainable city
Source: Lehmann (2013)

As highlighted by Ismaila Rimi and Yakubu Aliyu (2019), "*low carbon city is a sustainable urbanisation approach that centres on curtailing the anthropogenic carbon footprint of cities by means of minimising or abolishing the utilisation of energy sourced from fossil fuels. It combines the features of low carbon society and low carbon economy while supporting partnerships among governments, private sectors, and civil societies*".

LOW CARBON CITIES

At the 15th Conference of the Parties (COP 15), the United Nations Climate Change Conference in Copenhagen, Malaysia proposed reducing its CO2 emissions intensity by 40% by 2020, compared to 2005 levels. Since then, the Malaysian Government has actively advocated and promoted green and low carbon development, especially in cities. After years of steady progress toward mitigating climate change and reducing CO2 emissions, Malaysia pledged in the 21st Conference of Parties (COP21) in Paris to reduce the country's in-house gas emissions by 45% by 2030, compared to 2005 levels. To meet this ambitious goal, several policies have been introduced.

- The National Green Technology Policy (2010) aims to accelerate technology deployment through training. The policy is built on four pillars: (1) energy – seek to attain energy independence and promote efficient utilisation; (2) environment – conserve and minimise the impact on the environment; (3) economy – enhance the national economic development through the use of technology; and (4) social – improve the quality of life for all.
- The Renewable Energy Act (2011) aims to increase the generation of electricity from renewable sources of energy (solar photovoltaic, biogas, biomass and small hydropower) by establishing and implementing a feed-in-tariff system, which will allow producers and users to sell excess power to the national power grid.
- The National Energy Efficiency Action Plan (NEEAP) (2015) focuses on tackling issues pertaining to energy supply by managing demand efficiently. The Plan prescribes a path towards improving energy efficiency by pursuing the implementation of measures that are considered as "harvesting the low hanging fruits", as they are viable for the nation as well as the end users.
- The Low Carbon Cities Framework (LCCF) is developed to achieve sustainable development and the reduction of carbon emissions. The performance criteria for low carbon cities are measurable strategies to reduce carbon emission through policy control, better process and product management, development of technology, transformation in the procurement system, consumption strategies and carbon capture. In relation to this, the key elements identified, which are urban environment (Refer to Table 1), urban transportation (Refer to Table 2), and urban infrastructure (Refer to Table 3) and buildings (Refer to Table 4). In addition, another 15 performance criteria and 41 sub-criteria help the stakeholders comprehend the cities' carbon footprint and assist them in taking the applicable reduction measures in achieving the national climate aspirations.
- The Green Technology Application for the Development of Low Carbon Cities (GTALCC) is a 5-year project which facilitates the implementation of low carbon initiatives in Malaysian cities, showcasing a clear and integrated approach to low carbon urban development.

Table 1. Performance criteria and sub-criteria for urban environment

No	Performance criteria and sub criteria
Performance criteria 1: Site selection	
UE 1-1	Development within defined urban footprint
UE 1-2	Infill development
UE 1-3	Development within transit nodes and corridors
UE 1-4	Brownfield and greyfield redevelopment
UE 1-5	Hill slope development
Performance criteria 2: Urban form	
UE 2-1	Mixed-use development
UE 2-2	Compact development
UE 2-3	Road and parking
UE 2-4	Comprehensive pedestrian network
UE 2-5	Comprehensive cycling network
UE 2-6	Urban Heat Island (UHI) effect
Performance criteria 3: Urban greenery and environmental quality	
UE 3-1	Preserve natural ecology, water body and biodiversity
UE 3-2	Green open space
UE 3-3	Number of trees

Source: Ministry of Energy, Green Technology and Water (2017)

Table 2. Performance criteria and sub-criteria for urban transportation

No	Performance criteria and sub criteria
Performance criteria 4: Reduction use of private motorised transport on urban road network	
UT 1-1	Classified traffic volume urban road network
UT 1-2	Vehicle-km of travel by modes
Performance criteria 5: Increase in public transport	
UT 2-1	Public transport ridership
UT 2-2	Public transport system improvement and coverage
Performance criteria 6: Mode shift from private to public transport and non-motorised transport	
UT 3-1	Modal share of private, public, and non-motorised transport
Performance criteria 7: Use of low carbon transport	
UT 4-1	Use of more fuel efficient vehicles for passenger vehicles and green freight transport
UT 4-2	Number of charging stations
Performance criteria 8: Improvement to level of service of road links and junctions	
5-1	Performance of road links and junctions
5-2	Average link speeds and journey speeds
Performance criteria 9: Utilisation of Transit-Oriented-Development (TOD) approach	
UT 6-1	New development and redevelopment schemes incorporating TOD concept
UT 6-2	Walking and cycling facilities to support access and mobility to/from public transit nodes

Source: Ministry of Energy, Green Technology and Water (2017)

Table 3. Performance Criteria and Sub-criteria for Urban Infrastructure

No	Performance criteria and sub criteria
Performance criteria 10: Infrastructure provision	
UI 1-1	Land take for infrastructure and utility services
UI 1-2	Earthwork management
UI 1-3	Urban storm water management and flood mitigation
Performance criteria 11: Waste	
UI 2-1	Construction waste management
UI 2-2	Industrial waste management
UI 2-3	Municipal Solid Waste (MSW) management
Performance criteria 12: Energy	
UI 3-1	Energy optimisation
UI 3-2	Renewable energy
UI 3-3	Site-wide district cooling system
Performance criteria 13: Water management	
UI 4-1	Efficient water management

Source: Ministry of Energy, Green Technology and Water (2017)

Table 4. Performance criteria and sub-criteria for building

No	Performance criteria and sub criteria
Performance criteria 14: Sustainable energy management system	
B 1-1	Energy management system
B 1-2	Facility management
Performance criteria 15: Low carbon buildings	
B 2-1	Passive and active design
B 2-2	Operational energy consumption
B 2-3	Operational water consumption
B 2-4	Preserve existing building stock by retrofitting

Source: Ministry of Energy, Green Technology and Water (2017)

The Malaysian government has developed the National Low Carbon Cities Masterplan (Refer to Figure 5) in order to transform Malaysian cities into low carbon while driving low carbon development. In crafting the path forward to low carbon development in Malaysia, three key drivers, three key enablers, nine key directions and 24 key actions are recommended (Refer to Figure 6). A total of 33 local and regional governments have been chosen as targeted cities. Selection is determined primarily by the number of people living in the city/area; the total population must exceed 300,000 (Refer to Table 5) (Ministry of Environment and Water, 2021).

Figure 5. Framework of national low carbon cities masterplan

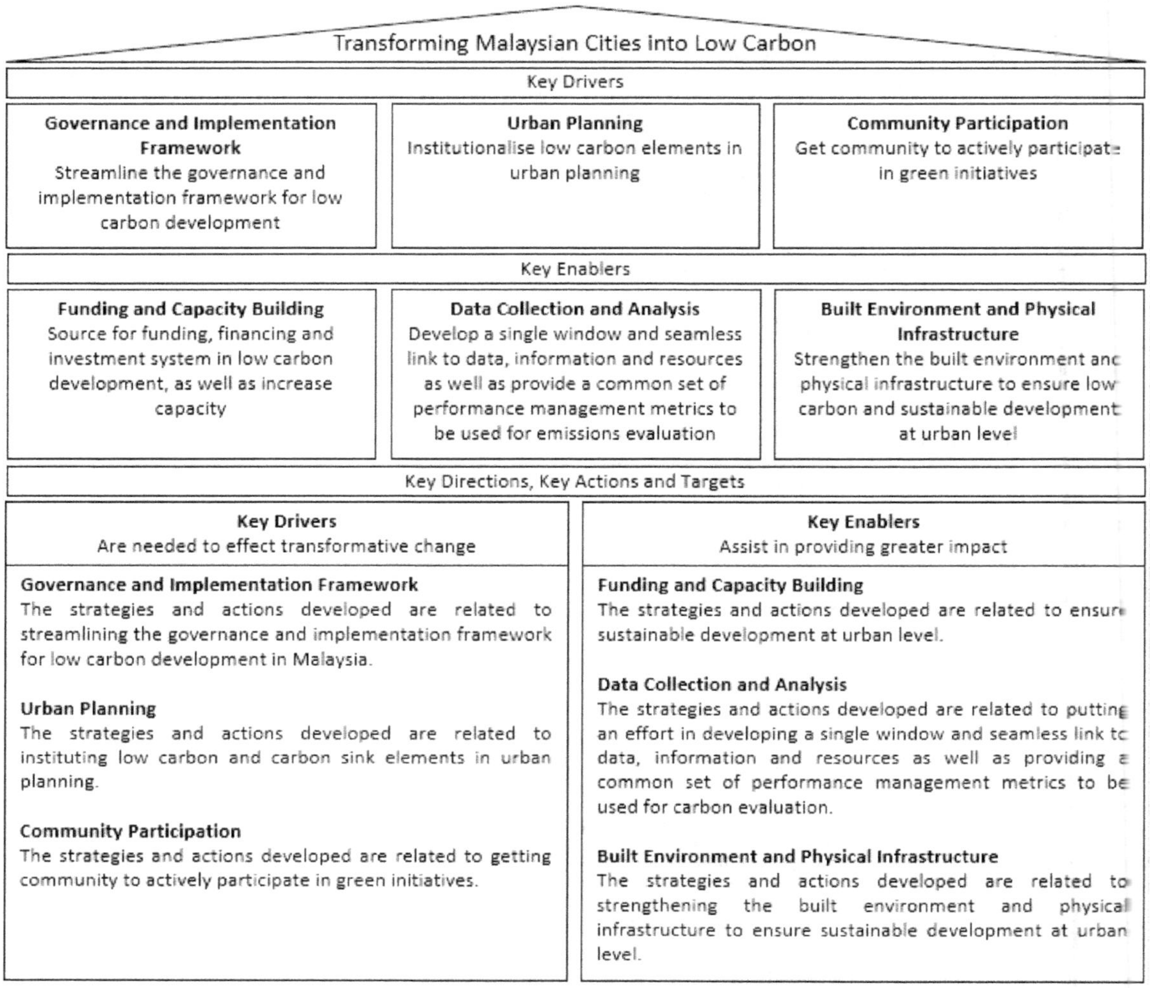

Figure 6. Key drivers and key enablers of National Low Carbon Cities Masterplan

Key Drivers & Key Enablers	Key Directions	Key Actions
Governance and Implementation Framework	Streamline and Integrate Related Low Carbon Policies and Regulations	• **Action 1.1** Align Existing Regulation and Laws to Support Low Carbon Cities Development • **Action 1.2** Align National Climate Change Policy (NCCP) to Support Low Carbon Cities Development • **Action 1.3** Establish Absolute Carbon Reduction Targets for Targeted Cities (2021 - 2050) • **Action 1.4** Establish Policies to Enable Top Down Approach for Low Carbon Implementation at State Level • **Action 1.5** Integrate Low Carbon Guidelines and Components into Existing and New Planning Development Documents • **Action 1.6** Promote Agriculture, Forestry and Other Land Uses (AFOLU) as Part of GHG Reduction Measures
	Strengthen the Institutional Framework and Implementation Mechanism at All Levels	• Action 2.1 Improve the Governance and Implementation Structure at Federal and State Levels • Action 2.2 Strengthen the Implementation Mechanism at the Ground Level
Urban Planning	Mainstream Low Carbon Urban Planning and Development	• Action 3.1 Embed Low Carbon Elements in Urban Planning and Development • Action 3.2 Develop Standard Guideline of GHG Emission Reduction Strategies for Easy and Consistent Implementation at Ground Level
Community Participation	Increase Community Participation in Low Carbon Development	• Action 4.1 Nurture Active Participation and Awareness through Effective Communication Plan • Action 4.2 Use Education to Foster Human Behavioural Changes to Sustainable Practices
Funding and Capacity Building	Provide Funding and Financing to Facilitate Low Carbon Development	• Action 5.1 Create Specific Low Carbon Development Fund and Budget to Implement Low Carbon Programmes and Initiatives • Action 5.2 Create Alternative Funding to Finance Low Carbon Initiatives and Programmes at Local Level
	Invest and Build Capacity to Act	• Action 6.1 Develop and Place Dedicated Officers at State and Local Levels to Increase Productivity and Create Holistic Manpower Support System • Action 6.2 Develop and Nurture Knowledge, Expertise and Skills in Low Carbon Development Area at State and Local Levels
Data Collection and Analysis	Improve Low Carbon Information and Data Management	• Action 7.1 Establish Proper and Efficient System of Data Collection and Management for GHG Inventory Purposes • Action 7.2 Develop Central Online System on GHG Emission Reporting and Data Management to be Used at All Levels
	Measure Low Carbon Performance	• Action 8.1 Align Performance-Based Tools to Global Protocol For Community-Scale Greenhouse Gas Emission Inventories (GPC)
Built Environment and Physical Infrastructure	Develop Citywide/ Sectoral Development Strategies on Low Carbon	• Action 9.1 Spatial Planning and Development • Action 9.2 Energy • Action 9.3 Transportation • Action 9.4 Waste

Table 5. Targeted cities for low carbon development in Malaysia

Category	Selection	Justification
City Council	18 out of 18	• All City Councils are selected as they meet the 2010 census data criteria of population exceeding 300,000
		• Under the Ministry of Housing & Local Government requirement, City Council must have a total number of population exceeding 500,000
Municipal Council	12 out of 36	12 local authorities are selected based on the selection criteria – with the exception of Kulai Municipal Council, Pasir Gudang City Council, Hang Tuah Jaya Municipal Council and Sepang Municipal Council.
District Council	1 out of 95	Pontian District Council (part of Iskandar Malaysia and participating city of the Green Technology Application for the Development of Low Carbon Cities (GTALCC) project).
Economic Region	1 out of 5	Iskandar Malaysia (participating city of the GTALCC project).
Modified Local Authority	1 out of 5	Putrajaya Corporation (participating city of the GTALCC project).
Group 1	Group 2	Group 3
Hang Tuah Jaya Municipal Council	Alor Setar City Council	Kota Bharu Municipal Council
Iskandar Malaysia	Ampang Jaya Municipal Council	Kota Kinabalu City Hall
Iskandar Puteri City Council	Ipoh City Council	Kuala Terengganu City Council
Johor Bahru City Council	Kajang Municipal Council	Kuantan City Council
Kuala Lumpur City Hall	Klang Municipal Council	Sandakan Municipal Council
Kulai Municipal Council	Kuching North City Hall	Sungai Petani Municipal Council
Melaka Historic City Council	Kuching South City Council	Tawau Municipal Council
Pasir Gudang City Council	Miri City Council	
Penang Island City Council	Selayang Municipal Council	
Petaling Jaya City Council	Seremban City Council	
Pontian District Council	Subang Jaya City Council	
Putrajaya Corporation		
Seberang Perai City Council		
Sepang Municipal Council		
Shah Alam City Council		

CONCLUSION

Malaysia embarked on an aggressive approach to sustainable development with the introduction of the New Economic Policy (NEP) in 1970. The New Economic Model (NEM) implemented in 2009 to strengthen sustainable development is based on three fundamental principles - high income, inclusiveness and sustainability. Due to increasing population growth in cities, Malaysia is struggling to separate economic growth and carbon emissions, or risk being locked in an unsustainable development path. As such, the government is taking measures to balance sustainable urban development with the formulation of policies related to low carbon cities with the hope of creating sustainable cities.

The commencement of discussions on reducing CO2 emissions at the 15th Conference of the Parties (COP 15) in Copenhagen, Malaysia began planning to reduce CO2 emissions by 40% in 2005. This was followed by the formation of several policies and plans such as the National Green Technology Policy (2010), the Renewable Energy Act (2011), the National Energy Efficiency Action Plan (NEEAP) (2015), the Low Carbon Cities Framework (LCCF) (2011), the Green Technology Application for the Development of Low Carbon Cities (GTALCC) (2016) and the National Low Carbon Cities Masterplan (NLCCM) (2021).

As low carbon city is still a relatively new concept in Malaysia, its development and operation require active promotion and use of green technologies. Furthermore, as Malaysia embarks on its journey towards a low carbon society, it must also address the issue of increasing awareness among Malaysians as well as reducing high levels of greenhouse gas emissions. Hence, a holistic approach should encompass not only energy policy but also social, economic, and ecological aspects of sustainable development. To realise this vision, the experts, the government, and political leadership all need to come together (Abdul Rahman, 2020).

REFERENCES

Abdul Rahman, H. (2020). Malaysia Commitment towards Low Carbon Cities. *International Journal of Academic Research in Business & Social Sciences*, *10*(15), 253–266. doi:10.6007/IJARBSS/v10-i15/8247

Afroz, R., Hassan, M. N., & Ibrahim, N. A. (2003). Review of Air Pollution and Health Impacts in Malaysia. *Environmental Research*, *92*(2), 71–77. doi:10.1016/S0013-9351(02)00059-2 PMID:12854685

Crowe. (n.d.). *Manufacturing*. https://www.crowe.com/my/industries/manufacturing

Department of Statistics Malaysia. (2021). *Pocket Stats Q2 2021*. https://www.dosm.gov.my/v1/uploads/files/7_Publication/Infographic/PocketStats/Negeri/Johor/ST1-2021/Poket_Stats_Johor_ST1_2021.pdf

Economic Planning Unit. (2017). Malaysia - Sustainable Development Goals Voluntary. *National Review*. https://sustainabledevelopment.un.org/content/documents/15881Malaysia.pdf

Economic Planning Unit. (n.d.). *Sustainable Development Goals*. https://www.epu.gov.my/en/sustainable-development-goals

Flint, J., & Raco, M. (Eds.). (2012). *The Future of Sustainable Cities: Critical Reflections*. The Policy Press.

Green Technology Application for the Development of Low Carbon Cities. (2019). *World Cities Day: Accelerating Low Carbon Cities in Malaysia through the GTALCC Project*. http://gtalcc.gov.my/2019/11/01/world-cities-day-accelerating-low-carbon-cities-in-malaysia-through-the-gtalcc-project

International Climate Initiative. (n.d.). *Sustainable Urban Development*. https://www.international-climate-initiative.com/en/issues/cross-cutting-topics/sustainable-urban-development

Ismaila Rimi, A., & Yakubu Aliyu, B. (2019). Low Carbon City: Strategies and Case Studies. In W. Leal Filho, A. Azul, L. Brandli, P. Özuyar, & T. Wall (Eds.), *Sustainable Cities and Communities, Encyclopedia of the UN Sustainable Development Goals*. Springer. doi:10.1007/978-3-319-71061-7_24-2

Jenks, M., & Dempsey, N. (Eds.). (2005). *Future Forms and Design for Sustainable Cities*. Routledge.

Lee, N. (2019). *Low Carbon Cities - Malaysia's Response to Global Climate Emergency*. United Nations Development Programme. https://www.my.undp.org/content/malaysia/en/home/news-centre/articles/2019/lowcarboncity.html

Lehmann, S. (Ed.). (2013). *Low Carbon Cities: More Than Just Buildings, Low Carbon Cities - Transforming Urban Systems*. Routledge.

Ministry of Energy, Green Technology, and Water. (2017). *Low Carbon Cities Framework, Version 2*. https://www.lccf.my/wp-content/uploads/2018/10/LCCF_Book-Version-2-2017.pdf

Ministry of Environment and Water. (2021). *National Low Carbon Cities Masterplan*. https://www.kasa.gov.my/resources/alam-sekitar/NLCCM.pdf

Müller, J. (2021). *Carbon monoxide emissions in Malaysia from 2012 to 2019*. Statista. https://www.statista.com/statistics/796326/carbon-monoxide-emissions-malaysia

Somasundram, S., Sambasivan, M., Rasiah, R., & Tee, P. L. (2018). Ranking the Challenges of the Urban Community in Malaysia. *Institutions and Economies*, *10*(4), 69–89.

Tang, H. T., & Lee, T. M. (2016). The Making of Sustainable Urban Development: A Synthesis Framework. *Sustainability*, *8*(5), 1–28. doi:10.3390u8050492

United Nations Department of Economic and Social Affairs. (2018). *The Speed of Urbanization Around the World*. https://population.un.org/wup/Publications/Files/WUP2018-PopFacts_2018-1.pdf

Usmani, R. S. A., Saeed, A., Abdullahi, A. N., Pillai, T. R., Jhanjhi, N. Z., & Hashem, I. A. T. (2020). Air Pollution and its Health Impacts in Malaysia: A Review. *Air Quality, Atmosphere & Health*, *13*(9), 1093–1118. doi:10.100711869-020-00867-x

While, A., Jonas, A., & Gibbs, D. (2010). From Sustainable Development to Carbon Control: Ecostate Restructuring and the Politics of Urban and Regional Development. *Transactions of the Institute of British Geographers*, *35*(1), 76–93. doi:10.1111/j.1475-5661.2009.00362.x

Wu, Y., Shen, L., Shuai, C., Jiao, L., Liao, S., & Guo, Z. (2021). Key Driving Forces on the Development of Low Carbon City (LCC) in China. *Ecological Indicators*, *124*, 107379. doi:10.1016/j.ecolind.2021.107379

Yigitcanlar, T. (Ed.). (2010). *Rethinking Sustainable Development*. IGI Global. doi:10.4018/978-1-61692-022-7

Yigitcanlar, T., & Teriman, S. (2015). Rethinking Sustainable Urban Development: Towards An Integrated Planning and Development Process. *International Journal of Environmental Science and Technology*, *12*(1), 341–352. doi:10.100713762-013-0491-x

Yuan, H., Zhou, P., & Zhou, D. (2011). What is Low-Carbon Development? A Conceptual Analysis. *Energy Procedia*, *5*, 1706–1712. doi:10.1016/j.egypro.2011.03.290

Chapter 11
Organizational Structural Construct Based on a Framework for Reliability, Safety, and Deployment of Organizational Resources

José G. Vargas-Hernández
https://orcid.org/0000-0003-0938-4197
Instituto tecnológico Mario Molina, Zapopan, Mexico & Unidad Zapopan, Mexico

ABSTRACT

This chapter has the purpose to analyze an organizational structural construct based on a framework for elements for reliability, safety, and deployment of organizational resources. It is assumed that theoretical and empirical studies in organizational resilience have limited contributions on the concepts of high-reliability organization applied to a diversity of entities and with a variety of characteristics. The method employed is the analytical reflective of the theoretical and empirical literature review. This study concludes that the emerging concept of organizational resilience confirms that the creation and development of an organizational resilience framework for structural construct can be supported by elements based on flexibility of organizational culture, organizational safety and reliability, the promotion elements, and the deployment of organizational resources.

INTRODUCTION

Organizations seek to improve resilience of structure and functions, assets and infrastructure against disruption, degradation, and destruction. Organizational resilience can be evaluated on its facilities, infrastructure, and supply chains (Kohno et al. 2012). Organizational resilience is considered as a second-order construct but manifests at the first-order level constructs identified by Richtnér and Löfsten (2014) as cognitive, structural and emotional resources linked to organizational creativity. Resilience is

DOI: 10.4018/978-1-7998-9590-9.ch011

also the considered as the ability to absorb, stabilize the system structure, achieve function and identity in the cope of shocks.

A methodology to develop organizational resilience is based on structures and processes aimed to enhance the ability to respond to disruptions and create opportunities (Denver, 2017, p. 20). Organizational resilience can be defined in terms of its outcome or what does, as "the maintenance of positive adjustment under challenging conditions such that the organization emerges from those conditions strengthened and more resourceful" (Sutcliffe & Vogus, 2003; Vogus & Sutcliffe, 2007).

Enhancing organizational resilience has a variety of concepts, principles, approaches, guidelines, and elements which combined enable to design a framework to be implemented at different organizational levels combined with different factors at each level, creating and developing a theoretical model to influence organizational resilience. The concept of organizational resilience can be a single at the organizational level or multi-level concept (Linnenluecke, 2017) constructed and achieved at different organizational collective levels. Organizational resilience from the perspective of individual level is based on the inference that the organization is resilience as its individuals (Coutu, 2002; Horne, 1997; Horne and Orr 1998; Mallak 1998; Shin *et al.* 2012).

The concept of organizational resilience emerges from cognitive and engineering sciences among others to create and develop a framework for structural construct of organizational resilience supported on elements based on flexibility of organizational culture, organizational safety and reliability, the promotion elements, and the deployment of organizational resources. All these issues include relevant literature studies, their differences, and aspects, which are explained in more detail in the following subtitles.

Organizational resilience constructs contribute to theoretical development and testing following the dialectical process of a lifecycle in construct development ion include both the validity police and the opposing perspective of an advocate perspective to achieve organizational effectiveness (Brahma 2009; Suddaby 2010; Hirsch and Levin 1999). A construct taxonomy and development based on methodological literature leads to assess and evaluate the literature (Law et al. 1998; Podsakoff et al. 2016; Wong et al. 2008).

This analysis is different to other approaches on organizational resilience structural construct evaluation in the sense that proposes an integrated new model of measurement based on the resilience performance of all the different organizational levels. This model is proposed to being structurally constructed at the different organizational levels through a hypothetical organizational resilience construct development and measurement from a multidisciplinary perspective and not to be confused with the criticized multidimensional constructs as a group of interrelated constructs. The organizational structural construct evaluation is supported by the attributes given by the attributes of the flexibility of the organizational culture, the organizational safety and reliability, the promotion elements for organizational resilience and the deployment of organizational resources.

This study begins by presenting an analysis of an organizational resilience framework leading to the development of a structural construct of organizational resilience for the evaluation of organizational resilience performance based on the attributes described an analyzed separately. The first attribute of this model is the flexibility of organizational culture, followed by the analysis of organizational safety and reliability, to continue with the promotion elements for organizational resilience and finally, the deployment of organizational resources.

FRAMEWORK OF ORGANIZATIONAL RESILIENCE

The concept of resilience is very promising theory and empirical research in organizational studies, despite that the conceptual and operational issues are considered of being fuzzy and the urgent need to develop taxonomies and construct frameworks (Clement and Rivera, 2017; DesJardine *et al.* 2017; Limnios, *et al.* 2014; Linnenluecke, 2017; Williams, *et al.* 2017). The constituent elements of the concept of organizational resilience are not clear under any specific discipline encompassing a set of diverse organizational disciplines and challenging the validity of unconnected concepts in a theoretical paradigm (Hirsch and Levin 1999).

There is a lack of a process framework for individual elements in different resilience phases. There is not an exhaustive list of elements and practices that constitutes organizational resilience which is contextualized in various settings. The definition of organizational resilience includes common elements and context-specific aspects. Definitions of resilience lack some common constituent elements (Aleksić et al. 2013). Organizations that experience collapse are more specific in benefits rather than a general organizational resilience frame (Hamel & Välikangas, 2003). The collapse of an organizations can be reframed as a process of resilience.

A comprehensive and integrated model that draws on various frameworks and approaches combines elements (Pasteur, 2011). Several factors improve organizational resilience which can be enhanced by the elements of people, core business systems and facilities (Foster and Dye 2005). An institutional, legal, organizational and procurement aspects of societal resilience are used as a framework to retrieve indicators and patterns able to identify critical issues (Becker, Abrahamsson, and Tehler, 2014; Herrera, *et al.* 2014; Van Der Beek, and Schraagen, 2015). The components of the organizational resilience framework may change depending on the cumulative or individual weather extremes. The multi-disciplinary perspective of organizational resilience inquires the contribution of organization science and developing more robust framework with reification of assumptions to benefit from adverse and disturbing events and conditions.

A rigid quantitative framework for assessing organizational resilience allow to compare the levels of resilience between organizations and improve their engagement. Indicators for social resilience developed by Cuthill et al. (2008) adopted the SMARTT framework referring to indicators being specific, measurable, achievable, reviewable, time-lined, and talking. Indicators of resilience may represent what is considered healthy and successful.

Hillman, and Guenther (2021) review systematically the literature on organizational resilience construct covering both conceptual and operational issues to discuss the critics about the concept of resilience for being fuzzy and analyze the taxonomies and construct development. Resilience has been constructed at different organizational levels which can be analyzed through the hypothetical organizational resilience construct development and measurement not to be confused with the criticized multidimensional constructs as a group of interrelated constructs (Hirsch and Levin 1999; Wong et al. 2008; Carpenter and Brock 2008). Development of hypothetical constructs and measurement scales of organizational resilience are confused sometimes as interrelated group of constructs (Hirsch and Levin 1999; Wong et al. 2008).

A multi-dimensional and latent reflective three first-order construct framework of organizational resilience developed by Richtnér and Löfsten (2014) applying conceptualizations of Sutcliffe and Vogus (2003), is based on factor analysis that identify structural resources, emotional resources, and cognitive resources, which are resources linked to organizational creativity. A framework of organizational research is developed by Williams et al. (2017) integrating two research streams related to resilience and crisis research.

This study is aimed to review the main concepts of the organizational resilience construct development as a framework for analysis. Findings from empirical research on organizational resilience led to Hillman, and Guenther (2021) to the conclusion that the concept of organizational resilience as a valuable construct for management research requires more clarity in terms of measurement.

A multilevel framework of structural construct of organizational resilience level emphasizes that it is constructed at different collective levels through workers and teams. A construct development following a life cycle needs to be supported by a dialectical process to includes the role of validity police and the opposing perspective (Hirsch and Levin 1999). A construct defined by the validity police perspective is relevant for a theoretical, conceptual, and methodological framework. Organizations use a resilience framework mindset to reinvent and reintegrate beyond former homeostasis. Key resilience practices are not always considered in many companies that might be reluctant towards establishing comprehensive and integrated resilience frameworks. The organizational resilience framework must be based on international best standards and practices.

STRUCTURAL CONSTRUCT OF ORGANIZATIONAL RESILIENCE

The operationalization of a measurement model for organizational resilience requires the development of a construct able to clarify the structural relationship of the dimensions involved, as essential to elaborate good research questions and theoretical parsimony (Law et al. 1998; Wong et al. 2008). In a reflective measurement model, any change in the construct as latent variable leads towards changes in the effect observable indicators while in a formative measurement model changes in indicators of the construct determine changes in the cause indicator as the latent variable (Diamantopoulos and Siguaw 2006; Edwards and Bagozzi 2000). T

From the systemic perspective Tierney (2003) organizational resilience is a structural construct with the dimensions of robustness, resourcefulness, redundancy, and rapidity. A three-dimension construct of organizational resilience based on robustness, agility and integrity was developed by Kantur and Iseri Say (2015). To evaluate resilience, Tompkins (2007) proposes robustness, responsiveness, resourcefulness, rapidity, and redundancy. The ways to increasing organizational resilience are the redundancy, flexibility, and cultural change, which intends to address the resilience of future known and unknown events. Resilience is the ability to recover from disruption and improve by building redundancy and flexibility (Sheffi and Rice 2005).

Potential threat scenarios provide specific organizational resilience, but not general resilience which can be supported through the organizational structure that encourages collaboration shared mission and enhance robustness. The organizational resilience of hazardous industries depends on reliability and robustness which determines their ability to avoid degradation, failure, and errors. Structural resilience includes factors such as physical strength and robustness.

Organizational resilience is the ability to maintain positive adjustment, that emerge from conditions strengthened and more resourceful under challenging conditions (Sutcliffe and Vogus, 2003). Mindset and engagement in resourcefulness and nature of social resources facilitate resilience (Williams and Shepherd 2016). Some leadership aspects are related to resilience such as integrity, accountability, resourcefulness, effective communications, etc. (Helwig, 2013).

The advantage of redundancy is the ability to increase organizational resilience in the face of failures. A resilience building approach after resource depletion in a post shock implies efficiency, supported by redundancy and overlap. Inter-organizational relationships in supply chain resilience enhances organizational resilience draw from the design principles of redundancy and flexibility (Linnenluecke 2017; Pettit et al. 2010; Sheffi and Rice 2005; Zsidisin and Wagner 2010; Ponomarov and Holcomb 2009).

A characterization of factors leading to impact resistance and rapidity elaborated by McDaniels et al. (2008) included several indicators ex-ante decisions and ex post adjustments of organizational resilience in the context of future climate variabilities and weather extremes.

Resilience can be fragile, antifragile and robust. Resilience relates to the concepts of fragility, antifragility, and robustness. Fragility is a broken system damaged by variations (Taleb, 2012; Taleb & Douady, 2013). Resilience is critical to organizational success during times of high disruption relying more on policies, procedures, enforcement, and accountability and moving towards agility and analytics. Antifragility is the property of a system to face challenges, failures, and volatility (Taleb 2012).

Resilience is the capacity of a system, organization, or person to maintain the core purpose and integrity in the face of dramatic changes of circumstances (Zolli and Healy, 2012). Responsibility lines in organizations fosters accountability and low tolerance for failure in potential conflict between specific and general resilience (Tetlock, 1985).

Collective leadership has a relevant role in organizational resilience and social responsibility. The motivation of employees may raise the level of organizational resilience to be able to behave responsively when facing unexpected situations (Dawson, 2010). Technological knowledge of systems supports specific resilience against known and unanticipated operations which can be balanced distribution of responsibilities and personnel programs in the organization.

Organizational resilience splits between defensive, progressive, consistent, and flexible behaviors forming a framework termed as the tension quadrant. However, a fifth strand termed fitness for purposes has emerged. An inflexible organization becomes unproductive as well as the excessive cost cutting impedes resilience. Resilience is a mental restoration ability characterized as the internal individual ability to flexibly cope with and recover from temporary mental illness because of unexpected contingency (Oshio, Nakatani, Kaneko and Nagamine, 2002).

Resilience is the physical ability to return and recover the original state, flexibility, and stability. Resilience is the ability of recovery flexibility minimizing the damages in coping with an unexpected event and recover from the negative effects. Technological resources are used by organizations to achieve flexibility as required by the organizational resilience under the technology-in-practice framework.

A flexible heuristics orientation may increase organizational resilience in adverse situations more than the efficient orientation of routines. In building strong and flexible processes, Fuzzy Resilience Grade is distinct that fuzzy Resilience Early Warning Grade (Omidvar et al. 2017). In the micro-foundations of resilience, the organizational information systems may have risk and enabling factors. Organizations require a balance between the two processes Disembodying the system optimizes control of operations, but resilience decreases du to inflexibility, while embedding increases resilience but damage the organization (Ignatiadis and Nandhakumar, 2007)

FLEXIBILITY OF ORGANIZATIONAL CULTURE

The hurdle to organizational resilience is the inflexibility of organizational culture (Wilkinson et al. 2003). The principle of organizational resilience encompasses the ethos, values, behaviors, and cultural change of the organization. Organizational resilience can be increased by the support of features such as organizational culture, social capital, leadership, communication (Castleden et al., 2011; Lewis, Donaldson-Feilder, & Pangallo, 2011). Resilience is the result of a combination of attitude, culture, process, and framework (Hiles 2011; and Daskon 2010)

The objectives of organizational resilience related to maturity levels in which the higher the level, the more organizational resilience. These levels are decline, survive, bounce back, and bounce forward within an integrated framework and the establishment of resilience culture. An organizational culture of resilience sets the foundations for recovery and sustainability (Alesi, 2008; Coles and Buckle, 2004). Cultures are dynamic and can influenced resilience levels in organizations. Culture has an influence on various model frameworks for measuring organizational resilience and societal resilience. Organizational resilience supports the equal involvement and participation of both women and men, subject to cultural influences.

Resilience focuses more on the cultural change to facilitate problems (Sutcliffe and Vogus, 2003). Resilience is an on-going process that relates the individual with the organizational cultures that have the potential to self-correct after traumatic experiences (Paton *et al.* 2000)

Cultural factors influence organizational resilience based on knowledge that enable to implement and operate correctly. Cultural factors influence resilience at organizational level and introduce appropriate action plans and solutions required to reduce the negative impact.

Active resilience motivates and inspires others with a manifesting compounding effect on the organization that provides a framework strengthen by culture and values to make decisions in difficult situations and required to survive, thrive, and stabilize.

Organizational resilience is optimized by developing and maintaining a resilience culture, (Valastro 2011, Hiles 2011, Pasteur 2011, Daskon 2010 and Somers 2009). The promotion of organizational resilience features has been already identified such as organizational culture, leadership, communication, resources, etc. (Crichton, Ramsay, & Kelly, 2009; Lengnick-Hall, Beck, & Lengnick-Hall, 2011; McManus et al.; Norris, Stevens, Pfefferbaum, Wyche, & Pfefferbaum, 2008; Stephenson, 2010).

Fostering organizational culture change to build commitment towards resilience. The organizational cultural change perspective that promotes the involvement of anybody in the needed concerns and issues without any barriers can enhance the organizational resilience. The individual resilience characteristics can be applied to organizational resilience which are essential to create a growing organizational culture of resilience.

Development of an organizational resilience approach is underpinned by organizational cultural change and branding built on sharing experiences and interactions with others. Organizational resilience requires training based on leadership, culture of trust, empathy, and acceptance. Organizations can build their own resilience leading to reduce stress in change Culture of organizational resilience building should be supported by the served individuals. Some new cultural identified trends need further investigation and can stimulate more in-depth research.

ORGANIZATIONAL SAFETY AND RELIABILITY

Organizational resilience is organizing for safety and reliability. The safety and reliability perspective of organizational resilience is a response to operate chaos without equilibria. Reliability and robustness determine organizational resilience when degradation, failure and error are no tolerated (Roberts, 1990). The system´s safety and reliability affect the dimensions of service aiming towards resilience.

Resilience is defined as the ability in difficult situations to stay safe and avoid accidents (Hale, 2006: 40). A framework for assessing resilience of systems and its components in a relationship of multiple risks to current operating parameters and the boundary of its safe operations is and indicator of resilience. Organizational resilience enact safety by handling exceptional events (Antunes 2011). Beyond the trade-offs between safety and production, and the link between the failure to balance production with safety risks and accidents, there are more to be studied and learnt about the enhancement of organizational resilience (Woods, 2003).

Create safety is inherent to resilience engineering perspective (Dekker et al. 2008). Employee enactment of safety to handle and deal unexpected events enhances organizational resilience (Antunes 2011; Borges and Menegon 2012; Carvalho et al. 2012) supported by information technology (Chewning et al. 2013; Gimenez et al. 2017).

More efficient and reliable organizations are also more committed to resiliency mindset to recognize and identify events that go wrong and resolve with the minimum of harm. The organizational resilience research links the reactions to unexpected events focusing on responses and organizational reliability dealing with mindfulness for the presence of unexpected events (Weick & Sutcliffe, 2007).

Organizational resilience is a positive perspective focusing on the enhancement of safety and reliability and the salotungenetic understanding of coping (Sutcliffe and Vogus 2003). The essential elements of organizational resilience in functional domains are the combination of the of people behavior, process reliability and product excellence to provide experience, trust, and reputation aimed to achieve information, supply, and operational resilience. Resilience can be integrated with operating reliability across a range of conditions. The organizational structures and procedures ensure reliability and facilitate organizational resilience.

Resilience has been analyzed in the context of high-reliability organizations (Weick & Sutcliffe, 2001) and in the context of responses to weather extremes events (Linnenluecke & Griffiths, 2012). Some assumptions of empirical studies in organizational resilience limit their contributions such as the concept of high-reliability organization applied to a diversity of entities with a variety of characteristics (La Porte & Consolini, 1998; Bigley & Roberts, 2001; La Porte & Thomas, 1995). A high reliable organization can learn from errors rather than rigidity (Weick & Sutcliffe, 2007) enabling to analyze the conditions of resilience in an interactionist perspective questioning the notion of organizational resilience. A high reliable organization exhibits resilience in unanticipated occurrences (Kendra & Wachtendorf, 2003: 14).

Organizations are more organizational resilience reliability-seeking then reliability-achieving (Linnenluecke 2017). The interdependent relationship between organizational and community reliability is basic for the resilience between the organization and community (Lee, Vargo, & Seville, 2013; McManus et al., 2008).

PROMOTION ELEMENTS FOR ORGANIZATIONAL RESILIENCE

Resilience promotes the mitigation and preparedness relying on the quantitative conception of determining the real probability risk of adverse events and the severity of their consequences (Gephart, Van Maanen, & Oberlechner, 2009: 143). Some factors promoting organizational resiliencies can be identified and assessed through different approaches. Some of the practices that are effective in enabling and fostering organizational resilience are to provide training and development of resiliency (Coutu, 2002).

Organizational resilience may be promoted by decentralization, redundancy, diversity, deployment of organizational resources and structures (Bruneau et al., 2003; Wildavsky, 1988; Vogus and Sutcliffe, 2007). From the same perspective, Akgün, & Keskin, (2014) there are several elements that integrate organizational resilience, among others, competence orientation, behavioral preparedness, social capital, original and unscripted agility, practical habits, and resource networks.

The resilience framework accommodates a qualitative capacity to absorb shocks and unexpected events maintaining the functions of recognition, recombination and renewal of organizational structures and processes. Networks are relational resources and protective factors that facilitate organizational resilience (Gittell et al. 2006; Kahn et al. 2013; Vogus and Sutcliffe 2007). The range of a personal network relationships is an antecedent of resilience that have influence in the availability of resources to recover from crises. The framework is the contextual resilience are characterized by the social capital and the resource network.

The communication systems using network theory are relevant to evaluate organizational resilience (Ruiz-Martin et al. 2017, Ruiz-Martin et al. 2015). Using a personal narrative helps credibility that fosters organizational resilience. Experience and expertise are the power that foster organizational resilience (Lengnick-Hall et al. 2011; Sutcliffe and Vogus 2003; Weick et al. 1999) in organic structures than contribute to improve resilience more than hierarchical and mechanistic management structures (Jaaron and Backhouse, 2014). The hierarchy composition principle determines the importance of the elements of organizational resilience.

The resilience processes considered as the ability of the system to absorb and recover from disruptions and shocks, transforming structures and means for functioning in the face of stresses (Van der Vegt et al., 2015: 972; Williams and Shepherd 2016). Organizational resilience support structural and contextual ambidexterity (Eltantawy 2016). A viable system model can be used to assess resilience and structural arrangements (Chan 2011). Tests on a structural model may provide empirical evidence of a set of exogenous variables to determine endogenous variables can be used to determine the antecedent and positive outcomes of organizational resilience.

An approach of organizational resilience from the internal structural and workflow articulation between occupational groups characterized by symbolic and identity values. Social network analysis (Borgatti et al., 2009; Borgatti, et al., 2018) is a tool to analyze the structure of interactions in organizational resilience. The different types of structures, actors and contents of networks may affect the organizational resilience.

Some of the distinct attributes used to define organizational resilience are closely related to structure. Organizational resilience is the ability to maintain a structural configurations (McCarthy *et al.* 2017), surviving and retaining the structure and functions (Lampel *et al.* 2014; Salwan and Gada 2018), business functions (Antunes, 2011; Clement and Rivera, 2017) above-average returns (de Oliveira Teixeira and Werther 2013). A loss of resilience of organizational structures and processes may have consequences with direct and indirect impacts for organizations (Wilbanks et al. 2007; O'Brien et al. 2004). Organizational interruption impacts determine losses from actual events with limited insights on predictive elements of future organizational resilience. Behavior has an impact on vulnerability from structural change impact of resilience (Gallopín, 2006).

Organizational resilience requires more distributed control with central coordination and not centralized control with distributed implementation. Functional decentralization as being simultaneously bureaucratic and decentralized facilitates organizational resilience in such a way that authority patterns shift to functional skills (Clarke 1993; La Porte and Consolini 1991: 31).

Diversity is the variability of features impacted by threat and unexpected events attacking species, physical attributes. Diversity provides increased resilience. Organizational diversity and variation are proactive in nature to ensure resilience. Some characteristics that can be used as indicators of resilience can be diversity, skills, physical substance, etc. Resilience rather than stability is supported by diversity (Brock et al., 2002: 272). Organizational resilience has indicators such as level of knowledge, adequacy of resources, diversity, information sharing, etc.

DEPLOYMENT OF ORGANIZATIONAL RESOURCES

Organizational resilience is multilevel related to resources, processes, and routines. The multi-level conception of organizational resilience across the organization, groups and individual interactions is related to the effective use of resources, processes, and routines dependent. Literature on organizational resilience is more based on normative and prescriptive methodology focusing on attributes, behaviors and resources (Boin and van Eeten, 2013; Duit, 2016; Sutcliffe and Vogus, 2003). Synergy between organizational resilience theory development and the ambiguous and resource constrained operating decision contexts may result in cyclical processes.

Contextual resilience integrates the resources and connections to provide the setting for using the behavioral and cognitive resilience. Collective sensemaking is a relevant element of cognitive resilience (Lengnick-Hall and Beck 2009; Lengnick-Hall et al. 2011; Linnenluecke et al. 2012; Maitlis, 2005; Patriotta, 2003; Maitlis and Christianson, 2014). Conceptualization of organizational resilience focus on typologies of specific behaviors (Coutu, 2002; Hamel and Välikangas, 2003; Horne and Orr, 1998; Ishak and Williams, 2018), to integrate resilient resources and behaviors (Lengnick-Hall and Beck, 2005; Sutcliffe and Vogus 2003; Vogus and Sutcliffe 2007).

The organizational resilience approach is likely where there are resources constraints. Organizations that must deal with unexpected events, identify resources, develop practices and processes to facilitate organizational bricolage leading to organizational resilience (Bechky and Okhuysen 2011).

The slack resources are a concept that is an antecedent to organizational resilience contributing to the problem solving of the organization (Acquaah *et al.* 2011; Gittell *et al.* 2006; Lengnick-Hall and Beck, 2005; Linnenluecke and Griffiths, 2012). In adverse events the resources are brought from external sources, regional and state level to support the organizational resilience in order that organizations can be able to bounce back (Carpenter et al. 2001). Organizational resources losses and the conditions of failure and hard times require organizational resilience leading to renewal and constant change.

Accessible financial, human and time resources are the foundation for adequate reactions under challenging situations (Hamel and Vaelikangas 2003; Lengnick-Hall and Beck 2009; Vogus and Sutcliffe, 2007). Human capital, social and financial resources are influencing factors that facilitate organizational resilience (Danes et al. 2009). The financial growth is an element of organizational resilience. Social resources such as social capital are a source of organizational resilience (Gittell et al. 2006; Powley, 2009; Sutcliffe and Vogus, 2003) in time of crisis and offer contextual benefits (Lengnick-Hall and Beck, 2009, Leana and van Buren, 1999; Faraj and Sproull, 2000; Gittell et al. 2006; McGuinness and Johnson, 2014).

Organizations foster resiliency by increasing the psychological resources and motivation through task autonomy and discretion of employees to build competences, self-efficacy, and confidence to respond during challenging situations (Sutcliffe & Vogus, 2003; Masten & Reed, 2002). Employees play relevant the role in resilience to deal with unexpected events and access to resources. Efficacy as an outcome of organizational resilience that enhances the ability to process feedback, rearrange and transfer resources and knowledge (Sutcliffe and Vogus, 2003). A low level of organizational resilience is present during the phase of release characterized by the rapid disbanding of the resources accumulated in the system. During the phase of reorganization, the organizational resilience increase characterized by the reassembly of resources and components of the system.

The ability of building organizational resilience against unanticipated and unexpected threats by organizations can increase their resilience with limited resources. Building and enhancing organizational resilience against unanticipated threats requires an ability to act outside of the response plans by investing some resources in risk-assessment and testing in the individual and system critical elements. Organizational work resilience empowers the human resources, the business model, and interactions (Foster & Dye 2005). Recovery operations may improve organizational resilience from testing and assuring availability of skilled human resources. Team and individual resilience can be developed and improved by training and human resources development (Lengnick-Hall et al. 2011).

Organizational resources make different contributions to resilience. Resource allocation decisions are made to support organizational resilience in anticipation of adverse conditions. The element of anticipation of organizational resilience emphasize to maintain effectiveness and avoiding degradation. Organizational resilience decisions on the use of resources requires a lot of sensitivity to carry on consequences. Sensing process helps the organizational resilience orientation to perceive threats and opportunities from emerging resource factors and options, partnerships, business models, etc. Organizational resilience requires a buffer to maximize the potential to regenerate allowing more time for the emergence of a better option to enhance resilience and maximize resources.

Resources and practices of organizational bricolage is relevant to resilience characterized by mindfulness (Bechky and Okhuysen 2011). The use of *salutogenic* lens, organizational resources, and assets as indicators for organizational resilience contribute to the evaluation and engagement of organizational contingency planning.

Entrepreneurial resilience is distinguished from organizational resilience in both theorizations and in practices in terms of resources, experiences, and slacks (Manfield and Newey, 2017). Resilience in family organizations is evaluated by the role clarity, decision authority ownership equality, fairness of compensation, failure to resolve conflicts, unfair workloads, and competition for resources (Danes et al. 2009). SMEs vulnerability and resilience are associated to resources, experiences, mindset, and risk taking (Kish-Gephart and Campbell 2015; Doern, 2016).

CONCLUSION

The reflective analysis of the concept of organizational resilience emerging from cognitive, ecology and engineering sciences, among others, confirms that the creation and development of an organizational resilience framework for structural construct can be supported by elements based on flexibility of organizational culture, organizational safety and reliability, the promotion elements, and the deployment of organizational resources.

The concept of organizational resilience is linked to the differing backgrounds of respondents despite their similarities, it is related as the ability to cope with risks and disturbances, planning and organizational structures. The structural arrangements of the working groups to cope with unexpected events question the boundaries to enhance the organizational resilience. Organizational resilience is dependent on the specific situation.

Resilience can be developed, practiced, and enhanced at large scale state-wide and international level frameworks. Organizational resilience requires commitment of all involved to transform and build upon characteristics of values and behaviors achieved through interactions and ongoing relationships that focus on the protection of resources and assets from the external threats.

REFERENCES

Acquaah, M., Amoako-Gyampah, K., & Jayaram, J. (2011). Resilience in family and nonfamily firms: An examination of the relationships between manufacturing strategy, competitive strategy, and firm performance. *International Journal of Production Research*, *49*(18), 5527–5544. doi:10.1080/00207543.2011.563834

Akgün & Halit Keskin. (2014). Organizational resilience capacity and firm product innovativeness and performance. *International Journal of Production Research*, *52*(23), 6918–6937.

Aleksić, A., Stefanović, M., Arsovski, S., & Tadić, D. (2013). An assessment of organizational resilience potential in SMEs of the process industry, a fuzzy approach. *J Loss Prevent Proc*, *26*, 1238–1245. doi 10.1016/j.jlp.2013.06.004

Alesi, P. (2008). Building enterprise-wide resilience by integrating business continuity capability into day-to-day business culture and technology. *Journal of Business Continuity & Emergency Planning*, *2*(3), 214–220.

Antunes, P. (2011). BPM and exception handling: Focus on organizational resilience. *IEEE Transactions on Systems, Man, and Cybernetics*, *41*, 383–392. doi:10.1109/TSMCC. 2010.20625 04

Bechky, B. A., & Okhuysen, G. A. (2011). Expecting the unexpected? How SWAT officers and film. *Academy of Management Journal*, *54*(2), 239–261.

Becker, P., Abrahamsson, M., & Tehler, H. (2014). An emergent means to assurgent ends: societal resilience for safety and sustainability. In Becom. Resilient. Ashgate Publishing, Ltd.

Boin, A., & van Eeten, M. J. B. (2013). The Resilient Organization—A critical appraisal. *Public Management Review*, *15*, 429–445.

Borgatti, S. P., Everett, M. G., & Johnson, J. C. (2018). Analyzing social networks. *Sage (Atlanta, Ga.)*.

Borgatti, S. P., Mehra, A., Brass, D. J., & Labianca, G. (2009). Network analysis in the social sciences. *Science*, *323*(5916), 892–895. doi:10.1126cience.1165821

Borges, F. M., & Menegon, N. L. (2012). Different roles in the quest for system resilience. *Work (Reading, Mass.)*, *41*, 3238–3245.

Carvalho, F. A., Koren, O., & Goodrich, J. K. (2012). Transient Inability to Manage Proteobacteria Promotes Chronic Gut Inflammation in TLR5-Deficient Mice. *Cell Host & Microbe*, *12*(2), 139–152. doi:10.1016/j.chom.2012.07.004

Brahma, S. S. (2009). Assessment of construct validity in management research. *Journal of Management Research, 9*, 59–71.

Brock, W. A., Mäler, K. G., & Perrings, C. (2002). Resilience and Sustainability: The Economic Analysis of Nonlinear Dynamic Systems. In L. H. Gunderson & C. S. Holling (Eds.), *Panarchy: Understanding Transformations in Human and Natural Systems* (pp. 261–289). Island Press.

Bruneau, M., Chang, S. E., Eguchi, R. T., Lee, G. C., O'Rourke, T. D., Reinhorn, A. M., Shinozuka, M., Tierney, K., Wallace, W. A., & von Winterfeldt, D. (2003). A framework to quantitatively assess and enhance the seismic resilience of communities. *Earthquake Spectra, 19*(4), 733–752. doi:10.1193/1.1623497

Carpenter, S., Walker, B., Anderies, J. M., & Abel, N. (2001). From metaphor to measurement: Resilience of what to what? *Ecosystems (New York, N.Y.), 4*, 765–781.

Castleden, M., McKee, M., Murray, V., & Leonardi, G. (2011, September). Resilience thinking in health protection. *Journal of Public Health, 33*(3), 369–377. doi:10.1093/pubmed/fdr027

Chan, J. K. (2011). Enhancing Organisational Resilience: Application of Viable System Model and MCDA in a Small Hong Kong Company. *International Journal of Production Research, 49*(18), 5545–5563. doi:10.1080/00207543.2011.563829

Chewning, L. V., Lai, C.-H., & Doerfel, M. L. (2013). Organizational resilience and using information and communication technologies to rebuild communication structures. *Management Communication Quarterly, 27*, 237–263. doi:10.1177/08933 18912 46581 5

Clarke, K. R. (1993). Non-parametric multivariate analyses of changes in community structure. *Austral Ecology, 18*(1), 117–143. doi:10.1111/j.1442-9993.1993.tb00438.x

Clement, V., & Rivera, J. (2017). From adaptation to transformation: An extended research agenda for organizational resilience to adversity in the natural environment. *Organization & Environment, 30*, 346–365. doi:10.1177/10860 26616 65833 3

Coles, E., & Buckle, P. (2004). Developing community resilience as a foundation for effective disaster recovery. *Australian Journal of Emergency Management, 19*(4), 6–15.

Coutu, D. L. (2002). How resilience works. *Harvard Business Review, 80*(5), 46–55.

Crichton, M. T., Ramsay, C. G., & Kelly, T. (2009). Enhancing organizational resilience through emergency planning: Learnings from cross-sectorial lessons. *Journal of Contingencies and Crisis Management, 17*, 24–37.

Cuthill, M., Ross, H., Maclean, K., Owens, K., & Witt, B. (2008). Reporting Social Outcomes of Development: An Analysis of Diverse Approaches. *The International Journal of Interdisciplinary Social Sciences: Annual Review, 3*, 145–158.

Danes, S. M., Lee, J., Amarapurkar, S., Stafford, K., Haynes, G., & Brewton, K. E. (2009). Determinants of family business resilience after a natural disaster by gender of business owner. *Journal of Developmental Entrepreneurship, 14*(4), 333–354. doi:10.1142/S1084946709001351

Daskon, C. (2010). Cultural resilience – the roles of cultural traditions in sustaining rural livelihoods: A case study from rural kandyan villages in central Sri Lanka. *Sustainability*, *2*(4), 1080–1100.

Dawson, C. S. (2010). *Leading culture change: what every CEO needs to know*. Stanford University Press.

Dekker, J. M., Funahashi, T., & Nijpels, G. (2008, April 1). Prognostic Value of Adiponectin for Cardiovascular Disease and Mortality. *The Journal of Clinical Endocrinology and Metabolism*, *93*(4), 1489–1496. doi:10.1210/jc.2007-1436

Denyer, D. (2017). *Organizational Resilience: A summary of academic evidence, business insights and new thinking*. BSI and Cranfield School of Management.

DesJardine, M., Bansal, P., & Yang, Y. (2017). Bouncing back: Building resilience through social and environmental practices in the context of the 2008 global financial crisis. *Journal of Management*, *26*. doi:10.1177/01492 06317 70885 4

Diamantopoulos, A., & Siguaw, J. A. (2006). Formative versus reflective indicators in organizational measure development: A comparison and empirical illustration. *British Journal of Management*, *17*, 263–282.

Doern, R. (2016). Entrepreneurship and Crisis Management: The Experiences of Small Business during the London 2011 Riots. *International Small Business Journal*, *34*(3), 276–302. doi:10.1177/0266242614553863

Duit, A. (2016). Resilience thinking: Lessons for Public Administration. *Public Administration*, *94*, 364–380.

de Oliveira Teixeira, E., & Werther, W.B. (2013). Resilience: Continuous renewal of competitive advantages. *Bus Horiz*, *56*, 333–342. https ://doi.org/ r.2013.01.009 doi:10.1016/j.busho

Edwards, J. R. (2001). Multidimensional constructs in organizational behavior research: An integrative analytical framework. *Organizational Research Methods*, *4*, 144–192.

Edwards, J. R., & Bagozzi, R. P. (2000). On the nature and direction of relationship between constructs and measures. *Psychological Methods*, *5*, 155.

Eltantawy, R. A. (2016). The role of supply management resilience in attaining ambidexterity: A dynamic capabilities approach. *Journal of Business and Industrial Marketing*, *31*(1), 123–134. doi:10.1108/JBIM-05-2014-0091

Faraj, S., & Sproull, L. (2000). Coordinating expertise in software development teams. *Management Science*, *46*, 1554–1568.

Foster, S., & Dye, K. (2005). Building continuity into strategy. *Journal of Corporate Real Estate*, *7*(2), 105–119.

Gallopín, G. C. (2006). Linkages between Vulnerability, Resilience and Adaptive Capacity. *Global Environmental Change*, *16*(3), 293–303.

Gephart, R. P., Van Maanen, J., & Oberlechner, T. (2009). Organizations and risk in late modernity. *Organization Studies*, *30*(2–3), 141–155. https://doi.org/ doi:10.1177/0170840608101474

Gimenez, R., Hernantes, J., Labaka, L., Hiltz, S. R., & Turoff, M. (2017). Improving the resilience of disaster management organizations through virtual communities of practice: A Delphi study. *Journal of Contingencies and Crisis Management*, *25*, 160–170. doi:10.1111/1468-5973.12181

Gittell, J. H., Cameron, K., Lim, S., & Rivas, V. (2006). Relationships, layoffs, and organizational resilience: Airline industry responses to September 11. *The Journal of Applied Behavioral Science*, *42*, 300–329.

Hale, A., & Heijer, T. (2006). Defining Resilience. In E. Hollnagel, D. D. Woods, & N. Leveson (Eds.), *Resilience Engineering: Concepts and Precepts* (pp. 35–40). Ashgate.

Hamel, G., & Välikangas, L. (2003). The quest for resilience. *Harvard Business Review, 81*(9), 52–63.

Helwig, K. R. (2013). Resilience: A responsibility that can't be delegated. *Frontiers of Health Services Management*, *30*(2), 31–35. https://www.ache.org/pubs/Frontiers/frontiers_index.cfm

Herrera, I. A., Pasquini, A., Ragosta, M., & Vennesland, A. (2014). The SCALES framework for identifying and extracting resilience related indicators: preliminary findings of a go-around case study. *SIDs 2014-Proc. SESAR Innov. Days, Eurocontrol.*

Hiles, A. (2011). *The Definitive Handbook of Business Continuity Management*. Wiley.

Hillman, J., & Guenther, E. (2021). Organizational Resilience: A Valuable Construct for Management Research? *International Journal of Management Reviews*, *23*, 7–44. doi:10.1111/ijmr.12239

Hirsch, P. M., & Levin, D. Z. (1999). Umbrella advocates versus validity police: A life-cycle model. *Organization Science*, *10*, 199–212.

Horne, J. F. (1997). The coming of age of organizational resilience. *Business Forum, 22*, 24–28.

Horne, J. F., & Orr, J. E. (1998). Assessing Behaviors that Create Resilient Organizations. *Employment Relations Today*, *24*, 29–39.

Ignatiadis, I. & Nandhakumar, J. (2007). The Impact of Enterprise Systems on Organizational Control and Drift: A Human-Machine Agency Perspective. *International Journal of Enterprise Information Systems, 3*(3), 36-51. DOI: doi:10.1057/palgrave.jit.2000087

Ishak, A. W., & Williams, E. A. (2018). A dynamic model of organizational resilience: Adaptive and anchored approaches. *Corporate Communications*, *23*, 180–196.

Jaaron, A. A. M., & Backhouse, C. J. (2014). Service organisations resilience through the application of the vanguard method of systems thinking: A case study approach. *International Journal of Production Research*, *52*, 2026–2041.

Kahn, W. A., Barton, M. A., & Fellows, S. (2013). Organizational crises and the disturbance of relational systems. *Academy of Management Review*, *38*, 377–396. doi:10.5465/amr.2011.0363

Kantur, D., & İşeri-Say, A. (2015). Measuring organizational resilience: A scale development. Journal of Business. *Economics & Finance*, *4*(3), 456–472.

Kendra, J. M., & Wachtendorf, T. (2003). Elements of Resilience after the World Trade Center Disaster: Reconstituting New York City's Emergency Operations Center. *Disasters*, *27*(1), 37–53.

Kish-Gephart, J. J., & Campbell, J. T. (2015). You Don't Forget Your Roots: The Influence of CEO Social Class Background on Strategic Risk Taking. *Academy of Management Journal*, *58*(6), 1614–1636. doi:10.5465/amj.2013.1204

Kohno, Y., Masuda, Y., Nagahashi, H., Tanaka, K., & Tashiro, K. (2012). Form development for self-rating an organization's vulnerability and resilience to disruption. *Journal of Disaster Research*, *7*(4), 392–407. doi:10.20965/jdr.2012.p0392

Lampel, J., Bhalla, A., & Jha, P. P. (2014). Does governance confer organisational resilience? Evidence from UK employee-owned businesses. *European Management Journal*, *32*, 66–72.

Law, K. S., Wong, C.-S., & Mobley, W. M. (1998). Toward a taxonomy of multidimensional constructs. *Academy of Management Review*, *23*, 741–755.

La Porte, T. R., & Consolini, P. M. (1998). Theoretical and operationalchallenges of "high-reliability organizations": Air-traffic control and aircraft carriers. *International Journal of Public Administration*, *21*(6–8), 847–852. doi:10.1080/01900699808525320

La Porte, T. R., & Thomas, C. W. (1995). Regulatory compliance and the ethos of quality enhancement: Surprises in nuclear power plant operations. *Journal of Public Administration Research and Theory. J-PART*, *5*(1), 109–137.

La Porte, T. R., & Consolini, P. M. (1991). Working in practice but not in theory: Theoretical challenges of "high-reliability organizations". *Journal of Public Administration Research and Theory. J-PART*, *1*(1), 19–48.

Leana, C. R., & van Buren, H. J. III. (1999). Organizational social capital and employment practices. *Academy of Management Review*, *24*, 538–555.

Lee, A. V., Vargo, J., & Seville, E. (2013). Developing a Tool to Measure and Compare Organizations' Resilience. *Natural Hazards Review*, *14*, 29–41. doi:10.1061/(ASCE)NH.1527-6996.0000075

Lengnick-Hall, C. A., & Beck, T. E. (2009). Resilience capacity and strategic agility: Prerequisites for thriving in a dynamic environment. In Resilience engineering perspectives, Volume 2. Preparation and restoration. Ashgate Publishing.

Lengnick-Hall, C. A., & Beck, T. E. (2005). Adaptive fit versus robust transformation: How organizations respond to environmental change. *Journal of Management*, *31*, 738–757.

Lengnick-Hall, C. A., Beck, T. E., & Lengnick-Hall, M. L. (2011). Developing a capacity for organizational resilience through strategic human resource management. *Human Resource Management Review*, *21*, 243–255.

Lewis, R., Donaldson-Feilder, E., & Pangallo, A. (2011). *Developing resilience*. Affinity Health at Work. Retrieved August 31, 2013, from https://www.cipd.co.uk/

Limnios, A. M., Mazzarol, T., Ghadouani, A., & Schilizzi, S. G. M. (2014). The Resilience Architecture Framework: Four Organizational Archetypes. *European Management Journal*, *32*(1), 104–116.

Linnenluecke, M. K. (2017). Resilience in business and management research: A review of influential publications and a research agenda. *International Journal of Management Reviews*, *19*(1), 4–30.

Linnenluecke, M. K., & Griffiths, A. (2012). Assessing organizational resilience to climate and weather extremes: Complexities and methodological pathways. *Climatic Change*, *113*, 933–947.

Maitlis, S. (2005). The social processes of organizational sensemaking. *Academy of Management Journal*, *48*, 21–49.

Maitlis, S., & Christianson, M. (2014). Sense making in organizations: Taking stock and moving forward. *The Academy of Management Annals*, *8*, 57–125. doi:10.1080/19416520.2014.873177

Mallak, L. A. (1998). Measuring resilience in health care provider organizations. *Health Manpower Management*, *24*(4), 148–152. doi:10.1108/09552069810215755

Manfield, R. C., & Newey, L. R. (2017). Resilience as an Entrepreneurial Capability: Integrating Insights from a Cross-Disciplinary Comparison. *International Journal of Entrepreneurial Behaviour & Research*. Advance online publication. doi:10.1108/IJEBR-11-2016-0368

Masten, A. S., & Reed, M. J. (2002). Resilience in development. In C. R. Snyder & S. Lopez (Eds.), Handbook of positive psychology (pp. 74-88). Oxford University Press.

McCarthy, I.P., Collard, M., & Johnson, M. (2017). Adaptive organizational resilience: an evolutionary perspective. *Curr Opin Environ Sustain, 28*, 33–40. https ://doi.org/t.2017.07.005 doi:10.1016/j.cosus

McDaniels, T., Chang, S., Cole, D., Mikawoz, J., & Longstaff, H. (2008). Fostering resilience to extreme events within infrastructure systems: Characterizing decision contexts for mitigation and adaptation. *Global Environmental Change*, *18*, 310–318.

McGuinness, M., & Johnson, N. (2014). Exploiting social capital and path-dependent resources for organisational resilience: Preliminary findings from a study on flooding. *Procedia Economics and Finance*, *18*, 447–455.

McManus, S., Seville, E., Vargo, J., & Brunsdon, D. (2008). Facilitated process for improving organizational resilience. *Natural Hazards Review*, *9*(2), 81–90. doi:10.1061/_ASCE_1527-6988_2008_9:2_81

O'Brien, K., Sygna, L., & Haugen, J. E. (2004). Vulnerable or resilient? A multi-scale assessment of climate impacts and vulnerability in Norway. *Climatic Change*, *64*, 193–225.

Omidvar, M., Mazloumi, A., Mohammad Fam, I., & Nirumand, F. (2017). Development of a framework for resilience measurement: Suggestion of fuzzy resilience grade (RG) and fuzzy resilience early warning grade (REWG). *WOR*, *56*, 463–474. doi:10.3233/WOR-17251 2

Oshio, S., Nakatani, M., Kaneko, M., & Nagamine, K. (2002). Negative na dekigoto karanotatchinaori-womichibikushinritekitokusei; seishintekikaihukuryokusyakudo nosakusei [The psychological properties that promote bounce back from negative states]. *Japanese Journal of Counseling Science*, *35*, 57–65.

Pasteur, K. (2011). *From Vulnerability to Resilience: A Framework for Analysis and Action to Build Community Resilience*. Practical Action Publishing.

Paton, D., Smith, L., & Violanti, J. (2000). Disaster response: Risk, vulnerability and resilience. *Disaster Prevention and Management*, *9*(3), 173–179.

Patriotta, G. (2003). Sensemaking on the shop floor: Narratives of knowledge in organizations. *Journal of Management Studies*, *40*, 349–375.

Powley, E. H. (2009). Reclaiming resilience and safety: Resilience activation in the critical period of crisis. *Human Relations*, *62*(9), 1289–1326.

Pettit, T. J., Fiksel, J., & Croxton, K. L. (2010). Ensuring supply chain resilience: Developmentof a conceptual framework. *Journal of Business Logistics*, *31*(1), 1–21.

Podsakoff, P. M., MacKenzie, S. B., & Podsakoff, N. P. (2016). Recommendations for creating better concept definitions in the organizational, behavioral, and social sciences. *Organizational Research Methods*, *19*, 159–203.

Richtnér, A., & Löfsten, H. (2014). Managing in turbulence: How the capacity for resilience influences creativity. *R & D Management*, *44*, 137–151.

Roberts, K. H. (1990). Some Characteristics of One Type of High Reliability Organization. *Organization Science*, *1*(2), 160.

Ruiz-Martin, C., Pérez Ríos, J., Wainer, G., Pajares, J., Hernández, C., & López-Paredes, A. (2017). The Application of the Viable System Model to Enhance Organizational Resilience. Advances in Management Engineering, 88–100. https://doi.org/ doi:10.1007/978-3-319-55889-9_5

Ruiz-Martin, C., López-Paredes, A., & Wainer, G. (2015). Applying complex network theory to the assessment of organizational resilience. *IFAC-PapersOnLine*, *48*(3), 1224–1229. doi:10.1016/j.ifacol.2015.06.251

Sahwan, P., & Gada, V. P. (2018). Antecedents of resilience: An investigation into bharat forge. *Indian Journal of Industrial Relations*, *53*, 449–461.

Sheffi, Y., & Rice, J. B. (2005). A supply chain view of the resilient enterprise. *MIT Sloan Management Review*, *47*, 41–48.

Shin, J., Taylor, M. S., & Seo, M.-G. (2012). Resources for change: The relationships of organizational inducements and psychological resilience to employees' attitudes and behaviors toward organizational change. *Academy of Management Journal*, *55*, 727–748.

Somers, S. (2009). Measuring resilience potential: An adaptive strategy for organizational crisis planning. *Journal of Contingencies and Crisis Management*, *17*(1), 12–23.

Suddaby, R. (2010). Editor's comments: Construct clarity in theories of management and organization. *Academy of Management Journal*, *35*, 346–357.

Sutcliffe, K. M., & Vogus, T. (2003). Organizing for resilience. In K. S. Cameron, J. E. Dutton, & R. E. Quinn (Eds.), *Positive organizational scholarship* (pp. 94–110). Berrett-Koehler.

Taleb, N. N., & Douady, R. (2013). Mathematical definition, mapping, and detection of (anti)fragility. *Quantitative Finance*, *13*(11), 1677–1689. doi:10.1080/14697688.2013.800219

Taleb, N. N. (2012). *Antifragile: Things that Gain from Disorder* (Vol. 3). Random House.

Tetlock, P. E. (1985, September). Accountability: A Social Check on the Fundamental Attribution Error. *Social Psychology Quarterly*, *48*(3), 227–236.

Tierney, K. J. (2003). *Conceptualizing and measuring organizational and community resilience: lessons from the emergency response following the September 11, 2001, attack on the World Trade Center*. Univ. of Delaware.

Tompkins, J. A. (2007). 4 Steps to business resilience. *Industrial Management (Norcross, Georgia)*, *49*(4), 14–18.

Valastro, J. (2011). Organisational resilience: a position paper for critical infrastructure. Commonwealth of Australia.

Van Der Beek, D., & Schraagen, J. M. (2015). ADAPTER: Analysing and developing adaptability and performance in teams to enhance resilience. *Reliability Engineering & System Safety*, 141.

van der Vegt, G. S., Essens, P., Wahlstrom, M., & George, G. (2015). Managing risk and resilience. *Academy of Management Journal*, *58*, 971–980.

Vogus, T. J., & Sutcliffe, K. M. (2007). *Organizational resilience: Towardsa theory and research agenda*. Paper presented at the Systems, Manand Cybernetics, 2007. ISIC. IEEE International Conference.

Weick, K. E., & Sutcliffe, K. M. (2007). Managing the unexpected: Resilient performance in an age of uncertainty (2nd ed.). Jossey-Bass.

Weick, K. E., & Sutcliffe, K. M. (2001). *Managing the unexpected: Assuring high performance in an age of complexity*. Jossey-Bass.

Weick, K. E., Sutcliffe, K. M., & Obstfeld, D. (1999). Organizing for High Reliability: Processes of Collective Mindfulness. In R. S. Sutton & B. M. Staw (Eds.), *Research in Organizational Behavior* (Vol. 1, pp. 81–123). Jai Press.

Williams, T. A., Gruber, D. A., Sutcliffe, K. M., Shepherd, D. A., & Zhao, E. Y. (2017). Organizational response to adversity: Fusing crisis management and resilience re-search streams. *The Academy of Management Annals*, *11*, 733–769.

Wong, C.-S., Law, K. S., & Huang, G.-H. (2008). On the importance of conducting construct-level analysis for multidimensional constructs in theory development and testing. *Journal of Management*, *34*, 744–764.

Woods, D. (2003). Creating Foresight: How Resilience Engineering Can Transform NASA' s Approach to Risky Decision Making. Testimony on the future of NASA for Committee of Commerce, Science and Transportation.

Wilbanks, T. J., & Romero Lankao, P. (2007). Industry, settlement, and society. In Climate change 2007: impacts, adaptation, and vulnerability: contribution of Working Group II to the Fourth Assessment Report of the Intergovernmental Panel on Climate Change. Cambridge University Press.

Wildavsky, A. B. (1988). *Searching for safety* (3rd ed.). Transaction Publishers.

Wilkinson, A., Elahi, S., & Eidinow, E. (2003). Section 2. Background and dynamics of the scenarios. *Journal of Risk Research*, *6*, 365–401.

Williams, T., & Shepherd, D. (2016). Building resilience or providing sustenance: Different paths of emergent ventures in the aftermath of the Haiti earthquake. *Academy of Management Journal*. Advance online publication. doi:10.5465/amj.2015.0682

Williams, T. A., Gruber, D. A., Sutcliffe, K. M., Shepherd, D. A., & Zhao, E. Y. (2017). Organizational response to adversity: Fusing crisis management and resilience research streams. *The Academy of Management Annals*, *11*, 733–769.

Zolli, A., & Healy, A. M. (2012). *Resilience: Why Things Bounce Back*. Simon and Schuster, Inc.

Chapter 12
Sustainable Luxury Fashion:
From Owning to Sharing

Fayrene Chieng
Curtin University, Malaysia

ABSTRACT

Changing consumer values and beliefs, particularly among Millennials, who have been identified as the most influential consumer group for luxury brands, has resulted in increased responsibility for sustainability. Furthermore, as the sharing economy becomes more popular, consumers are more likely to engage in non-ownership approaches to consumption, such as collaborative consumption. Luxury brands must consider making a significant shift toward sustainability efforts. However, literature is scarce on sustainable luxury. This chapter provides systematic review of current research on sustainable luxury marketing, focusing on consumer motivations and the relationship between luxury value and sustainability. This chapter will provide a deep understanding of the mechanisms underlying the successful combination of luxury and sustainability, which may help luxury brands achieve a shift toward more sustainable products.

INTRODUCTION

Sustainable development has received a lot of attention in the last few decades. According to World Commission on Environment and Development (WCED), the core of sustainable development as "meeting the needs of the present without jeopardizing future generations' ability to meet their own needs" (WCED, 1987, p. 8). Sustainability applications in business operations and marketing allow brands to differentiate their products and services (McDonagh and Prothero, 2014). In this sense, the brands should integrate the sustainability concept into their marketing strategies. A sustainable marketing strategy focuses on cultivating and sustaining long-term relationships with customers, the social environment, and the natural environment, to improve brand value for clients (Peattie and Belz, 2010).

One industry in the spotlight of sustainable marketing practices is luxury fashion (Franco, Hussain and McColl, 2019). In the past decade, the luxury fashion industry has been criticized for unsustainable conduct that negatively impacts social and ecological environments (Fletcher, 2008). It produces signifi-

DOI: 10.4018/978-1-7998-9590-9.ch012

cant waste and pollution from manufacturing, destroying unsold goods as a marketing tactic, involving animal abuse when testing new materials and the exploitation of employees (Henninger et al., 2017; Kerr and Landry, 2017). Despite these criticisms, the luxury fashion sector is expanding rapidly, with a retail market worth more than USD24 billion in 2020 and expected to reach USD51 billion by 2023. The key question is could luxury fashion be associated with sustainability? Incorporating sustainability into brand development is a challenge for luxury companies. Brand managers need a better understanding of the luxury values they can leverage to achieve successful sustainable marketing strategies.

The rise of the collaborative consumption or sharing economy has brought forward various forms of collaborative business across multiple industries, including hotels (eg: Airbnb), transportation (eg: Uber) and fashion retail industry (e.g., Rent the Runway). According to Time (2011), "one of the 10 ideas that will change the world" is sharing economy. In particular, collaborative consumption allows marketers to engage in the co-creation and co-innovation of products and services and thus, assist in the push for greater sustainability (Lim, 2020). As a result, 'fashion-sharing' has developed, which includes renting, exchanging, and sharing clothes (Perlacia, Duml and Saebi, 2017). However, little research has explored the impact of sharing economy on luxury fashion. As a result, a better understanding of sharing-based practices and platforms has been encouraged (Pantano and Stylos, 2020).

Accordingly, this chapter aims to examine the possibility of luxury fashion brands to initiate change towards a more sustainable fashion system. The objectives of the paper are threefold: (1) to explore luxury fashion values with the principles of sustainability; (2) to understand the roles of luxury fashion brands in supporting sharing economy (3) to address the sustainability challenges facing luxury fashion firms.

SUSTAINABILITY AND LUXURY FASHION

Sustainability Marketing

The academic interest in sustainability dates back to the 1990s when Elkington (1997) proposed the framework of Triple Bottom Line of economic (profits), social (people) and environment (planet). The Triple Bottom Line model encourages organizations to measure success based on sustainability performance. Sustainability is a new addition to the comprehensive development of marketing. Sustainable marketing refers to the process of planning, implementing, and controlling the development, pricing, promotion, and distribution of products in a way that meets customer needs, achieves organisational goals and is compatible with ecosystems (Fuller,1999). Sustainable marketing includes the concepts of environment marketing, green marketing and societal marketing (Trivedi et al., 2018; Kemper and Ballantine, 2019). Later, Peattie and Belz (2010) integrated traditional forms of marketing into sustainable marketing (Figure 1). The authors claimed that sustainability marketing necessitates a long-term focus on relationship building rather than the traditional short-term focus on transactions in modern marketing.

Figure 1. New concept of sustainability marketing
Source: (Peattie and Belz, 2010)

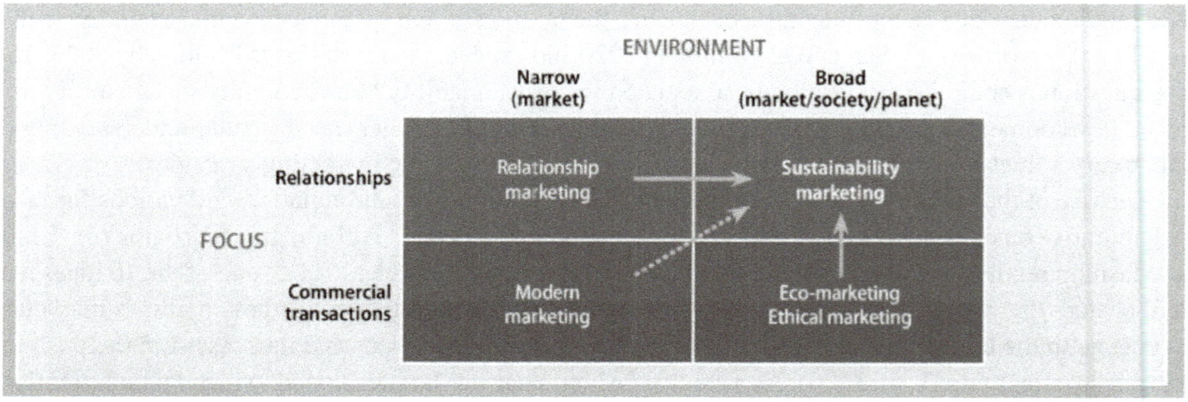

Sustainability in the fashion industry has begun to matter in the past decade. Hennings et al. (2017) explain that sustainability in fashion context refers to products that either contain environmentally friendly raw materials and/or are produced in a socially responsible manner. To add to the elaboration, Fletcher (2012) asserted that sustainability refers to products, practices, and relationships that promote environmental integrity and social quality. Fashion as a whole is perceived as incompatible with sustainability; it is characterized by short production runs and fast style cycles. Specifically, consumers eagerly await new products as soon as they are produced, and products are quickly coming to market. In the race to create the next big hit, designers ignore the life cycle of products and sustainability. This practice, in term conflicts with sustainability's long-term outlook. In response, fashion retailers have switched to more environmentally friendly materials and reduced the number of toxins they use in manufacturing and committed to social responsibility across all supply chains and greater transparency (Henninger et al., 2017; Joy et al. 2012).

The Essence of Luxury

Scholars from various disciplines have discussed the complicated nature of luxury, but there is no scientific consensus on what luxury is (Godart and Seong, 2017, Kapferer and Bastien, 2017). This perplexity may be due, in part, to its idiosyncratic nature (Kapferer, 1998), in which "what is luxury to one may be ordinary to another" (Phau and Prendergast, 2000, p. 123). Vigneron and Johnson (2004) linked luxury to the most prestigious brands, which are linked with status, rarity and rank. Luxury is something that is more than necessary (Bearden and Michael, 1982). Allérès (1997, as cited in Godart and Seong, 2017) explained luxury based on three hierarchical levels, each representing a different degree of accessibility. Inaccessible luxury refers to exclusive fashion or haute couture models, whereas intermediate luxury consists of specially tailored dresses that are wholly or partly duplicates of haute couture models at an expensive price. Accessible luxury, for example, ready-to-wear luxury brands corresponds to large production runs. In this chapter, luxury fashion is referred to exclusive ready-to-wear and fashion accessories.

Although luxury fashion is at odds with sustainability because it appeals more to desires than necessities. In this sense, it is somewhat hypocritical for the industry to advocate sustainability (Naderi and Strutton, 2015). Despite this, Kapferer (2010) asserted that the luxury industry displays sustainable qualities, referring to it as "the business of lasting value and permanence." In a similar vein, Hennings et al. (2017) considered a luxury as complementary to sustainability. The focus stems from the luxury value of heritage, timelessness, durability, and production in smaller batch sizes with a slow production cycle (Godart and Seong, 2017; Hennings et al., 2017; Joy et al, 2012). Most of the big luxury fashion retailers' have worked on sustainable initiatives and have made large investments to transform themselves into sustainable luxury (Adams et al., 2016).

SUSTAINABILITY IN LUXURY FASHION

As mentioned earlier, there is an assumption that the concepts of fashion and sustainability are contradictory, as the essence of fashion is innovation and constant change for a brand to remain fresh. This often means short production runs and fast style cycles, which can lead to waste. Sustainability, on the other hand, is considered as something of quality that endures over time. Luxury fashion retailers may be able to alleviate some of the challenges associated with fast fashion and provide leadership on sustainability concerns.

In essence, luxury fashion emphasizes longevity, durability, quality, authenticity, unique design aesthetic, and craftsmanship (Fionda and Moore, 2009; Hennings et al., 2017; Joy et al., 2012). Luxury fashion means much more to consumers than just a logo, its perception of rarity, privilege, and a first-class lifestyle (Kapferer and Bastien, 2012; Rolling and Sadachar, 2018). Since luxury fashion focuses on craftsmanship, longevity and durability, it is likely to complement the long-term perspective of sustainability (Arrigo, 2015; Hennings et al., 2017).

Inspired by the work of Wiedmann et al. (2007), this section explains consumer value perception concerning luxury fashion consumption and how it can be aligned with the principles of sustainability. Four dimensions of luxury values perceptions were discussed in the following sections: (1) functional, (2) individual, (3) social and (4) financial dimension of luxury values.

Functional Dimension of Luxury Fashion Value

As stated in Wiedmann et al. (2007), the functional dimension of luxury refers to the core benefits that drive the consumer-based luxury value. The essential values of a luxury fashion brand are durability, timeliness and artisanship and heritage (Godart and Seong 2017).

The Longevity of Luxury Fashion

Product longevity is an important dimension of sustainable consumption because it contributes to reduced waste (Sun, Bellezzqa and Paharia 2021). Durability and long-term value are inherently associated with luxury fashion (Athwal et al., 2019; Godart and Seong 2017; Sun et al., 2021). Luxury brands apply a long-term resource management strategy to produce high-quality products and thus are more sustainable (Amatulli et al., 2017; Athwal et al., 2019; Godart and Seong, 2017). In general, luxury products such as fine jewellery and bags can be used longer and are often passed down through generations due to their longevity (Wiedmann et al 2009). Such extended functional utility leads consumers to buy fewer luxury products and keep them longer. For example, Patagonia advertised the longevity of its products in its "Busy less, Demand more" campaign (Sun et al 2021). Luxurious products have a long life, thereby reducing waste and disposability problems. Therefore, buying luxury can be a unique way to engage in sustainable consumption.

The Artisanship of Luxury Fashion

In most cases, luxury fashion is synonymous with dream quality and a long history and heritage further enhance the strength of a brand (Joy et al., 2012). As an example, Louis Vuitton takes pride in its history of developing quality luggage for royalty for more than a century. The exceptional design aesthetics lend a sense of uniqueness to luxury fashion (Fionda and Moore, 2009; Joy et al., 2012; Phau and Prendergast, 2000). Because luxury fashion is produced in small quantities, it is scarce and exquisite. Luxury products are perceived by consumers as "rare products; when over diffused, they gradually lose their luxury character" (Dubois and Paternault, 1995, p. 72). A luxury product's production cycle is longer because skilled artisans use hand-picked, high-quality materials that are not mass-produced. Furthermore, when compared to fast fashion, luxury products are manufactured in smaller batch sizes (Hennings et al., 2017). In this sense, luxury products have limited availability, which restricts consumer consumption. Therefore, the artisanship and scarcity of luxury products may convey the idea that luxury brands encourage more reasonable, responsible consumption and help protect natural resources (Hennings et al., 2017; Kapferer, 2010; Ozdamar-Ertekin, 2019).

The Timeliness of Luxury Fashion

Luxury fashion brands are also known for their ability to transcend all eras of history (Joy et al., 2012). The stylistic longevity of their offerings demonstrates that their fashion will not quickly go out of style, reflecting its relevance (Fionda and Moore, 2009; Joy e al., 2012; Ozdamar-Ertekin, 2019). Slowing down the fashion cycle or the rate at which new collections are released can make it clear to consumers that they should value the product's longevity, timeliness, and craftsmanship. A commitment to quality craftsmanship and timeliness can propel luxury brands to the forefront of sustainability (Ozdamar-Ertekin, 2019). In other words, consumers are encouraged to use a high-quality, long-lasting product rather than something that is destined to the fashion trend.

Luxury product characteristics can be linked to sustainability, as consumers are hesitant to discard a product designed to last. As a result, Joy et al. (2012) argue that luxury fashion brands can be sustainable leaders by emphasizing product longevity, artisanship, and timeliness.

Individual Dimension of Luxury Fashion Value

The individual dimension describes the consumers' personal oriented value on luxury fashion consumption. These consumers emphasise self-expressive and hedonistic values (Jain, 2019). Hennigs et al. (2013) asserted that self-oriented sustainability value is associated with consumer's orientation.

Self-concept refers to an individual's inner aspect of self-perception (Sirgy, 2018). Individuals desire to view the self positively, they often reaffirm the positivity of the self-concept through consumption (Dunning, 2007). Due to such desire towards self, individuals often show self-defensive reactions, when they learn that their behaviours have negative environmental impacts (Feygina et al., 2010). Therefore, sustainable behaviours can be associated with self-concepts in achieving greater endorsement of sustainable actions (White, Habib, and Hardisty, 2019).

The self-concept also relates to sustainable behaviours in that the brand or product individuals own can become extensions of their identity (Belk, 1988). Consumers purchase the luxury fashion brand for its symbolic meaning as an expression of their concerns and aspirations for a better world (Bendell and Kleanthous, 2007; Kastanakis and Balabanis, 2014). They prefer the brand with the personality or image that is congruence with their self-concept (ie., self-congruity) and that consumers' self-concept affects purchasing behaviours (Sirgy, 2018). Self-congruity is proven to have a significant impact on luxury brand purchases (Wiedmann et al. 2007). In this sense, consumers include the personality of the luxury brand into their self-concept and use the brands to express and construct their self-concept (Sirgy, 2018; Vigneron and Johnson, 2004). Sustainability has gained importance in buyers' purchasing decisions (Atwal et al., 2019; Joy et al., 2012). A luxury brand that value artisanship and sustainability may encourage consumers to connect more deeply with sustainable value (Joy et al., 2012).

Consumers valued self-directed pleasure and perfection resulted in the consumption of luxury fashion brands that are high-quality, durable, and timeless (Wiedmann et al., 2007). Increasingly, these buyers are concerned about responsible consumption (Bendell and Kleanthous, 2007). In this sense, luxury purchases can also trigger negative emotional reactions, referred to as "guilty pleasure" (Cervellon and Shammas, 2013). Sustainable consumption acts as an incentive for luxury shoppers who want to feel good and are not guilty about buying a particular luxury brand (Kendall, 2010). They seek value beyond the product itself by investing in health and well-being (Hashmi, 2017). Sustainable luxury consumption offers greater emotional value to luxury buyers (Ki and Kim, 2016).

In a nutshell, consumers of high-end fashion, motivated by personal value, feel that sustainability and luxury are firmly linked (Cervellon and Shammas, 2013; Kapferer and Michaut-Denizeau, 2015). Consumers pay a premium for luxury goods because they anticipate higher quality, but they also expect luxury fashion merchants to contribute to sustainability. This emphasised that sustainability is an important aspect of luxury.

Social Dimension of Luxury Fashion Value

Luxury brands are used to represent one's social self (Beckham and Voyer, 2014). For some consumers, the key motivation of luxury consumption is 'buying to impress others' (Vigneron and Johnson, 1999; Wiedmann et al., 2007;). Hence, the social dimension pertains to how individuals perceive the utility that they acquire by consuming products or services that are recognized within their social group, such as conspicuousness and prestige value, which may significantly influence their evaluation and propensity to purchase (Wiedmann et al., 2007). Luxury brands act as a symbolic market for social group acceptance and conformity (Vigneron and Johnson, 2004). In recent years, sustainable consumption received increased consumer concern and has evolved as a new form of conspicuous consumption (Cervellon and Carey, 2011). According to Dugan (2008), traditionally people spent money to display their wealth, but now they spend on 'green to be seen". Consumers are willing to pay a premium for sustainable luxury products to demonstrate their commitment to sustainability (Cervellon and Shammas, 2013; Ramchandani and Coste-Maniere, 2012). It is the social pressure that prompt individuals to behave responsibly in the environment (Hustvedt and Dickson, 2009). With sustainability becoming the norm, consumers are increasingly engaged in a more sustainable consumption lifestyle to avoid social group rejection (Cvijanovich, 2011).

Financial Dimension of Luxury Fashion Value

The financial value of luxury fashion encompasses the monetary aspect of luxury. For luxury products, the price may have a positive role in determining the perception of high quality (Erickson and Johansson, 1985). In this regard, consumers, especially those status-conscious consumers are likely to use a price cue as a surrogate indicator of prestige (Groth and McDaniel, 1993). However, luxury consumers demand more value along with their luxury. As in Bendell and Kleanthous (2007), the economic value of luxury fashion refers to the durability of the luxury, maintaining the brand's heritage into the future (Bendell and Kleanthous, 2007). Research shows that consumers are willing to pay more for products that are perceived to be socially and environmentally responsible (Johnstone and Tan, 2015).

ROLE OF LUXURY FASHION BRANDS IN SUPPORTING COLLABORATIVE CONSUMPTION

The rise of collaborative consumption drives forces towards non-ownership and encourages the sharing, swapping and renting of a good or service. Increasingly, customers, who are more educated, smart, and want variety, prefer taking part in experiences rather than purchasing goods (Moeller and Wittkowski, 2010). As a result, rather than owning commodities, the consumer experience focuses on using them.

Through sharing and collaborative consumption, luxury fashion companies can develop innovative circular business models. For example, Kering is currently testing its own rental service on a subscription basis through a partnership with The Real Real and Yves Saint Laurent. Stella McCartney became the first luxury brand to boost the second-hand market (Niemtzow, 2018).

Understanding Sharing Economy

The sharing economy is described as an economic system based on individuals sharing underutilised assets or services for free or for a fee (Botsman, 2013). Eckhardt et al., (2019) defined sharing economy as "a scalable socio-economic system that employs technology-enabled platforms to provide users with temporary access to tangible and intangible resources that may be crowdsourced," (p. 7). The authors specified the characteristics of the sharing economy as (1) temporary access, (2) transfer of economic value, (3) platform mediation, (4) expanded consumer role, (5) crowdsources supply, (6) reputation systems, and (6) peer-to-peer exchanges. As a result of the creation of these new services, new business models focused on access rather than possession are emerging, with firms acting as crucial intermediates in the peer-to-peer market (Razeghian and Weber, 2019).

The sharing economy can be classified into three categories, according to Acquier et al., (2017). The first type of sharing economy is the assess economy, which focuses on sharing underutilised products. Second, there is the platform economy, which provides digital platforms for the intermediation of decentralised exchanges between individuals. The community-based economy, the third type of sharing economy, deal with the management of noncontractual and nonmonetized forms of interactions. Recent literature on sharing economy is mainly focused on transportation and accommodation. Sharing economy in the context of fashion may be different from other goods, as people tend to attach meaning to their fashion goods (Johnson, Kim, & Lennon, 2008). The following section identified luxury fashion sharing platforms.

Luxury Fashion Sharing Platforms

In recent years, there is a rapid change in the fashion industry, owing to the high demand for new products. These changes force the fashion companies to shorten the time taken to launch new collections (Cook and Yurchisin, 2017). Fashion items are considered as an investment because people's desire to make the best impression may lead them to turn to luxury brands, which in many cases imply top quality but also unaffordable price tags for middle- and working-class consumers (Watson & Yan, 2013). Collaborative forms of consumption would be more rewarding for consumers who are undecided about owing or not owing (Yuan & Shen, 2019). Accordingly, several collaborative consumption platforms have emerged to promote different forms of sharing, which may lead to affordability in product acquisition, consumer satisfaction, and minimizing waste (Pantano and Stylos, 2020). Some notable examples include Swap-Style, which allows people to swap fashion items all over the world; threadUp, which focuses on reselling children's clothing; and Rent the Runway (RTR), the most successful sharing economy enterprise in the industry, which provides consumers with temporary access to garments rather than ownership (Acquier et al., 2017).

By distinguishing between the transfer of ownership (temporary vs permanent) and retailer's role (distributor vs platform), Perlacia, Duml, Saebi (2017) identifies three types of fashion-sharing models: (1) fashion-rental, (2) platform-sharing model, and (3) e-commerce. According to the authors, fashion rentals provide customers with a fashion rental service to those who don't feel the need to own clothes but want to try out different styles continually. The 'fashion Netflix' model and 'fashion library' models are parts of this category. Platform-sharing models are those where the retailer's business model functions as an online platform for individuals to exchange clothing items between themselves. The 'Airbnb model' and 'swapping model' are examples of platform-sharing models. On the other hand, the retailer facilitates direct exchanges between buyers and sellers without owning second-hand items. Comparatively, to the above models (where items are rented or swapped), ownership is permanently transferred. These models serve as a roadmap for retailers to innovate and move towards collaborative consumption. They also encourage more sustainable business practices (e.g., swapping, renting or selling used items) that can help reduce the impact of consumption on the environment. Table 1 summarize types of fashion sharing models.

Table 1. Types of fashion-sharing models

	Fashion-Rental Model	Platform-Sharing Model	The E-Commerce Model
Sub-models	The Fashion *Netflix* Model Fashion Libraries	The Fashion *Airbnb* Model The Swapping Model	
Role of retailer	Distributor	Platform	Platform
Value proposition	Rent (optional buy) From luxury & haute couture to maternity or vintage clothing	Rent or swap Second-hand fashion items	Sell & buy Second-hand fashion items
Customer segments	Women & men	Women & men	Women, men & Kids
Channels	App, website & app management website, physical stores, events, blogs	App, website, physical stores, events	App, website physical stores, events, blogs
Cost / Revenue Structure	Revenues: Membership fees & Subscriptions; additional fees; events; sale Costs: Cleaning & shipping; salary; rent; website & app management	Revenues: Membership fee; additional fees; events Costs: Salary; rent; website & app management	Revenues: Sale and events Costs: Shipping; salary; rent;

Source: (Perlacia, Duml, Saebi, 2017)

Consumers' Concerns on Sharing

Engaging in sharing allows consumers to consume high-end brands at lower prices, enabling them to devote more of their spending to services and entertainment (Jain and Mishra 2020). Depending on various individual and societal factors, as well as the types of products or services sectors, different incentives may motivate consumers to engage in sharing. Jain and Mishra (2020) identified motivations for the consumption of luxury fashion goods in the context of sharing economy. These include extrinsic motivation such as economic benefits, social projection, fashion involvement and intrinsic motivation such as self-pleasing experience, perceived risk, and sustainable behaviour.

Extrinsic Motives

Prior studies have emphasized the relevance of economic benefits such as cost-cutting and usefulness as favoured considerations for using collaborative consumption (e,g, Roos & Hahn 2017; Hamari et al., 2016; Armstrong et al., 2016). Lower prices may act as a trigger for consumers to engage in collaborative consumption of high-fashion goods (Armstrong et al., 2016) because they make these goods more accessible to consumers (Jain and Mishra, 2020). It is not surprising that Hamari et al. (2016) concluded that sharing is both economically and environmentally beneficial.

Fashion has a 'symbolic power' that enhance one's social identity (O'Cass and McEwen, 2004). Involving and knowing the latest fashion trends drive fashion non-ownership mode of consumption (Moeller and Wittkowski 2010). Innovative fashion is regarded as one of the most important determinants of luxury fashion consumption (Lu & Pras, 2011). Sharing or collaborative consumption can extend the lifespan of fashion goods due to shared use by multiple people while also satisfying people's desire for variety and novelty-seeking without the burden of ownership.

Social projection is the most important factor predicting intention to acquire luxury fashion goods in the sharing economy (Jain and Mishra 2020). Consumers' use luxury brands, which are rich in status signalling, as extensions of their social identities (Kauppinen-Räisänen et al., 2018). Instead of buying expensive luxury goods, sharing economy mode may be a viable option for them. In the sharing economy, consumers can experiment with their personas, and project themselves in ways that they want, and explore alternative selves (Durgee and O'Connor, 1995).

Intrinsic Motives

Self-directed pleasure or enjoyment is one of the key drivers of luxury fashion consumption (Vigneron and Johnson 2004). Durgee and O'Connor (1995) emphasized that consumers find pleasure in using the product rather than having it. In a similar vein, Moeller and Wittkowski (2010) denoted that the non-ownership model allows customers to get access to an experiencing product for a set amount of time, during which they can use it for as long as it gives them joy and excitement.

Perceived risk is a critical aspect that determines customer value perception and, ultimately, purchases decisions in the digital marketplace (Teo and Yeong, 2003). Individuals might be reluctant to engage in sharing and utilising used fashion in the sharing economy due to the possible risks associated with it, such as contamination and germs and financial losses (Belk, 2014). Furthermore, some people may find it embarrassing to purchase pre-owned clothing (Iran and Geiger, 2018). There is a growing concern on privacy and security risk of participating in the sharing economy (Lee et al., 2018)

There is a growing trend towards socially and ecologically mindful consumption behaviour (Jain, 2019; Jang et al., 2012). The kinds of values that people have endorsed for their life and have an impact on their purchasing habits (Stern et al., 1999). People who engage in sustainable behaviour are more likely to recognize the benefits of their actions, which may motivate them to engage in more of the same in the future. (Khare, 2015). The sharing of products means that a product can be accessed and used simultaneously by multiple consumers, which can affect the number of products purchased and produced in the future. It is reasonable to conclude that sharing items is an "environmentally beneficial" mode of consumption. It is assumed that a reduction in production numbers corresponds to a reduction in environmental harm and non-renewable resource consumption. Consumers who are concerned about the environment may find sharing and collaboration consumption appealing (Hamari et al., 2013).

CHALLENGES OF SUSTAINABLE LUXURY FASHION

As argued, today's luxury fashion can be sustainable, but there are significant challenges. Luxury is thought to be timeless, whereas fashion is thought to be fleeting. A fashion item is typically used for a single season. A Chanel dress, for example, is no longer worn after a season. Historically, luxury was reserved for the wealthy and powerful, but this has changed due to the massification of luxury. Luxury brands began to offer more collections, product lines and ranges aimed at the middle class as a result of the success of high-street fast-fashion retailers. Luxury, which was historically associated with sustainability ideals by producing rare, high-quality products made by hand and with respect for tradition (Kapferer, 2010), has come to resemble consumer or fashion goods, designed for rapid obsolescence (Kapferer and Michaut-Denizeau, 2015). As a result, contemporary luxury fashion has begun to embody fast fashion principles (Ozdamar-Ertekin, 2016), and a segment of the luxury industry is now behaving like any fashionable mass retailer, putting additional strain on sustainability concerns. If the luxury sector attracts more customers, it may entice them to spend a large portion of their disposable income on objects or experiences that they do not need (Kapferer and Michaut-Denizeau, 2015). The long-term viability of this new form of mass luxury must be considered.

Godart and Seong (2017) identified six fashion principles and the sustainability challenges and opportunities associated with each. Table 2 explains luxury fashion's limitations and opportunities for sustainability.

Table 2. Luxury fashion's limitations and opportunities for sustainability

Principle	Opportunities for sustainability	Limitations for sustainability
Affirmation	Institutionalising the practice of sustainable fashion by changing consumers' perception of buying sustainable fashion items as a socially accepted or 'in fashion' practice	Consumers' desire to assert their individuality and social affiliation by being 'in fashion, which prompts regular changes of clothes. This leads to and is reinforced by, inflated production cycles
Convergence	Increasing consumers' preference for purchasing sustainable fashion items (principle 1: affirmation) to prompt the convergence of producers around producing sustainable fashion	Local styles converge with dominant fashion design trends that are formulated, updated and disseminated by big fashion capitals. These dominant designs are not always compatible with local climates
Autonomy	Encouraging actors within the fashion industry to develop aesthetically appealing designs that are also high on the eco-sustainability agenda	The fashion industry maintains its autonomy when it comes to the choice of fashion styles and designs. This autonomy makes it difficult for third party actors to push the sustainability agenda in the production process
Personalization	Encouraging each designer to use his/her autonomous influence to set a pro-sustainability trend and let it spill over from the fashion industry to other social spheres	Market audiences share their belief in individual fashion designers' creative autonomy. This makes it difficult for third party actors to push the sustainability agenda in the production process
Symbolisation	Encouraging each fashion brand to leverage, and reshape, its existing identity to include a proactive message on environmental issues	Fashion brands symbolise a powerful engine behind a stylistic trend change in the fashion industry. This may not go hand-in-hand with the notion of sustainability
Imperialization	Using the power of business groups to influence individual fashion brands and even other luxury segments via ripple effects to adopt and implement a large-scale sustainability agenda	Business groups play a major role in the industry. The sheer size and power centrality of these business groups can make adoption of changes in favour of sustainability difficult

Source: (Godart and Seong 2017)

Implementing a new sustainable paradigm may necessitate some changes to the existing industry structure, but it does not invalidate fashion's fundamental principles. Sustainability can be embraced in two ways by luxury fashion companies. Firstly, the luxury fashion firms can initiate an institutional change through slow luxury fashion. Slow fashion, as opposed to fast fashion, refers to long-lasting items with the seasonless or timeless design (Fletcher 2010). Slow fashion emphasises fewer, longer-lasting pieces that 'can dispel the notion that just because it's 'last season, it's devalued' (Sun et al., 2021). On the other hand, slow fashion products are typically more expensive than fast fashion, discouraging consumers from purchasing them (Yang et al., 2017). Another challenge for slow fashion could be reduced firm turnover due to the slowing of consumers' purchase cycles (Godart and Seong, 2017).

Luxury fashion firms may come up with innovative solutions for producing more sustainable fashion items. For example, Kering is supporting the Sustainable Cashmere Program, which allows for the regeneration of pasturelands, maintains healthy Mongolian grasslands and controls the proportion of goats and sheep (Noya Fibers, 2018). Another way for fashion luxury companies to ensure the availability of materials without harming the environment is to consider working with vegan raw materials. Stella McCartney is using a new technology called Mylo, created by Bolt Threats (a breakthrough biotech company). Mylo a sustainable material that looks and feels remarkably like animal leather and uses mycelium fibre, the underground root structure of mushrooms; it can be produced in days instead of years without the material waste of using animal hides (McCartney, 2019).

CONCLUSION

Sustainability and luxury fashion are closely related concepts that both inspire and complement one another (Henninger et al., 2017). Luxury fashion companies have increased their focus on implementing more sustainable practices in response to stakeholder demands (Jang et al., 2012). Leading luxury fashion houses such as Kering, Moët Hennessy Louis Vuitton (LVMH), Stella McCartney, and Vivienne Westwood have begun to promote more sustainable consumption through campaigns such as "buy less, buy better," as well as the sustainable or eco-fashion movement (Gwilt and Rissanen, 2012). Luxury brands with a history of high quality, heritage, artisanship, and durability are more likely to uphold social and environmental values (Hennings et al. 2013). Luxury fashion brands must credibly promote their true values to consumers so that they can understand how those values align with principles of sustainable development.

The rise of collaborative consumption drives forces towards non-ownership and encourages the sharing, swapping and renting of a good or service. Collaborative fashion consumption, also known as fashion sharing, brings about the tendency among consumers to engage with non-ownership approaches to fashion consumption. Fashion-sharing appears to be an ecological fight against waste and an economical alternative to purchases. Despite this, consumer mind sets are slow to change, which is an obvious barrier to fashion collaboration. Brand managers need to understand why consumers do (or do not) want to share luxury fashion. consumers' motives and practices to share. Instilling the value of mindful consumption in society is an important cornerstone of educating consumers about collaborative consumption and its benefits.

REFERENCES

Acquier, A., Daudigeos, T., & Pinkse, J. (2017). Promises and paradoxes of the sharing economy: An organizing framework. *Technological Forecasting and Social Change, 125*, 1–10. doi:10.1016/j.techfore.2017.07.006

Adams, R., Jeanrenaud, S., Bessant, J., Denyer, D., & Overy, P. (2016). Sustainability-oriented innovation: A systematic review. *International Journal of Management Reviews, 18*(2), 180–205. doi:10.1111/ijmr.12068

Amatulli, C., De Angelis, M., Costabile, M., & Guido, G. (2017). *Sustainable luxury brands: Evidence from research and implications for managers*. Palgrave Macmillan. doi:10.1057/978-1-137-60159-9

Armstrong, C. M., Niinimäki, K., Lang, C., & Kujala, S. (2016). A use-oriented clothing economy? Preliminary affirmation for sustainable clothing consumption alternatives. *Sustainable Development*, *24*(1), 18–31. doi:10.1002d.1602

Arrigo, E. (2015). Corporate Sustainability in Fashion and Luxury Companies. *Symphonya Emerging Issues in Management, 4*, 9-23.

Athwal, N., Wells, V. K., Carrigan, M., & Henninger, C. E. (2019). Sustainable luxury marketing: A synthesis and research agenda. *International Journal of Management Reviews*, *21*(4), 405–426. doi:10.1111/ijmr.12195

Bearden, W. O., & Michael, J. E. (1982). Reference group influence on product and Brand purchase decisions. *The Journal of Consumer Research*, *9*(2), 183–194. doi:10.1086/208911

Beckham, D., & Voyer, B. G. (2014). *Can sustainability be luxurious? A mixed-method investigation of implicit and explicit attitudes towards sustainable luxury consumption*. ACR North American Advances.

Belk, R. W. (1988). Possessions and the extended self. *The Journal of Consumer Research*, *15*(2), 139–168. doi:10.1086/209154

Belk, R. W. (2014). You are what you can access: Sharing and collaborative consumption online. *Journal of Business Research*, *67*(8), 1595–1600. doi:10.1016/j.jbusres.2013.10.001

Bendell, J., & Kleanthous, A. (2007). *Deeper luxury*. http://assets. wwf.org.uk/downloads/luxury_report.pdf

Botsman, R. (2013). *The sharing economy lacks a shared definition. Giving Meaning to the Terms*. https://www.fastcoexist.com/3022028/the-sharing-economy-lacks-a-shareddefinition

Cervellon, M. C., & Carey, L. (2011). Consumers' perceptions of 'green': Why and how consumers use eco-fashion and green beauty products. *Critical Studies in Fashion & Beauty*, *2*(1-2), 117–138. doi:10.1386/csfb.2.1-2.117_1

Cervellon, M. C., & Shammas, L. (2013). The value of sustainable luxury in mature markets: A customer-based approach. *Journal of Corporate Citizenship*, *2013*(52), 90–101. doi:10.9774/GLEAF.4700.2013.de.00009

Chow, P. S., & Li, C. K. Y. (2018). Towards Closed-Loop Fashion Supply Chains—Reflections from Retailer-Facilitated Used Apparel Collection Programs. In Contemporary Case Studies on Fashion Production, Marketing and Operations. Springer.

Cook, S. C., & Yurchisin, J. (2017). Fast fashion environments: Consumer's heaven or retailer's nightmare? *International Journal of Retail & Distribution Management*, *45*(2), 143–157. doi:10.1108/IJRDM-03-2016-0027

Cvijanovich, M. (2011). *Sustainable luxury: Oxymoron? Lecture in luxury and sustainability*. http://www.mcmdesignstudio. ch/files/ Guest%20professor%20Lucern%20School%20of%20Art%20%20and%20Design.pdf

Dubois, B., & Paternault, C. (1995). Understanding the world of international luxury brands: The dream formula. *Journal of Advertising Research*, *3*(4), 69–76.

Dunning, D. (2007). Self-image motives and consumer behavior: How sacrosanct self-beliefs sway preferences in the marketplace. *Journal of Consumer Psychology*, *17*(4), 237–249. doi:10.1016/S1057-7408(07)70033-5

Durgee, J. F., & Colarelli O'Connor, G. (1995). An exploration into renting as consumption behavior. *Psychology and Marketing*, *12*(2), 89–104. doi:10.1002/mar.4220120202

Eckhardt, G. M., Houston, M. B., Jiang, B., Lamberton, C., Rindfleisch, A., & Zervas, G. (2019). Marketing in the sharing economy. *Journal of Marketing*, *83*(5), 5–27. doi:10.1177/0022242919861929

Ecouterre. (2012). *Sh!t Dame Vivienne Westwood Says: Greatest Hits Edition*. http://www.ecouterre.com/shit-dame-viviennewestwood- says/vivienne-westwood-says-4/?extend=1

Elkington, J. (1997). *Cannibals with Forks: The triple bottom line of 21st century business*. Capstone.

Erickson, G. M., & Johansson, J. K. (1985). The role of price in multi-attribute product evaluations. *The Journal of Consumer Research*, *12*(2), 195–199. doi:10.1086/208508

Feygina, I., Jost, J. T., & Goldsmith, R. E. (2010). System Justification, the Denial of Global Warming, and the Possibility of 'System-Sanctioned Change,'. *Personality and Social Psychology Bulletin*, *36*(3), 326–338. doi:10.1177/0146167209351435 PMID:20008965

Fibers, N. (2018). *Experience the natural difference*. www.noyafibers.com/

Fionda, A. M., & Moore, C. M. (2009). The Anatomy of The Luxury Fashion Brand. *Journal of Brand Management*, *16*(5/6), 347–363. doi:10.1057/bm.2008.45

Fletcher, K. (2010). Slow fashion: An invitation for systems change. *Fashion Practice*, *2*(2), 259–265. doi:10.2752/175693810X12774625387594

Fletcher, K. (2012). Durability, Fashion, Sustainability: The Processes and Practices of Use. *Fashion Practice*, *4*(2), 221–238. doi:10.2752/175693812X13403765252389

Franco, J. C., Hussain, D., & McColl, R. (2019). Luxury fashion and sustainability: Looking good together. *The Journal of Business Strategy*, *41*(4), 55–61. doi:10 1108/JBS-05-2019-0089

Fuller, D. A. (1999). *Sustainable marketing: Managerial-ecological issues*. Sage Publications.

Godart, F., & Seong, S. (2017). Is Sustainable Luxury Fashion Possible? In M. A. Gardetti & A. L. Torres (Eds.), *Sustainable Luxury: Managing Social and Environmental Performance in Iconic Brands*. Routledge. doi:10.4324/9781351287807-2

Groth, J. C., & McDaniel, S. W. (1993). The exclusive value principle: The basis for prestige racing. *Journal of Consumer Marketing*, *10*(1), 10–16. doi:10.1108/07363769310026539

Gwilt, A., & Rissanen, T. (2012). *Shaping sustainable fashion: Changing the way we make and use clothes*. Routledge.

Hashmi, G. (2017). Redefining the essence of sustainable luxury management: The slow value creation model. In M. Gardetti (Ed.), *Sustainable management of luxury* (pp. 3–27). Springer. doi:10.1007/978-981-10-2917-2_1

Hennigs, N., Wiedmann, K. P., Klarmann, C., & Behrens, S. (2013). Sustainability as part of the luxury essence: Delivering value through social and environmental excellence. *Journal of Corporate Citizenship*, *52*(52), 25–35. doi:10.9774/GLEAF.4700.2013.de.00005

Henninger, C. E., Alevizou, P. J., Tan, J. L., Huang, Q., & Ryding, D. (2017). Consumption strategies and motivations of chinese consumers: The case of UK sustainable luxury. *Journal of Fashion Marketing and Management*, *21*(3), 419–434. doi:10.1108/JFMM-05-2017-0046

Hustvedt, G., & Dickson, M. A. (2009). Consumer likelihood of purchasing organic cotton apparel: Influence of attitudes and self-identity. *Journal of Fashion Marketing and Management*, *13*(1), 49–65. doi:10.1108/13612020910939879

Iran, S., & Geiger, S. M. (2018). To wear or to own? Influences of values on the attitudes towards and the engagement in collaborative fashion consumption. In M. Heuer & C. Becker-Leifhold (Eds.), *Eco-Friendly and Fair* (pp. 153–162). Routledge.

Jain, S. (2019). Factors affecting sustainable luxury purchase behavior: A conceptual framework. *Journal of International Consumer Marketing*, *31*(2), 130–146.

Jain, S., & Mishra, S. (2020). Luxury fashion consumption in sharing economy: A study of Indian millennials. *Journal of Global Fashion Marketing*, *11*(2), 171–189.

Jang, J., Ko, E., Chun, E., & Lee, E. (2012). A study of a social content model for sustainable development in the fast fashion industry. *Journal of Global Fashion Marketing*, *3*(2), 61–70.

Janssen, C., Vanhamme, J., Lindgreen, A., & Lefebvre, C. (2014). The Catch-22 of responsible luxury: Effects of luxury product characteristics on consumers' perception of fit with corporate social responsibility. *Journal of Business Ethics*, *119*(1), 45–57.

Johnson, K. K. P., Kim, M., & Lennon, S. J. (2008). Dress and human behavior: A review and critique. *Clothing & Textiles Research Journal*, *26*(3), 3–22.

Johnstone, M. L., & Tan, L. P. (2015). Exploring the gap between consumers' green rhetoric and purchasing behaviour. *Journal of Business Ethics*, *132*(2), 311–328.

Joy, A., Sherry, J. F., Venkatesh, A., Wang, F., & Chan, R. (2012). Fast Fashion, Sustainability, and the Ethical Appeal of Luxury Brands. *Fashion Theory*, *16*(3), 273–295.

Kapferer, J. M., & Michaut-Denizeau, A. (2015). *Are luxury purchasers insensitive to sustainable development? New insights from research. Sustainable luxury*. Greenleaf Publishing Limited.

Kapferer, J. N. (1998). Why are we seduced by luxury brands? *Journal of Brand Management*, *6*(1), 44–49.

Kapferer, J.-N. (2010). All that glitters is not green: The challenge of sustainable luxury. *European Business Review*. www.europeanbusinessreview.com/?p=2869

Kapferer, J. N., & Bastien, V. (2012). *The Luxury Strategy: Break the Rules of Marketing to Build Luxury Brands*. Kogan Page.

Kapferer, J. N., & Bastien, V. (2017). The specificity of luxury management: Turning marketing upside down. In J. N. Kapferer, J. Kernstock, T. Brexendorf, & S. Powell (Eds.), *Advances in Luxury Brand Management. Journal of Brand Management: Advanced Collections*. Palgrave Macmillan.

Kauppinen-Räisänen, H., Björk, P., Lönnström, A., & Jauffret, M. N. (2018). How consumers' need for uniqueness, self-monitoring, and social identity affect their choices when luxury brands visually shout versus whisper. *Journal of Business Research*, *84*, 72–81.

Kemper, J. A., & Ballantine, P. W. (2019). What do we mean by sustainability marketing? *Journal of Marketing Management*, *35*(3-4), 277–309.

Kendall, J. (2010). *Responsible Luxury: A report on the new opportunities for business to make a difference*. https://www.rapaportfairtrade.com/Docs/ CIBJO-responsible_luxury.pdf

Kerr, J., & Landry, J. (2017). *Pulse of the fashion industry. In Global Fashion Agenda*. The Boston Consulting Group.

Khare, A. (2015). Antecedents to green buying behaviour: A study on consumers in an emerging economy. *Marketing Intelligence & Planning*, *33*(3), 309–329.

Ki, C. W., & Kim, Y. K. (2016). Sustainable versus conspicuous luxury fashion purchase: Applying self-determination theory. *Family and Consumer Sciences Research Journal*, *44*(3), 309–323.

Kim, H., Choo, H. J., & Yoon, N. (2013). The Motivational Drivers of Fast Fashion Avoidance. *Journal of Fashion Marketing and Management*, *17*(2), 243–260.

Lee, Z. W., Chan, T. K., Balaji, M. S., & Chong, A. Y. L. (2018). Why people participate in the sharing economy: An empirical investigation of Uber. *Internet Research*.

Lim, W. M. (2020). The Sharing Economy: A Marketing Perspective. *Australasian Marketing Journal*, *28*(3), 4–13.

Lu, P., & Pras, B. (2011). Profiling mass affluent luxury goods consumers in China: A psychographic approach. *Thunderbird International Business Review*, *53*(4), 435–455.

McCartney, S. (2019). *The next chapter with BOLT threads: mylo material, rooted in nature*. www.stellamccartney.com/experience/en/the-next-chapter-with-bolt-threads-mylo-material-rooted-innature/

McDonagh, P., & Prothero, A. (2014). Sustainability marketing research: Past, present and future. *Journal of Marketing Management*, *30*(11-12), 1186–1219.

McNeill, L., & Moore, R. (2015). Sustainable fashion consumption and the fast fashion conundrum: Fashionable consumers and attitudes to sustainability in clothing choice. *International Journal of Consumer Studies*, *39*(3), 212–222.

Moeller, S., & Wittkowski, K. (2010). The burdens of ownership: Reasons for preferring renting. *Managing Service Quality*, *20*(2), 176–191.

Naderi, I., & Strutton, D. (2015). I support sustainability but only when doing so reflects fabulously on me: Can green narcissists be cultivated? *Journal of Macromarketing*, *35*(1), 70–83.

Niemtzow, E. (2018). *Disrupting luxury: creating resilient businesses in times of rapid change*. Business of Social Responsibility. Available at: www.bsr.org/en/our-insights/report-view/disrupting-luxury-creating-resilient-businesses-in-times-of-rapid-change

O'cass, A., & McEwen, H. (2004). Exploring consumer status and conspicuous consumption. *Journal of Consumer Behaviour: An International Research Review*, *4*(1), 25–39.

Ozdamar-Ertekin, Z. (2019). Can Luxury Fashion Provide a Roadmap for Sustainability? *Markets, Globalization & Developmental Review*, *4*(1).

Pantano, E., & Stylos, N. (2020). The Cinderella moment: Exploring consumers' motivations to engage with renting as collaborative luxury consumption mode. *Psychology and Marketing*, *37*(5), 740–753.

Pavione, E., Pezzetti, R., & Dalla, M. (2016). Emerging competitive strategies in the global luxury industry in the perspective of sustainable development: The case of Kering group. *Management Dynamics in the Knowledge Economy Journal*, *4*(2), 41–61.

Peattie, K., & Belz, F. M. (2010). Sustainability marketing—An innovative conception of marketing. *Marketing Review St. Gallen*, *27*(5), 8–15.

Perlacia, A. S., Duml, V., & Saebi, T. (2017). Collaborative consumption: Live fashion, don't own it. *BETA Bulletin of Experimental Treatments for AIDS*, *31*(1), 6–24.

Phau, I., & Prendergast, G. (2000). Consuming luxury brands: The relevance of the 'rarity principle'. *Journal of Brand Management*, *8*(2), 122–138.

Ramchandani, M., & Coste-Manière, I. (2012). Asymmetry in multi-cultural luxury communication: A comparative analysis on luxury brand communication in India and China. *Journal of Global Fashion Marketing*, *3*(2), 89–97.

Razeghian, M., & Weber, T. A. (2019). The advent of the sharing culture and its effect on product pricing. *Electronic Commerce Research and Applications*, *33*, 100801.

Rolling, V., & Sadachar, A. (2018). Are sustainable luxury goods a paradox for millennials? *Social Responsibility Journal*, *14*(4), 802–815.

Roos, D., & Hahn, R. (2019). Understanding collaborative consumption: An extension of the theory of planned behavior with value-based personal norms. *Journal of Business Ethics*, *158*(3), 679–697.

Rosenbaum, E., & Caminiti, S. (2020). *Coronavirus: How the pandemic has impacted luxury retail*. CNBC. https://www.cnbc.com/2020/09/19/coronavirus-how-the-pandemic-has-impacted-luxury-retail.html

Sirgy, M. J. (2018). Self-congruity theory in consumer behavior: A little history. *Journal of Global Scholars of Marketing Science*, *28*(2), 197–207.

Stern, P. C., Dietz, T., Abel, T., Guagnano, G. A., & Kalof, L. (1999). A value-belief-norm theory of support for social movements: The case of environmentalism. *Human Ecology Review*, *6*(2), 81–97.

Sun, J. J., Bellezza, S., & Paharia, N. (2021). Buy Less, Buy Luxury: Understanding and Overcoming Product Durability Neglect for Sustainable Consumption. *Journal of Marketing*, *85*(3), 28–43.

Teo, T. S., & Yeong, Y. D. (2003). Assessing the consumer decision process in the digital marketplace. *Omega*, *31*(5), 349–363.

Time. (2011). *10 ideas that will change the world*. Available at http://content.time. com/time/specials/packages/completelist/0,29569,2059521,00.html

Trivedi, K., Trivedi, P., & Goswami, V. (2018). Sustainable marketing strategies: Creating business value by meeting consumer expectation. *International Journal of Management Economics and Social Sciences*, *7*(2), 186–205.

Vigneron, F., & Johnson, L. W. (1999). A review and a conceptual framework of prestige- Seeking Consumer behavior. *Academy of Marketing Science Review*, *9*(1), 1–14.

Watson, M. Z., & Yan, R. N. (2013). An exploratory study of the decision processes of fast versus slow fashion consumers. *Journal of Fashion Marketing and Management*, *17*(2), 141–159.

WCED. (1987). *Our common future. The report of the World Commission on Environment and Development*. Oxford University Press.

White, K., Habib, R., & Hardisty, D. J. (2019). How to SHIFT consumer behaviors to be more sustainable: A literature review and guiding framework. *Journal of Marketing*, *83*(3), 22–49.

Wiedmann, K. P., Hennigs, N., & Siebels, A. (2007). Measuring consumers' luxury value perception: A crosscultural framework. *Academy of Marketing Science Review*, *11*, 1–21.

Wiedmann, K. P., Hennigs, N., & Siebels, A. (2009). Value-based segmentation of luxury consumption behavior. *Psychology and Marketing*, *26*(7), 625–651.

Yang, S., Song, Y., & Tong, S. (2017). Sustainable retailing in the fashion industry: A systematic literature review. *Sustainability*, *9*(7), 1266.

Yuan, Q., & Shen, B. (2019). Renting fashion with strategic customers in the sharing economy. *International Journal of Production Economics*, *218*, 185–195.

Chapter 13
Sustainable Resilience in Urban Land Use

José G. Vargas-Hernández
https://orcid.org/0000-0003-0938-4197
Instituto Tecnológico Mario Molina, Zapopan, Mexico

Elsa Patricia Orozco-Quijano
https://orcid.org/0000-0002-6616-3174
Laurentian University, Canada

ABSTRACT

Humanity is facing a series of important challenges, global warming being one of the most important. Consequently, sustainability and resilience have become key elements in providing a better response to the crisis and in maintaining an equilibrium between ecology, economics, and various social domains. The design and use of urban land should consider the inclusion of a multi-functional green infrastructure to obtain different benefits, from ecosystem services to value creation. Additionally, the urban land-use planning system contributes to economic growth, social development, and environmental sustainability, while biodiversity is able to provide renewal and reorganization capacities for changes in social-ecosystems. All these elements bring forth a different paradigm for the future decisions of communities.

INTRODUCTION

Human development has had a profound imprint on nature and co-evolving ecosystems. This has resulted in complex, economic-socio-ecological challenges for sustainability and future development. Human activity alters the dynamics of ecosystems with its important impact on the atmosphere, climate, land surface, forest, sea, and waters. Cities have been portrayed as predominantly monumental static and architectural structures of ever evolving and increasing ecological complexity. Disturbances change the resilient capacity of nature to supply ecosystem services, they can degrade socio-ecological systems and lead to social and economic vulnerability. Urban dwellers pose a high impact on ecosystem services with

DOI: 10.4018/978-1-7998-9590-9.ch013

their habits in trade and consumption, claiming support in waste absorption, carbon emissions, residential water use and wood for industrial purposes (Folke et al., 1997, Grimm et al., 2008).

According to Levin (1999), humans depend on fragile ecosystem services. A global health control of the ecosystems, published in 2005 by The United Nations Millennium Ecosystem Assessment (MA) observed that the technological advancement is the main cause of degradation of the Earth's ecosystem services, which are being used unsustainably. The growing eco-deterioration also impedes in the battle against poverty (Millennium Ecosystem Assessment (MA), 2005). The ecosystem and natural resources are controlled by a few people who do it for short-term economic gain.

The survival of humankind is also dependent on healthy and resilient social-ecological systems and sustainable environments. Meanwhile, human well-being, economic growth and social development are dependent on the interrelationships between and within regions and environmental sustainability (Arrow et al., 1995; Folke et.al., 1998). Uncertainty, diversity and variability of social-ecosystems are all factors that contribute to their diminishing capacity to cope with disturbance and change within functional groups in the adaptive capacity of ecosystems (Folke et al. 2002; Jackson et al. 2001; Scheffer et al. 2001).

In order to conserve ecological resources, it is essential to promote sustainable and resilient lifestyles in sustainable urban social-ecosystems. This can be done with various activities that range from the construction of green spaces, sustainable architecture, green housing, eco-villages, green business and green economic sectors, sustainable urban agriculture and farming, green technologies, renewable energies and designing reversible and flexible systems (Zhang and Babovic, 2012). Sustainable architecture or ecological economics, sustainable technology, and agriculture (Costanza and Patten, 1995) stand out as specific types of sustainable and resilient urban development. Thus, sustainable, environmental and ecological systems are being identified within resilient social-ecosystems as the elements that have the capacity to continue functioning despite being confronted with natural and anthropogenic disturbances, anticipating and preparing ahead for them.

The resilience approach provides a conceptual and theoretical framework for interdisciplinary collaboration with ecological economics, sustainable development and governance (Lambin, 2005). Contextual and conceptual factors of urban change can be assembled into a framework of ecological urban design. Adverse human impacts on the social-ecosystem and the biosphere can be minimized through the use of resilient and sustainable environmental approaches such as environmental resource management, conservation biology, environmental and ecological economics, bio economics, green technology, etc.

On the other hand, ecology refers to the paradigm, knowledge, methods and procedures of contemporary ecological science (Kolasa & Pickett, 2005), and is a multidimensional and complex concept that requires an interdisciplinary framework of analysis for its application in urban spaces (Pickett & Cadenasso, 2002). The dimensions of ecology are the notion, the models and the metaphors used to communicate assumptions, values and experiences (Cadenasso et al., 2006a)

Urban land-use is inextricably interrelated with resilient social-ecosystems, which is influenced by the behavior of individuals, groups, organizations and communities. Urban land-use is targeted at specific and limited functions of the city, such as biomass and water passage and accumulation. In recent population trends, urban land-use and vacancy patterns must consider their impacts on vacant land and structures. In densely populated areas, urban farming, agriculture and gardening offers an alternative use and integrates multiple functions. However, current land-use practices in urban sustainable planning prohibit agricultural and farming activities in urban spaces while there is a significant loss of farmland nearby (Pothukuchi & Kaufman, 1999; 2000).

Another important element is urban green space, or an underdeveloped piece of land located within the territorial context of a city and open to the public. Urban green spaces are pressured to provide economic, social, cultural and ecological functions. These spaces provide ecosystems services to human beings and must simultaneously meet the needs and preferences of local population.

Therefore, urban green spaces play a critical role in conserving biodiversity, mitigating the impacts of climate change, sequestering carbon, improving micro-climate, protecting water resources, conserving biodiversity, protecting water resources and supplying fresh food. Urban agriculture, farming and gardening have become increasingly necessary and are supported by sustainable urban planning and designing to improve the quality of life in the city. The benefits of urban agriculture are recognized for their multicultural traditions, recreational trends and poverty alleviation (Hough, 1995, p. 230).

Also, urban ecosystems are a potential solution for future ecological and environmental issues caused by the loss of natural landscapes. When the natural resources and the ecosystem are controlled by a few privileged people, the capacity of adaptive development is reduced, the resilience diminishes and there is more disequilibrium. The balance between natural and urban ecosystems and the surrounding regional landscape is limited. Urban ecosystem services are important in the conception of urban green spaces and the biodiversity, micro-climate control, carbon sequestration, soil infiltration, food production and recreation that it can contribute to its community.

Sustainable urban planning seeks to create attractive land-use combinations to meet the needs of residents and environmental challenges through initiatives like urban farming, agriculture and gardening. Urban planning seeks to create and incorporate attractive land-use combinations to sustainable development plans, and provide recreational, educational, cultural and agricultural resources, as well tourism, farming and gardening, urban forestry, aquaculture, health services and commerce, (van de Berg and van Veenhuizen, 2005; Deelstra et all, 2006).

However, the urban land-use planning and design authorities don't always consider the relevance of natural resources and land provision to support urban food production (except for urban planning policies that support gardening). Therefore, urban land-use policies and rules may have negative impacts on local food production and distribution (City of Portland, 2007).

Innovative types of land-use can offer benefits to vulnerable groups (Clement 2013, p. 76). The innovation of productive land-use as landscape typology is designated for local food production and, with innovation in ecological resilience, these open spaces require decommissioning of urban services, and encourage residents to seek employment in agriculture.

On the other hand, multi-functional urban planning involves the participation of various stakeholders in making decisions on green infrastructure planning. Furthermore, community greening initiatives are a community-based effort to transform underutilized sites and areas into valuable green spaces like community gardens (Tidball and Krasny 2009). Community organizations for nature conservation focus on the preservation of urban social-ecosystems and protect them from dysfunctional anthropogenic activities in order to adapt the development and achieve economic efficiency.

Innovative and integrated sustainable initiatives and strategies in urban land-use planning can contribute to green resilient economic growth, as well as social development issues such as inclusion and equality, and environmental sustainability.

For the implementation of strategies, it is important to create a typology of community land-use types based on vacancy characteristics, the income of the area's residents and vacancy market rates. This will allow the transformation of vacant spaces into resilient green spaces, and allow them to carry out their many inherent functions (Akers, 2013; Detroit Works Project, 2014, p. 51). Vacant land restoration should be an interdisciplinary approach that combines economic and socio ecosystem concerns from a holistic urban land use perspective.

SUSTAINABILITY AND GREEN SOCIAL-ECOSYSTEM RESILIENCE

Human beings have had a profound imprint on nature and now, we must deal with the resulting challenges. One of the most difficult realities is the phenomenon of global warming.Some options and practices drawn from sustainability and green social-ecosystem resilience could very well help communities in the fight against global warming.

Sustainability is a set of goals combining social equity, economic viability and ecological integrity (Curwell, Deakin, & Symes, 2005; Jenks & Jones, 2010). Sustainability is also defined by the capacity of a system or process to be preserved, enhanced, upheld, or maintained. It is the capacity of biological systems and processes to endure disturbances and remain vigorously diverse, remaining as the systematic combination of environmental science and sustainable development (Lynn et al., 2014).

One of the core values in sustainable practices is the sustainable development and interconnection in the domains of ecology, culture, politics, and economics (James, et al., 2015). From this social perspective, sustainability is a challenge that has an impact on economic efficiency, production, distribution, urbanization, transportation, lifestyles and ethical consumerism, and it involves local and global efforts to meet core human needs without distorting the ecosystem (Kates et al., 2005; IISD, 2009; EurActiv, 2004).

Sustainable development also implies proactive and responsible decision-making. It requires innovative processes that maintain balanced social and ecological systems between resilience, economic efficiency, social inclusion and equality, political justice and vibrant cultural values that work to ensure a lively, desirable and sustainable ecosystem for all of its residing species (Liam et al., 2013). Sustainability is also a normative social goal that can be promoted with the mechanisms of ecological resilience.

Resilience is defined as the capacity of socio-ecological systems to self-reorganize after any disturbance. Resilience is a concept and model framework used to operationalize normative sustainability (Childers, Pickett, Grove, Ogden, & Whitmer, 2014). It refers to the ability of an ecosystem to respond productively to significant disruptive change and adapt to external variables that threaten its existence.

At the same time, resilience is a system´s ability to adapt to any kind of disturbance and self-reorganize while undergoing transformation, and retaining its initial forms, roles, identity, and feedback characteristics (Walker et al., 2004).

The concept of resilience is defined by its capacities to absorb the uncertainty that follows any kind of shocking event or conflict, to maintain its primary functions, and to go through self-growth, renewal, development and re-organization. (Gunderson and Holling, 2002; Berkes et al., 2003).

Any disturbance of a strong and resilient socio-economic and ecological system can have the potential to create new opportunities for innovation and advancement. However, when the system is weak, any slight disturbance can be disastrous. (Adger, 2006).

SOCIAL ECOSYSTEM RESILIENCE

Resilience is also a dynamic process that forms symbiotic relationships within and between the social ecosystem and its environment. Social-ecosystem resilience is found in the continuous cycle of adaptation and transformation all while maintaining the system's integrity and viability. It is the reaction of the socio-ecological system towards disruption and destruction, and its capacity to recover and develop in a state of uncertainty, discontinuity, and emergency. Social-ecosystem resilience happens when self-organization and learning meet adaptation and persistence.

Resilience is concerned with the management of sustainable interactions between human-developed systems and natural ecosystems. Social resilience linked to social change is the communities' capacity to cope with extrinsic disturbances to their social infrastructure, such as political turbulence, socio-economic reforms, and environmental variability (Adger 2000; Anderies et al., 2004). Resilience can interfere and be in conflict with other beneficial social objectives, such as economic efficiency, due to the costs of redundancy. In other words, economic efficiency reduces resilience. The resilience of social-ecosystems requires more adaptability to stress while maintaining stability in the face of extrinsic disturbances and to find a solution to the conflict between stability and resilience for sustainable development in terms of complex system cycles.

Apart from representing the measures taken by a social-ecosystem to self-organize and cope with disturbances while still maintaining its inertia, attraction and capacities for learning and adaptation (Carpenter et al. 2001), resilience can also be an approach for cogitating and critiquing social–ecological systems, with policy implications for sustainable development (Folke et al., 2002).

Social-ecosystem resilience is an essential factor to cope with uncertain and complex systems for sustainable natural resources and ecosystem services (Gunderson and Holling 2002). Any disequilibrium between sustainability and development change leads to the collapse of ecosystems. In addition, it is extremely difficult to transform a resilient ecosystem into a more congenial one (Scheffer et al., 2001; Gunderson and Holling, 2002; Walker et al., 2004). In other words, it is possible to prevent degradation by promoting the system's congeniality with nature.

A sustainable and resilient social-ecosystem does not largely depend on human input or activity due to the fact that anthropogenic interferences can interrupt the provision of inputs. Instead, it is more reliant on the ways of nature.

The social ecosystem is currently threatened by anthropogenic activities that find themselves at the brink of collapse, and this requires prompt action. In the context of social-ecological systems, management and flexible collaboration are crucial; they help develop policy frameworks as a basis to build adaptive capacity. Nature should be strengthened to stimulate development through the interaction and interdependence with humankind to enhance resilience in social-ecosystems.

ECOLOGICAL RESILIENCE

On the other hand, resilience plays an important role in the field of ecology. (Holling, 1973; Wu & Wu, 2013) Ecological resilience is a concept that must be operationalized to be applied in urban environments and cities (Musacchio, 2008).

Older perspectives of resilience assumed that a stable and static equilibrium between socio-economic and ecological systems was required in order to adapt to nature. (Berkes et al., 2003, Smit and Wandel, 2006). Resilience has tools that were developed upon structured scenarios and adaptive management that can be used to build complex and uncertain systems. These tools increase the capacity to build ecological resilience.

Ecological resilience is the capacity of a site in an urban system to adjust and control its interactions with external vulnerabilities, disruptions and shock, thus ensuring a more sustainable urban component of the ecosystem. Ecological resilience is the ecosystem´s capacity to cope with disturbance all while maintaining its structure and functions. Unlike engineering resilience which has the capacity of returning to its previous existing state before perturbation, ecological resilience refers to patch ecology or landscape and the notion of metacity and experimental modeling and design.

Sources of natural resilience and complex adaptive systems are more than just the preservation of ecosystems and resistance to change. Traditional and dominant theoretical perspectives assume a certain stability and resilience in the environment, as well as a static equilibrium in the natural elements of the system after the external disturbances have been dealt with and removed from the system (Holling, 1973).

RESPONSE DIVERSITY

Resilience sustains the urban ecosystem under uncertain and complex situations. Because of this, human activity can have direct consequences and cause shifts in resilient social ecosystems.

Response diversity among species within a functional group is a component of resilience and is critical to ecosystem reorganization. It is a fundamental capacity of individuals, groups, organizations, and ecosystems to respond to significant disruptive changes.

Response diversity is the set of reactions among species belonging to one ecosystem, whose functions promote environmental change. Species and populations diversity within functional groups maintain ecological redundancy in ecosystem services (Luck et al. 2003). Resilience in relation to species should consider that the loss of species is non-random in relation to response diversity and the functions of the ecosystem. However, response diversity in ecosystem resilience is linked to ecosystem disturbances and environmental changes. Biological diversity is essential in social ecosystem resilience and in sustainable ecosystem change (Peterson et al. 1998). Biological diversity enhances the social ecosystem resilience and ensures the production of ecosystem services.

For this reason, resilience approaches the opportunities that arise from ecosystem changes in its structures, processes, emergence of great developments and in its coping with disturbances. Resilience is an essential factor for sustainable development, especially to maintain a dynamic equilibrium with the natural disturbances of the social–ecosystem's functioning. Response diversity as a method to sustain ecosystem states, functional groups and ecosystem services come together to face disturbances and environmental change. Response diversity operates across spatial and temporal scales.

High response diversity increases the insuring buffer for resilience and the effectiveness of ecosystem management policies and actions. Response diversity is relevant to resilience because the diversity of species contributing to an ecosystem's functions work towards the renewal and reorganization of environmental changes. In addition, it contributes to resilience when planning, managing and restoring social ecosystems. Finally, it provides adaptive capacity in uncertain and complex systems and human-dominated environments.

Moderate perturbations and disturbances on the stability of resilient social-ecosystems may either be absorbed by their ability to reorganize, or may bring small changes in resilience supported by response diversity (Deutsch et al. 2003). For example, response diversity helps maintain resilience in ecosystems that are affected by toxic chemicals and acidification, such as lakes (Carpenter and Cottingham 1997).

Response diversity does not necessarily support the notion that a high biodiversity is synonymous to high ecosystem resilience, and that the ecosystem is less vulnerable to environmental change. The migration of population to urban centers has led to a reduction in ecosystem biodiversity (MA, 2005; Sala et al., 2000). Biodiversity and response diversity, which is a variability in responses of species to environmental change, are both critical factors of social-ecosystems. On the other hand, cultural diversity and common property systems are linked to building resilience in urban socio-ecological systems. Urbanization processes have led to higher levels of cultural diversity in cities (Zanoni and Janssens, 2009).

URBAN AND ECOSYSTEM RESILIENCE

The terms "urban" and "city" are used to describe densely settled regions. These urban systems have spatial and functional contexts that combine social, biological, architectural and geophysical components (Graham & Marvin, 2001; Seto et al., 2010; Naveh, 2000; Pickett & Grove, 2009). Some of the main social dimensions of urban systems are economics of production and consumption, economic and political power, social inclusion, identity, equality and change, social justice and vulnerability, the nature of livelihood and lifestyle (Dow, 2000; Grove et al., 2006; Machlis, Force, & Burch, 1997).

Urban spaces have a direct influence on the environmental values of urban populations (Miller, 2005; Tidball et al., 2010). Urban spaces and territories are changing rapidly, becoming globally interconnected across contrasting types of landscapes and are always facing new environmental, demographic and social threats.

Additionally, urban green commons (UGCs) have the potential to facilitate civic participation and cultural integration, to manage urban land and biological diversity in urban spaces and promote urban resilience building (Colding and Barthel, 2012). Urban transformation is benefiting from the shift in the framework of urban ecology, which has seen an evolution from its earlier approach to metabolic urban energy budgets to that of city resilience, focusing on hybrid systems such as the biophysical - social structures and processes (Cadenasso et al., 2006b; Cadenasso & Pickett, 2013; Cadenasso & Pickett, 2008; Pickett, Cadenasso, & Grove, 2004).

Urban resilience in cities is the ecological approach used to analyze changes, disturbances, vulnerabilities and mutability of a city's development and its relationship with climate change.

On the other hand, sustainability measurement requires transparent accountability between the resources depleted and those used to replace them in the ecosystem. The accountability of natural resources in an ecosystem occurs through the adaptation process after an external disturbance. Adaptive processes contribute to the adaptive cycle in urban socio-ecological systems.

An ecosystem is a structural and functional unit of the biosphere. Ecosystems have complex interrelationships with human activities that constantly threaten their sustainability. The vulnerability of an ecosystem is related to the other organisms that exist within that functional group. Contraction of spatial resilience increases the disturbance to catastrophic levels (Nyström and Folke 2001).

Ecosystem resilience is the capacity to accommodate and adapt to disturbances, and the ability to buffer and persist in the face of external interference. In other words, it is the amount of disturbance that a system can absorb while still remaining in the same state and maintaining its attraction (Holling 1973, 1996). Ecosystem resilience also represents the degree of ability that a system has to learn, adapt and self-organize when confronted with external disturbances (Carpenter et al. 2001). The dynamic changes of ecosystem resilience are related to the diversity of species and functional groups (Walker 1992, 1997; Norberg et al. 2001).

Ecosystem resilience has a cross-scale response diversity. This means that biodiversity has an important role in formulating policy for sustained economic and socio-ecological development. Managing for resilience is to constantly work with uncertainty in the biosphere shaped by human action (Folke et al. 2002).

The preservation of congenital features leads to the robustness of the ecosystem, despite alterations in its behavior and changes in its environment. The resilience of ecosystems provides backups to replace failures in the species. This is done through the diversification and redundancy of biodiversity, which overlaps with ecological functions in natural ecosystems. Ecological functions of various kinds are often confronted with external disturbances. Ecological disruption occurs across a limited range of spatial and time scales allowing undisturbed scales to persist and ecological functions to operate.

GREEN RESILIENCE

The framework for sustainable planning in urban ecosystems draws notions from urban ecology, green resilience, green infrastructure, multifunctional and sustainable landscape planning, etc., with the purpose of creating and developing healthy and sustainable economic and social–ecological urban systems. Urban ecology is rooted in landscape ecology and combines principles from physical and atmospheric sciences, soil, hydrology and social sciences, etc. (Sukopp, 1990; Collins et al., 2000; McDonnell & Hahs, 2009; Pickett, Burch, Dalton, & Foresman, 1997; Redman, Grove, & Kuby, 2000). Green resilience deals with the coping of our planet with anthropogenic disturbances and ensures that it remains viable for future generations.

The concept of green resilience may be seen from a narrow interpretation to broader one of the socio-economic and ecological contexts. An ecological unit is the functioning of components and their relationships and interactions with each other, forming a complex and dynamic whole.

Sustainable and green resilience of ecosystems can be measured at event junctures, where naturally occurring regenerative forces interact with the energy released into disturbances.ESTA PARTE NO SE ENTIENDE PENSE EN REMOVERLA These regenerative forces are the solar energy, water, soil, atmosphere, vegetation, and biomass (Ben, 2013). Green resilience is an institutional capacity to cope and deal with stress and conflicts arising from climate change, unforeseen contingencies, unsustainable development to live and other emerging environmental issues within the ecosphere.

Green resilience sources intertwine with complex adaptive systems of dynamic changes in the ecosystem. The dynamic adaptive capacity of the ecosystem is provided by the connection between resilience, development change and sustainability (Smit and Wandel 2006). The key to coping with change in social systems is in anticipating and combating disturbances, in adaptive development and in integrating resilience in the interactions with ecological sustainable development. Adaptive development in the social ecosystems has the ability to carry out the ecological assessment of actual events and taking corrective action.

Sustainable development pretends to reduce social and ecological damage on both a local and a global scale through the operation of fairness and social inclusion, protection of the environment, and economic efficiency. Green resilience-building in complex, uncertain and unpredictable urban ecosystems is supported by structured scenarios and active adaptive management for sustainable development. Green resilience management enhances sustainable development in changing complex environments where the future is uncertain and unpredictable (Walker et al., 2004; Adger et al., 2005). The strategies in any system of urban green resilience focus on green infrastructure and aim to transform and adapt various resources to face future challenges such as climate change and food insecurity.

THE ISSUE OF LAND USE IN URBAN AREAS BASED ON KNOWLEDGE

The term "ecosystem", coined by Roy Clapham in 1930, describes the biological and physical environmental components that come together as a unit, and where all the elements coexist in relation to one another. The ecosystem was described as the interaction between the living creatures (biocenosis) and the environment where they live, or (biotope) (Tansley, 1935). According to the Convention on the Biological Diversity (1992), ecosystems are dynamic and complex systems, where communities of plants, animals and micro-organisms live in harmony with their non-living environment in a functional unit.

Other definitions of "ecosystems" define it as biological organizations formed by living organisms interacting with each other and in a symbiotic relationship with their environment. An ecosystem is capable of harnessing solar energy during photosynthesis and convert it into carbon dioxide and other inorganic chemicals that are essential to organic life. An ecosystem is an open system that requires a flow of energy and matter between diverse organisms and their environment, driving biogeochemical processes.

A functioning system has living and non-living components interacting with each other (Christopherson 1997). Therefore, any ecosystem has both living organisms and abiotic (non-living matter) elements. The biotic components are the living forms that inhabit the ecosystem and have a biogeochemical energy cycle. Actually, the term "ecosystem" refers to the bionic community of living organisms and biocenosis in continuous interaction with their environment or biotope and functioning in a space as a unit.

The abiotic elements represent the nonorganic material of the environment that determine which life forms can thrive in the ecosystem. Energetic processes in ecosystems are formed by tropic (anthropic? No se cual es la palabra) levels that are in turn, defined by the role of organisms and their flow of energy. Ecosystems fall between the extremes of biological complexity (Odum, 1971). In sum, living organisms are continuously interacting with environmental biotic and abiotic components (Golley, 1993).

Besides being complex and adaptive systems characterized by historical dependency and non-linear dynamics, ecosystems have multiple basins of attraction (Levin 1999). The biosphere is the largest ecosystem, and it interacts and exchanges matter and energy with the lithosphere, hydrosphere and atmosphere.

Ecosystem processes respond seasonally to solar activity, which represents the largest biogeochemical carbon cycle on the planet (Odum, 1971). An ecosystem-level process can be represented by a biogeochemical exchange cycle between organisms and their environment (Golley, 1993). Energy transfer and matter cycling processes are essential in determining ecosystem structures and functions of a wide diversity of species, as well as in defining the interactions between organisms and their environment (Golley, 1993). The living elements are continuously competing to reproduce and survive among each other. When the strength of dominant species begins to decline, other subdominant species in the same functional group are able to survive (Elmqvist et al. 2001).

The ability of a social ecosystem to sustain itself relies on its ability to adapt to the environmental changes that often occur in multiple-equilibrium systems and human-dominated environments (Folke et al. 1996; Norberg et al. 2001; Luck et al. 2003). Environmental change with low response diversity may result on extinct or ecologically insignificant functional groups that contribute to ecosystem services.

Protecting a social ecosystem from compounded perturbations requires the functional groups of species to be ready for renewal and reorganization (Lundberg and Moberg 2003).

Response diversity management sustains and enhances the flow of ecosystem services that are confronted with disturbances and that operate within and across spacial and temporal scales.

The impact of disturbances on the loss of species has many implications for social ecosystems and their flow of services (Zimov et al. 1995). The persistence of functional groups of species prevents shifts to ecosystem states and helps sustain the flow of ecosystem services. Species loss may entail low rates of ecosystem processes. Low or absent response diversity redirects ecosystem development into a different pathway. Stress-sensitive species populations tend to decline, and response diversity deteriorates while less sensitive species experience minimal changes in ecological processes (Schindler 1990; Frost et al. 1995, Rudd et al. 1988).

URBAN LAND USE

On the other hand, urbanization is rapidly expanding in cities, which are becoming frontiers for landscape ecology in urban ecosystem science.

Urban land is a natural resource-constraint threatening the prospect to meet the needs of increasing urban population, the economic prosperity and socio-political stability of the city, and is constantly influencing policy decisions. Resource depletion and pollution are two global issues that are directly related to land-use change.

The movement of people into more densely populated urban settlements can lessen pressure on urban and suburban sprawl and more remotely located ecosystems (Colding, 2011).

In regard to eco-oriented urban land uses, there has been an increasing emphasis on sustainable urbanization since metropolitan areas are engaged to upgrading land-use regulations, infrastructure, urban form and ecosystem services, etc. This has been done in an effort to protect urban biodiversity and to create a better urban resilient socio-ecosystem, capable of developing a sustainable urban environment with more social justice and economic growth, all while improving competitiveness and attractiveness of the city (de Jong et al. 2015).

Additionally, urban land maintains its relationships with the urban land market, local government regulations, management practices and with technology innovations. It is influenced by the complexity of societal processes and ignores the systemic consequences and effects on the resilient socio-ecosystem services.

Land use must prioritize nature and biodiversity in order to support the sustainable urban development in a territorial context. Networks of open urban spaces unite nature and gardening with the goal to build green and resilient cities inspired by nature and biodiversity (Quincerot & Weil, 2009, p. 175; Daune & Mongé, 2011). Land uses can be appropriate to develop a network of green open spaces for gardening in core areas of the city (Quincerot & Weil, 2009).

A contemporary and ecological movement advocates for principles of sustainable land use in urban planning even though this movement is not always involved in projects that demonstrate those principles (Seana, Johnson & Peters, 1999). Furthermore, the integration of land-use initiatives as formulated in urban planning are not always implemented or realized and can become negotiation spaces for less formalized land-use initiatives and practices.

A sustainable urban transportation system that uses renewable resources and energy and that operates efficiently and affordably helps minimize the use of land and limits emissions the emission of waste and noise in the atmosphere.

Biodiversity in suburbs constitutes both natural and semi-natural land with an increase in the semi-rural urban fringe (Blair, 2001; McKinney, 2002; Sukopp et al., 1979 Colding et al., 2006). Urban development emerges in high levels of biodiversity areas with high ecosystem productivity (Ricketts and Imhoff, 2003; Hansen et al., 2004; Ljungqvist et al., 2010).

In addition, cities that show a commitment to urban planning and to the implementation of ecosystem services in support of greening projects for transforming urban green infrastructure are likely to benefit from the value creation of these projects, which would in turn, be beneficial for all of the population. The modernist model of urban development is described as a life cycle of cities moving from commodity exchange and industrialization, through an ecological version that mitigates all the ills of the urban ecosystem. Therefore, urban design and planning take into account the coordination of resources, capacities and efforts to be implemented in comprehensive agendas across the city.

Landscape ecology comprises the concepts of landscape sustainability. It represents the capacity to consistently provide long-term and landscape-specific ecosystem services that are essential for maintaining and improving human well-being (Wu 2013) and ecosystem services in changing landscapes (Wu & Qu, 2013).

Urban green infrastructure is a strategically planned and manages an urban network of natural lands, working landscapes, and urban open green spaces that provide a range of diverse benefits. Ecosystem services for example, can offer many benefits to human beings. (Millennium Ecosystem Assessment 2005). The social-ecosystems capacity to minimize the impact of disturbances affects the flow of the services required for the well-being of its community. Landscape services can offer some benefits to the population because it functions as a structure–function-value chain to create landscape development (Termorshuizen Opdam 2009).

Urban planners and landscape designers can coordinate activities across different fields and urban functions, allowing these spaces to fulfill their full potential as multifunctional and sustainable spaces.

The multi-scale analysis of land-use compositions is a useful element for the planning of land use and for the design of policy for urban sustainability. This analysis of land uses may be conducted with a participatory design process of visioning, defining, relating the elements, elaborating the site plan and the implementation process. Multiple land-use scenarios simulate the future changes in composition of their functions, such as self-sufficiency in vegetable production. Changes in land use may lead to inaccurate counts of land abandonment and vacant land (Bowman and Pagano 2004).

Furthermore, multifunctional landscape frameworks are applied to both agroecosystems and planning urban ecosystems, and it provides beneficial production, ecological, and cultural functions, considering the needs and preferences of users and owners (Otte et al. 2007; Lovell et al. 2010).

A commitment to multifunctional urban green infrastructure brings value of ecosystem services to urban populations. The optimization of urban green space functions can be put to the test by using a multifunctional landscape framework for sustainable urban design and planning of green infrastructure. Multifunctional green infrastructure provides ecosystem services and the presence of biodiversity in urban areas can bring many benefits to the environment and society.

These urban ecosystem services are supplied through participatory planning processes that are focused on multifunctional green resilience infrastructure, and that are developed to contribute to sustainable ecological, social and economic welfare of the city. Ecosystem services transform urban green infrastructure through the integration of empowerment and creative processes into small-scale greening projects.

A multi-functional role of land uses can provide urban corridors of gardening spaces to preserve nature, agriculture and farming practices, and to perform educational and recreational activities that help protect biodiversity and the natural environment all while improving resilient socio ecosystems and inner-city densification.

The relationship between biological diversity and the various functions of an ecosystem is founded on the abilities of self-renewal and reorganization that biodiversity can bring to stimulate change and growth in social-ecosystems (Loreau et al. 2001; Kinzig et al. 2002). Despite the diversity in compositions and considerable species turnover, the organization and functioning of social-ecosystems can be seen as conservative due to patterns of species loss. (Schindler 1990; Kalin Arroyo et al. 1995; Forys and Allen 2002; Brown et al. 2001, Havlicek and Carpenter 2001). Otherwise, social-ecosystems may change when some species are lost or when there is an invasion of other new species (Estes and Duggins 1995; Terborgh et al. 2001; Vitousek and Walker 1989).

Some spaces can also be used for the reuse and recycling of waste. On a long-term basis, this specific type of land use can help reduce transportation and improve city management. Cities often struggle to manage opposing external and internal frontiers of land and should be more spontaneous in the decisions they make regarding land-use management of soils. (Berger 2007). This constant tension between the expansion of urban periphery and unused spaces has always existed in the internal frontier of the urban core. (Rusk 1993).

LAND USE CHANGE

The accelerated conversion and change of land use from arable or forested lands to urban land use is threatening the biodiversity, the species and the natural resources which have historically provided the sustenance, valuable goods and services, climate regulation, water recharging, nutrient recycling, agricultural products, timber, seafood and waste assimilation, etc. All of these benefits are in danger of extinction due to increasing urban land use. In response to the growing challenges posed by the conversion from agricultural to urban land uses, it is crucial that local governments formulate and implement urban development strategies that ensure more eco-efficient benefits in terms of economic growth and productivity as well as more socially equitable, inclusive and environmental sustainability.

Land-use issues require a multi-disciplined and cross-departmental approach that will have a direct impact on economic efficiency and urban growth, employment, social inclusion and equality, health and sustainable environment. Urban zoning, neighborhood plans, and the spatial-temporal patterns of inequality are other factors that have significant impact on land use.

However, the use of land for agriculture and farming are not broadly accepted by local governments because they believe that there are possible health risks associated to these practices. Urban agriculture and farming practices can sometimes be divisive within their societies, especially when the spaces could be used for other scarce economic activities. Urban land-use planning and zoning is growing exponentially and conflicts with other similar practices that question the usefulness of urban agriculture. Enhanced security is required around the physical limitations of the urban spaces, and although this has potential productive qualities, it also causes the spaces to become unbuildable and their urban parcels, underutilized. (Pagano and Bowman 2000) The high land prices, the exposure to pollution, the contamination of water, air and soil from industrial and commercial activities and traffic affect the land use for housing, education, recreation, agriculture, farming and gardening. This causes hampering investments and leads to poor land-use security (Mougeot 2000).

In addition, buildings and infrastructure put great pressure on urban land use. Vacant residential yards and industrial rooftop spaces are considered different land uses. Some land-use maps do not distinguish parking lots from other vacant spaces. A good example that was reported by Hui in 2011, is the abandoned land used to plant flowers, ornamental plants, herbs and vegetables, next to a government building.

However, urban land use for agriculture, farming and gardening have become quite attractive because of their potential to meet multiple needs of their community, such as supplying fresh and healthy food in neighborhoods with limited access, articulating the linkages between the built environment, food systems and health while offering opportunities to residents for employment, recreation and education (Hodgson et al., 2011; Redwood, 2011). Montreal for example, has the largest municipal urban agriculture program in Canada, and has effective land-use designation (Cosgrove, 2001).

Public actions can be taken to promote the social dimensions of urban public spaces as part of collective re-appropriated spaces for diversified uses of unused vacant land around housing areas. Recovered unused land is often used for agriculture, farming and temporary gardening projects created on constructible land and adapting to the demands of residents. These public actions for more integral city development are aimed to foster conviviality, proximity and social cohesion between residents (Canton de Genève, 2013), and enhance the urbanite social interaction and cohesion while improving quality of life.

The urban land-use planning system contributes to the economic growth, social development and environmental sustainability of a city. Vancouver's Food Action Plan (City of Vancouver, 2003) supported the land-use decision to serve as a public resource to support the city's commitments to sustainability. In states like Oregon, the land-use planning system demands that each city set an urban growth boundary to show the physical limits and control of "sagebrush subdivisions, coastal condo-mania, and the ravenous rampage of suburbia", and the protection of farm and forest lands (McCall, 1973).

The awareness of sustainable urban land-use planning reinforces the development and maintenance of a data-based development system. It manages issues of urban growth or decline as well as rundown and waste resources. (Carley, 1995; Curwell and Cooper, 1998; Department of the Environment, Transport and the Regions (DETR), 1998). The decision-making process around land use, urban development and parallel policies are made in support of sustainable planning. The policies are made based on an inventory of natural resources.

In most cities, urban land-use planning for commercial farming requires special permits and must follow zoning and building regulations and city codes for water sources, fire and energy as well as waste disposal.

Urban planning and food production policies developed by local authorities may connect the issues of land-use planning and sustainable development. Some cities have already implemented an urban land-use and comprehensive plan that includes urban farming and agriculture. In order to do so, they adjusted zoning and permission granting procedures and included infrastructure, materials, knowledge, and other resources in their city plans. (Mukherji and Morales 2010).

The land-use planning system fills the middle layer vacuum. Although land availability and land use are not statutory requirements for sustainable urban planning, they are at the center of the development of urban food production.

Land-use planning has an important role in urban policy as it delivers sustainable development ideas. Urban gardening for example, contributes to the growth of cities' economies by promoting health practices. (Hynes, 1996, p. 161). Urban land use policies and regulations are also used for the management of vacant city spaces, which in in turn, creates networks of sustainable urban spaces and provides better ecosystem services for the development of more sustainable cities. Long-term vacancy requires more oriented regeneration policies (National Land Use Database, 2000). Vacant buildings require the recording of reliable and comprehensive information.

The rights to access the city and its built environments are other key elements that grant citizens the right to part-take in the development of their community. It allows them to participate and help make democratic decisions about their city planning, and grants them the right to access, occupy and use urban spaces. (Lefebvre, 1996).

The term "built environment" refers to "the human-made structures that provide the setting for human activity such as buildings, parks and green spaces, neighborhoods and cities. The supporting infrastructures of built environments, such as water supply or energy networks is often incorporated within these environments. "The built environment is a material, spatial, and cultural product of human labor that combines physical elements and energy in forms for living, working, and playing." (Kaklauskas & Gudauskas, 2016, p.413). These concepts underline the communities' opportunity to care for their surroundings and increase the quality of life by providing the necessary elements to propitiate a resilient and sustainable environment.

CHALLENGES AND RECOMMENDATIONS

Pressures arising from climate change are related to some extent, to the increasing scarcity of land for urban use and other natural resources, such as water and natural nutrients. In many places, population is continuing to rise and becoming an important concern for the policy agenda. The orientation toward resilient and ecological land use is only one of municipal governments' challenges as they must work to converge the structures and processes of urban social-ecosystems with energy, fuel, climate, water and food. These challenges incorporate economic, social and environmental perspectives, and integrate initiatives of diverse stakeholders to invest in natural resources and capital projects and generate development of green resilience in the city.

The phenomenon of resilience in sustainable development may lead to some policy recommendations to improve the interrelationships between the economic efficiency and the social-ecosystems and biosphere, to develop flexible and innovative relationships of collaboration, and to achieve sustainability and its operationalization in the context of socio-ecological resilience. Other policy recommendations should focus on the development of indicators to measure any change in the level of resilience and to signal and monitor uncertainties of social–ecosystem variables and to manage diversity.

Human beings are living in a time of qualitative changes in many areas of urban life. These changes have a great impact on city management. Seemingly, now is the time to redefine the city's functional structure; many countries still operate under obsolete and ineffective functional and spatial divisions. In the face of significant changes in civilization, many existing regulations impose barriers and impede the rational development of communities; it's time to introduce new and innovative solutions. Notably, there are urban land-use plans that propose innovative and pro-environmental solutions that support green, resilient and eco-oriented uses of urban ecosystems and promote a better quality of life in the city. In sum, urban land is scarce, and it should be treated in a more sustainable manner.

City planners and landscape designers consider agricultural and farming landscapes to be important areas for the future of sustainable urban development. The urban agriculture and farming lands are inherently multi-functional and can offer many public benefits beyond the provision of sustainability and commodity outputs. The amount of vacant land in urban centers is increasing, especially where land-use densities are declining. This is the result of the decline seen by manufacturing activities after limits on employment creation and population density have been reached.

Urban land use scenarios are a tool that helps to allocate vacant urban spaces to vegetable production in residential green spaces like gardens and rooftops. Land-use control and building regulations constraint and limit farming and gardening in urban areas.

In order to determine the current characteristics of land uses, it is necessary to conduct some database analysis from primary and secondary sources. This approach allows cities to broaden their vision by considering the multiple functions of a specific site and defining its various components by comparing data with other cities. Then, land uses are identified for specific functions such as education and recreation, etc. Land-use components, their dimensions and locations are included in the proposals. This whole process serves to identify the needs and expectations of the urban community regarding land uses, spatial design and site plans.

Urban sustainable planning systems can encourage the use of urban land for more sustainable development like the production of local food. Sustainable urban planning fails to consider that the food system is its turf, pointing the responsibilities to land-use regulations and built environment. Dudo de este sentence tambien The temporal urban land-use plans that are applied to open green spaces have formalized the concept of urban gardening and farming initiatives to help provide more qualitative resilient ecosystem services that contribute to the development of more resilient cities.

In addition, land-use planning must meet the demands posed by the socio-economic activities and urban growth to ensure the effective management of value creation and environmental sustainability. However, farming and gardening may not always be alternatives in an urban setting, especially when other competing lands with higher value can meet the needs of the city. Urban agriculture, farming and gardening are integrated into the city's sustainable planning for land use and policy processes. These sustainable practices offer new frontiers for sustainable land use planners and landscape designers and offer endless possibilities for sustainable urban development and transformation of urban spaces.

City authorities and local governments should adopt innovative urban planning and sustainable development strategies based on the use of land, resource protection practices, environmental and ecological services, social inclusion and egalitarian issues, economic growth and efficiency, etc. A strategic orientation of initiatives could seriously obstruct zoning plans. On the other hand, sustainable urban planning aims to encourage urban agriculture, farming and gardening as an effective use of land. Land-use planning and landscape design should reconcile demands of socio-economic activities and urban growth.

Ultimately, new forms of value are ascribed to public and private urban properties in order to meet other land use priorities such as housing, commercial areas, urban green areas and open spaces, roads and other infrastructure. Efficiency of urban land use can be achieved through different means and variables, such as energy consumption, water, other natural resources and waste management.

Finally, urban land use has different applications for the multiple levels of society: from the entire city to small neighborhoods, from communities to small vacant lots, houses and buildings. Urban land use should be evaluated on a basis of landscape multi-functionality, and account for the various contributions, functions, services and benefits that it can provide.

The urban social-ecosystem's cultural functions, biodiversity, ecological services, economic efficiency, social inclusion and equality have the potential to bring great benefits to communities and neighborhoods and to society as a whole.

REFERENCES

Adger, W. N. (2006). Vulnerability. *Global Environmental Change, 16*(3), 268–281. doi:10.1016/j.gloenvcha.2006.02.006

Adger, W. N. (2000). Social and ecological resilience: Are they related? *Progress in Human Geography, 24*(3), 347–364. doi:10.1191/030913200701540465

Adger, W. N., Hughes, T. P., Folke, C., Carpenter, S. R., & Rockstrom, J. (2005). Social– ecological resilience to coastal disasters. *Science, 309*(5737), 1036–1039. doi:10.1126cience.1112122 PMID:16099974

Akers, J. (2013). Making markets: Think tank legislation and private property in Detroit. *Urban Geography, 34*(8), 1070–1095. doi:10.1080/02723638.2013.814272

Anderies, J. M., Janssen, M. A., & Ostrom, E. (2004). A framework to analyze the robustness of social-ecological systems from an institutional perspective. *Ecology and Society, 9*(1), 18. http://www. ecologyandsociety.org/vol9/iss1/art18/

Arrow, K., Bolin, B., Costanza, R., Dasgupta, P., Folke, C., Holling, C. S., Jansson, B. O., Levin, S., Mäler, K. G., Perrings, C., & Pimentel, D. (1995). Economic growth, carrying capacity and the environment. *Science, 268*(5210), 520–521. doi:10.1126cience.268.5210.520 PMID:17756719

Falk, B. (2013). The resilient farm and homestead. Chelsea Green Publishing.

Berger, A. (2007). *Drosscape: Wasting Land Urban America*. Princeton Architectural Press.

Berkes, F., Colding, J., & Folke, C. (Eds.). (2003). *Navigating Social–Ecological Systems: Building Resilience for Complexity and Change*. Cambridge University Press.

Blair, R. B. (2001). Birds and butterflies along urban gradients in two ecoregions of theU.S. In J. L. Lockwood & M. L. McKinney (Eds.), *Biotic Homogenization* (pp. 459–486). Kluwer. doi:10.1007/978-1-4615-1261-5_3

O Bowman, A. M., & Pagano, M.A., (2004). Terra Incognita: Vacant Land and Urban Strategies. Georgetown University Press.

Walker & Salt. (2012). *Resilience Practice: Building Capacity to Absorb Disturbance and Maintain Function*. Island Press.

Brown, J. H., Ernest, S. K. M., Parody, J. M., & Haskell, J. P. (2001). Regulation of diversity: Maintenance of species richness in changing environments. *Oecologia, 126*(3), 321–332. doi:10.1007004420000536 PMID:28547444

Cadenasso, M. L., & Pickett, S. T. A. (2008). Urbanprinciples for ecological landscape design and management: Scientific fundamentals. *Cities and the Environment, 1*(2), 4. doi:10.15365/cate.1242008

Cadenasso, M. L., & Pickett, S. T. A. (2013). Three tides: The development and state of the art of urban ecological studies. In S. T. A. Pickett, M. L. Cadenasso, & B. P. McGrath (Eds.), *Resilience in urban ecology and design: Linking theory and practice for sustainable cities* (pp. 29–46). Springer. doi:10.1007/978-94-007-5341-9_2

Cadenasso, M. L., Pickett, S. T. A., & Grove, J. M. (2006a). Dimensions of ecosystem complexity: Heterogeneity, connectivity, and history. *Ecological Complexity*, *3*(1), 1–12. doi:10.1016/j.ecocom.2005.07.002

Cadenasso, M. L., Pickett, S. T. A., & Grove, J. M. (2006b). Integrative approaches to investigating human-natural systems: The Baltimore Ecosystem Study. *Nature Sciences Sociétés*, *14*(1), 1–14. doi:10.1051/nss:2006002

Canton de Genève. (2013). Plan directeur cantonal 2030. A14: Promouvoir de nouvelles formes de jardins fa-miliaux et encourager la création de plantages. République et Canton de Genève.

Carley, M. (1995). The bigger picture: Organising for sustainable urban regeneration. *Town and Country Planning*, *64*(9), 236–239.

Carpenter, S. R., & Cottingham, K. L. (1997). Resilience and restoration of lakes. *Conservation Ecology*, *1*(1), 2. doi:10.5751/ES-00020-010102

Carpenter, S. R., Walker, B., Anderies, J. M., & Abel, N. (2001). From metaphor to measurement: Resilience of what to what? *Ecosystems (New York, N.Y.)*, *4*(8), 765–781. doi:10.100710021-001-0045-9

Childers, D. L., Pickett, S. T. A., Grove, J. M., Ogden, L., & Whitmer, A. (2014). Advancing urban sustainability theory and action: Challenges and opportunities. *Landscape and Urban Planning*, *125*, 320–328. doi:10.1016/j.landurbplan.2014.01.022

City of Portland. (2007). *ENN-1.01: Food Policy Council (Binding city policy)*. Retrieved September 24, 2007, from http://www.portlandonline. com/auditor/index.cfm?a=ihci&c=checj

City of Vancouver. (2003). *Action plan for creating a just and sustainable food system for the City of Vancouver (RTS Number: 3755)*. Author.

Clement, D. (2013). *The spatial injustice of crisis-driven neoliberal urban restructuring in Detroit* (Unpublished master's thesis). University of Miami. Retrieved from http://scholarlyrepository.miami.edu/oa_theses/406/

Christopherson, R. W. (1997). Geosystems: An Introduction to Physical Geography (3rd ed.). Prentice Hall Inc.

Colding, J. (2011). The role of ecosystem services in contemporary urban planning. In Urban Ecology. Patterns, Processes and Applications. Oxford University Press. doi:10.1093/acprof:oso/9780199563562.003.0028

Colding, J., & Barthel, S. (2012). *The potential of Urban Green Commons in the resilience building of cities*. Elsevier B.V.

Colding, J., Lundberg, J., & Folke, C. (2006). Incorporating green-area user groups in urbanecosystem management. *Ambio*, *35*(5), 237–244. doi:10.1579/05-A-098R.1 PMID:16989508

Collins, J. P., Kinzig, A., Grimm, N. B., Fagan, W. F., Hope, D., Wu, J., & Borer, E. T. (2000). A new urban ecology. *American Scientist*, *88*(5), 416–425. doi:10.1511/2000.5.416

Convention on the Biological Diversity. (1992). The Earth Summit. Held in Rio de Janeiro on 5 June 1992 and entered into force on 29 December 1993. United Nations, General Assembly.

Cosgrove, S. (2001). *Montréal's community gardening program*. Retrieved July 29, 2007, from http://www.cityfarmer.org/Montreal13.html

Costanza, R., & Patten, B. C. (1995). Defining and predicting sustainability. *Ecological Economics*, *15*(3), 193–196. doi:10.1016/0921-8009(95)00048-8

Curwell, S., & Cooper, I. (1998). The implications of urban sustainability. *Building Research and Information*, *26*(1), 17–28. doi:10.1080/096132198370074

Curwell, S., Deakin, M., & Symes, M. (Eds.). (2005). *Sustainable urban development, volume 1: The framework and protocols for environmental assessment*. Routledge. doi:10.4324/9780203299913

de Jong, M., Joss, S., Schraven, D., Zhan, Ch., & Weijnen, M. (2015). Sustainable–Smart–Resilient–Low Carbon–Eco–Knowledge Cities; Making Sense of a Multitude of Concepts Promoting Sustainable Urbanization. *Journal of Cleaner Production*, *109*(1), 25–38. doi:10.1016/j.jclepro.2015.02.004

Daune, L., & Mongé, N. (2011). L'agriculture urbaine, un fondement dans le projet de territoire. *Urbia—Les Cahiers du développement urbain durable, 12*, 85-105.

Deelstra, T., Boyd, D., & van den Biggelaar, M. (2006). *Multifunctional land use, promoting urban agriculture in Europe*. Academic Press.

DETR. (1998). *Sustainable Development: Opportunities for Change*. Department of the Environment, Transport and the Regions. Consultation Paper on a Revised UK Strategy, DETR.

Detroit Works Project. (2014). *Detroit future city: Detroit strategic framework plan*. Retrieved from http://detroitfuturecity.com/wp-content/uploads/2014/12/DFC_Full_2nd.pdf

Deutsch, L., Folke, C., & Skanberg, K. (2003). The critical natural capital of ecosystem performance as insurance for human well-being. *Ecological Economics*, *44*(2-3), 205–217. doi:10.1016/S0921-8009(02)00274-4

Dow, K. (2000). Social dimensions of gradients in urban ecosystems. *Urban Ecosystems*, *4*(4), 255–275. doi:10.1023/A:1015767231137

Elmqvist, T., Wall, M., & Berggren, A. L. (2001). Tropical forest reorganization after cyclone and fire disturbance in Samoa: remnant trees as biological legacies. *Cons Ecol, 5*, 10. http://www.consecol.org/vol5/iss2/art10

Estes, J. A., & Duggins, D. O. (1995). Sea otters and kelp forests in Alaska: Generality and variation in a community ecological paradigm. *Ecological Monographs*, *65*(1), 75–100. doi:10.2307/2937159

EurActiv. (2004). *Sustainable Development: Introduction*. Author.

Folke, C., Carpenter, S. R., Elmqvist, T., Gunderson, L., Holling, C. S., & Walker, B. (2002). Resilience and sustainable development: Building adaptive capacity in a world of transformations. *Ambio*, *31*(5), 437–440. doi:10.1579/0044-7447-31.5.437 PMID:12374053

Folke, C., Pritchard, L., Berkes, F., Colding, J., & Svedin, U. (1998). *The Problem of Fit Between Ecosystems and Institutions*. International Human Dimensions Programme (IHDP). IHDP Working Paper No 2. www.uni-bonn.de/IHDP/public.htm

Folke, C., Jansson, A., Larsson, J., & Costanza, R. (1997). Ecosystem appropriation by cities. *Ambio*, *26*, 167–172.

Folke, C., Holling, C. S., & Perrings, C. (1996). Biological diversity, ecosystems and the human scale. *Ecological Applications*, *6*(4), 1018–1024. doi:10.2307/2269584

Forys, E. A., & Allen, C. R. (2002). Functional group change within and across scales following invasions and extinctions in the Everglades ecosystem. *Ecosystems (New York, N.Y.)*, *5*(4), 339–347. doi:10.100710021-001-0078-0

Frost, T. M., Carpenter, S. R., Ives, A. R., & Kratz, T. K. (1995). Species compensation and complementarity in ecosystem function. In C. G. Jones & J. H. Lawton (Eds.), *Linking species and ecosystems*. Chapman & Hall. doi:10.1007/978-1-4615-1773-3_22

Golley, F. B. (1993). *A History of the Ecosystem Concept in Ecology: More Than the Sum of the Parts*. Yale University Press.

Graham, S., & Marvin, S. (2001). *Splintering urbanism: Networked infrastructures, technological mobilities and the urban condition*. Routledge.

Grimm, N. B., Faeth, S. H., Golubiewski, N. E., Redman, C. L., Wu, J., Bai, X., & Briggs, J. M. (2008). Global change and the ecology of cities. *Science*, *319*(5864), 756–760. doi:10.1126cience.1150195 PMID:18258902

Grove, J. M. (2009). Cities: Managing densely settled social–ecological systems. In F. S. Chapin III G. P. Kofinas, & C. Folke (Eds.), *Principles of ecosystem stewardship: Resilience-based natural resource management in a changing world* (pp. 281–294). doi:10.1007/978-0-387-73033-2_13

Gunderson, L. H., & Holling, C. S. (Eds.). (2002). *Panarchy: Understanding Transformations in Human and Systems*. Island Press.

Hansen, A. J., Defries, R., & Turner, W. (2004). Land use change and biodiversity: a syn-thesis of rates and consequences during the period of satellite imagery. In G. Gutman & C. Justice (Eds.), *Land Change Science: Observing, Monitoring, and Understanding Trajectories of Change on the Earth's Surface* (pp. 277–299). Springer Verlag.

Havlicek, T. D., & Carpenter, S. R. (2001). Pelagic species size distributions in lakes: Are they discontinuous? *Limnology and Oceanography*, *46*(5), 1021–1033. doi:10.4319/lo.2001.46.5.1021

Hodgson, K., Caton Campbell, M., & Bailkey, M. (2011). Urban agriculture: growing healthy, sustainable places. Washington, DC: American Planning Association.

Holling, C. S. (1996). Engineering resilience versus ecological resilience. In P. C. Schulze (Ed.), *Engineering within ecological constraints*. National Academy Press.

Holling, C. S. (1973). Resilience and stability of ecological systems. *Annual Review of Ecology and Systematics*, *4*(1), 1–23. doi:10.1146/annurev.es.04.110173.000245

Hough, M. (1995). *Cities and Natural Process*. Routledge. doi:10.4324/9780203292433

Hui, S. C. M. (2011). *Green roof urban farming for buildings in high-density urban cities*. Invited paper for the Hainan China World Green Roof Conference 2011, Hainan, China.

Hynes, H. P. (1996). *A Patch of Eden: America's Inner-city Gardeners*. Chelsea Green Publishing Company.

IISD. (2009). *What is Sustainable Development?* International Institute for Sustainable Development.

Jackson, J. B. C., Kirby, M. X., Berger, W. H., Bjorndal, K. A., Botsford, L. W., Bourque, B. J., Bradbury, R. H., Cooke, R., Erlandson, J., Estes, J. A., Hughes, T. P., Kidwell, S., Lange, C. B., Lenihan, H. S., Pandolfi, J. M., Peterson, C. H., Steneck, R. S., Tegner, M. J., & Warner, R. R. (2001). Historical overfishing and the recent collapse of coastal ecosystems. *Science*, *293*(5530), 629–638. doi:10.1126cience.1059199 PMID:11474098

James, P., Magee, L., Scerri, A., & Steger, M. B. (2015). *Urban Sustainability in Theory and Practice*. Routledge.

Jenks, M., & Jones, C. (Eds.). (2010). Dimensions of the sustainable city. Springer.

Kaklauskas, A., & Gudauskas, R. (2016). Intelligent decision-support systems and the Internet of Things for the smart built environment. In *Start-Up Creation* (pp. 413–449). Woodhead Publishing. doi:10.1016/B978-0-08-100546-0.00017-0

Kalin Arroyo, M. T., Zedler, P. H., & Fox, M. D. (Eds.). (1995). *Ecology and biogeography of Mediterranean ecosystems in Chile, California, and Australia*. Springer-Verlag. doi:10.1007/978-1-4612-2490-7

Kates, R., Parris, T., & Leiserowitz, A. (2005). What is Sustainable Development? Goals, Indicators, Values, and practice. *Environment*, *47*(3), 8–21. doi:10.1080/00139157.2005.10524444

Kinzig, A. P., Pacala, S. W., & Tilman, D. (Eds.). (2002). *The functional consequences of biodiversity*. Princeton University Press.

Kolasa, J., & Pickett, S. T. A. (2005). Changing academic perspectives of ecology: A view from within. In M. J. Mappin & E. A. Johnson (Eds.), *Environmental education and advocacy* (pp. 50–71). Cambridge University Press.

Lambin, E. F. (2005). Conditions for sustainability of human-environment systems: Information, motivation, and capacity. *Global Environmental Change*, *15*(3), 177–180. doi:10.1016/j.gloenvcha.2005.06.002

Lefebvre, H. (1996). The right to the city. *Writings on Cities, 63181*.

Levin, S. (1999). *Fragile dominion: complexity and the commons*. Perseus Books.

Liam, M., Andy, S., Paul, J., Thom, J. A., Padgham, L., Hickmott, S., Deng, H., & Cahill, F. (2013). Reframing social sustainability reporting: Towards an engaged approach. *Environment, Development and Sustainability*, *15*(1), 225–243. doi:10.100710668-012-9384-2

Ljungqvist, J., Barthel, S., Finnveden, G., & Sörlin, S. (2010). The Urban Anthropocene: Lessons for Sustainability from the Environmental History of Constantinople. In P. Sinclair, F. Herschend, C. Isendahl, & G. Nordquist (Eds.), *The Urban Mind, cultural and environmental dynamics Studies in Global Archaeology* (Vol. 15, pp. 368–394). University Press.

Loreau, M., Naeem, S., Inchausti, P., Bengtsson, J., Grime, J. P., Hector, A., Hooper, D. U., Huston, M. A., Raffaelli, D., Schmid, B., Tilman, D., & Wardle, D. A. (2001). Biodiversity and ecosystem functioning: Current knowledge and future challenges. *Science, 294*(5543), 804–808. doi:10.1126cience.1064088 PMID:11679658

Lovell, S. T., DeSantis, S., Nathan, C. A., Olson, M. B., Mendez, V. E., Kominami, H. C., Erickson, D. L., Morris, K. S., & Morris, W. B. (2010). Integrating agroecology and landscape multifunc-tionality in Vermont: An evolving framework to evaluate the design of agroecosystems. *Agricultural Systems, 103*(5), 327–341. doi:10.1016/j.agsy.2010.03.003

Luck, G. W., Daily, G. C., & Ehrlich, P. R. (2003). Population diversity and ecosystem services. *Trends in Ecology & Evolution, 18*(7), 331–336. doi:10.1016/S0169-5347(03)00100-9

Lundberg, J., & Moberg, F. (2003). Mobile link organisms and ecosystem functioning: Implications for ecosystem resilience and management. *Ecosystems (New York, N.Y.), 6*(1), 87–98. doi:10.100710021-002-0150-4

Kahle, L. R., & Gurel-Atay, E. (Eds.). (2014). *Communicating Sustainability for the Green Economy*. M.E. Sharpe.

Machlis, G. E., Force, J. E., & Burch, W. R. Jr. (1997). The human ecosystem. 1. The human ecosystem as an organizing concept in ecosystem management. *Society & Natural Resources, 10*(4), 347–367. doi:10.1080/08941929709381034

McCall, T. (1973). *Legislative address, Governor Tom McCall, Oregon, (1973).* Retrieved July 20, 2008, from http://arcweb.sos.state.or.us/governors/McCall/legis1973.html

McDonnell, M. J., & Hahs, A. (2009). Comparative ecology of cities and towns: Past, present and future. In M. J. McDonnell, A. Hahs, & J. Breuste (Eds.), *Ecology of cities and towns: A comparative approach* (pp. 71–89). Cambridge University Press. doi:10.1017/CBO9780511609763.006

McKinney, M. L. (2002). Urbanization, biodiversity, and conservation. *Bioscience, 52*(10), 883–890. doi:10.1641/0006-3568(2002)052[0883:UBAC]2.0.CO;2

Millennium Ecosystem Assessment (MA). (2005). *Synthesis.* Island Press. http://www.MAweb.org

Miller, J. R. (2005). Biodiversity conservation and the extinction of experience. *Trends in Ecology & Evolution, 20*(8), 430–434. doi:10.1016/j.tree.2005.05.013 PMID:16701413

Mukherji, N., & Morales, A. (2010). Zoning for urban Agriculture. *Zoning Practice, 3.*

Musacchio, L. R. (2008). Metropolitan landscape ecology: Using translational research to increase sustainability, resilience, and regeneration. *Landscape Journal, 27*(1), 1–8. doi:10.3368/lj.27.1.1

National Land Use Database. (2000). Previously Developed Land (PDL): Vacant Sites and Derelict Sites, and Other Previously Developed Land and Buildings that May be Available for Redevelopment, Data Specification, NLUD – a partnership. *Rethinking Urban Capacity.*

Naveh, Z. (2000). The total human ecosystem: Integrating ecology and economics. *Bioscience*, *50*, 357–361.

Nelson, D. R., Adger, W. N., & Brown, K. (2007). Adaptation to environmental change: Contributions of a resilience framework. *Annual Review of Environment and Resources*, *32*, 395–419.

Nyström, M., & Folke, C. (2001). Spatial resilience of coral reefs. *Ecosystems (New York, N.Y.)*, *4*(5), 406–417. doi:10.100710021-001-0019-y

Odum, E. P. (1971). *Fundamentals of Ecology* (3rd ed.). W. B. Saunders.

Otte, A., Simmering, D., & Wolters, V. (2007). Biodiversity at the landscape level: Recent concepts and perspectives for multifunctional land use. *Landscape Ecology*, *22*(5), 639–642. doi:10.100710980-007-9094-6

Pagano, M. A., & Bowman, A. (2000). Land in Cities: An Urban Resource. Brookings Institution, Center on Urban and Metropolitan Policy.

Peterson, G., Allen, C.R., & Holling, C.S. (1998). Ecological resilience, biodiversity, and scale. *Ecosystems, 1*, 6–18.

Pickett, S. T. A., & Cadenasso, M. L. (2002). Ecosystem as a multidimensional concept: Meaning, model and metaphor. *Ecosystems (New York, N.Y.)*, *5*(1), 1–10. doi:10.100710021-001-0051-y

Pickett, S. T. A., Burch, W. R. Jr, Dalton, S., & Foresman, T. (1997). Integrated urban ecosystem research: Themes, needs, and applications. *Urban Ecosystems*, *1*(4), 183–184. doi:10.1023/A:1018579628818

Pickett, S. T. A., Cadenasso, M. L., & Grove, J. M. (2004). Resilient cities: Meaning, models, and metaphor for integrating the ecological, socio-economic, and planning realms. *Landscape and Urban Planning*, *69*(4), 369–384. doi:10.1016/j.landurbplan.2003.10.035

Pickett, S. T. A., Groffman, P. M., Brush, G. S., Galvin, M. F., Grove, J. M., ... Troy, A. R. (2008). Exchanges across land-water-scape boundaries in urban systems: Strategies for reducing nitrate pollution. *Annals of the New York Academy of Sciences*, *1134*(1), 213–232. doi:10.1196/annals.1439.012 PMID:18566096

Pothukuchi, K., & Kaufman, J. (2000). The food system: A stranger to the planning field. *Journal of the American Planning Association*, *66*(2), 112–124. doi:10.1080/01944360008976093

Pothukuchi, K., & Kaufman, J. (1999). Placing the food system on the urban agenda: The role of municipal institutions in food systems planning. *Agriculture and Human Values*, *16*(2), 213–244. doi:10.1023/A:1007558805953

Quincerot, R., & Weil, M. (2009). *Genève 2020: Plan di-recteur communal de la Ville de Genève*. Ville de Genève.

Redman, C., Grove, J. M., & Kuby, L. (2000). *Toward a unified understanding of human ecosystems: Integrating social sciences into long-term ecological research* White Paper of the Long-Term Ecological Research. Albuquerque, NM: LTER Network.

Redwood, M., & Bahri, A. (2010). *Wastewater Irrigation and Health: Assessing and Mitigation Risks in Low-income Countries*. Earthscan/IDRC/IWMI.

Ricketts, T., & Imhoff, M. (2003). Biodiversity, urban areas, and agriculture: Locating prior-ity ecoregions for conservation. *Conservation Ecology*, *8*(2), 1. doi:10.5751/ES-00593-080201

Rudd, J. W. M., Kelly, C. A., Schindler, D. W., & Turner, M. A. (1988). Disruption of the nitrogen cycle in acidified lakes. *Science*, *240*(4858), 1515–1517. doi:10.1126cience.240.4858.1515 PMID:17793981

Rusk, D. (1993). *Cities without Suburbs*. The Woodrow.

Sala, O. E., Chapin, F. S. I., Armesto, J. J., Berlow, E., Bloomfield, J., Dirzo, R., Huber-Sanwald, E., Huenneke, L. F., Jackson, R. B., Kinzig, A., Leemans, R., Lodge, D. M., Mooney, H. A., Oesterheld, M., Poff, N. L., Sykes, M. T., Walker, B. H., Walker, M., & Wall, D. H. (2000). Global biodiversity scenarios for the year 2100. *Science*, *287*(5459), 1770–1774. doi:10.1126cience.287.5459.1770 PMID:10710299

Seana I., Johnson, L. & Peters, K. (1999). Community gardens and sustainable land use planning: A case-study of the Alex Wilson community garden. *Local Environment*, *4*(1), 33-46. doi:10.1080/13549839908725579

Seto, K. C., De Groot, R., Bringezu, S., Erb, K., Graedel, T. E., Ramankutty, N., & Skole, D. L. (2010). Stocks, flows, and prospects of land. In T. E. Graedel & E. van der Voet (Eds.), *Linkages of sustainability* (pp. 72–96). MIT Press.

Scheffer, M., Carpenter, S. R., Foley, J. A., Folke, C., & Walker, B. H. (2001). Catastrophic shifts in ecosystems. *Nature*, *413*(6856), 591–596. doi:10.1038/35098000 PMID:11595939

Schindler, D. W. (1990). Experimental perturbations of whole lakes as tests of hypotheses concerning ecosystem structure and function. *Oikos*, *57*(1), 25–41. doi:10.2307/3565733

Smit, B., & Wandel, J. (2006). Adaptation, adaptive capacity and vulnerability. *Global Environmental Change*, *16*(3), 282–292. doi:10.1016/j.gloenvcha.2006.03.008

Sukopp, H., Hejny, S., & Kowarik, I. (Eds.). (1990). *Urban ecology: Plants and plant communities in urban environments*. SPB Academic Publishing.

Sukopp, H., Trautmann, W., & Korneck, D. (1979). The soilflora and vegetation of Berlin'swastelands. In I. Laurie (Ed.), *Nature in Cities*. John Wiley.

Tansley, A. G. (1935). The use and abuse of vegetational concepts and terms. *Ecology*, *16*(3), 284–307. doi:10.2307/1930070

Terborgh, J., Lopez, L., Nunez, P., Rao, M., Shahabuddin, G., Orihuela, G., Riveros, M., Ascanio, R., Adler, G. H., Lambert, T. D., & Balbas, L. (2001). Ecological meltdown in predator-free forest fragments. *Science*, *294*(5548), 1923–1926. doi:10.1126cience.1064397 PMID:11729317

Termorshuizen, J. W., & Opdam, P. (2009). Landscape services as a bridge between landscape ecology and sustainable development. *Landscape Ecology*, *24*(8), 1037–1052. doi:10.100710980-008-9314-8

Tidball, G. K., Krasny, E. M., Svendsen, E., Cambell, L., & Helphand, K. (2010). Stewardship, learning and memory in disaster resilience. *Environmental Learning Research*, *16*(5–6), 591–609. doi:10.1080/13504622.2010.505437

Tidball, K. G., & Krasny, M. E. (2009). *From risk to resilience: what role for community greening and civic ecology in cities?* Wageningen Academic Publishers.

van de Berg, L., & van Veenhuizen, R. (2005). Multiple functions of urban Agriculture. *Urban Agriculture Magazine*, 14.

Walker, B. H., Holling, C. S., Carpenter, S. R., & Kinzig, A. P. (2004). Resilience, adaptability and transformability in social–ecological systems. *Ecology and Society, 9*(2), 5. http://www.ecologyandsociety. org/vol9/iss2/art5/

Wu, J., & Wu, T. (2013). Ecological resilience as a foundation for urban design and sustainability. In S. T. A. Pickett, M. L. Cadenasso, & B. McGrath (Eds.), *Resilience in ecology and urban design: Linking theory and practice for sustainable cities* (pp. 211–229). Springer. doi:10.1007/978-94-007-5341-9_10

Yohe, G., & Tol, R. S. J. (2002). Indicators for social and economic coping capacity – moving toward a working definition of adaptive capacity. *Global Environmental Change, 12*(1), 25–40. doi:10.1016/S0959-3780(01)00026-7

Zanoni, P., & Janssens, M. (2009). Sustainable DiverCities. In M. Janssens, D. Pinelli, D. C. Reyman, & S. Wallman (Eds.), *Sustainable Cities. Diversity, Economic Growthand Social Cohesion* (pp. 3–25). Edward Elgar.

Zhang, S. X., & Babovic, V. (2012). A real options approach to the design and architecture of water supply systems using innovative water technologies under uncertainty. *Journal of Hydroinformatics, 488*. www.frontiersinecology.org

Zimov, S. A., Chuprynin, V. I., Oreshko, A. P., Chapin, F. S. III, Reynolds, J. F., & Chapin, M. C. (1995). Steppe–tundra transition: An herbivore-driven biome shift at the end of the Pleistocene. *American Naturalist, 146*(5), 765–794. doi:10.1086/285824

KEY TERMS AND DEFINITIONS

Eco-Urban: Those urban environments that are characterized by having a series of characteristics that define them as sustainable and ecological.

Green Resilience: Green resilience is based on the infrastructure of urban green areas applied to cities and is that they have the capacity to prepare, resist and recover from a crisis.

Land Use: Encompasses the management and modification of the natural environment to convert it into agricultural land: arable fields, grasslands; or human settlements. The term land use is also used to refer to the different land uses in zoning.

Resilience: The word resilience refers to the ability to overcome critical moments and adapt after experiencing some unusual and unexpected situation. It also indicates return to normal.

Urban: Makes reference to that belonging to or relating to the city.

Urban Ecology: Is a discipline whose object of study is the interrelationships between the inhabitants of an urban agglomeration and its multiple interactions with the environment.

Urban Socio-Ecological Systems: Are a complex urban structures that can be analyzed considering the social subsystem and the ecological subsystem.

Chapter 14
The Future of Capability Building in Sustainable Development

Chabi Gupta
Christ University, India

ABSTRACT

Charting the future will entail leaders to look beyond the normal, to look for peculiarities and the unthinkable options in order to sustain in the long run. Leaders should seek to promote their employees' digital, cognitive, social, and emotional capabilities, as well as their adaptability and resilience. The working world will change dramatically over the next 10 years, and people in practically every function and industry will need to learn new skills to keep up. These changes have been expedited by the COVID-19 crisis. The authors look at how capability building will—and should—change in the coming years in this discussion about the next normal.

INTRODUCTION

Our working world will change dramatically over the next ten years, and people in practically every function and industry will need to learn new skills to keep up. These changes have been expedited by the COVID-19 crisis. We look at how capability building will—and should—change in the coming years in this discussion about The Next Normal.

Charting the future will entail leaders to look beyond the normal, to look for peculiarities and the unthinkable options in order to sustain in the long run. Leaders should seek to promote their employees' digital, cognitive, social, and emotional capabilities, as well as their adaptability and resilience (Figure 1).

DOI: 10.4018/978-1-7998-9590-9.ch014

Figure 1. Jobs that require technological, social and emotional skills

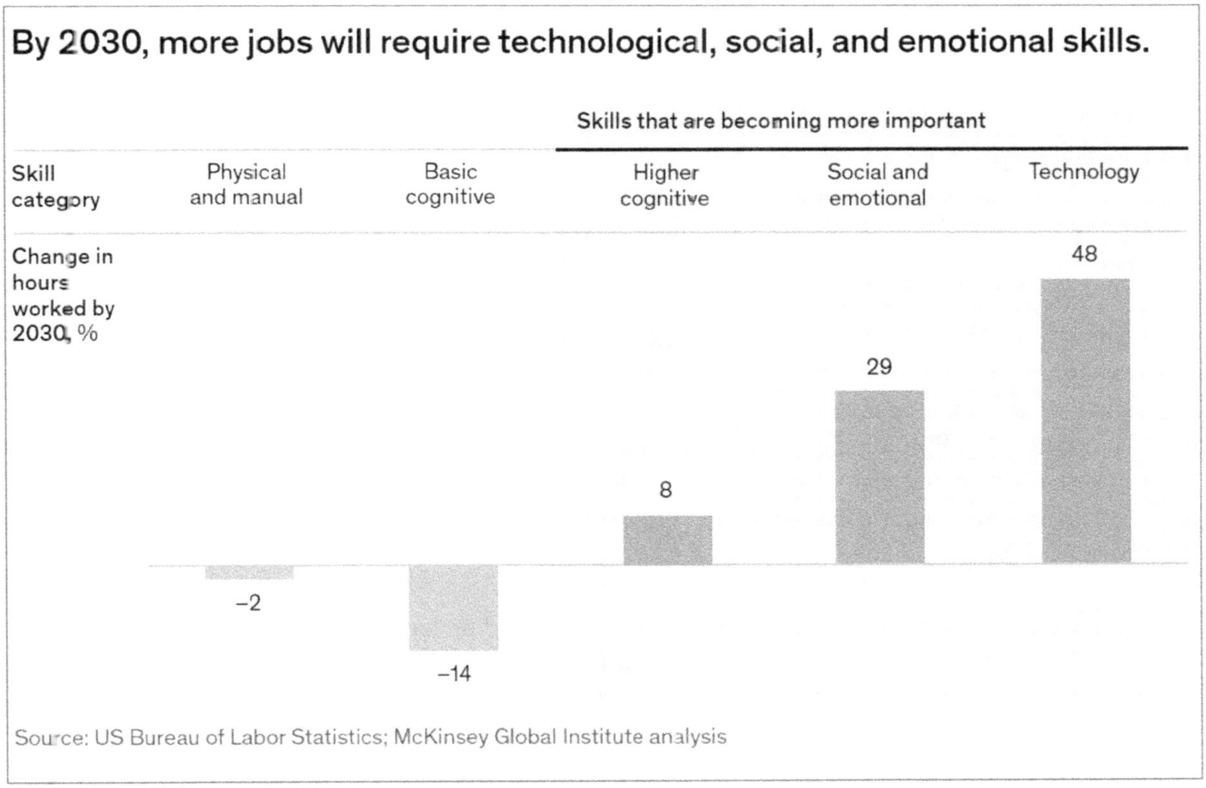

It has been widely acknowledged that putting equal focus on how a company produces money (performance) and how its leaders govern the place is the key to achieving long-term success (health). Companies that do so outperform their competitors by a factor of three. It has also been recently discovered that going one step further and focusing on performance and health at both the organisational and individual levels can help leaders capture even more value.

Even for the most seasoned leader, coordinating performance and health across levels is a difficult task. To do this properly, the new way of working must be embedded at all levels of the business. This can be accomplished by refocusing capability-building programmes to assist employees in developing knowledge, skills, and habits.

CAPABILITY BUILDING OR CAPABILITY BUILDING

The ability of an individual or organisation to effectively absorb change is referred to as "capability building" in the context of transformation. The concept of "changing assimilation points" proposed by Daryl Conner is a good way to think about capability. Each person has a limited number of "assimilation points," for example, 500 points. A new boss, for example, might cost 100 assimilation points, whereas a shift to a new office might cost 200 points, and so on. Conner employs a point analogy to demonstrate the underlying truth that people can only digest a certain amount of change before experiencing unpleasant overload symptoms. Burnout, sadness, and anxiety are just a few examples.

The idea is to keep change moving at a pace that corresponds to the individual's rate of assimilation. Individuals can renew and improve their ability to integrate change by developing resilience.

Understanding capability building at the organisational level is critical to an organization's ability to implement change effectively. Too often, the rate and scope of change outpaces the organization's ability to absorb it, like to throwing a gallon of water on a sponge that's already soaked. In such circumstances, identifying the capability issue and devising measures to address it is critical. This could involve the following:

1. Allowing employees more time to complete a task in order to facilitate assimilation.
2. Resourcing is bringing in more resources to relieve employees of their day-to-day responsibilities, allowing them to better absorb change.
3. Understanding: Providing psychological safety to employees by indicating that it is understood that change is tough and that tasks may take longer or have a greater error rate than usual.
4. Employees may require encouragement to manage their energy rather than just their time during periods of intense change.

Capability is thus a finite resource that can be replenished under certain conditions.

Capability building, on the other hand, refers to the skills and knowledge required for a specific undertaking. Although a company may have the ability to adapt, it may be lacking in certain crucial qualities. This was reported through empirical studies carried out by Worley, C. G., Feyerherm, A. E., & Knudsen, D. (2010)

Managers' ability to effectively lead change is a common example of a capability gap. Managers are frequently promoted to their roles as a result of technical aptitude and seniority, but they may not have been schooled in the craft of management, especially change leadership, as Henry Mintzberg has widely documented. This can create a lose-lose-lose situation: the manager is under-equipped, and her employees are under-trained. Gaps in capability can be filled by providing proper training and mentoring, especially in the specialist field of change leadership. This procedure should start with basic training, which can subsequently be supplemented with coaching.

The notions of change capability and capability building interact in an intriguing way. In many circumstances, boosting a team's knowledge and skills can actually assist in expanding capability. This is essentially the concept of working smarter, not harder, which is a good path to take as firms increasingly discover that dealing with change is the new normal. Two things become abundantly clear:

- In the future, teamwork will be more important than rivalry.
- The future will be as much about capabilities as it will be about products.

COMPETENCE AND CAPABILITY

While competency mapping is essential, capability takes things a step further. When we build capability in our people, we enable them to do their jobs more successfully today while also preparing them for future problems.

Competence describes a person's current state and includes the knowledge and abilities required to do a job. Capability, on the other hand, is about integrating knowledge and skills, as well as adapting and flexing to meet future demands. Shifting from a competency-based to a capability-based approach necessitates a mental shift. To successfully create, innovate, lead, and manage change as a future strategic leader, the organsations's talent development programmes must make people more learning agile and more devoted to continual learning & development. Until the late 1990s or early 2000s, most employees worked for only one or two companies during their careers. In reality, most European economies, as well as the industrial economies of the United States, were built on this talent paradigm, which included standard retirement and pension plans. The corporate landscape was significantly different at the time, with the top 20 firms employing about 10% of the workforce.

Everything has changed. Millennial workers are aspirational, and they are always on the search for better job opportunities. They look for work online, where there is a wealth of possibilities, and they interview for new jobs on a frequent basis throughout their careers. These millennials have a habit of changing jobs frequently. Millennials are uneasy and pessimistic about their employment, lives, and the world around them, according to Deloitte's Global Millennial Survey. They are pessimistic about the economy, to say nothing of their current jobs.

Because millennials will make up 75 percent of the workforce by 2025, it's clear that the organisation will need to adjust their employee training and development programmes to their likes and preferences.

And it's already taking place. Most large corporations today treat employee onboarding as a multi-month journey filled with various types of tangible milestones and learning activities.

Employee journeys have their own set of twists and turns, detours, and even a few bumps, but they are eventually full of memorable experiences. A company's employee experience is defined by these moments taken together. Employees now require various sorts of support and services at all times of the day – for example, outbound sales professionals who travel regularly want travel services, while those working remotely require modern computers, phones, and tablets, as well as VPN and file storage systems. Not only that, but in regulatory environments, personnel are required to clock in every day, take necessary courses, maintain certifications, and stay up to date on process changes on a regular basis. Furthermore, when a company combines, undergoes a big upgrade, or, for that matter, experiences a downturn, it takes a great deal of effort to incorporate these changes into the bodies and minds of employees.

All of these factors are important to employees. If we look at how employees assess their employers on sites like Glassdoor, Indeed, and Kununu, we can see that culture, management, and the work environment are frequently mentioned as the most significant characteristics at work.

DEVELOPING A CONTINUOUS CAPABILITY BUILDING MODEL

The state of employee engagement is changing. The amount of disruption caused by digital technology has been enormous and unparalleled in the last five years. As we have stated, the social and emotional significance of loyalty and longevity is evolving.

It's time to rethink and renew the employee experience strategy in this light. Several parties are involved in providing a positive employment experience:

- The hiring manager
- The supervisor
- The CEO of a company
- Processes, rules, and technology's intangible stakeholders

Organizations must formalise their approaches to maintaining and improving capabilities in order to capitalise on the skill-development work they are already doing. Despite this, few executives report that their companies perform well in this area. Almost half say that their organisations encourage staff to develop their skills. However as per the study conducted by Kumar, G., Subramanian, N., & Arputham, R. M. (2018). less than one in five people have a common knowledge of their human and business functions — a practise that increases the importance of skills development and also aligns learning goals with business needs. Those who report co-ownership most likely say it has been very efficient in all the support capacities we have asked for.

Companies which develop skills most effectively link these skills to achievement and to achieve their objectives (Figure 2).

Figure 2. The most effective capability builders take consistent action than others to maintain and improve the capabilities

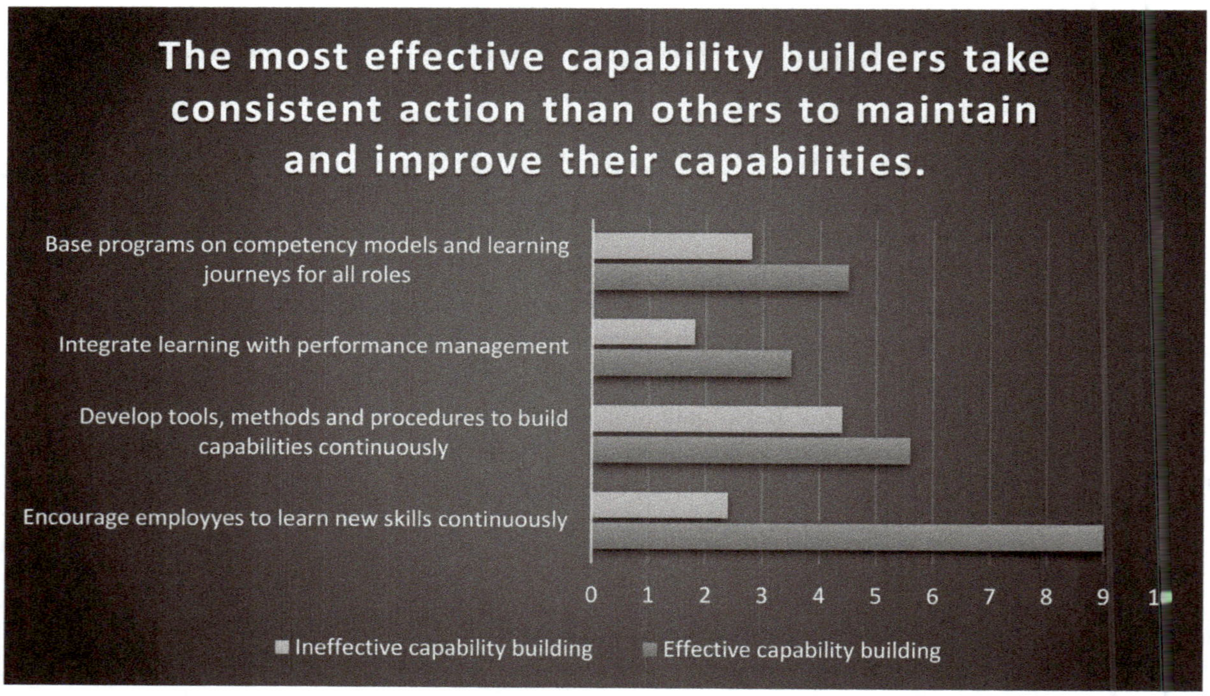

BUILDING ORGANISATIONAL CAPABILITIES

"Value does not come from the ability to manage and use such abilities by organisations. This might include rethinking the nature of the business model, business processes, skills and skills, behaviours, recompense systems, organisational structure, physical infrastructure, etc."

Few organisations can avoid the challenge of becoming central to value in the current economic climate. Although this statement may seem a well-used cliché of management, the fact is that many organisations continue to change the isolation of the business value they expect. for example the advantages.

The ability to deliver value through change investment has always been critical to organisations' success. In view of cost reduction, restrictions on investment funding, economic impacts, and increased regulation supervision, this becomes more and more important. The reality is that many organisations reduce their budgets for education and spend less discreetly on training and development.

Upstill-Goddard, J., Glass, J., Dainty, A., & Nicholson, I. (2016) in their research concluded that sufficient experience has demonstrated that everyone can implement a process to achieve benefits. This, of course, alone will not achieve success as many other factors – many of them behavioural – are needed for success. This report aims at challenging managers to manage and sustain their organisational capability to achieve benefits. It considers what can be done to better achieve the benefits and, above all, where to begin. It builds on the first report of the series, "winning hearts and minds" and examines practical actions that allow senior managers throughout the organisation to create a value-focused culture. It will not happen by itself to create sustained organisational capabilities to realise advantages. It requires a clear focus on time with strong leadership commitment (Figure 3).

Figure 3. Building organisational capabilities

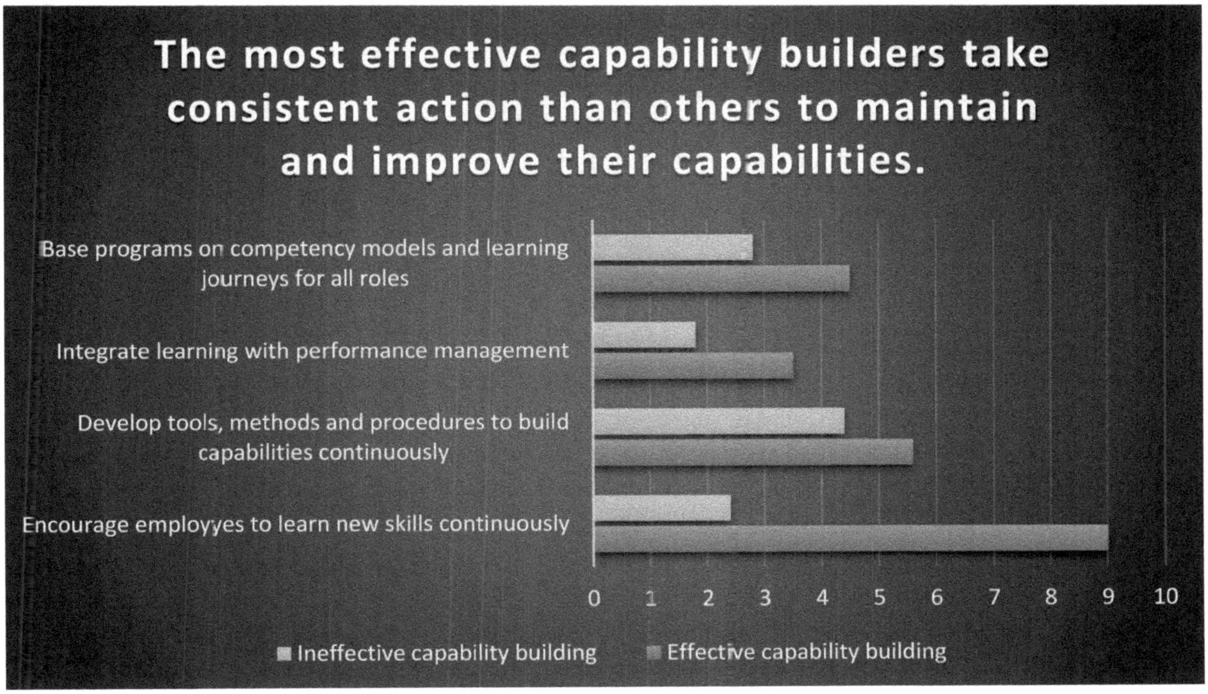

Capability to organise allows strategy. As a framework, people, systems, institutions, technology and culture can take different forms by drawing and aligning them. Capability building promotes innovation, transformation and change. However, the relevant question is how does the business (and human resources) identify, measure, and improve organisational capabilities? According to Michael Ehret, Vice President, Human Resources, Supply Chain at Johnson & Johnson, organisational competence is defined generally as "whatever an organisation does that generates real business results." And, in order to enable business strategy, Amui, L. B. L., Jabbour, C. J. C., de Sousa Jabbour, A. B. L., & Kannan, D. (2017) in their study concluded that it is necessary to concentrate on the core capabilities that will drive value difference and then dedicate the time and resources required to build and grow those capabilities.

IDENTIFICATION, ASSESSMENT, AND ADVANCEMENT OF CAPABILITIES

The Leader's Role in Capability Development

The process of determining skills is not something that can be done alone. The task of the leader, on the other hand, is to make them explicit.

Most leaders, together with their senior teams, devote a great deal of time and effort to developing strategy, communication, and the organization's mission and vision. Some leaders may be particularly skilled at expressing strategic intent to employees at all levels of the organisation.

Few leaders use capabilities to ensure that their strategies are carried out successfully. Companies that don't define strategy as capabilities frequently find themselves questioning, "Why isn't the strategy working?" Companies like Pzifer, American Express, and Boeing have realised that in debates about execution, the capability model has replaced organisational charts. According to a study carried out by Poapongsakorn, N., & Tonguthai, P. (2003), interviews, secondary research, and field immersion can all be used to assess capabilities.

While a list of capabilities is useful, capability models provide a more accurate picture of strategic success. Building out the core business and enabling models such as IT and HR can help leaders dramatically increase the organization's sustainability and agility.

Organizations rarely distinguish between business-critical capabilities and capabilities that transform or differentiate.

Capabilities contribute in diverse ways to achieving and executing strategy, and they should be fed and sourced accordingly. The ability to recognise and appreciate this distinction can help a company stand apart.

Munajat, Q., & Kurnia, S. (2015) through their empirical research concluded that some capabilities have a direct impact on the organization's financials and contribute directly to the customer value proposition. It's vital to have a shared understanding of why a company's customers value it. The value and benefits of capability-based planning must be communicated by leaders. The skills that must be explicitly stated will be highlighted during the business modelling phase. Leaders must "call out" and express the capabilities that the organisation "must have" in order to survive and prosper after they have been recognised. This aids in the dispersal of organisational politics and the funding of "the squeaky wheel."

All capabilities are not created equal. They have relative importance (Figure 4).

Figure 4. Capabilities

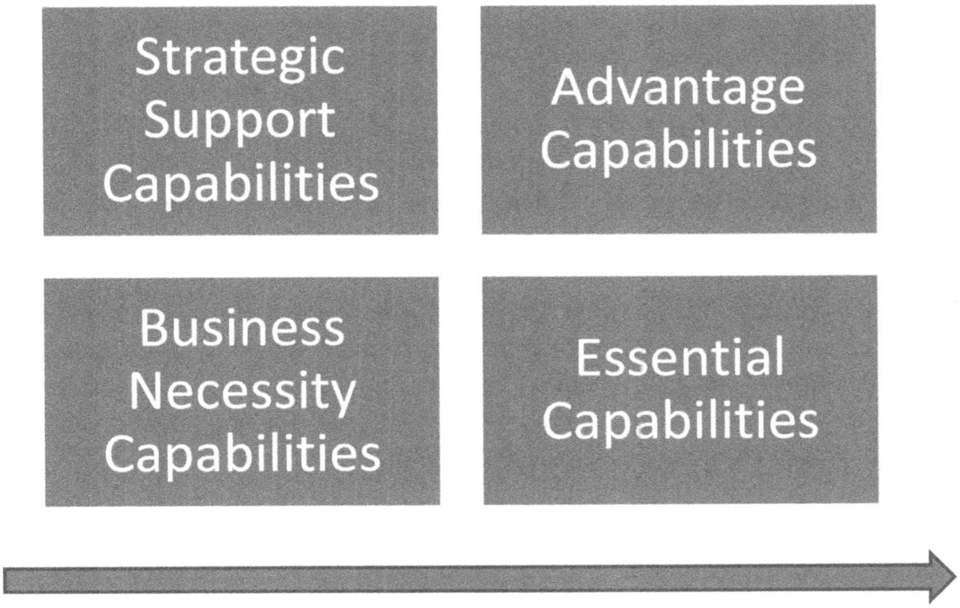

The next stage for a leader and his or her team is to determine how well the organisation is performing these capabilities and where there are gaps in capability.

As per the research reported by Reuter, C., Foerstl, K. A. I., Hartmann, E. V. I., & Blome, C. (2010) "Given our strategy, what work needs to be completed at world-class levels, and what work can be conducted at industry equivalents?" is the question to pose.

Organizations endure dysfunction when leaders fail to appraise the strategic importance of a capability, such as resource conflict, stopped execution, and confused project agendas.

Having determined if the organisation needs to invest in a capability, the next step for a leader is to evaluate the level of maturity the capability needs to perform and when the capability needs to be realised. Some capabilities need immediate improvement while others can be matured over many years in fact, there may be value in waiting.

In order to close the most critical gaps, a leader must make these actions explicit, convey the process to ensure alignment, and seek engagement from the rest of the organisation.

Experienced leaders must apply their knowledge and encourage a diverse group of stakeholders to participate in the root cause study of the capability gap. Involving the organisation in the analysis is a critical step in determining whether to bridge the gap by brokering, borrowing, constructing, or purchasing the capability.

BUILDING CAPABILITIES FOR SUSTAINABLE DEVELOPMENT

Development is more about capability building than it is about optimizing given resources (Lee and Mathews 2010). Because of its numerous long-term effects, capability building is valued and necessary. As an example, Capability-building strategies aim to reduce reliance on outside specialists as sources of information, resources, and solutions to community problems. Capability building encourages local people to take action on local issues by preventing a dependency connection with outsiders from growing. Capability building develops a sense of ownership and empowerment among community partners, allowing them to take more control over their own development. Increased confidence, skills, knowledge, and resources as a result of capability building activities on one project may help a community partner imagine and implement additional projects. Capability development efforts are more attentive to the nuances of local culture and context, resulting in more realistic and acceptable community solutions than approaches that do not focus on capability building. Growth, learning, and change are reciprocal in capability building approaches to community work; that is, both the organisation and the community should be different at the end of the collaborative community work (Figure 5).

Figure 5. Capability development process

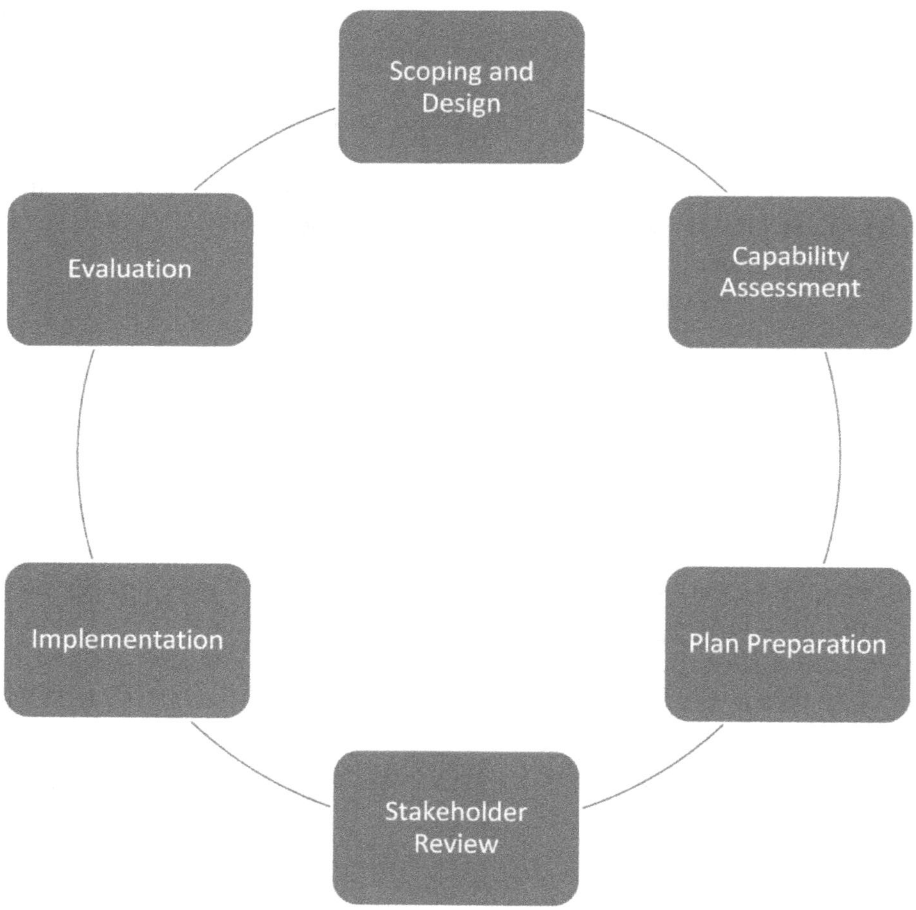

The Capability development process involves various stages. The success of any capability development program depends on the culture, context, and circumstances of the organization, and individuals involved, so the process should be adjusted to the context as required.

REFERENCES

Amui, L. B. L., Jabbour, C. J. C., de Sousa Jabbour, A. B. L., & Kannan, D. (2017). Sustainability as a dynamic organizational capability: A systematic review and a future agenda toward a sustainable transition. *Journal of Cleaner Production*, *142*, 308–322. doi:10.1016/j.jclepro.2016.07.103

Kumar, G., Subramanian, N., & Arputham, R. M. (2018). Missing link between sustainability collaborative strategy and supply chain performance: Role of dynamic capability. *International Journal of Production Economics*, *203*, 96–109. doi:10.1016/j.ijpe.2018.05.031

Munajat, Q., & Kurnia, S. (2015). Towards Sustainability Framework Development: Identifying Organisational Capability for Sustainability Practices. In PACIS (p. 106). Academic Press.

Poapongsakorn, N., & Tonguthai, P. (2003). Technological capability building and the sustainability of export success in Thailand's textile and electronics industries. In *Technological Capabilities and Export Success in Asia* (pp. 173–226). Routledge.

Reuter, C., Foerstl, K. A. I., Hartmann, E. V. I., & Blome, C. (2010). Sustainable global supplier management: The role of dynamic capabilities in achieving competitive advantage. *The Journal of Supply Chain Management*, *46*(2), 45–63. doi:10.1111/j.1745-493X.2010.03189.x

Upstill-Goddard, J., Glass, J., Dainty, A., & Nicholson, I. (2016). Implementing sustainability in small and medium-sized construction firms. *Engineering, Construction, and Architectural Management*, *23*(4), 407–427. doi:10.1108/ECAM-01-2015-0015

Worley, C. G., Feyerherm, A. E., & Knudsen, D. (2010). Building a collaboration capability for sustainability: How Gap Inc. is creating and leveraging a strategic asset. *Organizational Dynamics*, *39*(4), 325–334. doi:10.1016/j.orgdyn.2010.07.004

ADDITIONAL READING

FAO. (n.d.). *How to design capacity development interventions and ensure their sustainability*. https://www.fao.org/capacity-development/resources/practical-tools/design-capacity-development/zh/

James, V. U. (2018). *Capacity Building for Sustainable Development*. CABI. https://www.cabi.org/bookshop/book/9781780646169/

Chapter 15
Towards a Sustainable Future of Marketing Management Praxis in Rural Destination Spaces

Samuel Adeyinka-Ojo
Curtin University, Malaysia

ABSTRACT

The aim of this study is to explore and apply sustainable destination branding strategies and the roles of the relationship-building approach in understanding the future of marketing management praxis in rural tourism destinations. A review of the literature on tourism marketing, destination management, rural tourism, green marketing, sustainable tourism management, brand and destination branding shows that the application of sustainable destination branding using the relationship-based approach underpinned by relationship-based theories is lacking in the literature sources, especially in rural tourism destination marketing. Therefore, an understanding of sustainable destination branding and a relationship-based approach becomes indispensable for the sustainable future of marketing management in rural tourism destinations to achieve the goals of attracting quality tourist arrivals and becoming the destination of choice. Data analysis is based on 46 in-depth interviews and participant observations conducted over a period of four years in Bario, Sarawak, Malaysia.

INTRODUCTION

The application and adaptation of traditional marketing strategy in tourism destinations have become well known (Baker & Cameron, 2008). There have been increased international competitiveness, globalization and transaction costs across the globe due to over 2 million tourism destinations (Balakrishnan, 2008) in over 250 countries (Morgan, Hastings & Pritchard, 2012). As a result, these destinations that offer tourist opportunity to visit different place of choice has led tourism marketers and practitioners in recent times to differentiate tourism destinations using the branding strategies. A review of the extant literature indicates there are studies on green marketing, tourism destination branding and destination marketing. However, it appears that empirical research on sustainable destination branding (SDB) and

DOI: 10.4018/978-1-7998-9590-9.ch015

relationship building approach (RBA) underpinned by relationship-based theories are lacking in the future of marketing management especially in rural tourism destinations.

These views are consistent with Chen and Phou (2013) that relationship-based theories and relationship building to sustainable destination branding, especially in tourism destinations is emerging and is till at the formation stage. Similarly, it has been observed that there is still a lack of theoretical and empirical studies featuring relationship building process in developing a destination brand (Choi & Cai, 2012). In this regard, the purpose of this study is reduce the existing gap in the literature by exploring the future of marketing management in rural tourism destinations using sustainable destination branding strategies and relationship building praxis. In particular, the following questions guided this study: (1) What are the sustainable destination branding strategies specific to rural tourism destinations? and (2) What are the roles of relationship-based approach in the future of marketing management praxis of rural tourism destinations?

LITERATURE REVIEW

There are several studies over the years on tourism marketing management, sustainable tourism and destination branding in attracting tourist, increase the tourist arrivals and receipts. In order to highlight the existing gaps, this section dwells on the following extant different literature work on tourism over the years.

Tourism Destination Sustainability and Sustainable Destination Branding

It is commonly viewed that any description on 'sustainability' or 'sustainable practice' should take into account the triple-bottom line concepts of social, economic and environmental features as contained in the Brundtland Report of 1987 (Swarbrooke, 2006). The United Nations World Tourism Organisations [UNWTO] (2005, p.12) defined sustainable tourism as "tourism that takes full account of its current and future, social, economic and environmental impacts, addressing the needs of visitors, the industry, the environment and the host communities". Tourism destination sustainability has been described as the ability of a tourism destination to maintain and monitor the quality of its cultural, social, physical and natural endowment while competing with similar tourism destinations (Kayat, 2011). Similar studies on destination sustainability include preservation of tourism heritage (Azlan & Bagul, 2010); reuse and recycle of tourism resources (Eber, 1992); protect community environment (Choi & Sirakaya, 2005); and reduction in global tourism-related carbon dioxide emission particularly from aircraft (Cooper, 2012). There are several definitions on destination branding. In this study, the definition of destination branding as defined by Blain, Levy and Ritchie (2005) was adopted as:

Destination branding is the marketing activities that: (a) support the creation of a name, symbol, logo, word mark or other graphic that both identifies and differentiates a destination; (b) that consistently conveys the expectations of a memorable travel experience that is uniquely associated with the destination; (c) that serves to consolidate and reinforce the emotional connection between the tourist and the destination; and (d) reduces consumers search costs and perceived risk. (p. 337).

This definition appears to be holistic as it takes into consideration the basic elements of tourism destination and benefits of destination branding. Academic research on sustainable destination branding is very limited (Inch, 2011; Stole, 2011). Extant literature on the few related sustainable destination branding shows that there is generally a diversified definition of sustainable destination branding that has been adopted by many researchers. For example, Woodland and Acott (2007) have examined how local tourism branding in protected places of South Downs in England can be used in promoting destination sustainability of the New Park. Similarly, Maheshwari, Vandewalle and Bamber (2011) focused on the application of sustainable development in promoting place branding and used the city of Liverpool as a case study. Stole (2011)'s study is on sustainable green destination branding with the case studies of five major cities of Cape town, Copenhagen, Melbourne, Portland and Vancouver. It should be noted that these studies were conducted in places other than rural tourism destinations.

Stole (2011, p.33) described sustainable destination branding as different marketing activities that involved differentiating a tourism destination from similar or competing destinations that takes into consideration the social, economic and environmental responsibility and contribute to sustainable development of the tourism destinations. This definition was adopted in this study because it takes into consideration the characteristics of the sustainable system (i.e. the triple-bottom line) (Swarbrooke, 2006). This definition also shows that marketing and sustainable destination branding are interrelated because they are both activities-driven. Factors influencing sustainable destination branding include credibility (Stole, 2011; Insch, 2011; Ottman, 2011); transparent destination brand behaviour (Stole, 2011; Grant, 2008); and stakeholders' commitment (Stole, 2011). Sustainable destination branding must accommodate multiple stakeholder interests and all stakeholders must share a fundamental intrinsic value of the natural environment (Walker & Hanson, 1998). In other words, for future marketing management of rural tourism, sustainable destination branding requires stakeholders to take a shared responsibility of the destination.

Relationship-Based Building Approach

Relationship building approach is rooted in relationship-based theories such as stakeholder theory and social (relational exchange theory (Fyall, Garod & Wang, 2012). The use of relationship-based approach to study how a destination brand is developed is crucial to the sustainable tourism destination because destination branding requires collaboration with the stakeholders due to the complex process involved (Khanna, 2011; Insch, 2011; Cai, 2002). In relationship building, the roles of each of the tourism destination stakeholders are considered. The inclusion of the role of stakeholders argues for the rationale to adopt relationship building to develop sustainable tourism destination brand. This view is consistent with Szondi (2010) that the relationship-based approach to destination branding advocates that internal and external stakeholders should have control of the individual destination brand and future destination marketing management.

Relationship building is a unique approach that can be used in the formulation of future marketing management engagement in rural tourism destination because RBA is focused on the involvement of stakeholders and non-stakeholders. The concept of relationship-based approach is the perception of mutual benefit to all the parties that are involved in a relationship building process (Choi & Cai, 2012), and to plan for the future marketing activities of tourism destinations. These views are shared by Fyall, Callod and Edwards (2003) that those involved in relationship based concept will ensure that the relationship is maintained due to the expected benefits such as destination marketing advantage, building and managing the relationship. An understanding of future marketing management in rural tourism destinations through the relationship-based approach is indispensable. This is because the RBA emphasizes the need to take into cognizance the tourism destination peculiar characteristics in terms of people, culture, natural environment, location, values, tourism assets, social and economic sustainability. These opinions are consistent with Sheth and Sisodia (2005) that consumers (tourists) are advocating a marketing approach that is more relevant to the society which include tourism destination.

Stakeholder Theory and Stakeholders in Rural Destination Space

The relationship-based approach basically recognises the role of the multiple stakeholders in rural tourism destinations. Previous studies have applied the stakeholder theory in understanding the destination branding process and its relationship with the marketing of tourism destination (Marzano, 2007; Marzano & Scott, 2005). Richard Edward Freeman is widely acknowledged to have developed the stakeholder theory and provide two definitions of a stakeholder. A stakeholder is defined as "any group or individual who can affect or is affected by the achievement of an organisation's objectives" (Freeman, 1984, p. 46); and those groups who are vital to the survival of the organization (Freeman, Wicks and Parmar, 2004). There are other definitions of stakeholder conceptualized by researchers; however, Freeman's (1984) definition of stakeholder is adopted in this study because it is widely used in tourism studies (Musa, Noor, & Mohamad, 2013; Fyall et al., 2012, p.13; Kayat, 2011, p. 119; Marzano, 2007; Yuksel, Bramwell, & Yuksel, 1999). Moreover, Freeman (1984) developed stakeholder map which has been adapted to tourism destination marketing management, planning and branding (Sautter & Leisen, 1999) as presented in Figure 1. Jamal and Getz (1995) pointed out that there is no single entity that is capable of handling and developing destination branding process, and by extension the marketing of tourism destinations.

Figure 1. Rural destination space stakeholder map. adapted from Freeman (1984, p.55); Sautter and Leisen (1999, p.315); Quinlan (2008, p. 63)

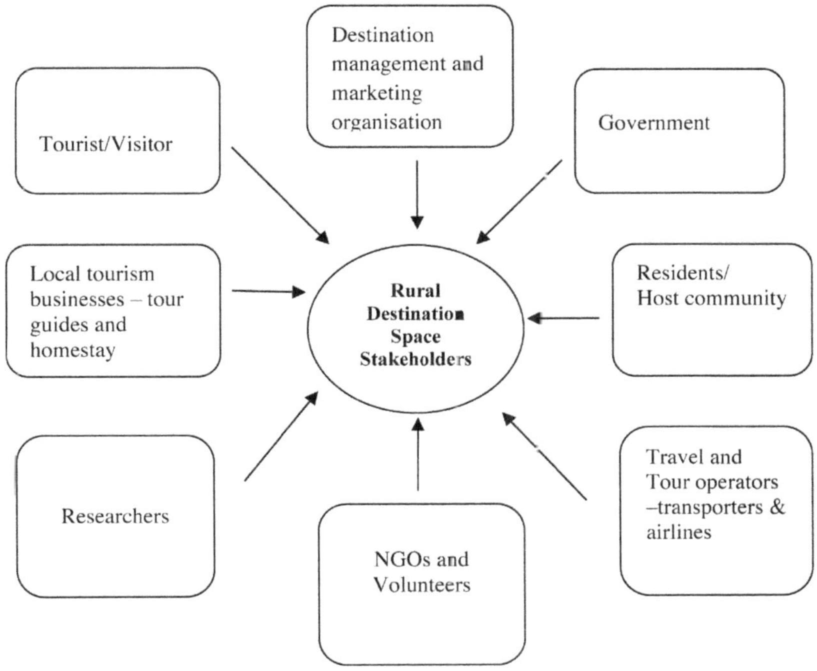

The roles of these eight groups of stakeholders is depicted in Figure 1 have not been fully explored in the future marketing management practices of rural tourism destinations. Most of the studies on the marketing of tourism destinations were focused on destination management and marketing organisations [DMMOs] (Adeyinka-Ojo et al. 2014; Pike & Page 2014, Fyall, Garrod & Wang, 2012; Wang 2011; UNWTO, 2007; Ritchie & Ritchie, 1998; Pearce, 1992). Besides that, Wang (2008) developed nine roles of DMOs and these roles were extended to 10 with the inclusion of tourism product developer by Adeyinka-Ojo et al. (2014, p. 155). Wang (2008) also developed a framework for the roles of destination marketing organisation which include advocate, organizer, network management organisation, catalyst, tourism product developer convener and facilitator, community brand builder, funding agent, information provider, partner and team builder. This framework did not take into cognizance the future marketing management of tourism especially in rural destinations.

Future of Marketing Management Praxis in Rural Tourism Destination

Globally, the marketing of tourism destination is increasingly becoming competitive (UNWTO, 2013; Tasci, 2011; Balakrishnan, 2008). According to Wang (2011), marketing of tourism destination is viewed as a complex issue, because of the competitions among the destination management and marketing organisations (DMMOs) to increase their individual market share by evolving unique destination marketing strategies (Hosany, Ekinci & Uysal, 2007; Adeyinka-Ojo, Khoo-Lattimore & Nair, 2014). Tourism is a service sector that applies services marketing to promote different tourism products (Weaver & Lawton, 2010). Studies on the future of marketing management in tourism destinations are emerging but challenging (Morrison, 2013). In a recent study conducted by the destination marketing association international (DMAI) and Karl Albrecht international (KAI) on the future of destination marketing by the destination marketing organisations (DMOs), there are three issues identified in the study. These strategic themes are related to DMOs functions in understanding and marketing tourism destinations which include the following: (a) relevance; (b) value proposition; and (c) visibility (Morrison, 2013).

On relevance, it was found that the space is becoming increasingly crowded and competitive due to new entrants and these have eroded the unique and traditional position of destination marketing functions of DMOs. In terms of value proposition, the core value proposition of the DMOs has been 'nibbling away' by the new players in the tourism destination marketing. On top of that is the visibility theme on DMOs in which the social media and internet sources on destination information marketing offered a superior job compared with the traditional DMOs functions (Morrison, 2013, p. 556-557). The DMAI Futures Study also identified eight 'super-trends' affecting the future of marketing management in tourism destinations. These are customer, competitor, economic, technological, social, political (funding), legal and geophysical (Morrison, 2013). The going green (geophysical) is much concerned about increasing emphasis on sustainable tourism development and green praxis (or sustainable destination branding) and in the current study the focus is on rural tourism destination.

Tourism destination marketing is fundamentally different from the marketing of goods due to the main characteristics that distinguish tourism services marketing from goods which are (a) intangibility; (b) inseparability; (c) variability; and (d) perishability (Bowen, Makens & Kotler, 2005; Weaver & Lawton, 2010, p. 183). In view of the unique attributes of marketing the tourism destination and challenges, it becomes imperative for the future marketing management in rural tourism destinations to adopt a proactive and innovative approach that will requires the engagement of sustainable destination branding and relationship-based approach. This is an emerging gap in the future marketing management of tourism especially in rural destinations and this study is positioned to contribute to the existing literature on tourism destination marketing.

METHODOLOGY

This study has adopted qualitative research methodology because it is the most appropriate in answering the research questions (Guba & Lincoln, 1994), and the researchers are interested in multiple realities, rather than one particular answer. The aim is to elicit rich, detailed data that can be used in the data analysis (Lofland & Lofland, 1984). This study also involved in-depth interviews and participant observation as the method of data collection which covered a period of three years from 2012 to 2014, and a follow up in February 2020 by visiting the study context – Bario, a rural tourism destination in Sarawak in east Malaysia. It is situated between 3,200 and 6,000 feet or at an altitude of about 1,100m above sea-level (Jiwan, Paul, Teo & Jiwan 2006) with a population of about 1,200 people (Malaysian Government 2011). The village is accessible via an 18 seater Otter aircraft twice a day depending on the weather condition. Alternatively, it takes 12 to 14 hours in a four-wheel drive on a logging road in and out of Bario to the major towns and cities (Jiwan et al. 2006) as quality of roads is poor. Bario is predominantly rice farming community without amenities such as good roads, water, electricity, hotels and modern houses.

The researchers' conducted in-depth interviews with 40 respondents in Bario until the point of data saturation were reached when the inclusion of additional data yields no new dimensions to the common ideas (Jennings, 2010; Strauss & Corbin, 2008). Besides that, we conducted a total of 12 days of participant observation in Bario which generated 15 pages of field notes. A semi-structured interview protocol was developed that focuses on the sustainable destination branding strategies, the roles of relationship-based building among the multiple stakeholders, destination stakeholders and their roles in rural tourism marketing management, and suggestion for the future of marketing practices in rural tourism especially at the study context. The in-depth interview session lasted an average of 50 minutes and digitally recorded (Rasmussen, Erik & Beckmann, 2006). Transcription was undertaken immediately after the conclusion of the interview (Gubrium and Holstein, 2001), so that the data collected from the participants would still be fresh in the researcher's mind (Prayag & Ryan, 2011). We adopted thematic analysis to analyse the in-depth interviews and content analysis to field notes from the participant observation.

Thematic content analysis was deemed fit because it is a qualitative analytic method that involves identifying themes by systematically reading the data very carefully and then re-reading the data several times (Fereday & Muir-Cochrane, 2006).This study also adopted the six stages of thematic analysis as recommended by Braun and Clarke (2006) which allows the researcher familiarising with the data, developing the initial codes or open codes, searching for the relevant themes, reviewing themes that have emerged, defining, labelling or naming the codes, and finally producing a report of the findings. This analytic method specifically identified codes and themes that provide answer to our four research questions. This study also followed the recommendation of Tilstone (1998) that the participant observation should address the context and content of the phenomenon being studied. In this case the context for observation refers to the date, time of the day, length of observation, and events which the researcher observed. On the other hand, the content of observation in this study refers to the process that led to the stakeholders' participation and involvement in activities that lead to marketing, sustainable branding and relationship building. Field notes from the participant observation were used as supplementary data and content analysed for the themes developed from the in-depth interviews.

FINDINGS AND DISCUSSION

This study presents an exploration of the future of marketing management through the sustainable destination branding strategies (SDBSs) and relationship-based approach (RBA) among the multiple stakeholders in rural tourism destination. This section presents the findings from the in-depth interviews conducted with the 46 participants presented in Table 1.

Table 1. Summary of participants interviewed

Year/ Respondents	2012	2013	2014	2020	Total
International tourists	2	3	8		13
Researcher	-	-	1		1
Local tourists	2	1	4		7
Local residents and homestay operators	4	3	4	6	17
Airline pilot	1	-	1		2
Ministry of tourism	-	-	1		1
Volunteers/NGOs	1	-	2		3
Destination marketing expert	-	-	1		1
Department of immigration	-	-	1		1
Total	**10**	**7**	**23**	**6**	**46**

Source: Developed for this study

The 46 respondents interviewed consist of 14 international tourists from Canada, Spain, France, Netherlands, Australia, United States of America, Japan, United Kingdom, Poland, New Zealand, and Germany. Similarly, 7 local tourists from Malaysia and 17 local residents and homestay operators, and the remaining 8 respondents were interviewed in Bario, Miri and Kuching. Overall, these participants came from 12 different countries. In addition, these respondents age ranged between 20 and 70 years old. Majority of the tourists are visiting Bario for the first time. Findings are presented in the following four different perspectives.

Sustainable Destination Branding Strategies for Rural Tourism Marketing Management

As mentioned in the previous section that the academic interest on sustainable destination branding is emerging. SDBSs involves different components which include the strategic stages, challenges, critical success factors (CSFs) and sustainable destination brand management. Findings based on the information elicited from the respondents in this study in relation to the SDBSs in rural tourism are presented in the following statements. When asked about the SDBSs in the future marketing management praxis of rural destination, a 28-year old local tourist from Kuching Malaysia echoed:

First is to know the tourism assets/attractions in Bario. There is also the need to identify which one appeals to the visitors and why it attracts them. The involvement of other stakeholders is very crucial for sustainable destination branding… and communicated the expected brand benefits in terms of rural destination marketing.

Of interest is the view that stakeholders should be involved and sustainable brand benefits should be communicated to them. This is different from tangible goods branding where the company does not need to inform its customers why its product is branded. A key informant from the department of immigration commented:

…First is to encourage the local people and other stakeholders to be involved and this will require strong leadership. Also there is a need to do marketing research …there should be brand planning to ascertain the quantity of resources which would be involved. The brand needs to be launched so that stakeholders can support the scheme.

Findings also indicate the need for a leadership that would drive the sustainable destination brand building process. Sustainable branding also requires large amount of resources such as human, financial and non-financial resources. The unique destination attractions and infrastructures development are vital resources in sustainable destination branding strategies for rural tourism marketing. A 65-year old tourist from New Zealand observed:

There should be stakeholder involvement, brand planning, brand benefits communication, launching and do a proper financial requirement for the branding programmes and get relevant government agencies' support. There is a need to develop destination logos and slogans for the community as a tourist destination to distinguish the place from competitors and for recall... purposes.

Notably, the support of the government through its several ministries and departments are important for the planning, communication of brands and implementation stage. This is because adequate funding is required to develop a sustainable destination branding strategies. In addition, a 54-year old tourist from the United States said:

Bario people… should work with the local authority and the state to promote sustainable destination branding strategies… and ensure that the destination image of Bario and its attractions are well communicated…the community has to build a kind of relationship that will draw support from the government… to preserve the culture and the environment and attractions.

Beside this, a researcher from the University of London and also a respondent in this study suggested:

There should be 'community protocol' – which must be put in place. Community protocol is very important because it will highlight the facilities available and services provided in Bario, the code of conduct and behaviours expected from the tourist. Similarly it will also state the tourist should expect if they visit Bario. This I think is crucial for a sustainable destination branding and future destination marketing...

Analyses of these findings include the following sustainable destination branding strategies specific to rural tourism destination. These include (a) strong local leadership and bottom-up approach; (b) community protocol; (c) provision of infrastructures and superstructures; (d) destination brand management and sustainability, and (e) non-stakeholders' involvement. These findings are uncovered in this study as potential contributions to the existing literature. However, the following findings are consistent with the existing literature (a) host community involvement and multiple stakeholders support (including government) involvement (Hankinson, 2009, 2010; Hanna & Rowley, 2011); (b) brand benefits communication to the core stakeholders (Baker & Cameron, 2008 p. 89); (c) destination brand planning (Baker & Cameron, 2008 p. 89); (d) marketing research and analysis of destination identity, awareness and image (Morgan & Pritchard, 2004, 2010, p. 69); (e) brand execution/implementation or launch (Baker & Cameron, 2008 p. 89; Anholt, 2010); (f) identify destination core tourism attractions/assets (Baker & Cameron, 2008 p. 89); and (g) destination logos and slogans, brand promise, management, monitoring and review (Baker & Cameron, 2008; Tasci, 2011). This study has uncovered 12 sustainable destination branding strategies in understanding the future of marketing management in rural tourism destinations.

Relationship Building and Future of Marketing Management in Rural Tourism Destination

This study has adopted the relationship-based building approach in understanding the future of marketing management in rural tourism destinations. This is important because the marketing of rural tourism destination goes beyond the core stakeholders but the contributions of interdependent individuals or non-stakeholders are needed (Jamal & Getz, 1995). These groups of people could be regarded as the potential friends of a particular rural tourism destination. Findings on the roles of relationship-based approach in the future of marketing management in rural tourism destinations and in particular the study context are presented in the following section. To start, a 68-year old local resident, retiree, farmer and volunteer in community service in Bario pointed out:

I think Bario has been very fortunate in terms of different stakeholders if we should go back to what I have said. The food and cultural festival was initiated by somebody from England, the e-Bario website was also initiated by another gentleman from outside Bario, the researchers from the University of Cambridge who worked on the megaliths and stone monuments were also not from Bario, the NGOs and volunteers they are not from Bario. ... So, relationship building through our hospitability and well meaningful people has worked for Bario ... So, I think for all these stakeholders they should build a progressive relationship among themselves especially we the community in Bario and this is what we need to make Bario a premium destination, as I said

The importance of relationship building cannot be overemphasised. Findings show that tourism destination stakeholders and non-stakeholders are involved in relationship building. This makes the relationship based approach important for the future of marketing management practise especially in a rural tourism destination. In a rural destination where government presence is not visibly seen, relationship building among the stakeholders will provide the needed social, economic and infrastructure facilities that will promote tourism and the marketing efforts. These views are corroborated vividly by one of the respondents, a community leader in Bario:

Most of the infrastructural development and projects we have … in Bario were to market and brand the place. I believe they came from the relationship building strategy we employed in the leadership. I mean for example, the Kelabits association where I was the president for three terms of three years each [9 years]. Through building and maintaining good relationships we have been able to attract and work with quite a good number of individuals and organisations in marketing tourism… as an industry in Bario,

These findings are revealing in terms of what relationship building among the stakeholders and non-stakeholders could achieve in the rural tourism destination marketing activities to boost its tourism and economic development. These findings are not in the existing studies on the rural destination marketing process which further justifies previous calls for the relationship-based approach to tourism destination marketing and branding (Szondi, 2010; Choi & Cai, 2012). Comments on relationship building from other participants include a 65- year old tourist from New Zealand:

… Bario is a very small destination; relationship building will help the place to develop its rural tourism marketing in the [future and enhance] its destination brand very fast through mutual relationship among the stakeholders …

One of the authors of the book "Bario Revival" and a community leader in Bario affirmed:

…Relationship building plays two important roles. First is to bring the main stakeholders to participate in the community development, tourism, future marketing and branding. The second is to liaise with non-stakeholders who can provide financial and networking with marketing and destination branding experts with experience to support the tourism branding and community development…

A tourist from the United States of America commented:

I think the basic thing is to establish effective communication, honesty and transparency among the stakeholders… in the relationship building in the [future marketing] potentials of Bario as a rural tourism destination.

Furthermore, a 40-year old marketing and branding expert observed:

I think relationship building would be an effective strategy to develop a future destination marketing and branding. However, another challenge here would be the process involved in getting an arrow head [local leadership] that would be the prime mover and give the direction to follow. To achieve this long term goal, the community association in Bario should take it upon themselves to establish a kind of rapport with other stakeholders.

As the participants rightly observed, the relationship concept is mainly used by the marketers especially in the promotion and marketing of physical products in order to gain customers and brand loyalty for their products. Notably, academic interest, marketing and destination practitioners' contributions on the relationship-based approach in the marketing and destination branding are less reported in the tourism destination marketing and sustainable brand building literature. This view is consistent with Choi and Cai's (2012) observation that there is a lack of theoretical and empirical studies featuring the relationship building process in connection with destination branding, and in particular the future marketing management of rural tourism destinations. Similarly, it has been suggested that the application of the relationship-based theory and relationship building to tourism destination branding, specifically tourism destinations marketing is emerging and is still a novel endeavour (Chen & Phou, 2013).

More importantly, this study produces new findings. For example, from the roles of relationship building in the future marketing management of rural tourism destination perspective the following are the new findings. First is the networking with non-stakeholders. They are individuals and corporate friends of the rural destination and, in particular, they were identified in Bario as members of the public who have sponsored corporate social responsibility (CSR) projects and provision of infrastructures facilities. These were achieved through relationship building among the tourism destination stakeholders and non- stakeholders.

Second is the progressive relationship, sense of ownership and trust among the stakeholders. This implies that relationship building should take into cognizance the interest of all the parties and actors involved, so that sense of ownership unlike the physical product can be entrenched. This is very important because one of the challenges of destination marketing and brand development is the issue of multiple stakeholders and lack of ownership. These views are corroborated by Baker and Cameron (2007) that there are multiple stakeholders involved in tourism destination marketing and branding, and there is no sole control over destination product and marketing (Morgan & Pritchard, 2004, 2010). Third is the sustainable destination brand development and marketing due to a sense of responsibility to ensure the continuous growth and maturity of the destination marketing. In addition, based on the thorough analysis of the respondents' views and their personal experience, relationship building is an indispensable strategy that should be employed by stakeholders in rural tourism destination specifically in Bario to develop its future marketing activities and management. These findings are very important to this study because of the relationship-based approach it has adopted.

Field Notes on Participant Observation

Findings from observations of stakeholders' involvement, participation and contribution to tourism and future destination marketing in rural tourism especially the case study context. In Bario, six stakeholders who participated in different tourism activities were observed namely: (a) volunteers and non-government organisations; (b) researchers; (c) government ministries; agencies and Forestry Department; (d) tourists; (e) local residents; and (f) MASwings Airline. The involvements of these six stakeholders were motivated by desire to develop a sustainable tourism destination brand and relationship building in marketing Bario as a tourism destination. These observations also confirmed findings from the in-depth interviews that stakeholders and non-stakeholders should engage in relationship-building efforts.

IMPLICATIONS AND CONCLUSION

This study has found that sustainable destination branding and relationship-based building approach are crucial in understanding the future marketing management and efforts especially in rural tourism destinations. This is mostly due to the increased marketing and branding competition from global tourism destinations. More importantly, new tourism destinations have emerged and industry players are adopting modern technology to provide destination information, offerings and incentives for the potential tourists. In this era of digital disruption and acceleration, several destinations have adopted social media and other digital platforms to promote their destinations. In this circumstance, most rural tourism destinations are at disadvantage due to lack of internet services and limited destination appeal. This view is corroborated by Cai (2002, p. 738) that the challenge of tourism marketing in rural tourism destination is its limited drawing power and "individual rural destinations are often too small to form a critical mass required of a primary destination". Similar view was expressed by Haven-Tang and Sedgley (2014) that the common characteristics of rural tourism products and rural destinations marketing is the lack of distinct differentiation or uniqueness of offerings which makes it a challenge to develop a sense of destination marketing identity. Nevertheless, this study has produced both theoretical contribution and implications for practice.

The theoretical contribution from this study is that it has developed a framework for a sustainable future of marketing management praxis in rural destination space. This framework is presented in Figure 2 which illustrated sustainable destination branding strategies specific to rural destinations and roles of relationship building approach in the marketing and branding functions of rural tourism highlighted in the previous section.

Figure 2. Framework for a sustainable future of marketing management praxis in rural destination space

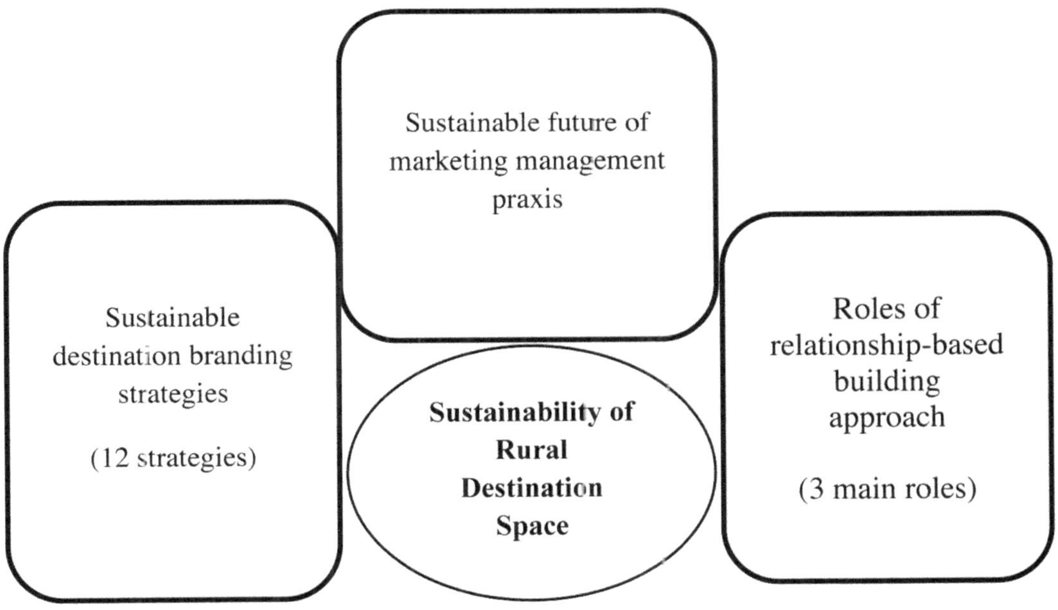

Managerial implications suggest that rural tourism destination managers, host community, and community association should evolve community protocol and code of conduct, involvement of multiple stakeholders and non-stakeholders in the future marketing praxis of rural tourism destinations. In order to ensure that the sustainable destination brand building and relationship building approach are done successfully in the future marketing of rural tourism destinations the role of community participation is important. Therefore, there is a need for the core destination stakeholders to understand that the starting point should be sustainable community-driven strategy through the local leadership using the bottom-up approach that is developed within the local community that will promote the destination marketing of rural destination rather than top-down approach from the government. The bottom-up approach has the potential to create a sense of belonging among the diverse stakeholders which could attract quality tourist arrivals and in particular such place becoming a preferred rural tourism destination among the visitors.

In conclusion, for three consecutive years between 2012 and 2014 and a follow-up in February 2020 before COVID-19 pandemic global lockdown, the researcher undertook six visits to Bario as a single case study that utilized triangulation of data sources to enhance the credibility of this study. However, it is acknowledged that the findings from this study may not be generalised to other rural tourism destinations due to different tourism destination offerings, geographic location, and accessibility appeal, behaviour of the host community and characteristics of core stakeholders. As a result, this study suggests that future studies should be conducted in multiple rural tourism destinations to validate the findings and implications resulting from this study.

ACKNOWLEDGMENT

The funding for this project is made possible through the research grant obtained from the Malaysian Ministry of Education Long Term Research Grant Scheme (LRGS) Programme [Reference No: JPT.S (BPKI)2000/09/01/015Jld.4(67)].

REFERENCES

Adeyinka-Ojo, S. F., Khoo-Lattimore, C., & Nair, V. (2014). A framework for rural tourism destination management and marketing organisations. *Procedia: Social and Behavioral Sciences*, *144*, 151–163. doi:10.1016/j.sbspro.2014.07.284

Anholt, S. (2010). *Handbook on tourism destination branding*. ETC/UNWTO.

Azlan, M. D. Z., & Bagul, A. H. B. (2010). Modernisation and its effects on heritage Tourism in Melaka. *TEAM Journal of Hospitality & Tourism*, *7*(1), 46–57.

Baker, B. (2007). *Destination branding for small cities: the essentials for successful place branding*. Portland, OR: Creative Leap books.

Baker, M. J., & Cameron, E. (2008). Critical success factors in destination marketing. *Tourism and Hospitality Research*, *8*(2), 79–97. doi:10.1057/thr.2008.9

Balakrishnan, M. S. (2008). Dubai – a star in the east. *Journal of Place Management and Development*, *1*(1), 62–91.

Blain, C., Levy, S., & Ritchie, J. R. B. (2005). Destination branding: Insight and practices from destination management organisations. *Journal of Travel Research*, *43*(4), 328–338. doi:10.1177/0047287505274646

Bowen, J., Makens, J., & Kotler, P. (2005). *Marketing for hospitality and tourism* (4th ed.). Prentice Hall.

Braun, V., & Clarke, V. (2006). Using thematic analysis in psychology. *Qualitative Research in Psychology*, *3*(2), 77–101. doi:10.1191/1478088706qp063oa

Cai, L. A. (2002). Cooperative branding for rural destination. *Annals of Tourism Research*, *29*(3), 720–742. doi:10.1016/S0160-7383(01)00080-9

Chen, C.-F., & Phou, S. (2013). A closer look at destination: Image, personality, relationship and loyalty. *Tourism Management*, *36*, 269–278. doi:10.1016/j.tourman.2012.11.015

Choi H. S. C., & Sirakaya, E. (2005). Measuring residents' attitude toward sustainable tourism: Development of sustainable tourism attitude scale. *Journal of Travel Research*, *43*(4), 380–394. doi:10.1177/0047287505274651

Choi, S. H., & Cai, L. A. (2012). Destination loyalty and communication – a relationship-based tourist behavioural model. *International Journal of Strategic Communication*, *6*(1), 45–58. doi:10.1080/1553118X.2011.634868

Cooper, C. (2012). *Essentials of Tourism*. Pearson Education Limited.

Fereday, J., & Muir-Cochrane, E. (2006). Demonstrating rigor using thematic analysis: A hybrid approach of inductive and deductive coding and theme development. *International Journal of Qualitative Methods*, *5*(1), 1–11. doi:10.1177/160940690600500107

Freeman, R. E. (1984). *Strategic management: A stakeholder approach*. Pitman.

Freeman, R. E., Wicks, A. C., & Parmar, B. (2004). Stakeholder theory and "The corporate objective revisited.". *Organization Science*, *15*(3), 364–369. doi:10.1287/orsc.1040.0066

Fyall, A., Callod, C., & Edwards, B. (2003). Relationship marketing: The challenge for destinations. *Annals of Tourism Research*, *30*(3), 644–659. doi:10.1016/S0160-7383(03)00046-X

Fyall, A., Garrod, B., & Wang, Y. (2012). Destination collaboration: A critical review of theoretical approaches to a multi-dimensional phenomenon. *Journal of Destination Marketing & Management*, *1*(1-2), 10–26. doi:10.1016/j.jdmm.2012.10.002

Grant, J. (2008). Green marketing. *Strategic Direction*, *24*(6), 25–27. doi:10.1108/02580540810868041

Guba, E. G., & Lincoln, Y. S. (1994). Competing paradigms in qualitative research. In N. K. Denzin & Y. S. Lincoln (Eds.), *Handbook of Qualitative Research*. Sage Publications Inc.

Gubrium, J. A., & Holsten, J. A. (2001). *Handbook of interview research: Context and method*. Sage. doi:10.4135/9781412973588

Hankinson, G. (2009). Managing destination brands: Establishing a theoretical foundation. *Journal of Marketing Management*, *25*(1-2), 97–115. doi:10.1362/026725709X410052

Hankinson, G. (2010). Place branding research: A cross disciplinary agenda and the views practitioners. *Place Branding and Public Diplomacy*, *6*(4), 300–315. doi:10.1057/pb.2010.29

Hanna, S., & Rowley, G. (2011). Towards a strategic place brand-management model. *Journal of Marketing Management*, *27*(5-6), 458–476. doi:10.1080/02672571003683797

Haven-Tang, C., & Sedgley, D. (2014). Partnership working in enhancing the destination brand of rural areas: A case study of made in Monmouthshire, Wales, UK. *Journal of Destination Marketing & Management*, *3*(1), 59–67. doi:10.1016/j.jdmm.2013.12.001

Hosany, S., Ekinci, Y., & Uysal, M. (2007). Destination image and destination personality. *International Journal of Culture, Tourism and Hospitality Research*, *1*(1), 62–81. doi:10.1108/17506180710729619

Insch, A. (2011). Conceptualization and anatomy of green destination brands. *International Journal of Culture, Tourism and Hospitality Research*, *5*(3), 282–290. doi:10.1108/17506181111156970

Jamal, T., & Getz, D. (1995). Collaboration theory and community tourism planning. *Annals of Tourism Research*, *22*(1), 186–204. doi:10.1016/0160-7383(94)00067-3

Jennings, G. (2010). Tourism research (2nd ed.). Wiley & Sons.

Jiwan, D., Paul, C. P. K., Teo, G. K., & Jiwan, M. (2006). Integrated highland development in Bario, Sarawak, Malaysia: an overview. *International Symposium Towards Sustainable Livelihoods and Ecosystems in Mountainous Regions*.

Kayat, K. (2011). *Homestay Programme as a Malaysian Tourism Product*. UUM Press.

Khanna, M. (2011). Destination branding: Tracking brand India. *Synergy*, *9*(1), 40–49.

Kotler, P., Bowen, J.T., & Makens, J.C. (2014). Marketing for hospitality and tourism (6th ed.). Pearson.

Lofland, J., & Lofland, L. H. (1984). Analysing social settings: A guide to qualitative observation and analysis (2nd ed.). Belmont, CA: Wadsworth.

Maheshwari, V., Vandewalle, I., & Bamber, D. (2011). Place branding's role in sustainable development. *Journal of Place Management and Development*, *4*(2), 198–213.

Malaysian Government. (2011). Population and housing census of Malaysia: preliminary count Report 2010. Author.

Marzano, G. (2007). *The effect of stakeholder power on a destination branding process: The GoldCoast VeryGC brand* (Doctoral Thesis). University of Queensland, Australia.

Marzano, G., & Scott, N. (2005). Stakeholder power in destination branding: a methodological discussion. *Proceedings of the Destination Branding and Marketing for Regional Tourism Development Conference*, 203-212.

Morgan, N., Hastings, E., & Pritchard, A. (2012). Developing a new DMO marketing evaluation framework: The case of visit Wales. *Journal of Vacation Marketing*, *18*(1), 73–89.

Morgan, N., & Pritchard, A. (2010). Meeting the destination branding challenge In N. Morgan, A. Pritchard, & R. Pride (Eds.), Destination Branding: Creating the unique destination proposition (2nd ed.). Elsevier Butterworth-Heinemann.

Morrison, A. M. (2013). *Marketing and managing tourism destinations*. Routledge.

Musa, N., Noor, S. D., & Mohamad, W. (2013). Developing destination brand identity: towards sustainability of tourism destination from the perspective of stakeholders and theory of social identity. *Proceedings of International Conference on Tourism Development.*

Ottman, J. A. (2011). *The new rules of green marketing strategies, tools, and inspiration for sustainable branding*. Greenleaf Publishing Limited.

Pearce, D. G. (1992). *Tourists Organisations*. Longman.

Pike, S., & Page, S. J. (2014). Destination marketing organisations and destination marketing: A narrative analysis of the literature. *Tourism Management*, *41*, 201–227.

Prayag, G., & Ryan, C. (2011). The relationship between the 'push' and 'pull' factors of a tourist destination: The role of nationality – an analytical qualitative research approach. *Current Issues in Tourism*, *14*(2), 121–143.

Quinlan, T. (2008). *A stakeholder approach to the branding of urban tourism destinations* (Master Thesis). Waterford Institute of Technology, Ireland.

Rasmussen, S. E., Ostergaard, P., & Beckmann, C.S. (2006). Essentials of social Science Research Methodology. Southern Denmark University Press.

Ritchie, J. R. B., & Ritchie, R. J. B. (1998). The branding of tourism destination: past achievements and future challenges. *Annual congress of the International Association of Scientific Experts in Tourism*, 89-116.

Sautter, E. T., & Leisen, B. (1999). Managing stakeholders: A tourism planning model. *Annals of Tourism Research*, *26*(2), 312–328.

Sheth, J., & Sisodia, R. (2005). A dangerous divergence: Marketing and society. *Journal of Public Policy & Marketing*, *24*(1), 160–162.

Stole, E. (2011). *The road to successful green destination branding* (Master's thesis). Department of Inter- national Economics and Management, Copenhagen Business School, Denmark.

Strauss, A. L., & Corbin, J. M. (2008). *Basics of qualitative research: Techniques and procedures for developing grounded theory*. Sage publications Limited.

Swarbrooke, J. (2006). *Sustainable tourism management*. CABI Publishing.

Szondi, G. (2010). From image management to relationship building: A public relations approach to nation branding. *Place Branding and Public Diplomacy*, *6*(4), 333–343.

Tasci, A. D. A. (2011). Destination branding and positioning. In Y. Wang & A. Pizam (Eds.), *Destination marketing and management theories and applications*. CABI.

Tilstone, C. (Ed.). (1998). *The technique of observation. In observing teaching and learning: principle and practice* (pp. 32–53). David Fulton Publishers.

United Nations World Tourism Organisation. (2005). *Making tourism more sustainable. A guide for policy makers*. UNWTO.

United Nations World Tourism Organisation. (2007). *A practical guide to tourism destination Management. UNWTO.*

United Nations World Tourism Organisation. (2013). World tourism barometer – tourism trends and marketing. Author.

Walker, R. H., & Hanson, D. J. (1998). Green Marketing and Green Places: A Taxonomy for the Destination Marketer. *Journal of Marketing Management*, *14*, 623–639.

Wang, Y. (2008). Collaborative destination marketing: Roles and strategies of convention and visitors bureaus. *Journal of Vacation Marketing*, *14*(3), 191–209.

Wang, Y. (2011). Destination marketing and management: scope, definition and structures. In Y. Wang & A. Pizam (Eds.), *Destination marketing and management: Theories and applications* (pp. 1–20). CAB International.

Weaver, D., & Lawton, L. (2010). *Tourism management* (4th ed.). John Wiley & Sons.

Woodland, M., & Acott, T. G. (2007). Sustainability and local tourism branding in England's South Downs. *Journal of Sustainable Tourism*, *15*(6), 715–724.

Yuksel, F. B., Bramwell, A., & Yuksel, A. (1999). Stakeholder interviews and tourism planning at Pamukkale, Turkey. *Tourism Management*, *20*(3), 351–360.

Chapter 16
Understanding How Entrepreneurship Innovation Solves Women's Challenges in the Arab Region:
Omani Women Entrepreneurs Model

Fadi Abdel Muniem Ahmad Abdel Fattah
https://orcid.org/0000-0002-4655-4777
A'Sharqiyah University, Oman

Hussam Al Halbusi
Ahmed Bin Mohammed Military College, Qatar

ABSTRACT

Sustainable economic growth is a top priority for Oman, aiming to lessen reliance on oil and increase economic diversification. The government sees entrepreneurship and innovation as vital players in creating jobs, diversifying the economy, and transforming the economy from a traditional to a knowledge-based economy. Under the Visions 2020-2040, the government has developed programs to enhance and encourage women's engagement in SMEs to maximize returns, create employment opportunities, and reduce the market and institutional failures. Lack of women engagement in SMEs is due to barriers of entrants and women who intend to start their own business can face challenges that lead to failure in their business endeavors. Among these challenges are government policies, financial support, supporting R&D, and culture. Further research is necessary to investigate factors that motivate Omanis to become entrepreneurs and overcome the obstacles. The main objective of this chapter is to develop a conceptual framework to highlight the main challenges that limit Omani women from participating in SMEs.

DOI: 10.4018/978-1-7998-9590-9.ch016

INTRODUCTION

Entrepreneurship is an important support system for economic growth in developed and developing countries (Al-Ghazali et al., 2013; Dickes et al., 2017; Hicks and Faulk, 2018; Lihn and Bjørnskov, 2017a; Schneider, 2017; Taqi, 2016; Yi and Duval-Couetil, 2018). In Oman, sustainable economic growth is the primary concern on its developing plans, aiming to reduce the reliance on oil and enhance economic diversification (Magd and McCoy, 2014). In the Oman Visions 2020-2040, the government is looking to entrepreneurship and innovation as a critical player to create jobs, diversify economics and transform the economy from a traditional to a knowledge-based economy. Many researchers acknowledge that Small and Medium Enterprises (SMEs) play an important role in countries' economic growth and development (AlMaimani and Johari, 2015; Mathew, 2010; Mohammed et al., 2016; Tamim et al., 2015). In general, women are considered critical economic players in many countries. The Omani government asserted, on different occasions, the vital role of women in influencing the country's economy (Magd and McCoy, 2014; Naguib and Jamali, 2015). Thus, enhancing the Omani women's role and participation in SMEs will impact influencing the economic growth and development of the country (Belwal and Belwal, 2014; Narayanasamy et al., 2016). Although in Arabic context as specific, and the world, in general, the men are more likely to start a business than women, and most of them owned businesses in Arabic contexts are owned by men, there is a growing trend from women as well to start and opened their business.

Indeed, Omani women's participation has increased due to government support (El Hamidi, 2017; Taqi, 2016); either this support is coming in hard or soft support. The government has developed programs to enhance and encourage women's engagement in SMEs to maximize returns and create employment opportunities (AlMaimani and Johari, 2015; Yi and Duval-Couetil, 2018), and add to that to reduce the market and institutional failures. Lack of women engagement in SMEs is often characterized by barriers to their entrants to the labor market (Lihn and Bjørnskov, 2017a). Researchers contend that women who intend to start their own business can face challenges that lead to failure in their business endeavors (Hicks and Faulk, 2018). Among these challenges are government policies, financial support, supporting R&D, culture, and tradition, which are the main constraints (Bade, 2018; Farhangmehr et al., 2016a; Tarabar, 2018). In the same vein, most women have difficulty accessing financial resources and end up depending on their families and relatives in securing a source of capital to start up their business (Belwal et al., 2014; Environment and Enterprises, 2016). The lack of financial resources limits entrepreneurs' ability to start a new business (Dickes et al., 2017; El Hamidi, 2017; Taqi, 2016). Furthermore, educational qualification, skills, experience, and lack of motivation are essential factors that often lead to the entrepreneur's failure (Mthanti and Ojah, 2018; Schneider, 2018).

Several studies were conducted in Oman to describe women's characteristics and barriers to business and employment. One of those studies in this regard was by (McElwee and Al-Riyami, 2003), who pointed out that further research is necessary to investigate factors that motivate Omanis to become entrepreneurs and overcome the obstacles that hinder such motivation. Like many parts of the developing world, Omani women face challenges that prevent them from starting their businesses. The main objective of this chapter is to develop a conceptual framework to highlight the main challenges that limit Omani women from participating in SMEs. We hope this framework will provide a road map to policymakers to embark on appropriate administrative regulations and laws to facilitate Omani women's involvement in entrepreneurship.

DESCRIPTION OF THE OMAN CONTEXT

Developing countries face problems of increasing unemployment as their working-age populations are growing. The public sector, especially in the GCC countries, plays an essential role in providing employment opportunities to their nationals. However, in almost all of these countries, the public sector is already reaching saturation. In that sense, the private sector can be the only key to ingesting a portion of the growing population of working age (Farzanegan, 2014). There is a substantial growth in the number of SMEs in Oman. According to (Riyada Annual Report, 2018), 37,289 companies were registered in the Authority Public for SMEs Development (Riyada) by the end of 2018 compared to 31,836 companies registered in 2017. Most of these SMEs are micro-enterprises which account for around 74% of total registered enterprises (Al-Abri et al., 2018). Despite this growth, the contribution of SMEs to Oman GDP is remaining at a modest level in comparison to other countries in GCC and around the world (Riyada Mapping Report, 2018), and the total contribution is estimated to be lower than 20% in 2017 (Al-Abri et al., 2018). The total number of enterprises established by women in Oman is lower than males. According to (Riyada Annual Report, 2017), the total number of enterprises established by women was 7,355 compared to 24,480 enterprises founded by males.

Entrepreneurship is the engine for many future changes in the economies of developing countries nowadays. In the GCC economies, most of the most prominent ownership of companies are owned by family-oriented firms or foreign ownership (Arouri et al., 2014). Many family-owned companies in the world have gone public, while they are still owned and managed privately in the GCC. According to Farzanegan (2014), there is a negative relationship between countries dependent on oil rents and the new business formation density. Most of the entrepreneurship-driven efforts in developing countries are "necessity entrepreneurship" and not opportunity-driven as there are "no better choices for work" (Reynolds, Bygrave, Autio, Arenius, & Monitor, 2004, p.2).

Oman is faced with several kinds of challenges in its attempts to foster entrepreneurship development: regulatory and administration issues, macroeconomic and market conditions, regulatory labor market, education and training, financial infrastructure, R&D infrastructure, society culture, and limited entrepreneurship support programs (Al-Shanfari, 2012). Today there are many programs in Oman, either provided by public or private sectors under the social responsibility programs, supporting the growing and accelerating entrepreneurship capacity in the country. Based on the Riyada Mapping Report (2018), there are numerous supporting programs focusing on cultivating entrepreneurship in Oman, like incubators, funding organizations, training and development programs. Nevertheless, the effectiveness of these programs is still questionable due to their funding sources and focus, as most of them are focusing on the early stages of SMEs start-ups (Riyada Mapping Report. 2018). Al-Abri et al. (2018) stated that SMEs in Oman have a wide range of support from the government and other initiatives programs from other institutions, but SMEs face obstacles that limit their growth and survival. However, we still do not know the actual situation of the country's entrepreneurship policy after Oman began promoting entrepreneurship and enhancing entrepreneurial activities. There is a lack of available studies that evaluate any entrepreneurship policies implemented in Oman, despite the introduction of support programs (Al Shukaili, 2017).

THE IMPORTANCE OF ENTREPRENEURSHIP TO DEVELOPING COUNTRIES

Many developing countries perceive entrepreneurship as a source of economic growth (Brixiova, 2013). Thus, many policymakers focus on entrepreneurial activities in developing countries to diversify income and reduce the risk of depending primarily on revenue from natural resources. Developing countries have faced the problem of increasing unemployment rate due to a growing population of individuals who are of working age. The public sector cannot provide for or meet all the employment needs of these individuals (Al Shukaili et al., 2018). Informal firms contribute heavily to economic activity in developing countries (Ayyagari et al., 2014) and are less efficient, productive, and socially beneficial than small formal firms in developing counties (Bennett, 2010). Therefore, SMEs have a significant role in developing countries regarding job generation, supporting innovation and creativity, economic growth, and development (Al Shukaili et al., 2016). According to Omani Youth Trends Book Report (2019), the job seekers need 25 months to get a job in 2019 compared to 42 months in 2015 which indicates that Omanis can currently find jobs better. The majority of Omani youth are looking to find job positions in the public sector (87% of job seekers), and women prefer to have a job in the public sector than in the private sector (NCSI, 2019). Furthermore, 11% of Omanis who secured a job have owned a business, while only 8% of job seekers are looking to start their own business. Indeed, these statistics show that women are more willing to start a business if they can balance their work and family duties and look for markets close to their homes (Belwal et al., 2014).

MARKET AND INSTITUTIONAL FAILURES

Although young firms can act as essential engines of change in developing countries, they face multiple markets and institutional challenges (Al Shukaili et al., 2018). They lack market and institutional mechanisms (that is, availability of skilled human capital, financial sources, and policy incentives), which seem to promote entrepreneurship in developed countries (González-Pernía et al., 2015). Similarly, Ayyagari, Demirguc-kunt, & Maksimovic (2014) argue that small firms in developing countries face many institutional obstacles such as limited access to finance sources, poorly functioning judicial systems, and legal enforcement, and weak property rights protection. Furthermore, a recent survey conducted by the World Bank (2014) showed a significant shortage in domestic credit provided by private financial markets to entrepreneurs in developing countries, in contrast to developed countries. We believe that the effect of entrepreneurship policy on entrepreneurial activity is not uniform across countries, and often, the presumed positive effect is questioned.

In the current study, Al-Abri et al. (2018) summarize the most challenges SMEs face in Oman based on the literature review for studies conducted about Oman between 2014 and 2017. They found that most of these obstacles that can limit the success of enterprises in Oman are; human capital, government support, financial capital, and technology. Al Shukaili et al. (2017) explored the reasons behind the stagnation of new ventures obtaining government financing support in Oman (a developing country). They found that many of the reasons behind this stagnation can be attributed to the following six profiles that characterize those new ventures and their owners: 1) female entrepreneurs who do not have a high-school education but had work experience; 2) female entrepreneurs who receive support from the government but lack high-school education; 3) lack of education for both male and female entrepreneurs; 4) male entrepreneurs without training and experience; 5) lack of working experience and training support despite an acceptable level of education; 6) firms run by male entrepreneurs with any school level of education and without training support from the government. According to Al Shukaili (2017) and Quatraro and Vivarelli (2013), the main challenge for developing countries is the need to address market failure and reduce bureaucracy, which tend to produce regulatory constraints for entrepreneurs. There are very few studies in the literature of developing countries concerned with addressing these issues from an entrepreneurship perspective.

SOCIETY PERCEPTION

Social perception is the interpretation and judgment of other people within a community or society based on that community's social traditions, rules, culture, and norms (Kennedy and Hill, 2016). Perception is defined as how people formulate impressions of others' personalities, behavior, and attitude (Friedman, 2011; Mashood et al., 2009). Women in Oman interact with several cultural, social, and traditional norms, which exhibit a barrier to their participation in the labor market (Al-Lamky, 2008; Belwal and Belwal, 2014). Gender discrimination is one of these barriers. Research suggests that men in Arab societies are given higher authority in the house and in the workplace, where they have the power to decide for women (Al-Lamky, 2008; Belwal and Belwal, 2014; Naguib and Jamali, 2015). However, in Oman nowadays, women have many top management job positions in some public and private institutions.

Family support and encouragement play an essential role in inducing women into entrepreneurship (Brush et al., 2009; Narayanasamy et al., 2016). However, family cultural values tend to limit women's orientation towards entrepreneurship (Al-Asfour et al., 2017; Panda, 2018). Narayanasamy et al. (2016) acknowledge that women are solely responsible for taking care of the family and raising children in compliance with social perception. Furthermore, social perception tends to be cruel towards women who work for a living outside the home instead of managing their houses. Hu et al. (2016) argue that women face the challenge of balancing personal life with work-life when they choose to be entrepreneurs. In Arabic contexts, specifically, men are not engaged much in helping women at home or sharing the duties inside the home. Therefore, women have to devote their work and home responsibilities. Social perception about women is that they are not capable of running a business with substantial financial resources because their mindset can get affected emotionally in situations where important decisions need to be made (Anderson, 2015; Hu et al., 2016; Pistrui and Sreih, 2010; Taqi, 2016). In addition, the Islamic ethics and values of running a business for women have also impacted the predation of entrepreneurship capacity among Muslim women. This perception tends to impact entrepreneurship-related activities directly, specifically in the Arab world when women are involved (Hu et al., 2016; Tlaiss, 2015).

ACCESS TO FINANCIAL RESOURCES

Access to the financial resource is the ability to secure money for a specific purpose by governments or private institutions (Dickes et al., 2017). Hicks and Faulk (2018) explain that the Omani government's funding aim primarily to maintain economic growth through funding support programs in order to ensure that higher levels of entrepreneurs are engaged in business activities as well as creating employment opportunities for other people (Christina et al., 2014; Dickes et al., 2017; Magd and McCoy, 2014; Report, 2014). Financial institutions (such as banks) will provide support to new businesses through providing credit and start-up capital (Lihn and Bjørnskov, 2017b; Youngberg, 2017). Designing and founding different financial sources like crowdfunding, venture capital, and angel investment is still new and not well used in the Omani context. Yusoff et al. (2018) argue that one of the difficulties entrepreneurs face is insufficient financial support and the high-interest rate provided by financial institutions.

Omani women entrepreneurs encounter difficulties when trying to access financial resources (Christina et al., 2014; Environment and Enterprises, 2016; Kumar, 2007). Kumar (2007) argues that one of those difficulties for Omani women is the limited available information on how to get access to those financial resources. These entrepreneurial women often lack the knowledge required to look for the financing institutions available to them (Christina et al., 2014; Mthanti and Ojah, 2018; Yusoff et al., 2018). More often than not, they depend on their families, friends, or assets to secure the required source of capital. Al-Rafad fund program is one of the Omani government's funding institutions to develop and promote SMEs through loans and other facilities for young entrepreneurs. There are also other institutions programs and social responsibilities initiatives from some companies that provide funding support such as the commercial and Islamic banks, Oman Development Bank, Oman Technology Fund, Sharakah Company (Youth Fund), SME Development Fund (Inma), and many others (Riyada Mapping Report, 2018) Notwithstanding these sources of assistance to entrepreneurs, research suggests that women entrepreneurs are not satisfied with the financial aspects of these facilities (Bade, 2018; El Hamidi, 2017; Youngberg, 2017) due to the high-interest rate charged which often drive women entrepreneurs to rely on their families for their start-up capital (Bade, 2018; Hicks and Faulk, 2018; Payne and Mervar, 2017).

Moreover, the complexity of administrative procedures and regulations coupled with high fees can also restrict entrepreneurial Omani women from developing their home-based businesses to real competitive enterprises (Youngberg, 2017). Many developing countries suffer from financial difficulties such as credit constraints, imperfect financial markets, and asymmetric information, which often lead to government intervention by designing initiatives such as government programs to address these problems (Levinsky, 1997; Al Shukaili, 2017). Al-Sadi et al. (2013) contend that the most common barriers that affect women entrepreneurs are "financial support, knowledge to collaborate, access to technology, industrial support, pressure to achieve, interacting with males, training opportunities, information on opportunities, and the time required for training" (p.72). Furthermore, Khan et al. (2005) argue that the main challenges for women entrepreneurs in Oman are that most of their business is concentrated in the service sector and run on a small size (capital and sales).

EDUCATIONAL QUALIFICATION: MISMATCH WITH JOB REQUIREMENT

Radwan (2014) points out that mismatching occurs when a job seeker is either overqualified or not qualified enough to meet a job requirement. Skills and knowledge mismatch are very costly for firms, workers, and society. Employers and policymakers face challenges aligning job seekers' qualifications and skills with job requirements, which illustrates the gap between supply and demand in the labor market (Al-Ani, 2017; Al-Azri, 2016; Ali et al., 2017; Radwan, 2014; U.E., 2014). The mismatching between qualifications and job requirements has been defined as an obstacle facing women's engagement in entrepreneurship. The level of education, skills, and relevant expertise is a cornerstone in establishing new businesses and succeeding in entrepreneurship (Barba-Sánchez and Atienza-Sahuquillo, 2018; Huang et al., 2012; Matriano and Suguku, 2015). As argued, a combination of education and entrepreneurship will help enhance the growth of an economy. Schneider (2017) contends that women often study disciplines that are not related to the knowledge required by businesses. As such, education presents an obstacle in the face of women's participation in entrepreneurship. The type of education possessed by women does not match the skills required by entrepreneurship activities (Schneider, 2018). Some researchers suggest that men have more opportunities (than women) to acquire technical and practical skills due to support from training institutions and families (Belwal et al., 2015). Ali and Muthuraman, (2017) argue that lack of education and experience in business disciplines held by women in Oman work as a disadvantage to their entrepreneurial aspirations, even though they strive to foster self-confidence and prove their active role in society.

One of the indicators of entrepreneurship success is in aligning education programs in higher education institutions and training programs that improve students' skills, knowledge (Ali and Muthuraman, 2017; AlMaimani and Johari, 2015; Matriano and Suguku, 2015; Schneider, 2018), and enable them to make the right decision in the right place when facing issues in the work environment (Sousa and Almeida, 2014). Many factors are responsible for Omani women's failure in entrepreneurship (Mohammed et al., 2016). The government does not provide sufficient training programs that qualify women to acquire the right skills and knowledge. Thus, they miss the competencies required to succeed in their entrepreneurial activities. New venture growth in developing economies needs more attention from institutions to reduce market failures (i.e., financial market failure) and improve the human capital of entrepreneurs who are the target of their support programs (Al Shukaili, 2018).

ENTREPRENEURIAL MOTIVATION

Entrepreneurial motivation is the willingness and drive of an individual or group of individuals to establish and develop a business or venture to achieve specific entrepreneurship goals (Mathew, 2010; Zeidan and Bahrami, 2011). Motivation has a significant role in enhancing the success of entrepreneurs; it is defined as the engine of passion in accomplishing the task well (Ismail et al., 2016). Motivation is necessary to achieve goals successfully (Farhangmehr et al., 2016b; Rosa et al., 2008). Yi and Duval-Couetil, (2018) argue that lack of educational qualification combined with negative social perception and difficulties in accessing financial resources impacts women entrepreneurs' motivation to establish their businesses. In addition to their responsibilities to raise children and take care of the house (Almobaireek and Manolova, 2013; Al-Riyami et al., 2010). Lack of family's appreciation and consideration of women's helpful role in entrepreneurship contribution (Al-Ghazali et al., 2013; Mathew, 2010) and socioeconomic development demotivate their orientation towards entrepreneurial activities (Almobaireek and Manolova, 2013). Self-fulfillment is one of the motivation drivers that create a sense of satisfaction. Kickul et al. (2009) contend that entrepreneurship provides the appropriate environment to achieve self-satisfaction through the management of the enterprise, the authority to make a decision, and the contribution to economic development. Researchers suggest that most small entrepreneurs in developing countries are motivated by their desire to survive in situations of limited employment opportunities (Rosa et al., 2008, Sultan, 2011), while in developed countries, entrepreneurs' motivation is to exploit an opportunity, innovate, and develop a venture (Al-Ghazali et al., 2013; Gitonga, 2017; Özsungur, 2019).

OMANI WOMEN FAILURE IN ENTREPRENEURSHIP

Entrepreneurship is a process that involves taking a risk in order to create a venture and explore and discover a new product or service (Kargwell, 2012 and Newell et al., 2015). Many factors are often involved in improving entrepreneurs' chances of success, such as government, financial institutions, education, and training institutions (Lihn and Bjørnskov, 2017b; Tarabar, 2018). Society culture and lack of adequate sources of finance restrict women's engagement in entrepreneurship (Lihn and Bjørnskov, 2017b; McElwee and Al-Riyami, 2003; Tamim et al., 2015). Women Entrepreneurs suffer from a lack of a network of entrepreneurial women. This disadvantage restricts sharing of knowledge between them and experience in the field of private business (DeGhetto et al., 2018; Kargwell, 2012). Tarabar (2018) contends that exchanging knowledge and discussing business issues are vital to entrepreneurs' success. Moreover, the lack of flexible procedures facilitated by government institutions, private sector, and financing institutions also play their part in restricting Omani women's engagement in entrepreneurship (Lihn and Bjørnskov, 2017b).

Tamim et al., (2015) argue that social support and encouragement are essential factors in motivating women to manage an enterprise and contribute positively to the economy and community while also taking care of their families (DeGhetto et al., 2018). Kargwell, (2012) explains that one of the essential difficulties challenging Omani women is interacting with men in the workplace, which goes against social tradition that expects women to be separated from men while at work (Lihn and Bjørnskov, 2017b). According to Al Shukaili et al. (2017), despite being beneficiaries of the government's loan support program, Omani women entrepreneurs' absence of formal education led to stagnation, regardless of their prior work experience or the other business training support received from the government. As explained above, Omani women's failure in entrepreneurship is attributed to obstacles related to their participation in the labor market (Campbell, 2012). Uneducated women or educated women with mismatching specialization lack the skills required to start up a business (Ali and Muthuraman, 2017; Matriano and Suguku, 2015; Sousa and Almeida, 2014). Research shows a mismatch between women's qualifications and the type of skills that entrepreneurship requires, which puts them at a disadvantage when financing their enterprises (Lihn and Bjørnskov, 2017b; McElwee and Al-Riyami, 2003; Tamim et al., 2015). Furthermore, Oman's conservative society demotivates Omani women by discouraging them from engagement in entrepreneurship (Al-Ghazali et al., 2013; Mathew, 2010).

CONCEPTUAL FRAMEWORK

As can be gleaned from the literature mentioned above, many factors impact entrepreneurial Omani women's ability to succeed in entrepreneurship. This can be summarized as follows: social perception, access to financial resources, and education qualification. Furthermore, entrepreneurial motivation tends to act as a mediating factor. We present the following conceptual framework as the basis for understanding this phenomenon. As illustrated below in Figure (1), the framework can be the basis for a future empirical study to test its validity.

Figure 1. Conceptual framework

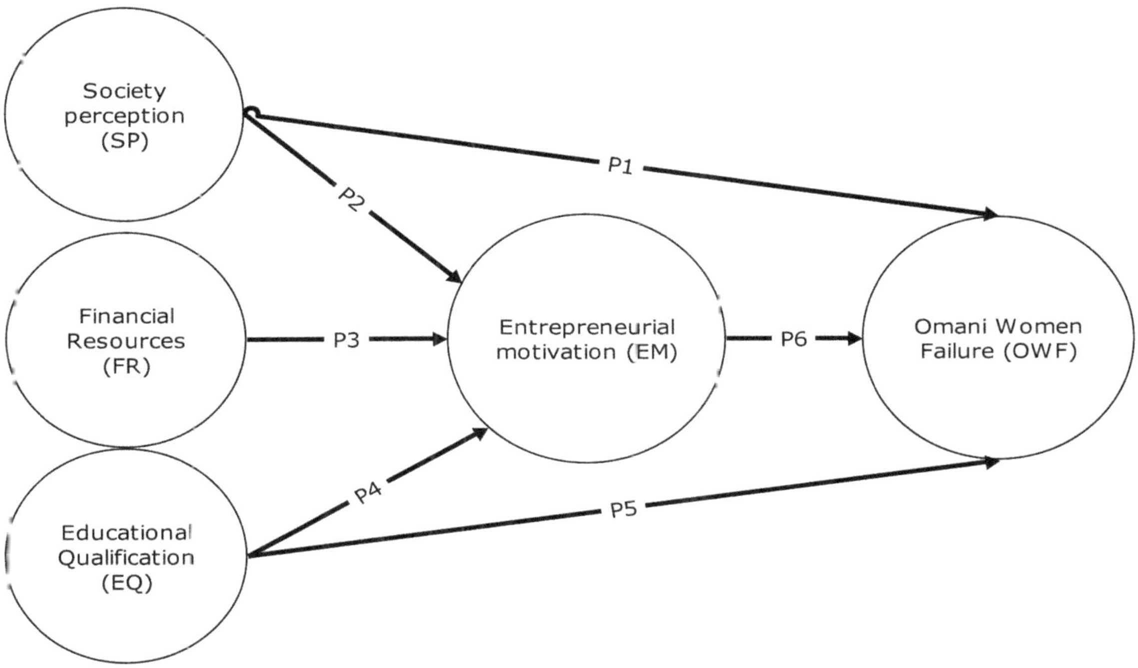

**S.P.: Society Perception; F.R.: Financial Resources; E.Q.: Education Qualification; EM: Entrepreneurial motivation; OWF: Omani Women Failure. Thus, research propositions are as follows:

- **P-1:** There is a positive relationship between social perception and Omani women's failure in entrepreneurship.
- **P-2:** There is a positive relationship between access to financial resources and Omani women's failure in entrepreneurship.
- **P-3:** There is a positive relationship between educational qualifications mismatch with job requirements and Omani women's failure in entrepreneurship.
- **P-4:** There is a positive relationship between entrepreneurial motivation and Omani women's failure in entrepreneurship.

CONCLUSION AND RECOMMENDATIONS

The Omani government has high hopes for the role that entrepreneurship in Oman can play in supporting the country's development plans to maintain sustainable economic growth. It has devoted plenty of resources and efforts to achieve that objective. However, Omani women's participation in entrepreneurship is limited by many challenges such as inadequate financial resources, lack of skills, and educational qualification mismatch with job requirements. This chapter highlights the key challenges that impede Omani women's success in entrepreneurship and limit their entrance to the SME market. Public and private sector institutions must provide the appropriate environment for Omani women to reduce the obstacles they face and succeed in their businesses. This chapter provides a road map to policymakers to embark on appropriate administrative regulations and laws to facilitate Omani women's involvement in entrepreneurship. Moreover, higher education institutes' cooperation is required by providing education that imparts relevant business skills to students to help with their entrepreneurial objectives and dreams.

LIMITATIONS AND SUGGESTIONS FOR FUTURE RESEARCH

This conceptual study paves the way for further research to enhance Omani women's role in entrepreneurship. Nevertheless, this chapter has its limitation, such as the absence of a methodology approach to collect data, limiting the ability to investigate the reliability of the studied concepts. Further research needs to be conducted to collect and analyze data that investigate the challenges facing Omani women's participation in entrepreneurship and to (possibly) include other variables in the conceptual framework. We recommend including women entrepreneurs in data collection to verify factors impeding them in starting up their own business in future research.

REFERENCES

Al-Abri, M. Y., Rahim, A. A., & Hussain, N. H. (2018). Entrepreneurial ecosystem: An exploration of the entrepreneurship model for SMEs in Sultanate of Oman. *Mediterranean Journal of Social Sciences*, *9*(6), 193–193. doi:10.2478/mjss-2018-0175

Al-Abri, M. Y., Rahim, A. A., & Hussain, N. H. (2018). Entrepreneurial ecosystem: An exploration of the entrepreneurship model for SMEs in Sultanate of Oman. *Mediterranean Journal of Social Sciences*, *9*(6), 193–193. doi:10.2478/mjss-2018-0175

Al Amri, S., Neelufer, A., & Christina, B. (2014). Challenges and barriers encountered by the SMEs owners in Muscat. *International Journal of Small Business and Entrepreneurship Research*, *2*(3), 1–13.

Al-Ani, W. (2017). Alternative education needs in Oman: Accommodating learning diversity and meeting market demand. *International Journal of Adolescence and Youth*, *22*(3), 322–336. doi:10.1080/02673843.2016.1179204

Al-Asfour, A., Tlaiss, H. A., Khan, S. A., & Rajasekar, J. (2017). Saudi women's work challenges and barriers to career advancement. *Career Development International*, *22*(2), 184–199. doi:10.1108/CDI-11-2016-0200

Al-Azri, A. K. H. (2016). *Academics', students', employers', and graduates' perceptions towards business management and administration undergraduate employability: implications for higher education and industry in Oman* (Doctoral dissertation). Brunel University London.

Al-Ghazali, B. M., Yusoff, R. M., & Sadi, M. A. (2013). Women entrepreneurs in Bahrain: Motivations and barriers. *Jurnal Teknologi*, *64*(2). Advance online publication. doi:10.11113/jt.v64.2251

Al-Riyami, R., Warren, L., & McElwee, G. (2002). Opportunities and challenges for Omani women entrepreneurs. *International Journal of Entrepreneurship and Innovation*, *3*(2), 133–144. doi:10.5367/000000002101299123

Al-Sadi, R., Belwal, R., & Al-Badi, R. (2011). Woman entrepreneurship in the Al-Batinah region of Oman: An identification of the barriers. *Journal of International Women's Studies*, *12*(3), 58–75.

Al-Shanfari, D. A. (2012). Entrepreneurship in Oman: A snapshot of the main challenges. *Proceedings of the United Nations Conference on Trade and Development: Multi-year expert meeting on enterprise development policies and capacity-building in science, technology, and innovation (STI).*

Al Shukaili, A. (2017). *Constraining Factors for Effective Entrepreneurship Policy Implementation in a Developing Economy: Evidence from Oman (Doctor of Philosophy).* University of Deusto.

Al Shukaili, A. (2018). *Entrepreneurship Policy for Transforming Local Contexts In A Developing Economy: Evidence From Oman*. Presented at the Majan International Conference 2018, Muscat, Oman.

Al Shukaili, A., Cucculelli, M., González-Pernía, J. L., & Legazkue, I. P. (2016). Government Loan Support and Entrepreneurship in A Developing Economy: The Context of Oman. In *ICSB World Conference Proceedings* (pp. 1-8). International Council for Small Business (ICSB).

Al Shukaili, A., Madanoglu, M., González-Pernía, J. L., & Legazkue, I. P. (2017). Entrepreneurship policy and stagnation of new ventures in the context of a developing economy (Interactive Paper). *Frontiers of Entrepreneurship Research*, *37*(14), 5.

Ali, Y., Nusair, M. M., Alani, F., Khan, F. R., & Al Badi, L. (2017). Employment in the private sector in Oman: Sector-based approach for localization. *Humanities & Social Sciences Reviews, 5*(1), 1-20.

AlMaimani, J., & Johari, F. B. (2015). Enhancing active participation of SMEs and Islamic Banks towards economic diversification in Oman. *Procedia Economics and Finance*, *31*, 677–688. doi:10.1016/S2212-5671(15)01156-9

Almobaireek, W. N., & Manolova, T. S. (2013). Entrepreneurial motivations among female university youth in Saudi Arabia. *Journal of Business Economics and Management*, *14*(sup1), S56-S75.

Anderson, B. B. (2015). World Journal of Entrepreneurship, Management, and Sustainable Development Corrupting activities and economic development Article information. *World Journal of Entrepreneurship, Management and Sustainable Development*, *11*(1), 64–70. doi:10.1108/WJEMSD-07-2014-0020

Arouri, H., Hossain, M., & Badrul Muttakin, M. (2014). Effects of the board and ownership structure on corporate performance: Evidence from GCC countries. *Journal of Accounting in Emerging Economies*, *4*(1), 117–130. doi:10.1108/JAEE-02-2012-0007

Ayyagari, M., Demirguc-kunt, A., & Maksimovic, V. (2014). Who creates jobs in developing countries? *Small Business Economics*, *43*(1), 75–99. doi:10.100711187-014-9549-5

Bade, M. (2018). Bargaining over crowdfunding benefits. *J. Entrep. Public Policy*, *7*, 166–177.

Barba-Sánchez, V., & Atienza-Sahuquillo, C. (2018). Entrepreneurial intention among engineering students: The role of entrepreneurship education. *European Research on Management and Business Economics*, *24*(1), 53–61. doi:10.1016/j.iedeen.2017.04.001

Belwal, R., Al Balushi, H., & Belwal, S. (2015). Students' perception of entrepreneurship and enterprise education in Oman. *Education + Training*, *57*(8/9), 924–947. doi:10.1108/ET-12-2014-0149

Belwal, S., & Belwal, R. (2014). Work-life balance, family-friendly policies and quality of work-life issues: Studying employers' perspectives of working women in Oman. *Journal of International Women's Studies*, *15*(1), 96–117.

Belwal, S., Belwal, R., & Saidi, F. A. (2014). Characteristics, motivations, and challenges of women entrepreneurs in Oman's Al-Dhahira region. *Journal of Middle East Women's Studies*, *10*(2), 135–151. doi:10.2979/jmiddeastwomstud.10.2.135

Bennett, J. (2010). Informal firms in developing countries: Entrepreneurial stepping stone or consolation prize? *Small Business Economics*, *34*(1), 53–63. doi:10.100711187-009-9194-6

Brixiova, Z. (2013). Modeling productive entrepreneurship in developing countries. *Small Business Economics*, *41*(1), 183–194. doi:10.100711187-011-9410-z

Brush, C. G. A., de Bruin, A., & Welter, F. (2009). A Gender-Aware Framework for Women's Entrepreneurship. *International Journal of Gender and Entrepreneurship*, *1*(1), 8–24. doi:10.1108/17566260910942318

Campbell, N., & Mitchell, D. T. (2012). A (partial) review of entrepreneurship literature across disciplines. *Journal of Entrepreneurship and Public Policy*, *1*(2), 183–199. doi:10.1108/20452101211261453

DeGhetto, K., Sutton, T., & Zorn, M. L. (2018). Institutional drivers of born-public ventures. *Journal of Entrepreneurship and Public Policy*, *7*(1), 14–33. doi:10.1108/JEPP-D-17-00012

El HamidiF. (2017). Women Entrepreneurs in the MENA Region: Opportunities or a Mirage? Ssrn. doi:10.2139/ssrn.3060881

Environment, T. E., & Enterprises, S. (2016). *Access To Financial Resources - The Enabling Environment for*. Suzana Radulovic.

Evetts, J. (1998). Managing the technology but not the organization: Women and career in engineering. *Women in Management Review*, *13*(8), 283–290. doi:10.1108/09649429810243144

Farzanegan, M. R. (2014). Can oil-rich countries encourage entrepreneurship? *Entrepreneurship and Regional Development*, *26*(9-10), 706–725. doi:10.1080/08985626.2014.981869

Friedman, A. (2011). Perception : A Cognitive Sociological Approach. *Social Cognition*, 1–23.

Gitonga, A. N. (2017). *Factors influencing entrepreneurial motivation on university student's intentions of becoming entrepreneurs: A case of United States International University–Africa (USIU-A)* (Doctoral dissertation). United States International University-Africa.

González-Pernía, J. L., Jung, A., & Peña, I. (2015). Innovation-driven entrepreneurship in developing economies. *Entrepreneurship and Regional Development*, *27*(9-10), 555–573. doi:10.1080/08985626.2015.1075602

Hicks, M., & Faulk, D. G. (2018). Do entrepreneur-focused facility incentives create economic impacts? Evidence from Indiana. *Journal of Entrepreneurship and Public Policy*, *7*(3), 222–234. doi:10.1108/JEPP-D-18-00013

Hmedat, W., Ali, M., & Muthuraman, B. (2017). A Study on Entrepreneurial Initiatives among MBA Students in Sultanate of Oman. *International Journal of Management, Innovation & Entrepreneurial Research, 3*(2).

Hu, Q., Kapucu, N., & O'Byrne, L. (2014). Strategic planning for community-based small nonprofit organizations: Implementation, benefits, and challenges. *The Journal of Applied Management and Entrepreneurship, 19*(1), 83–101. doi:10.9774/GLEAF.3709.2014.ja.00007

Huang, K. H., Mas-Tur, A., & Yu, T. H. K. (2012). Factors affecting the success of women entrepreneurs. *The International Entrepreneurship and Management Journal, 8*(4), 487–497. doi:10.100711365-012-0233-4

Ismail, I., Husin, N., Rahim, N. A., Kamal, M. H. M., & Mat, R. C. (2016). Entrepreneurial success among single mothers: The role of motivation and passion. *Procedia Economics and Finance, 37*, 121–128. doi:10.1016/S2212-5671(16)30102-2

Kargwell, S. A. (2012). Women entrepreneurs breaking through: Push and pull within UAE cultural context. *International Journal of Business and Social Science, 3*(17).

Kennedy, K. (2016). Employee Job Satisfaction and Engagement: Revitalizing a Changing Workforce. A research report by The Society for Human Resource Management.

Khan, S. A., Ghosh, A. P., & Myers, D. A. (2005). Women entrepreneurship in Oman. *Proceedings of 50th World Conference of the International Council for the Small Business (ICSB),* 15–18.

Kickul, J., Gundry, L. K., Barbosa, S. D., & Whitcanack, L. (2009). Intuition versus analysis? Testing differential models of cognitive style on entrepreneurial self–efficacy and the new venture creation process. *Entrepreneurship Theory and Practice, 33*(2), 439–453. doi:10.1111/j.1540-6520.2009.00298.x

Levitsky, J. (1997). SME guarantee schemes: A summary. *Financier-Burr Ridge, 4*, 5–11.

Lihn, J., & Bjørnskov, C. (2017). Economic freedom and veto players jointly affect entrepreneurship. *Journal of Entrepreneurship and Public Policy, 6*(3), 340–358. doi:10.1108/JEPP-D-17-00007

Magd, H. A., & McCoy, M. P. (2014). Entrepreneurship in Oman: Paving the way for a sustainable future. *Procedia Economics and Finance, 15*, 1632–1640. doi:10.1016/S2212-5671(14)00634-0

Mashood, N., Verhoeven, H., & Chansarkar, B. (2009). Emiratisation, Omanisation and Saudisation–common causes: common solutions. In *10th International Business Research Conference, Dubai, UAE* (pp. 1-12). Academic Press.

Mathew, V. (2010). Women entrepreneurship in the Middle East: Understanding barriers and use of ICT for entrepreneurship development. *The International Entrepreneurship and Management Journal, 6*(2), 163–181. doi:10.100711365-010-0144-1

Matriano, M. T., & Suguku, D. (2015). Entrepreneurship Growth in Oman: Position, Prospects, and Growth of Entrepreneurial Education. *International E-Journal of Advances in Education, 1*(2), 127–131. doi:10.18768/ijaedu.58791

McElwee, G., & Al-Riyami, R. (2003). Women entrepreneurs in Oman: Some barriers to success. *Career Development International*, *8*(7), 339–346. doi:10.1108/13620430310505296

Millennium Research Group. (2000). Annual industry report. *Implant Dentistry*, *9*, 192–194. doi:10.1097/00008505-200009030-00003

Mohammed, S., Uddin, M. A., & Ahmad, M. (2016). Factors affecting entrepreneur's development in Oman. *Corporate Ownership and Control*, *13*(2), 66–70. doi:10.22495/cocv13i2p7

Mthanti, T., & Ojah, K. (2018). Institutions, human capital, and entrepreneurial orientation: Implications for growth policy. *J. Entrep. Public Policy*, *7*(2), 135–160. doi:10.1108/JEPP-D-18-00002

Naguib, R., & Jamali, D. (2015). Female entrepreneurship in the UAE: A multi-level integrative lens. *Gender in Management*, *30*(2), 135–161. doi:10.1108/GM-12-2013-0142

Narayanasamy, K., Rasiah, D., & Jacobs, C. J. (2011). An empirical study of factors influencing gender differences in entrepreneurship. *International Business & Economics Research Journal*, *10*(10), 17–30. doi:10.19030/iber.v10i10.5976

Newell, G. D., & Holian, M. J. (2017). An agent-based model of entrepreneurship: Examining the role of alertness and transaction costs. *Journal of Entrepreneurship and Public Policy*, *6*(2), 259–270. doi:10.1108/JEPP-01-2015-0003

Özsungur, F. (2019, May). Research on women's entrepreneurship motivation: Sample of Adana Province. *Women's Studies International Forum*, *74*, 114–126. doi:10.1016/j.wsif.2019.03.006

Panda, S. (2018). Constraints faced by women entrepreneurs in developing countries: Review and ranking. *Gender in Management*, *33*(4), 315–331. doi:10.1108/GM-01-2017-0003

Payne, J. E., & Mervar, A. (2017). The entrepreneurship-unemployment nexus in Croatia. *Journal of Entrepreneurship and Public Policy*, *6*(3), 375–384. doi:10.1108/JEPP-D-17-00013

Pistrui, D., & Fahed-Sreih, J. (2010). Islam, entrepreneurship, and business values in the Middle East. *International Journal of Entrepreneurship and Innovation Management*, *12*(1), 107–118. doi:10.1504/IJEIM.2010.033170

Quatraro, F., & Vivarelli, M. (2015). Drivers of entrepreneurship and post-entry performance of newborn firms in developing countries. *The World Bank Research Observer*, *30*(2), 277–305. doi:10.1093/wbro/lku012

Radwan, D. M. (2014). *Education for employment: Omani graduates' perspective toward the 'work readiness' competencies needed in the labour market* (Doctoral dissertation). The British University in Dubai (BUiD).

Riyada Annual Report. (2017). *Public Authority for SME Development (Riyad) Annual Report 2017*. Academic Press.

Report, R. A. (2018). Public Authority for SME Development (Riyada) Annual Report 2018. Academic Press.

Report, R. M. (2018). *Mapping The SME Ecosystem in Oman 2018. Public Authority for SME Development*. Riyada.

Reynolds, P. D., Bygrave, W. D., Autio, E., Cox, L. W., & Hay, M. (2004). *Global entrepreneurship monitor 2003. Executive Report, Babson College/Ewing Marion Kauffman Foundation*. London Business School.

Rosa, P., Kodithuwakku, S. S., & Balunywa, W. (2006, December). Entrepreneurial motivation in developing countries: what does' necessity'and'opportunity'entrepreneurship really mean? *Babson College Entrepreneurship Research Conference (BCERC).*

Sarmento, M. F. P. G. M. (2016). Predicting entrepreneurial motivation among university students: The role of entrepreneurship education. *Education + Training*, *58*(7/8), 861–881.

Schneider, K. (2017). Entrepreneurial competencies of women entrepreneurs of micro and small enterprises. *Science Journal of Education*, *5*(6), 252–261. doi:10.11648/j.sjedu.20170506.14

Shukaili, A. A., Cucculelli, M., González-Pernía, J. L., & Legazkue, I. P. (2018). Entrepreneurship policy to overcome barriers to new firm growth in a developing economy: Evidence from Oman. *International Journal of Entrepreneurship and Small Business*, *35*(4), 511–537. doi:10.1504/IJESB.2018.096173

Sousa, M. J., & Almeida, M. do R. (2014). Entrepreneurial Skills Development. *6th Int. Conf. Appl. Econ. Business Dev.*, 135–138.

Sultan, N. (2011). Making a Difference in a Troubled Country: The Case of Entrepreneurial and Female Leadership in Yemen. *Leadership Development in the Middle East*, 297-327.

Tamim, M., Foisal, M., & Sagar, A. H. (2015). Factors Affecting the Women Entrepreneurship Development in Small and Medium Enterprises (SME) in Bangladesh- An Evaluative Study. *European Journal of Business and Management*, *7*, 153–161.

Taqi, N. (2016). *The Challenges Facing Women Entrepreneurs : A Study On Gulf Cooperation Council (GCC) Countries Evidence from the Kingdom of Bahrain, United Arab Emirates, and Saudi Arabia* (PhD thesis). Najma Taqi.

Tarabar, D. (2018). Regional integration and entrepreneurship: Evidence from European Union. *J. Entrep. Public Policy*, *7*(2), 117–134. doi:10.1108/JEPP-D-18-00003

Tlaiss, H. (2015). Islamic work-related values and entrepreneurship: Evidence from the Middle East. *Journal of Business Ethics*, *129*(4), 859–877. doi:10.100710551-014-2138-3

World Bank. (2014). *World Development Indicators*. Author.

Yi, S., & Duval-Couetil, N. (2018). What drives engineering students to be entrepreneurs? Evidence of validity for an entrepreneurial motivation scale. *Journal of Engineering Education*, *107*(2), 291–317. doi:10.1002/jee.20199

Youngberg, D. (2017). Using predictive decision-making to implement technology prizes. *Journal of Entrepreneurship and Public Policy*, *6*(3), 274–289. doi:10.1108/JEPP-D-17-00004

Zeidan, S., & Bahrami, S. (2011). Women entrepreneurship in GCC: A framework to address challenges and promote participation in a regional context. *International Journal of Business and Social Science*, *2*(14), 100–107.

Chapter 17
Unlock the Next Level of Green:
GREEFE for Organizational Sustainable Innovation

Ying Ying Tiong
Curtin University, Malaysia

ABSTRACT

This study aims to encourage organisational "safeness" during and after the pandemic by integrating green practices and a safe approach for sustainable innovation. The hotel industry was referred considering (1) the COVID-19 pandemic had a significant impact on the industry, (2) safe stay is the current trend which is expected will persist for an extended period, and (3) hotel environmental friendliness is a competitive advantage. The pandemic has redirected customer attention away from hotel features and onto the "safest" hotel that is practically Coronavirus-free. While recognising the negative environmental impact created by the industry, this research proposed a GREEFE framework to connect the fundamental elements of hotel marketing (green marketing mix: green products, green price, green promotion, and green place) with safety measures. The systematic review supported that green is associated with being clean and safe. Therefore, the hoteliers are recommended to ensure a safe hotel stay by going green during and after the pandemic.

THE ISSUES

Environmental deterioration is a persistent problem and one of the most pressing challenges in the world, since it cannot be completely resolved despite several attempts at solutions. According to the prior research, the environmental problem in Malaysia has recorded a long history (Khalil, Husin, Mahat and Nasir, 2011). It began a century ago when the tin mining industry had just started, and the problems expanded when the nation penetrated the other sectors. Later, as reported by the Ministry of Environment in 1996, the environmental issues worsen when the government shifted the nation's core of economic development to Industrialisation. Even though these sectors brought in many benefits such as more new jobs, greater opportunities for foreign investment, and improved economic growth, the environmental problem that caused almost all types of pollution is the downside of industrialisation. Consequently, the

DOI: 10.4018/978-1-7998-9590-9.ch017

country faces a difficult situation, as reconciling environmental sustainability and economic growth is practically impossible.

Remedies to the problem were offered along with the environmental problems. The Malaysian government recognized the environmental components long ago, in early 1976 (Hezri and Nordin, 2006). The implementation of environmental policies, on the other hand, has been significantly delayed. There was no particular policy in place until 2009, when the notion of environmental sustainability was restored and enhanced in the National Green Technology Policy (Borhan and Ahmad, 2012). In particular to the green hotel development in Malaysia, the industry is undoubtedly not maintaining its infancy stage, but it is still a long way from maturity. It is ironic when there are only 24 rated green hotels and resorts recorded throughout Malaysia to date (Ministry of Tourism, Arts and Culture Malaysia, 2021). Other hotels are unrated, and some claim themselves as environmentally friendly hotel without being rated or certified. This number is particularly intolerable since Malaysia promotes eco-tourism and receives more than 28 million tourists per year (Malaysia Tourism, 2021).

This alert-less behaviour of the industry requires attention as the environmental behaviour and the trend of travel green is on the rise. However, the previous researchers explained that this phenomenon as a burden to firms is deemed understandable. Most of the hotel firms in Malaysia found attempts of transforming into the green firm as an additional cost to the organisation (Zeenat and Mariam, 2014). The green investment requiring green purchasing equipment, technology acquisition, and skilled human resources are additional costs (Eneizan et al., 2016). The other researchers further argued the outcomes of hotel's green practice as unable to guarantee environmental ramifications as expected (Longoni and Caliano, 2018) despite the initiative of the hotel in practising green to reduce the environmental degradation is always plausible (Inman and Green, 2018; Hartman and Vachon, 2018). These criticisms contradict the main stream studies (Bokolo et al., 2018; Chen et al., 2018; Molina-Azorin et al., 2015), where the capabilities of green hotel practices are being doubted.

However, there are also other group of Hoteliers who are actively going green to protect the environment whilst tackling green market opportunities. They realised that the value of being green is not limited to satisfying market demand, but also to obtaining cost savings and, in the long term, addressing the environmental problem through resource efficiency. The organization's environmentally friendly strategy allows for more efficient manufacturing and the elimination of needless operating expenditures, which saves money for businesses (Bokolo et al., 2018; Chen et al., 2018; Molina-Azorin et al., 2015). Thus, this logic supports the assumption that that waste reduction has resulted in cost savings, which has reduced environmental problems both directly and indirectly. According to Klassen and Mclaughlin (1996), firms concerned about reducing the negative environmental impacts of their production processes can expand their business and stay competitive.

Aside from that, the consumer attitude towards green has gradually gone beyond the environmental value to associate it with the benefit of human health (Xu, Wang and Yu, 2020; Alhosseini Tabataba'i-Nasab et al., 2019). As a result of greater public awareness of the environmental situation, a "buy green" movement has also evolved. Consumers' preferences are evolving toward greener products and services, and they are willing to pay a premium for green products and services (Costa, Montemurro and Giuliani, 2018). This is also applicable to travellers who have a high degree of environmental behavioural intention that they are more likely to pay for their hotel stay or return to the same hotel. They are also more inclined to spread good word of mouth about the hotel's outstanding environmental performance and recommend it to their friends and family (Namkung and Jang, 2007).

However, following the initial outbreak of COVID-19, the whole hotel industry has altered its attention. Di Marco et al. (2020) have suggested pandemic risk to be taken into account for environmentally sustainable development. The suggestion was made mainly to measure human's heath along with the consideration of a devastating economic situation. The pandemic had indeed put global businesses in a very challenging position. There is a need to include the social dimension in the business recovery measure as one of the essential criteria. It was reported that the practice of social distancing and isolation that is essential to be implemented during the pandemic had indeed weakened the wellbeing of a particular group of people and led to long term consequences (Veira et al., 2020). Many people have felt under extreme stress levels towards anxiety (Roy et al., 2020), in which the heightened stress level will not be diminished with the recovery of a crisis (Veira et al., 2020). Such pandemic fallout is expected to impact the tourism industry even after the pandemic negatively.

The top resolution that can assure greenness and cleanliness should be "safety-related" measures. It is not only the "entry-requirements" that travellers must choose, but it is also an essential element for the hotel's internal operation to shape employee safety behaviour (for example, compliance, participation, and adaptation); belief restoration partially mediated the influence of safety leadership on safety behaviour (Zhang et al., 2020). With the increased knowledge of the importance of safety, it is not uncommon for the world to have the same concern for hotel stay following the pandemic, with all forms of safety measures among the most popular. To name a few, there is the "Health and Safety Pledge" (Radisson Hotels), "Shangri-La Cares" (Shang-La Hotels), "Hilton Travel Flexibility and Safety Standards" (Hilton Hotels), "Covid-19: Stay Safe with Avani" (Avani Hotels), "Commitment to Clean" (Marriot International) and so on. The tourism industry needs people to travel with less hesitation, even only via the assurance of peace of mind (Tourism Malaysia, 2020).

With an emphasis on environmental protection and sustainability, the author propose a review of hotels' green marketing approaches; safety measures; and their integration as sustainable innovations during and after COVID-19. The literature review are provided in the following sections.

SUSTAINABLE INNOVATION I: GREENING THE FUNDAMENTAL "PS"

"P" has long been associated with the marketing mix, making it seem "market-oriented" and "marketing-related". In fact, each P denotes a distinct component of an organisation over which a company has some level of control. These components are essential given their purpose in keeping a firm's operation running, which is a significant enhancer to satisfying the consumer who may be a repeat customer or those who are possibly creating a long-term relationship (Brown et al., 1991). Typically, P was classified into four components: product, pricing, location of distribution, and promotion, known as the marketing mix (McCarthy, 1960). The four Ps are a collection of controlled marketing variables that organisations may use to elicit desired responses from their target market (Kotler and Armstrong, 1989). However, "P" does not have a fixed meaning and could be represented, or "Ps", on the other hand, does not have a defined meaning and could be represented and substituted by any P.

Likewise, there is no specific meaning assigned to green Ps in the context of green, leaving it with boundless possibility. Researchers often developed a new definition by putting environmental meaning into the marketing mix to make it sound more environmentally friendly. Bradley (1989), who presented a checklist with four additional marketing mix components, including the package, advertising, sales force, and after-sales service, in addition to the four Ps components previously mentioned, may have been the first to establish the green marketing mix concept in the 1980s. However, the marketing mix he had proposed did not fully embrace the notion of all Ps. A later study by Ginsberg and Bloom (2004) blended environmental concepts into an organisation's Ps and limited the focus to the four primary Ps - product, price, promotion, and place - and identified these "Ps" as organisational strategies.

Why does green Ps matter? The environmental crisis has progressively shifted consumers' consumption patterns from unsustainable to sustainable (Kumar, Kumar, Rahman et al., 2011). It was a critical decision for the organisation to embrace Ps in environmentally friendly ways because the customers' mental images could alter due to the greened Ps image (Hashem and Al-Rifai, 2011). Considering consumer preference is generally linked to a brand's image, incorporating environmental elements within the Ps increases customer perception. Consumers, for example, are more inclined to buy from a business that strives to protect the environment than those that do not express anything about the environment (Sudalakshmi and Chinnadorai, 2014). Aside from that, implementing green "Ps" may help a company maintain its reputation and achieve a competitive edge through cost-cutting, employee satisfaction, waste reduction, and social welfare (Kumar et al., 2011).

Another question is, would an organisation achieve its objective of developing an environmentally friendly image without using green for its Ps? The answer is no, at least for the environmental-oriented organisations. Environmental orientation, according to the researchers, has no favourable effect on an organisation's competitive advantage through green image until the firm implements a green Ps strategy (Rahmawati et al., 2014). In general, the green Ps strategy directly impacts the growth of market share (Abzari et al., 2013) and the firm's financial performance (Constantinos et al., 2012). For instance, green products and distribution strategies positively impact business product market performance. Green pricing and promotion strategies, on the other hand, are directly related to a company's return on assets. By emphasising a firm base for the business, the fundamental marketing mix - 4Ps that are directly related to the business's operation are highlighted.

The Sneak Peek into Green Ps: The Fundamental of Marketing Mix

Green Products: The term "green product" refers to goods or services offered to the market with the most negligible negative impact on the environment. Green products are those products that use the fewest natural resources, do no harm or contamination to the environment, and the products are recyclable and conservable (Shamdasani, Lin and Richmond, 1993). The core premise of green products is recyclable and conservable. However, it might only be in a limited sense. Prakash (2002) brought the six Rs principles to the manufacturing line, including repaired, reconditioned, remanufactured, reused, recycled, and reduced to provide a clear vision of green products. Green products are typically made in several methods, including remanufacturing from recycled materials or simple reuse. These products are credited with preserving natural resources effectively, which in the meantime is money-saving (Eneizan and Wahad, 2016).

In light of this, green products should be manufactured so that efficient raw material consumption is achieved, particularly for non-renewable elements (Bradley, 2007). Alternatively, it should conserve natural resources to guarantee that the manufacturing process causes the least amount of environmental damage (Eneizan and Wahab, 2016). Given the significance of product features and physical appearance in influencing consumer preferences (Peter and Bonnelley, 2015), green product quality should meet, if not exceed, customer expectations (Larashati et al., 2012). Additionally, government intervention has an essential effect on green consumer attitudes. According to a prior study, positive consumer attitudes about green products are influenced mainly by government support, which the green consumers see as the government's role in environmental preservation (Tan and Lau, 2010).

Green Price: As reflected by its name, Green price is designed to charge environmentally friendly products. Products had been customised into environmentally friendly ways to lessen the negative influence on the environment. By investigating the value of green pricing, researchers described it as bringing better value to both consumers and organisations (Martin and Schouten, 2012). The researchers also suggested weighting both economic and non-economic of the environmental cost of production. Green pricing has two negative aspects: premium pricing and decreased pricing. Going green is expensive due to higher expenditures of technology acquisition, equipment, additional staff, and the external element for the green conversion (Eneizan et al., 2016). Green production occasionally needs innovation. Therefore, organisations sometimes charge a premium for the new market segment (Porter and Linde, 1995).

Price is a dynamic variable closely linked to customer behavior. The consumer's actual behaviour may not require him or her to pay for the green product (Solaiman et al., 2015). When consumers are aware of the pricing offered by alternative products that are comparably less expensive than the green product offer, the price disparity that leads to attitude and behaviour becomes more prominent (Kumar and Rohtak, 2014). Nevertheless, consumers will pay extra if green products provide added value that other alternatives cannot be obtained or substituted. It says that green pricing is not a complete failure of marketing strategy. Green products with high environmental value at a premium price will continue to be consumers' first choice. As a result, green pricing, which charges based on the value of green products will benefit organisational performance as it grows the return on assets (Leonidou et al, 2013).

Green Promotion: Promotion in a green way is regarded as transmitting crucial environmental information to consumers, which necessitates changes in goods, processes, and organisational focuses that create meaningful linkages to business operations (Solaiman et al, 2015). In short, green promotion comprises all of the methods that may be utilized to inform the market about its offerings through promotional tools such as advertising, publicity, public relations, and other activities (Chan, 2013). Firms should transparently transmit the green message through promotional activities to be accurately translated into green consumers' minds and enhance the firm's image. As a result, advertising is critical to the organisation, primarily if the organisation has invested money in environmental protection or green products (Kumar and Rohtak, 2014).

Incorporation of tools and techniques such as green advertising (Maulani, 2015), eco-labelling (Zuhairah and Noor, 2015; Chan, 2013), green sponsorship (Nadini and Deshpande, 2011), sales promotion, public relation activityinto the communication of green product has been highly recommended to enhance firm's image (Chan, 2013; Rex and Baumann, 2007). These promotional tools have a lot in common when it comes to promoting ways to lessen the negative influence on the environment. For example, rather than focusing on the green content, the green advertisement should advertise in a greener way, such as using recycled paper for the brochure advertisement (Maulani, 2015). In terms of green labelling, numerous researchers have highlighted the ISO14001 certification as firm labelling to embrace the green agenda improving green image (Zuhairah and Noor, 2015; Chan, 2013).

Green Place: The term "green place" refers to an environmentally friendly place or distribution that focuses on reducing environmental deterioration to reduce carbon footprint (Leonidou et al., 2013; Abzari et al., 2013; Hashem and Al-Rifai, 2011). Aside from environmental efficiency, one of the goals of green distribution is to present a green image (Kumar and Rohtak, 2014). It has been defined as an appropriate gateway to handle green products for the customer, including delivery facilitation and cycling procedures assurance in an environmentally friendly way (Hashem and Al-Rifai, 2011). Other research emphasised the safety of transportation of goods to reduce the possible harm to the environment. Therefore, green distribution is also defined as the channel selected to reduce the damage caused to the environment (Arseculeratne and Yazdanifard, 2014).

SUSTAINABLE INNOVATION II: SAFETY MEASURES

The hotel industry due to its dynamic is one of the most challenging industries. Simply put, lodging as the key elements for the tourism sector has a wide range of alternatives, whereby one alternative itself has arrays of options available in the market. Even worse, the industry is getting fragile when the high-contextuality of the tourism sector requires individual involvement throughout the service delivery process, which is easily influenced by peoples and incidents take place within or even beyond its geographical boundaries. For instance, the terrorist attacks at New York, London or Thailand; natural disaster such as Indian Ocean Tsunami; to the recent contagious disease like Influenza A (H1N1), Ebola epidemic and COVID-19 pandemic had hit the tourism market hard with travel risk, either in real or perception (Neuburger and Egger, 2020), disrupted the tourism sector worldwide.

Drawing particular attention to the most recent COVID-19 pandemic, the lockdowns at almost all countries in the world have seriously curbed tourism growth. Although many people would still expect to travel as planned without any action being taken on their vacation booked, and a small number of people claimed that they will continue their vacation plan as schedule (Kourgiantakis et al., 2020), individual's willingness to travel has indeed been budged during and after the pandemic. Health and safety will remain the top priority for travelling decision during and after the pandemic. Most of the hoteliers in the world had started promoting 'travel in safe' striving for '*safecation*' to promise visit made cleared for safe. Health and safety are expected will remain the top priority for travelling decision during and after the pandemic. As a way forward, most of the hoteliers had started promoting 'travel in safe' striving for 'safecation' to make all visits cleared for safe (Travelocity, 2020).

Safe in this context apply to 'clean' or 'hygiene' as part of the requirement of *safecation*. Malaysia Association of Hotels (MAH) has launched a 'Clean and Safe' certification program to attest the safe working guideline of hotels employees through a clear approach across a hotel's servicescape and work to meet the regulatory standards and guidelines of the World Health Organization (WHO) to improve hotel's hygiene and safety standard (MAH, 2020). Likewise, the Portugal National Tourist Authority had established 'Clean and Safe' seal of approval to provide cleanliness protocols in maintaining effective hygiene measure and to distinguish 'Clean and Safe' tourism activities for the prevention of COVID-19 infectious disease (Turismo DE Portugal, 2020). These programmes are expected will boost the travellers' confidence to travel again with the physical safety and peace of mind assured (Tourism Malaysia, 2020).

Since the COVID-19 outbreak, the Top Hotel brands in the world, as ranked by Brand Directory (2021), have made safety the top priority of their business operations. Each of the hotels have designed its very own safety campaign, the top 3 hotel brands in the world, for instance:

Example 1: Hilton

Hyatt has the following campaign on Hilton ClaenStay as their strategy to attract more travellers during and after the pandemic, as adopted from https://www.hilton.com/en/p/what-to-expect/:

We've taken additional measures beyond our industry-leading cleaning standards by partnering with Reckitt, maker of Lysol & Dettol, to develop our Hilton CleanStay program. This innovative program builds upon our already rigorous cleaning standards by providing enhanced training for Team Members, increased cleaning of public areas and adjusted food & beverage service, to ensure our guests enjoy a worry-free stay.

Using the same quality brands you trust in your home, Hilton CleanStay builds on our already rigorous cleaning standards to provide complete peace of mind when you stay with any of Hilton's 18 brands.

Our promise to you is to deliver the same level of reliable and friendly service you'd expect from Hilton, but with the added confidence of industry-leading hygiene practices created to keep you safe.

Figure 1 below illustrates the screenshot of Hilton Hotels CleanStay, a cleaner stay from check in to check out campaign.

Figure 1. Screenshot of Hilton CleanStay

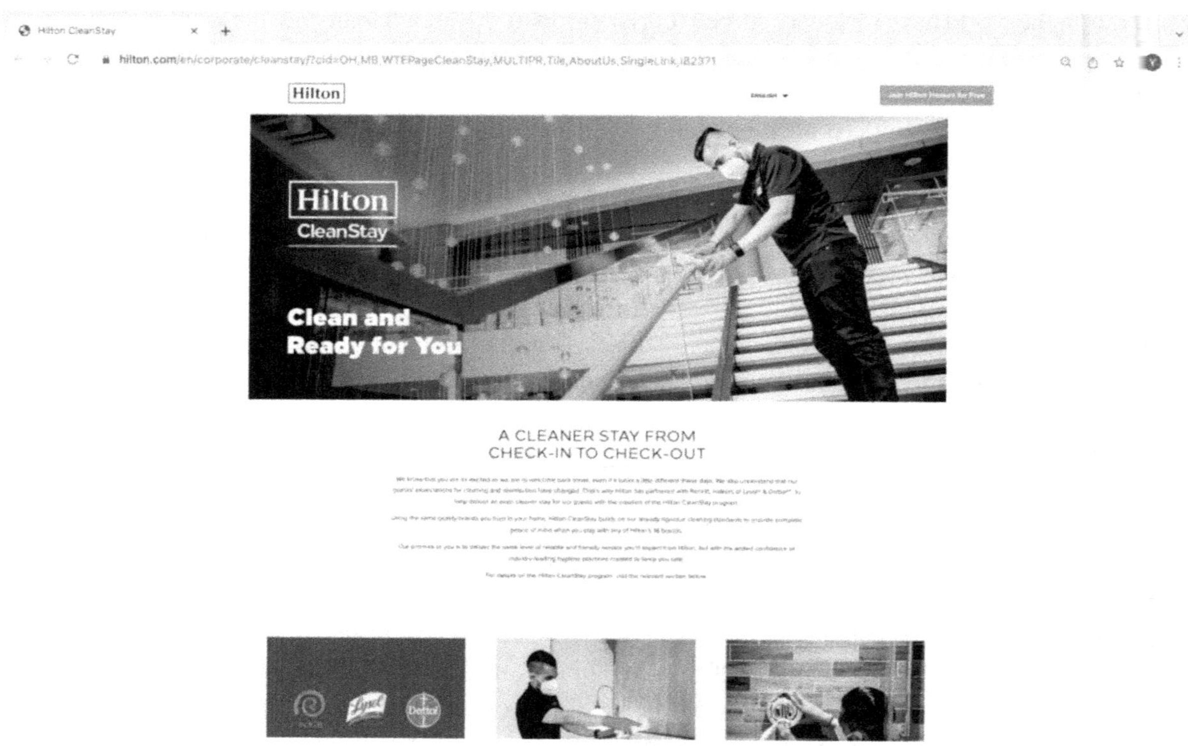

Example 2: Hyatt

As adopted from https://www.hyatt.com/info/care-and-cleanliness-americas, Hyatt has the following campaign on their safety first, wellbeing always as part of their pandemic recovery plan: *"One of our highest priorities for welcoming guests and colleagues back to Hyatt properties is doing it safely, with your wellbeing in mind. Guided by our purpose of care and experience delivering world-class hospitality for more than 60 years, Hyatt's Global Care & Cleanliness Commitment builds on our existing rigorous safety and cleanliness protocols and includes:*

GBAC STARTM cleanliness and training accreditation process through the Global Biorisk Advisory Council (GBAC) at all Hyatt hotels. Trained Hygiene & Wellbeing Leader or team at all locations, responsible for their hotel adhering to new operational protocols and training. Cross-functional panel of trusted medical and industry advisors—including experts from Cleveland Clinic—to help us fine-tune safety protocols and consider various aspects of the entire hotel experience.

As we welcome you back, you can have peace of mind knowing we are taking precautionary measures across Hyatt hotels worldwide in an effort to maintain a safe environment for our guests, customers and colleagues. Due to COVID-19, some locations may have travel restrictions in place including national, local and health advisories and requirements. Learn more.

Specifically, here are some enhanced cleanliness and wellbeing measures that you will see and experience at Hyatt hotels in the Americas:*

- *Cleaning & Sanitization*
- *Temperature & Wellbeing Checks*
- *Hand Hygiene & Social Distancing*
- *Masks & Gloves*

At all Hyatt hotels in the U.S., guests who are unvaccinated are required to wear face masks or coverings in hotel indoor public areas, as well as outdoors where social distancing is not feasible (with some limited exceptions). Hotel colleagues who are not vaccinated are still required to wear face masks indoors and outdoors.

All hotels are required to follow state and local requirements, if stricter than Hyatt's recommended guidance. In light of the latest CDC guidance, Hyatt requests that fully vaccinated guests and colleagues wear face coverings in hotel indoor public areas at Hyatt hotels in the U.S. that are located in counties with substantial or high COVID-19 transmission rates, as designated by the CDC. Learn more about CDC transmission rate designations here. Guests are encouraged to contact their hotel directly to learn more about specific safety mandates and travel restrictions that may be in place at their hotel. Guests with questions regarding their reservations or upcoming stay may contact a Hyatt Global Contact Center.

In all other countries across the Americas region, all guests are still required to wear face masks or coverings in hotel indoor public areas and when moving around in outdoor areas (with some limited exceptions). For more details and specific requirements, guests may visit our COVID-19 Travel Updates page, contact their hotel directly, or visit the hotel website. Hyatt colleagues are required to wear face masks or coverings, as well as additional personal protective equipment based on job specifications. From front desk associates to housekeeping, spa therapists and kitchen staff, colleagues are trained on the importance of wearing protective gear and are taking additional safety precautions for guests and each other.

Knock and Go Room Service

To promote safety for our guests and colleagues, all room service orders will be delivered to the door, unless otherwise indicated by the hotel. To minimize contact, our colleagues will knock on your door or ring your doorbell to notify you upon the delivery of your order. At some properties, grab-and-go options will be available.

Food Safety Protocols

Our teams are implementing precautionary measures starting with food preparation to set-up and service, and enhancing food safety and hygiene protocols for restaurants, room service, and group meetings and events. We are frequently disinfecting kitchen surfaces, and colleagues are wearing masks and gloves when plating and serving made-to-order dishes. We have temporarily shifted many restaurants with a buffet offering to à-la-carte menus and made-to-order options.

International Standards

All Hyatt hotels around the world continue to follow procedures and protocols developed in consideration of guidance and information shared by various health organizations including the World Health Organization (WHO), Centers for Disease Control and Prevention (CDC), local authorities and other leading experts and organizations like the Global Biorisk Advisory Council (GBAC). Our GBAC cleanliness and training accreditation process focuses on establishing hotel environments that are sanitary, safe and healthy.

These processes and procedures have been developed for Hyatt hotels in the Americas. A global cross-functional COVID-19 response team is closely monitoring new information and regularly updates the guidance on appropriate processes and procedures for all Hyatt hotels globally. Safety and cleanliness procedures implemented at each hotel may be adjusted in consideration of local practices, government requirements and guidance, and the situation where the hotel is located."

Figure 2 below illustrates the screenshot of Hyatt Hotels Safety First, Wellbeing Always campaign.

Figure 2. Screenshot of Hyatt safety first, wellbeing always

Example 3: Holiday Inn

The third example, from Holiday Inn Club, demonstrates the need of being "safe" during and after a pandemic. The Safe Travels campaign was adapted from https://holidayinnclub.com/safe-travels: *"Holiday Inn Club Vacations® is committed to giving you vacation experiences you'll love and a safe stay you can trust. That's why we implemented Safe Travels, a program that "checks the boxes" on the higher safety standards we've all come to expect. Our strengthened commitment to cleanliness and safety starts with the IHG Clean Promise and continues throughout your entire stay.*

Extra Safety Measures

With enhanced practices and services, Safe Travels brings an extra level of cleanliness and peace of mind to the owners, Club members and guests visiting our resorts. This includes:

- *Even higher villa cleaning standards that follow CDC best practices*

- *Using hospital-grade disinfectant on surfaces, shared areas and amenities*

- *Virtual check-in queues and contactless express check-outs*

- *Thorough safety training for all team members*
- *Hand-sanitizer stations within reach throughout the resorts*

Plenty of Space to Spread Out

And as always, our resorts are designed to give you all the comforts of home and all the joys of vacation. With expansive properties and large home-like villas, our resorts provide lots of living space, added flexibility and plenty of fun."

Figure 3 below illustrates the screenshot of Holiday Inn Club, Safe Travels campaign.

Figure 3. Screenshot of Holiday Inn Club, Safe Travels

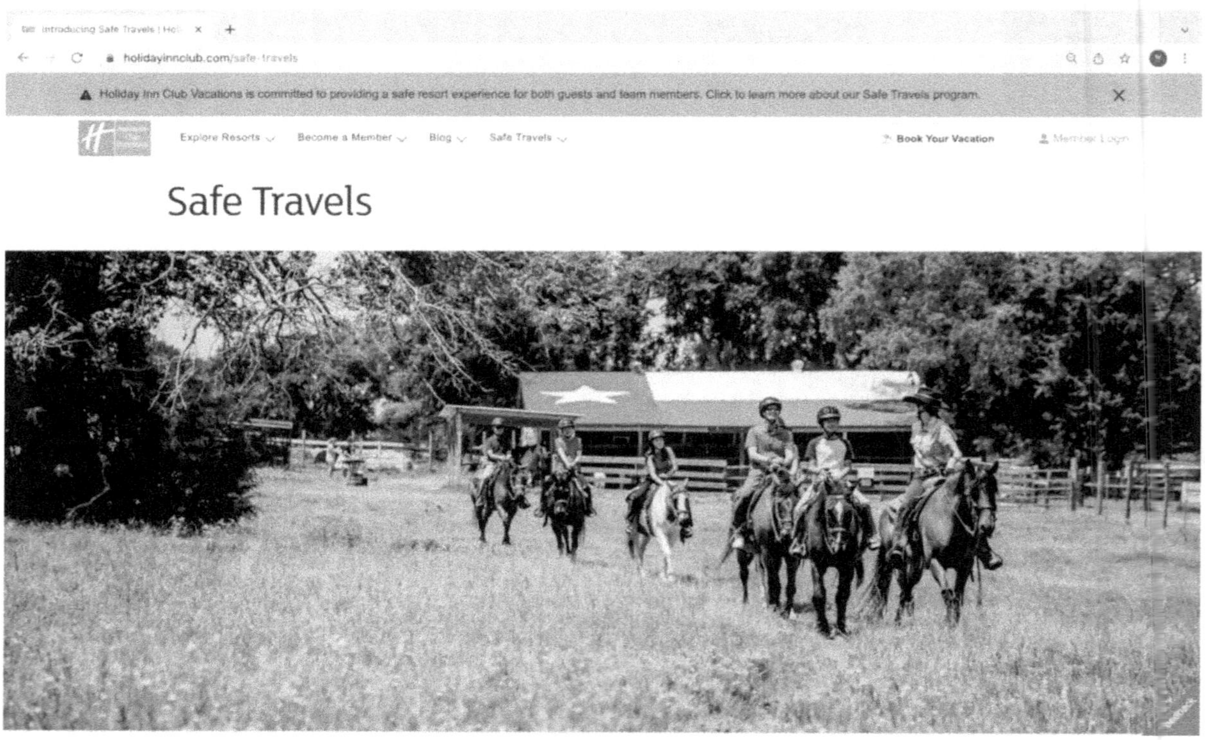

However, these safety measures does not emphasise or at least explicitly referring to the environmental safety. Therefore, the authors argued that the concept of clean and safe should go beyond the hygiene measure to also include the environmental aspects in the long run. There is intriguingly little to none of the hotels had referred their ongoing green practices as part of the safe guideline despite the positive performance implication of green as hotel safe operation has been confirmed (Tiong, Sondoh, Tanakinjal and Iggau, 2020).

SUSTAINABLE INNOVATION III: GREEN AND SAFE FOR GREEFE

A Systematic Review

The review of the literature shows a lack of research to date has measured the linkage of green to the perception of safe. To integrate and synthesize the extant knowledge on green or sustainable innovation, a systematic review was suggested to evaluate the association between green and safe or environmental and safe or green/environmental and clean and safe. The keywords "clean" have been noted given the authorities have considered it in majority of policies and guidelines as part of the essential element to determine hotel safeness. Taking Dengelico and Vocalelli's (2015) recommendation, the authors sourced all journal articles from Business Source Complete (EBSCO) and Web of Sciences due to its large collection of academic peer-reviewed articles especially in the field of business and social sciences. The authors searched the relevant title and proceed with identifying relevancy through abstract using a single or a combination of keywords. In the situation where the abstract did not portray the keywords, the entire paper was reviewed to either confirm its validity or confirm the other potential paper.

The previous researches had provided significant evidence on the implication of green on 'clean' in terms of environment (Vujcic et al., 2017; Ho et al., 2004). However, due to the specificity of the present research focus that is to examine the effect of green on the hotel safeness to contagious disease prevention, the concept of 'safe' which originally indicated the environment is free from pollution has been extended to highlight the environmental hygiene with an expectation to benefit human's health (Tambi and Atemnkeng, 2018). As such, the authors did not include 'green and clean' or 'environmental and clean' in the search list. Further to the evaluation of the association between the green brand and the value generated, the keywords 'green brand and value' were included. To avoid biases, the authors proceed with articles inclusion and exclusion based on a few specific criteria (Kitchenham, 2001).

Firstly, the search criteria were limited to include scientific papers published from 2003 to 2020. The year 2003 is a remarkable year for Secure Acute Respiratory Syndrome (SARS) outbreak that affected 26 countries worldwide. The authors intended to refer to a similar case of global outbreak aimed at exploring the possibilities of green participation in 'clean and safe' and 'green stay' after the incidents. Secondly, only full-text article published in peer-reviewed journals with the main research focus on environmental studies that are written in the English language were chosen due to the completeness and common language proficiency of the authors. Thirdly, the possibility of duplicate papers was checked to avoid duplication of information.

A total of 120 research articles were excluded from the list as these articles were found to be more relevant to pure science, or the terms found to inadequately explain the meaning of either 'green', 'environment', 'clean', 'safe' or 'hygiene'. Some of the keywords such as 'greener' and 'cleaner' are accepted as long as the original meaning is conveyed. However, keywords such as 'cleaning' that generated from 'clean' and keywords that used as the name of an object have been omitted because a different idea is indicated. In contrast, none of the studies was deleted for 'green brand and perceived value' keyword search. The authors proceed with an in-depth analysis of the articles by referring to the filtered list. As a result, 3 research papers were chosen for the synthesis analysis of hoteliers' perspective and 4 for the travellers' perspective.

Table 1 shows the search result of the keywords on both EBSCO and Web of Science Databases with the exclusion of duplicate analysis.

Table 1. Search results of keywords

Single Keyword and Its Combinations	Database		
	Business Source Complete	Web of Science	Total
Green ***and*** Safe Green ***and*** Clean ***and*** Safe Green ***and*** Hygiene Environmental ***and*** Safe Environmental ***and*** Clean ***and*** Safe Environmental ***and*** Hygiene	15 2 0 11 1 8	25 3 6 67 16 5	**154**
	38	116	

The Synthesis Analysis for Green and Safe

Due to the specificity of the current study that focuses on the effect of green on the prevention and cure of contagious diseases, 78% of the research papers collected during the original search have been removed. 3 peer-reviewed papers were chosen from the remaining 34 articles using Moher, Shamseer, Clarke et al. (2009) PRISMA Protocol. In summary, articles have been synthesised according to the specified indicators such as green or environmental, hygiene and clean. The outcome indicates a lack of study exploring the impact of green on 'clean and safe', and its association with 'hygiene'. However, the selected studies are sourced on the basis that the researchers had either addressed environmental protection and hygiene or indirectly relates hotel with green and contagious disease.

The first finding had drawn attention on the public environmental facilities in the tourism destination as the cue for tourists' environmental behaviour and an indicator for long term sustainability (Wang, Zhang, Sun et al., 2019). The second finding is aligned with the findings of Medina-Rodríguez et al. (2020), had elucidated the significance of the use of eco-friendly disinfectant during COVID-19 for environmental safety for the prevention of contagious disease. Lastly, the third findings disclosed the significant contribution of healthy nature to human health (Jiang and Wen, 2020). It is, therefore suggested that hoteliers should move beyond the antecedent perspective of clean and safe by incorporating green after the COVID-19 pandemic. Of all the 3 papers analysed, 2 articles are qualitative based review-papers (Daverey and Dutta, 2020; Jiang and Wen, 2020) and the remaining paper applied a quantitative approach through the survey questionnaire (Wang, Zhang, Sun et al., 2019). Figure 4 below depicted the PRISMA diagram for the synthesis analysis of hoteliers' perspective.

Figure 4. PRISMA diagram for the synthesis analysis

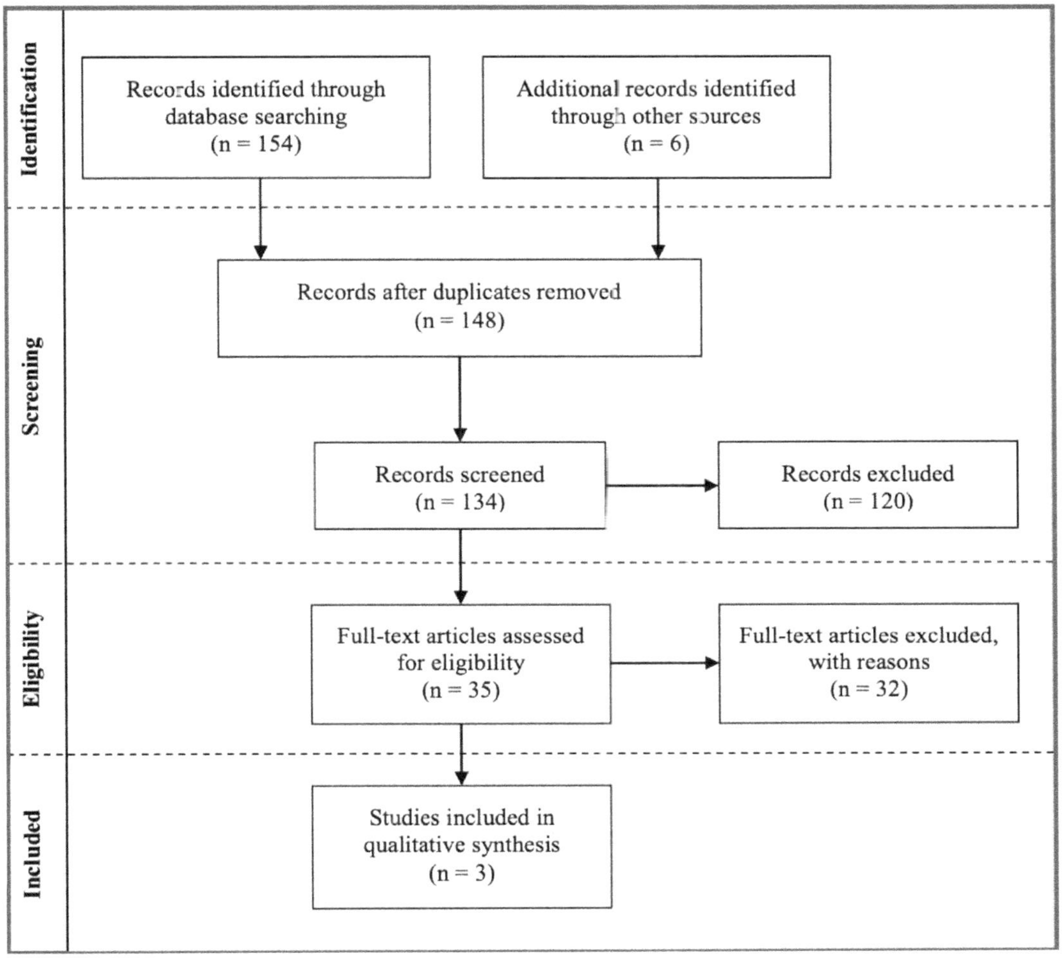

Recommendation: Unlock the Next Level of Green: Combining Green and Safe

Increasing attention is required for this issue as going green has been an existing practice of most hoteliers, but its value towards "safe" has been neglected. It is worth noting that green, while not directly associated with hygienic or clean outcomes, was discovered to be a moderator of travellers' environmental behaviour that serve as a hygienic factor in a tourism destination (Wang et al., 2020). For example, a hotel placing waste segregation bins in the public area would cue travellers' behaviour to segregate their waste based on its type. As a result, proper waste disposal improves hotel hygiene and effectively reduces the spread of contagious disease. Aside from that, incorporating "safe" into "green" is not difficult, but it is necessary to make this additional effort to secure the safety of the environment and people. Hotels might utilise green disinfectant as a replacement for alcohol- or chemical-based disinfectant, maintaining the environment sanitised, hygiene, and healthy by avoiding the use of chemicals (Medina-Rodrguez et al., 2020; Jiang and Wen, 2020).

Based on the current systematic review and analysis of the literature, hotel firms are recommended to consider incorporating safety measures into their existing green marketing mix (green products, green price, green promotion, and green place), at least as the foundation of their initial GREEFE attempt. To begin, hoteliers should consider green ingredients and/or raw materials (toiletries, amenities, food and beverages) and/or packaging, as well as safety precautions to avoid contagious coronavirus, as a requirement in the design and development of green hotel services. Second, to ensure that GREEFE approach is profitable and sustainable, hoteliers should quantify all costs incurred and charge a premium for the highest GREEFE quality. GREEFE pricing that guarantees both environmental benefits and safe stay might encourage and capture the demands of green travellers while also educating more "safe-oriented" consumers to embrace green.

Following that, GREEFE promotion must explicitly communicate the hotels' green and safety benefits. Hoteliers should reposition themselves by emphasising their role in reducing environmental impact and enhancing traveller well-being. The promotions encompass all types of marketing programmes such as advertising, direct marketing, personal selling, public relations, and sales promotion, and the GREEFE message should be transmitted to travellers through any of these programmes and marketing channels. Last but not least, the place element denotes both physical operating sites and distribution channels. The concept of GREEFE should be entrenched in supply chains to provide environmentally friendly after-use arrangements, collaborative commitment and direction, safety movement, and safe locations to conserve the environment and ensure a safe stay. Safety precautions are critical in green distribution since viruses can be spread during the transportation of goods, which endangering the health and safety of the travellers.

Figure 5. GREEFE framework

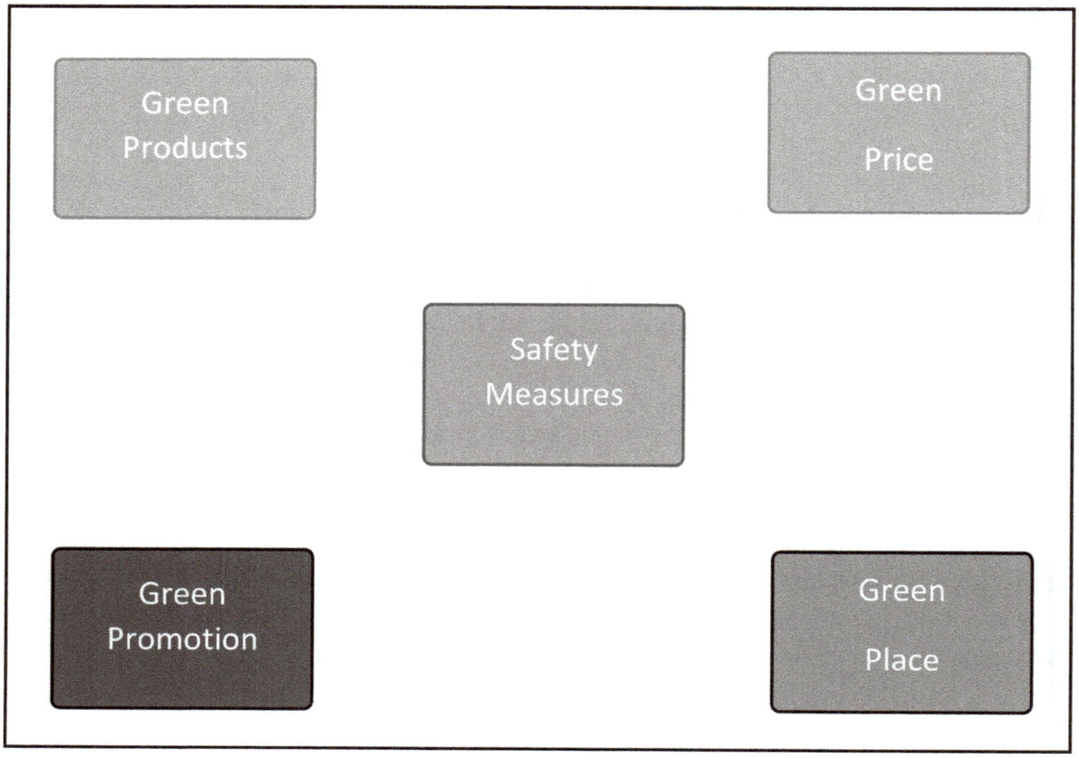

Figure 5 illustrates the GREEFE framework with green marketing mix as the fundamental elements. Aside from the aforementioned fundamental elements, practitioners and future scholars are encouraged to expand the existing framework to include other factors that align to the businesses' operational objectives and goals.

CONCLUSION

Green brands were perceived by travellers as more trustworthy and high-quality (Delafrooz and Goli, 2015), with "safety measures" being a must-have criterion for hotels during and after the epidemic. GREEFE hotels that adhere to green standard operating procedures, while conforming to clean and healthy standards, provide the impression that they are committed to preserving the hotel's hygiene while safeguarding the environment. In the minds of the travellers, this implies not only their health and safety are guaranteed but also part of their environmental responsibilities. This commitment contributes to the brand's trustworthiness and quality, which leads to increased confidence in travel among green travellers, clean-oriented travellers, and, eventually, GREEFE travellers.

REFERENCES

Abzari, M., Shad, F., Sharbiyani, A., & Morad, A. (2013). Studying the effect of the green marketing mix on market share increase. *European Online Journal of Natural and Social Sciences*, *2*(3), 641–653.

Ahn, J., & Kwon, J. (2020). Green hotel brands in Malaysia: Perceived value, cost, anticipated emotion, and revisit intention. *Current Issues in Tourism*, *23*(12), 1559–1574. doi:10.1080/13683500.2019.1646715

Alhosseini Almodarresi, S. M., Tabataba'i-Nasab, S. M., Bagheri Garabollagh, H., & Mohammadi, F. (2019). Does citizenship behavior have a role in changing attitude toward green products? *International Journal of Management Science and Engineering Management*, *14*(4), 284–292. doi:10.1080/17509653.2018.1563874

Arseculeratne, D., & Yazdanifard, R. (2014). How green marketing can create a sustainable competitive advantage for a business. *International Business Research*, *7*(1), 130.

Bokclo, A. J., Mazlina, A. M., & Awanis, R. (2018). A Proposed Model for Green Practice Adoption and Implementation in Information Technology Based Organizations. *Problems of Sustainable Development*, *1*(1), 95–112.

Borhan, H. B., & Ahmed, E. M. (2012). Simultaneous Model of Pollution and Income in Malaysia. *International Journal of Economic Perspectives*, *6*(1).

Bradley, N. (1989). *The Green Marketing Mix*. Industrial Marketing Research Association News. Available at: https://www.wmin.ac.uk/marketingresearch/Marketing/greenmix.htm

Bradley, N. (2007). *The green marketing mix*. Available at http:// www.wmin.ac.uk/marketingresearch/marketing/greenmix.htm

Brown, S., Gummesson, E., Edvardsson, B., & Gustavsson, B. (1991). Service quality: Multidisciplinary and multinational perspectives. New York: Lexington.

Chan, E. (2013). Managing green marketing: Hong Kong hotel managers' perspective. *International Journal of Hospitality Management*, *34*, 442–461. doi:10.1016/j.ijhm.2012.12.007

Chen, S., Chen, H. H., Zhang, K. Q., & Xu, X. L. (2018). A comprehensive theoretical framework for examining learning effects in green and conventionally managed hotels. *Journal of Cleaner Production*, *174*, 1392–1399. doi:10.1016/j.jclepro.2017.10.321

Constantinos, N. L., Constantine, S. K., & Neil, A. M. (2012). "Greening" the marketing mix: Do firms do it and does it pay off? *Journal of the Academy of Marketing Science*, *41*(2), 151–170.

Costa, E., Montemurro, D., & Giuliani, D. (2019). Consumers' willingness to pay for green cars: A discrete choice analysis in Italy. *Environment, Development and Sustainability*, *21*(5), 2425–2442. doi:10.100710668-018-0141-z

Dangelico, R. M., & Vocalelli, D. (2017). "Green Marketing": An analysis of definitions, strategy steps, and tools through a systematic review of the literature. *Journal of Cleaner Production*, *165*, 1263–1279. doi:10.1016/j.jclepro.2017.07.184

Daverey, A., & Dutta, K. (2021). COVID-19: Eco-friendly hand hygiene for human and environmental safety. *Journal of Environmental Chemical Engineering*, *9*(2), 104754. doi:10.1016/j.jece.2020.104754 PMID:33200069

Delafrooz, N., & Goli, A. (2015). The factors affecting the green brand equity of electronic products: Green marketing. *Cogent Business & Management*, *2*(1), 1079351. doi:10.1080/23311975.2015.1079351

Di Marco, M., Baker, M. L., Daszak, P., De Barro, P., Eskew, E. A., Godde, C. M., ... Karesh, W. B. (2020). Opinion: Sustainable development must account for pandemic risk. *Proceedings of the National Academy of Sciences of the United States of America*, *117*(8), 3888–3892. doi:10.1073/pnas.2001655117 PMID:32060123

Eneizan, B., & Wahab, K. A. (2016). Effects of green marketing strategy on the financial and non-financial performance of firms: A conceptual paper. *Arabian Journal of Business Management Review*, *6*, 254.

Eneizan, B., Wahab, K. A., Zainon, M. S., & Obaid, T. F. (2016). Effects of green marketing strategies on sales volume of green cars. *Singapore Journal of Business Economics, and Management Studies*, *5*(30), 41–54. doi:10.12816/0031491

Ginsberg, J. M., & Bloom, P. N. (2004). Choosing the right green marketing strategy. *MIT Sloan Management Review*, *46*(1), 79–84.

Hartmann, J., & Vachon, S. (2018). Linking environmental management to environmental performance: The interactive role of industry context. *Business Strategy and the Environment*, *27*(3), 359–374. doi:10.1002/bse.2003

Hashem, T., & Al-Rifai, N. (2011). The influence of applying green marketing mix by chemical industries companies in the three Arab States in West Asia on consumer's mental image. *International Journal of Business and Social Science*, *2*(3), 92–102.

Hezri, A., & Hasan, N. (2006). Towards sustainable development? The evolution of environmental policy in Malaysia. *Natural Resources Forum*, *30*(1), 37–50. doi:10.1111/j.1477-8947.2006.00156.x

Inman, R. A., & Green, K. W. (2018). Lean and green combine to impact environmental and operational performance. *International Journal of Production Research*, *56*(14), 1–17. doi:10.1080/00207543.2018.1447705

Jiang, Y., & Wen, J. (2020). Effects of COVID-19 on hotel marketing and management: A perspective article. *International Journal of Contemporary Hospitality Management*, *32*(8), 2563–2573. doi:10.1108/IJCHM-03-2020-0237

Khalil, N., Husin, H. N., Mahat, N., & Nasir, N. (2011). Sustainable environment: Issues and solutions from the perspective of facility managers. *Procedia Engineering*, *20*, 458–465. doi:10.1016/j.proeng.2011.11.188

Kitchenham, B. (2010). What's up with software metrics? A preliminary mapping study. *Journal of Systems and Software*, *83*(1), 37–51. doi:10.1016/j.jss.2009.06.041

Klassen, R. D., & McLaughlin, C. P. (1996). The impact of environmental management on firm performance. *Management Science*, *42*(8), 1199–1214. doi:10.1287/mnsc.42.8.1199

Kotler, P., Armstrong, G., & Starr, R. G. (1989). Principles of marketing. Prentice-Hall. Inc.

Kourgiantakis, M., Apostolakis, A., & Dimou, I. (2021). COVID-19 and holiday intentions: The case of Crete, Greece. *Anatolia*, *32*(1), 148–151. doi:10.1080/13032917.2020.1781221

Kumar, D., Kumar, I., Rahman, Z., Yadav, S., & Goyal, P. (2011). Green Marketing Mix: Competitive advantage during climate change. *International Journal of the Computer, the Internet and Management*, (19), 62.1-62.5.

Larashati, H., Hudrasyah, H., & Chandra, N. (2012). 7Ps of green marketing as factors influencing willingness to buy towards environmentally friendly beauty products. *Proceedings of International Conference on Business Management & IS*, *1*(1).

Leonidou, C. N., Katsikeas, C. S., & Morgan, N. A. (2013). "Greening" the marketing mix: Do firms do it and does it pay off? *Journal of the Academy of Marketing Science*, *41*(2), 151–170. doi:10.100711747-012-0317-2

Longoni, A., & Cagliano, R. (2018). Inclusive environmental disclosure practices and firm performance: The role of green supply chain management. *International Journal of Operations & Production Management*, *38*(9), 1815–1835. doi:10.1108/IJOPM-12-2016-0728

Malaysia Hotel Association. (2020). *Clean & Safe Malaysia*. Available at: https://group.bureauveritas.com/newsroom/malaysian-association-hotels-mah-has-appointed-bureau-veritas-deploy-their-clean-safe#:~:text=The%20Malaysian%20Association%20of%20Hotels,members%20spread%20across%2013%20states

Martin, D., & Schounten, J. (2012). *Sustainable Marketing*. Prentice Hall.

Maulani, T. S. (2015). Green banking: A service product innovation in brand image enhancement through the marketing mix. *First International Conference on Economics and Banking ICEB-15*, 39-43. 10.2991/iceb-15.2015.7

McCarthy, E. J. (1960). *Basic Marketing: A Managerial Approach*. Richard D. Irwin, Inc.

Medina-Rodríguez, A. C., Ávila-Sierra, A., Ariza, J. J., Guillamón, E., Baños-Arjona, A., Vicaria J. M., & Jurado, E. (2020). Clean-in-place disinfection of dual-species biofilm (Listeria and Pseudomonas) by a green antibacterial product made from citrus extract. *Food Control*, *118*, 107422. doi:10.1016/j.foodcont.2020.107422

Ministry of Tourism. (2021). *Tourist Arrival*. Available at https://www.tourism.gov.my/statistics

Ministry of Tourism, Arts, and Culture Malaysia. (2021). *Rated Tourist Accommodation Premises*. Available at https://www.motac.gov.my/en/check/hotel

Moher, D., Shamseer, L., Clarke, M., Ghersi, D., Liberati, A., Petticrew, M., Shekelle, P., & Stewart, L. A. (2015). Preferred reporting items for systematic review and meta-analysis protocols (PRISMA-P) 2015 statement. *Systematic Reviews*, *4*(1), 1–9. doi:10.1186/2046-4053-4-1 PMID:25554246

Molina-Azorin, J., Tari, J., Pereira-Moliner, J., López-Gamero, M. D., & Pertusa-Ortega, E. M. (2015). The effects of quality and environmental management on competitive advantage: A mixed methods study in the hotel industry. *Tourism Management*, *50*, 41–54. doi:10.1016/j.tourman.2015.01.008

Namkung, Y., & Jang, S. S. (2013). Effects of restaurant green practices on brand equity formation: Do green practices really matter? *International Journal of Hospitality Management*, *33*, 85–95. doi:10.1016/j.ijhm.2012.06.006

Neuburger, L., & Egger, R. (2021). Travel risk perception and travel behaviour during the COVID-19 pandemic 2020: A case study of the DACH region. *Current Issues in Tourism*, *24*(7), 1003–1016. doi:10.1080/13683500.2020.1803807

Peter, J., & Donnelly, J., Jr. (2015). A preface to marketing management (14th ed.). New York: McGraw Hill.

Porter, M. E., & Van der Linde, C. (1995). Toward a new conception of the environment-competitiveness relationship. *The Journal of Economic Perspectives*, *9*(4), 97–118. doi:10.1257/jep.9.4.97

Prakash, A. (2002). Green marketing, public policy and managerial strategies. *Business Strategy and the Environment*, *11*(5), 285–297. doi:10.1002/bse.338

Rahmawati, R., Hadiwidjojo, D., & Noermijati, S. (2014). Green Marketing Mix as Strategy to Improve Competitive Advantage in Real Estate Developer Companies. *International Journal of Business and Management*.

Rex, E., & Baumann, H. (2007). Beyond ecolabels: What green marketing can learn from conventional marketing. *Journal of Cleaner Production*, *15*(6), 567–576.

Roy, D., Tripathy, S., Kar, S. K., Sharma, N., Verma, S. K., & Kaushal, V. (2020). Study of knowledge, attitude, anxiety & perceived mental healthcare need in Indian population during COVID-19 pandemic. *Asian Journal of Psychiatry*, *51*, 102083. doi:10.1016/j.ajp.2020.102083 PMID:32283510

Shamdasani, P., Lin, G. C., & Richmond, D. (1993). Exploring green consumers in an oriental culture: Rolle of personal and marketing mix. *Advances in Consumer Research. Association for Consumer Research (U. S.)*, *20*, 488–493.

Solaiman, M., Osman, A., & Halim, M. S. (2015). Green marketing: A marketing mix point of view. *International Journal of Business and Technopreneurship*, *5*(1), 87–98.

Sudhalakshimi, K., & Chinnadorai, K. (2014). Green marketing mix - A social responsibility of manufacturing companies. *Global Journal of Commerce and Management Perspective*, 109-112.

Tambi, M. D., & Atemnkeng, J. T. (2018). Measuring the effect of environmental hygiene on child health outcomes in Cameroon. *Journal of Economics & Management*, *32*, 118–137.

Tan, B. C., & Lau, T. C. (2010). Attitude towards the environment and green products. *Management Science and Engineering*, *4*(2), 27–39.

Tiong, Y. Y., Sondoh, S. L. Jr, Tanakinjal, G. H., & Iggau, O. A. (2021). Cleaner operations in hotels: Recommendation for post-pandemic green recovery. *Journal of Cleaner Production*, *283*, 124621. doi:10.1016/j.jclepro.2020.124621 PMID:33071479

Travelocity. (2020). *Travelocity predicts 'Safecations' will be summer 2020's newest travel trend*. Available at https://www.travelocity.com/pressroom/travelocity-predicts- safecations-will-be-summer-2020s-newest-travel- trend/#:~:text=Travelocity%20predicts%20'Safecations'%20will%20be%20summer%2 02020's%20newest%20travel%20trend,-DALLAS%2C%20Texas%20(June&text=In%20fact%2C%20 Boomers%20were%20tw ice,and%20significant%20other%20(76%25

Vieira, C. M., Franco, O. H., Restrepo, C. G., & Abel, T. (2020). COVID-19: The forgotten priorities of the pandemic. *Maturitas*, *136*, 38–41. doi:10.1016/j.maturitas.2020.04.004 PMID:32386664

Vujcic, M., Tomicevic-Dubljevic, J., Grbic, M., Lecic-Tosevski, D., Vukovic, O., & Toskovic, O. (2017). Nature based solution for improving mental health and well-being in urban areas. *Environmental Research*, *158*, 385–392. doi:10.1016/j.envres.2017.06.030 PMID 28688269

Wang, C., Zhang, J., Sun, J., Chen, M., & Yang, J. (2020). Public environmental facilities: Hygiene factors for tourists' environmental behaviour. *Environmental Science & Policy*, *106*, 40–47. doi:10.1016/j.envsci.2020.01.009

Xu, X., Wang, S., & Yu, Y. (2020). Consumer's intention to purchase green furniture: Do health consciousness and environmental awareness matter? *The Science of the Total Environment*, *704*, 135275. doi:10.1016/j.scitotenv.2019.135275 PMID:31796272

Zeenat, B., & Mariam, J. (2014). Barriers of Malaysian green hotels and resorts. *Procedia: Social and Behavioral Sciences*, *153*, 501–509. doi:10.1016/j.sbspro.2014.10.083

Zhang, J., Xie, C., Wang, J., Morrison, A. M., & Coca-Stefaniak, J. A. (2020). Responding to a major global crisis: The effects of hotel safety leadership on employee safety behavior during COVID-19. *International Journal of Contemporary Hospitality Management*, *32*(11), 3365–3389. doi:10.1108/IJCHM-04-2020-0335

Zuhairah, H., & Noor, A. (2015). The Impact of Green Marketing Strategy on the Firm's Performance in Malaysia. *Procedia: Social and Behavioral Sciences*, 463–470.

Compilation of References

Abdul Rahman, H. (2020). Malaysia Commitment towards Low Carbon Cities. *International Journal of Academic Research in Business & Social Sciences*, *10*(15), 253–266. doi:10.6007/IJARBSS/v10-i15/8247

Abdulrazak, S., & Quoquab, F. (2018). Exploring consumers' motivations for sustainable consumption: A self-deterministic approach. *Journal of International Consumer Marketing*, *30*(1), 14–28. doi:10.1080/08961530.2017.1354350

Abzari, M., Shad, F., Sharbiyani, A., & Morad, A. (2013). Studying the effect of the green marketing mix on market share increase. *European Online Journal of Natural and Social Sciences*, *2*(3), 641–653.

Acquaah, M., Amoako-Gyampah, K., & Jayaram, J. (2011). Resilience in family and nonfamily firms: An examination of the relationships between manufacturing strategy, competitive strategy, and firm performance. *International Journal of Production Research*, *49*(18), 5527–5544. doi:10.1080/00207543.2011.563834

Acquier, A., Daudigeos, T., & Pinkse, J. (2017). Promises and paradoxes of the sharing economy: An organizing framework. *Technological Forecasting and Social Change*, *125*, 1–10. doi:10.1016/j.techfore.2017.07.006

Adams, R., Jeanrenaud, S., Bessant, J., Denyer, D., & Overy, P. (2016). Sustainability-oriented innovation: A systematic review. *International Journal of Management Reviews*, *18*(2), 180–205. doi:10.1111/ijmr.12068

Adawiyah, W. R. (2017). Determinants Of green Marketing quality practices among Small Medium Enterprises (SMEs). *Jurnal Ekonomi Dan Keuangan Ekuitas*, *1*(2), 240–258.

Adeyinka-Ojo, S. F., Khoo-Lattimore, C., & Nair, V. (2014). A framework for rural tourism destination management and marketing organisations. *Procedia: Social and Behavioral Sciences*, *144*, 151–163. doi:10.1016/j.sbspro.2014.07.284

Adger, W. N. (2000). Social and ecological resilience: Are they related? *Progress in Human Geography*, *24*(3), 347–364. doi:10.1191/030913200701540465

Adger, W. N. (2006). Vulnerability. *Global Environmental Change*, *16*(3), 258–281. doi:10.1016/j.gloenvcha.2006.02.006

Adger, W. N., Hughes, T. P., Folke, C., Carpenter, S. R., & Rockstrom, J. (2005). Social– ecological resilience to coastal disasters. *Science*, *309*(5737), 1036–1039. doi:10.1126cience.1112122 PMID:16099974

Adhya, A., Plowright, P., & Stevens, J. (2011). Defining sustainable urbanism: towards a responsive urban design. In *Proceedings of the conference on sustainability and the built environment*. King Saud University.

Afroz, R., Hassan, M. N., & Ibrahim, N. A. (2003). Review of Air Pollution and Health Impacts in Malaysia. *Environmental Research*, *92*(2), 71–77. doi:10.1016/S0013-9351(02)00059-2 PMID:12854685

Agarwal, S., & Garg, A. (2012). The importance of communication within organizations: A research on two hotels in Uttarakhand. *Journal of Business and Management*, *12*, 30–49.

Ahmad, A. H. (2006). Auditing communication satisfaction among academic staff: An approach to managing academic excellence. *Business Review (Federal Reserve Bank of Philadelphia)*, *5*(1), 330–333.

Ahn, J., & Kwon, J. (2020). Green hotel brands in Malaysia: Perceived value, cost, anticipated emotion, and revisit intention. *Current Issues in Tourism*, *23*(12), 1559–1574. doi:10.1080/13683500.2019.1646715

Akers, J. (2013). Making markets: Think tank legislation and private property in Detroit. *Urban Geography*, *34*(8), 1070–1095. doi:10.1080/02723638.2013.814272

Akgün & Halit Keskin. (2014). Organizational resilience capacity and firm product innovativeness and performance. *International Journal of Production Research*, *52*(23), 6918–6937.

Akmajian, A., Farmer, A. K., Bickmore, L., Demers, R. A., & Harnish, R. M. (2017). *Linguistics: An introduction to language and communication*. MIT press.

Akroyd, C., Narayan, S., & Sridharan, V. (2009). The use of control systems in new product development innovation: advancing the'help or hinder'debate. *ICFAI Journal of Knowledge Management, 7*(5-6), 70-90.

Akter, S., Krupnik, T., & Khanam, F. (2017). Climate change skepticism and index versus standard crop insurance demand in coastal Bangladesh. *National Center for Biotechnology Information, 17*, 2456-2466.: doi:10.1007/s10113-017-1174-9

Al Amri, S., Neelufer, A., & Christina, B. (2014). Challenges and barriers encountered by the SMEs owners in Muscat. *International Journal of Small Business and Entrepreneurship Research*, *2*(3), 1–13.

Al Shukaili, A. (2018). *Entrepreneurship Policy for Transforming Local Contexts In A Developing Economy: Evidence From Oman*. Presented at the Majan International Conference 2018, Muscat, Oman.

Al Shukaili, A., Cucculelli, M., González-Pernía, J. L., & Legazkue, I. P. (2016). Government Loan Support and Entrepreneurship in A Developing Economy: The Context of Oman. In *ICSB World Conference Proceedings* (pp. 1-8). International Council for Small Business (ICSB).

Al Shukaili, A. (2017). *Constraining Factors for Effective Entrepreneurship Policy Implementation in a Developing Economy: Evidence from Oman (Doctor of Philosophy)*. University of Deusto.

Al Shukaili, A., Madanoglu, M., González-Pernía, J. L., & Legazkue, I. P. (2017). Entrepreneurship policy and stagnation of new ventures in the context of a developing economy (Interactive Paper). *Frontiers of Entrepreneurship Research*, *37*(14), 5.

Al-Abri, M. Y., Rahim, A. A., & Hussain, N. H. (2018). Entrepreneurial ecosystem: An exploration of the entrepreneurship model for SMEs in Sultanate of Oman. *Mediterranean Journal of Social Sciences*, *9*(6), 193–193. doi:10.2478/mjss-2018-0175

Al-Ani, W. (2017). Alternative education needs in Oman: Accommodating learning diversity and meeting market demand. *International Journal of Adolescence and Youth*, *22*(3), 322–336. doi:10.1080/02673843.2016.1179204

Al-Asfour, A., Tlaiss, H. A., Khan, S. A., & Rajasekar, J. (2017). Saudi women's work challenges and barriers to career advancement. *Career Development International*, *22*(2), 184–199. doi:10.1108/CDI-11-2016-0200

Alawni, M. S., Yusoff, R. Z., Al-Swidi, A. K., & Al-Matari, E. M. (2015). The relationship between communication, customer knowledge and customer loyalty in Saudi Arabia insurance industry companies. *Mediterranean Journal of Social Sciences*, *6*(1), 315–318. doi:10.5901/mjss.2015.v6n1p318

Al-Azri, A. K. H. (2016). *Academics', students', employers', and graduates' perceptions towards business management and administration undergraduate employability: implications for higher education and industry in Oman* (Doctoral dissertation). Brunel University London.

Albertini, E. (2021). What are the environmental capabilities, as components of the sustainable intellectual capital, that matter to the CEOs of European companies? *Journal of Intellectual Capital.*

Albors-Garrigos, J., Igartua, J. I., & Peiro, A. (2018). Innovation management techniques and tools: Its impact on firm innovation performance. *International Journal of Innovation Management*, *22*(06), 1850051. doi:10.1142/S1363919618500512

Aleksić, A., Stefanović, M., Arsovski, S., & Tadić, D. (2013). An assessment of organizational resilience potential in SMEs of the process industry, a fuzzy approach. *J Loss Prevent Proc*, *26*, 1238–1245. doi:10.1016/j.jlp.2013.06.004

Alesi, P. (2008). Building enterprise-wide resilience by integrating business continuity capability into day-to-day business culture and technology. *Journal of Business Continuity & Emergency Planning*, *2*(3), 214–220.

Alfasi, N., & Portugali, J. (2007). Planning rules for a self-planned city. *Planning Theory*, *6*(2), 164–182. doi:10.1177/1473095207077587

Al-Fedaghi, S. (2012). A conceptual foundation for the Shannon-Weaver model of communication. *International Journal of Soft Computing*, *7*(1), 12–19. doi:10.3923/ijscomp.2012.12.19

Al-Ghazali, B. M., Yusoff, R. M., & Sadi, M. A. (2013). Women entrepreneurs in Bahrain: Motivations and barriers. *Jurnal Teknologi*, *64*(2). Advance online publication. doi:10.11113/jt.v64.2251

Alhosseini Almodarresi, S. M., Tabataba'i-Nasab, S. M., Bagheri Garabollagh, H., & Mohammadi, F. (2019). Does citizenship behavior have a role in changing attitude toward green products? *International Journal of Management Science and Engineering Management*, *14*(4), 284–292. doi:10.1080/17509653.2018.1563874

Ali, W., Jun, W., Hussain, H., Khan, N., Younas, M., & Jamil, I. (2021). Does green intellectual capital matter for green innovation adoption? Evidence from the manufacturing SMEs of Pakistan. *Journal of Intellectual Capital.*

Ali, Y., Nusair, M. M., Alani, F., Khan, F. R., & Al Badi, L. (2017). Employment in the private sector in Oman: Sector-based approach for localization. *Humanities & Social Sciences Reviews, 5*(1), 1-20.

Allen, C., & Clouth, S. (2012). *A guidebook to the green economy*. UNDESA.

Alleyne, C., Kakabadse, A., & Kakabadse, N. (2007). Using the HR intranet: An exploratory analysis of its impact on managerial satisfaction with the HR function. *Personnel Review*, *36*(2), 295–310. doi:10.1108/00483480710726154

AlMaimani, J., & Johari, F. B. (2015). Enhancing active participation of SMEs and Islamic Banks towards economic diversification in Oman. *Procedia Economics and Finance*, *31*, 677–688. doi:10.1016/S2212-5671(15)01156-9

Almobaireek, W. N., & Manolova, T. S. (2013). Entrepreneurial motivations among female university youth in Saudi Arabia. *Journal of Business Economics and Management*, *14*(sup1), S56-S75.

Al-Riyami, R., Warren, L., & McElwee, G. (2002). Opportunities and challenges for Omani women entrepreneurs. *International Journal of Entrepreneurship and Innovation*, *3*(2), 133–144. doi:10.5367/000000002101299123

Al-Sadi, R., Belwal, R., & Al-Badi, R. (2011). Woman entrepreneurship in the Al-Batinah region of Oman: An identification of the barriers. *Journal of International Women's Studies*, *12*(3), 58–75.

Al-Shanfari, D. A. (2012). Entrepreneurship in Oman: A snapshot of the main challenges. *Proceedings of the United Nations Conference on Trade and Development: Multi-year expert meeting on enterprise development policies and capacity-building in science, technology, and innovation (STI).*

Amatulli, C., De Angelis, M., Costabile, M., & Guido, G. (2017). *Sustainable luxury brands: Evidence from research and implications for managers*. Palgrave Macmillan. doi:10.1057/978-1-137-60159-9

Amiri, M. (2015). Internal communication: Perception and opinions of bank employees. *Academie Royale Des Sciences D Outre-mer Bulletin Des Seances, 4*(5), 17-22.

Ammari, G., Alkurdi, B., Alshurideh, A., & Alrowwad, A. (2017). Investigating the impact of communication satisfaction on organizational commitment: A practical approach to increase employees' loyalty. *International Journal of Marketing Studies*, *9*(2), 113–133. doi:10.5539/ijms.v9n2p113

Amores-Salvadó, J., Cruz-González, J., Delgado-Verde, M., & González-Masip, J. (2021). Green technological distance and environmental strategies: the moderating role of green structural capital. *Journal of Intellectual Capital.*

Amui, L. B. L., Jabbour, C. J. C., de Sousa Jabbour, A. B. L., & Kannan, D. (2017). Sustainability as a dynamic organizational capability: A systematic review and a future agenda toward a sustainable transition. *Journal of Cleaner Production*, *142*, 308–322. doi:10.1016/j.jclepro.2016.07.103

Anderies, J. M., Janssen, M. A., & Ostrom, E. (2004). A framework to analyze the robustness of social-ecological systems from an institutional perspective. *Ecology and Society, 9*(1), 18. http://www. ecologyandsociety.org/vol9/iss /art18/

Anderson, B. B. (2015). World Journal of Entrepreneurship, Management, and Sustainable Development Corrupting activities and economic development Article information. *World Journal of Entrepreneurship, Management and Sustainable Development*, *11*(1), 64–70. doi:10.1108/WJEMSD-07-2014-0020

Anholt, S. (2010). *Handbook on tourism destination branding*. ETC/UNWTO.

Animashaun, A., Tunkarimu, T., & Dastane, O. (2016). Customer perceived value towards convenience stores in malaysia: The influence on customer satisfaction, loyalty and retention. *Journal of Marketing and Consumer Behaviour in Emerging Markets*, *2*(4), 4–27.

Antunes, P. (2011). BPM and exception handling: Focus on organizational resilience. *IEEE Transactions on Systems, Man, and Cybernetics*, *41*, 383–392. doi:10.1109/TSMCC. 2010.20625 04

Aral, S., Dellarocas, C., & Godes, D. (2013). Introduction to the special issue—social media and business transformation: A framework for research. *Information Systems Research*, *24*(1), 3–13. doi:10.1287/isre.1120.0470

Armstrong, C. M., Niinimäki, K., Lang, C., & Kujala, S. (2016). A use-oriented clothing economy? Preliminary affirmation for sustainable clothing consumption alternatives. *Sustainable Development*, *24*(1), 18–31. doi:10.1002d. 602

Arouri, H., Hossain, M., & Badrul Muttakin, M. (2014). Effects of the board and ownership structure on corporate performance: Evidence from GCC countries. *Journal of Accounting in Emerging Economies*, *4*(1), 117–130. doi:10.1108/JAEE-02-2012-0007

Arrigo, E. (2015). Corporate Sustainability in Fashion and Luxury Companies. *Symphonya Emerging Issues in Management, 4*, 9-23.

Arrow, K., Bolin, B., Costanza, R., Dasgupta, P., Folke, C., Holling, C. S., Jansson, B. O., Levin, S., Mäler, K. G., Perrings, C., & Pimentel, D. (1995). Economic growth, carrying capacity and the environment. *Science*, *268*(5210), 520–521. doi:10.1126cience.268.5210.520 PMID:17756719

Arseculeratne, D., & Yazdanifard, R. (2014). How green marketing can create a sustainable competitive advantage for a business. *International Business Research*, *7*(1), 130.

Asheim B. T., Smith, H. L., & Oughton, C. (2011). Regional innovation systems: Theory, empirics and policy. *Regional Studies*, *45*(7), 875–891. doi:10.1080/00343404.2011.596701

Athwal, N., Wells, V. K., Carrigan, M., & Henninger, C. E. (2019). Sustainable luxury marketing: A synthesis and research agenda. *International Journal of Management Reviews*, *21*(4), 405–426. doi:10.1111/ijmr.12195

Austin, E. W., & Pinkleton, B. E. (2015). *Strategic public relations management: Planning and managing effective communication campaigns*. Routledge. doi:10.4324/9781315754833

Awang, Z. (2012). Research methodology and data analysis (2nd ed.). UiTM Press.

Ayyagari, M., Demirguc-kunt, A., & Maksimovic, V. (2014). Who creates jobs in developing countries? *Small Business Economics*, *43*(1), 75–99. doi:10.100711187-014-9549-5

Azjen, I. (1991). The Theory of Planned Behaviour. *Organizational Behavior and Human Decision Processes*, *50*(2), 179–211. doi:10.1016/0749-5978(91)90020-T

Azlan M. D. Z., & Bagul, A. H. B. (2010). Modernisation and its effects on heritage Tourism in Melaka. *TEAM Journal of Hospitality & Tourism*, *7*(1), 46–57.

B. K. A., Mahato, A., Thapa, S., Rai, A., & Devkota, N. (2019). Achieving Nepal's sustainable development goals (SDGs) by effective compliance of corporate governance. *Quest Journal of Management and Social Sciences*, *1*(1), 50–72. doi:10.3126/qjmss.v1i1.25974

Bade M. (2018). Bargaining over crowdfunding benefits. *J. Entrep. Public Policy*, *7*, 166–177.

Bag, S., & Gupta, S. (2019). Examining the effect of green human capital availability in adoption of reverse logistics and remanufacturing operations performance. *International Journal of Manpower*, *41*(7), 1097–1117. doi:10.1108/IJM-07-2019-0349

Baker, B. (2007). *Destination branding for small cities: the essentials for successful place branding*. Portland, OR: Creative Leap books.

Baker, M. J., & Cameron, E. (2008). Critical success factors in destination marketing. *Tourism and Hospitality Research*, *8*(2), 79–97. doi:10.1057/thr.2008.9

Balakrishnan, M. S. (2008). Dubai – a star in the east. *Journal of Place Management and Development*, *1*(1), 62–91.

Balıkçıoğlu, B., & Karacaoğlu, K. (2007). Sosyal Bir Ürün Olarak Topluma Pazarlanan Hayırseverlik: Stratejik Hayırseverlik [Philanthropy that Is Marketed to Society as A Social Product: Strategic Philanthropy]. *Gazi Üniversitesi İktisadi ve İdari Bilimler Fakültesi Dergisi*, *9*(2), 121–141.

Banstola, A. (2007). Prospects and challenges of e-banking in Nepal. *Journal of Nepalese Business Studies*, *4*(1), 96–104. doi:10.3126/jnbs.v4i1.1034

Banyte, J., Salciuviene, L., Dovaliene, A., Piligrimiene, Z., & Sroka, W. (2020). Sustainable Consumption Behavior at Home and in the Workplace: Avenues for Innovative Solutions. *Sustainability Mdpi Journal*, *12*, 6564.

Barba-Sánchez, V., & Atienza-Sahuquillo, C. (2010). Integration of the environment in managerial strategy: Application of the resource-based theory of competitive advantage, dynamic capabilities, and corporate social responsibilities. *African Journal of Business Management*, *4*(6), 1155–1165.

Barba-Sánchez, V., & Atienza-Sahuquillo, C. (2018). Entrepreneurial intention among engineering students: The role of entrepreneurship education. *European Research on Management and Business Economics*, *24*(1), 53–61. doi:10.1016/j.iedeen.2017.04.001

Baresel-Bofinger, A., Ketikidis, P., Koh, S., & Cullen, J. (2011). Role of 'green knowledge' in the environmental transformation of the supply chain: The case of Greek manufacturing. *International Journal of Knowledge-Based Development*, *2*(1), 107–128. doi:10.1504/IJKBD.2011.040628

Bashir, M. A., Sheng, B., Doğan, B., Sarwar, S., & Shahzad, U. (2020). Export product diversification and energy efficiency: Empirical evidence from OECD countries. *Structural Change and Economic Dynamics*, *55*, 232–243. doi:10.1016/j.strueco.2020.09.002

Batty, M. (2013). *A new science of cities*. MIT Press. doi:10.7551/mitpress/9399.001.0001

Bearden, W. O., & Michael, J. E. (1982). Reference group influence on product and Brand purchase decisions. *The Journal of Consumer Research*, *9*(2), 183–194. doi:10.1086/208911

Bechky, B. A., & Okhuysen, G. A. (2011). Expecting the unexpected? How SWAT officers and film. *Academy of Management Journal*, *54*(2), 239–261.

Becker, P., Abrahamsson, M., & Tehler, H. (2014). An emergent means to assurgent ends: societal resilience for safety and sustainability. In Becom. Resilient. Ashgate Publishing, Ltd.

Beckham, D., & Voyer, B. G. (2014). *Can sustainability be luxurious? A mixed-method investigation of implicit and explicit attitudes towards sustainable luxury consumption*. ACR North American Advances.

Beiser-McGrath, L., & Bernauer, T. (2021). *Current surveys may underestimate climate change skepticism evidence from list experiments in Germany and the USA*. Academic Press.

Belk, R. W. (1988). Possessions and the extended self. *The Journal of Consumer Research*, *15*(2), 139–168. doi:10.1086/209154

Belk, R. W. (2014). You are what you can access: Sharing and collaborative consumption online. *Journal of Business Research*, *67*(8), 1595–1600. doi:10.1016/j.jbusres.2013.10.001

Belu, C., & Manescu, C. (2013). Strategic corporate social responsibility and economic performance. *Applied Economics*, *45*(19), 2751–2764. doi:10.1080/00036846.2012.676734

Belwal, R., Al Balushi, H., & Belwal, S. (2015). Students' perception of entrepreneurship and enterprise education in Oman. *Education + Training*, *57*(8/9), 924–947. doi:10.1108/ET-12-2014-0149

Belwal, S., & Belwal, R. (2014). Work-life balance, family-friendly policies and quality of work-life issues: Studying employers' perspectives of working women in Oman. *Journal of International Women's Studies*, *15*(1), 96–117.

Belwal, S., Belwal, R., & Saidi, F. A. (2014). Characteristics, motivations, and challenges of women entrepreneurs in Oman's Al-Dhahira region. *Journal of Middle East Women's Studies*, *10*(2), 135–151. doi:10.2979/jmiddeastwomstud.10.2.135

Bendell, J., & Kleanthous, A. (2007). *Deeper luxury*. http://assets. wwf.org.uk/downloads/luxury_report.pdf

Benner, M. J., & Tushman, M. L. (2003). Exploitation, exploration, and process management: The productivity dilemma revisited. *Academy of Management Review*, *28*(2), 238–256. doi:10.5465/amr.2003.9416096

Bennett, J. (2010). Informal firms in developing countries: Entrepreneurial stepping stone or consolation prize? *Small Business Economics*, *34*(1), 53–63. doi:10.100711187-009-9194-6

Berger, A. (2007). *Drosscape: Wasting Land Urban America*. Princeton Architectural Press.

Berger, A. A. (2018). *Media and communication research methods: An introduction to qualitative and quantitative approaches*. Sage Publications.

Berkes, F., Colding, J., & Folke, C. (Eds.). (2003). *Navigating Social–Ecological Systems: Building Resilience for Complexity and Change*. Cambridge University Press.

Bhattacharyya, S. S. (2010). Exploring the concept of strategic corporate social responsibility for an integrated perspective. *European Business Review*, *22*(1), 82–101. doi:10.1108/09555341011009025

Bhattacharyya, S. S., Sahay, A., Arora, A. P., & Chaturvedi, A. (2008). *A toolkit for designing firm-level strategic corporate social responsibility (CSR) initiatives*. Social Responsibility. doi:10.1108/17471110810892802

Biondi, L., & Galli, R. (1992). Technological trajectories. *Futures*, *24*(6), 580–592. doi:10.1016/0016-3287(92)90118-Y

Birkmann, J., Garschagen, M., Kraas, F., & Quang, N. (2010). Adaptive urban governance: New challenges for the second generation of urban adaptation strategies to climate change. *Sustainability Science*, *5*(2), 185–206. doi:10.100711625-010-0111-3

Blain, C., Levy, S., & Ritchie, J. R. B. (2005). Destination branding: Insight and practices from destination management organisations. *Journal of Travel Research*, *43*(4), 328–338. doi:10.1177/0047287505274646

Blair, R. B. (2001). Birds and butterflies along urban gradients in two ecoregions of theU.S. In J. L. Lockwood & M. L. McKinney (Eds.), *Biotic Homogenization* (pp. 459–486). Kluwer. doi:10.1007/978-1-4615-1261-5_3

Blythe, J. (2008). *Essentials of marketing*. Pearson Education.

Bocock, R. (1993). *Consumption* (1st ed.). Routledge. doi:10.4324/9780203313114

Boin, A., & van Eeten, M. J. B. (2013). The Resilient Organization—A critical appraisal. *Public Management Review*, *15*, 429–445.

Bokolo, A. J., Mazlina, A. M., & Awanis, R. (2018). A Proposed Model for Green Practice Adoption and Implementation in Information Technology Based Organizations. *Problems of Sustainable Development*, *1*(1), 95–112.

Boleti, E., Garas, A., Kyriakou, A., & Lapatinas, A. (2021). Economic Complexity and Environmental Performance: Evidence from a World Sample. *Environmental Modeling and Assessment*, *26*(3), 251–270. doi:10.100710666-021-09750-0

Bonner, J. M. (2005). The influence of formal controls on customer interactivity in new product development. *Industrial Marketing Management*, *34*(1), 63–69. doi:10.1016/j.indmarman.2004.07.004

Boons, F., Montalvo, C., Quist, J., & Wagner, M. (2013). Sustainable innovation, business models and economic performance: An overview. *Journal of Cleaner Production*, *45*, 1–8. doi:10.1016/j.jclepro.2012.08.013

Borgatti, S. P., Everett, M. G., & Johnson, J. C. (2018). Analyzing social networks. *Sage (Atlanta, Ga.)*.

Borgatti, S. P., Mehra, A., Brass, D. J., & Labianca, G. (2009). Network analysis in the social sciences. *Science*, *323*(5916), 892–895. doi:10.1126cience.1165821

Borges, F. M., & Menegon, N. L. (2012). Different roles in the quest for system resilience. *Work (Reading, Mass.)*, *41*, 3238–3245.

Borhan, H. B., & Ahmed, E. M. (2012). Simultaneous Model of Pollution and Income in Malaysia. *International Journal of Economic Perspectives*, *6*(1).

Borucke, M., Moore, D., Cranston, G., Gracey, K., Iha, K., Larson, J., Lazarus, E., Morales, J. C., Wackernagel, M., & Galli, A. (2013). Accounting for demand and supply of the biosphere's regenerative capacity: The National Footprint Accounts' underlying methodology and framework. *Ecological Indicators*, *24*, 518–533. doi:10.1016/j.ecolind.2012.08.005

Botsman, R. (2013). *The sharing economy lacks a shared definition. Giving Meaning to the Terms*. https://www.fastcoexist.com/3022028/the-sharing-economy-lacks-a-shareddefinition

Bowen, J., Makens, J., & Kotler, P. (2005). *Marketing for hospitality and tourism* (4th ed.). Prentice Hall.

Braczyk, H.-J., Cooke, P. N., Heidenreich, M., & Krauss, G. (1998). *Regional innovation systems: the role of governances in a globalized world*. Psychology Press.

Brad Maddock and Dr Jeana Kriewaldt. (2014). *Post-primary education and energy literacy: an analysis of the potential for geography curricula to contribute to Australian students' energy literacy* (Vol. 27). Geographical Education.

Bradley, N. (1989). *The Green Marketing Mix*. Industrial Marketing Research Association News. Available at https://www.wmin.ac.uk/marketingresearch/Marketing/greenmix.htm

Bradley, N. (2007). *The green marketing mix*. Available at http:// www.wmin.ac.uk/marketingresearch/marketing/greenmix.htm

Brahma, S. S. (2009). Assessment of construct validity in management research. *Journal of Management Research*, *9*, 59–71.

Braun, V., & Clarke, V. (2006). Using thematic analysis in psychology. *Qualitative Research in Psychology*, *3*(2), 77–101. doi:10.1191/1478088706qp063oa

Brixiova, Z. (2013). Modeling productive entrepreneurship in developing countries. *Small Business Economics*, *41*(1), 183–194. doi:10.100711187-011-9410-z

Brock, W. A., Mäler, K. G., & Perrings, C. (2002). Resilience and Sustainability: The Economic Analysis of Nonlinear Dynamic Systems. In L. H. Gunderson & C. S. Holling (Eds.), *Panarchy: Understanding Transformations in Human and Natural Systems* (pp. 261–289). Island Press.

Brown, S., Gummesson, E., Edvardsson, B., & Gustavsson, B. (1991). Service quality: Multidisciplinary and multinational perspectives. New York: Lexington.

Brown, J. H., Ernest, S. K. M., Parody, J. M., & Haskell, J. P. (2001). Regulation of diversity: Maintenance of species richness in changing environments. *Oecologia*, *126*(3), 321–332. doi:10.1007004420000536 PMID:28547444

Brown, R. L., Durbin, J., & Evans, J. M. (1975). Techniques for Testing the Constancy of Regression Relationships over Time Source. *Journal of the Royal Statistical Society. Series B. Methodological*, *37*(2), 149–192. doi:10.1111/j.2517-6161.1975.tb01532.x

Bruneau, M., Chang, S. E., Eguchi, R. T., Lee, G. C., O'Rourke, T. D., Reinhorn, A. M., Shinozuka, M., Tierney, K., Wallace, W. A., & von Winterfeldt, D. (2003). A framework to quantitatively assess and enhance the seismic resilience of communities. *Earthquake Spectra*, *19*(4), 733–752. doi:10.1193/1.1623497

Brush, C. G. A., de Bruin, A., & Welter, F. (2009). A Gender-Aware Framework for Women's Entrepreneurship. *International Journal of Gender and Entrepreneurship*, *1*(1), 8–24. doi:10.1108/17566260910942318

Bryson, C., & Hand, L. (2007). The role of engagement in inspiring teaching and learning. *Innovations in Education and Teaching International*, *44*(4), 349–362. doi:10.1080/14703290701602748

Bucăţa, G., & Rizescu, A. M. (2017). The role of communication in enhancing work effectiveness of an organization. *Land Forces Academy Review*, *22*(1), 49–57. doi:10.1515/raft-2017-0008

Burewoy, M. (1991). Reconstructing social theories. In *Ethnography Unbound*. University of California Press.

Buysse, K., & Verbeke, A. (2003). Proactive environmental strategies: A stakeholder management perspective. *Strategic Management Journal*, *24*(5), 453–470. doi:10.1002mj.299

Cadenasso, M. L., & Pickett, S. T. A. (2008). Urbanprinciples for ecological landscape design and management: Scientific fundamentals. *Cities and the Environment*, *1*(2), 4. doi:10.15365/cate.1242008

Cadenasso, M. L., & Pickett, S. T. A. (2013). Three tides: The development and state of the art of urban ecological studies In S. T. A. Pickett, M. L. Cadenasso, & B. P. McGrath (Eds.), *Resilience in urban ecology and design: Linking theory and practice for sustainable cities* (pp. 29–46). Springer. doi:10.1007/978-94-007-5341-9_2

Cadenasso, M. L., Pickett, S. T. A., & Grove, J. M. (2006a). Dimensions of ecosystem complexity: Heterogeneity, connectivity, and history. *Ecological Complexity*, *3*(1), 1–12. doi:10.1016/j.ecocom.2005.07.002

Cadenasso, M. L., Pickett, S. T. A., & Grove, J. M. (2006b). Integrative approaches to investigating human-natural systems: The Baltimore Ecosystem Study. *Nature Sciences Sociétés*, *14*(1), 1–14. doi:10.1051/nss:2006002

Cagnazzo, L., Taticchi, P., & Botarelli, M. (2008). A literature review on innovation management tools. *Revista de Administração da Universidade Federal de Santa Maria*, *1*(3), 316–330.

Cai, L. A. (2002). Cooperative branding for rural destination. *Annals of Tourism Research*, *29*(3), 720–742. doi:10.1016/S0160-7383(01)00080-9

Camagni, R. (1991). *Innovation networks: spatial perspectives*. Belhaven-Pinter.

Campbell, N., & Mitchell, D. T. (2012). A (partial) review of entrepreneurship literature across disciplines. *Journal of Entrepreneurship and Public Policy*, *1*(2), 183–199. doi:10.1108/20452101211261453

Can, M., Dogan, B., & Saboori, B. (2020). Does trade matter for environmental degradation in developing countries? New evidence in the context of export product diversification. *Environmental Science and Pollution Research International*, *27*(13), 14702–14710. doi:10.100711356-020-08000-2 PMID:32052330

Can, M., & Gozgor, G. (2017). The impact of economic complexity on carbon emissions: Evidence from France. *Environmental Science and Pollution Research International*, *24*(19), 16364–16370. doi:10.100711356-017-9219-7 PMID:28547378

Canton de Genève. (2013). Plan directeur cantonal 2030. A14: Promouvoir de nouvelles formes de jardins fa-miliaux et encourager la création de plantages. République et Canton de Genève.

Carley, M. (1995). The bigger picture: Organising for sustainable urban regeneration. *Town and Country Planning*, *64*(9), 236–239.

Carpenter, S. R., & Cottingham, K. L. (1997). Resilience and restoration of lakes. *Conservation Ecology*, *1*(1), 2. doi:10.5751/ES-00020-010102

Carpenter, S., Walker, B., Anderies, J. M., & Abel, N. (2001). From metaphor to measurement: Resilience of what to what? *Ecosystems (New York, N.Y.)*, *4*, 765–781.

Carrillo-Hermosilla, J., Del Río, P., & Könnölä, T. (2010). Diversity of eco-innovations: Reflections from selected case studies. *Journal of Cleaner Production*, *18*(10-11), 1073–1083. doi:10.1016/j.jclepro.2010.02.014

Carroll, A. B. (1991). The pyramid of corporate social responsibility: Toward the moral management of organizational stakeholders. *Business Horizons*, *34*(4), 39–48. doi:10.1016/0007-6813(91)90005-G

Carter, C. F., & Williams, B. R. (1958). *Investment in innovation*.

Carvalho, F. A., Koren, O., & Goodrich, J. K. (2012). Transient Inability to Manage Proteobacteria Promotes Chronic Gut Inflammation in TLR5-Deficient Mice. *Cell Host & Microbe*, *12*(2), 139–152. doi:10.1016/j.chom.2012.07.004

Castleden, M., McKee, M., Murray, V., & Leonardi, G. (2011, September). Resilience thinking in health protection. *Journal of Public Health*, *33*(3), 369–377. doi:10.1093/pubmed/fdr027

Cavallone, M., & Modina, M. (2013). Customer perception of bank communication: Evidence and implications. *Corporate Ownership and Control*, *10*(4), 299–307. doi:10.22495/cocv10i4c3art1

Cervellon, M. C., & Carey, L. (2011). Consumers' perceptions of 'green': Why and how consumers use eco-fashion and green beauty products. *Critical Studies in Fashion & Beauty*, *2*(1-2), 117–138. doi:10.1386/csfb.2.1-2.117_1

Cervellon, M. C., & Shammas, L. (2013). The value of sustainable luxury in mature markets: A customer-based approach. *Journal of Corporate Citizenship*, *2013*(52), 90–101. doi:10.9774/GLEAF.4700.2013.de.00009

Chance, T. (2009). Towards sustainable residential communities; the Beddington zero energy development (BedZED) and beyond. *Environment and Urbanization*, *21*(2), 527–544. doi:10.1177/0956247809339007

Chan, E. (2013). Managing green marketing: Hong Kong hotel managers' perspective. *International Journal of Hospitality Management*, *34*, 442–461. doi:10.1016/j.ijhm.2012.12.007

Chang, C. (2016). The determinants of green product innovation performance. *Corporate Social Responsibility and Environmental Management*, *23*(2), 65–76. doi:10.1002/csr.1361

Chang, C., & Chen, Y. (2012). The determinants of green intellectual capital. *Management Decision*, *50*(1), 74–94. doi:10.1108/00251741211194886

Chan, J. K. (2011). Enhancing Organisational Resilience: Application of Viable System Model and MCDA in a Small Hong Kong Company. *International Journal of Production Research*, *49*(18), 5545–5563. doi:10.1080/00207543.2011.563829

Chappells, H., & Trentmann, F. (2015). Sustainable consumption in history: Ideas, resources and practices. In L. A. Reisch & J. Thøgersen (Eds.), *Handbook of research on sustainable consumption* (pp. 51–70). Edward Elgar. doi:10.4337/9781783471270.00011

Charter, M., & Polonsky, M. (2017). *A Global Perspective on Greening Marketing Practice* (1st ed.). Routledge.

Chen, C.-F., & Phou, S. (2013). A closer look at destination: Image, personality, relationship and loyalty. *Tourism Management*, *36*, 269–278. doi:10.1016/j.tourman.2012.11.015

Chen, C., Tomsovic, K., & Aydeniz, M. (2014, July). Filling the Pipeline: Power System and Energy Curricula for Middle and High School Students Through Summer Programs. *IEEE Transactions on Power Systems*, *29*(4), 1874–1879. doi:10.1109/TPWRS.2013.2293752

Chenhall, R. H., & Moers, F. (2015). The role of innovation in the evolution of management accounting and its integration into management control. *Accounting, Organizations and Society*, *47*, 1–13. doi:10.1016/j.aos.2015.10.002

Chen, S., Chen, H. H., Zhang, K. Q., & Xu, X. L. (2018). A comprehensive theoretical framework for examining learning effects in green and conventionally managed hotels. *Journal of Cleaner Production*, *174*, 1392–1399. doi:10.1016/j.jclepro.2017.10.321

Chen, Y. (2008). The positive effect of green intellectual capital on competitive advantages of firms. *Journal of Business Ethics*, *77*(3), 271–286. doi:10.100710551-006-9349-1

Chen, Y., & Chang, C. (2013). Utilize structural equation modeling (SEM) to explore the influence of corporate environmental ethics: The mediation effect of green human capital. *Quality & Quantity*, *47*(1), 79–95. doi:10.100711135-011-9504-3

Chesbrough, H. W. (2006). The era of open innovation. *Managing Innovation and Change, 127*(3), 34-41.

Chetty, S. (1996). The case study method for research in small-and medium-sized firms. *International Small Business Journal*, *15*(1), 73–85. doi:10.1177/0266242696151005

Chewning, L. V., Lai, C.-H., & Doerfel, M. L. (2013). Organizational resilience and using information and communication technologies to rebuild communication structures. *Management Communication Quarterly*, *27*, 237–263. doi:10.1177/08933 18912 46581 5

Childers, D. L., Pickett, S. T. A., Grove, J. M., Ogden, L., & Whitmer, A. (2014). Advancing urban sustainability theory and action: Challenges and opportunities. *Landscape and Urban Planning*, *125*, 320–328. doi:10.1016/j.landurbplan.2014.01.022

Choi, H. S. C., & Sirakaya, E. (2005). Measuring residents' attitude toward sustainable tourism: Development of sustainable tourism attitude scale. *Journal of Travel Research*, *43*(4), 380–394. doi:10.1177/0047287505274651

Choi, S. H., & Cai, L. A. (2012). Destination loyalty and communication – a relationship-based tourist behavioural model. *International Journal of Strategic Communication*, *6*(1), 45–58. doi:10.1080/1553118X.2011.634868

Choshaly, S. H. (2019). Applying innovation attributes to predict purchase intention for the eco-labeled products. *International Journal of Innovation Science*, *11*(4), 583–599.

Chow, P. S., & Li, C. K. Y. (2018). Towards Closed-Loop Fashion Supply Chains—Reflections from Retailer-Facilitated Used Apparel Collection Programs. In Contemporary Case Studies on Fashion Production, Marketing and Operations. Springer.

Christensen, R., & Knezek, G. (2015). The Climate Change Attitude Survey: Measuring Middle School Student Beliefs and Intentions to Enact Positive Environmental Change. *International Journal of Environmental and Science Education*, *10*(5), 773–788.

Christopherson, R. W. (1997). Geosystems: An Introduction to Physical Geography (3rd ed.). Prentice Hall Inc.

ChuangI.HoA. (2016). *HarvardX and MITx: Four years of open online courses—fall 2012-summer 2016*. Available at SSRN 2889436. doi:10.2139/ssrn.2889436

City of Portland. (2007). *ENN-1.01: Food Policy Council (Binding city policy)*. Retrieved September 24, 2007, from http://www.portlandonline. com/auditor/index.cfm?a=ihci&c=checj

City of Vancouver. (2003). *Action plan for creating a just and sustainable food system for the City of Vancouver (RTS Number: 3755)*. Author.

Clarke, K. R. (1993). Non-parametric multivariate analyses of changes in community structure. *Austral Ecology*, *18*(1), 117–143. doi:10.1111/j.1442-9993.1993.tb00438.x

Clement, D. (2013). *The spatial injustice of crisis-driven neoliberal urban restructuring in Detroit* (Unpublished master's thesis). University of Miami. Retrieved from http://scholarlyrepository.miami.edu/oa_theses/406/

Clement, V., & Rivera, J. (2017). From adaptation to transformation: An extended research agenda for organizational resilience to adversity in the natural environment. *Organization & Environment*, *30*, 346–365. doi:10.1177/10860 26616 65833 3

ClimateAction. (2021). *WWF: Huge rise in demand for sustainable goods during Pandemic - Climate Action*. https://www.climateaction.org/news/wwf-huge-rise-in-demand-for-sustainable-goods-during-pandemic

Cohen, J., & Stewart, I. (1994). *The collapse of chaos: discovering simplicity in a complex world*. Penguin Group Ltd.

Cohn, S. (2013). A firm-level innovation management framework and assessment tool for increasing competitiveness. *Technology Innovation Management Review*, *3*(10), 6–15. doi:10.22215/timreview/731

Colding, J. (2011). The role of ecosystem services in contemporary urban planning. In Urban Ecology. Patterns, Processes and Applications. Oxford University Press. doi:10.1093/acprof:oso/9780199563562.003.0028

Colding, J., & Barthel, S. (2012). *The potential of Urban Green Commons in the resilience building of cities*. Elsevier B.V.

Colding, J., Lundberg, J., & Folke, C. (2006). Incorporating green-area user groups in urbanecosystem management. *Ambio*, *35*(5), 237–244. doi:10.1579/05-A-098R.1 PMID:16989508

Coles, E., & Buckle, P. (2004). Developing community resilience as a foundation for effective disaster recovery. *Australian Journal of Emergency Management*, *19*(4), 6–15.

Collins, J. P., Kinzig, A., Grimm, N. B., Fagan, W. F., Hope, D., Wu, J., & Borer, E. T. (2000). A new urban ecology. *American Scientist*, *88*(5), 416–425. doi:10.1511/2000.5.416

Constantinos, N. L., Constantine, S. K., & Neil, A. M. (2012). "Greening" the marketing mix: Do firms do it and does it pay off? *Journal of the Academy of Marketing Science*, *41*(2), 151–170.

Contractor, F. J., & Lorange, P. (1988). Why should firms cooperate? The strategy and economics basis for cooperative ventures. *Cooperative Strategies in International Business, 1*, 3-30.

Contractor, F., Yang, Y., & Gaur, A. S. (2016). Firm-specific intangible assets and subsidiary profitability: The moderating role of distance, ownership strategy and subsidiary experience. *Journal of World Business*, *51*(6), 950–964. doi:10.1016/j.jwb.2016.09.002

Convention on the Biological Diversity. (1992). The Earth Summit. Held in Rio de Janeiro on 5 June 1992 and entered into force on 29 December 1993. United Nations, General Assembly.

Cook, S. C., & Yurchisin, J. (2017). Fast fashion environments: Consumer's heaven or retailer's nightmare? *International Journal of Retail & Distribution Management*, *45*(2), 143–157. doi:10.1108/IJRDM-03-2016-0027

Cooper, C. (2012). *Essentials of Tourism*. Pearson Education Limited.

Cooper, R. (2001). *Winning at New Products; Accelerating the Process from Idea to Launch*. Perseus Books.

Cosgrove, S. (2001). *Montréal's community gardening program*. Retrieved July 29, 2007, from http://www.cityfarmer.org/Montreal13.html

Costa, E., Montemurro, D., & Giuliani, D. (2019). Consumers' willingness to pay for green cars: A discrete choice analysis in Italy. *Environment, Development and Sustainability*, *21*(5), 2425–2442. doi:10.100710668-018-0141-z

Costanza, R., & Patten, B. C. (1995). Defining and predicting sustainability. *Ecological Economics*, *15*(3), 193–196. doi:10.1016/0921-8009(95)00048-8

Cotton, D. R. E., Miller, W., Winter, J., Bailey, I., & Sterling, S. (2015). Developing students' energy literacy in higher education. *International Journal of Sustainability in Higher Education*, *16*(4), 456–473. doi:10.1108/IJSHE-12-2013-0166

Coutu, D. L. (2002). How resilience works. *Harvard Business Review*, *80*(5), 46–55.

Crichton, M. T., Ramsay, C. G., & Kelly, T. (2009). Enhancing organizational resilience through emergency planning: Learnings from cross-sectorial lessons. *Journal of Contingencies and Crisis Management*, *17*, 24–37.

Crowe. (n.d.). *Manufacturing*. https://www.crowe.com/my/industries/manufacturing

Curwell, S., & Cooper, I. (1998). The implications of urban sustainability. *Building Research and Information*, *26*(1), 17–28. doi:10.1080/096132198370074

Curwell, S., Deakin, M., & Symes, M. (Eds.). (2005). *Sustainable urban development, volume 1: The framework and protocols for environmental assessment*. Routledge. doi:10.4324/9780203299913

Cuthill, M., Ross, H., Maclean, K., Owens, K., & Witt, B. (2008). Reporting Social Outcomes of Development: An Analysis of Diverse Approaches. *The International Journal of Interdisciplinary Social Sciences: Annual Review*, *3*, 145–158.

Cvijanovich, M. (2011). *Sustainable luxury: Oxymoron? Lecture in luxury and sustainability*. http://www.mcmdesign-studio ch/files/ Guest%20professor%20Lucern%20School%20of%20Art%20%20and%20Design.pdf

Dandagi, S., Bhushi, U., Bagodi, V., & Sinha, D. (2016). Strategic management of technical university: Structural equation modelling approach. *Journal of Modelling in Management*, *11*(1), 75–90.

Danes, S. M., Lee, J., Amarapurkar, S., Stafford, K., Haynes, G., & Brewton, K. E. (2009). Determinants of family business resilience after a natural disaster by gender of business owner. *Journal of Developmental Entrepreneurship*, *14*(4), 333–354. doi:10.1142/S1084946709001351

Dangelico, R. M., & Vocalelli, D. (2017). "Green Marketing": An analysis of definitions, strategy steps, and tools through a systematic review of the literature. *Journal of Cleaner Production*, *165*, 1263–1279. doi:10.1016/j.jclepro.2017.07.184

Dangelico, R., Pujari, D., & Pontrandolfo, P. (2017). Green Product Innovation in Manufacturing Firms: A Sustainability-Oriented Dynamic Capability Perspective. *Business Strategy And The Environment, Wiley Blackwell*, *26*(4), 490–506.

Dankbaar, B. (2003). *Innovation management in the knowledge economy* (Vol. 7). World Scientific. doi:10.1142/p288

Darnton, A. (2007). *15 Principles for Practice from Behavioural Theory*. Andrew Darnton for the Energy Saving Trust.

Daskon, C. (2010). Cultural resilience – the roles of cultural traditions in sustaining rural livelihoods: A case study from rural kandyan villages in central Sri Lanka. *Sustainability*, *2*(4), 1080–1100.

Dastane, O. (2020). Impact of Digital Marketing on Online Purchase Intention: Mediation Effect of Customer Relationship Management. *Journal of Asian Business Strategy*, 142-158.

Daune, L., & Mongé, N. (2011). L'agriculture urbaine, un fondement dans le projet de territoire. *Urbia—Les Cahiers du développement urbain durable*, *12*, 85-106.

Davenport, T., & Prusak, L. (1998). *Working knowledge: How organizations manage what they know*. Harvard Business Press.

Deverey, A., & Dutta, K. (2021). COVID-19: Eco-friendly hand hygiene for human and environmental safety. *Journal of Environmental Chemical Engineering*, *9*(2), 104754. doi:10.1016/j.jece.2020.104754 PMID:33200069

Dawson, C. S. (2010). *Leading culture change: what every CEO needs to know*. Stanford University Press.

Daylight, R. (2017). Saussure and the model of communication. *Semiotica*, *2017*(217), 173–194. doi:10.1515em-2016-0038

de Jong, M., Joss, S., Schraven, D., Zhan, Ch., & Weijnen, M. (2015). Sustainable–Smart–Resilient–Low Carbon–Eco–Knowledge Cities; Making Sense of a Multitude of Concepts Promoting Sustainable Urbanization. *Journal of Cleaner Production*, *109*(1), 25–38. doi:10.1016/j.jclepro.2015.02.004

de Oliveira Teixeira, E., & Werther, W.B. (2013). Resilience: Continuous renewal of competitive advantages. *Bus Horiz, 56*, 333–342. https ://doi.org/ r.2013.01.009 doi:10.1016/j.busho

De Roo, G., Hillier, J., & van Wezemael, J. (Eds.). (2020). *Complexity and planning: systems, assemblages and simulations*. Ashgate Publishing. doi:10.4337/9781786439185

Deelstra, T., Boyd, D., & van den Biggelaar, M. (2006). *Multifunctional land use, promoting urban agriculture in Europe*. Academic Press.

DEFRA. (2003). *Changing patterns: UK government framework for sustainable consumption and production*. DEFRA.

DeGhetto, K., Sutton, T., & Zorn, M. L. (2018). Institutional drivers of born-public ventures. *Journal of Entrepreneurship and Public Policy*, *7*(1), 14–33. doi:10.1108/JEPP-D-17-00012

Dekker, J. M., Funahashi, T., & Nijpels, G. (2008, April 1). Prognostic Value of Adiponectin for Cardiovascular Disease and Mortality. *The Journal of Clinical Endocrinology and Metabolism*, *93*(4), 1489–1496. doi:10.1210/jc.2007-1436

Delafrooz, N., & Goli, A. (2015). The factors affecting the green brand equity of electronic products: Green marketing. *Cogent Business & Management*, *2*(1), 1079351. doi:10.1080/23311975.2015.1079351

Delgado-Verde, M., Amores-Salvad6, J., Martín-de Castro, G., & Navas-López, J. E. (2014). Green intellectual capital and environmental product innovation: The mediating role of green social capital. *Knowledge Management Research and Practice*, *12*(3), 261–275. doi:10.1057/kmrp.2014.1

Denyer, D. (2017). *Organizational Resilience: A summary of academic evidence, business insights and new thinking*. BSI and Cranfield School of Management.

Department of Statistics Malaysia. (2021). *Pocket Stats Q2 2021*. https://www.dosm.gov.my/v1/uploads/files/7_Publication/Infographic/PocketStats/Negeri/Johor/ST1-2021/Poket_Stats_Johor_ST1_2021.pdf

DesJardine, M., Bansal, P., & Yang, Y. (2017). Bouncing back: Building resilience through social and environmental practices in the context of the 2008 global financial crisis. *Journal of Management*, *26*. doi:10.1177/01492 06317 70885 4

DETR. (1998). *Sustainable Development: Opportunities for Change*. Department of the Environment, Transport and the Regions. Consultation Paper on a Revised UK Strategy, DETR.

Detroit Works Project. (2014). *Detroit future city: Detroit strategic framework plan*. Retrieved from http://detroitfuturecity.com/wp-content/uploads/2014/12/DFC_Full_2nd.pdf

Deutsch, L., Folke, C., & Skanberg, K. (2003). The critical natural capital of ecosystem performance as insurance for human well-being. *Ecological Economics*, *44*(2-3), 205–217. doi:10.1016/S0921-8009(02)00274-4

DeWaters, J. (2009). Energy literacy survey: A broad assessment of energy-related knowledge. Attitudes and Behaviors. Clarkson University.

DeWaters, J., & Susan, E. (2011). Powers, Energy literacy of secondary students in New York State (USA): A measure of knowledge, affect, and behavior. *Energy Policy*, *39*(3), 1699–1710. doi:10.1016/j.enpol.2010.12.049

Dharmavaram, V., & Nittala, R. (2018). Service quality and customer satisfaction in online banking. *International Journal of Online Marketing*, *8*(2), 45–56. doi:10.4018/IJOM.2018040103

Di Marco, M., Baker, M. L., Daszak, P., De Barro, P., Eskew, E. A., Godde, C. M., ... Karesh, W. B. (2020). Opinion: Sustainable development must account for pandemic risk. *Proceedings of the National Academy of Sciences of the United States of America*, *117*(8), 3888–3892. doi:10.1073/pnas.2001655117 PMID:32060123

Diamantopoulos, A., & Siguaw, J. A. (2006). Formative versus reflective indicators in organizational measure development: A comparison and empirical illustration. *British Journal of Management*, *17*, 263–282.

Dickey, D. A., & Fuller, W. A. (1979). Distribution of the Estimators for Autoregressive Time Series With a Unit Root. *Journal of the American Statistical Association*, *74*(366), 427. doi:10.2307/2286348

Dietz, S., & Neumayer, E. (2007). Weak and strong sustainability in the SEEA: Concepts and measurement. *Ecological Economics*, *61*(4), 617–626. doi:10.1016/j.ecolecon.2006.09.007

Docter, J., & Stokman, C. (1987). *Innovation strategies of small industrial companies. In Innovation: Adaptation and Growth*. Elsevier.

Dodgson, M. (1993). Learning, trust, and technological collaboration. *Human Relations*, *46*(1), 77–95. doi:10.1177/001872679304600106

Doern, R. (2016). Entrepreneurship and Crisis Management: The Experiences of Small Business during the London 2011 Riots. *International Small Business Journal*, *34*(3), 276–302. doi:10.1177/0266242614553863

Dogan, B., Madaleno, M., Tiwari, A. K., & Hammoudeh, S. (2020). Impacts of export quality on environmental degradation: Does income matter? *Environmental Science and Pollution Research International*, *27*(12), 13735–13772. doi:10.100711356-019-07371-5 PMID:32030594

Doğan, B., Saboori, B., & Can, M. (2019). Does economic complexity matter for environmental degradation? An empirical analysis for different stages of development. *Environmental Science and Pollution Research International*, *26*(31), 31900–31912. doi:10.100711356-019-06333-1 PMID:31489548

Donaldson, L. (2001). The contingency theory of organizations. *Sage (Atlanta, Ga.)*.

Donatiello, J. E. (2015). The world's population: An encyclopedia of critical issues, crises, and ever-growing countries. *Reference and User Services Quarterly*, *54*(4), 85. doi:10.5860/rusq.54n4.85b

Donni, R., Dastane, O., Haba, H. F., & Selvaraj, K. (2018). Consumer perception factors for fashion M-commerce and its impact on loyalty among working adults. *Business and Economic Review*, *8*(2), 168–192.

Dosi, G., & Orsenigo, L. (1994). Macrodynamics and microfoundations: an evolutionary perspective. Economics of Technology, 91-123.

Dow, K. (2000). Social dimensions of gradients in urban ecosystems. *Urban Ecosystems*, *4*(4), 255–275. doi:10.1023/A:1015767231137

Dowrick, S. (1995). *Economic approaches to innovation*. Edward Elgar Publishing.

Drage, C., Calantone, R., Agrawal, M., & MacKoy, R. (1993). The consumption culture and its critiques: A framework for analysis. *Journal of Macromarketing*, *13*(Fall), 32–45. doi:10.1177/027614679301300205

Drury, F. (2019). *Enchanting photos of the abandoned village taken over by hippies living in fairytale houses in the Spanish mountains*. MailOnline. http://www.dailymail.co.uk/news/article-3139295/Enchanting-photos-abandoned-village-taken-Spanish-hippies-living-fairytale-houses-mountains.html

Dubois, B., & Paternault, C. (1995). Understanding the world of international luxury brands: The dream formula. *Journal of Advertising Research*, *3*(4), 69–76.

Duit, A. (2016). Resilience thinking: Lessons for Public Administration. *Public Administration*, *94*, 364–380.

Dunleavy, J., & Milton, P. (2008). Student engagement for effective teaching and deep learning. *Education Canada*, *48*(5), 4–8.

Dunning, D. (2007). Self-image motives and consumer behavior: How sacrosanct self-beliefs sway preferences in the marketplace. *Journal of Consumer Psychology*, *17*(4), 237–249. doi:10.1016/S1057-7408(07)70033-5

Durgee, J. F., & Colarelli O'Connor, G. (1995). An exploration into renting as consumption behavior. *Psychology and Marketing*, *12*(2), 89–104. doi:10.1002/mar.4220120202

Dyllick, T., & Hockerts, K. (2002). Beyond the business case for corporate sustainability. *Business Strategy and the Environment*, *11*(2), 130–141. doi:10.1002/bse.323

Eckhardt, G. M., Houston, M. B., Jiang, B., Lamberton, C., Rindfleisch, A., & Zervas, G. (2019). Marketing in the sharing economy. *Journal of Marketing*, *83*(5), 5–27. doi:10.1177/0022242919861929

Economic Planning Unit. (2017). Malaysia - Sustainable Development Goals Voluntary. *National Review*. https://sustainabledevelopment.un.org/content/documents/15881Malaysia.pdf

Economic Planning Unit. (n.d.). *Sustainable Development Goals*. https://www.epu.gov.my/en/sustainable-development-goals

Ecouterre. (2012). *Sh!t Dame Vivienne Westwood Says: Greatest Hits Edition*. http://www.ecouterre.com/shit-dame-viviennewestwood- says/vivienne-westwood-says-4/?extend=1

Edwards, J. R. (2001). Multidimensional constructs in organizational behavior research: An integrative analytical framework. *Organizational Research Methods*, *4*, 144–192.

Edwards, J. R., & Bagozzi, R. P. (2000). On the nature and direction of relationship between constructs and measures. *Psychological Methods*, *5*, 155.

El HamidiF. (2017). Women Entrepreneurs in the MENA Region: Opportunities or a Mirage? Ssrn. doi:10.2139/ssrn.3050881

Elkington, J. (1997). *Cannibals with Forks: The triple bottom line of 21st century business*. Capstone.

Elmqvist, T., Wall, M., & Berggren, A. L. (2001). Tropical forest reorganization after cyclone and fire disturbance in Samoa: remnant trees as biological legacies. *Cons Ecol, 5*, 10. http://www.consecol.org/vol5/iss2/art10

Eltantawy, R. A. (2016). The role of supply management resilience in attaining ambidexterity: A dynamic capabilities approach. *Journal of Business and Industrial Marketing*, *31*(1), 123–134. doi:10.1108/JBIM-05-2014-0091

Emekci, S. (2019). Green consumption behaviours of consumers within the scope of TPB. *Journal of Consumer Marketing*, *36*(3), 410–417.

Eneizan, B., & Wahab, K. A. (2016). Effects of green marketing strategy on the financial and non-financial performance of firms: A conceptual paper. *Arabian Journal of Business Management Review*, *6*, 254.

Eneizan, B., Wahab, K. A., Zainon, M. S., & Obaid, T. F. (2016). Effects of green marketing strategies on sales volume of green cars. *Singapore Journal of Business Economics, and Management Studies*, *5*(30), 41–54. doi:10.12816/0031491

Environment, T. E., & Enterprises, S. (2016). *Access To Financial Resources - The Enabling Environment for*. Suzana Radulovic.

Erickson, G. M., & Johansson, J. K. (1985). The role of price in multi-attribute product evaluations. *The Journal of Consumer Research*, *12*(2), 195–199. doi:10.1086/208508

Estes, J. A., & Duggins, D. O. (1995). Sea otters and kelp forests in Alaska: Generality and variation in a community ecological paradigm. *Ecological Monographs*, *65*(1), 75–100. doi:10.2307/2937159

EurActiv. (2004). *Sustainable Development: Introduction.* Author.

Eveleens, C. (2010). Innovation management; a literature review of innovation process models and their implications. *Science*, *800*, 900–916.

Evetts, J. (1998). Managing the technology but not the organization: Women and career in engineering. *Women in Management Review*, *13*(8), 283–290. doi:10.1108/09649429810243144

Fagerberg, J., Fosaas, M., & Sapprasert, K. (2012). Innovation: Exploring the knowledge base. *Research Policy*, *41*(7), 1132–1153. doi:10.1016/j.respol.2012.03.008

Falk, B. (2013). The resilient farm and homestead. Chelsea Green Publishing.

Fang, J., Gozgor, G., Lu, Z., & Wu, W. (2019). Effects of the export product quality on carbon dioxide emissions: Evidence from developing economies. *Environmental Science and Pollution Research International*, *26*(12), 12181–12193. doi:10.100711356-019-04513-7 PMID:30835064

Faraj, S., & Sproull, L. (2000). Coordinating expertise in software development teams. *Management Science*, *46*, 1554–1568.

Farzanegan, M. R. (2014). Can oil-rich countries encourage entrepreneurship? *Entrepreneurship and Regional Development*, *26*(9-10), 706–725. doi:10.1080/08985626.2014.981869

Fath, B. D., Jørgensen, S. E., & Cole, M. (Eds.). (2020). *Managing Human and Social Systems.* CRC Press. doi:10.1201/9781003053514

Featherstone, M. (1991). *Consumer culture and postmodernism.* Sage.

Felipe, J., Kumar, U., Abdon, A., & Bacate, M. (2012). Product complexity and economic development. *Structural Change and Economic Dynamics*, *23*(1), 36–68. doi:10.1016/j.strueco.2011.08.003

Fereday, J., & Muir-Cochrane, E. (2006). Demonstrating rigor using thematic analysis: A hybrid approach of inductive and deductive coding and theme development. *International Journal of Qualitative Methods*, *5*(1), 1–11. doi:10.1177/160940690600500107

Feygina, I., Jost, J. T., & Goldsmith, R. E. (2010). System Justification, the Denial of Global Warming, and the Possibility of 'System-Sanctioned Change,'. *Personality and Social Psychology Bulletin*, *36*(3), 326–338. doi:10.1177/0146167209351435 PMID:20008965

Fibers, N. (2018). *Experience the natural difference.* www.noyafibers.com/

Fionda, A. M., & Moore, C. M. (2009). The Anatomy of The Luxury Fashion Brand. *Journal of Brand Management*, *16*(5/6), 347–363. doi:10.1057/bm.2008.45

Flensburg, P. (2009). An enhanced communication model. *The International Journal of Digital Accounting Research*, *9*(15), 31–43.

Fletcher, K. (2010). Slow fashion: An invitation for systems change. *Fashion Practice*, *2*(2), 259–265. doi:10.2752/175693810X12774625387594

Fletcher, K. (2012). Durability, Fashion, Sustainability: The Processes and Practices of Use. *Fashion Practice*, *4*(2), 221–238. doi:10.2752/175693812X13403765252389

Flint, J., & Raco, M. (Eds.). (2012). *The Future of Sustainable Cities: Critical Reflections.* The Policy Press.

Florin, J., Lubatkin, M., & Schulze, W. (2003). A social capital model of high-growth ventures. *Academy of Management Journal, 46*(3), 374–384.

Folke, C., Pritchard, L., Berkes, F., Colding, J., & Svedin, U. (1998). *The Problem of Fit Between Ecosystems and Institutions*. International Human Dimensions Programme (IHDP). IHDP Working Paper No 2. www.uni-bonn.de/IHDP/public.htm

Folke, C., Carpenter, S. R., Elmqvist, T., Gunderson, L., Holling, C. S., & Walker, B. (2002). Resilience and sustainable development: Building adaptive capacity in a world of transformations. *Ambio, 31*(5), 437–440. doi:10.1579/0044-7447-31.5.437 PMID:12374053

Folke, C., Holling, C. S., & Perrings, C. (1996). Biological diversity, ecosystems and the human scale. *Ecological Applications, 6*(4), 1018–1024. doi:10.2307/2269584

Folke, C., Jansson, A., Larsson, J., & Costanza, R. (1997). Ecosystem appropriation by cities. *Ambio, 26*, 167–172.

Fook, A. C. W., & Dastane, O. (2021). Effectiveness of Loyalty Programs in Customer Retention: A Multiple Mediation Analysis. *Jindal Journal of Business Research, 10*(1), 7–32.

Forys, E. A., & Allen, C. R. (2002). Functional group change within and across scales following invasions and extinctions in the Everglades ecosystem. *Ecosystems (New York, N.Y.), 5*(4), 339–347. doi:10.100710021-001-0078-0

Foster, S., & Dye, K. (2005). Building continuity into strategy. *Journal of Corporate Real Estate, 7*(2), 105–119.

Franco, J. C., Hussain, D., & McColl, R. (2019). Luxury fashion and sustainability: Looking good together. *The Journal of Business Strategy, 41*(4), 55–61. doi:10.1108/JBS-05-2019-0089

Freeman, C. (1991). Networks of innovators: A synthesis of research issues. *Research Policy, 20*(5), 499–514. doi:10.1016/0048-7333(91)90072-X

Freeman, R. E. (1984). *Strategic management: A stakeholder approach*. Pitman.

Freeman, R. E., Wicks, A. C., & Parmar, B. (2004). Stakeholder theory and "The corporate objective revisited.". *Organization Science, 15*(3), 364–369. doi:10.1287/orsc.1040.0066

Freytag, T., Gössling, S., & Mössner, S. (2019). Living the green city: Freiburg's Solarsiedlung between narratives and practices of sustainable urban development. *Local Environment, 19*(6), 644–659. doi:10.1080/13549839.2013.868872

Friedman, A. (2011). Perception : A Cognitive Sociological Approach. *Social Cognition*, 1–23.

Frost, T. M., Carpenter, S. R., Ives, A. R., & Kratz, T. K. (1995). Species compensation and complementarity in ecosystem function. In C. G. Jones & J. H. Lawton (Eds.), *Linking species and ecosystems*. Chapman & Hall. doi:10.1007/978-1-4615-1773-3_22

Fuchs, D. A., & Lorek, S. (2005). Sustainable consumption governance: A history of promises and failures. *Journal of Consumer Policy, 28*(3), 261–288. doi:10.100710603-005-8490-z

Fuller, D. A. (1999). *Sustainable marketing: Managerial-ecological issues*. Sage Publications.

Fyall, A., Callod, C., & Edwards, B. (2003). Relationship marketing: The challenge for destinations. *Annals of Tourism Research, 30*(3), 644–659. doi:10.1016/S0160-7383(03)00046-X

Fyall, A., Garrod, B., & Wang, Y. (2012). Destination collaboration: A critical review of theoretical approaches to a multi-dimensional phenomenon. *Journal of Destination Marketing & Management, 1*(1-2), 10–26. doi:10.1016/j.jdmm.2012.10.002

Gaire, A. K. S. (2018). Effectiveness of internet banking system and clients satisfaction: evidence from Surkhet, Nepal. *Technology, 1*(1), 10-21.

Gajurel, D. P., & Pradhan, R. S. (2012). Concentration and competition in Nepalese banking. *Journal of Business. Economics, 1*(1), 5–16.

Galbreath, J. (2009). Building corporate social responsibility into strategy. *European Business Review, 21*(2), 109–127. doi:10.1108/09555340910940123

Galli, A., Wackernagel, M., Iha, K., & Lazarus, E. (2014). Ecological Footprint: Implications for biodiversity. *Biological Conservation, 173*, 121–132. doi:10.1016/j.biocon.2013.10.019

Gallopín, G. C. (2006). Linkages between Vulnerability, Resilience and Adaptive Capacity. *Global Environmental Change, 16*(3), 293–303.

Ganganaboina, A., & Riaz, S. (2017). *Communication of Green Marketing Strategies for Creating Consumer Awareness: A study of grocery retail sector in Sweden*. University of Gavle.

Gann, D. (2000). *Building innovation: complex constructs in a changing world*. Thomas Telford. doi:10.1680/bicciacw.25967

Gaur, A. S., Kumar, V., & Singh, D. (2014). Institutions, resources, and internationalization of emerging economy firms. *Journal of World Business, 49*(1), 12–20. doi:10.1016/j.jwb.2013.04.002

Gautam, T., & Dhital, M. S. (2004). Customer satisfaction in Nepalese commercial banks. *Journal of Management and Development Review, 1*(2), 1–18.

Geiger, S. M., Fischer, D., & Schrader, U. (2018). Measuring what matters in sustainable consumption: An integrative framework for the selection of relevant behaviors. *Sustainable Development, 26*(1), 18–33. doi:10.1002d.1688

George, D., & Mallery, M. (2010). *SPSS for Windows Step by Step: A Simple Guide and Reference* (10th ed.). Pearson.

Gephart, R. P., Van Maanen, J., & Oberlechner, T. (2009). Organizations and risk in late modernity. *Organization Studies, 30*(2–3), 141–155. https://doi.org/ doi:10.1177/0170840608101474

Gerbner, G. (1956). Toward a general model of communication. *Audio Visual Communication Review*, 171-199.

Gilinsky, A. Jr, Newton, S., & Vega, R. (2016). Sustainability in the global wine industry: Concepts and cases. *Agriculture and Agricultural Science Procedia, 8*, 37–49. doi:10.1016/j.aaspro.2016.02.006

Gimenez, R., Hernantes, J., Labaka, L., Hiltz, S. R., & Turoff, M. (2017). Improving the resilience of disaster management organizations through virtual communities of practice: A Delphi study. *Journal of Contingencies and Crisis Management, 25*, 160–170. doi:10.1111/1468-5973.12181

Ginsberg, J. M., & Bloom, P. N. (2004). Choosing the right green marketing strategy. *MIT Sloan Management Review, 46*(1), 79–84.

Girardet, H. (1996). *The GAIA atlas of cities: new directions for sustainable urban living*. Gaia Books Limited.

Gitonga, A. N. (2017). *Factors influencing entrepreneurial motivation on university student's intentions of becoming entrepreneurs: A case of United States International University–Africa (USIU-A)* (Doctoral dissertation). United States International University-Africa.

Gittell, J. H., Cameron, K., Lim, S., & Rivas, V. (2006). Relationships, layoffs, and organizational resilience: Airline industry responses to September 11. *The Journal of Applied Behavioral Science, 42*, 300–329.

Global Footprint Network National Footprint Accounts. (2020). http://data.footprintnetwork.org

Global Footprint Network. (2021). *Open Data Platform.* https://data.footprintnetwork.org/#/countryTrends?type=BCpc,EFCpc&cn=223

Glynn Mangold, W., Miller, F., & Brockway, G. R. (1999). Word-of-mouth communication in the service marketplace. *Journal of Services Marketing*, *13*(1), 73–89. doi:10.1108/08876049910256186

Godart, F., & Seong, S. (2017). Is Sustainable Luxury Fashion Possible? In M. A. Gardetti & A. L. Torres (Eds.), *Sustainable Luxury: Managing Social and Environmental Performance in Iconic Brands*. Routledge. doi:10.4324/9781351287807-2

Godin, B. (2009). National innovation system: The system approach in historical perspective. *Science, Technology & Human Values*, *34*(4), 476–501. doi:10.1177/0162243908329187

Golley, F. B. (1993). *A History of the Ecosystem Concept in Ecology: More Than the Sum of the Parts*. Yale University Press.

Gomes, L. A. V., & Salerno, M. S. (2010). Modelo que integra processo de desenvolvimento de produto e planejamento inicial de spin-offs acadêmicos. *Gestão & Produção*, *17*(2), 245–255. doi:10.1590/S0104-530X2010000200003

González-Pernía, J. L., Jung, A., & Peña, I. (2015). Innovation-driven entrepreneurship in developing economies. *Entrepreneurship and Regional Development*, *27*(9-10), 555–573. doi:10.1080/08985626.2015.1075602

Goode, M., & Moutinho, L. (1996). The effects of consumers age on overall satisfaction: An application to financial services. *Journal of Professional Services Marketing*, *13*(2), 93–112. doi:10.1300/J090v13n02_07

Goodhue, D. L., & Loiacono, E. T. (2002, January). Randomizing survey question order vs. grouping questions by construct: An empirical test of the impact on apparent reliabilities and links to related constructs. In *Proceedings of the 35th Annual Hawaii International Conference on System Sciences* (pp. 3456-3465). IEEE. 10.1109/HICSS.2002.994385

Gozgor, G., & Can, M. (2016). Export product diversification and the environmental Kuznets curve: Evidence from Turkey. *Environmental Science and Pollution Research International*, *23*(21), 21594–21603. doi:10.100711356-016-7403-9 PMID:27519900

Gozgor, G., & Can, M. (2017). Does export product quality matter for CO2 emissions? Evidence from China. *Environmental Science and Pollution Research International*, *24*(3), 2866–2875. doi:10.100711356-016-8070-6 PMID:27838907

Graham, S., & Marvin, S. (2001). *Splintering urbanism: Networked infrastructures, technological mobilities and the urban condition*. Routledge.

Granger, C. W. J., & Yoon, G. (2002). *Hidden Cointegration*. SSRN Electronic Journal. doi:10.2139srn.313831

Grant, J. (2008). Green marketing. *Strategic Direction*, *24*(6), 25–27. doi:10.1108/02580540810868041

Green Technology Application for the Development of Low Carbon Cities. (2019). *World Cities Day: Accelerating Low Carbon Cities in Malaysia through the GTALCC Project*. http://gtalcc.gov.my/2019/11/01/world-cities-day-accelerating-low-carbon-cities-in-malaysia-through-the-gtalcc-project

Grimm, N. B., Faeth, S. H., Golubiewski, N. E., Redman, C. L., Wu, J., Bai, X., & Briggs, J. M. (2008). Global change and the ecology of cities. *Science*, *319*(5864), 756–760. doi:10.1126cience.1150195 PMID:18258902

Griskevicius, V., & Douglas, T. K. (2013). Fundamental motives: How evolutionary needs influence consumer behavior. *Journal of Consumer Psychology*, *23*(3), 372–386. doi:10.1016/j.jcps.2013.03.003

Grossman, G. M., & Krueger, A. B. (1991). *Environmental Impacts of a North American Free Trade Agreement*. National Bureau of Economic Research Working Paper Series. No. 3914. doi:10.3386/w3914

Groth, J. C., & McDaniel, S. W. (1993). The exclusive value principle: The basis for prestige racing. *Journal of Consumer Marketing*, *10*(1), 10–16. doi:10.1108/07363769310026539

Grove, J. M. (2009). Cities: Managing densely settled social–ecological systems. In F. S. Chapin III, G. P. Kofinas, & C. Folke (Eds.), *Principles of ecosystem stewardship: Resilience-based natural resource management in a changing world* (pp. 281–294). doi:10.1007/978-0-387-73033-2_13

Guba, E. G., & Lincoln, Y. S. (1994). Competing paradigms in qualitative research. In N. K. Denzin & Y. S. Lincoln (Eds.), *Handbook of Qualitative Research*. Sage Publications Inc.

Gubrium, J. A., & Holsten, J. A. (2001). *Handbook of interview research: Context and method*. Sage. doi:10.4135/9781412973588

Gültekin, N. (2015). Sosyal Sorumluluk: Fedakarlık Mı? Stratejik Mi? [Evaluatıon Of Socıal Responsıblıty Applıcatıons Of Private Educatıon Instıtutıons]. *Ekonomi ve Yönetim Araştırmaları Dergisi*, *4*(1), 10–30.

Gunderson, L. H., & Holling, C. S. (Eds.). (2002). *Panarchy: Understanding Transformations in Human and Systems*. Island Press.

Guo, Y. (2018). Implementing relationship banking strategies and techniques and improving customer value. *Finance and Market, 2*(2).

Gürcl, Y., Büyükbalcı, P., Yasemin, B. A. L., & Berkin, E. (2010). Kurumsal Sosyal Sorumluluk Kavramı Ve Gelişmekte Olan Ülkelerde Konuya Bakış [Concept of Corporate Social Responsibility and a Perspective on the Issue in Abstract Developing Country Context]. *İstanbul Üniversitesi Siyasal Bilgiler Fakültesi Dergisi*, (43), 135-162.

Guthey, G., & Whiteman, G. (2009). Social and ecological transitions: Winemaking in California. *Emergence*, *11*(3), 37–48.

Gwilt, A., & Rissanen, T. (2012). *Shaping sustainable fashion: Changing the way we make and use clothes*. Routledge.

Habitat, I. I. I. (2016). *Revised zero draft of the new urban agenda*. https://www.habitat3.org/zerodraft

Hagedoorn, J. (1990). Organizational modes of inter-firm co-operation and technology transfer. *Technovation*, *10*(1), 17–30. doi:10.1016/0166-4972(90)90039-M

Hair, J. F. (2010). *Multivariate data analysis: a global perspective*. Person Prentice Hall.

Hair, J. F., Black, W. C., Babin, B. J., Anderson, R. E., & Tatham, R. L. (2006). *Multivariate data analysis* (Vol. 6). Pearson Prentice Hall.

Hair, J., Hult, T., Ringle, C., & Sarstedt, M. (2014). *A Primer on Partial Least Squares Structural Equation Modeling (PLS-SEM)*. Sage Publications, Inc. (Thousand Oaks).

Hale, A., & Heijer, T. (2006). Defining Resilience. In E. Hollnagel, D. D. Woods, & N. Leveson (Eds.), *Resilience Engineering: Concepts and Precepts* (pp. 35–40). Ashgate.

Hale, L. A. (2018). At home with sustainability: From green default rules to sustainable consumption. *Sustainability*, *10*(1), 249. doi:10.3390u10010249

Hamel, G., & Välikangas, L. (2003). The quest for resilience. *Harvard Business Review, 81*(9), 52–63.

Hankinson, G. (2009). Managing destination brands: Establishing a theoretical foundation. *Journal of Marketing Management*, *25*(1-2), 97–115. doi:10.1362/026725709X410052

Hankinson, G. (2010). Place branding research: A cross disciplinary agenda and the views practitioners. *Place Branding and Public Diplomacy*, *6*(4), 300–315. doi:10.1057/pb.2010.29

Hanna, S., & Rowley, G. (2011). Towards a strategic place brand-management model. *Journal of Marketing Management, 27*(5-6), 458–476. doi:10.1080/02672571003683797

Hansen, A. J., Defries, R., & Turner, W. (2004). Land use change and biodiversity: a syn-thesis of rates and consequences during the period of satellite imagery. In G. Gutman & C. Justice (Eds.), *Land Change Science: Observing, Monitoring, and Understanding Trajectories of Change on the Earth's Surface* (pp. 277–299). Springer Verlag.

Han, Y., & Hansen, H. (2012). Determinants of sustainable food consumption: A meta-analysis using a traditional and a structural equation modeling approach. *International Journal of Psychological Studies, 4*(1), 22–45. doi:10.5539/ijps.v4n1p22

Hargie, O., Tourish, D., & Wilson, N. (2002). Communication audits and the effects of increased information: A follow-up study. *The Journal of Business Communication, 39*(4), 414-436.

Haron, S. A., Paim, L., & Yahya, N. (2005). Towards sustainable consumption: An examination of environmental knowledge among Malaysians. *International Journal of Consumer Studies, 29*(5), 426–436. doi:10.1111/j.1470-6431.2005.00460.x

Haroon, H., & Malik, H. D. (2018). The Impact of organizational communication on organizational performance. *Journal of Research in Social Sciences, 2*(1), 140–156.

Hartley, D. (2006). Excellence and enjoyment: The logic of a 'contradiction'. *British Journal of Educational Studies, 54*(1), 3–14. doi:10.1111/j.1467-8527.2005.00331.x

Hartman, D. (2013). A global comparative perspective on innovation and economic diversification in Turkey. In İstanbul Policy Center (pp. 1–28). Istanbul Policy Center (IPC).

Hartmann, D., Guevara, M. R., Jara-Figueroa, C., Aristarán, M., & Hidalgo, C. A. (2017). Linking Economic Complexity, Institutions, and Income Inequality. *World Development, 93*, 75–93. doi:10.1016/j.worlddev.2016.12.020

Hartmann, J., & Vachon, S. (2018). Linking environmental management to environmental performance: The interactive role of industry context. *Business Strategy and the Environment, 27*(3), 359–374. doi:10.1002/bse.2003

Hashem, T., & Al-Rifai, N. (2011). The influence of applying green marketing mix by chemical industries companies in the three Arab States in West Asia on consumer's mental image. *International Journal of Business and Social Science, 2*(3), 92–102.

Hashmi, G. (2017). Redefining the essence of sustainable luxury management: The slow value creation model. In M. Gardetti (Ed.), *Sustainable management of luxury* (pp. 3–27). Springer. doi:10.1007/978-981-10-2917-2_1

Hausmann, R., & Hidalgo, C. A. (2011). The network structure of economic output. *Journal of Economic Growth, 15*(4), 309–342. doi:10.100710887-011-9071-4

Hausmann, R., Hidalgo, C. A., Bustos, S., Coscia, M., Simoes, A., & Yildirim, M. A. (2014). *The Atlas of Economic Complexity: Mapping Paths to Prosperity*. The MIT Press. doi:10.7551/mitpress/9647.001.0001

Haven-Tang, C., & Sedgley, D. (2014). Partnership working in enhancing the destination brand of rural areas: A case study of made in Monmouthshire, Wales, UK. *Journal of Destination Marketing & Management, 3*(1), 59–67. doi:10.1016/j.jdmm.2013.12.001

Havlicek, T. D., & Carpenter, S. R. (2001). Pelagic species size distributions in lakes: Are they discontinuous? *Limnology and Oceanography, 46*(5), 1021–1033. doi:10.4319/lo.2001.46.5.1021

Haws, K. L., Naylor, R. W., Coulter, R., & Bearden, W. O. (2012). Keeping it all without being buried alive: Understanding product retention tendency. *Journal of Consumer Psychology, 22*(2), 224–236.

Haws, K., Winterich, K., & Naylor, R. (2014). Seeing the world through GREEN-tinted glasses: Green consumption values and responses to environmentally friendly products. *Journal of Consumer Psychology*, *24*(3).

Hayes, R. H., & Abernathy, W. J. (1980). Managing our way to economic decline. Harvard Bus. Rev., 58(4).

Helwig, K. R. (2013). Resilience: A responsibility that can't be delegated. *Frontiers of Health Services Management*, *30*(2), 31–35. https://www.ache.org/pubs/Frontiers/frontiers_index.cfm

Henderson, R. M., & Clark, K. B. (1990). Architectural innovation: The reconfiguration of existing product technologies and the failure of established firms. *Administrative Science Quarterly*, *35*(1), 9–30. doi:10.2307/2393549

Hennigs, N., Wiedmann, K. P., Klarmann, C., & Behrens, S. (2013). Sustainability as part of the luxury essence: Delivering value through social and environmental excellence. *Journal of Corporate Citizenship*, *52*(52), 25–35. doi:10.9774/GLEAF.4700.2013.de.00005

Henninger, C. E., Alevizou, P. J., Tan, J. L., Huang, Q., & Ryding, D. (2017). Consumption strategies and motivations of chinese consumers: The case of UK sustainable luxury. *Journal of Fashion Marketing and Management*, *21*(3), 419–434. doi:10.1108/JFMM-05-2017-0046

Herrera, I. A., Pasquini, A., Ragosta, M., & Vennesland, A. (2014). The SCALES framework for identifying and extracting resilience related indicators: preliminary findings of a go-around case study. *SIDs 2014-Proc. SESAR Innov. Days, Eurocontrol.*

Herr, P. M., Kardes, F. R., & Kim, J. (1991). Effects of word-of-mouth and product-attribute information on persuasion: An accessibility-diagnosticity perspective. *The Journal of Consumer Research*, *17*(4), 454–462. doi:10.1086/208570

Hertsgaard, M. (2010). What climate change means for wine industry. *Wired Science.*

Hertwich, E. (2002). Life-cycle approaches to sustainable consumption. *Workshop Proceedings Interim Report, International Institute for Applied Systems Analysis.*

Heslin, P. A., & Ochoa, J. D. (2008). Understanding and developing strategic corporate social responsibility. *Organizational Dynamics*, *37*(2), 125–144. doi:10.1016/j.orgdyn.2008.02.002

Hezri, A., & Hasan, N. (2006). Towards sustainable development? The evolution of environmental policy in Malaysia. *Natural Resources Forum*, *30*(1), 37–50. doi:10.1111/j.1477-8947.2006.00156.x

Hicks, M., & Faulk, D. G. (2018). Do entrepreneur-focused facility incentives create economic impacts? Evidence from Indiana. *Journal of Entrepreneurship and Public Policy*, *7*(3), 222–234. doi:10.1108/JEPP-D-18-00013

Hidalgo, C. A., & Hausmann, R. (2009). The building blocks of economic complexity. In *Proceedings of the National Academy of Sciences of the United States of America* (Vol. 106, Issue 26). 10.1073/pnas.0900943106

Hiles, A. (2011). *The Definitive Handbook of Business Continuity Management*. Wiley.

Hillman, J., & Guenther, E. (2021). Organizational Resilience: A Valuable Construct for Management Research? *International Journal of Management Reviews*, *23*, 7–44. doi:10.1111/ijmr.12239

Hill, N., & Alexander, J. (2001). Handbook of customer satisfaction and loyalty measurement. *International Journal of Retail & Distribution Management*, *29*(7), 347–347. doi:10.1108/ijrdm.2001.29.7.347.1

Hirsch, P. M., & Levin, D. Z. (1999). Umbrella advocates versus validity police: A life-cycle model. *Organization Science*, *10*, 199–212.

Hmedat, W., Ali, M., & Muthuraman, B. (2017). A Study on Entrepreneurial Initiatives among MBA Students in Sultanate of Oman. *International Journal of Management, Innovation & Entrepreneurial Research, 3*(2).

Hodgson, K., Caton Campbell, M., & Bailkey, M. (2011). Urban agriculture: growing healthy, sustainable places. Washington, DC: American Planning Association.

Hoe, J., Dastane, O., & Selvaraj, K. (2018). Predicting consumer perception and its impact on purchase intention for residential property market. *Journal of Technology Management and Business*, *5*(2).

Holling, C. S. (1973). Resilience and stability of ecological systems. *Annual Review of Ecology and Systematics*, *4*(1), 1–23. doi:10.1146/annurev.es.04.110173.000245

Holling, C. S. (1996). Engineering resilience versus ecological resilience. In P. C. Schulze (Ed.), *Engineering within ecological constraints*. National Academy Press.

Hoque, M. E., Nik Hashim, N. M. H., & Razzaque, M. A. (2018). Effects of communication and financial concerns on banking attitude-behaviour relations. *Service Industries Journal*, *38*(13-14), 1017–1042. doi:10.1080/02642069.2018.1428954

Horne, J. F. (1997). The coming of age of organizational resilience. *Business Forum, 22*, 24–28.

Horne, J. F., & Orr, J. E. (1998). Assessing Behaviors that Create Resilient Organizations. *Employment Relations Today*, *24*, 29–39.

Horne, R. E. (2009). Limits to labels: The role of eco-labels in the assessment of product sustainability and routes to sustainable consumption. *International Journal of Consumer Studies*, *33*, 175–182.

Hosany, S., Ekinci, Y., & Uysal, M. (2007). Destination image and destination personality. *International Journal of Culture, Tourism and Hospitality Research*, *1*(1), 62–81. doi:10.1108/17506180710729619

Hough, M. (1995). *Cities and Natural Process*. Routledge. doi:10.4324/9780203292433

Huang, C., & Kung, F. (2011). Environmental consciousness and intellectual capital management: Evidence from Taiwan's manufacturing industry. *Management Decision*, *49*(9), 1405–1425. doi:10.1108/00251741111173916

Huarng, K. H., Mas-Tur, A., & Yu, T. H. K. (2012). Factors affecting the success of women entrepreneurs. *The International Entrepreneurship and Management Journal*, *8*(4), 487–497. doi:10.100711365-012-0233-4

Hubert, M., & Kenning, P. (2008). A Current overview of Consumer Neuroscience. Journal of Consumer Behavior, 7(4-5), 272-292.

Hui, S. C. M. (2011). *Green roof urban farming for buildings in high-density urban cities.* Invited paper for the Hainan China World Green Roof Conference 2011, Hainan, China.

Hui, S. C. S., Dastane, O., Johari, Z., & Roslee, M. (2021). Enhancing Online Repurchase Intention via Application of Big Data Analytics in E-Commerce. In *Handbook of Research on Innovation and Development of E-Commerce and E-Business in ASEAN* (pp. 395–434). IGI Global.

Hu, Q., Kapucu, N., & O'Byrne, L. (2014). Strategic planning for community-based small nonprofit organizations: Implementation, benefits, and challenges. *The Journal of Applied Management and Entrepreneurship*, *19*(1), 83–101. doi:10.9774/GLEAF.3709.2014.ja.00007

Husted, B. W., & Allen, D. B. (2007). Strategic corporate social responsibility and value creation among large firms: Lessons from the Spanish experience. *Long Range Planning*, *40*(6), 594–610. doi:10.1016/j.lrp.2007.07.001

Hustvedt, G., & Dickson, M. A. (2009). Consumer likelihood of purchasing organic cotton apparel: Influence of attitudes and self-identity. *Journal of Fashion Marketing and Management, 13*(1), 49–65. doi:10.1108/13612020910939879

Hynes, H. P. (1996). *A Patch of Eden: America's Inner-city Gardeners*. Chelsea Green Publishing Company.

Iammarino, S. (2005). An evolutionary integrated view of regional systems of innovation: Concepts, measures and historical perspectives. *European Planning Studies, 13*(4), 497–519. doi:10.1080/09654310500107084

Ignatiadis, I. & Nandhakumar, J. (2007). The Impact of Enterprise Systems on Organizational Control and Drift: A Human-Machine Agency Perspective. *International Journal of Enterprise Information Systems, 3*(3), 36-51. Doi:10.1057/palgrave.jit.2000087

IISD. (2009). *What is Sustainable Development?* International Institute for Sustainable Development.

Inman, R. A., & Green, K. W. (2018). Lean and green combine to impact environmental and operational performance. *International Journal of Production Research, 56*(14), 1–17. doi:10.1080/00207543.2018.1447705

Insch, A. (2011). Conceptualization and anatomy of green destination brands. *International Journal of Culture, Tourism and Hospitality Research, 5*(3), 282–290. doi:10.1108/17506181111156970

International Climate Initiative. (n.d.). *Sustainable Urban Development*. https://www.international-climate-initiative.com/en/issues/cross-cutting-topics/sustainable-urban-development

IPCC. (2014). Climate Change 2014: Synthesis Report. Contribution of Working Groups I, II and III to the Fifth Assessment Report of the Intergovernmental Panel on Climate Change. IPCC.

Iqbal, N., Abbasi, R., Shinwari, R., Guangcai, W., Ahmad, M., & Tang, K. (2021). Does exports diversification and environmental innovation achieve carbon neutrality target of OECD economies? *Journal of Environmental Management, 291*, 112648. doi:10.1016/j.jenvman.2021.112648 PMID:33940360

Iran, S., & Geiger, S. M. (2018). To wear or to own? Influences of values on the attitudes towards and the engagement in collaborative fashion consumption. In M. Heuer & C. Becker-Leifhold (Eds.), *Eco-Friendly and Fair* (pp. 153–162). Routledge.

Ishak, A. W., & Williams, E. A. (2018). A dynamic model of organizational resilience: Adaptive and anchored approaches. *Corporate Communications, 23*, 180–196.

Ishaq Bhatti, M., Zafarullah, M., Awan, H. M., & Bukhari, K. S. (2011). Employees' perspective of organizational service quality orientation: Evidence from Islamic banking industry. *International Journal of Islamic and Middle Eastern Finance and Management, 4*(4), 280–294. doi:10.1108/17538391111186537

Ismaila Rimi, A., & Yakubu Aliyu, B. (2019). Low Carbon City: Strategies and Case Studies. In W. Leal Filho, A. Azul, L. Brandli, P. Özuyar, & T. Wall (Eds.), *Sustainable Cities and Communities, Encyclopedia of the UN Sustainable Development Goals*. Springer. doi:10.1007/978-3-319-71061-7_24-2

Ismail, I., Husin, N., Rahim, N. A., Kamal, M. H. M., & Mat, R. C. (2016). Entrepreneurial success among single mothers: The role of motivation and passion. *Procedia Economics and Finance, 37*, 121–128. doi:10.1016/S2212-5671(16)30102-2

Jaaron, A. A. M., & Backhouse, C. J. (2014). Service organisations resilience through the application of the vanguard method of systems thinking: A case study approach. *International Journal of Production Research, 52*, 2026–2041.

Jabbour, C., De Sousa Jabbour, A., & Sarkis, J. (2019). Unlocking effective multi-tier supply chain management for sustainability through quantitative modeling: Lessons learned and discoveries to be made. *International Journal of Production Economics, 217*, 11–30. doi:10.1016/j.ijpe.2018.08.029

Jackson, J. B. C., Kirby, M. X., Berger, W. H., Bjorndal, K. A., Botsford, L. W., Bourque, B. J., Bradbury, R. H., Cooke, R., Erlandson, J., Estes, J. A., Hughes, T. P., Kidwell, S., Lange, C. B., Lenihan, H. S., Pandolfi, J. M., Peterson, C. H., Steneck, R. S., Tegner, M. J., & Warner, R. R. (2001). Historical overfishing and the recent collapse of coastal ecosystems. *Science*, *293*(5530), 629–638. doi:10.1126cience.1059199 PMID:11474098

Jacobs, D., & Snijders, H. (2008). *Innovation routine: how managers can support repeated innovation*. Stichting Management Studies.

Jain, S. (2019). Factors affecting sustainable luxury purchase behavior: A conceptual framework. *Journal of International Consumer Marketing*, *31*(2), 130–146.

Jain, S., & Mishra, S. (2020). Luxury fashion consumption in sharing economy: A study of Indian millennials. *Journal of Global Fashion Marketing*, *11*(2), 171–189.

Jamali, D. (2007). The case for strategic corporate social responsibility in developing countries. *Business and Society Review*, *112*(1), 1–27. doi:10.1111/j.1467-8594.2007.00284.x

Jamal, T., & Getz, D. (1995). Collaboration theory and community tourism planning. *Annals of Tourism Research*, *22*(1), 186–204. doi:10.1016/0160-7383(94)00067-3

James, P., Magee, L., Scerri, A., & Steger, M. B. (2015). *Urban Sustainability in Theory and Practice*. Routledge.

Jang, J., Ko, E., Chun, E., & Lee, E. (2012). A study of a social content model for sustainable development in the fast fashion industry. *Journal of Global Fashion Marketing*, *3*(2), 61–70.

Janssen, C., Vanhamme, J., Lindgreen, A., & Lefebvre, C. (2014). The Catch-22 of responsible luxury: Effects of luxury product characteristics on consumers' perception of fit with corporate social responsibility. *Journal of Business Ethics*, *119*(1), 45–57.

Jardon, C., & Dasilva, A. (2017). Intellectual capital and environmental concern in subsistence small businesses. *Management of Environmental Quality*, *28*(2), 214–230. doi:10.1108/MEQ-05-2015-0085

Jardon, C., & Martos, M. (2012). Intellectual capital as competitive advantage in emerging clusters in Latin America. *Journal of Intellectual Capital*, *13*(4), 462–481. doi:10.1108/14691931211276098

Jenks, M., & Jones, C. (Eds.). (2010). Dimensions of the sustainable city. Springer.

Jenks, M., & Dempsey, N. (Eds.). (2005). *Future Forms and Design for Sustainable Cities*. Routledge.

Jennings, G. (2010). Tourism research (2nd ed.). Wiley & Sons.

Jesuthasan, M. (2021). *Explainer: The Climate Crisis and Singapore*. New Naratif.

Jiang, Y., & Wen, J. (2020). Effects of COVID-19 on hotel marketing and management: A perspective article. *International Journal of Contemporary Hospitality Management*, *32*(8), 2563–2573. doi:10.1108/IJCHM-03-2020-0237

Jirawuttinunt, S. (2018). The Relationship between Green Human Resource Management and Green Intellectual Capital of Certified ISO 14000 Businesses in Thailand. *St. Theresa. Journal of the Humanities and Social Sciences*, *4*(1), 20–37.

Jiwan, D., Paul, C. P. K., Teo, G. K., & Jiwan, M. (2006). Integrated highland development in Bario,Sarawak, Malaysia: an overview. *International Symposium Towards Sustainable Livelihoods and Ecosystems in Mountainous Regions*.

Johnson, K. K. P., Kim, M., & Lennon, S. J. (2008). Dress and human behavior: A review and critique. *Clothing & Textiles Research Journal*, *26*(3), 3–22.

Johnstone, M. L., & Tan, L. P. (2015). Exploring the gap between consumers' green rhetoric and purchasing behaviour. *Journal of Business Ethics*, *132*(2), 311–328.

Joshi, R., & Rahman, Z. (2015). Factors affecting green purchase behaviour and future research directions. *International Strategic Management Review*, *3*(1-2), 128–143. doi:10.1016/j.ism.2015.04.001

Joy, A., Sherry, J. F., Venkatesh, A., Wang, F., & Chan, R. (2012). Fast Fashion, Sustainability, and the Ethical Appeal of Luxury Brands. *Fashion Theory*, *16*(3), 273–295.

Kahle, L. R., & Gurel-Atay, E. (Eds.). (2014). *Communicating Sustainability for the Green Economy*. M.E. Sharpe.

Kahn, W. A., Barton, M. A., & Fellows, S. (2013). Organizational crises and the disturbance of relational systems. *Academy of Management Review*, *38*, 377–396. doi:10.5465/amr.2011.0363

Kaklauskas, A., & Gudauskas, R. (2016). Intelligent decision-support systems and the Internet of Things for the smart built environment. In *Start-Up Creation* (pp. 413–449). Woodhead Publishing. doi:10.1016/B978-0-08-100546-0.00017-0

Kalin Arroyo, M. T., Zedler, P. H., & Fox, M. D. (Eds.). (1995). *Ecology and biogeography of Mediterranean ecosystems in Chile, California, and Australia*. Springer-Verlag. doi:10.1007/978-1-4612-2490-7

Kantur, D., & İşeri-Say, A. (2015). Measuring organizational resilience: A scale development. Journal of Business. *Economics & Finance*, *4*(3), 456–472.

Kapferer, J.-N. (2010). All that glitters is not green: The challenge of sustainable luxury. *European Business Review*. www.europeanbusinessreview.com/?p=2869

Kapferer, J. M., & Michaut-Denizeau, A. (2015). *Are luxury purchasers insensitive to sustainable development? New insights from research. Sustainable luxury*. Greenleaf Publishing Limited.

Kapferer, J. N. (1998). Why are we seduced by luxury brands? *Journal of Brand Management*, *6*(1), 44–49.

Kapferer, J. N., & Bastien, V. (2012). *The Luxury Strategy: Break the Rules of Marketing to Build Luxury Brands*. Kogan Page.

Kapferer, J. N., & Bastien, V. (2017). The specificity of luxury management: Turning marketing upside down. In J. N. Kapferer, J. Kernstock, T. Brexendorf, & S. Powell (Eds.), *Advances in Luxury Brand Management. Journal of Brand Management: Advanced Collections*. Palgrave Macmillan.

Kapoor, K. K., & Dwivedi, Y. D. (2020). Sustainable consumption from the consumer's perspective: Antecedents of solar innovation adoption. *Resources, Conservation and Recycling*, *152*(1), 1–12. doi:10.1016/j.resconrec.2019.104501

Karasoy, A. (2019). Drivers of carbon emissions in Turkey: Considering asymmetric impacts. *Environmental Science and Pollution Research International*, *26*(9), 9219–9231. doi:10.100711356-019-04354-4 PMID:30721434

Kargwell, S. A. (2012). Women entrepreneurs breaking through: Push and pull within UAE cultural context. *International Journal of Business and Social Science*, *3*(17).

Kates, R., Parris, T., & Leiserowitz, A. (2005). What is Sustainable Development? Goals, Indicators, Values, and practice. *Environment*, *47*(3), 8–21. doi:10.1080/00139157.2005.10524444

Kauppinen-Räisänen, H., Björk, P., Lönnström, A., & Jauffret, M. N. (2018). How consumers' need for uniqueness, self-monitoring, and social identity affect their choices when luxury brands visually shout versus whisper. *Journal of Business Research*, *84*, 72–81.

Kayat, K. (2011). *Homestay Programme as a Malaysian Tourism Product*. UUM Press.

Kay, R. (2011). Evaluating learning, design, and engagement in web-based learning tools (WBLTs): The WBLT Evaluation Scale. *Computers in Human Behavior*, *27*(5), 1849–1856. doi:10.1016/j.chb.2011.04.007

Keeble, D., & Wilkinson, F. (2017). *High-technology clusters, networking and collective learning in Europe*. Routledge. doi:10.4324/9781315188904

Kemper, J. A., & Ballantine, P. W. (2019). What do we mean by sustainability marketing? *Journal of Marketing Management*, *35*(3-4), 277–309.

Kendall, J. (2010). *Responsible Luxury: A report on the new opportunities for business to make a difference*. https://www.rapaportfairtrade.com/Docs/ CIBJO-responsible_luxury.pdf

Kendra, J. M., & Wachtendorf, T. (2003). Elements of Resilience after the World Trade Center Disaster: Reconstituting New York City's Emergency Operations Center. *Disasters*, *27*(1), 37–53.

Kennedy, K. (2016). Employee Job Satisfaction and Engagement: Revitalizing a Changing Workforce. A research report by The Society for Human Resource Management.

Kennedy, C., Cuddihy, J., & Engel-Yan, J. (2020). The changing metabolism of cities. *Journal of Industrial Ecology*, *11*(2), 43–59. doi:10.1162/jie.2007.1107

Kennedy, C., Pincetl, S., & Bunje, P. (2010). The study of urban metabolism and its applications to urban planning and design. *Environmental Pollution*, *159*(8–9), 1965–1973. PMID:21084139

Kerr, J., & Landry, J. (2017). *Pulse of the fashion industry. In Global Fashion Agenda*. The Boston Consulting Group.

Khalil, N., Husin, H. N., Mahat, N., & Nasir, N. (2011). Sustainable environment: Issues and solutions from the perspective of facility managers. *Procedia Engineering*, *20*, 458–465. doi:10.1016/j.proeng.2011.11.188

Khan, S. A., Ghosh, A. P., & Myers, D. A. (2005). Women entrepreneurship in Oman. *Proceedings of 50th World Conference of the International Council for the Small Business (ICSB)*, 15–18.

Khanna, M. (2011). Destination branding: Tracking brand India. *Synergy*, *9*(1), 40–49.

Khare, A. (2015). Antecedents to green buying behaviour: A study on consumers in an emerging economy. *Marketing Intelligence & Planning*, *33*(3), 309–329.

Kharel, S., Magar, S., Chaurasiya, N., Maharjan, S., & Rijal, C. P. (2019). Transparency and accountability in the Nepalese corporate sector: A critical assessment. *Quest Journal of Management and Social Sciences*, *1*(1), 1–25. doi:10.3126/qjmss.v1i1.25972

Khatri, J. R., & Upadhyaya-Dhungel, K. (2013). Internet banking in Nepal: Use and challenges. *Banking Journal*, *3*(2), 57–77. doi:10.3126/bj.v3i2.8544

Ki, C. W., & Kim, Y. K. (2016). Sustainable versus conspicuous luxury fashion purchase: Applying self-determination theory. *Family and Consumer Sciences Research Journal*, *44*(3), 309–323.

Kickul, J., Gundry, L. K., Barbosa, S. D., & Whitcanack, L. (2009). Intuition versus analysis? Testing differential models of cognitive style on entrepreneurial self–efficacy and the new venture creation process. *Entrepreneurship Theory and Practice*, *33*(2), 439–453. doi:10.1111/j.1540-6520.2009.00298.x

Kim, H., Choo, H. J., & Yoon, N. (2013). The Motivational Drivers of Fast Fashion Avoidance. *Journal of Fashion Marketing and Management*, *17*(2), 243–260.

Kim, M., Kim, B., & Oh, S. (2018). Relational benefit on satisfaction and durability in strategic corporate social responsibility. *Sustainability*, *10*(4), 1104. doi:10.3390u10041104

Kinzig, A. P., Pacala, S. W., & Tilman, D. (Eds.). (2002). *The functional consequences of biodiversity*. Princeton University Press.

Kirakosyan, K., & Dănăiață, D. (2014). Communication management in electronic banking. Better communication for better relationship. *Procedia: Social and Behavioral Sciences*, *124*, 361–370. doi:10.1016/j.sbspro.2014.02.497

Kish-Gephart, J. J., & Campbell, J. T. (2015). You Don't Forget Your Roots: The Influence of CEO Social Class Background on Strategic Risk Taking. *Academy of Management Journal*, *58*(6), 1614–1636. doi:10.5465/amj.2013.1204

Kitchenham, B. (2010). What's up with software metrics? A preliminary mapping study. *Journal of Systems and Software*, *83*(1), 37–51. doi:10.1016/j.jss.2009.06.041

Klassen, R. D., & McLaughlin, C. P. (1996). The impact of environmental management on firm performance. *Management Science*, *42*(8), 1199–1214. doi:10.1287/mnsc.42.8.1199

Kline, S. J., & Rosenberg, N. (1986). An overview of innovation. The positive sum strategy: Harnessing technology for economic growth. *The National Academy of Science, USA*, *35*, 36.

Kohno, Y., Masuda, Y., Nagahashi, H., Tanaka, K., & Tashiro, K. (2012). Form development for self-rating an organization's vulnerability and resilience to disruption. *Journal of Disaster Research*, *7*(4), 392–407. doi:10.20965/jdr.2012.p0392

Kolasa, J., & Pickett, S. T. A. (2005). Changing academic perspectives of ecology: A view from within. In M. J. Mappin & E. A. Johnson (Eds.), *Environmental education and advocacy* (pp. 50–71). Cambridge University Press.

Kotler, P., Armstrong, G., & Starr, R. G. (1989). Principles of marketing. Prentice-Hall. Inc.

Kotler, P., Bowen, J.T., & Makens, J.C. (2014). Marketing for hospitality and tourism (6th ed.). Pearson.

Kotsemir, M., Abroskin, A., & Meissner, D. (2013). *Innovation concepts and typology–an evolutionary discussion.* Higher School of Economics Research Paper No. WP BRP, 5.

Kourgiantakis, M., Apostolakis, A., & Dimou, I. (2021). COVID-19 and holiday intentions: The case of Crete, Greece. *Anatolia*, *32*(1), 148–151. doi:10.1080/13032917.2020.1781221

Kreimer, A., Arnold, M., & Carlin, A. (Eds.). (2003). *Building safer cities: the future of disaster risk*. The International Bank for Reconstruction and Development/The World Bank.

Kumar, D., Kumar, I., Rahman, Z., Yadav, S., & Goyal, P. (2011). Green Marketing Mix: Competitive advantage during climate change. *International Journal of the Computer, the Internet and Management*, (19), 62.1-62.5.

Kumar, G., Subramanian, N., & Arputham, R. M. (2018). Missing link between sustainability collaborative strategy and supply chain performance: Role of dynamic capability. *International Journal of Production Economics*, *203*, 96–109. doi:10.1016/j.ijpe.2018.05.031

Kurland, N. B., & Bailey, D. E. (2000). Telework: The advantages and challenges of working here, there, anywhere, and anytime. *IEEE Engineering Management Review*, *28*(2), 49–60.

Kurucz, E. C., Colbert, B. A., & Wheeler, D. (2008). The business case for corporate social responsibility. The Oxford handbook of corporate social responsibility, 83-112.

Kwiatkowski, D., Phillips, P. C. B., Schmidt, P., & Shin, Y. (1992). Testing the null hypothesis of stationarity against the alternative of a unit root. How sure are we that economic time series have a unit root? *Journal of Econometrics*, *54*(1–3), 159–178. doi:10.1016/0304-4076(92)90104-Y

La Porte, T. R., & Consolini, P. M. (1991). Working in practice but not in theory: Theoretical challenges of "high-reliability organizations". *Journal of Public Administration Research and Theory. J-PART*, *1*(1), 19–48.

La Porte, T. R., & Consolini, P. M. (1998). Theoretical and operationalchallenges of "high-reliability organizations": Air-traffic control and aircraft carriers. *International Journal of Public Administration*, *21*(6–8), 847–852. doi:10.1080/01900699808525320

La Porte, T. R., & Thomas, C. W. (1995). Regulatory compliance and the ethos of quality enhancement: Surprises in nuclear power plant operations. *Journal of Public Administration Research and Theory. J-PART*, *5*(1), 109–137.

Lambin, E. F. (2005). Conditions for sustainability of human-environment systems: Information, motivation, and capacity. *Global Environmental Change*, *15*(3), 177–180. doi:10.1016/j.gloenvcha.2005.06.002

Lampel, J., Bhalla, A., & Jha, P. P. (2014). Does governance confer organisational resilience? Evidence from UK employee-owned businesses. *European Management Journal*, *32*, 66–72.

Langendahl, P.-A., Cook, M., & Potter, S. (2016). Sustainable innovation journeys: Exploring the dynamics of firm practices as part of transitions to more sustainable food and farming. *Local Environment*, *21*(1), 105–123. doi:10.1080/13549839.2014.926869

Lantos, G. P. (2001). The boundaries of strategic corporate social responsibility. *Journal of Consumer Marketing*, *18*(7), 595–632. doi:10.1108/07363760110410281

Larashati, H., Hudrasyah, H., & Chandra, N. (2012). 7Ps of green marketing as factors influencing willingness to buy towards environmentally friendly beauty products. *Proceedings of International Conference on Business Management & IS*, *1*(1).

Lassar, W. M., Manolis, C., & Winsor, R. D. (2000). Service quality perspectives and satisfaction in private banking. *Journal of Services Marketing*, *14*(3), 244–271. doi:10.1108/08876040010327248

Laukkanen, T., Sinkkonen, S., & Laukkanen, P. (2009). Communication strategies to overcome functional and psychological resistance to Internet banking. *International Journal of Information Management*, *29*(2), 111–118. doi:10.1016/j.ijinfomgt.2008.05.008

Law, K. S., Wong, C.-S., & Mobley, W. M. (1998). Toward a taxonomy of multidimensional constructs. *Academy of Management Review*, *23*, 741–755.

Leana, C. R., & van Buren, H. J. III. (1999). Organizational social capital and employment practices. *Academy of Management Review*, *24*, 538–555.

Lee, N. (2019). *Low Carbon Cities - Malaysia's Response to Global Climate Emergency*. United Nations Development Programme. https://www.my.undp.org/content/malaysia/en/home/news-centre/articles/2019/lowcarboncity.html

Lee, A. V., Vargo, J., & Seville, E. (2013). Developing a Tool to Measure and Compare Organizations' Resilience. *Natural Hazards Review*, *14*, 29–41. doi:10.1061/(ASCE)NH.1527-6996.0000075

Lee, K. M. (2014). Predictors of sustainable consumption among young educated consumers in Hong Kong. *Journal of International Consumer Marketing*, *26*(3), 217–238. doi:10.1080/08961530.2014.900249

Lee, Z. W., Chan, T. K., Balaji, M. S., & Chong, A. Y. L. (2018). Why people participate in the sharing economy: An empirical investigation of Uber. *Internet Research.*

Lefebvre, H. (1996). The right to the city. *Writings on Cities, 63181.*

Lehmann, S. (Ed.). (2013). *Low Carbon Cities: More Than Just Buildings, Low Carbon Cities - Transforming Urban Systems*. Routledge.

Lengnick-Hall, C. A., & Beck, T. E. (2009). Resilience capacity and strategic agility: Prerequisites for thriving in a dynamic environment. In Resilience engineering perspectives, Volume 2. Preparation and restoration. Ashgate Publishing.

Lengnick-Hall, C. A., & Beck, T. E. (2005). Adaptive fit versus robust transformation: How organizations respond to environmental change. *Journal of Management*, *31*, 738–757.

Lengnick-Hall, C. A., Beck, T. E., & Lengnick-Hall, M. L. (2011). Developing a capacity for organizational resilience through strategic human resource management. *Human Resource Management Review*, *21*, 243–255.

Lenka, U., Suar, D., & Mohapatra, P. K. (2009). Service quality, customer satisfaction, and customer loyalty in Indian commercial banks. *The Journal of Entrepreneurship*, *18*(1), 47–64. doi:10.1177/097135570801800103

Lenski, W. (2010). Information: A conceptual investigation. *Information (Basel)*, *1*(2), 74–118. doi:10.3390/info1020074

Levin, S. (1999). *Fragile dominion: complexity and the commons*. Perseus Books.

Levitsky, J. (1997). SME guarantee schemes: A summary. *Financier-Burr Ridge*, *4*, 5–11.

Lewis, R., Donaldson-Feilder, E., & Pangallo, A. (2011). *Developing resilience*. Affinity Health at Work. Retrieved August 31, 2013, from https://www.cipd.co.uk/

Liam, M., Andy, S., Paul, J., Thom, J. A., Padgham, L., Hickmott, S., Deng, H., & Cahill, F. (2013). Reframing social sustainability reporting: Towards an engaged approach. *Environment, Development and Sustainability*, *15*(1), 225–243. doi:10.100710668-012-9384-2

Lihn, J., & Bjørnskov, C. (2017). Economic freedom and veto players jointly affect entrepreneurship. *Journal of Entrepreneurship and Public Policy*, *6*(3), 340–358. doi:10.1108/JEPP-D-17-00007

Limnios, A. M., Mazzarol, T., Ghadouani, A., & Schilizzi, S. G. M. (2014). The Resilience Architecture Framework: Four Organizational Archetypes. *European Management Journal*, *32*(1), 104–116.

Lim, W. M. (2020). The Sharing Economy: A Marketing Perspective. *Australasian Marketing Journal*, *28*(3), 4–13.

Lin, D., Hanscom, L., Murthy, A., Galli, A., Evans, M., Neill, E., Mancini, M., Martindill, J., Medouar, F.-Z., Huang, S., & Wackernagel, M. (2018). Ecological Footprint Accounting for Countries: Updates and Results of the National Footprint Accounts, 2012–2018. *Resources*, *7*(3), 1–22. doi:10.3390/resources7030058

Linnenluecke, M. K. (2017). Resilience in business and management research: A review of influential publications and a research agenda. *International Journal of Management Reviews*, *19*(1), 4–30.

Linnenluecke, M. K., & Griffiths, A. (2012). Assessing organizational resilience to climate and weather extremes: Complexities and methodological pathways. *Climatic Change*, *113*, 933–947.

Liu, C. (2010, October). Developing green intellectual capital in companies by AHP. In *2010 8th International Conference on Supply Chain Management and Information* (pp. 1-5). IEEE.

Ljungqvist, J., Barthel, S., Finnveden, G., & Sörlin, S. (2010). The Urban Anthropocene: Lessons for Sustainability from the Environmental History of Constantinople. In P. Sinclair, F. Herschend, C. Isendahl, & G. Nordquist (Eds.), *The Urban Mind, cultural and environmental dynamics Studies in Global Archaeology* (Vol. 15, pp. 368–394). University Press.

Lofland, J., & Lofland, L. H. (1984). Analysing social settings: A guide to qualitative observation and analysis (2nd ed.). Belmont, CA: Wadsworth.

Longhi, C., & Keeble, D. (2017). High-technology clusters and evolutionary trends in the 1990s. *High-technology clusters, networking and collective learning in Europe*, 21-56.

Longoni, A., & Cagliano, R. (2018). Inclusive environmental disclosure practices and firm performance. *International Journal of Operations & Production Management*, *38*(9), 1815–1835. doi:10.1108/IJOPM-12-2016-0728

López-Gamero, M., Zaragoza-Sáez, P., Claver-Cortés, E., & Molina-Azorín, J. (2011). Sustainable development and intangibles: Building sustainable intellectual capital. *Business Strategy and the Environment*, *20*(1), 18–37. doi:10.1002/bse.666

Loreau, M., Naeem, S., Inchausti, P., Bengtsson, J., Grime, J. P., Hector, A., Hooper, D. U., Huston, M. A., Raffaelli, D., Schmid, B., Tilman, D., & Wardle, D. A. (2001). Biodiversity and ecosystem functioning: Current knowledge and future challenges. *Science*, *294*(5543), 804–808. doi:10.1126cience.1064088 PMID:11679658

Lovell, S. T., DeSantis, S., Nathan, C. A., Olson, M. B., Mendez, V. E., Kominami, H. C., Erickson, D. L., Morris, K. S., & Morris, W. B. (2010). Integrating agroecology and landscape multifunc-tionality in Vermont: An evolving framework to evaluate the design of agroecosystems. *Agricultural Systems*, *103*(5), 327–341. doi:10.1016/j.agsy.2010.03.003

Luck, G. W., Daily, G. C., & Ehrlich, P. R. (2003). Population diversity and ecosystem services. *Trends in Ecology & Evolution*, *18*(7), 331–336. doi:10.1016/S0169-5347(03)00100-9

Lundberg, J., & Moberg, F. (2003). Mobile link organisms and ecosystem functioning: Implications for ecosystem resilience and management. *Ecosystems (New York, N.Y.)*, *6*(1), 87–98. doi:10.100710021-002-0150-4

Lu, P., & Pras, B. (2011). Profiling mass affluent luxury goods consumers in China: A psychographic approach. *Thunderbird International Business Review*, *53*(4), 435–455.

Luthra, S., Garg, D., & Haleem, A. (2016). The impacts of critical success factors for implementing green supply chain management towards sustainability: An empirical investigation of Indian automobile industry. *Journal of Cleaner Production*, *121*, 142–158. doi:10.1016/j.jclepro.2016.01.095

Macdiarmid, J. I., Douglas, F., & Campbell, J. (2016). Eating like there's no tomorrow: Public awareness of the environmental impact of food and reluctance to eat less meat as part of a sustainable diet. *Appetite*, *96*, 487–493. doi:10.1016/j.appet.2015.10.011 PMID:26476397

Machlis, G. E., Force, J. E., & Burch, W. R. Jr. (1997). The human ecosystem. 1. The human ecosystem as an organizing concept in ecosystem management. *Society & Natural Resources*, *10*(4), 347–367. doi:10.1080/08941929709381034

Magd, H. A., & McCoy, M. P. (2014). Entrepreneurship in Oman: Paving the way for a sustainable future. *Procedia Economics and Finance*, *15*, 1632–1640. doi:10.1016/S2212-5671(14)00634-0

Maheshwari, V., Vandewalle, I., & Bamber, D. (2011). Place branding's role in sustainable development. *Journal of Place Management and Development*, *4*(2), 198–213.

Maitlis, S. (2005). The social processes of organizational sensemaking. *Academy of Management Journal*, *48*, 21–49.

Maitlis, S., & Christianson, M. (2014). Sense making in organizations: Taking stock and moving forward. *The Academy of Management Annals*, *8*, 57–125. doi:10.1080/19416520.2014.873177

Malaysia Hotel Association. (2020). *Clean & Safe Malaysia*. Available at: https://group.bureauveritas.com/newsroom/malaysian-association-hotels-mah-has-appointed-bureau-veritas-deploy-their-clean-safe#:~:text=The%20Malaysian%20Association%20of%20Hotels,members%20spread%20across%2013%20states

Malaysian Government. (2011). Population and housing census of Malaysia: preliminary count Report 2010. Author.

Malik, S., Cao, Y., Mughal, Y., Kundi, G., Mughal, M., & Ramayah, T. (2020). Pathways towards sustainability in organizations: Empirical evidence on the role of green human resource management practices and green intellectual capital. *Sustainability*, *12*(8), 3228. doi:10.3390u12083228

Mallak, L. A. (1998). Measuring resilience in health care provider organizations. *Health Manpower Management*, *24*(4), 148–152. doi:10.1108/09552069810215755

Manasakis, C., Mitrokostas, E., & Petrakis, E. (2014). Strategic corporate social responsibility activities and corporate governance in imperfectly competitive markets. *Managerial and Decision Economics*, *35*(7), 460–473. doi:10.1002/mde.2635

Manfield, R. C., & Newey, L. R. (2017). Resilience as an Entrepreneurial Capability: Integrating Insights from a Cross-Disciplinary Comparison. *International Journal of Entrepreneurial Behaviour & Research*. Advance online publication. doi:10.1108/IJEBR-11-2016-0368

Mansfield, E. (1995). Innovation, technology and the economy. *Management Science*, *34*(10), 6.

Mansoor, A., Jahan, S., y Riaz, M. (2021). Does green intellectual capital spur corporate environmental performance through green workforce? *Journal of Intellectual Capital*.

Mansour, I. H. F., Eljelly, A. M., & Abdullah, A. M. (2016). Consumers' attitude towards e-banking services in Islamic banks: The case of Sudan. *Review of International Business and Strategy*, *26*(2), 244–260. doi:10.1108/RIBS-02-2014-0024

Marinova, D., & Phillimore, J. (2003). Models of innovation. In S. L. Vautor (Eds.), The international handbook on innovation (pp. 44-53). Elsevier. doi:10.1016/B978-008044198-6/50005-X

Martin, D., & Schounten, J. (2012). *Sustainable Marketing*. Prentice Hall.

Marzano, G. (2007). *The effect of stakeholder power on a destination branding process: The GoldCoast VeryGC brand* (Doctoral Thesis). University of Queensland, Australia.

Marzano, G., & Scott, N. (2005). Stakeholder power in destination branding: a methodological discussion. *Proceedings of the Destination Branding and Marketing for Regional Tourism Development Conference*, 203-212.

Marzouk, O. A., & Mahrous, A. A. (2020). Sustainable consumption behavior of energy and water-efficient products in a resource-constrained environment. *Journal of Global Marketing*, *33*(5), 1–19. doi:10.1080/08911762.2019.1709005

Mashood, N., Verhoeven, H., & Chansarkar, B. (2009). Emiratisation, Omanisation and Saudisation–common causes: common solutions. In *10th International Business Research Conference, Dubai, UAE* (pp. 1-12). Academic Press.

Masten, A. S., & Reed, M. J. (2002). Resilience in development. In C. R Snyder & S. Lopez (Eds.), Handbook of positive psychology (pp. 74-88). Oxford University Press.

Mathew, V. (2010). Women entrepreneurship in the Middle East: Understanding barriers and use of ICT for entrepreneurship development. *The International Entrepreneurship and Management Journal*, *6*(2), 163–181. doi:10.100711365-010-0144-1

Matriano, M. T., & Suguku, D. (2015). Entrepreneurship Growth in Oman: Position, Prospects, and Growth of Entrepreneurial Education. *International E-Journal of Advances in Education, 1*(2), 127–131. doi:10.18768/ijaedu.58791

Maulani, T. S. (2015). Green banking: A service product innovation in brand image enhancement through the marketing mix. *First International Conference on Economics and Banking ICEB-15*, 39-43. 10.2991/iceb-15.2015.7

Ma, Y., Chen, S., & Ruangkanjanases, A. (2021). Understanding the Antecedents and Consequences of Green Human Capital. *SAGE Open, 11*(1), 1–11. doi:10.1177/2158244020988867

McCall, T. (1973). *Legislative address, Governor Tom McCall, Oregon, (1973).* Retrieved July 20, 2008, from http://arcweb.sos.state.or.us/governors/McCall/legis1973.html

McCarthy, I.P., Collard, M., & Johnson, M. (2017). Adaptive organizational resilience: an evolutionary perspective. *Curr Opin Environ Sustain, 28*, 33–40. https ://doi.org/t.2017.07.005 doi:10.1016/j.cosus

McCarthy, E. J. (1960). *Basic Marketing: A Managerial Approach.* Richard D. Irwin, Inc.

McCartney, S. (2019). *The next chapter with BOLT threads: mylo material, rooted in nature.* www.stellamccartney.com/experience/en/the-next-chapter-with-bolt-threads-mylo-material-rooted-innature/

McDaniels, T., Chang, S., Cole, D., Mikawoz, J., & Longstaff, H. (2008). Fostering resilience to extreme events within infrastructure systems: Characterizing decision contexts for mitigation and adaptation. *Global Environmental Change, 18*, 310–318.

McDonagh, P., & Prothero, A. (2014). Sustainability marketing research: Past, present and future. *Journal of Marketing Management, 30*(11-12), 1186–1219.

McDonnell, M. J., & Hahs, A. (2009). Comparative ecology of cities and towns: Past, present and future. In M. J. McDonnell, A. Hahs, & J. Breuste (Eds.), *Ecology of cities and towns: A comparative approach* (pp. 71–89). Cambridge University Press. doi:10.1017/CBO9780511609763.006

McElhaney, K. (2009). A strategic approach to corporate social responsibility. *Leader to Leader, 52*(1), 30–36. doi:10.1002/ltl.327

McElwee, G., & Al-Riyami, R. (2003). Women entrepreneurs in Oman: Some barriers to success. *Career Development International, 8*(7), 339–346. doi:10.1108/13620430310505296

McGuinness, M., & Johnson, N. (2014). Exploiting social capital and path-dependent resources for organisational resilience: Preliminary findings from a study on flooding. *Procedia Economics and Finance, 18*, 447–455.

McKinney, M. L. (2002). Urbanization, biodiversity, and conservation. *Bioscience, 52*(10), 883–890. doi:10.1641/0006-3568(2002)052[0883:UBAC]2.0.CO;2

McManus, S., Seville, E., Vargo, J., & Brunsdon, D. (2008). Facilitated process for improving organizational resilience. *Natural Hazards Review, 9*(2), 81–90. doi:10.1061/_ASCE_1527-6988_2008_9:2_81

McNeill, L., & Moore, R. (2015). Sustainable fashion consumption and the fast fashion conundrum: Fashionable consumers and attitudes to sustainability in clothing choice. *International Journal of Consumer Studies, 39*(3), 212–222.

McNown, R., Sam, C. Y., & Goh, S. K. (2018). Bootstrapping the autoregressive distributed lag test for cointegration. *Applied Economics, 50*(13), 1509–1521. doi:10.1080/00036846.2017.1366643

McWilliams, A., Siegel, D. S., & Wright, P. M. (2006). Corporate social responsibility: Strategic implications. *Journal of Management Studies, 43*(1), 1–18. doi:10.1111/j.1467-6486.2006.00580.x

Medina-Rodríguez, A. C., Ávila-Sierra, A., Ariza, J. J., Guillamón, E., Baños-Arjona, A., Vicaria, J. M., & Jurado, E. (2020). Clean-in-place disinfection of dual-species biofilm (Listeria and Pseudomonas) by a green antibacterial product made from citrus extract. *Food Control*, *118*, 107422. doi:10.1016/j.foodcont.2020.107422

Meissner, D., & Kotsemir, M. (2016). Conceptualizing the innovation process towards the 'active innovation paradigm'—Trends and outlook. *Journal of Innovation and Entrepreneurship*, *5*(1), 1–18. doi:10.118613731-016-0042-z

Michaud, C., & Llerena, D. (2010). Green Consumer Behaviour: An Experimental Analysis of Willingness to Pay for Remanufactured Products. *Business Strategy and the Environment*.

Michelon, G., Boesso, G., & Kumar, K. (2013). Examining the link between strategic corporate social responsibility and company performance: An analysis of the best corporate citizens. *Corporate Social Responsibility and Environmental Management*, *20*(2), 81–94. doi:10.1002/csr.1278

Miles, M., & Huberman, A. (1994). *Qualitative Data Analysis. An Expanded Sourcebook* (2nd ed.). Sage.

Millennium Ecosystem Assessment (MA). (2005). *Synthesis*. Island Press. http://www.MAweb.org

Millennium Research Group. (2000). Annual industry report. *Implant Dentistry*, *9*, 192–194. doi:10.1097/00008505-200009030-00003

Miller, J. R. (2005). Biodiversity conservation and the extinction of experience. *Trends in Ecology & Evolution*, *20*(8), 430–434. doi:10.1016/j.tree.2005.05.013 PMID:16701413

Ministry of Energy, Green Technology, and Water. (2017). *Low Carbon Cities Framework, Version 2*. https://www.lccf.my/wp-content/uploads/2018/10/LCCF_Book-Version-2-2017.pdf

Ministry of Environment and Water. (2021). *National Low Carbon Cities Masterplan*. https://www.kasa.gov.my/resources/alam-sekitar/NLCCM.pdf

Ministry of Tourism, Arts, and Culture Malaysia. (2021). *Rated Tourist Accommodation Premises*. Available at https://www.motac.gov.my/en/check/hotel

Ministry of Tourism. (2021). *Tourist Arrival*. Available at https://www.tourism.gov.my/statistics

Mishra, B. B. (2008). *The development of e-payment and challenges in Nepal*. Academic Press.

Moeller, S., & Wittkowski, K. (2010). The burdens of ownership: Reasons for preferring renting. *Managing Service Quality*, *20*(2), 176–191.

Mogles, N., Walker, I., Ramallo-González, A. P., Lee, J., Natarajan, S., Padget, J., Gabe-Thomas, E., Lovett, T., Ren, G., Hyniewska, S., & Coley, D. (2017). How smart do smart meters need to be? *Building and Environment*, *125*, 439–450. doi:10.1016/j.buildenv.2017.09.008

Mohammed, S., Uddin, M. A., & Ahmad, M. (2016). Factors affecting entrepreneur's development in Oman. *Corporate Ownership and Control*, *13*(2), 66–70. doi:10.22495/cocv13i2p7

Moher, D., Shamseer, L., Clarke, M., Ghersi, D., Liberati, A., Petticrew, M., Shekelle, P., & Stewart, L. A. (2015). Preferred reporting items for systematic review and meta-analysis protocols (PRISMA-P) 2015 statement. *Systematic Reviews*, *4*(1), 1–9. doi:10.1186/2046-4053-4-1 PMID:25554246

Mohr, J., & Nevin, J. R. (1990). Communication strategies in marketing channels: A theoretical perspective. *Journal of Marketing*, *54*(4), 36–51. doi:10.1177/002224299005400404

Molina-Azorin, J., Tari, J., Pereira-Moliner, J., López-Gamero, M. D., & Pertusa-Ortega, E. M. (2015). The effects of quality and environmental management on competitive advantage: A mixed methods study in the hotel industry. *Tourism Management*, *50*, 41–54. doi:10.1016/j.tourman.2015.01.008

Montaño, D. E., & Kasprzyk, D. (2015). Theory of reasoned action, theory of planned behavior, and the integrated behavioral model. *Health behavior: Theory, research and practice, 70*(4), 231.

Mont, O., & Plepys, A. (2008). Sustainable consumption progress: Should we be proud or alarmed? *Journal of Cleaner Production*, *16*(4), 531–537. doi:10.1016/j.jclepro.2007.01.009

Moore, P. M., Rivera, S., Bravo-Soto, G. A., Olivares, C., & Lawrie, T. A. (2018). Communication skills training for healthcare professionals working with people who have cancer. *Cochrane Database of Systematic Reviews*, *2018*(7), 1–120. doi:10.1002/14651858.CD003751.pub4 PMID:30039853

Moran, D. D., Wackernagel, M., Kitzes, J. A., Goldfinger, S. H., & Boutaud, A. (2008). Measuring sustainable development— Nation by nation. *Ecological Economics*, *64*(3), 470–474. doi:10.1016/j.ecolecon.2007.08.017

Morgan, N., & Pritchard, A. (2010). Meeting the destination branding challenge In N. Morgan, A. Pritchard, & R. Pride (Eds.), Destination Branding: Creating the unique destination proposition (2nd ed.). Elsevier Butterworth-Heinemann.

Morgan, N., Hastings, E., & Pritchard, A. (2012). Developing a new DMO marketing evaluation framework: The case of visit Wales. *Journal of Vacation Marketing*, *18*(1), 73–89.

Moroni, S. (2015). Complexity and the inherent limits of explanation and prediction: Urban codes for self-organising systems. *Planning Theory*, *14*(3), 248–267. doi:10.1177/1473095214521104

Morrison, A. M. (2013). *Marketing and managing tourism destinations*. Routledge.

Mowery, D., & Rosenberg, N. (1979). The influence of market demand upon innovation: A critical review of some recent empirical studies. *Research Policy*, *8*(2), 102–153. doi:10.1016/0048-7333(79)90019-2

Mthanti, T., & Ojah, K. (2018). Institutions, human capital, and entrepreneurial orientation: Implications for growth policy. *J. Entrep. Public Policy*, *7*(2), 135–160. doi:10.1108/JEPP-D-18-00002

Mukherji, N., & Morales, A. (2010). Zoning for urban Agriculture. *Zoning Practice, 3*.

Müller, J. (2021). *Carbon monoxide emissions in Malaysia from 2012 to 2019*. Statista. https://www.statista.com/statistics/796326/carbon-monoxide-emissions-malaysia

Munajat, Q., & Kurnia, S. (2015). Towards Sustainability Framework Development: Identifying Organisational Capability for Sustainability Practices. In PACIS (p. 106). Academic Press.

Munthiu, C. M. (2009). The buying decision process and types of buying decision behaviour. *Sibiu Alma Mater University Journals*, *2*(4), 27–33.

Musacchio, L. R. (2008). Metropolitan landscape ecology: Using translational research to increase sustainability, resilience, and regeneration. *Landscape Journal*, *27*(1), 1–8. doi:10.3368/lj.27.1.1

Musa, N., Noor, S. D., & Mohamad, W. (2013). Developing destination brand identity: towards sustainability of tourism destination from the perspective of stakeholders and theory of social identity. *Proceedings of International Conference on Tourism Development*.

Muyeed, M. A. (2012). Customer perception on service quality in retail banking in developing countries-a case study. *International Journal of Marketing Studies*, *4*(1), 116–122. doi:10.5539/ijms.v4n1p116

Naderi, I., & Strutton, D. (2015). I support sustainability but only when doing so reflects fabulously on me: Can green narcissists be cultivated? *Journal of Macromarketing*, *35*(1), 70–83.

Naguib, R., & Jamali, D. (2015). Female entrepreneurship in the UAE: A multi-level integrative lens. *Gender in Management*, *30*(2), 135–161. doi:10.1108/GM-12-2013-0142

Namkung, Y., & Jang, S. S. (2013). Effects of restaurant green practices on brand equity formation: Do green practices really matter? *International Journal of Hospitality Management*, *33*, 85–95. doi:10.1016/j.ijhm.2012.06.006

Narayanasamy, K., Rasiah, D., & Jacobs, C. J. (2011). An empirical study of factors influencing gender differences in entrepreneurship. *International Business & Economics Research Journal*, *10*(10), 17–30. doi:10.19030/iber.v10i10.5976

Narteh, B., & Odoom, R. (2015). Does internal marketing influence employee loyalty? Evidence from the Ghanaian banking industry. *Services Marketing Quarterly*, *36*(2), 112–135. doi:10.1080/15332969.2015.1014237

Narula, S. A., & Desore, A. (2016). Framing green consumer behavior research: Opportunities and challenges. *Social Responsibility Journal*, *12*(1), 1–22.

Natalicchio, A., Ardito, L., Savino, T., & Albino, V. (2017). Managing knowledge assets for open innovation: A systematic literature review. *Journal of Knowledge Management*, *21*(6), 1362–1383. doi:10.1108/JKM-11-2016-0516

National Land Use Database. (2000). Previously Developed Land (PDL): Vacant Sites and Derelict Sites, and Other Previously Developed Land and Buildings that May be Available for Redevelopment, Data Specification, NLUD – a partnership. *Rethinking Urban Capacity.*

Naveh, Z. (2000). The total human ecosystem: Integrating ecology and economics. *Bioscience*, *50*, 357–361.

Neagu, O. (2019). The Link between Economic Complexity and Carbon Emissions in the European Union Countries: A Model Based on the Environmental Kuznets Curve (EKC) Approach. *Sustainability*, *11*(17), 1–27. doi:10.3390u11174753

Neagu, O. (2020). Economic Complexity and Ecological Footprint: Evidence from the Most Complex Economies in the World. *Sustainability*, *12*(21), 1–18. doi:10.3390u12219031

Neagu, O., & Teodoru, M. (2019). The Relationship between Economic Complexity, Energy Consumption Structure and Greenhouse Gas Emission: Heterogeneous Panel Evidence from the EU Countries. *Sustainability*, *11*(2), 1–29. doi:10.3390u11020497

Nekmahmud, M., & Fekete-Farkas, M. (2020). Why Not Green Marketing? Determinates of Consumers' Intention to Green Purchase Decision in a New Developing Nation. *Sustainability Mdpi Journal*, *12*, 7880.

Nelson, D. R., Adger, W. N., & Brown, K. (2007). Adaptation to environmental change: Contributions of a resilience framework. *Annual Review of Environment and Resources*, *32*, 395–419.

Nelson, R. R. (1993). *National innovation systems: A comparative analysis*. Oxford University Press on Demand.

Nepal Rastra Bank. (2016). *Directives, Notification: Banks & FIs Regulation, Categorization of Banks.* Retrieved from https://www.nrb.org.np/bfr/bfrdirectives.php?vw=15

Nepal Rastra Bank. (2018). *Directives, Notification: Banks & FIs Regulation.* Retrieved from https://www.nrb.org.np/bfr/bfrdirectives.php?vw=15

Neuburger, L., & Egger, R. (2021). Travel risk perception and travel behaviour during the COVID-19 pandemic 2020: A case study of the DACH region. *Current Issues in Tourism*, *24*(7), 1003–1016. doi:10.1080/13683500.2020.1803807

Newell, G. D., & Holian, M. J. (2017). An agent-based model of entrepreneurship: Examining the role of alertness and transaction costs. *Journal of Entrepreneurship and Public Policy*, *6*(2), 259–270. doi:10.1108/JEPP-01-2015-0003

Nguyen, D., & Slater, S. (2010). Hitting the sustainability sweet spot: Having it all. *The Journal of Business Strategy*, *31*(3), 5–11. doi:10.1108/02756661011036655

Niemtzow, E. (2018). *Disrupting luxury: creating resilient businesses in times of rapid change*. Business of Social Responsibility. Available at: www.bsr.org/en/our-insights/report-view/disrupting-luxury-creating-resilient-businesses-in-times-of-rapid-change

Niosi, J. (1999). Fourth-generation R&D: From linear models to flexible innovation. *Journal of Business Research*, *45*(2), 111–117. doi:10.1016/S0148-2963(97)00230-0

Nupur, J. M. (2010). E-banking and customers' satisfaction in Bangladesh: An analysis. *International Review of Business Research Papers, 6*(4), 145-156.

Nyström, M., & Folke, C. (2001). Spatial resilience of coral reefs. *Ecosystems (New York, N.Y.)*, *4*(5), 406–417. doi:10.100710021-001-0019-y

O'Bowman, A. M., & Pagano, M.A., (2004). Terra Incognita: Vacant Land and Urban Strategies. Georgetown University Press.

O'Brien, K., Sygna, L., & Haugen, J. E. (2004). Vulnerable or resilient? A multi-scale assessment of climate impacts and vulnerability in Norway. *Climatic Change*, *64*, 193–225.

O'cass, A., & McEwen, H. (2004). Exploring consumer status and conspicuous consumption. *Journal of Consumer Behaviour: An International Research Review*, *4*(1), 25–39.

O'Reilly, N. M., Robbins, P., & Scanlan, J. (2019). Dynamic capabilities and the entrepreneurial university: A perspective on the knowledge transfer capabilities of universities. *Journal of Small Business and Entrepreneurship*, *31*(3), 243–263. doi:10.1080/08276331.2018.1490510

Odum, E. P. (1971). *Fundamentals of Ecology* (3rd ed.). W. B. Saunders.

OEC. (2021a). *Economic Complexity Legacy Rankings (ECI) Legacy Rankings | OEC - The Observatory of Economic Complexity*. https://oec.world/en/rankings/legacy/eci

OEC. (2021b). *OEC - The Observatory of Economic Complexity*. https://oec.world/en/resources/methods#eci

OECD. (1997). *Oslo manual—Guidelines for collecting and interpreting innovation data* (2nd ed.). OECD.

OECD. (2002a). *Policies to promote sustainable consumption: An overview. Policy Case Studies Series*. OECD.

OECD. (2002b). *Towards sustainable household consumption: Trends and policies in OECD countries. Policy Case Studies Series*. OECD.

OIV. (2004). *Resolution CST 1/2004-Develpment of Sustainable Vitivinivulture*. Pareis.

OIV. (2008). *Resolution CST/2008-OIV Guidelines for Sustainable Vitiviniculture: Production, Processing and Packaging of Products*. Verone/it.

OIV. (2016). *Resolution CST 518/2016-OIV General Principles of Sustainable Vitiviniculture - Environmental - Social - Economic and Cultural Aspects*. Brento Gonçalves.

Oliva, F. L., & Kotabe, M. (2019). Barriers, practices, methods and knowledge management tools in startups. *Journal of Knowledge Management*.

Omidvar M., Mazloumi, A., Mohammad Fam, I., & Nirumand, F. (2017). Development of a framework for resilience measurement: Suggestion of fuzzy resilience grade (RG) and fuzzy resilience early warning grade (REWG). *WOR*, *56*, 463–474. doi:10.3233/WOR-172512

Orlitzky M., Siegel, D. S., & Waldman, D. A. (2011). Strategic corporate social responsibility and environmental sustainability. *Business & Society*, *50*(1), 6–27. doi:10.1177/0007650310394323

Ortt, J. R., & Smits, R. (2006). Innovation management: Different approaches to cope with the same trends. *International Journal of Technology Management*, *34*(3-4), 296–318. doi:10.1504/IJTM.2006.009461

Oshio, S., Nakatani, M., Kaneko, M., & Nagamine, K. (2002). Negative na dekigoto karanotatchinaoriwomichibikushinritekitokusei; seishintekikaihukuryokusyakudo nosakusei [The psychological properties that promote bounce back from negative states]. *Japanese Journal of Counseling Science*, *35*, 57–65.

Otte, A., Simmering, D., & Wolters, V. (2007). Biodiversity at the landscape level: Recent concepts and perspectives for multifunctional land use. *Landscape Ecology*, *22*(5), 639–642. doi:10.1007/10980-007-9094-6

Ottman, J. A. (2011). *The new rules of green marketing strategies, tools, and inspiration for sustainable branding.* Greenleaf Publishing Limited.

Ozdamar-Ertekin, Z. (2019). Can Luxury Fashion Provide a Roadmap for Sustainability? *Markets, Globalization & Developmental Review*, *4*(1).

Özsungur, F. (2019, May). Research on women's entrepreneurship motivation: Sample of Adana Province. *Women's Studies International Forum*, *74*, 114–126. doi:10.1016/j.wsif.2019.03.006

Paavola, J. (2001). Towards sustainable consumption: Economics and ethical concerns for the environment in consumer choices. *Review of Social Economy*, *59*(2), 227–248. doi:10.1080/00346760110036175

Paço, D., Shiel, A., & Alves, C. (2019). H. A new model for testing green consumer behaviour. *Journal of Cleaner Production*, *207*, 998–1006.

Pagano, M. A., & Bowman, A. (2000). Land in Cities: An Urban Resource. Brookings Institution, Center on Urban and Metropolitan Policy.

Panayotou, T. (1993). *Empirical tests and policy analysis of environmental degradation at different stages of economic development* (Wep 2-22, WP:238; ILO Working Papers). International Labour Organization. https://econpapers.repec.org/RePEc:ilo:ilowps:992927783402676

Panda, S. (2018). Constraints faced by women entrepreneurs in developing countries: Review and ranking. *Gender in Management*, *33*(4), 315–331. doi:10.1108/GM-01-2017-0003

Pant, B. (2016). *Financial Inclusion in Nepal: Policy Review and Prescriptions* (No. 34). NRB Working Paper.

Pantano, E., & Stylos, N. (2020). The Cinderella moment: Exploring consumers' motivations to engage with renting as collaborative luxury consumption mode. *Psychology and Marketing*, *37*(5), 740–753.

Parajuli, S., Paudel, U. R., & Devkota, N. (2020). Banking Communications: A Perceptual Study of Customer Relations. *South Asian Journal of Social Studies and Economics*, *8*(3), 23–34. doi:10.9734ajsse/2020/v8i330212

Parajuli, S., Rajbhandari, S., Joshi, A., Sujan, K. C., & Bhandari, U. (2019). Transforming corporate governance through effective corporate social responsibility (CSR) and social entrepreneurship orientation in Nepal. *Quest Journal of Management and Social Sciences*, *1*(1), 26–49. doi:10.3126/qjmss.v1i1.25973

Park, H. J., & Lin, L. M. (2020). Exploring attitude–behavior gap in sustainable consumption: Comparison of recycled and upcycled fashion products. *Journal of Business Research*, *117*, 623–628. doi:10.1016/j.jbusres.2018.08.025

Pasteur, K. (2011). *From Vulnerability to Resilience: A Framework for Analysis and Action to Build Community Resilience*. Practical Action Publishing.

Paton, D., Smith, L., & Violanti, J. (2000). Disaster response: Risk, vulnerability and resilience. *Disaster Prevention and Management*, *9*(3), 173–179.

Patriotta, G. (2003). Sensemaking on the shop floor: Narratives of knowledge in organizations. *Journal of Management Studies*, *40*, 349–375.

Paudel, U. R., Parajuli, S., Devkota, N., & Mahapatra, S. K. (2020). What determines customers' perception of banking communication? An empirical evidence from commercial banks of Nepal. *Global Economy Journal*, *20*(4), 1–21. doi:10.1142/S2194565920500190

Paudel, U. R., Puri, S., Parajuli, S., Devkota, N., & Bhandari, U. (2021). Measuring Cultural Diversity Impact in Hospitality Industry Leadership: Managerial Communication Perspective from Five Star Hotels in Kathmandu Valley, Nepal. *Journal of Tourism & Adventure*, *4*(1), 75–88. doi:10.3126/jota.v4i1.40680

Pavione, E., Pezzetti, R., & Dalla, M. (2016). Emerging competitive strategies in the global luxury industry in the perspective of sustainable development: The case of Kering group. *Management Dynamics in the Knowledge Economy Journal*, *4*(2), 41–61.

Payne, J. E., & Mervar, A. (2017). The entrepreneurship-unemployment nexus in Croatia. *Journal of Entrepreneurship and Public Policy*, *6*(3), 375–384. doi:10.1108/JEPP-D-17-00013

Pearce, D. G. (1992). *Tourists Organisations*. Longman.

Peattie, K., & Belz, F. M. (2010). Sustainability marketing—An innovative conception of marketing. *Marketing Review St. Gallen*, *27*(5), 8–15.

Peattie, K., & Crane, A. (2005). Green marketing: Legend, myth, farce or prophesy? *Qualitative Market Research*, *8*(4), 357–370.

Pei, T. J., & Dastane, O. (2021). Digital Technology in Retail: Impact on Shopper Satisfaction. In Handbook of Research on Disruptive Innovation and Digital Transformation in Asia (pp. 187-213). IGI Global.

Perlacia, A. S., Duml, V., & Saebi, T. (2017). Collaborative consumption: Live fashion, don't own it. *BETA Bulletin of Experimental Treatments for AIDS*, *31*(1), 6–24.

Pesaran, M. H., Shin, Y., & Smith, R. J. (2001). Bounds testing approaches to the analysis of level relationships. *Journal of Applied Econometrics*, *16*(3), 289–326. doi:10.1002/jae.616

Peter, J., & Donnelly, J., Jr. (2015). A preface to marketing management (14th ed.). New York: McGraw Hill.

Peter, R., & Colm, O. G. (2016). Innovation processes: Do they help or hinder new product development outcomes in Irish SMEs? *Irish Journal of Management*, *35*(1), 104–107.

Peterson, G., Allen, C.R., & Holling, C.S. (1998). Ecological resilience, biodiversity, and scale. *Ecosystems, 1*, 6–18.

Pettit, T. J., Fiksel, J., & Croxton, K. L. (2010). Ensuring supply chain resilience: Developmentof a conceptual framework. *Journal of Business Logistics*, *31*(1), 1–21.

Phau, I., & Prendergast, G. (2000). Consuming luxury brands: The relevance of the 'rarity principle'. *Journal of Brand Management*, *8*(2), 122–138.

Phillips, P. C. B., & Perron, P. (1988). Testing for a Unit Root in Time Series Regression. *Biometrika*, *75*(2), 335–346. doi:10.1093/biomet/75.2.335

Phyper, J., & MacLean, P. (2009). *Good to green: managing business risks and opportunities in the age of environmental awareness*. John Wiley & Sons.

Pickett, S. T. A., Burch, W. R. Jr, Dalton, S., & Foresman, T. (1997). Integrated urban ecosystem research: Themes, needs, and applications. *Urban Ecosystems*, *1*(4), 183–184. doi:10.1023/A:1018579628818

Pickett, S. T. A., & Cadenasso, M. L. (2002). Ecosystem as a multidimensional concept: Meaning, model and metaphor. *Ecosystems (New York, N.Y.)*, *5*(1), 1–10. doi:10.100710021-001-0051-y

Pickett, S. T. A., Cadenasso, M. L., & Grove, J. M. (2004). Resilient cities: Meaning, models, and metaphor for integrating the ecological, socio-economic, and planning realms. *Landscape and Urban Planning*, *69*(4), 369–384. doi:10.1016/j.landurbplan.2003.10.035

Pickett, S. T. A., Groffman, P. M., Brush, G. S., Galvin, M. F., Grove, J. M., ... Troy, A. R. (2008). Exchanges across land-water-scape boundaries in urban systems: Strategies for reducing nitrate pollution. *Annals of the New York Academy of Sciences*, *1134*(1), 213–232. doi:10.1196/annals.1439.012 PMID:18566096

Pike, S., & Page, S. J. (2014). Destination marketing organisations and destination marketing: A narrative analysis of the literature. *Tourism Management*, *41*, 201–227.

Pikkarainen, T., Pikkarainen, K., Karjaluoto, H., & Pahnila, S. (2004). Consumer acceptance of online banking: An extension of the technology acceptance model. *Internet Research*, *14*(3), 224–235. doi:10.1108/10662240410542652

Piligrimiene, Z., Zukauskaite, A., Korzilius, H., Banter, J., & Dovalien, A. (2020). Internal and external determinants of consumer engagement in sustainable consumption. *Sustainability*, *12*(4), 1–20. doi:10.3390u12041349

Pirić, V., Martinović, M., & Barac, Z. (2018). A study on customer's perception of Croatia's banking industry. *UTMS Journal of Economics (Skopje)*, *9*(2), 169–180.

Pistrui, D., & Fahed-Sreih, J. (2010). Islam, entrepreneurship, and business values in the Middle East. *International Journal of Entrepreneurship and Innovation Management*, *12*(1), 107–113. doi:10.1504/IJEIM.2010.033170

Pittayachawan, S., Abareshi, A., Hon Kam, B., & Teo, L. (2014). Green consumerism: a study on the prospect of consumers participation in corporate environmental management programs. *Conference Paper.*

Poapongsakorn, N., & Tonguthai, P. (2003). Technological capability building and the sustainability of export success in Thailand's textile and electronics industries. In *Technological Capabilities and Export Success in Asia* (pp. 173–226). Routledge.

Podsakoff, P. M., MacKenzie, S. B., & Podsakoff, N. P. (2016). Recommendations for creating better concept definitions in the organizational, behavioral, and social sciences. *Organizational Research Methods*, *19*, 159–203.

Pollach, I. (2015). Strategic corporate social responsibility: The struggle for legitimacy and reputation. *International Journal of Business Governance and Ethics*, *10*(1), 57–75. doi:10.1504/IJBGE.2015.068685

Porter, M. E., & Kramer, M. R. (2006). The link between competitive advantage and corporate social responsibility. *Harvard Business Review*, *84*(12), 78–92. PMID:17183795

Porter, M. E., & Kramer, M. R. (2011). Creating shared value. *Harvard Business Review.*

Porter, M. E., & Van der Linde, C. (1995). Toward a new conception of the environment-competitiveness relationship. *The Journal of Economic Perspectives*, *9*(4), 97–118. doi:10.1257/jep.9.4.97

Porter, M., & Van der Linde, C. (1995). Green and competitive: Ending the stalemate. *Harvard Business Review*, *72*(3/5), 97–118.

Pothukuchi, K., & Kaufman, J. (1999). Placing the food system on the urban agenda: The role of municipal institutions in food systems planning. *Agriculture and Human Values*, *16*(2), 213–244. doi:10.1023/A:1007558805953

Pothukuchi, K., & Kaufman, J. (2000). The food system: A stranger to the planning field. *Journal of the American Planning Association*, *66*(2), 112–124. doi:10.1080/01944360008976093

Power, M., & Rienstra, B. (1999). Internal communication in new corporate conglomerates: Developing a corporate communication model for loosely coupled businesses in local government. *International Journal of Public Sector Management*, *12*(6), 501–515. doi:10.1108/09513559910301757

Powley, E. H. (2009). Reclaiming resilience and safety: Resilience activation in the critical period of crisis. *Human Relations*, *62*(9), 1289–1326.

Prakash, A. (2002). Green marketing, public policy and managerial strategies. *Business Strategy and the Environment*, *11*(5), 285–297. doi:10.1002/bse.338

Prayag, G., & Ryan, C. (2011). The relationship between the 'push' and 'pull' factors of a tourist destination: The role of nationality – an analytical qualitative research approach. *Current Issues in Tourism*, *14*(2), 121–143.

Prendergast, G. P., & Tsang, A. S. L. (2019). Explaining socially responsible consumption. *Journal of Consumer Marketing*, *36*(1), 146–154. doi:10.1108/JCM-02-2018-2568

Princen, T. (2003). Principles for sustainability: From cooperation and efficiency to sufficiency. *Global Environmental Politics*, *3*(1), 33–50. doi:10.1162/152638003763336374

Qandile, Y. A., & Sabry, M. A. (1998). Guidelines for the treatment of solar energy topics in the unified science curricula of the Gulf Arab States. *Renewable Energy*, *14*(1–4), 401–414. doi:10.1016/S0960-1481(98)00096-2

Quatraro, F., & Vivarelli, M. (2015). Drivers of entrepreneurship and post-entry performance of newborn firms in developing countries. *The World Bank Research Observer*, *30*(2), 277–305. doi:10.1093/wbro/lku012

Quincerot, R., & Weil, M. (2009). *Genève 2020: Plan di-recteur communal de la Ville de Genève*. Ville de Genève.

Quinlan, T. (2008). *A stakeholder approach to the branding of urban tourism destinations* (Master Thesis). Waterford Institute of Technology, Ireland.

Quoquab, F., & Mohammad, J. (2017). Managing sustainable consumption: Is it a problem or panacea? In W. L. Filho, D. M. Pociovalisteanu, & A. Q. Al-Amin (Eds.), *Sustainable Economic Development: Green Economy and Green Growth*. Springer. doi:10.1007/978-3-319-45081-0_7

Radwan, D. M. (2014). *Education for employment: Omani graduates' perspective toward the 'work readiness' competencies needed in the labour market* (Doctoral dissertation). The British University in Dubai (BUiD).

Rafols, I., Leydesdorff, L., O'Hare, A., Nightingale, P., & Stirling, A. (2012). How journal rankings can suppress interdisciplinary research: A comparison between innovation studies and business & management. *Research Policy*, *41*(7), 1262–1282.

Rahmawati, R., Hadiwidjojo, D., & Noermijati, S. (2014). Green Marketing Mix as Strategy to Improve Competitive Advantage in Real Estate Developer Companies. *International Journal of Business and Management*.

Ramchandani, M., & Coste-Manière, I. (2012). Asymmetry in multi-cultural luxury communication: A comparative analysis on luxury brand communication in India and China. *Journal of Global Fashion Marketing*, *3*(2), 89–97.

Rasmussen, S. E., Ostergaard, P., & Beckmann, C.S. (2006). Essentials of social Science Research Methodology. Southern Denmark University Press.

Razeghian, M., & Weber, T. A. (2019). The advent of the sharing culture and its effect on product pricing. *Electronic Commerce Research and Applications*, *33*, 100801.

Redman, C., Grove, J. M., & Kuby, L. (2000). *Toward a unified understanding of human ecosystems: Integrating social sciences into long-term ecological research*. White Paper of the Long-Term Ecological Research. Albuquerque, NM: LTER Network.

Redwood, M., & Bahri, A. (2010). *Wastewater Irrigation and Health: Assessing and Mitigation Risks in Low-income Countries*. Earthscan/IDRC/IWMI.

Rehman, S., Kraus, S., Shah, S., Khanin, D., & Mahto, R. (2021). Analyzing the relationship between green innovation and environmental performance in large manufacturing firms. *Technological Forecasting and Social Change*, *163*, 120481. doi:10.1016/j.techfore.2020.120481

Reisch, L., Eberle, U., & Lorek, S. (2013). Sustainable food consumption: an overview of contemporary issues and policies. *Sustainability: Science, Practice and Policy*, *9*(2), 7–25.

Report, R. A. (2018). Public Authority for SME Development (Riyada) Annual Report 2018. Academic Press.

Report, R. M. (2018). *Mapping The SME Ecosystem in Oman 2018. Public Authority for SME Development*. Riyada.

Reuter, C., Foerstl, K. A. I., Hartmann, E. V. I., & Blome, C. (2010). Sustainable global supplier management: The role of dynamic capabilities in achieving competitive advantage. *The Journal of Supply Chain Management*, *46*(2), 45–63. doi:10.1111/j.1745-493X.2010.03189.x

Rex, E., & Baumann, H. (2007). Beyond ecolabels: What green marketing can learn from conventional marketing. *Journal of Cleaner Production*, *15*(6), 567–576.

Reynolds, P. D., Bygrave, W. D., Autio, E., Cox, L. W., & Hay, M. (2004). *Global entrepreneurship monitor 2003. Executive Report, Babson College/Ewing Marion Kauffman Foundation*. London Business School.

Rezvani, Z., Jansson, J., & Bengtsson, M. (2018). Consumer motivations for sustainable consumption: The interaction of gain, normative and hedonic motivations on electric vehicle adoption. *Business Strategy and the Environment*, *27*(8), 1272–1283. doi:10.1002/bse.2074

Richtnér, A., & Löfsten, H. (2014). Managing in turbulence: How the capacity for resilience influences creativity. *R & D Management*, *44*, 137–151.

Ricketts, T., & Imhoff, M. (2003). Biodiversity, urban areas, and agriculture: Locating prior-ity ecoregions for conservation. *Conservation Ecology*, *8*(2), 1. doi:10.5751/ES-00593-080201

Rijal, S. (2006). Application of management control system in Nepalese commercial banks. *Journal of Nepalese Business Studies*, *3*(1), 92–99. doi:10.3126/jnbs.v3i1.486

Ritchie, J. R. B., & Ritchie, R. J. B. (1998). The branding of tourism destination: past achievements and future challenges. *Annual congress of the International Association of Scientific Experts in Tourism*, 89-116.

Riyada Annual Report. (2017). *Public Authority for SME Development (Riyad) Annual Report 2017*. Academic Press.

Roberts, K. H. (1990). Some Characteristics of One Type of High Reliability Organization. *Organization Science*, *1*(2), 160.

Rogers, E. M. (1995). Diffusion of Innovations: modifications of a model for telecommunications. In *Die diffusion von innovationen in der telekommunikation* (pp. 25–38). Springer. doi:10.1007/978-3-642-79868-9_2

Roggema, R. (2012a). *Swarm planning: the development of a spatial planning methodology to deal with climate adaptation* [PhD thesis]. Delft University of Technology.

Roggema, R. (2012c). Shifting paradigms. In R. Roggema (Ed.), *The design charrette: ways to envision sustainable futures*. Springer.

Roggema, R. (2014). Towards enhanced resilience in city design: A proposition. *Land (Basel)*, *3*(2), 460–481. doi:10.3390/land3020460

Roggema, R. (2015). Three urbanisms in one city: Accommodating the paces of change. *Journal of Environmental Protection*, *6*(09), 946–956. doi:10.4236/jep.2015.69084

Rolling, V., & Sadachar, A. (2018). Are sustainable luxury goods a paradox for millennials? *Social Responsibility Journal*, *14*(4), 802–815.

Romero, J. P., & Gramkow, C. (2021). Economic complexity and greenhouse gas emissions. *World Development*, *139*, 105317. doi:10.1016/j.worlddev.2020.105317

Roos, D., & Hahn, R. (2019). Understanding collaborative consumption: An extension of the theory of planned behavior with value-based personal norms. *Journal of Business Ethics*, *158*(3), 679–697.

Rosa, P., Kodithuwakku, S. S., & Balunywa, W. (2006, December). Entrepreneurial motivation in developing countries: what does' necessity'and'opportunity'entrepreneurship really mean? *Babson College Entrepreneurship Research Conference (BCERC).*

Rosenbaum, E., & Caminiti, S. (2020). *Coronavirus: How the pandemic has impacted luxury retail.* CNBC. https://www.cnbc.com/2020/09/19/coronavirus-how-the-pandemic-has-impacted-luxury-retail.html

Rosenberg, N. (1976). *Perspectives on technology*. CUP Archive. doi:10.1017/CBO9780511561313

Rothwell, G., Rothwell, R., & Zegveld, W. (1985). *Reindustrialization and technology*. ME Sharpe.

Rothwell, R. (1991). External networking and innovation in small and medium-sized manufacturing firms in Europe. *Technovation*, *11*(2), 93–112. doi:10.1016/0166-4972(91)90040-B

Rothwell, R. (1992). Developments towards the fifth generation model of innovation. *Technology Analysis and Strategic Management*, *4*(1), 73–75. doi:10.1080/09537329208524080

Rothwell, R. (1994). Towards the fifth-generation innovation process. *International Marketing Review*, *11*(1), 7–31. doi:10.1108/02651339410057491

Roy, D., Tripathy, S., Kar, S. K., Sharma, N., Verma, S. K., & Kaushal, V. (2020). Study of knowledge, attitude, anxiety & perceived mental healthcare need in Indian population during COVID-19 pandemic. *Asian Journal of Psychiatry*, *51*, 102083. doi:10.1016/j.ajp.2020.102083 PMID:32283510

Rudd, J. W. M., Kelly, C. A., Schindler, D. W., & Turner, M. A. (1988). Disruption of the nitrogen cycle in acidified lakes. *Science*, *240*(4858), 1515–1517. doi:10.1126cience.240.4858.1515 PMID:17798981

Ruiz-Martin, C., Pérez Ríos, J., Wainer, G., Pajares, J., Hernández, C., & López-Paredes, A. (2017). The Application of the Viable System Model to Enhance Organizational Resilience. Advances in Management Engineering, 88–100. https://doi.org/ doi:10.1007/978-3-319-55889-9_5

Ruiz-Martin, C., López-Paredes, A., & Wainer, G. (2015). Applying complex network theory to the assessment of organizational resilience. *IFAC-PapersOnLine*, *48*(3), 1224–1229. doi:10.1016/j.ifacol.2015.06.251

Runhaar, H., Tigchelaar, C., & Vermeulen, W. J. (2008). Environmental leaders: Making a difference. A typology of environmental leaders and recommendations for a differentiated policy approach. *Business Strategy and the Environment*, *17*(3), 160–178. doi:10.1002/bse.520

Rusk, D. (1993). *Cities without Suburbs*. The Woodrow.

Rus, S., Mocan, M., Ardelean, B. O., Ivascu, L., & Cioca, L. I. (2016). Conceptualization and examination of success factors in the banking system. *Procedia Economics and Finance*, *39*, 679–684. doi:10.1016/S2212-5671(16)30289-1

Sadia, A., Salleh, B. M., Kadir, Z. A., & Sanif, S. (2016). The relationship between organizational communication and employees productivity with new dimensions of effective communication flow. *Journal of Business and Social Review in Emerging Economies*, *2*(2), 93–100. doi:10.26710/jbsee.v2i2.35

Sahal, D. (1981). Alternative conceptions of technology. *Research Policy*, *10*(1), 2–24. doi:10.1016/0048-7333(81)90008-1

Sako, M. (1992). *Price, quality and trust: Inter-firm relations in Britain and Japan*. Cambridge University Press. doi:10.1017/CBO9780511520723

Sala, O. E., Chapin, F. S. I., Armesto, J. J., Berlow, E., Bloomfield, J., Dirzo, R., Huber-Sanwald, E., Huenneke, L. F., Jackson, R. B., Kinzig, A., Leemans, R., Lodge, D. M., Mooney, H. A., Oesterheld, M., Poff, N. L., Sykes, M. T., Walker, B. H., Walker, M., & Wall, D. H. (2000). Global biodiversity scenarios for the year 2100. *Science*, *287*(5459), 1770–1774. doi:10.1126cience.287.5459.1770 PMID:10710299

Salerno, M. S., de Vasconcelos Gomes, L. A., Da Silva, D. O., Bagno, R. B., & Freitas, S. L. T. U. (2015). Innovation processes: Which process for which project? *Technovation*, *35*, 59–70. doi:10.1016/j.technovation.2014.07.012

Salwan, P., & Gada, V. P. (2018). Antecedents of resilience: An investigation into bharat forge. *Indian Journal of Industrial Relations*, *53*, 449–461.

Sam, C. Y., McNown, R., & Goh, S. K. (2019). An augmented autoregressive distributed lag bounds test for cointegration. *Economic Modelling*, *80*, 130–141. doi:10.1016/j.econmod.2018.11 001

Santini, C., Cavicchi, A., & Casini, L. (2013). Sustainability in the wine industry: Key questions and research trends a. *Agricultural and Food Economics*, *1*(1), 1–14. doi:10.1186/2193-7532-1-9

Sapkota, N., Paudel, N., Subedi, D. K., Bhattarai, R., & Shrestha, R. (2018). Role of information communication technology (ICT) in Nepalese banking industry. *American Scientific Research Journal for Engineering, Technology, and Sciences*, *42*(1), 75–88.

Sarmento, M. F. P. G. M. (2016). Predicting entrepreneurial motivation among university students: The role of entrepreneurship education. *Education + Training*, *58*(7/8), 861–881.

Saunders, M., Lewis, P., & Thornhill, A. (2016). *Research Methods for Business Students* (7th ed.). Pearson.

Sautter, E. T., & Leisen, B. (1999). Managing stakeholders: A tourism planning model. *Annals of Tourism Research*, *26*(2), 312–328.

Schaefer, A., & Crane, A. (2005). Addressing sustainability and consumption. *Journal of Macromarketing*, *25*(1), 76–92. doi:10.1177/0276146705274987

Scheffer, M., Carpenter, S. R., Foley, J. A., Folke, C., & Walker, B. H. (2001). Catastrophic shifts in ecosystems. *Nature*, *413*(6856), 591–596. doi:10.1038/35098000 PMID:11595939

Schindler, D. W. (1990). Experimental perturbations of whole lakes as tests of hypotheses concerning ecosystem structure and function. *Oikos*, *57*(1), 25–41. doi:10.2307/3565733

Schlich, B. (2012). *The customer takes control: global consumer banking survey 2012.* Ernst & Young.

Schneider, K. (2017). Entrepreneurial competencies of women entrepreneurs of micro and small enterprises. *Science Journal of Education*, *5*(6), 252–261. doi:10.11648/j.sjedu.20170506.14

Seana I., Johnson, L. & Peters, K. (1999). Community gardens and sustainable land use planning: A case-study of the Alex Wilson community garden. *Local Environment*, *4*(1), 33-46. doi:10.1080/13549839908725579

Searns, R. M. (1995). The evolution of greenways as an adaptive urban landscape form. *Landscape and Urban Planning*, *33*(1), 65–80. doi:10.1016/0169-2046(94)02014-7

Seebode, D., Jeanrenaud, S., & Bessant, J. (2012). Managing innovation for sustainability. *R & D Management*, *42*(3), 195–206. doi:10.1111/j.1467-9310.2012.00678.x

Şeitan, R. (2017). Organizational discourses-A literature review. *Acta Universitatis Danubius Communication, 11*(2).

Sert, N. Y. (2012). Benefit Perception About the Understanding of Corporate Social Responsibility in Private Sector in Turkey: Using Web Sites for Announcing of Corporate Social Responsibility Activities. AJIT-e. *Bilişim Teknolojileri Online Dergisi*, *3*(9), 31–50.

Seto, K. C., De Groot, R., Bringezu, S., Erb, K., Graedel, T. E., Ramankutty, N., & Skole, D. L. (2010). Stocks, flows, and prospects of land. In T. E. Graedel & E. van der Voet (Eds.), *Linkages of sustainability* (pp. 72–96). MIT Press.

Shabbir, M., Sulaiman, M., Al-Kumaim, N., Mahmood, A., & Abbas, M. (2020). *Green Marketing Approaches and Their Impact on Consumer Behavior towards the Environment—A Study from the UAE.* Sustainability Mdpi Journal.

Shafiea, F. A., Dasimah, O., & Karuppannanb, S. (2013). Urban metabolism: a research methodology in urban planning and environmental assessment. *Proceedings of the 1st international conference on research methodology for built environment and engineering.*

Shahbaz, M., Gozgor, G., & Hammoudeh, S. (2019). Human capital and export diversification as new determinants of energy demand in the United States. *Energy Economics*, *78*, 335–349. doi:10.1016/j.eneco.2018.11.016

Shahbaz, M., & Sinha, A. (2019). Environmental Kuznets curve for CO2 emissions: A literature survey. *Journal of Economic Studies (Glasgow, Scotland)*, *46*(1), 106–168. doi:10.1108/JES-09-2017-0249

Shahzad, U., Doğan, B., Sinha, A., & Fareed, Z. (2021). Does Export product diversification help to reduce energy demand: Exploring the contextual evidences from the newly industrialized countries. *Energy*, *214*, 118881. doi:10.1016/j.energy.2020.118881

Shahzad, U., Fareed, Z., Shahzad, F., & Shahzad, K. (2021). Investigating the nexus between economic complexity, energy consumption and ecological footprint for the United States: New insights from quantile methods. *Journal of Cleaner Production*, *279*, 123806. doi:10.1016/j.jclepro.2020.123806

Shahzad, U., Ferraz, D., Doğan, B., & Aparecida do Nascimento Rebelatto, D. (2020). Export product diversification and CO2 emissions: Contextual evidences from developing and developed economies. *Journal of Cleaner Production*, *276*, 124146. doi:10.1016/j.jclepro.2020.124146

Shahzad, U., Lv, Y., Doğan, B., & Xia, W. (2021). Unveiling the heterogeneous impacts of export product diversification on renewable energy consumption: New evidence from G-7 and E-7 countries. *Renewable Energy*, *164*, 1457–1470. doi:10.1016/j.renene.2020.10.143

Shamdasani, P., Lin, G. C., & Richmond, D. (1993). Exploring green consumers in an oriental culture: Rolle of personal and marketing mix. *Advances in Consumer Research. Association for Consumer Research (U. S.)*, *20*, 488–493.

Sharifi, A. (2016). From garden city to eco-urbanism: The quest for sustainable neighborhood development. *Sustainable Cities and Society*, *20*, 1–16. doi:10.1016/j.scs.2015.09.002

Sharif, N. (2006). Emergence and development of the National Innovation Systems concept. *Research Policy*, *35*(5), 745–766. doi:10.1016/j.respol.2006.04.001

Sharma, H. (2011). Bankers' perspectives on e-banking. *Global Journal of Research in Management*, *1*(1), 71-85.

Sharma, R., Shahbaz, M., Kautish, P., & Vo, X. V. (2021). Analyzing the impact of export diversification and technological innovation on renewable energy consumption: Evidences from BRICS nations. *Renewable Energy*, *178*, 1034–1045. doi:10.1016/j.renene.2021.06.125

Sharma, S., & Ruud, A. (2003). On the path to sustainability: Integrating social dimensions into the research and practice of environmental management. *Business Strategy and the Environment*, *12*(4), 205–214. doi:10.1002/bse.366

Sheffi, Y., & Rice, J. B. (2005). A supply chain view of the resilient enterprise. *MIT Sloan Management Review*, *47*, 41–48.

Shenhar, A. J. (2001). One size does not fit all projects: Exploring classical contingency domains. *Management Science*, *47*(3), 394–414. doi:10.1287/mnsc.47.3.394.9772

Sheth, J., & Sisodia, R. (2005). A dangerous divergence: Marketing and society. *Journal of Public Policy & Marketing*, *24*(1), 160–162.

Shin, Y., Yu, B., & Greenwood-Nimmo, M. (2014). Modelling Asymmetric Cointegration and Dynamic Multipliers in a Nonlinear ARDL Framework. In R. C. Sickles & W. C. Horrace (Eds.), Festschrift in Honor of Peter Schmidt (Vol. 44, Issue 0, pp. 281–314). Springer New York. doi:10.1007/978-1-4899-8008-3_9

Shin, J., Taylor, M. S., & Seo, M.-G. (2012). Resources for change: The relationships of organizational inducements and psychological resilience to employees' attitudes and behaviors toward organizational change. *Academy of Management Journal*, *55*, 727–748.

Shoaib, M., Abbas, Z., Yousaf, M., Zámečník, R., Ahmed, J., & Saqib, S. (2021). The role of GHRM practices towards organizational commitment: A mediation analysis of green human capital. *Cogent Business & Management*, *8*(1), 1870798. doi:10.1080/23311975.2020.1870798

Shove, E. (2003). *Comfort, Cleanliness and Convenience*. Routledge.

Shrestha, P. (2018). Service quality and customer satisfaction: Evidence of Nepalese banks. *NCC Journal*, *3*(1), 121–133. doi:10.3126/nccj.v3i1.20254

Shrestha, S., Devkota, N., Paudel, U., Bhandari, U., & Parajuli, S. (2020). Bankers' Communication Know-how: An Analysis from Commercial Banks of Kathmandu valley. *Quest Journal of Management and Social Sciences*, *2*(1), 80–99. doi:10.3126/qjmss.v2i1.29023

Shrestha, S., Thapa, S., Mangrati, L., Devkota, P., Rai, R., & Adhikari, K. (2019). Quality of work life (QWL) situation in the Nepalese corporate sector. *Quest Journal of Management and Social Sciences*, *1*(1), 119–145. doi:10.3126/qjmss.v1i1.25977

Shukaili, A. A., Cucculelli, M., González-Pernía, J. L., & Legazkue, I. P. (2018). Entrepreneurship policy to overcome barriers to new firm growth in a developing economy: Evidence from Oman. *International Journal of Entrepreneurship and Small Business*, *35*(4), 511–537. doi:10.1504/IJESB.2018.096173

Shukla, S. (2021). Green Marketing: Promoting Green Consumerism for Sustainable Development. *Prestige E-Journalof Management And Research*, *2*(1), 2350–1316.

Siegel, D. S., & Vitaliano, D. F. (2007). An empirical analysis of the strategic use of corporate social responsibility. *Journal of Economics & Management Strategy*, *16*(3), 773–792. doi:10.1111/j.1530-9134.2007.00157.x

Siegrist, M., Visschers, V. H., & Hartmann, C. (2015). Factors influencing changes in sustainability perception of various food behaviors: Results of a longitudinal study. *Food Quality and Preference*, *46*, 33–39. doi:10.1016/j.foodqual.2015.07.006

Sikdar, P., Kumar, A., & Makkad, M. (2015). Online banking adoption: A factor validation and satisfaction causation study in the context of Indian banking customers. *International Journal of Bank Marketing*, *33*(6), 760–785. doi:10.1108/IJBM-11-2014-0161

Sirgy, M. J. (2018). Self-congruity theory in consumer behavior: A little history. *Journal of Global Scholars of Marketing Science*, *28*(2), 197–207.

Slater, D. (1997). *Consumer culture and modernity*. Polity Press.

Smit, B., & Wandel, J. (2006). Adaptation, adaptive capacity and vulnerability. *Global Environmental Change*, *16*(3), 282–292. doi:10.1016/j.gloenvcha.2006.03.008

Smythe, J. (1996). The changing role of internal communication in tomorrow's company. *Managing Service Quality*, *6*(2), 41–44. doi:10.1108/09604529610109756

Solaiman, M., Osman, A., & Halim, M. S. (2015). Green marketing: A marketing mix point of view. *International Journal of Business and Technopreneurship*, *5*(1), 87–98.

Solomon, M. R. (1995). *Consumer behaviour: Buying, having and being*. Allyn & Bacon.

Solow, R. M. (1957). Technical change and the aggregate production function. *The Review of Economics and Statistics*, *39*(3), 312–320. doi:10.2307/1926047

Somasundram, S., Sambasivan, M., Rasiah, R., & Tee, P. L. (2018). Ranking the Challenges of the Urban Community in Malaysia. *Institutions and Economies*, *10*(4), 69–89.

Somers, S. (2009). Measuring resilience potential: An adaptive strategy for organizational crisis planning. *Journal of Contingencies and Crisis Management*, *17*(1), 12–23.

Song, W., Yu, H., & Xu, H. (2020). Effects of green human resource management and managerial environmental concern on green innovation. *European Journal of Innovation Management*, *24*(3), 951–967. doi:10.1108/EJIM-11-2019-0315

Sousa Filho, J. M. D., Wanderley, L. S. O., Gómez, C. P., & Farache, F. (2010). Strategic corporate social responsibility management for competitive advantage. *BAR - Brazilian Administration Review*, *7*(3), 294–309. doi:10.1590/S1807-76922010000300006

Sousa, M. J., & Almeida, M. do R. (2014). Entrepreneurial Skills Development. *6th Int. Conf. Appl. Econ. Business Dev.*, 135–138.

Stern, P. C., Dietz, T., Abel, T., Guagnano, G. A., & Kalof, L. (1999). A value-belief-norm theory of support for social movements: The case of environmentalism. *Human Ecology Review*, *6*(2), 81–97.

Stole, E (2011). *The road to successful green destination branding* (Master's thesis). Department of Inter- national Economics and Management, Copenhagen Business School, Denmark.

Strauss, A. L., & Corbin, J. M. (2008). *Basics of qualitative research: Techniques and procedures for developing grounded theory*. Sage publications Limited.

Suddaby, R. (2010). Editor's comments: Construct clarity in theories of management and organization. *Academy of Management Journal*, *35*, 346–357.

Sudhalakshimi, K., & Chinnadorai, K. (2014). Green marketing mix - A social responsibility of manufacturing companies. *Global Journal of Commerce and Management Perspective*, 109-112.

Sukopp, H., Hejny, S., & Kowarik, I. (Eds.). (1990). *Urban ecology: Plants and plant communities in urban environments*. SPB Academic Publishing.

Sukopp, H., Trautmann, W., & Korneck, D. (1979). The soilflora and vegetation of Berlin'swastelands. In I. Laurie (Ed.), *Nature in Cities*. John Wiley.

Sultan, N. (2011). Making a Difference in a Troubled Country: The Case of Entrepreneurial and Female Leadership in Yemen. *Leadership Development in the Middle East*, 297-327.

Sun, J. J., Bellezza, S., & Paharia, N. (2021). Buy Less, Buy Luxury: Understanding and Overcoming Product Durability Neglect for Sustainable Consumption. *Journal of Marketing*, *85*(3). 28–43.

Sutcliffe, K. M., & Vogus, T. (2003). Organizing for resilience. In K. S. Cameron, J. E. Dutton, & R. E. Quinn (Eds.), *Positive organizational scholarship* (pp. 94–110). Berrett-Koehler.

Svensson, G. (2004). Interactive service quality in service encounters: Empirical illustration and models. *Managing Service Quality*, *14*(4), 278–287. doi:10.1108/09604520410546815

Swarbrooke, J. (2006). *Sustainable tourism management*. CABI Publishing.

Szondi, G. (2010). From image management to relationship building: A public relations approach to nation branding. *Place Branding and Public Diplomacy*, *6*(4), 333–343.

Taleb, N. N. (2012). *Antifragile: Things that Gain from Disorder* (Vol. 3). Random House.

Taleb, N. N., & Douady, R. (2013). Mathematical definition, mapping, and detection of (anti)fragility. *Quantitative Finance*, *13*(11), 1677–1689. doi:10.1080/14697688.2013.800219

Tambi, M. D., & Atemnkeng, J. T. (2018). Measuring the effect of environmental hygiene on child health outcomes in Cameroon. *Journal of Economics & Management*, *32*, 118–137.

Tamim, M., Foisal, M., & Sagar, A. H. (2015). Factors Affecting the Women Entrepreneurship Development in Small and Medium Enterprises (SME) in Bangladesh- An Evaluative Study. *European Journal of Business and Management*, *7*, 153–161.

Tan, L., Johnstone, M., & Yang, L. (2016). Barriers to green consumption behaviours: The roles of consumers' green perceptions. Australian And New Zealand Marketing Academy, 1441-3582.

Tan, B. C., & Lau, T. C. (2010). Attitude towards the environment and green products. *Management Science and Engineering*, *4*(2), 27–39.

Tang, H. T., & Lee, T. M. (2016). The Making of Sustainable Urban Development: A Synthesis Framework. *Sustainability*, *8*(5), 1–28. doi:10.3390u8050492

Tan, M., & Teo, T. S. (2000). Factors influencing the adoption of Internet banking. *Journal of the Association for Information Systems*, *1*(1), 5–14. doi:10.17705/1jais.00005

Tansley, A. G. (1935). The use and abuse of vegetational concepts and terms. *Ecology*, *16*(3), 284–307. doi:10.2307 1930070

Taqi, N. (2016). *The Challenges Facing Women Entrepreneurs : A Study On Gulf Cooperation Council (GCC) Countries Evidence from the Kingdom of Bahrain, United Arab Emirates, and Saudi Arabia* (PhD thesis). Najma Taqi.

Tarabar, D. (2018). Regional integration and entrepreneurship: Evidence from European Union. *J. Entrep. Public Policy*, *7*(2), 117–134. doi:10.1108/JEPP-D-18-00003

Tasci, A. D. A. (2011). Destination branding and positioning. In Y. Wang & A. Pizam (Eds.), *Destination marketing and management theories and applications*. CABI.

Teberga, P. M. F., Oliva, F. L., & Kotabe, M. (2018). Risk analysis in introduction of new technologies by start-ups in the Brazilian market. *Management Decision*, *56*(1), 64–86. doi:10.1108/MD-04-2017-0337

Teece, D. J., Pisano, G., & Shuen, A. (1997). Dynamic capabilities and strategic management. *Strategic Management Journal*, *18*(7), 509–533. doi:10.1002/(SICI)1097-0266(199708)18:7<509::AID-SMJ882>3.0.CO;2-Z

Teece, D., Peteraf, M., & Leih, S. (2016). Dynamic capabilities and organizational agility: Risk, uncertainty, and strategy in the innovation economy. *California Management Review*, *58*(4), 13–35. doi:10.1525/cmr.2016.58.4.13

Teo, T. S., & Yeong, Y. D. (2003). Assessing the consumer decision process in the digital marketplace. *Omega*, *31*(5), 349–363.

Terborgh, J., Lopez, L., Nunez, P., Rao, M., Shahabuddin, G., Orihuela, G., Riveros, M., Ascanio, R., Adler, G. H. Lambert, T. D., & Balbas, L. (2001). Ecological meltdown in predator-free forest fragments. *Science*, *294*(5548), 1923–1926. doi:10.1126cience.1064397 PMID:11729317

Termorshuizen, J. W., & Opdam, P. (2009). Landscape services as a bridge between landscape ecology and sustainable development. *Landscape Ecology*, *24*(8), 1037–1052. doi:10.100710980-008-9314-8

Tetlock, P. E. (1985, September). Accountability: A Social Check on the Fundamental Attribution Error. *Social Psychology Quarterly*, *48*(3), 227–236.

Tezer, A., & Bodur, H. (2020). The Green consumption Effect: How Using Green Products Improves Consumption Experience. *The Journal of Consumer Research*, *47*. Advance online publication. . doi:10.1093/jcr/ucz045

Thøgersen, J. (2007). The motivational roots of norms for environmentally responsible behaviour. *Proceedings of the Nordic Consumer Policy Research Conference*, 1-16.

Thomas, G. F., Zolin, R., & Hartman, J. L. (2009). The central role of communication in developing trust and its effect on employee involvement. *The Journal of Business Communication, 46*(3), 287-310.

Thomson, K., & Hecker, L. (2001). Value-adding communication: Innovation in employee communication and internal marketing. *Journal of Communication Management (London)*, *5*(1), 48–58. doi:10.1108/13632540110806668

Thussu, D. K. (2018). *International communication: Continuity and change*. Bloomsbury Publishing.

Tidball, G. K., Krasny, E. M., Svendsen, E., Cambell, L., & Helphand, K. (2010). Stewardship, learning and memory in disaster resilience. *Environmental Learning Research*, *16*(5–6), 591–609. doi:10.1080/13504622.2010.505437

Tidball, K. G., & Krasny, M. E. (2009). *From risk to resilience: what role for community greening and civic ecology in cities?* Wageningen Academic Publishers.

Tidd, J., & Bessant, J. (2018). Innovation management challenges: From fads to fundamentals. *International Journal of Innovation Management*, *22*(05), 1840007. doi:10.1142/S1363919618400078

Tidd, J., & Thuriaux-Alemán, B. (2016). Innovation management practices: Cross-sectorial adoption, variation, and effectiveness. *R & D Management*, *46*(S3), 1024–1043. doi:10.1111/radm.12199

Tierney, K. J. (2003). *Conceptualizing and measuring organizational and community resilience: lessons from the emergency response following the September 11, 2001, attack on the World Trade Center.* Univ. of Delaware.

Tilstone, C. (Ed.). (1998). *The technique of observation. In observing teaching and learning: principle and practice* (pp. 32–53). David Fulton Publishers.

Time. (2011). *10 ideas that will change the world.* Available at http://content.time. com/time/specials/packages/completelist/0,29569,2059521,00.html

Tiong, Y. Y., Sondoh, S. L. Jr, Tanakinjal, G. H., & Iggau, O. A. (2021). Cleaner operations in hotels: Recommendation for post-pandemic green recovery. *Journal of Cleaner Production*, *283*, 124621. doi:10.1016/j.jclepro.2020.124621 PMID:33071479

Tisdell, E. J. (1995). *Creating inclusive adult learning environments: Insights from multicultural education and feminist pedagogy.* DIANE Publishing.

Tlaiss, H. (2015). Islamic work-related values and entrepreneurship: Evidence from the Middle East. *Journal of Business Ethics*, *129*(4), 859–877. doi:10.100710551-014-2138-3

Tompkins, J. A. (2007). 4 Steps to business resilience. *Industrial Management (Norcross, Georgia)*, *49*(4), 14–18.

Travelocity. (2020). *Travelocity predicts 'Safecations' will be summer 2020's newest travel trend.* Available at https://www.travelocity.com/pressroom/travelocity-predicts- safecations-will-be-summer-2020s-newest-travel-trend/#:~:text=Travelocity%20predicts%20'Safecations'%20will%20be%20summer%202020's%20newest%20travel%20trend,-DALLAS%2C%20Texas%20(June&text=In%20fact%2C%20Boomers%20were%20tw ice,and%20significant%20other%20(76%25

Trevlopoulos, N., Tsalis, T., Evangelinos, K., Tsagarakis, K., Vatalis, K., & Nikolaou, I. (2021). The influence of environmental regulations on business innovation, intellectual capital, environmental and economic performance. *Environment Systems & Decisions*, *41*(1), 163–178. doi:10.100710669-021-09802-6

Trivedi, K., Trivedi, P., & Goswami, V. (2018). Sustainable marketing strategies: Creating business value by meeting consumer expectation. *International Journal of Management Economics and Social Sciences*, *7*(2), 186–205.

Trudel, R. (2019). Sustainable consumer behavior. *Counselling Psychology Review*, *2*(1), 85–96.

Ullah, H., Wang, Z., Bashir, S., Khan, A., Riaz, M., & Syed, N. (2021). Nexus between IT capability and green intellectual capital on sustainable businesses: Evidence from emerging economies. *Environmental Science and Pollution Research International*, *28*(22), 27825–27843. doi:10.100711356-020-12245-2 PMID:33515153

UN. (2017). *SDG Index and Dashboards report 2017 – Global Responsibilities, International spill-overs in achieving the goals.* BertelsmannStiftung. Available at: https://sdgs.un.org/sites/default/files/publications/24862017SDGIndexandDashboardsReportfull.pdf

United Nations Department of Economic and Social Affairs. (2018). *The Speed of Urbanization Around the World.* https://population.un.org/wup/Publications/Files/WUP2018-PopFacts_2018-1.pdf

United Nations World Tourism Organisation. (2005). *Making tourism more sustainable. A guide for policy makers.* UNWTO.

United Nations World Tourism Organisation. (2007). *A practical guide to tourism destination Management. UNWTO.*

United Nations World Tourism Organisation. (2013). World tourism barometer – tourism trends and marketing. Author.

Upstill-Goddard, J., Glass, J., Dainty, A., & Nicholson, I. (2016). Implementing sustainability in small and medium-sized construction firms. *Engineering, Construction, and Architectural Management, 23*(4), 407–427. doi:10.1108/ECAM-01-2015-0015

Usmani, R. S. A., Saeed, A., Abdullahi, A. N., Pillai, T. R., Jhanjhi, N. Z., & Hashem, I. A. T. (2020). Air Pollution and its Health Impacts in Malaysia: A Review. *Air Quality, Atmosphere & Health, 13*(9), 1093–1118. doi:10.1007/s11869-020-00867-x

Valastro, J. (2011). Organisational resilience: a position paper for critical infrastructure. Commonwealth of Australia.

van de Berg, L., & van Veenhuizen, R. (2005). Multiple functions of urban Agriculture. *Urban Agriculture Magazine*, 14.

Van Der Beek, D., & Schraagen, J. M. (2015). ADAPTER: Analysing and developing adaptability and performance in teams to enhance resilience. *Reliability Engineering & System Safety*, 141.

van der Duin, P. A., Ortt, J. R., & Aarts, W. T. (2014). Contextual Innovation Management Using a Stage-Gate Platform: The Case of P hilips S having and B eauty. *Journal of Product Innovation Management, 31*(3), 489–500. doi:10.1111/jpim.12109

van der Vegt, G. S., Essens, P., Wahlstrom, M., & George, G. (2015). Managing risk and resilience. *Academy of Management Journal, 58*, 971–980.

Van Eemeren, F. H., & Grootendorst, R. (2016). *Argumentation, communication, and fallacies: A pragma-dialectical perspective*. Routledge. doi:10.4324/9781315538662

Van Staden, E., Marx, S., & Erasmus-Kritzinger, L. (2007). *Corporate communication: getting the message across in business*. VanSchaik.

Verloop, J., & Wissema, J. G. (2004). *Insight in innovation: Managing innovation by understanding the laws of innovation*. Elsevier.

Vermeir, I., & Verbeke, W. (2006). Sustainable food consumption: Exploring the consumer "attitude-behavioral intention" gap. *Journal of Agricultural & Environmental Ethics, 19*(2), 169–194. doi:10.100710806-005-5485-3

Victor, V., Thoppan, J., Nathan, R., & Maria, F. (2018). Factors Influencing Consumer Behavior and Prospective Purchase Decisions in a Dynamic Pricing Environment—An Exploratory Factor Analysis Approach. *Social Sciences Mdpi Journal, 7*(153).

Vieira, C. M., Franco, O. H., Restrepo, C. G., & Abel, T. (2020). COVID-19: The forgotten priorities of the pandemic. *Maturitas, 136*, 38–41. doi:10.1016/j.maturitas.2020.04.004 PMID:32386664

Vigneron, F., & Johnson, L. W. (1999). A review and a conceptual framework of prestige- Seeking Consumer behavior. *Academy of Marketing Science Review, 9*(1), 1–14.

Visa, I., Perniu, D., Alimisis, D., Visa, M., Cardon, L., & Bakay, E. (2008). Integrated Approach of Sustainable Energy Education and Research for Pre-University Curricula. *Bulletin of the Transilvania University of Brasov, Series I. Engineering and Science*, *1*(50), 287–292.

Vogus, T. J., & Sutcliffe, K. M. (2007). *Organizational resilience: Towardsa theory and research agenda.* Paper presented at the Systems, Manand Cybernetics, 2007. ISIC. IEEE International Conference.

Vohora, A., Wright, M., & Lockett, A. (2004). Critical junctures in the development of university high-tech spinout companies. *Research Policy*, *33*(1), 147–175. doi:10.1016/S0048-7333(03)00107-0

Vringer, K., Heijden, E. V. D., Soest, D. V., Vollebergh, H., & Dietz, F. (2017). Sustainable consumption dilemmas. *Sustainability*, *9*(6), 942. doi:10.3390u9060942

Vujcic, M., Tomicevic-Dubljevic, J., Grbic, M., Lecic-Tosevski, D., Vukovic, O., & Toskovic, O. (2017). Nature based solution for improving mental health and well-being in urban areas. *Environmental Research*, *158*, 385–392. doi:10.1016/j.envres.2017.06.030 PMID:28688269

Vyas, V., & Raitani, S. (2014). Drivers of customers' switching behaviour in Indian banking industry. *International Journal of Bank Marketing*, *32*(4), 321–342. doi:10.1108/IJBM-04-2013-0033

Walker & Salt. (2012). *Resilience Practice: Building Capacity to Absorb Disturbance and Maintain Function.* Island Press.

Walker, B. H., Holling, C. S., Carpenter, S. R., & Kinzig, A. P. (2004). Resilience, adaptability and transformability in social–ecological systems. *Ecology and Society*, *9*(2), 5. http://www.ecologyandsociety. org/vol9/iss2/art5/

Walker, R. H., & Hanson, D. J. (1998). Green Marketing and Green Places: A Taxonomy for the Destination Marketer. *Journal of Marketing Management*, *14*, 623–639.

Walther, J. B. (1988). Communication satisfaction in the bank: An audit evaluation. *The Journal of Business Communication*, *25*(3), 79-86.

Wang, C., & Juo, W. (2021). An environmental policy of green intellectual capital: Green innovation strategy for performance sustainability. *Business Strategy and the Environment*, *30*(7), 1–14. doi:10.1002/bse.2800

Wang, C., Zhang, J., Sun, J., Chen, M., & Yang, J. (2020). Public environmental facilities: Hygiene factors for tourists' environmental behaviour. *Environmental Science & Policy*, *106*, 40–47. doi:10.1016/j.envsci.2020.01.009

Wang, Y. (2008). Collaborative destination marketing: Roles and strategies of convention and visitors bureaus. *Journal of Vacation Marketing*, *14*(3), 191–209.

Wang, Y. (2011). Destination marketing and management: scope, definition and structures. In Y. Wang & A. Pizam (Eds.), *Destination marketing and management: Theories and applications* (pp. 1–20). CAB International.

Wang, Z., Ben Jebli, M., Madaleno, M., Doğan, B., & Shahzad, U. (2021). Does export product quality and renewable energy induce carbon dioxide emissions: Evidence from leading complex and renewable energy economies. *Renewable Energy*, *171*, 360–370. doi:10.1016/j.renene.2021.02.066

Waterman, R. H., & Peters, T. J. (1982). *In search of excellence: Lessons from America's best-run companies.* Harper & Row.

Watson, M. Z., & Yan, R. N. (2013). An exploratory study of the decision processes of fast versus slow fashion consumers. *Journal of Fashion Marketing and Management*, *17*(2), 141–159.

WCED. (1987). *Our common future. The report of the World Commission on Environment and Development.* Oxford University Press.

WCED. (1987). World commission on environment and development. *Our Common Future*, *17*(1), 1–91.

Weaver, D., & Lawton, L. (2010). *Tourism management* (4th ed.). John Wiley & Sons.

Webster, C., & Lai, L. W. C. (2003). *Property rights, planning and markets*. Edward Elgar.

Weick, K. E., & Sutcliffe, K. M. (2007). Managing the unexpected: Resilient performance in an age of uncertainty (2nd ed.). Jossey-Bass.

Weick, K. E., & Sutcliffe, K. M. (2001). *Managing the unexpected: Assuring high performance in an age of complexity*. Jossey-Bass.

Weick, K. E., Sutcliffe, K. M., & Obstfeld, D. (1999). Organizing for High Reliability: Processes of Collective Mindfulness. In R. S. Sutton & B. M. Staw (Eds.), *Research in Organizational Behavior* (Vol. 1, pp. 81–123). Jai Press.

While, A., Jonas, A., & Gibbs, D. (2010). From Sustainable Development to Carbon Control: Ecostate Restructuring and the Politics of Urban and Regional Development. *Transactions of the Institute of British Geographers*, *35*(1), 76–93. doi:10.1111/j.1475-5661.2009.00362.x

White, K., Habib, R., & Hardisty, D. J. (2019). How to SHIFT consumer behaviors to be more sustainable: A literature review and guiding framework. *Journal of Marketing*, *83*(3), 22–49.

White, K., & Simpson, B. (2013). When do (and don't) normative appeals influence sustainable consumer behaviors? *Journal of Marketing*, *77*(2), 78–95.

Widener, S. (2006). Associations between strategic resource importance and performance measure use: The impact on firm performance. *Management Accounting Research*, *17*(4), 433–457. doi:10.1016/j.mar.2005.10.002

Wiedmann, K. P., Hennigs, N., & Siebels, A. (2007). Measuring consumers' luxury value perception: A crosscultural framework. *Academy of Marketing Science Review*, *11*, 1–21.

Wiedmann, K. P., Hennigs, N., & Siebels, A. (2009). Value-based segmentation of luxury consumption behavior. *Psychology and Marketing*, *26*(7), 625–651.

Wilbanks, T. J., & Romero Lankao, P. (2007). Industry, settlement, and society. In Climate change 2007: impacts, adaptation, and vulnerability: contribution of Working Group II to the Fourth Assessment Report of the Intergovernmental Panel on Climate Change. Cambridge University Press.

Wildavsky, A. B. (1988). *Searching for safety* (3rd ed.). Transaction Publishers.

Wilkie, W. (1994). *Consumer behavior*. John Wiley & Sons,Inc.

Wilkinson, A., Elahi, S., & Eidinow, E. (2003). Section 2. Background and dynamics of the scenarios. *Journal of Risk Research*, *6*, 365–401.

Williams, T. A., Gruber, D. A., Sutcliffe, K. M., Shepherd, D. A., & Zhao, E. Y. (2017). Organizational response to adversity: Fusing crisis management and resilience research streams. *The Academy of Management Annals*, *11*, 733–769.

Williams, T. A., Gruber, D. A., Sutcliffe, K. M., Shepherd, D. A., & Zhao, E. Y. (2017). Organizational response to adversity: Fusing crisis management and resilience re-search streams. *The Academy of Management Annals*, *11*, 733–769.

Williams, T., & Shepherd, D. (2016). Building resilience or providing sustenance: Different paths of emergent ventures in the aftermath of the Haiti earthquake. *Academy of Management Journal*. Advance online publication. doi:10.5465/amj.2015.0682

Wilson, C., & Dowlatabadi, H. (2007). Models of Decision Making and Residential Energy Use. *Annual Review of Environment and Resources*, *32*(1), 169–203. doi:10.1146/annurev.energy.32.053006.141137

Wolff, F., & Schönherr, N. (2011). The impact evaluation of sustainable consumption policy instruments. *Journal of Consumer Policy*, *34*(1), 43–66. doi:10.100710603-010-9152-3

Wolman, A. (1965). The metabolism of cities. *Scientific American*, *213*(3), 179–190. doi:10.1038cientificamerican0965-178 PMID:14338520

Wong, C.-S., Law, K. S., & Huang, G.-H. (2008). On the importance of conducting construct-level analysis for multidimensional constructs in theory development and testing. *Journal of Management*, *34*, 744–764.

Woodland, M., & Acott, T. G. (2007). Sustainability and local tourism branding in England's South Downs. *Journal of Sustainable Tourism*, *15*(6), 715–724.

Woods, D. (2003). Creating Foresight: How Resilience Engineering Can Transform NASA' s Approach to Risky Decision Making. Testimony on the future of NASA for Committee of Commerce, Science and Transportation.

Wood, W., & Hayes, T. (2012). Social influence on consumer decisions: Motives, modes, and consequences. *Journal of Consumer Psychology*, *22*(3), 324–328. doi:10.1016/j.jcps.2012.05.003

World Bank. (2014). *World Development Indicators*. Author.

World Commission on Environment and Development. (1987). *Our common future*. Oxford University Press.

Worley, C. G., Feyerherm, A. E., & Knudsen, D. (2010). Building a collaboration capability for sustainability: How Gap Inc. is creating and leveraging a strategic asset. *Organizational Dynamics*, *39*(4), 325–334. doi:10.1016/j.orgdyn.2010.07.004

Wu, J., & Wu, T. (2013). Ecological resilience as a foundation for urban design and sustainability. In S. T. A. Pickett, M. L. Cadenasso, & B. McGrath (Eds.), *Resilience in ecology and urban design: Linking theory and practice for sustainable cities* (pp. 211–229). Springer. doi:10.1007/978-94-007-5341-9_10

Wu, Y., Shen, L., Shuai, C., Jiao, L., Liao, S., & Guo, Z. (2021). Key Driving Forces on the Development of Low Carbon City (LCC) in China. *Ecological Indicators*, *124*, 107379. doi:10.1016/j.ecolind.2021.107379

Xu, A. (2019). Study on human resource management of sewage treatment enterprises. *Fresenius Environmental Bulletin*, *28*(12), 10035–10039.

Xu, X., Wang, S., & Yu, Y. (2020). Consumer's intention to purchase green furniture: Do health consciousness and environmental awareness matter? *The Science of the Total Environment*, *704*, 135275. doi:10.1016/j.scitotenv.2019.135275 PMID:31796272

Yadiati, W., Nissa, N., Paulus, S., Suharman, H., & Meiryani, M. (2019). The role of green intellectual capital and organizational reputation in influencing environmental performance. *International Journal of Energy Economics and Policy*, *9*(3), 261–268. doi:10.32479/ijeep.7752

Yang, S., Song, Y., & Tong, S. (2017). Sustainable retailing in the fashion industry: A systematic literature review. *Sustainability*, *9*(7), 1266.

Yang, Y.-C., & Zhao, X. (2019). Exploring the relationship of green packaging design with consumers' green trust, and green brand attachment. *Social Behavior and Personality*, *47*(8), e8181.

Yaseen, S. G., & El Qirem, I. A. (2018). Intention to use e-banking services in the Jordanian commercial banks. *International Journal of Bank Marketing*, *36*(3), 557–571. doi:10.1108/IJBM-05-2017-0082

Yigitcanlar, T. (Ed.). (2010). *Rethinking Sustainable Development*. IGI Global. doi:10.4018/978-1-61692-022-7

Yigitcanlar, T., & Teriman, S. (2015). Rethinking Sustainable Urban Development: Towards An Integrated Planning and Development Process. *International Journal of Environmental Science and Technology*, *12*(1), 341–352. doi:10.100713762-013-0491-x

Yi, S., & Duval-Couetil, N. (2018). What drives engineering students to be entrepreneurs? Evidence of validity for an entrepreneurial motivation scale. *Journal of Engineering Education*, *107*(2), 291–317. doi:10.1002/jee.20199

Yohe, G., & Tol, R. S. J. (2002). Indicators for social and economic coping capacity – moving toward a working definition of adaptive capacity. *Global Environmental Change*, *12*(1), 25–40. doi:10.1016/S0959-3780(01)00026-7

Yönet, E. (2005). Kurumsal Sosyal Sorumluluk Anlayışında Son Dönemeç: Stratejik Sorumluluk [The Last Turn Of Corporate Socıal Responsıbılıty: Strategıc Responsibility]. *Balıkesir Üniversitesi Sosyal Bilimler Enstitüsü Dergisi*, *8*(13), 239–264.

Yong, J., Yusliza, M., Jabbour, C., & Ahmad, N. (2019a). Exploratory cases on the interplay between green human resource management and advanced green manufacturing in light of the Ability-Motivation-Opportunity theory. *Journal of Management Development*, *39*(1), 31–49. doi:10.1108/JMD-12-2018-0355

Yong, J., Yusliza, M., Ramayah, T., & Fawehinmi, O. (2019). Nexus between green intellectual capital and green human resource management. *Journal of Cleaner Production*, *215*, 364–374. doi:10.1016/j.jclepro.2018.12.306

Youngberg, D. (2017). Using predictive decision-making to implement technology prizes. *Journal of Entrepreneurship and Public Policy*, *6*(3), 274–289. doi:10.1108/JEPP-D-17-00004

Yuan, H., Zhou, P., & Zhou, D. (2011). What is Low-Carbon Development? A Conceptual Analysis. *Energy Procedia*, *5*, 1706–1712. doi:10.1016/j.egypro.2011.03.290

Yuan, Q., & Shen, B. (2019). Renting fashion with strategic customers in the sharing economy. *International Journal of Production Economics*, *218*, 185–195.

Yue, B., Sheng, G., She, S., & Xu, J. (2020). Impact of Consumer Environmental Responsibility on Green Consumption Behavior in China: The Role of Environmental Concern and Price Sensitivity. *Sustainability Mdpi Journal, 12*(2074).

Yuen, K. F., & Lim, J. M. (2016). Barriers to the implementation of strategic corporate social responsibility in shipping. *The Asian Journal of Shipping and Logistics*, *32*(1), 49–57. doi:10.1016/j.ajsl.2016.03.006

Yuksel, F. B., Bramwell, A., & Yuksel, A. (1999). Stakeholder interviews and tourism planning at Pamukkale, Turkey. *Tourism Management*, *20*(3), 351–360.

Yu, S. H., & Liang, W. C. (2020). Exploring the determinants of strategic Corporate social responsibility: An empirical examination. *Sustainability*, *12*(6), 2368. doi:10.3390u12062368

Yusliza, M., Yong, J., Tanveer, M., Ramayah, T., Faezah, J., & Muhammad, Z. (2020). A structural model of the impact of green intellectual capital on sustainable performance. *Journal of Cleaner Production*, *249*, 119334. doi:10.1016/j.jclepro.2019.119334

Yusoff, Y., Omar, M., Zaman, M., & Samad, S. (2019). Do all elements of green intellectual capital contribute toward business sustainability? Evidence from the Malaysian context using the Partial Least Squares method. *Journal of Cleaner Production*, *234*, 626–637. doi:10.1016/j.jclepro.2019.06.153

Zanoni, P., & Janssens, M. (2009). Sustainable DiverCities. In M. Janssens, D. Pinelli, D. C. Reyman, & S. Wallman (Eds.), *Sustainable Cities. Diversity, Economic Growthand Social Cohesion* (pp. 3–25). Edward Elgar.

Zaragoza-Sáez, P., Claver-Cortés, E., Marco-Lajara, B., & Úbeda-García, M. (2020). Corporate social responsibility and strategic knowledge management as mediators between sustainable intangible capital and hotel performance. *Journal of Sustainable Tourism*, 1–23. doi:10.1080/09669582.2020.1811289

Zeenat, B., & Mariam, J. (2014). Barriers of Malaysian green hotels and resorts. *Procedia: Social and Behavioral Sciences*, *153*, 501–509. doi:10.1016/j.sbspro.2014.10.083

Zeidan, S., & Bahrami, S. (2011). Women entrepreneurship in GCC: A framework to address challenges and promote participation in a regional context. *International Journal of Business and Social Science*, *2*(14), 100–107.

Zhang, J., Xie, C., Wang, J., Morrison, A. M., & Coca-Stefaniak, J. A. (2020). Responding to a major global crisis: The effects of hotel safety leadership on employee safety behavior during COVID-19. *International Journal of Contemporary Hospitality Management*, *32*(11), 3365–3389. doi:10.1108/IJCHM-04-2020-0335

Zhang, S. X., & Babovic, V. (2012). A real options approach to the design and architecture of water supply systems using innovative water technologies under uncertainty. *Journal of Hydroinformatics*, *488*. www.frontiersinecology.org

Zhao, W., & Scroeder, P. (2010). Sustainable consumption and production: trends, challenges and options for the Asia-Pacific region. *National Resources Forum*, *34*, 4-15.

Zhao, G., Geng, Y., Sun, H., Tian, X., Chen, W., & Wu, D. (2020). Mapping the knowledge of green consumption: A meta-analysis. *Environmental Science and Pollution Research International*, *27*, 44937–44950. PMID:33001398

Zhu, Q., Sarkis, J., & Lai, K. H. (2013). Institutional-based antecedents and performance outcomes of internal and external green supply chain management practices. *Journal of Purchasing and Supply Management*, *19*(2), 106–117. doi:10.1016/j.pursup.2012.12.001

Zimov, S. A., Chuprynin, V. I., Oreshko, A. P., Chapin, F. S. III, Reynolds, J. F., & Chapin, M. C. (1995). Steppe–tundra transition: An herbivore-driven biome shift at the end of the Pleistocene. *American Naturalist*, *146*(5), 765–794. doi:10.1086/285824

Zolli, A., & Healy, A. M. (2012). *Resilience: Why Things Bounce Back*. Simon and Schuster, Inc.

Zuhairah, H., & Noor, A. (2015). The Impact of Green Marketing Strategy on the Firm's Performance in Malaysia. *Procedia: Social and Behavioral Sciences*, 463–470.

About the Contributors

Fadi Abdel Fattah is currently an Assistant Professor in Management, College of Business Administration (COBA) in A'Sharqiyah University (ASU), Ibra, Sultanate of Oman. He has published in several international indexed journals. Also, He has been appointed as an advisory board and editorial member in international journals and top associations in his domain. Dr. Fadi secured several research grants. He also supervised MBA students and served as an external and internal examiner for graduate students. His research interests in Consumer Behavior, Service quality, Knowledge Management, and Healthcare Management. Through his career in teaching, he has taught several courses at the undergraduate and graduate levels. He pays special attention to students' involvement and engagement to help them become more proactive and participative. He has chaired several committees and initiatives at his current and previous positions. Dr. Fadi and his team create three undergraduate and postgraduate programs that attract more than 200 students.

Samuel Adeyinka-Ojo is a senior lecturer and Head of Department of Management, Marketing & Digital Business at Curtin University, Malaysia. His research interests include tourism destination marketing and branding, hospitality marketing, visitor behaviour, food festivals and events management, social media, digital marketing, quality management, human resources management in hospitality and tourism, financial accounting and hospitality revenue management, sustainable rural and ecotourism destination.

Hussam Al Halbusi holds a Ph.D. in Management and Administration, currently working as Assistant Professor at Management Department, Ahmed Bin Mohammed Military College (ABMMC), Doha, Qatar. Hussam received my BSc degree with first-class honors from the University of Al Anbar in 2011. After completing my BSc in Business Management, he was awarded a Master's degree in Business policy from Fatih University Istanbul, Turkey 2015. He obtained my Ph.D. from the Faculty of Business and Accountancy (UMFBA), University of Malaya, Malaysia 2020. My research interests lie in the areas of Strategic Management, Business Ethics, Leadership, Human Resources Management, Organizational Psychology, Organizational Sociology, Innovation, Entrepreneurship, SMEs, Technology Adaption, and Technology Addiction. He has published numerous scientific journal articles and conference papers. He is a regular reviewer of numerous prestigious journals. During his career, he was engaged in more than 50 projects.

Haneen Allataifeh is a Ph.D. student at the Faculty of Business & Accountancy at the University of Malaya. Her interest focuses on innovation management and the digitalization impact on innovation practices.

Fayrene Chieng is currently a Lecturer at Curtin University Malaysia. She earned her doctorate in Marketing from Curtin University, Australia. Her research interest focuses on consumer behaviour, experiential consumption, and sustainability marketing.

Omkar Dastane obtained his PhD (Business) from Curtin University. Omkar's research mainly emphasizes digital consumers and the technological impact on businesses. His extensive research interests are mobile commerce, customer perceived value, internet marketing, and online consumer behaviour. Dr Omkar is a founder member of the ASCENT international conference series and has a comprehensive publication track record on his credit. He is also an active reviewer for several Journals, including the International Journal of Asian Business and Information Management, International Journal of E-Business Research, Connection Science, Frontiers in Psychology among others. Dr Omkar is actively engaged in commercial research, industry consultancy and advanced research coaching. His prior academic appointment was as Head – Centre for Postgraduate Studies at one of the leading HEI offering UK franchisee programs in Malaysia.

Niranjan Devkota is an economist with the special focus behavioral economics linking agriculture, climate change and other contemporary issues over a decade. He is now working as coordinator of Research Management Cell at Quest International College affiliated to Pokhara University, Nepal. His research is focused on perception and behavioral studies for people. He has presented his research ideas in different conferences/seminars and workshops. He has published in various journals and performed as reviewer for several journals. He is also engaged in various development projects.

Herman Fassou Haba is an analyst for BMO financial group and researcher conducts research in business management, marketing, project management and finance. Having BSC in accounting and finance and an MBA from Anglia Ruskin University, UK. Herman is currently pursuing MSC in project management research studies at L'université du Québec à Trois-Rivières, Canada.

Maria Jesus Garcia Garcia is a visiting fellow at the Open University, UK.

Chabi Gupta is an alumnus from Shri Ram College of Commerce Delhi University. She has completed recently an executive program in Business Analytics from Wharton School of Business, University of Pennsylvania. She has over 19 years of rich teaching and industrial experience of working in reputed universities, bank, and financial institutions. To her credit there are several national, international publications and presentations in conferences. Her research areas of interest are Finance, Banking and Analytics.

Mikail Kar is working as an academic at Bursa Uludag University, Department of Economics. He completed his undergraduate degree at Istanbul Marmara University, his master's degree at the State University of New York, and his PhD degree at Bursa Uludag University. He mainly works on economic theory, market analysis, methodological issues, economic policy, industrial economics. He has many book chapters and articles published in distinguished international publishing houses and journals in these fields of study. He is still continuing his academic studies at Bursa Uludag University and giving lectures in the field of economic theory.

Alper Karasoy is a research assistant (Ph.D.) in the Department of Economics at Afyon Kocatepe University, Turkey. His research interests include, but are not limited to, environmental economics, energy economics, applied econometrics, the drivers, and the impacts of remittances. His research has been published in International Migration, Environmental Science and Pollution Research, Management of Environmental Quality: An International Journal, Natural Resources Forum, and OPEC Energy Review.

Yeşim Kurt received her bachelor's, master's and doctoral degrees from Anadolu University Aviation Management Department. She is currently working at Kırlareli University, Lüleburgaz Faculty of Aeronautics and Astronautics. In addition to her areas of interest such as airline management, airport management, and aviation safety management, she also works on corporate social responsibility, sustainability, human resources, organizational theories, and leadership.

Bartolomé Marco-Lajara (PhD) is Professor at the University of Alicante. His research interests are strategic management and tourism management. He is the author of several books, book chapters and international articles related to the areas above mentioned. He is a member of the Tourism Research Institute at the University of Alicante since its foundation and the main researcher of the European project 'Next Tourism Generation Alliance' at his University, as well as of the public competitive project for the creation of the Tourist Observatory of the Valencian Community (Spain). He has taken part in others public and private projects, such as the development of the strategic plan of the Alicante province for the period 2010-2020. He is the Head of the Department of Management at the University of Alicante, and previously was the Assistant Dean of the Economics Faculty for the Business Degree.

Javier Martínez-Falcó is Assistant Professor in the Department of Management at the University of Alicante. In the field of research, he focuses his interest on issues related to the Strategic Management of the Company, specifically in the areas of Knowledge Management and Corporate Sustainability of wine companies, on which he has written several publications in the form of articles, book chapters and contributions to conferences. He has also participated in several national research projects and teaches Strategic Management on the ADE, TADE and DADE degree courses.

Sedigheh Moghavvemi is Associate Professor of Technology Management and Entrepreneurship at the Faculty of Business & Accountancy at the University of Malaya. Her research experience includes business and management, technology adoption, innovation management, smart tourism, and social media. She has worked on different research and consultancy projects pertaining to entrepreneurship, marketing, tourism, human resource, the results of which have been published in peer-reviewed journals.

Elsa Patricia Orozco Quijano is a Research Professor in Marketing, International Management and expert in Work integrated Learning with over 15 years' experience teaching in post-secondary institutions in Canada and beyond.

Udaya Raj Paudel is a PhD scholar in TU, Kathmandu, Nepal- working in the field of English and Communication. His research works reflect communication, ethics, business and culture with latest practices worldwide. More than two decades of educational institution management and teaching English and Communication has propelled him as communication consultant in various organizations. Mr. Paudel projects commitments in research and ethical communication. He has presented his research ideas in different conferences/seminars and workshops. He has published in various journals and performed as reviewer for several journals.

Alfonso P. Ramallo-González received the Ph.D. degree in building physics from the University of Exeter, U.K., with a scholarship from the Wates Foundation. He has worked as a Postdoctoral Researcher on two EPSRC funded projects at the Department of Architecture and Civil Engineer, University of Bath, U.K. He is currently a Savedra-Fajardo Research Fellow at the Faculty of Computer Science, University of Murcia, and PI of three years project ThermaSim.

José A. Ruipérez-Valiente received the B.Eng. degree in telecommunications from Universidad Católica de San Antonio de Murcia, and the M.Eng. degree in telecommunications and the M.Sc. and Ph.D. degrees in telematics from Universidad Carlos III of Madrid while conducting research with Institute IMDEA Networks in the area of learning analytics and educational data mining. He was a postdoctoral associate with MIT. He has received more than 20 academic/research awards and fellowships, has published more than 80 scientific publications in high impact venues, and participated in over 18 funded projects. He currently holds the prestigious Spanish Fellowship Juan de la Cierva with the University of Murcia.

Eduardo Sánchez García (PhD) is an assistant professor in the Department of Business Organization at the University of Alicante (Spain). His research is in the field of strategic management of the company. Specifically, he focuses on the study of the territorial agglomeration of companies in clusters and the absorptive capacity, and its influence on the innovative performance and entrepreneurial orientation of companies. He is co-author of several papers presented at conferences, both national and international, as well as several articles and book chapters related to his field of research.

Stella Tan has recently acquired MBA from Anglia Ruskin University, UK. Prior to that she holds Advanced Diploma and Bachelors Degree in accounting. Stella's research interest include green marketing, sustainability and consumer behaviour. Stella is responsible for Business Partnerships in Singapore and China market for Bitget. Stella spent several years for gaining experience and establishing herself as an administrative professional prior joining Bitget. She is a performance-driven, self-motivated worker with strong work ethics and excellent communication skills and a proven ability to achieve and exceed her goals. These experiences have shaped her into an experienced Partner Operation Executive with a track record of performance in a responsible manner with thorough and skillful support of upper management.

Ying Ying Tiong obtained her PhD in green marketing strategy from the Universiti Sabah Malaysia and had started her journey with Curtin University in 2019. Her research interest includes environmental studies, marketing strategy, branding, competitive advantage and firm performance.

José G. Vargas-Hernández, M.B.A., Ph.D., Member of the National System of Researchers of Mexico and a research professor at University Center for Economic and Managerial Sciences, University of Guadalajara. Professor Vargas-Hernández has a Ph. D. in Public Administration and a Ph.D. in Organizational Economics. He has undertaken studies in Organisational Behaviour and has a Master of Business Administration, published four books and more than 200 papers in international journals and reviews (some translated to English, French, German, Portuguese, Farsi, Chinese, etc.) and more than 300 essays in national journals and reviews. He has obtained several international Awards and recognition.

Patrocinio Zaragoza-Sáez (PhD, University of Alicante, Spain) is a Professor at the Department of Management at the University of Alicante, Spain. She is the Coordinator of the University Master's Degree in Tourism Management and Planning. Her primary research interests are strategic management, knowledge management and intellectual capital, tourist districts, ambidexterity and tourism industry. She has published research papers in international journals including Journal of Business Research, Journal of Knowledge Management, Journal of Intellectual Capital, Journal of Sustainable Tourism, Current Issues in Tourism, Tourism Management, International Journal of Contemporary Hospitality Management, Knowledge Management Research and Practice and Business Strategy & Environment, among others.

Index

G

H

I

L

M

N

O

P

R

S

T

U

V

W

www.ingramcontent.com/pod-product-compliance
Lightning Source LLC
LaVergne TN
LVHW060409300926
849162LV00006B/1381
9781799895909